DATE DUE

The House of Commons, 1604–1610

THE HOUSE OF COMMONS 1604-1610

by Wallace Notestein

Yale University Press
New Haven and London, 1971

Designed by Sally Sullivan,
set in Linotype Baskerville type,
and printed in the United States of America by
Vail-Ballou Press, Inc., Binghamton, N.Y.

Distributed in Great Britain, Europe, and Africa by
Yale University Press, Ltd., London; in Canada by
McGill-Queen's University Press, Montreal; in Mexico
by Centro Interamericano de Libros Académicos,
Mexico City; in Central and South America by Kaiman &
Polon, Inc., New York City; in Australasia by Australia and
New Zealand Book Co., Pty., Ltd., Artarmon, New South
Wales; in India by UBS Publishers' Distributors Pvt.,
Ltd., Delhi; in Japan by John Weatherhill, Inc.,
Tokyo.

Contents

Publisher's Note

Wallace Notestein was at work on this book when he died. The manuscript, therefore, had to be sent to press without his aid in revising final copy, checking footnotes and references, reading proof, and compiling the index.

The study was too good to set aside; even an unpolished book by Notestein should, we felt, be made available to interested readers. However, its publication would never have been possible, so quickly and so surely, without the persistent and dedicated professional assistance of the author's friends, Elizabeth Read Foster at Bryn Mawr and Basil Duke Henning at Yale. Mr. Henning was especially helpful in assuming the author's burdens during the last critical months of preparing the manuscript for press.

Everyone concerned with the manuscript in its various stages has tried to preserve both its substance and the individual style which enlivens all of Notestein's writing.

Yale University Press

Abbreviations

Add.	Additional Manuscripts, British Museum, London.
Adv.	Manuscripts, National Library of Scotland, Edinburgh.
Birch	Birch, Thomas, *The Court and Times of James the First,* ed. with an introduction and notes by [R. F. Williams], London 1848.
Bowyer	Willson, David Harris, ed., *The Parliamentary Diary of Robert Bowyer 1606–1607,* Minneapolis, 1931.
Carte	Carte Manuscripts, Bodleian Library, Oxford.
Cecil papers, Hatfield	Cecil Manuscripts, collection of the Marquess of Salisbury, Hatfield House, Hatfield, Herts.
CJ	*Journals of the House of Commons,* London, 1803–.
CSP Dom.	*Calendar of State Papers, Domestic Series,* London, 1857–59, 1872.
CSP Ven.	*Calendar of the State Papers and Manuscripts relating to English Affairs existing in the Archives and Collections of Venice and in other Libraries in Northern Italy,* 17 vols., London, 1900–25.
D'Ewes	D'Ewes, Sir Simonds, *The Journals of all the Parliaments during the reign of*

	Queen Elizabeth, both of the House of Lords and House of Commons, London, 1682.
DNB	Leslie, Sir Stephen, and Lee, Sir Sidney, eds., *The Dictionary of National Biography*, 22 vols., Oxford, 1960.
Folger	Manuscripts, Folger Shakespeare Library, Washington, D.C.
Foster	Foster, Elizabeth Read, *Proceedings in Parliament 1610*, New Haven and London, 1966.
Harl.	Harleian Manuscripts, British Museum, London.
H.L.R.O.	House of Lords Record Office, London.
HMC	*Historical Manuscripts Commission.*
Holdsworth	Holdsworth, W. S., *A History of English Law*, 12 vols., Boston, 1926.
Lansd.	Lansdowne Manuscripts, British Museum, London.
LJ	*Journals of the House of Lords*, 22 vols., London, 1846.
Parl. Debates 1610	Gardiner, Samuel Rawson, ed., *Parliamentary Debates in 1610*, 1st series, vol. 81, Camden Society, London, 1861.
Rawl.	Rawlinson Manuscripts, Bodleian Library, Oxford.
Royal	Royal Manuscripts, British Museum, London.
Rutland	Rutland Manuscripts, Belvoir Castle.
Somers Tracts	Scott, Walter, ed., *A Collection of Scarce and Valuable Tracts, selected from an infinite number in print and manuscript*, 13 vols., London, 1809–15.
SP	State Papers, Public Record Office, London.
Spedding	James Spedding, *The Letters and the Life of Francis Bacon*, London, 1861–74.

Stowe   Stowe Manuscripts, British Museum, London.

Titus   Titus Manuscripts, British Museum, London.

Winwood   *Memorials of Affairs of State in the Reigns of Q. Elizabeth and K. James I Collected (chiefly) from the Original Papers of the Right Honorable Sir Ralph Winwood, Kt.,* 3 vols., London, 1725.

Introduction

I   T HIS is a history of the House of Commons during the years 1604 to 1610. Intentionally I have made it a narrative account. More than that, I have been at pains to preserve as far as possible the quality of the debate. To do that completely is, of course, not feasible since a member repeated on Friday what he had said on the preceding Monday and possibly a fortnight earlier. I hope, nevertheless, to retain something of the character and flavor of the discussion. S. R. Gardiner used to maintain that the historian needs to know above all else the exact order in which events happened. The same may be said of speeches in the House of Commons. A member's paragraphs and sentences gain meaning and interest if we know what was said just before on the same topic. Such debates, if it is at all possible to present them in narrative form, reveal, as do few types of sources, the way the minds of members worked as they dealt with measures and policies; they thus afford many clues concerning the feel of the time.

But devising a scheme that would maintain the sequence of the debate has not been easy. In a single morning the Commons might discuss wardship, purveyance, and the union with Scotland. The narrator cannot follow such debates without confusing the reader. What I have done is divide the book into seven chapters. Chapters 1, 2, and 3 cover the first three sessions, respectively. Chapters 4 and 5 cover the fourth and fifth sessions, which are really one session with a summer interval. Chapter 6 deals with the committee system and Chapter 7 with the speakership throughout all the sessions. In the first five chapters, when I deal with each session separately, I have chosen the most significant topics of that session and then followed each of those topics through the session. In the third session the union with Scotland happened to be the one major topic discussed by the House; thus I follow only the debates on that subject in Chapter 3. In Chapters 4 and 5 I deal chronologically with grievances, subsidies, and impositions; that plan does not work perfectly because the three topics are so involved with one another, but it seemed better than any other plan.

I have had to limit speeches as well as topics. I have tried to summarize the pivotal speeches as well as those that raise interesting points not brought up by others. But in order to present an orderly narrative, it has been necessary to omit many less significant speeches and less relevant parts of speeches, even those by well-known members.

It is surprising how few men out of the whole body made speeches.[1] Some two score to three score members did most of the talking. Among them were such men as Sir Edwin Sandys, Sir Francis Bacon, Sir Julius Caesar, Richard Martin, Henry Yelverton, Fuller, Wingfield, Hastings, Owen, Lawrence Hyde, Sir Edward Montague, Sir Henry Montague, Hoskins, Hakewill, Brooke of York, Wentworth of Oxford, Nathaniel Bacon, Hare, Holles, Doddridge, Francis Moore, Alford, Thomas James of Bristol, D. James of Newport, Isle of Wight, Harley, Hitcham, Poole, Strode, Hesketh, Dyott, Holcroft, Samuel Lewknor, Twysden, Wiseman, Myddleton (Hugh?), Winch, Fleetwood, Sir John Savile, Dr. Paddy, Sir Edward Greville, Sir Thomas Beaumont, Sir Henry Beaumont, Tate, and Richard Spencer. Each spoke often enough that it is usually possible to gain some notion of his outlook and prejudices.

For the opposition, Sir Edwin Sandys and Richard Martin eventually became the two most significant figures. Sir Francis Bacon was easily the most entertaining spokesman for His Majesty, but Sir George More carried more weight with the average country gentleman. Members must have given an ear to every word uttered by John Hoskins as he condemned crooked paten-

tees. Occasionally an obscure speaker, a Samuel Lewknor for
Bishops Castle in Shropshire, a John Bond for Taunton, a Thomas
Dannet (or Damet) for Yarmouth, provided the House with interesting interludes. But of all the Commoners, Sandys was perhaps the most persuasive.

Now and then it has seemed best to sum up the arguments
without naming the speakers (except in footnotes). The reader
can then weigh the case without referring to the men involved.

The speeches by His Majesty to Parliament I have set down in
some detail; they reveal an unusual personality and exhibit a
point of view that the Commons had constantly to consider.

The other speakers were, three times out of four, old parliamentary hands who had been saying some of the same things in 1597
and 1601 that they were to say from 1604 to 1610. In the later
period, however, their speeches had more drive; they were directed
against a few major grievances that eventually became issues to be
supported. Thus their speeches—the attacks, rebuttals, and coun-
terattacks—occasionally comprise a story, but seldom one with a
happy ending.

It is our misfortune that we have to depend upon so few sources.
For some speeches the only source is the jottings of the Clerk of
the Commons as he scribbled fragments of sentences as fast as he
could. The meaning of some of those fragments is not always clear.
I have tried to interpret such passages, if essential, while at the
same time indicating my own uncertainties.

The debates were sometimes not unlike a tennis game, and it
required a sharp and shifting eye to follow the ball as it was
knocked back and forth. To the narrator it appears that few of
these men had Sir Francis Bacon's gift for summing up the debate
or for answering point by point those on the other side. Most debaters seemed to use the methods taught them in the grammar
school, to start with a premise and work forward from that. Others
worked forward by going over the whole case for one side and
thus repeating much of what had already been said. Nevertheless,
a casual critic of debating is inclined to suspect that the speakers
during the reign of James I were more effective than those of

mid-Elizabethan days but not so accomplished as the orators of the Long Parliament. If there was progress in debating, one is inclined to give less credit for this to the grammar schools and universities than to the accretion of talent, especially legal talent, in the Commons.

The observer of the Jacobean Lower House has to reckon with many types of speechmakers. He will soon discover that not a few who addressed the House were less concerned to convince their hearers than to exhibit their learning, some of it recently acquired. Some could hardly conceal their country simplicity, were given to overstatement about the abuses of which they complained, and liked to alarm their fellows (one member warned the Commons that if they knew what he knew they would tremble for their country).

There were also members who were markedly individual and might have been regarded by their fellows as characters—John Bond, the schoolmaster-physician from Taunton; Walter Gawyn, "a plain fellow" from Wiltshire; and Samuel Lewknor, an M.P. for Bishops Castle and a onetime military man.

Most of the members were serious-minded gentlemen who did not easily shed their gravity. There was no Nicholas Breton in the House to bring smiles with droll phrases. Ned Wymark was counted a wag, but his amusing comments were usually afterthoughts. John Hoskins was called a wit, but he could be deadly serious in St. Stephen's Chapel. It is possible indeed to be deceived about these men; few records remain, and the men who kept them were seldom those who would have appreciated, or have thought to set down on paper, the whimsical interpolation of some inconspicuous squire. The Commons would not have savored subtle words; they would have laughed at those who bored them, or with those who were rudely satirical.

Yet those Roman senators—for so some of them thought of themselves—however sober in manner, were not to be despised. They were typical of what may be called the upper middle classes, or the minor aristocracy, and they were not incapable of arriving at wise decisions. They interest the historian, for their kind dominated English public life from the last decades of Elizabeth's reign till the first decades of Victoria's. In the reign of James I, when public opinion had few means of expression, they were the voice of England. Mixed in among them were a few businessmen from London and country towns, the men from the towns possibly of somewhat the same type as Shakespeare's father but more well to do. They were often knowledgeable and could speak to the point.

The experience of the country gentlemen was not bad preparation for lawmaking. Many of them had been justices of the peace and had discovered for themselves the vagueness and inadequacy of many statutes and the wrongs still to be found in the common law. Many of the M.P.'s were investors in the trading companies and thus likely to gain some notion of the economic problems of the nation. But most M.P.'s had not experienced foreign travel and acquaintance with men beyond the Channel and the North Sea.

Their education did less to help them adapt to parliamentary activities than did their experience. In the grammar schools and in the schools now known as public schools, they were drilled in the classics and especially in Latin grammar. If they were sent as young men to one of the universities, they acquired facility in reading and writing Latin prose and familiarity with logic. The only history they were taught was in connection with the classics— Greek and Roman. From the schools and universities many of them went to the Inns of Court in London, where they learned to prepare cases and to argue and debate. They might pick up a little English history as it entered into their legal studies.

If they learned little history, they were heir to much. From the years of the first two Henrys the English people were accustomed to local self-government; from the early Edwards they had been sending representatives to Westminster. By the middle of Elizabeth's reign some of the members were looking forward to a day when they might share in policy making. They hoped to do more than rubber-stamp the proposals of the Privy Council, but the great Queen would not agree. With the new monarch, however, they hoped to assert themselves and gain some of the influence at Westminster they had in Barsetshire.

If history has any logic—a disputable if—the logic of the English past called for more influence by the knights of the shire and the burgesses. That was roughly what Hakewill and Whitelocke were to talk about in 1610, their historical heritage. At long last it was beginning to become something more than a dream.

It was to be three generations or more before that dream began to be realized. The English move slowly. If the men needed in Parliament were in short supply, if the members were sometimes children when it came to practical statesmanship, then there was a case for strong kingship. James VI of Scotland, now James I of England, felt himself abundantly qualified for that role. Moreover, had the Crown availed itself of the talent at hand, it was possibly better fitted than 80 percent of the Commons for making decisions. Robert Cecil, a long-time member of the Commons, now Earl of Salisbury, was well qualified to guide the state in foreign affairs and not without imagination in domestic matters. But he aimed to be, and had to be, the shadow of his sovereign, and that handicapped him.

The historian would find out much about the membership, but in addition he would learn who pulled the strings; who directed the program of those upholding the Crown and of those in opposition. The many volumes of the Cecil Correspondence and the State Papers Domestic at the Public Record Office afford answers to many questions about the spokesmen for the Crown. It is not easy, however, to discover the plans of those in opposition. The members who schemed to hold His Majesty in check set down little on paper, or at least little of which we know. The student of these limited sources comes to suspect that the power of the opposition rested first upon the leadership of Sir Edwin Sandys and those associated with him and second upon the domination in committees of members determined to render the House useful and significant.

How Sandys attained his influence over the Lower House within two sessions remains a mystery. He was in his mid-forties, that is, past middle age, as they reckoned then. A quiet man, he seemed hardly to have lifted his finger to gain his ascendancy. We must not forget, however, that we have little evidence upon which to base this assumption. In his portrait he looks less like a parliamentarian than a philosopher. In his motions and speeches he was a moderate given neither to overstatement nor to enthusiasm. He might indeed have flourished in the eighteenth century. It is a temptation to say that he was not gifted with words, and yet, in two of his most important speeches, he found the words that suited the situation. He had a greater gift for paragraphs: they were clear, orderly, and effective. He did not appear to play up to his audience, either to the gentlemen of the fields or to those of his own kind who had Cicero and Plutarch and Diodorus Siculus on their shelves. Yet he had a knack for drawing men along with him in a common pursuit of reason and of English liberty. Liberty was one of his favorite terms, and reason his watchword. When he spotted the next thing to do, he moved deliberately to accomplish it. He was not one to jump into the fray nor to carry the flag in front. Some of his everyday wisdom he probably gained from his old teacher and friend, Richard Hooker, author of *Ecclesiastical Polity*. Above all, through travel and the exchange of ideas with English and continental friends he learned to use the past and look to the future.

Richard Martin was of another breed. His quick and apt answers won the notice of Salisbury. Moreover, he had the gift, rare then, of being "facete," and his facetiousness seems to have proved no hindrance to his parliamentary career. Among his friends were Ben Jonson and Sir Henry Wotton. Members would choose him to be Chairman or Moderator of the Committee of the Whole House. In debate he stuck to the main point and made no long discourse. Only once did he—in his anticlerical zeal—fly off at a tangent, and he was so useful a House-of-Commons man that the episode is best overlooked.

Under the leadership of Sandys, Martin, and their allies, the majority group in the Commons moved toward increased influence. It did not always seem so, and there were discouraging intervals, but they had good cards and, when they realized this, played them slowly and cannily. The constant referral of matters to committees and subcommittees took time and enabled them to draw upon the maturest judgment of every committeeman. They moved with more dignity and assurance than they had in the days of the Queen. It must be admitted that, after the Gunpowder Plot, the wilder men in the House asserted themselves; they pressed for harsher laws against recusants and would have taken children over nine from their Catholic parents. The Commons could still lose their heads. They grew excited over Dr. Cowell's *The Interpreter* and were about to punish him. Happily, the leaders of the House decided that the antiquarian with a good deal of uncoordinated learning in his head was not a threat to the Commonwealth. It was easier to arrive at this decision, because the King agreed with it. Reports were brought into the House that members were being denounced in the universities for disloyalty to the Crown, but the matter was not pursued. The leaders of the House were not going to worry about mere dons. The McCarthys of that day were allowed to make their speeches, and Dr. Cowell was left to his folios. The Establishment—it would be wrong to use the term before 1607—in St. Stephens' tolerated only a modicum of nonsense.

The Establishment, in its use of committees and subcommittees, was only continuing a system that had developed rapidly during the reign of the Queen. By 1610 subcommittees were becoming a conspicuous feature of procedure. Unfortunately, we do not have the elaborate parliamentary diaries that illuminate the procedural methods of the 1620s, but we have enough evidence to make us look over the activities of the subcommittees with curiosity. The Great Committee, the Grand Committee, and more often now the Committee of the Whole House, usually met in the afternoon [2] and dealt with more significant matters, with decisions concerning policy, for example. The announcement of those decisions was often left to subcommittees. The subcommittee was likely to include Sandys, Martin, Fuller, Nathaniel Bacon, and others, a considerable proportion of whom were not to be regarded as followers of the Court. In other words, members who formed the backbone of the opposition were engaged in the wording of bills, petitions, and resolutions. We shall never know for certain what happened. It is unlikely that many more parliamentary diaries with details concerning the membership and proceedings of subcommittees will turn up. If we examine the situation closely, we can piece together a good deal that suggests rather than proves explanations of the success of those working with Sandys.

In the first place, whenever bills and petitions were to be formulated, there was a need for lawyers, and they were quickly placed on subcommittees. But the lawyers, and in particular those in the Commons, were protagonists of the common-law courts and resented alike the church and administrative courts. They were likely to align themselves with those who wished to see grievances abolished.

It was not only lawyers who were inclined to worry over grievances but also country gentlemen, many of whom were justices of the peace. They soon discovered that those patents granted by His Majesty and the special courts that had sprung up interfered with the order they, as justices of the peace, sought to maintain in their communities and that the courts nullified policies they were sworn to carry out. In consequence, they were likely to vote with Sandys and his group in Parliament.

The method of setting up subcommittees tended to work against His Majesty's influence in the Commons. When a subcommittee was proposed, the leaders of the House would sometimes name in the motion those who were to constitute the membership, or the members of the large committee may have called out the names of those who would form the subcommittee. For some reason, most of the men named were not likely to follow the lead of the Crown. We may guess that Privy Councillors, with their many duties, often failed to attend the large afternoon committees and thus missed the chance to nominate members of the subcommittees. On the other hand, such supporters of His Majesty as Bacon, Caesar, Sir George More, and Sir Walter Cope were often active on large committees and would probably have called out names for the subcommittees.

There were other reasons why the large committee might have

selected members of what might be called the opposition. The extreme wing among the Puritan members of Parliament formed an active and aggressive group, and other members with bees in their bonnets were likely to be present at the committee in the afternoon. Less zealous members would find the morning sessions quite enough for the day; they would perhaps slip back to their inns in the City and thus be missing when subcommittees were being nominated.

On one occasion Sandys gave away his interest in the membership of subcommittees. On May 18, 1610, the King demanded an answer from the committee as to whether they would give him satisfaction. His Majesty was on his high horse and might in a fury dismiss Parliament. The House resolved in committee to name a subcommittee to draw up an answer to the King. Sandys moved that the subcommittee might be chosen by a viva-voce vote on each name proposed, as had been done in choosing members to serve on the Commission for the Union. This suggestion, doubtless put forward by Sandys to ensure a subcommittee to his liking, was resisted. It was proposed instead that every man who had spoken should be on the committee. That was old custom, and Sandys could do nothing but assent.

His proposal was probably unnecessary. The Committee on Grievances (now a Grand Committee, or a Great Committee, or a Committee of the Whole House) was becoming increasingly important, and its method of procedure tended to fill subcommittees with those very men who wanted to see grievances done away with. In the large committee, which considered only those grievances brought in by members, the grievances presented were debated at length. If considerable differences of opinion developed about a given grievance, it would be referred to an appropriate subcommittee. Those who had spoken about the grievance were naturally given places on the subcommittee, and they were likely to be those most troubled by the grievance. Those who defended the grievance were often men who had a patent or monopoly, or their friends. These men, who had profited from the grievance, were likely to ask for a delay until counsel could be called to present the case for those connected with the grievance. In most instances they were not anxious for the limelight; hence the subcommittee sometimes had an impressive majority for abolishing the grievance.

The work of the subcommittees was seldom revised, either by the Committee of the Whole House or by any Grand Committee. Those who objected to something the subcommittee had put into a document would soon find out that the phrasing adopted by that subcommittee was not to be changed by the large committee in the afternoon. The decisions of that large committee, or of the Committee of the Whole House, were passed in the House, and such passage became a mere formality. The result was that in nearly every case the work of a subcommittee was not modified in any particular.

From such evidence as we now have, it would appear possible that Sandys, Martin, Croft, Fuller, Strode, Wentworth, and others were winning because they could command majorities in the afternoon session and thus fill subcommittees with those upon whom they could depend.

The historian who attempts a chronological account of the House of Commons meets with problems that are not easy to solve. For example, how should he deal with special episodes? On March 28, 1607, the members of the Lower House were debating whether the Scots could be induced to make concessions when Bacon remarked that no beast or bird was taught anything until it had been fed. Here was a piece of natural history, and we can imagine that it suddenly awakened the men from the shires. Sir Roger Owen took up at once the ornithological problem, which was of more vital interest to them than were the Scots. Should the historian put the bird-feeding story into his record? Or mention it in his introduction?

Several times the Clerk recorded a long silence in the House. That body was worried and was expressing its discontent in its own negative way. No doubt it is also true that the members were at a loss as to what they should do next and were not quite ready to offer suggestions.

Once a member was addressing the House when he suddenly realized that his colleagues were looking at one another as if to ask, "Did you hear what was just said?" At another time a member, censured sharply for what he had said the day before, gave an angry retort. The Clerk usually omitted such interludes from his minutes, but they were recorded briefly by Bowyer or by some gossipy letter writer such as Beaulieu or Samuel Calvert. Do they belong in this narrative? The answer depends upon whether the episode was typical of what took place in the Commons.

It has been impossible without a considerable staff of research assistants to examine the wills of members of the 1604–1610 Parliament and to find out the financial status of each member, how much land he held and on what tenures, where and to what degree he was educated, and what were his prejudices about politics and religion. I have a card catalogue of the members and have set down many chronological data and records of speeches made in the House in Elizabethan and early Jacobean days. In introducing a member I have been at pains to indicate in a phrase or sentence something of his personality and outlook. But the facts I might gather would be few compared with those available to the Parliament Trust, which will, I hope, in due time deal with the early Stuart period and will be able to command new source materials from all over England.

Many of the members had powerful patrons who by their influence had found seats for them in the House of Commons. Such men as the Earls of Salisbury, Northampton, Bedford, and great nobles arranged for the election of a considerable number of the M.P.'s. Yet the *Commons Journals* and other records would seem to show that, however much great landed gentlemen intervened to send certain adherents to the House of Commons, those members made less effort than might have been expected to vote as their patrons would have wished. No doubt some great lords now and then put pressure to bear upon members, but evidence of such pressure is hard to find.

Economic considerations, of course, played a role in the voting of members. The Bill of Assarts was carried in the Lower House, in spite of strong opposition from the Government. Members were afraid that some of their titles to land as against their overlord, the King, were not too secure. The passage of the Bill of Assarts would make them rest easy in their beds. The Free Trade Bill of 1604, in its final form, had the backing of many country gentlemen who were making investments in the joint-stock companies rather than in the "regulated companies." [3]

Only once, so far as I can recall, was an important motion passed by a narrow plus or minus majority. The resolution to take up and vote on the Subsidy Bill of March 18, 1606, received a majority of one. Many bills less agreeable to His Majesty passed with a majority of twenty or thirty. The opposition, to call it by that name, had a working majority of about that number.

One must ask questions about the considerable minority who supported their King. The many speeches against wardship, purveyance, and the other serious abuses of the time demonstrate that nearly half the members voted against reform when it came to a showdown.

There were good reasons for standing by the King: knighthoods, baronetcies, and even peerages to be had by the faithful. Perhaps equally effective were the many pensions granted by the King, the wardships bestowed, and the recusancy fines farmed out to the loyal. Fortunes could be made by the well-disposed. One of the well-to-do Myddletons remarked that the activities of the Government were calculated to take money from the poor and funnel it into the hands of the rich. Many of the latter had overspent themselves in keeping up with the Court and hoped to be compensated by it.

It was not wholly economic advantage that moved members to vote with the courtiers. The abuses discussed were not new: some dated back to the time of their grandfathers. These men feared "innovation," but there was more to it than that. A deep sense of loyalty to the throne, even when its occupant was a Scot whose ways were not always those of the English, moved many a member. One has only to read Shakespeare to understand the pervasive loyalty to the sovereign.

There were a few members, at least, who exhibited a loyalty to certain political principles. They shied away, for example, from legislation that might have limited personal freedom. On June 6, 1604, a bill against popish books was brought in, and Sir Edward Grevill argued that such a measure would take away the freedom of the individual.[4] Sir Henry Beaumont declared that the bill would set up an inquisition. It was, however, committed by a majority of ten votes. On November 6, 1610, when His Majesty was asking for a great deal of money, much more than the Commons believed they could possibly grant him, Sir Thomas Beaumont asserted that the needs of the King could not be supplied without driving the people to great want. Then he went on to say that the statute of Elizabeth, which was intended only for the repressing of papists, now served to "check other men," meaning that out of that statute had arisen church courts that had become a threat to the liberty of the individual. It is interesting that opposition to Puritan legislation was not unconnected with the fear of interference with liberty. When a bill was brought in from a committee to restrain arrests on the Sabbath, Hakewill pronounced it the "absurdest bill that ever passed from a committee." Sabbatarian legislation was steadily resisted in the last days of the great Queen by a Parliament that was, in general, Puritan, and it was not included among the many Puritan measures proposed in the first year of James's Parliament. Even Bacon admitted that the King's greatest honor was to govern subjects "moderately free."

II   T HE speech of the new sovereign at the opening of Parliament in 1604 enabled members to form some estimate of his mind and outlook. He had been in England for the better part of a year and was still elated by the way in which he had been received. His address to the two Houses had been carefully prepared and revealed a personage of learning with a capacity to state his views clearly, if not briefly. He was ready to set forth at once his policy concerning religion, and it was not one that pleased the more zealous Puritans. Nor were they comforted by what he said about the Catholic Church. That body was, he declared, the mother church, and he seemed to hope for a Christian union. He did not wish to persecute Roman Catholics who were loyal to the Crown, but he was unwilling to tolerate those who believed that the Pope should have authority over kings.

To Parliament he offered a certain amount of advice—he was never wanting in that commodity—urging them as magistrates and judges to be impartial. They were answerable to him, and he to God.

This was the first of many speeches and messages addressed to Parliament. They were full of allusions to himself and of generalizations about kingship, a subject to which he had given thought and on which he had read. He did not minimize its significance. Such wisdom as he had—the Speaker of the Lower House had alluded to him as a Solomon—he had picked up from books rather than from the close observation of his fellowmen in action.

As a king of Scotland he had a good record: by hook or crook he had established his rule over the unruly. Yet he had no gift for winning the public. He had none of the late Queen's sincere delight in meeting her subjects of every class. He was too enclosed within himself to be greatly interested in others, and his indifference was soon sensed. Moreover, he had known enough of conspiracies to be afraid of crowds. The cynical whispered that he was more interested in the deer he hunted than in the crowds around him.

In Parliament he soon encountered resistance of a kind to which he was unaccustomed, and he lost patience with it. He never understood the English way of threshing things out, which many English country gentlemen had learned in their long experience with local government. The tedious debates in Parliament seemed to him a waste of time. After all, he could tell them what to do. Had he not ordered matters in Scotland by the stroke of his pen? As the debates went on week after week, he became so enraged, wrote the French ambassador, that he could neither eat nor sleep. He really wanted to be reasonable, but his whole experience had convinced him that royal power was best. He steadily lost the good opinion of his subjects that he seemed to have had at the beginning. The same French ambassador wrote of the decline of the King's prestige: "What must be the state and condition of a Prince whom the preachers publicly assailed, whom the comedians . . . bring upon the stage, whose wife attends these representations to enjoy the laugh against her husband." On March 25, 1605, Samuel Calvert wrote to Winwood: "The plays do not forbear to present upon their stage the whole course of this present time, not sparing either King, State, or religion, in so great absurdity, and with such liberty that any would be afraid to hear them." Whether these reports from two different sources were exaggerations, I do not know. My friends among the scholars of the English drama do not recall and plays that fit the descriptions given here. It would have been a dangerous business openly to satirize the King, but it is not impossible that some actor or actors in playing a royal role imitated the mannerisms of James I. His gait, his way of talking, and his marked Scottish accent would have lent themselves to imitation.

His unpopularity with the English public was accentuated by stories of his extravagance. It was said that he spent £100,000 a year on his household, as against £50,000 spent before. Cecil apparently said or wrote something to the King about the expenses of the Court, for His Majesty wrote him: "It is a horror to me to think upon the weight of my place, the greatness of my debts, and the smallness of my means." He hoped that Cecil, as a good physician, would find the cure, so that he would be able to subsist with honor and credit, that is, find him more money. Meanwhile he went on distributing gifts with a free hand. In October 1606 Cecil learned that the King had been told by Lord Dunbar (formerly Sir George Home) that Cecil saw a fatality in the state, that it would never be rich. The King was assured by Cecil that he was busy with the problems of the Exchequer and was doing his best to find possible sources of income.

Even more immediate in His Majesty's view than the need for money was the confirmation of the union of the two kingdoms by Parliament. He had assumed that his scheme for union would be ratified quickly by both Houses, but when Parliament moved with deliberation, he became "very melancholious." The Venetian ambassador wrote to the Doge that James had assumed that the opposition was confined to the Lower House, but had learned that some in the Upper House were urging the Commons to be firm.[5]

It is possible to make allowances for James. He never did understand about landed gentlemen, of whom the House of Commons largely consisted, and their place in the English scene. He liked good-looking young men and noblemen of long lineage. He had no second sight as to who would prove wise and who useful. At times he behaved as if he were afraid of the English. On one occasion he alluded scornfully to kings who were afraid of their subjects, as if subconsciously he were aware of such a weakness in himself. The least slur upon the Scots roused his resentment.

In his brief *Memoirs,* Sir Robert Carey, later earl of Monmouth, gave clues as to the ways of the King. He quoted an acquaintance as having said to him that he knew the King better than Carey and that, if His Majesty perceived in him a discontented mind, he would never give him favor. The judgment coincided with that of an Irish Lord at the English Court who said of James: "He loved those he talked to to be as jovial as himself, especially when he was conscious that he had given them occasion to be otherwise."

The Court was full of old hands who watched the comings and goings at Whitehall and who became almost professional appraisers of the King's moods and fancies. To them James was no mystery. He preferred men whom he could tease and expected them to join in the laughter against themselves. The King liked to be the center of a merry party, preferably with several Scots around. He would poke fun at his servants, the lowly and the great, and they dared not answer. His humor could become bawdy, but was seldom really funny—at least to our ears—and never subtle.

His Majesty had no sixth sense as to the kind of man to whom he was writing. Week in and week out he sent off letters from his hunting headquarters to Cecil in London. He had not the least notion of the sensitive gentleman to whom he was offering in detail his opinions and jests. His Majesty was not "of the better sort," as the discerning John Chamberlain would have put it. He patronized his minister in a way that must have required Cecilian fortitude to endure. When James condescended, wrote a French ambassador later in the reign, he was vulgar.

We learn much about the King from the French ambassadors at his Court, who wrote many letters to Henry IV and to Villeroy. The French King and his minister were naturally interested in James I. What kind of man was this Scot who had become King of England? In what direction would he jump, toward an entente with France, or one with Spain? The ambassadors wrote at length giving details of their interviews with the King. Their narratives are so vivid that the historian feels he is eavesdropping behind an arras. One can hear the ambassador pouring out honeyed words about the greatness of James and the awe with which he was regarded in continental courts. One can almost witness the glow of satisfaction coming over His Majesty's face; it did not escape the ambassador. He threw out more line, and the King swallowed it eagerly. His Majesty had a sudden conviction; he was determined to take the action worthy of a great and powerful sovereign. Were not he and Henry IV the two great Kings of the last hundred years? The story the ambassador told the King of France made Henry and Villeroy laugh in a most unchristian way.

James once remarked that no king in the world was so little subject to flattery as he. Yet he was so easily overwhelmed by it that his courtiers should have seen to it that he was not exposed alone to wily ambassadors. Henry IV discovered that the ruler of England was naïve and undependable. Eventually the French King was to characterize his fellow sovereign as a "fraudulent trickster from his birth." It is better to say that he was a weak man, easily swayed by those near him.

The new English King was unsure of himself. He had moved into a world he knew not of. Some of the English at Court and the gentry who flocked to Whitehall to pay their respects were more sophisticated and worldly wise than the Highland nobles and Lowland lairds he had known in Edinburgh. James talked and talked to these new acquaintances, as an insecure man would do. The English courtiers listened and seldom interrupted. The more they heard, the more they thought of the greatness and high majesty of their late Queen and the contrast between the two monarchs. They learned that the King was inclined to listen, when he stopped talking, to the last man who had been able to gain his attention. Sir Robert believed that he had been promised an office that paid handsomely in fees and required little attention, only to learn, a fortnight later, that the office had been given to Sir John.

It was much the same with matters of general concern. His Majesty would promise that this or that abuse would be corrected. No doubt he meant well, but courtiers who suddenly realized that their patents or concessions were endangered would appeal to the kindly Scot, and the promises would be forgotten.

His weakness, indeed, was in part that he could not make up his mind about the various policies urged upon him. Samuel Calvert, an observer of the Court, suggested that James would sometimes leave town for hunting trips because he could not decide which policy to pursue. The result was that he often shifted course and could not be depended upon. He was fortunate in that few would venture to accuse him openly of duplicity. An occasional matter-of-fact speechmaker might suggest to the Commons, when His Majesty had offered to remedy a certain grievance, that he had made the same offer before, and that nothing had come of it. Some of the more active Puritans hinted in their writings that the King had a weak memory. Loyal Catholics, who deserved well of their sovereign, would have told, and now and then did tell, about his talent for forgetting his promises to them when he no longer needed their support. Thus it is not surprising, when quid pro quos were under discussion, that Members of Parliament demanded security from the King regarding his part of the bargain. It is hard for the best of administrators, when pushed by factions at cross-purposes, to be utterly truthful, and James was no administrator.

Members of Parliament were decently reticent about the ways of

His Majesty, but ambassadors from abroad, and even his own somewhat indiscreet Queen, put him down as a weak ruler. James may have picked up that judgment of him from some candid countryman of the North, for he once declared that he did not intend to go down to posterity as a weak king.

Had he been a strong sovereign, had he pursued a consistent policy, had he steadily said no to the Commons in the firm but not unfriendly manner of the great Queen, he might have kept them in subjection and possibly have put off for a generation or more the troubles and struggles that were to come.

Had he been consistent in another direction, had he been able to understand that country gentlemen who had some sway in their respective shires craved it also at Westminster and that they had the future with them, had he been willing to go part of the way with them, he might have awakened one day to find himself a popular leader of his people. After all, Sandys, Martin, and other figures in the opposition were moderate and reasonable men, and I suspect they would have played ball with him.

For he was not wholly in the wrong. For all his weakness, want of imagination, and high-flown language, he had a case and could state it. In October 1604 he wrote Cecil: "This far only I recommend to your consideration, that the King's old prerogative in continual possession may be as great security as a private subject's old possession, and that the abuse of the King's predecessor be not ground to deprive his successor of his lawful and rightly-used privileges." He said much else in favor of his own absolutist philosophy. We need not go into the backgrounds of that; they have been traced by students of political theory. Of course, James was an egoist by nature and inheritance, and his self-importance fitted in nicely with his notions of government.

There is an obvious and not ingenious paradox concerning the Scottish King and the English Queen before him. She had little to say about her royal prerogative, but in her later years laid down the law to Parliament and shut off, for brief periods, those who ventured to speak up. James talked at length and often of his great power; he confided to the French ambassador that he could do what he liked and that none could say him nay. Sandys said of James, knowing no doubt that his words would reach the royal ears: "As his Majesty in all his speeches was pleased to term himself the powerfulest King in all the world." Whether Sandys was poking a little fun at his sovereign we shall never know. But we can guess that the King would not have resented the quotation and would not have regarded it as humorous.

It was part of the King's nature that he could not take opposition calmly or even reasonably. In December 1610 he wrote to the Privy Council because he was annoyed with his advisers in that body. They had done nothing to the speechmakers in the House of Commons, whose complaints he resented. "We are sure no House save the House of hell could have found so many."

> Our ill fortune is this, that having lived so long in the Kingdom where we were born, we came out of it with an unstained reputation and without any grudge in the people's hearts, but for wanting of us. Wherein we have misbehaved ourself here we know not, nor can we ever yet learn. . . . In short the Lower House . . . have imperilled and annoyed our health, wounded our reputation, emboldened all ill-natured people, encroached upon many of our privileges, and plagued our purse with their delays.

With all his high-and-mighty attitudes, he once in a while stepped down from his throne. He was used to addressing Cecil as "my little beagle," and in one letter he signed himself, "Your fellow hound." On another occasion he wrote Cecil: "God knows I am but a man and in many ways inferior to many other men." God may have known it, but James recognized it only at rare intervals.

It will be seen in later chapters that the King was constantly hectoring the House of Commons. Now he was a schoolmaster talking to misbehaving boys, now a minister preaching the gospel of kingship, then an angry god from Olympus, and occasionally a kindly father willing to forgive foolish children. In all these roles he patronized proud gentlemen, and I suspect that this attitude hurt him most with the M.P.'s. He patronized men because he did not know better; he had none near, not even an oncoming Scot, to talk with as one man to another. Such a relationship he would not have encouraged.

He did, however, encourage those who offered him undiscriminating adulation, such as Henry Howard, Earl of Northampton. If others failed, he could even flatter himself. "Never any King," he confided to Parliament, "was willinger to observe the laws than I, who will go down to my grave with this honor to me, that I never gave unjust sentence." That self-satisfaction, so characteristic of his speeches, is also to be seen in the portraits of him.

When the Great Contract failed, Sir Thomas Lake quoted the King as saying that it was not unknown how far his honor had been wounded in this Parliament. That body had made itself into a confederacy and a bulwark for the protection of extravagant humors and conceits; his name, his dignity, his sovereignty, and all things else had been so tossed, questioned, and censored as seldom had been done to any monarch. He could not determine its scope unless there was some design to lay the foundation for a popular state.

His Majesty was overwrought. He would have found it hard to name a single M.P. who did not support a monarchy, in some degree limited, of course, by Parliament. Sir Henry Neville, looking back three and a half years later, observed that the King and Parliament had parted with distaste and acrimony and that apprehensions as to the future were common both at home and abroad. He maintained, nevertheless, that he knew the leaders of the Commons, that he had lived and conversed with them and was familiar with their inmost thoughts. They had not acted, he believed, out of evil feeling toward His Majesty; they had wished to do the King a service. Neville was, I am inclined to believe, right in his diagnosis. The leaders of the Commons were not enthusiastic about the King, but he was their King, and they would have been glad to support him, if they could. It is true that they were troubled about certain long-existing and serious abuses, wardship and purveyance, outworn relics of another age and long overdue for reform. The Commons had been able to do little with the aging Queen. Now was the time to push for changes. Had His Majesty been in earnest about doing away with these abuses, he might have been voted, in spite of his extravagance, the subsidies he needed.

By the end of 1610 the King was beginnng, I suspect, to lose his hold on affairs of state. By 1614 his changeableness and his confusion were becoming evident. More and more he was leaning upon Somerset and then upon George Villiers, later duke of Buckingham. His speeches were no longer the reasoned arguments of his first years as King of England. He was going downhill intellectually.

III   FEW men brought more experience to the office of Secretary of State than Robert Cecil. His father, the great Lord Burghley of Elizabeth's reign, had taken pains to coach his younger and more promising son for some such post as he himself had held. From 1584 to 1601 the son had served in six Parliaments. He had lived abroad long enough to familiarize himself with the French language and to become conversant with the politics and diplomacy of the major European courts. For several years he carried on for the Queen the labors of a Secretary of State and in 1596 was formally named to that exacting post. On the death of his father in 1598 he became the Privy Councillor closest to the Queen. Cecil played a major role in putting James VI of Scotland on the English throne and became James's Principal Secretary of State. He had to deal with administrative problems and at the same time to speak in Parliament for the King. In that capacity he had to cultivate the arts of persuasion and to look back and forward.

Here we are concerned with his relation to Parliament. He had to stand well with the House of Commons, where money grants originated, and thus he had to think of money, of its acquisition and expenditure. That was no light assignment at a time when the cost of government, as of everything else, was rising rapidly. What was more serious, he had to contend with a King who believed that he had come into his own, a wealthy kingdom, and that he could, and should, be generous to his followers. For some time Cecil was able to keep on the good side of his master, who at first appreciated his efforts to economize. Cecil was told that His Majesty said of him: "There was never a King in the world had such a servant as I have of him; he is passionate and angry when I give in an irresponsible suit, but yet he is careful to have me give what for my honor I must give." That was not all of the story. Now and then Cecil was able to stop grants by the King; more often he did not hear of them until it was too late. If he complained in the mildest terms of the waste in the King's service, his words were quickly relayed to the sovereign, who was not always as pleased as he had seemed at first. Cecil had to offer the best explanations he could, but it was something of a handicap that he was now in the Upper House. In May 1604 he was created Baron Cecil of Essendine; in August of the same year he was made Viscount Cranborne; and in May 1605 he was named Earl of Salisbury. For the sake of convenience, I shall continue to call him Cecil.

Of his activities in the Lords we know a great deal from two manuscripts that have lately come into circulation, but they help us only for the session of 1610. From them it is easy to determine that by that time Cecil had the Upper House in the hollow of his hand. Lord Zouch, Lord Saye and Sele, an archbishop, and a bishop or two might differ with Cecil now and then, but in general the peers listened to him and voted with him.

Why were the peers, most with titles older than that of Cecil and not unaware of their dignified and stately role, ready to follow the lead of a newcomer to their circle? The Upper House was slowly becoming less active than the Lower. Moreover, with the decline of their old feudal dominance in the shires, many of the peers had lost some of their interest in political affairs. A more urgent reason why they listened to Cecil was that many of them were in debt to the Crown, or to others, and those debts were in many instances long overdue. Meanwhile, at Court the peers observed the new King dispensing largess to those who flattered him. Here was no parsimonious Queen, but a beneficent King. Great earls, viscounts, and barons formed in line to receive. In one instance James promised a peer a thousand pounds a year and was told that such a sum was not nearly enough; his debts ran into thousands of pounds. It was prudent for peers to stand well with Cecil, who might speak a word for them.

It was not so easy for Cecil from a seat in the Lords to get his way with the Commons. He could, however, in the conferences of the joint committees of the two Houses be heard by fifty or one hundred men from the Commons, some of them the leaders of the House. Furthermore, his speeches in the conferences were relayed within a day or two to the whole House.

It was for the critical fourth session of Parliament, that of the first half of 1610, that Cecil, who by now had had long experience with the Commons, made ready. It was necessary, he realized, to conciliate the Commons—to persuade them, if possible, of the immediate needs of His Majesty. Hence he prepared facts and figures for the use of the Privy Council. He put forward proposals, the most important being that for a contribution by way of subsidies. He foresaw, he wrote to the Council, that the Commons, or at least some of them, would move to put off consent to any subsidy until they were assured that the King would offer "retribution," that is, would do away with the major abuses of which they complained.

Cecil anticipated that members would come to Parliament with as many arguments as wit and will could muster. To meet those arguments would become the duty of those in the King's service. Unfortunately, those officials had other pressing obligations and distractions. Further, at the moment when Cecil was preparing a memorandum, there was no time left for officials to assemble and arm themselves against "prepared and studied arguments." The arguments likely to be brought forward in the Commons were not to be answered by "fair tales and promises." Cecil's words suggested that he was aware of the King's habit of putting off or of forgetting promises. Cecil was making ready, but he was far from cheerful about the outlook and aware of his own inadequacy. Some things, he had to admit, were beyond his exact remembrance; he had come into the winter of his age (he was forty-seven). A member of the Lower House might put a case that would be hard for him to refute offhand. Nothing had been done, he remarked, to satisfy the country. He then alluded to the abuse of purveyance; it was still used in as many offices as ever and by the same mean instruments, that is, by irresponsible officials.

In anticipation of the same Parliament, Cecil drew up a statement for His Majesty. He wished to fill in the financial picture: what had been the expenses; what expenses could not be avoided; what extraordinary expenses had come up, and which of them might come up again; what debts the King had incurred; what Crown lands had been saved and what improvements in financing had been initiated since His Majesty had mounted the English throne. He hoped to see prepared a docket of the objections that might be raised in Parliament and of the answers that should be offered. What course should be pursued to preserve His Majesty from sudden necessity? He looked forward "to the furtherance of all other things which may give ornament to the Kingdom, to an increase to the industry of the people. All of which may be apprehended under the title of general policy, too much neglected in this State, where we have a King and Country so well composed for such a work." He seemed to implying that England had the advantage of a King and Council working in cooperation with Parliament. After a close consultation with Sir Julius Caesar of the Exchequer, he undertook to elucidate the financial situation in his first long speech before Parliament. For an imaginative program of what ought to be done, he found little support from the Privy Council and less from the King. Planning ahead was not the fashion in high places. Moreover the few Privy Councillors in the Lower House were not men who looked ahead and who could make debates significant. Any plans Cecil might have dreamed of to make over the state and put it on a firm financial basis were destined to be frustrated.

He was given no free hand, but he had influence. Despite his reservations about himself, he was a debater skilled in making a case for his royal master. His speeches were orderly and easy to follow. He had little faith in eloquence in a popular assembly; by eloquence he meant, I assume, fine talk, classical allusions, and mellifluous words. Cecil believed in plainness, in sincerity, and, above all, in the use of reason. But reason is not always simple, and it became necessary at times to set forth the deeper meaning behind events and public statements. In doing so he was occasionally too subtle for his audience.

Cecil asked that debates be kept on a high plane. In his first long speech, on February 15, 1610, he remarked: "There is no commonwealth but is full of grievances . . . lay them open, deal in them with respect to sovereignty, and speak without bitterness, and we [the Lords, for whom he professed to be speaking] will join with you." He was asking for moderation. He pleaded, too, for some dignity in debate: "For we are not carried by sense and affections in this Senate as are particular persons in their private wrongs." He also appealed for patriotism. On June 11, 1610, when begging for money, he said: "Think of the motion with some compassion for the strange state of England." At that one point he came close to using emotional appeal, but he seldom failed, nevertheless, to put his case cogently. Dudley Carleton wrote to Edmondes, then ambassador in Brussels, that in the dispute over the Great Contract Cecil was handicapped because those opposed to him came well prepared, but Cecil nevertheless gave "extraordinary contentment." He could speak to the point on the spur of the moment because of his thorough grasp of the subjects likely to come up. I suspect that the peers spoke so rarely—of which Cecil complained —because they had found out by experience that he was better informed than they. At one time Cecil told the Lords that in matters legal they were not able to meet with the Lower House, but admitted that in matters of government and state it was otherwise. On May 4, 1610, he informed the Commons that the offers they had put forward were not equivalent to the concessions the King was proposing to make. As for the subsidy, he assured them that they did not pay one-twentieth part of their estates, that is, as I understand it, one-twentieth part of the annual rentals they received.

He had to speak plainly and often; many times he must have become discouraged at the response of the Commons. It was the policy of the committee members in conference not to engage in the give-and-take for which Cecil was always pleading, but merely to listen and report back to the House what had been said. Cecil suspected that the Commons were reluctant to share in the cut-and-thrust of argument because they stood in awe of the greatness of the Lords. It was the force of the argument, he insisted, that counted.

Another problem, which he did not mention, must have worried him. The Lower House included few members competent and willing to make the case for His Majesty. It seemed that some of the dullest and most pontifical members arose to speak for their sovereign, but there were exceptions. Francis Bacon, who spoke frequently, was vivid and entertaining and occasionally reached the heights of common sense. Yet I am not sure that he carried weight either with country gentlemen who found him too facile or with his fellows of the legal profession who possibly missed the citations they expected. Dudley Carleton offered interesting motions and supported them adequately and with a light touch, which was not too common. Sir George More was persuasive because he was conciliatory and reasonable. But, alas, the forceful debaters were on the other side. James had need of what he dubbed slightingly "nimble antiquaries." A half-dozen Sir George Mores would have been useful to Cecil.

If Cecil had to be cook and captain and a bold mate of the royal brig, he was fortunate in the friends he had in the Lower House. His cousin Bacon—not a devoted cousin—observed that Cecil had a party in each House. Cecil was proud of the "benignity" with which the Commons had long treated him. From the Cecil correspondence it becomes evident that such men as Wingfield, Croft, Sir William Strode, and Richard Martin, none of whom could be reckoned among the King's supporters, were on friendly terms with the King's Minister. Even Sir Edwin Sandys had been reckoned as part of the Cecilian entourage.

But the debates, in particular those of 1610, when the tension between King and Commons was mounting, indicate that on the vexed question of the royal prerogative, the spokesman for His Majesty was making significant admissions. When discussing the security sought by the Commons that the proposed promises of the King as to wardship and purveyance would be honored, in return for a vote of subsidies, Cecil remarked: "I leave it to you whether the King may not bind himself by an Act of Parliament. I know not what an Act of Parliament may not do." The King's friends could hardly have listened to such words without misgivings. That was not all. In speaking for his master about Dr. Cowell's recently published handbook on legal and political terms, which had started the hornets buzzing in the House of Commons, Cecil declared that nothing should be written that would touch the fundamental laws of the commonwealth. The King, he asserted, did not consider it safe in a settled state and commonwealth "to touch the foundation." The word "foundation" sounds in this connection strangely like the later word "constitution."

When discussing subsidies in March 1610, he said that the King accepted ("holdeth") the view that subsidies belonged to him not by right but as an expression of the love of his subjects. On the same day he remarked that His Majesty would not want anyone to think that he could make laws without the three estates. "The King and the States are twins and they . . . grow and consolidate together."

Earlier in the same session Cecil asserted: "Kings, be they never so great, ought not to do what they like, and subjects, when there is need, ought not to deny out of humor." On April 28 of the same session he went further: "When Princes ask taxes more than the subjects can bear, they must bear with benignity, and they may be refused." Cecil was laying down limitations upon the prerogative less significant than those put forward by more outspoken members of the Lower House, but they were not unimportant.

He was, of course, speaking for the Lower House to overhear; he needed their help. Yet not all his statements supported the parliamentary case. At another time he declared: "True necessity must not be disputed;" that is, when the King was in desperate need, he had to be granted subsidies. He would have maintained that the state was above all, but he was careful with words. He was doubtless prepared to prove, to his own satisfaction, that his several statements were not inconsistent. Cecil was not given to throwing out isolated principles; like a good chess player, he would have his pieces support one another. He was never unaware of the strength of the other side and what might be said in their favor.

He must, nevertheless, have lain awake nights worrying about the admissions he had made, wondering what his master would say. So far as I know, His Majesty did not betray his spokesman. Once the subsidies were in hand, the admissions might be forgotten or given a royal gloss.

Cecil did more than enunciate what we would call constitutional principles. He praised the House of Commons: "You have so commended yourself [*sic*] and their judgment that sent you as you need no praise, your actions commending you." When he could, he liked to insist that the differences between the two Houses over various issues were of minor consequence. He went further and told the Commons that he owed as much to their House as they did. Was he not implying that he was an old House-of-Commons man and that his own philosophy of government had been affected by his years of association with that body? His words could not but warm the hearts of many members.

Cecil not only made admissions; he went out of his way to correct a statement by the King. On March 31, 1610, James discussed in a speech to Parliament the powers of kings and alluded to the possibility of an evil sovereign. At that time members may have listened anxiously to hear whether a tyrant was to be tolerated. James told them: "*Preces et lacrimae* are the means you can use." Those words were not forgotten. Cecil did what he could to blot out the memory by saying that the King was "far from the opinion of the Jesuits that *arma militiae* are *solum preces et lacrimae* [their arms were only prayers and tears]." Cecil attributed the words to the Jesuits. He deserved the goodwill of the Commons. In the delicate situation in 1610, when the House was becoming more recalcitrant and His Majesty more indignant and annoyed even with his faithful servants in the Privy Council, Cecil took a stand on the matter of privilege that must have pleased the Commons: he was the defender of free speech. He was very concerned with the liberty of the subject, wrote Bishop Goodman years later It is dangerous to argue from negatives, but I think Cecil's attitude toward Thomas Wentworth of Oxford (son of Peter Wentworth) is revealing. Wentworth had been speaking his mind about royal policy. Cecil might have recalled the instructions the King had given him before Parliament met that charged him with preventing all occasions of scandal and grudge: he was to see that members were purged of ill and prepared for good; he was to sound out their true intentions. In the case of Wentworth, Cecil failed to follow those instructions. In December 1610 James was eager to see Wentworth punished, and, when nothing happened, he criticized his Privy Councillors. It was not Northampton, his nephew Suffolk, nor the Scots hovering about His Majesty who put off indefinitely the imprisonment of Wentworth. Those men believed in the use of force and had no sympathy for freedom of speech. It is hard not to assume that Cecil was behind the failure to act.

Cecil said little about free speech, doubtless in deference to his master's strong views, but in Parliament he proved himself ready to listen to those who disagreed with him. On April 2, 1610, he was opposed in the Lords by the bishop of St. Asaph, and, when answering him, concluded: "Yet I commend him for speaking his conscience."

The whole history of Cecil's tenure suggests that the high hand was more often threatened by the King than applied by his Minister. One of the more zealous Puritans commented: "His Majesty hath also yielded them [the Puritans] greater liberty even in this kind than this House hath for years enjoyed."

In dealing with the Commons Cecil was not above acting a part.

At the end of February 1610, after he had finished his long discourse on the needs of His Majesty, he was asked what "retribution" would be given in return for subsidies. He registered surprise—he had expected them to open their hearts and vote the
King money. When that had been done, everyone could air his
griefs. He promised that "his Majesty would redress the same and
give them all satisfaction therein, as far as lay in his power." The
qualifying phrase was not to be overlooked. Cecil was no fool; he
knew that although the King was prepared to make those concessions already sketched by Cecil, in other matters in which the
Commons were vitally interested—wardship, purveyance, and nonconforming clergymen—His Majesty would yield little, if anything. No wonder Cecil hoped to see the glimmer of silver first.

In the matter of purveyance, the Lord Treasurer played a role
that did not become him. He had, as we have seen, expressed himself vigorously about the evils of purveyance. But when that old
but still active agitator, John Hare, who had exposed the crooked-
ness of the purveyors in Elizabethan days, reported from the conference and set forth the abuses the committee had uncovered,
Cecil turned on him for behaving like a tribune of the people.
This seemed rather unnecessary because Cecil was aware that the
King himself had been astonished at the practices of the purveyors
and had promised reform. Alas, His Majesty, perhaps under pressure from the Board of Green Cloth, reversed his field, and Cecil
had to go along with him. He aimed, he wrote in another connection, to be the shadow of the King's mind.[6]

He also played a part in the union of the two kingdoms. When
Sandys made it clear that the Commons were not prepared to yield
to the Lords about the difference between how those Scots born
before and those born after the accession of James to the English
throne were to be regarded, Cecil moved dramatically to end the
conference. From long experience with the Commons in Elizabethan days he may have hoped that the Lower House would be
taught a lesson by his gesture and that, within a few days, they
would request another conference and prove more amenable, but
the Lords had to make the first move.

It has been seen that Cecil was willing to concede more to Parliament than the King would, under ordinary circumstances, have accepted. It has been seen, too, that Cecil exercised a certain guile in his dealings with the Commons. If they resented this, they never said as much, so far as I know. It is impossible to follow the proceedings of the Commons from 1604 to 1610 without realizing that they did not trust the King and that they appear to have had a certain quiet confidence in Cecil. The man who mistrusted Cecil was the accomplished spokesman for His Majesty in the Lower House, Francis Bacon. Soon after Cecil's death in 1612, he wrote the King: "Lastly I cannot excuse him that is gone of an artificial animating of the Negative, which infusion or influence now ceasing, I have better hope." It was safe to accuse a dead man. Bacon must have known he was misrepresenting Cecil. Cecil had fought a long, heartbreaking battle to induce the Commons to vote some of the money the Government sorely needed, and it was for that money that he had offered concessions. He had stood for his King and yet retained, by some legerdemain consisting of well-chosen words and a gracious manner, the goodwill of a considerable proportion of the Commons. Was it all legerdemain and personality? Or did the Commons suspect that Cecil favored them as much as he dared?

His friends knew that he worried about his own future,[7] as well he might. He knew how changeable James VI of Scotland and James I of England had been, and he was aware, also, that his own attitude toward the Commons was not likely to endear him to the King. He had been able, during two sessions of Parliament, to retain the favor of His Majesty, but it had required considerable effort. When Hutton, the archbishop of York, asked Cecil to censure the King for his extravagance, for his waste of time in hunting, and for his religious policy, Cecil answered the letter by stating his own attitude toward the English Church and toward those clergy who refused to conform, an attitude that differed in no respect from that of His Majesty. It was hardly by chance that a copy of the letter was forwarded to the Earl of Worcester, who was in attendance upon the King in the country, and that James read the letter. At this point he still had confidence in his "little beagle." It was in 1606, when the King called upon Cecil during an illness, that James remarked that if Cecil should ever fail him there would be no safe hunting for the King of England. Cecil continued to hold the King's favor in the third session. But the Commons proved slow to act on the royal plan for the union, and when things went wrong for James, it was always the fault of his servants.

It was, however, in connection with the spending of money that Cecil always risked the danger of offending his King. At the same time the new methods he was developing to raise money were likely to make him enemies in the House of Commons. He set about to regularize the income from Crown lands. From the time of Edward III and perhaps earlier the Crown had been "arrenting" wastelands and woodlands to those who would improve them. Most such lands were known as "assarted" lands, and, in time, with the decline in the value of money over the centuries, the income from rentals amounted to so little that the sheriffs were no longer required to collect them. In consequence, hundreds of gentlemen held lands from the King for which they paid no rents. In the words of Cecil's understudy, Sir Walter Cope, there was a "revenue whch seemeth decayed by descent of time and worn out of all knowledge and remembrance, but by his Lordship's [Cecil's] care many of them have been lately revived by your Majesty's Commission of Assarts." There was an immediate need for such a commission.[8] In counties such as Northamptonshire, Wiltshire, and no doubt others, at the beginning of the new reign, reputable and well-known country gentlemen were breaking down fences and helping themselves to Crown lands on the margin of their own holdings. For example, Sir Edward Montague, of an old governing family, who had opened the attack on grievances in the parliamentary session of 1604 and was a zealous Puritan, had been fencing in Crown lands in Northamptonshire.

The Commission on Assarts was initiated by Cecil, and it was headed by the Lord Chancellor (Ellesmere), the Lord Treasurer, Cecil, and others. It was their function to take over for the King's use arrented and assarted lands "until the owners have made composition to us for the same, both by fine and rent." Cecil made it clear that those who compounded would find the rent small.

But this plan roused opposition. The Treshams and the Spencers in Northamptonshire started an action in the Exchequer through Serjeant Tanfield to "break the ice for them all," that is, for the hundreds of men who held assarted lands and had no letters patent from the King. They had an advantage in that many records had been lost and Crown lands and private lands were often hopelessly intermixed. Meanwhile a bill was introduced into the Commons to give security to those who had been in possession for a hundred years and a day, who had been reputed the lawful owners, and who had usually paid a rent. They were to hold the lands forever as assarted lands, as firmly as if they had been granted them by the King's progenitors. If, however, there were no documents to prove "tenure or service named," then the persons seized of the said assart lands should hold the lands by free socage, as of the manor of Greenwich. As has been said, the bill was badly drawn, and the language I have quoted from the proposed act is not at all clear. What I think is meant is that those who had recently encroached upon Crown lands were to hold them in free socage as of the manor of Greenwich.

It is interesting that Cecil, whose idea had been to raise money and at the same time to give security to those holding assarted lands, never, so far as I know, discussed the problem of assarts in Parliament. Nor was his name mentioned in the debates. He did not fight unnecessary battles; he could trust the Lords to put the bill about assarted lands to sleep.

In 1608, as Secretary, he was involved in another and larger scheme for raising money. The Lord Treasurer (Dorset) called together a selected group of merchants and gained their seeming support for a plan to levy impositions on a considerable number of imported commodities. The new tariffs were put largely upon luxury goods so that the poor would suffer as little as possible. It will be remembered that the Lord Treasurer died suddenly, and Cecil (Salisbury) had to carry on. Moreover he had to find the money, and quickly. But impositions without consent of Parliament roused the Commons to battle. Cecil assumed the blame as a loyal subordinate was bound to do. With great care he explained to Parliament that it was necessary to raise money without delay. It was, he maintained, the only antidote against future mischief.

Cecil never showed to better advantage than in his long effort during the two sessions of 1610 to persuade the Commons to give the King money. He was loyal to his sovereign and yet conciliatory to the Lower House. He told them:

> You offer so slowly as neither his Majesty, nor we [the Lords] know whether you are to bring anything. . . . The cause, I conceive, is not out of want of love and duty, but to great diffidence, and, although, according to the great variety of the subject and fear of the charge, some spoke for it, yet none that spake meant ill.

"none . . . meant ill." It was such seeming consideration for opposing views that commended Cecil to members and doubtless won some votes for the King. In June 1610 Cecil had declared that he would rather the Great Contract should fail than that the subjects should pay for anything "and the same spring up again." It was because the Commons feared that the abuses might spring up again that they hesitated to vote money, and Cecil knew it. If he occasionally turned sharp corners, he was moving in a single direction: to get money for the King. He hoped, if possible, to retain the goodwill of the Commons.

It was the general public, unaware of his action at firsthand, who blamed him for the failures of his master. After Cecil's death Sir Walter Cope, who knew the details of his various schemes for raising money, wrote to the King: "He never thought himself well but when he was bringing wax and honey to the hive. He lost the love of your people for your sake, and for your service."

It is sad to think that in Elizabethan days he had taken a great deal of honey for his own hive, using his position as Master of the Wards to make money for himself (so much that he tried to cover up some of his arrangements in complicated ways, as Hurstfield [9] has brought out). There is some evidence, Hurstfield believes, that he was less avaricious in his Jacobean days and also that he had twinges of conscience, especially when he realized how badly the King needed the income from the sale of wardships. It was an age of corruption, as Neale has pointed out and as every student of the period knows. The servants of the Crown were more or less expected to supplement their salaries by giving favors for money, and the post of Master of the Wards was desirable because of the great possibilities for what we would call graft. Cecil took a disproportionately large cut for himself and was able to build a monumental house at Hatfield that is still occupied by Cecils. Probably he did become less acquisitive in the reign of James,[10] but he still dealt with such crooks as William Typper, apparently on behalf of His Majesty. In some degree, however, he proved an illustration of the old adage: "Get on, get honor [office], get honest."

That he was a great Minister of State few of his contemporaries would have questioned. It was said that he had a "headpiece of great content" and that he could distinguish between truth and falsehood and pierce through the mists and walls of the darkest causes. In that day men spoke of the ability to see through a mill stone. Cecil could do that and find out what was behind or underneath. He had men posted here and there who furnished him with intelligence, and he knew how and when to use it. One who has to read scores of his letters, even when he recalls his financial dealings, finds it hard not to like him.[11] He had more to contend with than his illustrious father; he had to deal with a changeable and childish sovereign.

His biographer in the *Dictionary of National Biography* implied that Cecil was almost without personal friends. It is true that he had a formidable array of enemies. The Earl of Northampton felt for Cecil, living and dead, unmitigated hatred. So did many others who had been thwarted by him. He was in an impossible position; he could not avoid refusing favors. In order to remain in office, he had to keep the goodwill of the Scots around the King. Those English who disliked the Scots and coveted the offices and pensions bestowed upon them looked upon Cecil as a renegade and hoped to see him turned out of office. Cecil had to function in a Court where enemies were waiting for any misstep he might make and were disparaging him to the King. He was blamed for the laws passed against recusants; indeed, he was threatened with assassination. His secret agents brought him "pasquils" (lampoons posted in public places) denouncing him. It was asserted that five different men had sworn on the holy sacrament to compass his death if he did not shift his policy toward Catholics.

Yet it is a mistake to suppose that in a seemingly hostile world Cecil was without friends. His capacity for friendship enabled him to win what support he had in the House of Commons, and that capacity is revealed in letters to and from him. He wrote as one who felt far from friendless, as one who liked many people and assumed that they liked him.

Sir Roger Aston wrote of him: "The little beagle had run a true and perfect scent, which brought the rest of the hounds to a perfect tune." Fulke Greville wrote to him on August 30, 1597: "So happily are you tempered for other men." Another wrote of his "sweet and grave presence." Lord Dunbar considered him as friendly as any man living. His affability was recognized by his contemporaries, and Cecil did not hesitate to trust old friends with his inmost thoughts. To Sir John Harington, he wrote:

> You know all my former steps, good Knight, rest content, and give heed to one that hath sorrowed in the bright lustre of a Court, and gone heavily even to the best-seeming fair ground. 'Tis a great task to prove one's honesty and yet not spoil one's fortune. You have tasted a little hereof in our blessed Queen's time, who was more than a man and (in troth) some time less than a woman. I wish I waited now in her presence chamber, with ease at my food, and rest in my bed. I am pushed from the shore of comfort and know not where the winds and waves of a Court will bear me. I know it bringeth little comfort on earth, and he is, I reckon, no wise man that looketh this way to heaven.

In other words, heaven was a haven that statesmen could hardly hope to attain. Cecil had been considering that question when he wrote Harington that it was "a great task to prove one's honesty and yet not spoil one's fortune." He had elected not to spoil his fortune, and yet, as we have seen, his conscience troubled him. He would be honest with the Commons, after his own fashion.

About the same time things went sour between the "two kings," as James and Cecil were sometimes called by those who resented Cecil's share in power. In 1607 and especially in 1610, when the Great Contract failed to come off, the friendly words to Cecil from his master ceased. James wrote Cecil:

> It is true that I have found that by the perturbations of your own mind ye have broken forth in more passionate and strange discourses these last two sessions of Parliament than ever ye were wont to do. . . . For your greatest error hath been that ye expected to draw honey out of gall, being a little blended with the self-love of your own counsel.

It is conceivable that in his passionate discourses with his master he had as tactfully as possible presented the case for the Commons.

Cecil was a proud man, he behaved with dignity, and with none of that loathsome humility common among courtiers of the time. He became accustomed to the royal tantrums. He was called by the King, or so the gossips told him, a fool, a parrotmonger, a monkeymonger, "and twenty other names," and he was patronized unbearably. Moreover, he had been fearfully misrepresented to the King by his supposed friend, Sir Thomas Lake. Lake had picked up a silly story, probably fathered by Robert Carr, the future favorite and earl of Somerset, that Parliament was devising a scheme to send the Scots back to their own realm. The yarn was doubtless designed to harden the heart of the King against Parliament. James became angry that Cecil had not informed him of the plot. Lake knew that he had deeply wronged Cecil, but the harm was done. Cecil was blunt with Lake, but at the same time was careful that Lake's foolishness should not cost him his post. Relations were never the same again between Cecil and the King.

But Cecil was a sick man, and death was not far away. He must have been almost glad to leave the scene.

IV

PROBABLY a large majority of the House of Commons in 1604–1610 was Puritan in outlook. To prove it by an examination of the religion of each member would be difficult. A man of extreme Puritan convictions could be identified easily by his motions and speeches, but a moderate Puritan would seldom have revealed his religious views unless by his vote in the House, and information about that is scarce.

Unpublished writings of zealous Puritans show that efforts were made to see that M.P.'s were chosen "well affected" and that "very many were chosen." This seems to imply some effort at organization by Puritans, but there is not sufficient evidence to prove much save zeal.

There is, however, other evidence of the strength of the Puritans in Parliament. The Venetian ambassador wrote home in December 1604 that the Parliament contained many Puritans and that Privy Councillors were afraid that the Puritans in the country would appeal to Parliament. A Puritan writing of the silenced ministers observed that in the Commons they had a "senate consisting of men that are of special note for their jealous love of the gospel." Moreover, Sir Robert Wingfield, in addressing the Commons, estimated that three parts (presumably of four) were Puritan. James wrote: "I did not think that they [the Puritans] had been so great, so grand, and so dominant in your House." These were opinions; the clearest proof of Puritan power in the Commons was the speed with which measures about pluralities, nonresidence, a learned ministry, and "scandalous ministers" were approved by committees and passed by the Lower House, apparently with futile opposition. There are manuscripts, also, in which members of the House were exhorted to see that the "well-minded" should be present at all sessions so that no good bill should be overthrown. Members were to be prepared "in behalf of the freedom of the gospel to hazard their estates rather than leave their posterity to perpetual thraldom." [12] Instruction was offered as to when members should rise to speak and when they should push motions. Lawyers were enjoined to make ready "penned statutes." In another manuscript is a list of "Things Grievous to the Church of England," among them, "unpreaching ministers," bribery (probably by those seeking livings), the ex-officio oath, exactions from poor ministers by chancellors, commissaries, and other diocesan officials, and "the dissoluteness of noblemen, knights, and gentlemen not cohabiting with their wives." [13]

The documents I have been quoting represent minority opinion of the extreme Puritans. The vast majority of those known as Puritans were thoroughly Protestant and were not impressed by ritual and ceremony, nor favorable to the Brownist or to "sectaries." They hoped to see a clergyman, an educated one, in every parish, but the majority of them were not inclined to form a party. Most were probably more interested in doing away with the abuses of wardship and purveyance than in religious differences.

There were indeed so many questions before the Commons that in 1604 there was as yet no center around which those more or less in opposition could gather and no driving force behind such a possible group. It has already been suggested that the old leaders left over from Elizabethan days were largely moderates.[14] Usually the extremists create an active opposition quickly, and there were not enough of them.

The past, with its feudal remnants, had not yet lost its hold on the M.P.'s. They were accustomed to going along with the Government in most matters, to listening to Privy Councillors, and to endeavoring in general to please the Queen. They were not quite ready to unite on a program of legislation to correct abuses.

Such zealous Puritans as Nicholas Fuller and Sir Francis Hastings were not giving up; they were overlooking no chance to promote their cause. Sir Francis was of a Leicestershire family active in Elizabethan days on behalf of Puritan preachers. He was himself an old hand in the House, having entered it in 1571. He had proved himself a useful member, concerned to prevent enclosures and depopulation in the country, to improve the workings of the poor law, and to tax the poor as little as possible. He was a zealot, but hardly an extremist.

What distressed the Puritans most in 1604 was that the new canons passed by convocation had deprived some Puritan ministers of their livings: those who refused to conform in the matter of wearing a surplice and of making the sign of the cross in baptism. In Puritan quarters it was generally believed that between two and three hundred clergymen had been put out of their livings. S. B. Babbage has shown that the number was between eighty and ninety.[15] In general the Puritans maintained that the new canons had no validity unless ratified by Parliament; they based this theory upon the statute of 13 Eliz., cap. xii, which provided that those who received livings should declare their assent and subscribe to all the Articles of Religion, "which only concern the confession of the true Christian faith and the doctrine of the sacraments," that is, the doctrinal articles. But they were not bound to subscribe to the other articles.[16] Since the new canons enacted in 1604 by convocation had not been ratified by Parliament, it was held that those canons were not valid and did not bind clergymen. If clergymen refused to conform to the new canons, it was maintained that under the statute of 13 Eliz., cap. xii, it was within their right.[17] When we examine that statute we find nothing to justify the opinion that, to be lawful, canons must have been enacted by Parliament. Indeed the archbishop declared in 1610 that by 18 Hen. VIII power was given to the King and his successors forever by act of Parliament that "what canons the King shall ratify . . . shall be as good as though they were made in Parliament." [18] But when we look at 25 Hen. VIII, cap. xix, we find that clergy could make no canons without royal assent, and it was to that, I think, that the archbishop was referring. The statute seems to imply that the clergy could, with royal assent, make canons. In other words, the Puritan contention that Parliament had final control over the making of canons could be disputed. But some Puritans may have assumed that, since the Reformation Parliament had played so large a part in establishing the Church of England as independent from Rome, it might justly claim the authority to confirm canons.

The Puritans made other claims that were more readily justified. At the very beginning of the parliamentary session in 1604 Sir Edward Montague, it will be remembered, called attention to various grievances in his part of the country, among them the burden, vexation, and charge of the commissary courts. These courts were held by minor ecclesiastical officials and dealt with infractions of church practice, with the failures of churchwardens, and with the morals of parishioners. These officials were often accused of doing well for themselves financially. After Montague's speech a general committee and a special committee or subcommittee for commissary courts were set up. His Majesty was soon informed of this committee, probably by the archbishop, and, on April 16, 1604, he sent a message that complaints were being made against the commissary courts. Before they intermeddled with those matters, he hoped the committees would confer with convocation,[19] but that is what the Commons were unwilling to do. They maintained that there was no precedent for a conference between the Commons and convocation but were willing to confer with the Upper House and with the bishops in that body. The attitude of the Commons made the King restive. On April 17, 1604, he sent a message saying that he wanted an "absolute reformation," meaning thereby, I infer, that the reform should be initiated through the absolute power of the Supreme Head of the Church, the sovereign.

The message proved confusing. His Majesty had given power by letters patents to convocation "to debate, consider, and determine." But at almost the same time the Speaker told the Commons that the King would make no new precedents, that he would protect the Commons in those they had. Here was a pretty mess; here was a state of things. It was the typical performance of a vacillating sovereign. The Commons asked for a conference with the Lords, who were slow to reply. Meanwhile the Commons had set up a committee to prepare articles to be handled with the Lords in the coming conference.

On May 7, 1604, the committee drew up six articles "to establish unity in a middle course between the bishops and the ministers." By the first article the doctrinal parts of the statute of 13 Eliz., cap. xii, were to be explained, perfected, and established by Parliament. By the second article ministers should be bachelors of arts, or such as were deemed sufficient to instruct the people. The third article provided that no dispensation could be given to anyone to hold two or more benefices, and those who held benefices where they were not resident should furnish allowance to maintain a preacher. It provided, also, that where any living was under £20 a year an increase should be made in the living. The sixth article provided that faithful ministers who conducted themselves dutifully and taught the people diligently were not to be deprived, silenced, suspended, or imprisoned for not using the cross in baptism or for not wearing the surplice. The Lords were finally induced to have a conference with the Commons about religion, and Sir Francis Hastings, "with twenty more such other as are pleased to accompany him," were to meet with a committee of the Lords.

Hastings had no success with the Lords. On June 9, 1604, he reported that the bishops refused to join in a petition to the King. A report of what happened in the conference was made to the Commons: "An Instrument read by a bishop. A mislike that the Commons House should deal in any matters of religion. A mislike of the bishops' conference with us. That it prejudges the liberties of the Church." Convocation threatened that if the bishops would not desist from conferring with the Commons they would appeal to the King, "who has given them authority to deal only in these matters." The bishop of London, Richard Bancroft, virtually primate during the interval between the death of Whitgift and his own election, brought in the so-called Instrument. The Church was taking the offensive.

Sir Walter Cope, who looked to Salisbury as his patron, and who was a member for Westminster, reminded the House on June 8, 1604, of the steps taken by Parliament against the exorbitant claims of the Church in the reign of Henry IV. It was resolved that a subcommittee of the Great Committee for Religion should search precedents that might warrant the House in meddling with matters ecclesiastical.

Near the end of the session, for some reason, Bancroft poured oil on the troubled waters. He said that they (presumably the Lords) conceived that the privileges of Parliament stood upright,[20] and that there was to be no more ado about it.

In the session of 1605/06 the Commons busied themselves drawing up grievances, and it was decided to separate ecclesiastical grievances from others. On April 5, Fuller reported from the Committee for Grievances four articles concerning ecclesiastical grievances. The first article provided that ministers were to do no more than was required by the statute of 13 Eliz., cap. xii. The second article was directed against High Commissions "whereby divers bishops have, and all may have, more authority," than belonged to the archbishop in his ordinary jurisdiction. There were to be only two commissions, those for the provinces of Canterbury and York. The third article provided that anyone summoned before an ecclesiastical court should be given a statement of the case against him. The fourth article was to prevent excommunication for trifling offenses.

The Lords professed to find the articles "of great moment," but seemed in no haste to arrange a conference. On April 17, 1606, Bacon reported from the second conference with the Lords. The archbishop of Canterbury had assured the Commons that the deprived ministers might be restored to their livings if they would take the subscription. The bishop of Winchester had told the conference that the judgment of the High Commission was without appeal and without redress. On May 8 the Commons passed a bill "to restrain the execution of canons ecclesiastical (not confirmed by Parliament)." That bill was twice read in the Upper House, but there was no chance that the Lords would pass it.

On May 13, 1606, there was a report of another conference with the Lords, this one about the four ecclesiastical grievances. It was reported that the speech of the Lord Chancellor had been "short and rough." The first grievance was given a quick negative. The second grievance was left to "those who had authority in that behalf." To the third grievance, that men cited before church courts were not informed of the cause against them, the Lords answered that the grievance would be redressed "otherwise" where there was an abuse, presumably by pressure on the bishops from the Privy Council. This grievance included the ex-officio oath, an oath sometimes required in church courts, that those examined would answer all questions put to them. To this the Lords returned a negative. About the fourth grievance, that of excommunication for trivial causes, the Lords told the Commons that order had been taken for the Lords to join in a petition for reformation.

By this time it should have been evident to the Commons that a majority of the Upper House wished to see abuses corrected by the King and Privy Council, if at all. But the Puritans never lost hope. Before they knew the outcome of the four grievances they had begun bringing in one measure after another to accomplish some of the same purposes, and they did not weary in doing so. The bill against nonresidence and the plurality of benefices, the bill for a learned and godly ministry, the bill against scandalous and unworthy ministers, and that against simony were all expressions of Puritan zeal and activity. Some of the bills were doubtless former bills reintroduced. The bills were committed to new committees, or to those already set up, committees in which such members as Hastings, Fuller, Nathaniel Bacon, Wingfield, Wentworth, Yelverton, Strode, and others of like views were included. Some of the bills never got off the ground; others reached the Lords and were delayed there indefinitely.

About the grievances brought forward by the Puritans, there was, in the session of 1610, nothing very new or surprising. There was, of course, another appeal that deprived ministers be allowed to preach if they had permission of the bishop and if they lived peaceably and quietly. There was a new appeal about the abuse of excommunication for trivial offenses; in 1604 the King had been encouraging about reform in that respect, but apparently nothing had happened.

In answer to the ecclesiastical grievances presented in 1610, His Majesty told the Puritans that they should not meddle with the main point of government. That was his craft. Then he talked more hopefully. If any gentleman of the Lower House should come to him about a particular minister who had been long in the ministry and who was learned and peaceable, he would give him a reasonable answer. He admitted, as he had before, abuses in excommunication and suggested that the critics devise some form of coercion for the ecclesiastical courts to use. As for the Court of High Commission, he would listen to complaints and, if necessary, redress them.[21] He said it was not convenient to make changes concerning pluralities and nonresidence until provision was made for adequate livings.

V   THE historian, being above all curious, asks himself what took place before the events he is about to narrate. This is a question relevant to the Parliament that met in 1604 and to the debates that ensued. Were the members elected to that assembly making any preparations for the session ahead? It is not easy to collect information concerning this, but two interesting manuscripts dealing with legislation to be introduced afford a few clues. One of them—"A Calendar of Laws which may be Thought on, out of which Some may be Chosen to be Propounded for the Good of the Kingdom"—is found at Alnwick Castle in the Duke of Northumberland's archives. The phrasing suggests that the list presented was to be regarded as tentative. The other manuscript—"Acts to be Considered of against the next Parliament"—is among the State Papers Domestic in the PRO in London.

Comparison of the two manuscripts rouses more curiosity. The two lists of desirable measures are nearly the same, although arranged in a different order, and not always worded in precisely the same way. The two manuscripts have fifty-three items in common. The manuscript at Alnwick contains seven proposals not to be found in the one in the PRO and the latter includes eight items not found in the former. In other words, the two manuscripts embody in a considerable degree the same materials in a different arrangement; they are really a single document.

Who drew up that document, and why are its materials arranged so differently—indeed, in both manuscripts, rather haphazardly? I had hoped that in some castle, or modest country house, or local history repository related manuscripts would turn up, and that may yet happen. The only item I have come upon so far that has any relation to the two manuscripts is among the Gawdy manuscripts of the *HMC*.

On April 23, 1604, Sir Edward Mountford, himself not an M.P., wrote to Sir Bassingbourne Gawdy, M.P. for Thetford in Norfolk, that he heard that Sir Bassingbourne had a note of such statutes as were to be debated in the present Parliament, and requested a copy. If several copies of a well-known program of legislation (with variant readings) were in circulation, as seems not unlikely, one is tempted to guess how the program originated. The Government in Cecil's day collected documents of every kind that reflected public or parliamentary opinion, whether favorable or otherwise. The version of the document at the PRO might have been picked up by any one of Cecil's several agents. The version at Alnwick Castle might have come into possession of the then Earl of Northumberland, Henry Percy, in one of two ways. Francis Moore, an M.P. for Boroughbridge in 1588–89 and for Reading in 1597, 1601, and 1604, was a lawyer and a figure respected in the House of Commons, one of its most useful members. He had been in the service of the Earl of Northumberland and could have given him a copy of the document, for Moore might well have had a hand in writing it. Or the manuscript might have been presented to the Earl by Dudley Carleton, M.P. for St. Mawes in Cornwall, who served for some time as secretary to the Earl. I think it more likely that the manuscript came from Moore.

How did the document originate? It is conceivable that two, three, or more M.P.'s confabulating together about the coming session of Parliament set themselves to hammer out a list of reforms deemed desirable and that, having completed such a list, they passed it around among their parliamentary colleagues who made copies for themselves. Those colleagues perhaps volunteered suggestions and marked bills for inclusion or exclusion. In this way we could account for the likenesses and differences between copies.

The likenesses between the two versions are most evident in the first seven of the articles. In both versions, the first article proposed an "Act for the Recognition of his Majesty's Right to the Throne." The second article in the Alnwick manuscript (third in PRO manuscript) proposed an "Act declaring the Rights and State of the Principality of Wales and the Appanages and Preeminences appertaining to the King's Children." The fourth article in the Alnwick version (fifth in the PRO version) suggested an "Act for the Confirmaton of the Great Charter, with some Additions of Liberties of his Majesty's ['princely' added in the PRO version] Grace." Then followed two articles, one advocating the "Privileges and Preeminences of the Nobility in Parliament," and the other "Propounding the Privileges, Liberties, and Orders of the Commons House in Parliament."

The second article in the PRO version was an "Act for Disannulling of the Sentence given against the late Prince of famous Memory, Marie, Queen of Scotland, and the Defacing of all Records and Memories thereof." This article may have been inserted at the request of Scots in the royal entourage, possibly with the approval of the new sovereign. That it is not found in the Alnwick version is interesting. I do not recall that any bill about Mary, Queen of Scots, was introduced into the House.

Both manuscript versions included among the first set of articles (fourth in the PRO version and seventh in the Alnwick version) an "Act for the Reduction, Plantation, and Better Policy of the Kingdom of Ireland." In the PRO version after the word Ireland was added "and Scotland."

One would like to know more about the proposed "Act for the Confirmation of the Great Charter, with Additions." On March 26, 1604, a bill read in the Commons confirmed the ancient liberties. On March 29 what I assume was the same bill was read a second time and committed to nearly forty members. On April

12 the committee was appointed to meet on that afternoon, and on April 18 Humphrey Winch, M.P. for the borough of Bedford for the fourth time, reported from the committee that the bill was thought fit to sleep, and a new bill was offered by him to "Confirm to the Commons their Freedom and Liberties." That is the last that was heard of it, but the matter was raised again in 1610 when a bill about Magna Carta was given a first reading.

It was to be expected that in any program for the making of new laws the interests of the landed classes would not be overlooked. The "Bill for the Confirmation of Ancient Possessions as against Titles of Concealment and the Like" was designed to protect landowners against informers who searched for parcels of land once belonging to His Majesty that had in the past decades, or perhaps during the past three centuries, been quietly taken over by acquisitive gentlemen and retained by their heirs. The "Bill for the Better Establishment of the Assurance of the Realm and the Taking away of Perpetuities," that is, for securing the validity of conveyances of land and doing away with nonalienable lands, would make it easier for the gentry, when they wished to sell lands to pay debts, or to find money for dowries. The object of the bill concerning the Earl Marshal's Court (a proposal found only in the Alnwick manuscript) was probably to limit the exorbitant fees sometimes imposed by heralds for funerals and other ceremonial occasions in which county families took part, fees that accentuated the natural reluctance to die. At this time there seems to have grown up an earlier Parkinson's Law by which clerks proceeded to exact fees for services that they were bound in duty to give. A "Bill against the Assignment of Remainders to the Crown" was perhaps put on the list by country gentlemen. It does not appear in the PRO version.

Economic measures, some against business practices of the time, were perhaps sponsored by representatives from the larger boroughs: an act against usury, brokers, and other "greedy courses of gain" (possibly directed against those moneylenders who exacted high rates of interest); an act for the truer making of cloth; an act against engrossing merchandise (probably against those who arranged local monopolies); an act to prevent retail operations by aliens within the realm; an act to keep treasure within the realm; and an act to establish banks of money in fit places.

The legal measures proposed were possibly suggested by lawyers in the House and were directed against those who made ill use of the law. An act for limiting and defining the jurisdiction of the King's courts was probably intended to uphold the regular common-law courts as against Chancery, as against the ecclesiastical courts that were constantly reaching out for more power, and as against the new courts that had been developed to support administrative bodies, such as the Court of Green Cloth. An act against unjust vexations was designed to penalize persons who brought suits against those too poor to go to court and thus worried such unfortunates into the surrender of their properties. About the act for taking away certain formalities in pleadings and delays in process, the language speaks for itself. A proposed bill for reforming procedures in the Remembrancer's Office in the Exchequer was intended to do away with charges laid upon sheriffs when they entered their accounts. Both manuscripts contain a proposal for a law about treason: in the PRO version the article reads, "An Act for Declaring the Law in certain cases of Treason, that the Intent shall be inquired of as matter of fact and taken by Intendment of Laws." [22]

Four of the proposed statutes would benefit the subjects in general, those concerning purveyors, penal laws, monopolies, and informers. The evils of purveyance will be dealt with in later chapters. The measure for declaring, repealing, reviving, compounding, and limiting of divers penal laws struck at once at one of the conspicuous abuses of the time. The Crown enhanced its income by dispensing with certain laws in particular cases, in return, of course, for money, and gained a profit also from fining men for transgressing laws long since obsolete. James realized that it was an abuse and hoped at some future time to do away with it, but cash at once was deemed more necessary than exact justice. The third measure declared that the common law was against monopolies and privileges. The fourth dealt with abuses of informers.

Social reformers—to use a modern term—had been introducing bills into Parliament during the Queen's last years that were

designed to help the poor and unfortunate. In late Elizabethan
Parliaments we cannot but observe that certain men, such as Sir
Walter Ralegh and Sir Francis Hastings in particular, but also
Richard Martin, Francis Moore, Sir Robert Wroth, Sir Robert
Wingfield, Lawrence Hyde, John Hare, and doubtless others, were
concerned to give the underdog a chance. They evidently had
considerable support in the House. There were gentlemen of
landed estates, such as Wroth, but more often they were men who
were coming up, civil servants and well-to-do burgesses from
country towns who were accustomed to think of the poor,[23] and
there were also lawyers, such as Francis Moore and William
Hakewill, who knew how much the laws favored the landed
classes. Most of them were Puritans; it is often said that Puritans
came from the bourgeois classes. One cannot read the borough
records, more of which are being published, without learning how
much was being done in towns to look after their poor. Nor were
country gentlemen as justices of the peace altogether forgetful
of the hard-pressed farm laborers. The poor had to be helped lest
they die under hedges. The social reformers of various classes must
have had their say in the confabulations over the proposed program.

The program included much: decayed cities, boroughs, and
towns were to be repaired and reedified, by what means we are not
informed, but provision was to be made for the increase of population and of cottages; the poor and maimed soldiers, back from
Ireland and the Netherlands, were to be helped; the population was
to be protected against plagues and pestilence, how it is hard to
say; secret marriages without the consent of parents and friends
were to be restrained; excesses of apparel, of diet, and of buildings
and coaches, and "sumptuous expenses," were to be discouraged by
law; frays and duels were to be put down; excessive drinking was
to be dealt with, and tippling houses were to be limited in number; lewd and filthy houses were to be closed. These reformers,
as most reformers, were more idealistic than realistic.

The educational reformers managed to insert in the program an
article proposing the visiting of universities and the reforming of
certain points in their administration. About this bill I know

nothing. In 1597 a Mr. Davies—of what constituency I do not know—brought up the corruption among Masters of Colleges in Oxford and Cambridge, who appropriated to themselves funds bequeathed to the college. Davies asked for the assistance of lawyers in the House to draw the bill, and the House appointed Francis Moore and Mr. Boys, a lawyer from Canterbury. Whether the measure proposed in the program of 1604 had any relation to Davies's plan I do not know.[24] It is true, though, that bills were carried over from one Parliament to the next two or three.

A considerable body of ecclesiastical legislation was proposed, some of which will be dealt with in the following chapters. An "Act against Extortion by commissary courts" and an "Act against the Profanation of the Sabbath" were included in the program.

From other proposals made, one would suspect that some of those who took part in preparing this document were not without imagination. An "Act to declare the Privileges, Liberties, and Orders of the House of Commons" may have been a plan to give statutory sanction to what had been common practice in procedure. More surprising was a proposal for the new erecting of divers boroughs with privileges to send burgesses to Parliament; the same act was to suppress "decayed" boroughs. Here was something new. As early as 1571 the abuse of the nomination of members by decayed boroughs and the influence of patronage on the elections had been the subject of discussion in the House, but nothing seems to have come of it. A general proposal for a better system of representation had not yet been formulated.

A third proposal of an imaginative kind was for "Reforming the Year Books and the Courts of Common Law and the Establishment of Reporters and other Remedying of the Incertainty of laws."

There were a number of other measures in the new program. It was suggested that a market should be set up at Ipswich "or at some such place," doubtless for goods coming and going to and from Dutch and German ports. Garners for the provision of corn (wheat) were to be provided. The inning and recovering of marshes and overflown grounds was put down as desirable. Navigation was to be encouraged, as was the discovery of new lands (only in the Alnwick manuscript). The seas were to be made safe against piracy.

The curious reader who compares this program with the records of the Commons for the reign of Elizabeth will soon discover that many of the measures proposed in 1604 had been brought into the House as bills during her reign, particularly in the last decades of that reign. In the end the bills had been allowed to die in the House or had been held up by the Privy Councillors, by the Queen's "black husband," the archbishop of Canterbury, or by the Queen herself. Elizabeth could move quickly to stop such measures or to silence those who were responsible for bringing them in. She could do so without rousing great opposition, so great was her prestige by virtue of her successes in foreign affairs. With age she grew more high handed. Members of Parliament sometimes talked about freedom of speech, but got nowhere.

The legislative program embodied in the two manuscripts thus constitutes a kind of bridge between Elizabethan and early Jacobean Parliaments. They were a brief statement of what had been hoped for by the vocal part of the country, and was to be hoped for again. Vain hopes and courage vain! But all was not lost. Public attention was called to a considerable number of desirable reforms. In 1624 and a generation later some of them were to appear on the statute book.

What was left out of the program for legislation deserves mention. Not a word was given to the greatest of grievances, wardship. Nor was there any mention of the desirability of a bill for free trade. Nor was anything said for or against Cecil's scheme to restore assart lands to the Crown. The legislative union of England and Scotland, which the King had most at heart, was only touched upon in the Alnwick manuscript and omitted from the PRO version. In the Alnwick version the measure reads, "An Act for the Better Grounding of the Union." The word "grounding" sounds significant. Were the planners for legislation interested in accomplishing the ends in view, not by royal declaration but by Parliament?

Chapter 1

The First Session, 1603/04

James I, King of England

WHEN a new sovereign mounts the throne, there is usually a honeymoon period when he receives nothing but praise, when all is enthusiasm. James himself described, not without glee, the reception he received:

> Shall it ever be blotted out of my mind how at my first entry into this kingdom, the people of all sorts rid and ran, nay rather flew to meet me; their eyes flaming nothing but sparkles of affection, their mouths and tongues uttering nothing but sounds of joy, their hands, feet, and all the rest of their members in their gestures discovering a passionate longing and earnestness to meet and embrace their new Sovereign? [1]

It was roses, roses all the way. Men who had nothing else in common suddenly felt a community of emotion.

England had had two queens in succession, and now there was to be a man on the throne, a young, vigorous, and able man, it was reported.[2] It would be possible to fill pages with the poetry and prose of rejoicing. The poet, John Davies, wrote:

> Now wisest men with mirth do seem stark mad
> And cannot choose, their hearts are all so glad.

55

Thomas Lake, who, like hundreds of others, hoped for favors, wrote early in April to Cecil: "He is very facile, using no great majesty, no solemnities on the access, but witty to conceive and very ready of speech." [3] Ralph Winwood, who also looked for benefits, sent word to the States General:

> He hath sent us a King in the flower and strength of his years, a prince wise, sober, discreet, nowise debauched, or given over to pleasures, pious and religious, more learned in all kinds of good letters than any prince whatsoever of whom stories either ancient or modern have left us any memory. [4]

John Chamberlain wrote to Carleton:

> The King uses all very graciously. . . . These bountiful beginnings raise all men's spirits and put them in great hopes, inso much that not only protestants but papists and puritans and the very poets with their idle pamphlets promise themselves a great part in his favor. [5]

It will be observed, however, that Chamberlain really said little more than that men were hoping to gain favors from the new King.

On May 28 the French ambassador, who had thus far seen but little of the new English sovereign, wrote that his visage showed a certain sweetness of nature, that his countenance was simple and without majesty, and that his conversation and his familiarity showed his good sense and freedom. [6] Even as late as July Rosny had good words for James. The King had a great spirit, and he did not ignore learning. He liked to talk of affairs of state and to hear about great undertakings, to examine all the circumstances connected with them, and to be told of all the advantages and disadvantages. [7]

Seldom was the honeymoon of goodwill shorter than that enjoyed by James I. He had, he believed, a blessed mission to unite the English and the Scots, a more arduous undertaking, as it proved, than he had expected. It coud not be brought about overnight, but James was in a hurry. He did not understand the English. They were not as eager to hear or tell some new thing as St.

Paul's Athenians; they liked to look all around that new thing and then they might, in time, accept it and even make much of it.[8]

The honeymoon might have continued for a while, but, excited by his good fortune in having come into a new and wealthy kingdom, the King talked too much. He was a learned man of fairly wide interests, who could converse fluently and quote from continental theologians to admiring listeners. But the wiser English soon discovered that he lacked any consistent policy.

To the spokesmen of Henry IV he confided that not for a long time, indeed not for a century, had two kings of such quality been found,[9] a historical judgment that the ambassador relayed at once to Paris. To others, James explained that during the last few years of the reign of Elizabeth he had really been ruling England,[10] thus exposing himself to ridicule. In the English Court were men and women of a sophistication to which he was not accustomed.

Nor did he have any sense of the fitness of things. As he came down from the border through northern England, he remarked that he was impressed by the damage done to forests and parks [11] and feared that England had been injured more by forty-four years of peace than by ten years of war, a sly thrust at the late Queen whose fame he could seldom refrain from minimizing.

In his first address to Parliament he betrayed his self-esteem. He alluded to "the blessings which God hath in my person bestowed upon you all, wherein I protest I do more glory at the same for your weal than for any particular respect of mine own reputation or advantage therein." [12]

He was too fond of talking about religion, at least for his more worldly English audience.[13] At the dining table he suggested casually that the Pope was antichrist,[14] a thought that would not have been well received by Catholic subjects to whom he had been holding out the hope of more toleration. He discussed the subject of monarchy with the French ambassador, remarking that he and Henry IV were absolute monarchs in their dominion and in no respect dependent upon the counsels of their subjects.[15]

The two French ambassadors—the regular ambassador, de Beaumont, and the ambassador extraordinary, Rosny—were, of course, watching the new King with intense interest. It was of the first importance for Henry IV to be able to appraise the man with whom he hoped to negotiate. How far he could depend upon James in matters connected with Spain and the Low Countries was what de Beaumont and Rosny had to determine, if possible.

Rosny soon learned that the King's popularity was on the wane. When he went to make his first formal call upon James at Greenwich, he was escorted by Henry Percy, Earl of Northumberland, who had recently been made a Privy Councillor. After the presentation the Earl was accompanying Rosny back to his barge when he ventured to mention his own friendship with the King of France and to request a private conference with the ambassador. Rosny wrote that the Earl was one of the most able, powerful, and courageous men in England. But he went on to say that the Earl was dissatisfied with the present government and found fault with the actions and the conduct of the King.[16] A few days later Northumberland sent his secretary to tell Rosny that a faction at Court was devoted to Spain and hoped to see Britain and Spain allied in an offensive and defensive league. Such a league would demand, so Northumberland asserted, that France give Brittany and Burgundy to Spain, and Normandy, Guienne and Poitou to England, as these territories had once belonged to them.[17] Northumberland was right in saying that a pro-Spanish faction existed at the Court. But his other statement as to the lands to be taken from France may be largely discounted, although it was also mentioned by the Venetian ambassador.[18] Lord Cobham and Sir Walter Ralegh were said to have corroborated Northumberland's information.[19]

In time Rosny lost his enthusiasm for Northumberland and those associated with him. He considered them "meddlesome, crafty, and inventive" and their ideas extravagant and difficult to carry out.

Rosny, although accustomed to courts and their intrigues, was apparently surprised at what he heard of the jealousies and quarrels in the English Court. He was more interested in the almost total lack of confidence in the leadership of the Government. Both

Rosny and de Beaumont filled letters to Paris with stories of the situation. The upper classes, they wrote, were furious against the Scots.[20] Cecil was hated by some because he was believed to have allied himself with the Scottish interest. As for the common people, they were said to have contempt for the person of the King. Rosny had a good deal to say about the English, part of which is worth quoting because it is to a considerable degree doubtless a criticism of the King, of those around him, and, perhaps, of those who opposed him. The English, he wrote, were as inconstant as the ocean around them; they were extraordinarily uneven in their deliberations and were given to actions out of all relation to their words. Driven by pride and presumption, they took their fancies for truth and reality. They did not balance things, nor did they measure the present by the past or consider the situation of the people with whom they had to deal or the ways by which they could arrive at their ends, but they acted from arrogance and nonchalance.[21]

How French! From the Hundred Years' War to World War I the French had uttered opinions of that kind about the English; they are a rational people who believe that policy should be logical and consistent.

Of course, Rosny appraised English policy at a bad time. There had been better times. Elizabeth's policy, thanks to Walsingham and Burghley, had been not illogical.

James was anything but consistent. No one knew what his policy was, least of all the King himself. He had opposed peace with Spain and then, for a while, favored a treaty with that nation. At other times, however, he listened to the persuasive arguments of the French ambassador and was almost ready to collaborate with France in action against Spain. But in the end the friends of Spain, several of them well pensioned by the Spanish ambassador, prevailed: James turned pro-Spanish and came to consider himself the great patron of peace. Rosny was inclined to blame the English for the failures of James.[22] De Beaumont, the permanent ambassador, understood matters better and laid the blame where it belonged.

The King was devoted to hunting and would sacrifice the need for immediate decisions to the call of the field. His health, he persuaded himself, demanded an outdoor life. Ambassadors from foreign countries had to wait until he returned from a week or a fortnight in the field. The Venetian ambassador reported the distribution of papers accusing the King of neglecting the state.[23] The letter from Hutton, archbishop of York, to Cecil, censuring His Majesty on various matters, has already been mentioned in my introduction. Hutton asked for "more moderation in the lawful exercise of hunting" and that "the poor man's corn may be less spoiled." [24] Within nine months after his accession, James had probably lost the goodwill of many of his more intelligent subjects, those who were likely to know what was going on.[25] Nothing did more to make him unpopular than the favors shown the Scots. To the English the followers of the King who came down from the north seemed men of low caliber, men with outstretched hands, who did not command respect. To such men James gave places in the Privy Council craved by the highest English nobility; upon such men he bestowed Crown lands and profitable offices both in the country and in London.

The less important classes were also anti-Scot, and they quickly lost their enthusiasm for their Scottish sovereign. Queen Elizabeth had welcomed the friendly crowds that quickly gathered as she progressed through street and lane. James was reluctant to show himself to the people [26] and scarcely gracious. No doubt he feared assassination.

Parliament Begins: The Goodwin-Fortescue Case

THE first Parliament of the new reign met in March 1603/04. It was three years since there had been a Parliament, and changes in the membership of the Commons were to be expected, but the leadership, at the beginning, was slightly altered. Of course, Sir Robert Cecil, easily the first man in the sessions of 1597 and 1601, was now in the Upper House, and he had left no one to take his place in the

Commons, either as a general overseer or as a persuasive talker.

Sir Francis Bacon was a significant and even glamorous figure. A less important but far from negligible supporter of the Crown was Sir George More of Loseley near Guildford, the borough he represented. Like his father, Sir William, he had been in the good books of the great Queen, and he was to receive marks of favor from the new sovereign. His value as a spokesman for the royal point of view was enhanced by his moderation and seeming reasonableness. Not least among his parliamentary talents was that of being ready to suggest what to do in the confused situations that arose.

A more independent member, Sir Edward Hoby, represented Rochester (Kent), but in late Elizabethan Parliaments he had sat for the counties of Kent and Berkshire and the borough of Queenborough. Hoby was a diplomat, as his father had been before him. A cousin of Sir Robert Cecil, a son-in-law of the first Lord Hunsdon, and long on good terms with James VI of Scotland, Hoby had important connections and made full use of them. He also had the advantage of an impressive appearance and affable manners. During the days of the great Queen and the first years of her successor he was a frequent speaker in Parliament. Versed in the learning of his time, he had a clear head and a knowledge of parliamentary history and usage.

Four very considerable figures in Elizabethan Parliaments still active in the Parliament of 1604 were Francis Moore, Richard Martin, Sir Robert Wingfield, and Sir Francis Hastings. All of them had opposed Elizabeth in the matter of monopolies and were likely, if necessary, to stand up against the Privy Council of the new sovereign.

A member of greater political stature than any of them was Sir Edwin Sandys, son of an archbishop and at one time a pupil and assistant to the judicious Hooker at Corpus College, Oxford. Sandys had served in the Parliaments of 1588 and 1593 without attracting much attention, had then traveled on the Continent observantly, and had written a discriminating treatise, from the Protestant point of view, on the state of religion in Europe. In the new Parliament of 1604 he was to play a part, especially in connection with free trade and wardship. In the second session (1605/06) he became even more important. It was in the third session that he assumed the leadership of the House on the question of the Union.

On March 19 Parliament was addressed by His Majesty.[1] His coming, he declared, meant peace with foreign nations, where there had been war. There was also peace at home where two nations were now joined. He hoped that the blessing of his person would bring outward peace for years to come.

At his coming he had found one religion, but also papists and Novelists. The Puritans were always discontented with the government and did not wish to tolerate any superiority.[2] On matters of conscience, he did not wish to straighten out the minds of his subjects; he did not want to persecute them nor to increase their burdens. He had been considering the laws against recusants, and he thought the judges had enforced the laws too rigorously. He would make a distinction between lay papists and clergy: the laymen he would hesitate to punish unless they incited sedition; those clergy who maintained the supremacy of the Pope over kings could not be allowed to remain in the kingdom.

James proceeded to develop a notion characteristic of him—that he might be the means of bringing about a Christian union in religion. It would have gratified this ambitious ruler to have gathered all Christians into one flock. His own religion, he remarked, was indeed the true, ancient Catholic faith.

Then, off on another tack, he warned the papists not to presume too much upon his lenity. To their persons he was friendly, but he would pronounce mortal war against their errors. He could not permit them to increase their numbers without betraying himself and his posterity.

Turning his attention to Parliament, he urged the members not to make too many laws. Good judges had been planted over the realm to carry out the laws. He warned those judges not to make distinctions between persons and not to accept bribes, but to maintain a middle course. The welfare of his subjects would always be his greatest care. Had he not enlarged his favors to his subjects more than any sovereign before him? He hoped, however, that his subjects would show restraint in asking such favors. He concluded with an apology for his want of eloquence, by reason of the great weight of state affairs. These words must have amused those who were aware of how he neglected those affairs.

The long-winded response of the Speaker need not detain us long. The Parliament and the King, he pronounced, had two powers, one ordinary and the other absolute—ordinary in the proceedings of the Lords and Commons, but in His Highness absolute, either negatively to frustrate or affirmatively to confirm but not to institute. Apparently he left the initiation of legislation to Parliament. The Speaker deigned to praise the late Queen, but to the King he offered adulation. Then he presented five petitions, only three of which are given in the finished *Commons Journals*. All five, including the request for free speech, are mentioned in the less finished *Commons Journals*.[3]

On March 23 Sir Robert Wroth and Sir Edward Montague raised the question of grievances, doubtless by arrangement with some of the leaders of the House and with the Speaker. The choice of men was interesting. Neither Wroth nor Montague was a man of unusual parts, but each had force of character and had shown courage. More important, they were men of wide acres and long and honorable lineage, whose opinions would thus carry weight. Sir Robert Wroth, senior knight from Middlesex, had served in the Commons since 1562/63 and had, with his father, been a Marian exile. He talked about the abuses of wardship, purveyance, monopolies, penal statutes, the transportation of ordnance to foreign countries, and the writs of *Quo titulo ingressus*.[4]

He was followed by Sir Edward Montague, who had won disfavor with the new sovereign by supporting the petition from his county for the dismissed clergymen.[5] Four abuses were discussed by Montague. "The cry of the country," he exclaimed, "called upon me and my fellow companion [Sir Valentine Knightley] . . . to beg your assistance for their relief." Montague apologized for his infirmity of speech and thanked the members for listening. He spoke of the intolerable burden and charge of the commissary courts, and he alluded to the suspension of grave, learned, and sober-minded ministers for "not observing some ceremonies long amongst many disused." Ministers had been ejected, too, for "maintaining the truth against Popish doctrines, opinions, and ceremonies." He complained of depopulation and the excessive conversion of tillage into pastures, "notwithstanding some laws lately made against them." [6]

The motions by Wroth and Montague led to the naming of two large committees, which included many of the leaders of the Lower House: Francis Moore, Sir Francis Bacon, Richard Martin, Sir Francis Hastings, Nicholas Fuller, Lawrence Hyde, Sir Edward Hoby, Sir Edward Montague, Sir Robert Wingfield, Sir Thomas Ridgeway, Sir George More, John Hare, Sir Herbert Croft, Serjeant Doddridge, and others.

On March 26 Bacon reported from the committee named as a result of Wroth's motion. It was the hope of that committee, he said, that not only the King but also those Lords who had feudal tenants would yield their rights of wardship. In the committee there had been differences as to whether they should offer the King the whole proposal plotted out or whether they should ask him first for liberty to treat of wardship. They decided that the second alternative was preferable. Before they asked the King for permission to deal with wardship, they hoped to have a conference with the Lords in order to ask them to join in the petition.

The next day Bacon reported that the Lords agreed with the Commons about wardship and that they suggested that respite of homage be coupled with wardship in the petition to the King. As if by afterthought, they asked that in the next conference the committee consider the question of the election of Sir Francis Goodwin.

To explain this, we must retrace our steps to March 22, when the King and the Speaker addressed the House. On that day, as soon as the Speaker and the Commons were settled in their places, Sir William Fleetwood, knight of the shire for Buckinghamshire, had offered a motion on behalf of his colleague, Sir Francis Goodwin. Goodwin had been elected, but the return made by the sheriff had been refused by the Clerk of the Crown because Goodwin had been outlawed. On the sending out of a second writ, Sir John Fortescue, once Chancellor of the Exchequer and now Chancellor of the duchy of Lancaster, had been elected. Fleetwood asked that the return might be examined and that Goodwin might be received as a member of the House. He proposed that the Clerk of the Crown be asked to appear the next day at 8:00 a.m., bringing with him all writs of summons, indentures, and returns of elections for the county of Buckinghamshire for this Parliament. Further, he wished Goodwin to appear in person and to state his own case.

The next day, March 23, after the speeches by Wroth and Montague and the naming of committees to deal with the grievances mentioned by those members, the Clerk of the Crown appeared with the documents about the Buckinghamshire election. A debate followed by "sundry learned and grave members," [7] and then, after much dispute as to the form of the question to be put, it was finally voted that Goodwin had been lawfully elected and should be received as a member of the House. That this action was taken so quickly, without a great deal of consideration, would suggest that some of the leaders had met together and had resolved to lose no time in making a decision. From their own point of view they were right. They were now in a position to say, when royal pressure was brought to bear on them, that it was impossible for a court to change its decision.

It was on March 27 that the Lords, in agreeing to go along with the Commons in the matter of the petition to the King about wardship, asked that at the next conference between the two Houses the election of Sir Francis Goodwin might be considered. That startling request led several members to take the floor. It seemed to be the general opinion that the judgment of the House of Commons ought not to be questioned,[8] that "the like had never been before heard or seen that they should deliver a reason unto the Lords why they did it." [9] Mr. Attorney and others were called in by the Speaker to receive the message. Apparently the Attorney did not know, and we may assume that the Lower House did not realize, that the Lords, in their motion for a conference, had acted at "the King's pleasure." [10] Information to that effect was apparently whispered through the House and may have led to the resolution (not precisely in accord with the message they had just ordered to be sent) that "in all humbleness they would attend the King at his appointment and yield him their reasons why they did it." [11] Thereupon the House sent Sir John Stanhope and Sir John Herbert "about the said cause." Those messengers did not return to the House until that body was about to leave at 3:00 p.m. The two gentlemen brought an answer from the King wherein His Majesty thought himself "touched in honor," and wished to confer with a group from the Commons. [12]

The House considered what was to be done. [13] They arranged for a meeting of lawyers and gentlemen with the King on the following day at 8:00 a.m. and ordered that the House itself should meet at 6:00 a.m. "to treat of something to be delivered that morning . . . to the King." [14] Meanwhile they named a committee of about thirty-two to meet that afternoon at 4:00 p.m. "to set down the effect of that which Mr. Speaker was to deliver from the House to the King." [15]

When the House met the next day at 6:00 a.m. ("being for the most part come together"), [16] Sir John Herbert delivered a report about the message that he and Sir John Stanhope had given the King at the direction of the House. [17] Herbert told the Commons that

> the King was by information much moved against the proceedings of the House about Sir Francis Goodwin, whose privileges [that is, of the House] he meant by all ways and means as much to maintain and confirm as ever any of his predecessors had done, but desired that twelve lawyers and three-score knights and burgesses with the Speaker might come to him to the Court at Whitehall to satisfy him in that point, which was done, but what they should deliver to the King after much debate was that we did as of ourselves come unto his Majesty, not to give

the reasons of our judgment in that case, but to satisfy him of the irrevocableness of our judgments in so high a Court, being never before demanded an account of our proceedings there, and so the Court brake up at viii the clock, and the lawyers with the 60 gentlemen went to the Court.[18]

On March 29, the Speaker related the story of the message delivered to the King and of the reply of His Majesty. The Commons had held the election of Goodwin justified. Two outlawries there had been against him, one for £69 and one for £16. Both debts had been paid by Goodwin and a discharge received from the creditors. The Speaker had cited instances in the time of Elizabeth where outlawries had not prevented membership in the House.[19]

The Speaker went on to give the answer of His Majesty. The King regretted the "contestation" and was indifferent as to whether Goodwin or Fortescue were chosen. He had no special feeling ("affection"). The bringing in of a new writ had been the work of a Privy Councillor.[20] James could assume a judicious attitude, but he could not hold the pose for long. He compared the Commons to the Israelites and, by inference, himself to God, and then he told them that they had mistaken the law and had acted rashly in failing to consult the judges. As for precedents, those set in times of tyrants,[21] of women, and of simple kings were not to be taken seriously (an allusion to the Elizabethan precedents cited). He could have developed a more convincing argument had he been well advised by students of English history. He did say that the Commons should not meddle with returns which were made in Chancery, where they should be reformed and corrected. He turned to a weaker argument. All the privileges of the Commons, he insisted, came from him and should not be used against him.

Then he called upon the Lord Chief Justice, Sir John Popham, who declared upon his loyalty and oath as a judge that the House ought not to meddle with returns of writs, for they were made to His Majesty in the Court of Chancery. Popham cited a case in 35 Hen. VI where an outlaw was refused membership in Parliament. He mentioned, further, a resolution by the judges in 35 Eliz. to the effect that a person outlawed was not *idoneus*. Further, the Chief Justice asserted that even if a Member of Parliament had paid the debts incurred he was not free from the outlawry until he sued out a writ of scire facias.[22]

The King drew out the Chief Justice as to whether the outlawry was not void for want of a proclamation. He was told that the outlawry was not void except by a declaratory judgment of the court.[23]

The King asked if the outlawry was not void by virtue of two general pardons, as had been the opinion of Justice Williams.[24] Williams replied that he had been of that opinion but had since changed his mind.

The King then made three requests of the Commons: (1) that they should debate the question and resolve it among themselves, (2) that they agree to a conference with the judges, and (3) that they make a report of their proceedings to the Privy Council.[25] For the last two requests it would have been hard to discover any precedent. To have accepted the third proposal would have been to subordinate the Commons to the Privy Council.

The next morning the question was debated in the House. Sir Robert Wingfield, the first speaker, had been an M.P. for Stamford in Lincolnshire since 1586 and probably owed his seat to the influence of the Cecil family. His mother had been a sister of the first Lord Burghley. Notwithstanding this connection, Wingfield had opposed the Queen on at least two issues and seemed ready to break a lance with the new sovereign. The King, he explained to the House, had too many misinformers, which, he prayed God, might be removed.[26] If the King and the Council were to choose the Members of Parliament, free elections would mean nothing. The case of Sir Francis Goodwin and Sir John Fortescue became the case of the whole kingdom. Wingfield suggested that the endorsement of outlawry on the sheriff's return of Goodwin was "cogged in," that is, was put in by fraud. Against such an abuse he would speak without fear as a faithful member of the House.[27] The House, he declared, had advised and then resolved. To reverse its judgment would be childish.[28]

As for a conference with the judges, he was opposed to it. The judges were but judges of the law, not of Parliament.[29] Old lawyers would sometimes forget and interpret the law to suit the time in which they were living.[30] Did he mean that the judges would succumb to royal pressure? "If law be as they interpret, in what woeful case we be." [31] He exhorted the Commons to maintain the privileges which their ancestors had left them and which they ought to pass on to their posterity.[32]

This was plain speaking, and Wingfield, later called to account for it, set forth an explanatory statement concerning what he had said that was somewhat less emphatic than was reported at the time.[33]

Wingfield was followed by Sir George More who used conciliatory words designed to win the Commons. He commended Wingfield's speech, but urged the Commons to offer the King satisfaction. Let them confer with the judges, not as Parliament men but as counselors. Not a question of reversing errors but of being better informed, it could do no harm and might do good.[34] It would be unfortunate if this difference between the King and his people were noised abroad.[35] Let them ask the King for permission to make a law for the banishment of all outlaws from the Parliament and one allowing members of Parliament to retain all their privileges. In this last suggestion he came close to forecasting the outcome.

Bacon followed in More's steps. The House should not contest with the King. He quoted the Roman saying that it was best not to dispute with one that is master of thirty legions.[36] The problem was to give the King satisfaction and at the same time to retain their privileges. He favored a conference; they would lose no privilege, and they might gain something. The Lords were jealous of the honor of a Privy Council or (Fortescue), the Commons of the freedom of election to their body. The House was a Court of Record, but it would be desirable to have a law to declare their privileges. The King, through his Court of Chancery, was a judge of returns before the House had met, but not after it was in session; then the House was judge. There was no precedent, Bacon asserted, for a man being put out of the House for outlawry.

Four questions, Bacon said, were raised: (1) whether the House had the right to take notice of a return made before it was in session, (2) whether men could be outlawed by the House, (3) whether one who was pardoned but who had neglected to sue out a writ of scire facias may be called in question, (4) whether the writ was returned on February 17 or not.[37] The last point supported the parliamentary case. The Crown Office had sent out the new writ before the first had been returned.

Bacon's analysis was not wholly one-sided. He would have liked to have been the honest broker, stating the case for each side with skill and bringing opposing groups together.

Sir John Mallory, M.P. for Ripon, of Yorkshire family, had served on the Council of the North and was now in his second Parliament. He stood against any conference with the Lords and stoutly against any reversal of the position taken by the Commons.[38]

He was followed by Francis Moore, M.P. for Reading, who in 1601 had ventured to say: "And to what purpose is it to do anything by Act of Parliament when the Queen will undo the same by her prerogative?" [39] He was said to have drafted the Statute of Charitable Uses [1601]. At this point he declared that there were precedents that outlawry had been tolerated in Members of Parliament. As for a conference with the judges he favored it.[40]

Richard Martin had entered Parliament in 1601 as an M.P. for Barnstaple, and he now represented Christchurch in Hampshire and may have been given the nomination by Cecil. He opposed royal policies in the early years of James's reign but with such grace and humor that he did not bring down any rebuke upon himself and was finally given the Recordership of London. In this debate he asserted that an outlaw was allowed to serve as an executor for another and thus ought to prove a useful member.[41]

Henry Yelverton, son of an Elizabethan judge and M.P. for the borough of Northampton, was said, in what was probably his maiden speech, to have spoken "with great applause for gravity, boldness, and judgment." [42] That he was emphatic did not lessen the attention of his audience. As he marked some "dejected countenance" before him, he declared himself "distracted," not as to what he should think, but as to what he should say. To waver and vacillate in their resolution, he told the members, would not cause later generations to reverence and remember them; rather, it would make their acts a curse and scorn to posterity and make them guilty of levity, cruelty, and cowardice.[43] No court could reform its own judgments, even if those judgments were erroneous. Never had the Commons passed an act and then reversed it. If they did not now set forth their rights manfully, they would lose them.[44]

A former speaker (Bacon) had declared that exceptions taken before the House had assembled should be judged by the Lord Chancellor by rule of law but that exceptions taken after the House was in session were to be governed by rule of Parliament. To give way to that opinion would be to open a gap to thrust them into the Petty Bag (control by Chancery). A future Chancellor might force the country to vary their choices at his pleasure, and they might find themselves a Chancellor's Parliament, which God forbid.[45] Any suggestion by an individual might lead the Chancery to issue a new writ. Up to that point no elected member had ever been known to perish in Chancery on his way to the House.

The privilege to determine elections was "a flower of the Crown, royally imparted to their ancestors and . . . left by them to descend to us." "Prescription of time hath established the Prince's grace into the subjects' right. . . . Let us not faint but keep that flower fresh."

He warned them that they should not fear the greatness of Sir John Fortescue, whom he also for many respects had just cause to honor. Nor should they assume that the King willed "otherwise than the establishing of all the privileges of that House, for so he the King most royally willed the committees to . . . consider of their resolution, wishing they might justify their former proceedings, and if they could not among themselves resolve, then to confer with the Judges and so resolve." [46] Here Yelverton was putting the best possible gloss on the message the King had sent.

It was said, Yelverton continued, that the opinion of the judges was not a thing newly conceived by them. In 35 Hen. VI the judges resolved that no outlawed man ought to be admitted.[47] Within "four years after the first resolution, when it was yet fresh, namely 35 Hen. VI did oversway it in Parliament that a man outlawed might be, and was a member of this House, and so hath it run in precedent ever since." [48]

To unseat Goodwin would be to defraud the people. "I had rather depart from a Parliament where no law should be made," he concluded, "than sit in a Parliament where this privilege should be destroyed." He urged the Commons to return to their first resolution.

Thomas Crew, a Gray's Inn man and M.P. for Lichfield, who was later to make himself unpopular with the King, insisted upon the irregularity of the issue of the second writ before the day of the return of the first, an irregularity that troubled other members. Crew was opposed to any conference with the judges, but hoped that the consideration of the matter by the Commons would be delivered to the Privy Council for the satisfaction of the King.[49]

Thomas Hedley, M.P. for the borough of Huntingdon, declared that the Commons were not contesting with the King, whose honor was not involved. The King's inferior officers were to blame.[50]

Hext from Somerset, Barrington, of a great landed family in Essex, and Nicholas Fuller wished to see the Commons confer with the judges. Lawrence Hyde, who was most at home in opposition, hoped the Commons would come to a resolution and then inform the Councilors in writing.[51] William Wiseman, a London merchant and an old-timer in the Commons, was of much the same opinion.

Finally the House resolved that their judgment could not be altered and that their reasons should be set down in writing to be delivered to the Privy Council, and that a committee should be appointed of those who had spoken and of ten others to "consult of the resolution for the answer to the Lords of the Council," [52] to meet at 2:00 p.m. that day and to report next morning to the House for their comment.

Meanwhile King James had written to his Privy Council:

> Notwithstanding our more than loving proposition to the Lower House . . . and our more than fatherly conclusion with them, that if they were in the wrong towards us they should not be ashamed to acknowledge it,[53] but submit themselves to the opinion of the Judges. . . . We hear that they do persist in their former purpose . . . which seemeth so strange to us, as we have thought good to require you to signify unto them in our name that we expect they shall in that matter either give us satisfaction, or else deliver up by writing to you, there, or send to us what further doubt they find in that matter. . . . Our express pleasure is that this be the first thing they take in hand, and that no other matter be dealt in until it be determined.[54]

On April 2, the examination of the sheriff of Buckinghamshire by a select committee revealed that the sheriff had expected no contest and had sent word to Sir Francis Goodwin that he did not need to bring any freeholders to help him with their votes. Goodwin was running as second man to Sir John Fortescue.

As soon, however, as the sheriff reached Brickhill, the rendezvous substituted for Aylesbury because of the plague there, he was told by Sir George Throckmorton and by others that the first voice would be given for Goodwin. He answered that he hoped that it would not be so and requested every gentleman to deal with the freeholders on behalf of Fortescue. When it came to voting time at 8:00 a.m., he propounded Fortescue and Goodwin. The freeholders cried, "A Goodwin, a Goodwin." Every justice said "A Fortescue, a Fortescue," and came down from the bench and begged the freeholders to name him for the first place. Goodwin was summoned and "earnestly persuaded with the freeholders," saying Sir John was his good friend. He asked them not to do Sir John such an injury. But the opinion, according to the sheriff, was that Goodwin received between two and three hundred votes and Fortescue about sixty. I take it that Sir William Fleetwood was elected with Goodwin. For some reason the freeholders did not wish to choose Fortescue and were not heeding the advice of the gentry.

The sheriff was asked by the committee why he had made a second return so long before the Parliament met. He blamed what had happened on the Attorney General, the Clerk of the Crown, Sir George Coppin, and Sir John Fortescue. They had cooperated in turning over to him a new writ sealed, and apparently they had taken the old writ from him. It would seem that Sir John Fortescue had not been inactive in his own behalf.[55]

On April 3 the reasons penned by the committee to be presented to the King were brought in by Francis Moore. The Commons had never thought, or so they said, to offend His Majesty. As for the first objection—that since parliamentary writs were returned into Chancery the returns had to be examined there, "and not by us"—the committee answered that until the seventh year of Henry IV all parliamentary writs were returnable into Parliament, "as appeareth by many precedents of record." For this statement the committee offered no proof.

As one reads the act of 7 Hen. IV, cap. xv, it appears that the writs were returned into *Cancellaria nostra.* The committee declared that, although the writ had been somewhat altered, the power of Parliament "to examine and determine of elections remaineth, for so the statute hath been always expounded ever sithence by use, to this day." [56]

For the explanation that the writ had been so expounded, the committee offered no scintilla of evidence and one wonders where the evidence was to be found. That this writ, as quoted in the statute, was possibly based on earlier usage does not seem to have been considered by the committee.

The committee went on to cite a few Elizabethan precedents that proved little. Those toward the end of the reign were indeed significant; they indicated that the Commons were now aware, whether they had been earlier or not, of the importance of controlling the returns of elections.

As one examines D'Ewes, the returns in the early years of the great Queen and still earlier returns mentioned by D'Ewes, one wonders how much historical evidence exists to prove that the Commons in early Tudor days or earlier had control of the returns of elections. It has to be said that the parliamentary committee had seldom put out a weaker statement.[57] Why was it not pounced upon at once by the friends of the King? It would appear that few around the King were well versed in parliamentary history and precedents. Those who believe that before the third decade of the Queen's reign the Commons had control over their membership, need to prove their case.

In their statement to the King the House dealt also with the matter of outlawry. They cited instances where outlaws had served in Parliament; they said, also, that Goodwin had never been legally outlawed. A party outlawed, they maintained, had to be proclaimed an outlaw five times in the sheriff's court. A writ of exigent had been taken out in order to force payment of debts; the money had been paid, and the writ of exigent [58] had never been certified by a writ of certiorari. The committee made a further claim. A new clerk had come into office lately and made entries, since this election, signifying that Goodwin was outlawed.

On April 5 the Speaker apologized for his absence and brought a message from the King. His Majesty had received a parchment from the House, "whether it were an absolute resolution, or reason to give him satisfaction, he knew not." He was as anxious as any to maintain their privileges, but he had seen the judges and he was distracted as to his judgment. As a king he commanded that there should be a conference between the House and the judges and that his counsel might be present.[59]

The House was taken by surprise. Yelverton, who had with reasoned arguments and no little courage supported the case for Goodwin's election, now rose and declared that the Prince's command was like a thunderbolt or the roaring of a lion, a remarkable shift of position for one who with idiomatic phrases and telling sentences had begged the Commons not to reverse themselves.

The Speaker was not slow to put the question whether to confer with the judges, and it was so voted. A committee of twenty-one lawyers and sixteen gentlemen was named, and it was resolved, on the suggestion of Lawrence Hyde, that the committee should insist only upon the fortification and explanation of the reasons given His Majesty and should proceed to no other argument.[60] Hyde was doing his best to forestall any concession to the Crown on the question. On Martin's initiative, it was moved that the Commons should ask the King to be present.[61]

The Councilors consulted the King who gave the committee audience in the Council Chamber. His Majesty offered a solution. The judges urged that the first writ was not yet well returned and that neither Goodwin nor Fortescue should be returned. His Majesty ordered that a new writ should go forth. It was written in the margin of Montague's minutes that His Majesty had not only pardoned those who had spoken most and stoutest in this cause, but thought the best of them.[62] This all happened in committee. At the end of the morning the Speaker announced that the King had adjourned the House until April 11. It may be that the King had arranged such a cooling-off period before he met the committee and had not expected such an easy resolution of the controversy.

On April 11 the Commons met and Sir Francis Bacon reported the result, no doubt already known to many members. Bacon expatiated on the eloquence of the King. His Majesty had declared that he would not receive anything from his subjects, by which he meant that he was not asking a subsidy from them.[63] The King added that he would confirm all their just privileges. The word "just" would allow him a good deal of leeway. He continued that as Parliament had power, so had the Chancery. "The Court first judging should not be controlled," which would seem to mean that its judgment would have precedence. Then Bacon, on behalf of the Commons, appears to have answered that "Chancery [was] a confidentiary Court to the use of this Parliament during the time." [64] He said, further, that the Parliaments of England were not to be bound by the sheriff's return. Finally the King ordered that neither Goodwin nor Fortescue might have place. Montague stated in his minutes that the King ordered that a new writ should be granted to go out of the Lower House.[65] His Majesty, declared Bacon, had met the Commons halfway.

The King had been not a little excited when on April 5 he commanded as an absolute king. Now he had veered suddenly and offered a compromise. How did it happen? Was it possible that Cecil had not been wholly unsympathetic with the complaints of the men from the shires and that he had advised his master to meet the Commons part way? It is interesting that some of those members who spoke up for parliamentary privileges and rights, as they believed, were on good terms with Cecil, and some of them owed their seats to the influence of the Cecil family. Cecil had to support royalty or lose his place, but he could say a word in season and, if it was the last word, it might prevail.

It was the opinion of the Venetian ambassador [66] that the King was so intent upon the union of the two kingdoms that he would do what he could to secure unanimity on other issues. The Venetian ambassador concluded: "His Majesty is inclined to be favorable to the Lords but the Commons show great firmness in standing by their privilege." In his next letter Molin reported that the King was returning from his hunting sojourn and regretted the extremity to which the Goodwin-Fortescue controversy had been pushed, "for he sees that he must either give or receive considerable damage." [67]

Not everyone in the House was pleased at the outcome. It was moved that the Commons should declare that what was done was "at the request of the King." [68] Such a motion must have been made with a view to winning public opinion to the side of Parliament. The same speaker added that Parliament lost more at a session than it would have gained in a battle, by which I think he meant in terms of rights and privileges. The committee, it was said, had power only to fortify what had been agreed upon by the House, that is, to give reasons in favor of their action to seat

Goodwin. The committee, Brooke maintained,[69] had exceeded its
commission and had shown inconstancy and levity. He wished
them called to the bar. "But the acclamation of the House was
that it was a testimony of our duty and no levity." [70] The Commons resolved that a new writ should be issued, but the election
was for the first place only; Sir William Fleetwood had been
elected to the second place. In place of Fortescue, Christopher
Pigott was elected.

Brooke and three friends who disapproved of the compromise
did not realize that time was on the side of Parliament. To them
the King seemed to have gotten the best of the compromise solution.[71] From that day on, the right of the Commons to determine
the election of members was rarely questioned. Had the King
stuck to his claims, his successors would soon have had the battle
to fight again. The men in the House of Commons would not long
have submitted to the determination of their membership in
Chancery, for they had discovered that they did not have to submit. In the long run the compromise forced upon them turned out
to be a complete victory. It did not appear so, at the time, but it
proved the first of many defeats for the Stuarts.

Preliminary Discussions
of the Union

THE conclusion of the
Goodwin-Fortescue episode
seemed to leave the King
and the Commons in good spirits. James sent word that now the
House should treat of matters for the commonwealth and for himself: the union, bills for the commonwealth, and the "Reformation
of Ecclesiastical Discipline." [1]

He suggested that the plan for the union should now be prepared so that it would be ready for the next session, the last words
being significant. It was April 13, and the King, who had hoped
for immediate action, was now reconciled to a delay until the
next session of Parliament. The Lords made the first move; they
asked for a conference with the Commons touching the union.

The Commons named a hundred of their own House to meet with forty from the Lords that Saturday at 2:00 p.m.

On Monday, April 16, Sir Henry Montague reported the declaration of the Lords. They recognized that the use of two distinct names for the two kingdoms was an offense and proposed that the two nations might now be styled Great Britain.[2] As for the laws, rites, customs, and ceremonies, they should be considered by commissioners to be named from the lords, bishops, and men of all sorts. The commissioners would report to Parliament where matters would be concluded.

In the debate that followed Bacon touched upon the problems involved, the relation of the English Parliament and Privy Council to the united kingdoms, the trade between the two kingdoms and that with foreign countries, and other matters. As to the name of "Great Britain" for the newly united kingdoms, Bacon found some majesty in its style. Another member proposed the name "Britanny." Bacon suggested also that the King might be called emperor, a suggestion that may have originated in a higher quarter.

On April 19, it was proposed that the Commons confer with the Lords—"sentinels," as Bacon called them—who understood matters of state. He went on to catalogue objections to the name of Britain; the English would lose the ancient name of England, so famous and victorious. Yet it was as Britain that the nation held tack with (was matched with) the Romans in their greatness.[3] Names were but airy and volatile things.

Sir Edwin Sandys did not agree with that remark of Bacon. The cause now before them was the weightiest that had come or could come before them. Let them proceed with a leaden foot. Names involved the nature of things. The English House of Commons could not make laws to bind Britannia. "England sits here representatively only." It was the duty of the Commons to leave their successors free. Was he implying that the union might interfere with the historic rights of Englishmen in Parliament?

Secretary Herbert talked about the union in name and govern-

ment as honorable, profitable, and possible. He announced, no
doubt with authority, that they were to debate freely and without
limitation.

Francis Moore urged, as others, caution about the name.
Richard Martin feared that the name would "inwrap the matter."
By changing her name, England would lose that precedence in
the courts of Europe that was most dear to all nations.

The debate on April 20 added little to what had been said.
No enthusiasm developed for the name "Great Britain." Secretary
Herbert tried to meet the rising opposition by maintaining that
the name Britain would not take away England; it would take
away no dignities or privileges from either nation, "The government of other countries [Ireland and Scotland] to be brought to
ours."

It was resolved to confer with the Lords but to conclude nothing. All the committeemen for the conference were to meet with
the King at 2:00 p.m. Any man was free to accompany the committee to His Majesty.

On the following morning Bacon reported the speech of the
King to the Commons. His Majesty had no intention of altering
the fundamental laws, privileges, and customs of the realm, but he
hoped that all sorts of statutes and customs might be welded
("welled," in text) into one. He had not expected so much discourse and dispute. The Commons had found knots in rushes
and straws. The question of the union had become alehouse
talk. He deserved their attention because of his place and the
matter. True it was that England was famous, victorious, and
glorious, but she had been conquered; Scotland never had. His
ancestors, when they were lions and not sluggish, were ever
victorious.

The change of name was nothing serious, he continued. Lord
Walden suffered no diminution when he became Earl of Suffolk.
The benefit of a single name would extinguish the seeds of dis-
sension and prove a demonstration of the union to follow. He had
no intention that the Scots should encroach upon the English.

What he hoped for was that uniformity of manners and customs which God in his providence had begun.

As for the bill itself, he did not undertake to prescribe to Parliament what precise words they should use. He realized that doubts and questions of law were involved in the use of a new title. All that he was willing to omit for the time being. What he feared were the doubts aroused by the curious carping of some and the misinterpretation of the law. He hoped that his loyal subjects would help him not to be overruled by willfulness where he could not be convinced by reason.[4]

On April 23 Bacon reported that in the conference the Lords had recommended a commission of English and Scottish members who were to debate but not to conclude anything. Richard Percival, M.P. for Richmond in Yorkshire, who had been honored by the late Queen for his skill in translating ciphers and was said to have discovered the intention of the Spaniards to invade England, made a long speech, in which he let a cat out of the bag. Men of sufficiency (competency?) and learning, he asserted, ought not to be forestalled from speaking openly, the same point made by Crew. Was a rumor going around that men were being silenced in advance? Percival went on to talk of Mother England who had "nursed, bred, brought us up to be able to serve at home for justice, abroad for victories." He pointed out, also, a special difficulty under the union of the two kingdoms: what would be the number of the regnal year? He was afraid of the word "incorporation." Then he implied that, if Scots continued to move to England and pick up offices and lands, the English would have nothing of their own.

Sir Edwin Sandys opposed the title of emperor. The name of king was a sweet name. He reverted to an earlier suggestion that they beseech His Majesty for a proviso that none but the English should be given offices from the Crown. He hoped that the next session of Parliament would be a continuation of the present session, that is, with the same membership.

The warnings of Percival and Crew about freedom of speech

were observed by Privy Councilors. On the next day, April 24, the King sent word that in the matter of the union he allowed freedom and liberty to all. The implication that in some matters he would not allow such freedom was not commented upon, so far as we know.

On April 25 Bacon summarized the objections to the union under thirteen heads, making separate heads of what might have been put together. He saw no advantage in a new name. The present name had become dear to the English. If they altered the King's title, they would have to alter all things else. Wherever diplomats met, England would lose precedence. The change in name would bring confusion in records, in writs, and thus in the King's courts. The more we wade, the more we doubt, he exclaimed, as if in sympathy with the doubters. He continued that public opinion was to be regarded. "Kings have used to do it." What that meant, I assume, was that the public seemed opposed to change and that its opposition should be taken into account.

The next day Sandys made an analytical answer to Bacon and then went on to offer examples of unions, by marriage, election, and conquest, maintaining that there had never been any uniting in a third name. If there was no precedent, then the question of union had to be examined by reason, on which the law of nations was grounded. "We can give no laws to Britain because we are but parcel. Scotland cannot because it is another part. Together we cannot, because several corporations." That had consequences on English liberties:

> The King by oath at his coronation tied to maintain our liberties, etc. The subject by oath of allegiance tied to serve the King, to maintain all rights annexed to the Crown, etc. He [as King of Britain] may exact another oath of us. We have no warrant to require any of him.

The problem of union was difficult and should be approached with care and judgment and without passion.

It was the speech of a thinking man, but so hurriedly recorded by the Clerk that we cannot be sure that the argument is precisely stated.

At the conference with the Lords on May 1 the committeemen from the Upper House were inclined, ignoring the wishes of the King's supporters, to drop, for the time being at least, the matter of the name of Britain. They were, however, ready to proceed with the choosing of commissioners to meet with commissioners from Scotland. The Lords proposed a subcommittee of the two Houses to digest and frame the act for a commission.

Another conference followed on the same day, and the next morning Bacon reported that nominations were to be made for membership on the commission, which was to include lawyers, civilians, men of state, and merchants. It is interesting that merchants were recognized.

On May 1 a letter from His Majesty informed the Commons that he had treated them with sincerity and clearness and had been too little regarded. Either the Commons were jealous of him or distrusted him. When the commission had considered the union and reported, he wrote, "then will ye be your own cooks to dress it as ye list." He hoped that they would not be transported with the "curiosity of a few giddy heads." Few heads were less giddy than those of Sandys, Francis Moore, and Hakewill. It was possible for members, he continued, to blaspheme in God's face by preferring war to peace, trouble to quietness, hatred to love, weakness to greatness, and division to union. They could sow seeds of discord and dishonor to their King and to all his posterity.

This was a typical Jamesian statement. He felt himself en rapport with the Supreme Being and failed even to touch upon those real difficulties about union that worried the Commons. He presumed that he was right and that opposition to his program was perverse.

Hyde and Wingfield moved that the King be informed how they took his letter to heart. Strode feared that the King had been misinformed. It was suggested that every man who had access to the sovereign should purge himself of tales either to the King or to any Privy Councilor. It was also suggested that the Speaker should go to His Majesty to "satisfy" him. Then a committee was named to consider what the Speaker should say to His Majesty, a committee that included several of those who had spoken, Yelverton, Sandys, Sir George More, and Sir Henry Montague.

Would that we knew the explanation of what happened next. Late on the same day it was "resolved upon question to forbear to proceed in this committee, or to attend his Majesty in this matter." [5] On the next day came a message from the King, who recognized that their forbearance proceeded from love; therefore he gave it precedence in his thoughts. If they had come, he would have explained his position and endeavored to give them satisfaction. The King had a way of rushing forward and then drawing back. Probably the Privy Councilors knew that he was about to change his course and persuaded the members to refrain from sending a committee to see him.

Meanwhile the House busied itself with naming the committee to confer with the Lords about framing the bill for the Commission for the Union. A question was made of every one of the names of the commissioners proposed and each one approved by a separate vote.

Conferences between the two Houses over the commissioners continued during the month of May. The Commons were determined that the commissioners should have no final say, and on that point the Lords did not differ from them. There were differences, however, as to whether the commissioners should be named before the instructions for them were fully worked out. The Commons were intent that the commissioners who, as commissioners, had voted a certain way, might, when the results of their labors with the Scottish commissioners had been laid before the English Parliament, find it possible to vote otherwise if they so wished. About several details in the instructions there was sharp discussion. It was said that the bill, like winter fruit, "ripens slowly." [6] On June 2 the bill passed the Commons.

In his final speech His Majesty rebuked the Commons. In Scotland he had been treated as a counselor.

Contrary here, nothing but curiosity from morning to evening, to find fault with my propositions. There all things warranted that came from me. Here all things suspected. I will begin with the newest, the greatest, and the first, the Union. Look not that I will sing a palinode. Whatsoever hath been spread to distaste this Union, I set no frame to you but the matter, I avow, and more I avow the name Britanny. Else were I a rebel and a traitor to God and nature. . . . He that doth not love a Scotchman as his brother, or the Scotchman that loves not an Englishman as his brother is a traitor to God and the King. . . . He merits to be buried in the bottom of the sea that shall but think of a separation, where God hath made such a Union. I am not ashamed of my project, neither have I deferred it (I'll deal plainly) out of a liking of the Judges's reasons, or yours. . . . I have remitted the name till after the thing be done, lest quirks in law might take other hold than is meant.[7]

The King avoided the real issue as to laws and writs, and diplomatic status. He called names. He allowed himself, as he did so often, to lose his temper and his dignity.

Wardship

THE English landowning classes had long suffered from the abuses of wardship. Their failure to make an issue of it in Elizabethan Parliaments, as members had done with monopolies and had tried to do with purveyance, may be explained in part as owing to fear of change or, in other words, to sheer conservatism. So accustomed were the English to feudal burdens that they did not readily envisage the possibility of freeing themselves from them. Yet the State Papers Domestic, the calendars of the Cecil Manuscripts, and the letters and memoirs of the late Tudor and early Stuart decades prove that wardship had become a running sore in society and in the body politic. The sovereign had various rights, duties, and dues he could expect from his tenants in chief, most of them the nobility and gentry of England.

One of the King's rights, when a tenant in chief died and left an heir who was a minor, was to name a guardian for the ward. The guardian had to provide for the upbringing and education of the ward according to his state, but he could annex for himself, if he also gained the wardship of the land, the remaining income of the heir's lands until the heir came of age, paying only a fixed rent to the Crown. The guardianship of a ward thus became a profitable investment: the Crown could make money from the sale of wardships; it could also dispense wardships as rewards for service rendered in the past and possible service in the future and to bestow gifts on favorites.

The results were not always fortunate. The nobility, the gentry, and the hangers-on at Court were, many of them, importunate and brazen beggars for the guardianship of wards. Whenever a landed gentleman with an heir in his minority fell ill, the eager suitor hurried off letters to a Secretary of State, a Privy Councilor, or a royal favorite, setting forth his record of service to the Crown and his need for money. In a time when the gentle class, aside from younger sons, expected to live from their income and did not expect to take posts (except highly honorable ones in the government, the burdens of which could be carried by a subordinate), many gentlemen assumed that it was incumbent upon His Majesty to see to it that his wellborn subjects enjoyed a comfortable income.

It was not only the less well-endowed gentlemen who sought guardianships, but those on their way to wealth. The acquisition of wardships was recognized as one of the ways of getting on. To use a nineteenth-century phrase, wardships were a form of out-of-door relief for the privileged classes. The bestowal of such favors put additional power in the hands of the sovereign, power that carried political implications. Those Members of Parliament who needed financial rehabilitation or coveted more acres were unlikely to vote in the Commons in a way to offend that giver of all good things, His Majesty.

There was a feminine side to the question. If the tenant in chief left only an heiress, the King had the right to pick a husband for her under the old feudal principle that a woman could not perform military service and the overlord wished her to marry someone who was not his enemy and who could be of service to him. In practice the sovereign was likely to sell the heiress to the highest bidder. This sale of heiresses became an unwholesome feature of English life. A playwright of the time, George Wilkins, wrote a play, *The Miseries of Inforst Marriage* (1607), and writers and pamphleteers represented the sale of heiresses as a sign of something wrong in the state of England.

As feudal law developed, the overlord—the King in this case—came to control the marriages not only of heiresses but of male heirs. From this right His Majesty could derive additional revenue.[1]

It would appear that not only the statutes but the common law gave the wards the worst of it. If a man held any land *in capite,* then his heir was a ward not only for the land *in capite* but for all his land. If his father had accumulated debts, the guardian might draw all the profits, except the allowance for the upkeep and education of the ward, and leave the debts unsatisfied, with the result that the ward, when he came of age, would be forced to pay them.

The guardian was likely to prove overthrifty about the upkeep and education of the ward. He was likely, also, to draw all the immediate profit he could from the ward's lands. The ward, when he came of age, wrote Sir Thomas Smith, would find his "woods decayed, old houses, stock wasted, land ploughed to the bare." [2]

The abuses of wardship were so much in the minds of the landed class that Henry Percy, the Earl of Northumberland, broached it in one of those letters that he wrote to James VI of Scotland in reference to the succession of that sovereign to the English throne:

The burden that the gentility repines at chiefly is wardships, a law first instituted for preserving them in time of their minorities, now become the ruin almost of all men's houses once in a three descents, a commodity small in the Prince's coffers, when the accounts are cast up; neither doth this so far move them to discontent that they will venture the loss of all to redress this one, both because custom hath made them obedient to it, and hopes give them belief that they may be freed upon easier conditions hereafter.[3]

At the beginning of the reign of James, the Lord Treasurer, the Earl of Dorset, put forward, according to Sir Roger Wilbraham, a four-point plan:

1. To sell all copyholders their freeholds
2. To grant leases for sixty years of all the King's lands or fee farms, taking small fines and doubling or trebling the rents
3. To accept a composition for respite or homage
4. To accept an annual rent for wardship [4]

Sir Roger put the fourth point in this way: "The Master of the Wards said he was to have the wards turned to a certain annual rent to be propounded in Parliament." The Master of the Wards was Cecil. It was he who sent out word to feodaries in the shires to tell tenants by knight service that fathers might, if they so wished, buy out in their own lifetime the wardships and marriages of their heirs then living. By buying out the marriages Cecil meant that the father might pay a composition in place of fees due to the King for permission to the heir to marry. This message from Cecil was publicly read at Bodmin and at Truro in October 1603.[5] Letters such as those sent to Cornwall were sent out to feodaries in all counties.[6] It would appear that the Master of the Court of Wards was working hand in hand with the Lord Treasurer, and with the approval of the King, to raise ready money for the Crown and at the same time to offer some relief from wardship to the King's tenants in chief.

Wardship and purveyance were the two grievances that festered most in the minds of country gentlemen and thus of Members of Parliament. Agitation over wardship led to the framing of the Apology of 1604, and eventually to the proposed Great Contract and to the fiasco of the late autumn of 1610. It is true that voices of those who called for ecclesiastical reforms were insistent and that the feelings of those who disliked the Scots and feared the union of the two kingdoms were not easily quieted. But it was the burden of wardship and of purveyance that solidified opposition to the King in the Commons. Cecil's plan had apparently come to nothing.

Thus it is not surprising that as soon as Parliament met in March 1604 the problem of wardship was raised. It will be recalled that on March 23, the first day of discussion, Sir Robert Wroth mentioned matters that needed attention, most of them abuses, and wardship was among them. He urged "that the wardship of gentlemen's sons may be considered of, being a great servitude . . . to all the subjects of this Kingdom."[7]

The committee nominated to deal with Wroth's motion included most of the well-known figures of the House of Commons of the last years of Elizabeth. Among them were Sir Henry Neville, Sir Francis Bacon, Nathaniel Bacon, Sir Herbert Croft, Sir Thomas Crompton the well-known civilian, Sir Hugh Beeston, Nicholas Fuller, Lawrence Hyde, Francis Moore, John Hare (clerk of the Court of Wards), Sir Edward Hoby, Sir Francis Hastings, Sir Peter Manwood, Sir Thomas Holcroft, Sir Edward Lewknor, and Sir Edwin Sandys.

On March 26 Sir Francis Bacon reported from the committee. The King, he declared, might "be answered to his contentment" by granting him a yearly rent in place of wardship.[8] If he would accept that, it would amount to such sum as had never been offered to the King since tenures were set up.

Somewhat rashly, Bacon ventured to offer a historical explanation. Wardship was grounded, he asserted, on scutage.[9] Scutage had been "invented to defend the King and this Realm against the Scots."[10] With the two kingdoms joined, the case for wardship, livery, and *primer seizin* came to an end.[11] Parliament had granted, he said, to Henry VIII, Edward VI, and Mary the right to dissolve the Court of Wards.[12]

In the discussion that followed it was said that if the abolition of wardship was a matter of common justice, the Commons ought to proceed by bill; if it were a matter of grace, they ought to go to the King by way of petition. To the House it seemed that a petition was the most honorable way of proceeding.[13]

Before going further the Commons decided to ask for a conference with the Lords and chose a committee for that conference of twenty-four members, the Privy Councilors of the House, Bacon, Sandys, Francis Moore, Sir Edward Montague, and others. That committee went up to the Lords and received a favorable answer. The Lords proposed that, in addition to wardship, respite of homage [14] and licenses of alienation [15] should be considered. They proposed to send to the conference a committee of thirty to meet at 2:00 p.m. The Commons added thirty-six more names to the original twenty-four, and the conference was held that afternoon.[16]

That the Lords were cooperative probably means that the King was not averse to the proposition, at least not at this time. It was in keeping with the plan already put forward by the Lord Treasurer and the First Secretary as coming from His Majesty.

That same afternoon the committees of the Lords and the Commons met, "but the chamber was filled with as many more of the Lower House as was nominated, but the Lords misliked of it and so most were put out, and they only called by bill that were nominated." [17] Bacon asked the Lords to join with the Commons, and was told by the Lords' committee that they would raise the question in their House and give an answer. Then the Lords brought up the questions of respite of homage, licenses of alienation, and purveyance.

On March 27 Bacon reported from the conference. It was a grief, he declared, but not a wrong, that the heir of every man who held lands from the King by knight service was by prerogative to be in ward to the King for his body and lands. This situation the King was to be asked to remedy, not as a wrong but merely as an act of grace to his subjects. It was realized, Sir Francis went on to say, that the proposal concerned the King in revenue and reward, and consequently the Commons would be expected to compensate His Majesty for the losses he would incur and also to reward the

King's servants, those officials who administered wardship and would lose their positions.

For a time, the question of wardship was dropped; the Goodwin-Fortescue controversy had to be settled. On April 3, however, a few new names were added to the large committee nominated on March 23, a committee that was to deal with wardship and other grievances. By April 16, the Goodwin-Fortescue question being settled, the Commons were engaged in discussing the proposed union with Scotland.[18]

On May 16, after a long interval, Sir Maurice Berkeley brought wardship up again, and a debate ensued. Sir Thomas Ridgeway urged that the question of wardship should be treated in the conference with the Lords about the union—an untimely suggestion, since the union was still the topic of debate.

The problem before the House was whether the topic of wardship should go to the House of Lords by itself or hand in hand with that of purveyance. The decision was that wardship should go by itself; the problem of the composition for wardship was utterly different from that of composition for purveyance.

On May 19 Sandys was sent up to the Lords about a bill for free trade and at the same time he proposed to move the Lords that they should join with the Commons in a petition to His Majesty. They hoped to treat with the Lords regarding a composition for the abolition of wardship, *primer seizin,*[19] and respite of homage. On May 21 the Lords sent a message that they would appoint thirty committeemen to discuss the petition with His Majesty.

The next day it was ordered by the Commons that the committee named originally on March 23 should meet "for the matter of wardships only." On May 26 Sandys asked the House if they would be prepared to approve the directions set down by the committee. The directions, which were approved, were:

First, what we desire.
Secondly, the reasons for our desire.
Thirdly, the removing of impediments which may be objected to.

Fourthly, what course to be taken for the levying and assessing of our composition, if it please his Majesty to assent unto it.

The committee, asserted Sandys, wished to take away the tenures *in capite* and knight service and the burdens depending upon them, as wardship of lands and body, licenses of alienation, marriage of wards, liveries, respite of homage, *primer seizin,* reliefs, etc. Sandys continued about the abolition of wardship: "It is but a restitution unto the original right of all men, by the law of God and Nature, which is that children should be brought up by their parents and next of kin and by them be directed in their marriages." [20] The situation that existed was a grievance and a damage to the subject in his estate; it disabled him to serve his Prince and his country; it resulted in ill-suited marriages, a reproach to the nation.

Sandys went over the reasons of the Commons and explained why, more than their progenitors, they desired the abolition of wardship. There had been hope that at His Majesty's entry the Commons would be eased of the burden of wardship and that hope had been increased by His Majesty's benign offer of the last summer that men might beforehand compound for the marriages of their children. The Commons now hoped that the King, out of his gracious and noble disposition, would ease their burden.

Sandys went on to discuss the impediments to the abolition of wardship. What was to be done, he asked, about the wards of subjects? Were they also to be compounded for at such reasonable rates either of money or of yearly rent as might give satisfaction to the several Lords? Secondly, were pensions to be granted to His Majesty's officers who lost their occupation?

The problem of how to levy and assess the composition would have to be considered when His Majesty had assented to the composition. Some believed, admitted Sandys, that the difficulties were insuperable. "If their Lordships desire any project thereof, this may be proposed by way of overture, to occasion their Lordships to think of a better and more exquisite [one]." For this session all that was necessary was to agree with His Majesty as to the general sum to be raised and about commissioners to be chosen for the assessment of the revenue. Those commissioners were first to inform themselves what lands were in knight service (*in capite*), held by His Majesty in every shire. They were then to set down a proportionable rate to be raised from those lands. The commissioners were next to consider the proportion of ward lands in every shire and, when they had compared the same with the whole quantity, were to allot what should be raised out of every shire. Then they were to divide themselves in the several shires and subdivide every shire in such a way as to tax equitably the lands of every man. When they had done all this, they were to bring their findings before the next Parliament "which [may proceed] to a final conclusion."

It was a complicated scheme and would have involved elaborate machinery to make inquiries and to determine the proper assessments; many Members of Parliament would have been justifiably afraid that such close inquiries would provide evidence that they held concealed or assart lands which the Crown might recover from them.

Sir Robert Wroth suddenly spoke up in the House in apparent despair. It is probable that rumors that the King had changed his mind had reached the House. It was impossible, Wroth believed, that any good could come from the course they were taking. He had foreseen the outcome. He moved therefore that every man by his last will and testament should dispose of his child, paying the like fine, and that some bill should be brought in to that effect. Sir Robert's idea was a simple one, that everyone should provide in his will a composition for the wardship of his son and daughter.

The Lords had possibly heard, too, that the King had shifted his position. That very afternoon a conference was held by the joint committees of the two Houses about wardship and respite of homage.

The Lords moved the Commons to forbear any further dealing about wardship and not to offer any further petitions for it to the King. It was unfit and unreasonable to bring such a matter up in His Majesty's first Parliament.

That afternoon the two Houses adjourned until May 30. When the Commons resumed sitting on that day, they were requested by the Speaker to attend the King.

Of James's speech to them there is no copy nor account, so far as I know. Perhaps somewhere in the British Museum or in the Public Record Office a report of it may yet turn up. What we know is that the House "conceived some grief" [21] at the speech. The Clerk put down: "Many particular actions and passages of the House were objected unto them, with taxation and blame." [22]

On June 1 Sir Edwin Sandys reported on the conference with the Lords. He said the reply of the Lords had been threefold, covering expostulation or friendly reprehension, answers to the reasons, and admonition. Their words might have come from the King; they alluded to the dangers avoided in March of 1603 when everyone feared civil war. Instead of strife, however, there was now stability and a sovereign seated firmly on the throne. The Commons, instead of showing their pleasure, spent their time on matters of privilege, purveyance, etc. As for wardship, it was not characteristic of England alone, but was known in Scotland and France. The last commission for compounding had brought in only £4,000, but wardship had amounted to about £31,000. Respite of homage and alienations would prove less profitable to His Majesty than wardship.

This sudden turnabout of the Lords must have been a blow to the Commons. Various members took the floor. Sir Thomas Ridgeway, who was later said to have been "strong with his Devonshire crew," [23] moved a committee to take a survey of the proceedings of the House and to set down something in writing for His Majesty's satisfaction. It was finally resolved to name a committee to survey the proceedings that had been opposed and thus free the House from the scandal of levity, and also to seek some satisfaction about wardship and other problems. The committee named on March 23 was to have six more members, in addition to those added at other times. That resolution included this significant phrase: "Since it appeared his Majesty had made such an impression of mislike of the proceedings of the House in general, as also, that the grounds conceived touching wardship and

matters of that nature seemed to be so weakened and impugned."
Thus ended, or practically ended, the first lesson for those who
hoped to do away with wardship.

Wardship was brought up once more in the Apology, which
resulted from the work of the committee nominated to "consider of some satisfaction in the matter of wardship." With that
Apology I shall deal later. Drawn up with care and in some parts
with precision of language, it was never passed by the Commons
and hence was never presented to the King. About wardship the
Apology said:

> We cannot forget . . . how your Majesty in a former most
> gracious speech in your gallery at Whitehall advised us for un-
> just burthens to proceed against them by bill; but for such as
> were just, if we desired any ease, that we should come to your-
> self, by way of petition, with tender of such countervailable
> composition in profit as for the supporting of your royal state
> was requisite. . . . We prepared a petition . . . for leave to
> treat with your Highness touching a perpetual composition to
> be raised by yearly revenue out of the lands of your subjects, for
> wardships and other burthens depending upon them . . .
> wherein we first entered into this dutiful consideration, that
> this prerogative of the Crown, which we desire to compound for,
> was matter of mere profit and not of any honor at all or princely
> dignity . . . we entered into a second degree of consideration,
> with how great grievance and damage of the subject, to the decay
> of many houses and disabling of them to serve their Prince and
> country; with how great mischief also by occasion of many
> forced and ill-suited marriages; and lastly with how great con-
> tempt and reproach of our nation in foreign countries how
> small a commodity now was raised to the Crown, in respect of
> that which with great love and joy and thankfulness for the
> restitution of this original right in disposing of our children, we
> would be content and glad to assure unto your Majesty.[24]

Why had the King changed his policy? No doubt he was disappointed and even indignant that his statesmanlike schemes for the
union had not been received with enthusiasm. He probably

realized by now that there was little chance that the Commons, in return for concessions about wardship and purveyance, would vote him a composition which he could regard as an adequate equivalent.

The Purveyors in 1604

ONE of the prerogatives of royalty was the right to buy provisions for the royal household and to have the use of carts and horses for the conveyance of the provisions to the royal palaces or to the Court when the King was on a progress. The prices to be paid were fixed by the King's purveyors, and, having been fixed in medieval times, were not often changed, with the result that the King's purveyors paid only a fraction of the prices current during the reigns of Elizabeth and James I. It was a system that led to abuses. From the reign of Edward I on, statute after statute was passed to protect subjects from the rapacity of purveyors. Throughout the reign of Elizabeth and in earlier reigns, complaint had been made in Parliament about the purveyors, and bills had been introduced into the House of Commons. The abuse was certain to be put forward by some of the leaders in the new Parliament. Indeed, Cecil (Lord Cranborne), in writing the King a long letter intended for the eyes of Privy Councillors, touched upon the question: "Who does not know that purveyance is used in as many offices and by as mean instruments as ever it was! Nay what country gentleman can you speak withal that is not able to show you continual abuses." [1] He wished they had three or four weeks' time to make better arrangements about purveyance.

Cecil's words were confirmed by Wroth when, on March 23, he and Sir Edward Montague raised the matter of grievances. Wroth characterized the purveyors as the "hellhounds of England." [2] Committees of "gentlemen of good sort," [3] were nominated to deal with all seven grievances. Thee days later Sir Francis Bacon made a report. Four men—Lawrence Hyde, John Hare, Nicholas Fuller, and Lawrence Tanfield—presumably a subcommittee, were named to draw up a bill for the restraint of purveyors. They were also to consider a bill prepared by Hyde, to peruse all former statutes—a large assignment—and to report on the following Wednesday.

Hyde represented Marlborough in Wiltshire and had earlier represented other Wiltshire constituencies. In Elizabethan Parliaments he had spoken now and then and had been named to various committees.[4] A "very learned gentleman," Robert Bowyer called him.[5] Sir Edward Hoby, one of the spokesmen of the late Elizabethan Parliaments, wrote Sir Thomas Edmondes that Hyde and Hare had "represented the tribunes of the people." [6]

Hare, a member from Morpeth in Northumberland, had represented Horsham (Sussex) in six sessions and West Looe (Cornwall) in 1601. Clerk of the Court of Wards, he had been long concerned about the abuses of purveyors, and in 1589 he had introduced a bill for dealing with them and had served on a committee for the bill along with Wroth.[7] Usually in opposition, he was in 1606 characterized by Speaker Phelips as "an unconsiderate firebrand." [8] He seems, nevertheless, to have looked to Cecil as his patron.[9]

Nicholas Fuller, the son of a London merchant and a barrister of Gray's Inn, had been a member for a Cornish constituency in 1593. A zealous Puritan, he would be imprisoned in 1607 by Archbishop Bancroft for questioning the power of the Court of High Commission.

Tanfield, now member for Oxfordshire, who had represented New Woodstock, northwest of Oxford, since 1584, had not been a conspicuous figure in the House. So far as we can learn from D'Ewes and Townshend he had made one short speech and served on four committees.[10] But he had entertained James I at his house at Burford and was presumably on good terms with him. In his own community he was not trusted by all.[11]

The committee of four lost little time. On March 31 Hyde brought in a bill for the "Better Executing of Sundry Statutes touching Purveyors," as drawn and allowed, he asserted, by the General Committee. After a second reading, the bill was referred back to the General Committee who deemed it best to consult with the Officers of Green Cloth in charge of purveyance.

On April 14 the question was raised in the House as to whether they should carry on with the bill or proceed by petition to the King. In spite of Hyde's opposition, the latter policy was determined upon (the bill to be deferred for a time). On April 18 the petition drafted by the committee (the small committee?) was "so pressed to a reading as the House grew to a division about it." [12] By thirty votes it was carried that the petition should not be read then, but rather the next morning. It was, and then it was delivered back to the committee, to Francis Moore.[13]

The opponents of the purveyors were evidently not having things their own way. Hyde apologized for a sharp speech of the day before. But the attack nevertheless continued. It was decided that the Commission to the Purveyors should be delivered by the Clerk of the Crown to the committee, and that the committee was to meet in the afternoon. The Officers of Green Cloth, who had seemed in no hurry to meet with the committee, were summoned to attend it with such books as might afford instruction about the rates of composition used in the shires.[14]

On April 27 (possibly April 28) the petition was presented to the King by Bacon, accompanied by a committee selected for the purpose. In the petition it was specified that at least thirty-six laws had been enacted about purveyance,[15] and that, nevertheless, the Officers of Green Cloth did "check, charge, and imprison" His Majesty's subjects. The Commons had no mind to take away His Majesty's right but wished rather to confirm and put in execution the statutes already on the books. It was evident that the Commons had been worried by the words of an Officer of Green Cloth, who had told the committee plainly that they must not pass any laws on the matter of purveyance. It was possibly on account of such opposition that they had framed a petition.

In that petition to His Majesty the abuses of the purveyors were amply set forth. When they needed to supply the King with three hundred carts they levied from eight hundred to one thousand and at times gave back those they did not require, but only when bribed to do so. They would take money to ease the hundreds and the villages from the burdens of purveyance and then charge the whole sum upon others. They would demand carriages for others than the King, the Queen, and the Prince. They would take quarterly stipends from carts and wains coming into London. They would send out requests to borrow money, promising favors in return, and those who did not lend money received warrants to furnish carts. If the King "removed," merely to take dinner, the purveyors charged "near as many carts as at a full remove." It was further alleged that the country was heavily charged for wood, coal, hay, straw, timber, and other commodities, so much so that many people were charged more than if they paid five or six subsidies. The purveyors would requisition horses and then return them to their owners in such a state that they died within two or three days. They would take horses away from post service, from service with carts, and from service on the highways.

Purveyance was made, the petition read, according to the will of the purveyor. The price paid for the commodities was often not one-fourth of their true value.

According to law the constables and four others were to appraise the goods taken by the purveyors, but again and again the purveyors, "misliking the price," were said to have made new valuations of their own at the Court gate. It would have been easy for royal officials to overawe petty constables.

The officials did worse. They would stop farmers on the highway on their way to market and take what they wanted; they would stop men in the night, "where there is not and cannot be appraisement." Sometimes they would not show their commissions but merely send warrants for goods they fancied. The purveyors, the petition continued, took timber, compelled people to bring it to the waterside, and then sold it for their own profit.[16]

In reading this petition to the King, Bacon had a good deal to say, offering concrete examples and interesting generalizations: "There is no pound profit which redoundeth to your Majesty in this course but induceth and begetteth three pound damage upon your subjects, besides the discontentment." [17]

For the moment, at least, the King seemed impressed. He would, he assured them, ease the burden of his subjects. He was sorry that the general expectation of relief should be frustrated by these men.

He was glad to understand about them, and he would not neglect punishment. The last summer, as his Privy Councilors could testify, he had taken care that definite prices should be paid for his provision. He asked the Commons to consult Privy Councilors.

The Officers of the Household seem to have interrupted the proceedings. If abuses existed, they asserted, why did not those harmed complain to the justices of the peace? [18] When complaint was made to the officers, they maintained, they did justice.[19] They themselves were following old usage, always an argument of weight in that day. Unless they did so, they maintained, they would find it impossible to serve the King.[20]

It may be conjectured that His Majesty's answer did not wholly satisfy the Commons. His assumption that he had set the matter right the preceding summer was an indication that he was not likely to take further action. For once the Lords seemed to go along with the Commons. On May 5 they sent word that they had become sensible of the grief of the Commons and would be ready to further a remedy. The charges of the household were now greater, they stated, than they had been since the time of Henry VIII.[21] On the following Monday, May 7, Hare reported from the latest conference that the Officers of Green Cloth had issued to purveyors "unjust, unlawful, and untrue commissions." Such commissions, used since the days of Henry VIII, were "altogether against the law." "We," declared Hare, speaking presumably for his fellows in the Lower House, are "not after the purveyors, but after the Officers [of Green Cloth]." [22]

The attack was pressed. On May 9 Bacon, reporting from a conference with the Lords, declared that the "scope" of the Lords was to "exterminate all purveyors." The law was on their side, he maintained, that is, against the purveyors, and His Majesty's means were increased.[23] "Therefore the subject doth expect he will not press upon the people." To that assertion it was replied, apparently in the conference, that it would be impossible for the King to meet his charges unless he had some help "in this kind," that is, from purveyance.[24] In his behalf it was said further that he did not press all the penal laws from which he could gain money.

Thus "he looketh for the like measure of us," that is, he was asking his subjects to give him credit for not enforcing against them obsolete laws. He had great expenses in Ireland, it was added, and on account of the Cautionary Towns in the Low Countries; [25] he was losing money, too, by the peace with Spain.[26]

Bacon had a remedy, a proportion from the subject, £50,000 per annum. The sum named had perhaps been suggested to Bacon by Cecil, who, with reference to bargaining, would have put his sights high. "The shires," continued Bacon, "27000*li* composition. Supplies in specie 10,000*li*. . . ."[27] The Lords and Clergy should be assessed." [28]

On May 11 a composition of £20,000 was proposed by Hare. He would have £20,000 given to the King and "one entire subsidy presently." What he meant was, I think, that Parliament should offer the King £20,000 for the abolition of purveyance and then later vote him one subsidy in addition, which Hare may have assumed the Commons were likely to do in any case. Actually they did not grant His Majesty a subsidy at the end of the session; nor did he ask for it, realizing, doubtless, that he would not get it.

Hyde, who had been on the committee of four with Hare, spoke up against the imposition on the subjects of any annual sum.[29] The Commons, he said further, could enact no law to extirpate purveyors, nor to bind the King. Yet he seemed to believe that the bill before the House should be put through. Did he mean, as I think, that any law doing away with purveyance would not bind the Crown? Was he saying that the bill proposed for the "Better Executing of sundry Statutes touching Purveyors" would be a wiser move, since it would reinforce the limitations already laid down by former statutes on the unfair practices of purveyors?

Why did the Commons not jump at the proposal for composition made earlier by Bacon and now by Hare (at a smaller figure)? Many of those in the House may have watched, during the last years of Burghley, the workings of composition in certain counties and should have been ready for a composition, even at a high price, if it would rid them utterly of purveyors. I suspect the

trouble was that they had observed that, in spite of the compositions (all limited to certain commodities), purveyors persisted and
plundered hardworking farmers of their best corn, their prize
calves, and their fattest geese to afford dainty dinners for courtiers
in London, as they enviously suspected. Another reason why the
Commons did not press more eagerly for composition may have
been that country gentlemen, while they suffered from purveyors
on their home farms, did not suffer as much as yeomen. In some
way country gentlemen usually had the best of it. They were in
a position to meet the demands of the purveyors and did not
lie awake nights thinking about the hardships of their humbler
neighbors.

Once more it was resolved by a House undecided as to the next
move, to have a committee,[30] to which should be brought a note of
all compositions (those already in use in shires) and information
touching the royal demesnes and pastures and who occupied
them. Were the Commons considering the possibility of using on
a national scale the local machinery already set up in many counties? Or were they playing with the notion of putting a special
rental on Crown lands?

In the last weeks of May the question of composition was raised
again. Once more Hare spoke for a composition with the King.
This time he failed to mention the additional subsidy that he had
earlier proposed should go along with the composition. Fleetwood
named the same sum, £20,000. Upon the whole question of what
to do there was difference of opinion. Any form of composition
meant a heavy burden of work on justices of the peace, and many
M.P.'s were as well J.P.'s. The members also differed about
whether the "buying of justice" (a composition?) and whether the
matter of wardship should be referred, as Sandys had moved, to
the committee on purveyors. The motion was defeated.

On May 19 the House received a formal answer from the
Officers of His Majesty's Household. The large number of carts, up
to one thousand (as had been charged), was demanded at the very
beginning of the reign, the officers asserted, when the King, on his
entrance into the realm, had a considerable following.[31] Later the

number of carts had been cut down to three hundred. The officers said, further, that they had sent out letters to the justices of the peace asking them to report abuses, but they had received no answer. Possibly the letters had been sent after the officers had come under fire, and there had been little time for replies. If they had received complaints, the officers asserted, they would have punished the guilty. Fewer commissions, they maintained, were sent out at this time than in an earlier day. As for the payments for goods taken, they were the same as they had been for three hundred years. Here was the nub of the matter. The price of goods three hundred years earlier had little relation to their value at this time.

It may be that the answer of the Officers of His Majesty's Household affected the attitude of the Lords. The Commons seemed to proceed slowly about purveyance as if they feared a rough road ahead and could not decide how to move forward. On May 23 Sir George More asked for a report of the proceedings of the committee "which Mr. Hare had undertaken." [32] Hare reported that two questions should be put to the House. The first was whether they should answer the Lords that they knew no necessity of composition but desired to know it that they might better understand how to satisfy the King. The committee was in doubt about the next move and was asking some lead from the Lords and the King. There was not as yet much leadership in the Commons. If the Lords did not wish to satisfy them, then they proposed to be suitors to the King. The second question was whether a composition of £20,000 yearly should be offered to get rid of purveyance of every kind.

At that point Hyde proposed that the bill against purveyors be read.[33] After debate it was determined that the bill should be forborne and that "the former committees [committee members]" for purveyance should meet the next day in the afternoon "for something to satisfy the King, and every particular country [county] to consider, and inform what they think fit for themselves." [34]

On June 2 Sir George More wished it to be considered whether it were not the fittest and best for the subject to give an annual composition and not to continue any longer subject to purveyance. He proposed an act for the levying of "rateable contributions" toward compositions for the King's house "so long as they hold." [35] By the last phrase, I take it he meant if such a course were legal, if Parliament could devise a feasible plan for composition, a possibility that had been questioned.

Hare proposed that two subsidies should be voted to the King in order to be rid of the purveyors. The plan of subsidies was supported and opposed. Sir Walter Cope, a retainer of Cecil's, it will be recalled, suggested making trial of a composition of £30,000, a compromise between the £50,000 first mentioned and the £20,000 later mentioned.

It was moved to confer with the Lords about composition and, when that motion was voted on, it was disputed whether the yeas were the greater number. In the end the whole matter was put off until the next session. Of this action the Lords were informed.

On June 29 Hyde moved that since the bill of purveyors was to sleep till the next session, an order might be conceived that the justices of the peace should execute the laws already made. I have no evidence that this proposal came to anything.

In reflecting upon the fortunes of the issue of purveyance from March to early July, one asks why that issue was shoved aside for other matters, particularly for the union. The abuses of the purveyors worried members of the House, especially those from the home counties where exactions by purveyors were most felt. One would suppose that such abuses would be given a "high priority" place among evils to be remedied.

As we have seen, things looked hopeful for a while. The Commons received encouragement from the Upper House and a certain tepid sympathy from the King. Men talked about a composition with the King—that is, of making a regular payment instead of giving commodities. They would kill the dragon rather than cut off its fangs. But it proved hard to devise a plan for the composition, and His Majesty lost his first fine impulse—ceased, indeed, to support any scheme about purveyors. He was interested, above all, in the union, and on that question the Commons had failed to respond quickly or heartily to his wishes. The honeymoon was over, and those who raised doubts in the Commons were being listened to attentively.

It may be that the smoothly operating Cecil, who had guided the Commons in the last years of the great Queen, was not pulling the switches to keep the question of union on the main line and to shunt wardship and purveyance over to sidings. Meanwhile the Commons were to be kept in a state of hopefulness. Had not the King talked as if he were just about to offer concessions about purveyance? Had he not spoken of hanging an errant purveyor? The men around him, Privy Councilors and courtiers, were in no hurry for change. Moreover, there were Councilors near the King who were ready with advice that would blunt the edge of whatever good resolutions James might have made.

It is possible, too, that a considerable body of the membership of the Commons were less interested in the abuses of purveyance than in those of wardship. The Commons as yet lacked leadership. In time the members would fall into the habit of listening to Sandys and of going along with him. But Sandys was as yet only on the way to leadership, and he had indicated little interest in the topic of purveyance. Bacon had the ability and skill in speaking to win influence, but he did not carry the House with him. He was not sufficiently interested in other people to command a following of friends. Sir George More had been on good terms with the late Queen and was to prove useful to James. He was a man of moderate views and had the goodwill of the House. So had Sir Edward Hoby, but he was getting older and took less part in the debates. Francis Moore, Richard Martin, Sir Francis Hastings, and Sir Robert Wingfield had figured in the last Parliaments of Elizabeth, and all of them were inclined in the new reign to press for reform in state and church. Martin and Francis Moore had been particularly useful in the framing of laws and remained, in the reign of James, quietly competent in that capacity. Hyde and Hare, two men who tried to make some headway with the question of purveyance, did not work together, and neither was capable of gaining any general support. Wroth and Montague, as became great country gentlemen, had started things going very deliberately. But Wroth was old and tired, and Montague was neither magnetic nor persuasive.

Free Trade

*All the world choppeth and chang-
eth, runneth and raveth after marts,
markets, and merchandising.*
    John Wheeler, *A Treatise of Com-
    merce* (1601)

WARDSHIP and purveyance were abuses deeply rooted in the English past and not easily eradicated. Free trade was something different—the watchword of those who hoped to break the control of London big business over trade to foreign countries or, in other words, to curb the power of the Merchant Adventurers and of other great companies. To some degree it was an assault upon the Government, which had favored the great companies. The story goes beyond 1604, into 1605 and 1606. It begins, however, toward the end of April 1604 when, on April 18, more than three weeks after the House had assembled, a bill for free trade was introduced, apparently by merchants.[1]

The text of the original bill for free trade is to be found neither in the Lords' Record Office, nor in the Public Record Office. Among the Lansdowne Manuscripts,[2] however, is an "Act for Free Trade for all Merchants into all Countries beyond Seas." This version of the bill for free trade is presumably a copy of one in the Cottonian Manuscripts, originally collected by Sir Robert Cotton. It seems probable that the bill in the Lansdowne Manuscripts was a copy of the bill that was considered by the committee for the Free Trade Bill and that it may include two bills: (1) the "Bill for Merchants to have Free Liberty to Trade into all Countries, as is Used in all other Nations," and (2) a "Bill for the Enlargement of Trade for his Majesty's Subjects into Foreign Countries."

From Sandys's report from the committee on the bill, it seems likely that the two bills were fused into one. That document alludes in such various ways to the bills before the committee that we can be fairly sure that the Lansdowne version is a copy of the

Commons bill after, I think, it had gone through the committee. Whether it is just the same as the bill that had two readings in the Lords with amendments made in conference with the Commons, I cannot be sure. The reader who questions these speculations is urged to examine for himself the *Commons Journals* from April 18 to July 7 and the *Lords Journals* from June 29 to the end of the session.

The bill, if this is the right one, was carelessly drawn, was not in every respect clear, and was occasionally inconsistent. Sandys apologized for its form: "The bill is a good bill, though not in all points perhaps so perfect as it might be, which defects may be soon remedied . . . in future Parliaments." [3]

The bill, as we have it in the Lansdowne version, alludes to the statute of 12 Hen. VII, which I shall presently summarize. In the text of the bill it is asserted that, in spite of the statute of Henry VII, the said fraternity (the Merchant Adventurers) have procured to themselves and have so wrought with the officials of customs and those of ports that they refuse to accept for customs goods of English merchants who are not members of the said fraternity, thus depriving them of the benefit of the said law. Meanwhile other companies had gained charters for the sole trade into Russia, Eastland, East India, and Turkey, and had been inhibiting all other Englishmen from trading with those countries, "to the common impoverishing of the clothiers and abating of the price of such staple goods and commodities," to the decay of shipping and the ruin of merchant towns and sea towns other than London. [4]

It was therefore to be enacted that it was lawful for all His Majesty's subjects, "not being clothiers, retailers, inn-holders, farmers, mariners, nor using any handicraft" to have free passage and trade in the way of merchandise into Flanders, Holland, Zeeland, Brabant, and "into other countries and kingdoms whatsoever," which seems to have meant all nations. Heavy penalties were set down for those who delayed the goods of such merchants or molested them. [5]

Three provisos were included in the bill, as we have it. The first was that all grants, agreements, etc. of any society, fraternity, or company tending to a privilege or monopoly should be void. This seems inconsistent with the report of the committee [6] that the act "dissolveth no company, taketh away no good government."

It was provided, secondly, that anyone using the trade of merchandise beyond seas contrary to this act should forfeit one-half of the goods to the King and the other half to the informers.

The third provision was that those who wished to take advantage of this act should contribute to the necessary charges to be imposed upon the merchants of that kind "for the better government in those places." Those who refused to pay were to forfeit £40, one-half to the King, the other half to the informers.

That this bill had not been sponsored by well-known country gentlemen means something. When Sir Robert Wroth and Sir Edward Montague had laid before the House at its beginning the two lists of grievances to be dealt with, they had said nothing about free trade. Moreover, in the extensive program of measures deserving of attention in the coming Parliament of 1604 to be found in the Northumberland manuscript at Alnwick Castle, there is no allusion to free trade, nor to any measure that would affect the Merchant Adventurers. Yet we shall see later that many country gentlemen must have been responsible for the sweeping vote by which the bill for free trade passed the Commons. It is no more than a guess that some of the country gentlemen did not wake up to the possibilities of the free trade bill until its advantages had been presented by Sandys's report from the committee.

The bill was something new. I cannot recall that any bill of a similar nature had been offered to an Elizabethan Parliament. The Elizabethan Privy Council had been at pains to preserve the special privileges of the Merchant Adventurers, and they had ignored the act passed in the reign of Henry VII.

The statute of 12 Hen. VII, cap. vi, about the Merchant Adventurers had not minced matters. It had referred to the marts where all Englishmen and divers other nations in time past "have used to resort there to sell . . . the commodities of their countries and freely to buy again such things as seemed them most necessary and expedient for their profit." But of late, the statute continued, the Merchant Adventurers by a confederacy among themselves and

> of their incharitable and inordinate covetise . . . have . . . made an ordinance and constitution . . . that no Englishman . . . shall neither buy ne [*sic*] sell any goods, wares, or merchandises there, except he first compound and make fine with the said fellowship of merchants of London, and to their said confederates.

It was pointed out that this fine was increased so much that all merchants withdrew from the said marts, causing the King's subjects to lose their occupation and the poor people their living. It was further provided that every Englishman was to have free passage, resort, course, and recourse into the "said coasts of Flanders, Holland, Zeeland, Brabant, and other places thereto nigh adjoining under the obeisance of the said Archduke . . . there to buy and sell." Since that law was made, there had been charters and grants to companies that looked in another direction and granted special privileges, but the statute itself had never been repealed.

Whatever the laws had been, the Tudor sovereigns and their Councilors lent their support to the Merchant Adventurers, probably because they believed that such an organization was the surest means of protecting and promoting English trade abroad, a judgment for which there was much to be said. Queen Elizabeth had reason to be grateful to the company. When, early in her reign, the financial position of her Government had been seriously threatened, Sir Thomas Gresham forced the Merchant Adventurers (even by holding up their shipping) to make large loans to her and thus prevented what might have proved a crisis. It became the fixed policy of the Elizabethan Government to advance the fortunes of the Merchant Adventurers, particularly against their old rival, the Hanseatic League. Of course such an ambitious company, with privileges at home and abroad, drew upon itself no little envy and did not endear itself to the outports and the lesser merchants.

Take Bristol, for example. The London merchants were mo-
nopolizing the trade through the Straits of Gibraltar, where
Bristol merchants had been wont to send their ships. Even more
annoying, Londoners had gone into the country around Bristol
and, by offering long credits, had driven the Bristol cloth men out
of their own tributary territories.[7] When in 1595 the Corporation
and merchants of Bristol were asked to equip three ships for clearing the Channel of pirates, they complained that the Londoners
had increased infinitely their possessions at the expense of others.
That the Londoners, wealthy and strong, should press the Queen
to secure their gains as against the "poor purses" of Bristol was
a great wonder. They prayed that their sighs might be heard and
that Londoners might be commanded to receive them into "a community of trade." [8] Was it possible that not only high fees but
other forms of exclusion worried Bristol merchants?

In spite of all that could be said against its policies, the Merchant Adventurers was a well-run company, the most successful
of all English companies until the East India Company became a
rival. The Merchant Adventurers was broadly based. It was open
apparently to all qualified merchants in the realm who could
afford the entrance fees; it had allied subsidiary companies in
Bristol, Exeter, Norwich, Ipswich, York, Hull, and Newcastle. But
they were dubbed a monopoly, and monopolies were under fire, as
the debates on free trade prove. The word "monopoly" had gained
ill repute, as "Establishment" has today, and such words are sometimes explosive in their effects. The merchants of the outports
could not but regard the Merchant Adventurers and other companies, such as the Muscovy Company, as monopolies. They had
observed the pressure put upon Elizabeth and her final surrender.
They had seen Cecil suspend monopolies at the beginning of the
new reign. Was it not a favorable moment to introduce into the
Commons a bill for free trade? In the report of the committee for
the free-trade bill Sandys had written:

But the times being well altered from war to peace, this mischief [that under free trade, companies such as the Merchant

Adventurers might give over, as they were said to have done in
1588] would be but short, and other merchants soon grow to
take their places, if they should as (being rich) they may, forsake them.

Peace would have wide consequences.

Under our gracious Solomon, a prince of wisdom and peace,
we are like to be in league or amity with all nations whereby, as
there will be greater freedom abroad to trade to all places, so
fit to have greater at home for all persons to trade. . . . And as
there will be greater opportunity abroad, so also much greater
necessity at home, for what else shall become of gentlemen's
younger sons, who cannot live by arms, when there is no wars.

Astrid Friis in her ground-breaking monograph on the Cockayne Project puts forth the suggestion that one reason why the
bill was brought in at this particular time was because many merchants in the West Country had been doing well by preying on
Spanish shipping and realized that peace with Spain meant an end
to a profitable form of war. They hoped to find new outlets for
their activity by shipping goods to the nearer parts of Europe, and
the monopoly of the Merchant Adventurers stood in their way.⁹

The general discontent in the country and the widespread hope
that a new monarch would bring in a new broom and sweep out
the many cobwebs (a hope not quite dashed in 1604) made men
of initiative eager for changes, and not least for economic changes.
In Shakespeare's and Hakluyt's world such men were not uncommon.

It will be recalled that the bill for free trade had been first read
on April 18. The next day another bill was read for the "Enlargement of Trade for his Majesty's Subjects into Foreign Countries."
What the relation of the second bill was to the first I do not know.
On April 24 the two bills were committed to the same large committee. Sandys's name headed the list of members. Sir Thomas
Smith, governor of the recently formed East India Company and
a member of the Muscovy Company, whose grandfather had been

a Wiltshire clothier and whose father was a haberdasher in London, was the second name on the committee. Among other members were Francis Moore, that shrewd lawyer, alert to the ills of the commonwealth; John Prowse of Exeter, a figure in that city and later governor of the French Company; Sir Richard Hawkins, son of Sir John; Sir Thomas Ridgeway, well known in Devon; Lawrence Hyde, a Wiltshire M.P. and thus interested in cloth, who was critical of the royal government; Sir George More, an Elizabethan still going strong; Sir Henry Yelverton, son of an Elizabethan Speaker of the Commons and less judicious than his father; Sir Henry Neville, once ambassador to France, later entangled in the Essex episode, and now in his sixth Parliament; and Sir Robert Wroth, who was now in attendance at his ninth Parliament and who had led off the struggle about grievances on March 23, 1604. The committee included also the barons of the Cinque Ports and all the burgesses from cities and port towns; it must have had more than a hundred members. Theodore Rabb, in the article upon which I shall later draw, points out that only five merchants from the outports and one from a provincial port were members of the committee. But the M.P.'s from the outports, even when they were country gentlemen, were likely to listen to their merchant constituencies and to have been interested in the free-trade bill.

It was not until May 21 that Sir Edwin Sandys brought in from the committee a long report, "penned by himself." The first part of it put forward the case against the Merchant Adventurers. That statement was followed by a summary of the arguments on both sides, as if the committee had been sharply divided and had compromised by presenting an analysis of their debates. For five afternoons a week the committee had heard the statements drawn up by companies and by individuals. The country merchants, especially those from the west of England, had appeared in numbers and had testified against the restrictions imposed upon the cloth trade. It was said that even in London three-fourths of the merchants, doubtless the smaller men, were in sympathy with the proposed measure. Opposed to it were the principal aldermen of the City.[10] In support of the bill it was maintained that it was against the right and natural liberty of the subjects of England, a sly suggestion of the superior quality of liberty enjoyed by the English.

The report cited the example of other nations; it was said that they had no such organization as the Merchant Adventurers, a generalization denied at that time,[11] and denied in recent times by no less an authority than the late Sir William R. Scott.[12]

It was further asserted in the report that a more equal distribution of the wealth of the kingdom would prove a stabilizing influence and a source of strength, an unusual comment for that time. Sandys was not without his own political philosophy. London, it was declared, had been given too many favors. The customs and imports of that city amounted to £110,000, and those of the rest of England to £17,000, too great a difference.

The restraint of trade by the companies worked against the increase of shipping and thus against the increase of mariners; indeed, it led to the decreased employment of mariners. But, if war should break out, what the country would need above all would be mariners, many of them.

Free trade would mean increased customs duties and increased subsidies for the King. It would make possible greater opportunities for younger sons. All that was left to younger sons at that time was to become serving men, "a poor inheritance." Sandys's report tabulated the reasons for the restraint of trade by the companies and summarized the answers to those reasons.

The defenders of the Merchant Adventurers maintained that it was not a monopoly. A monopoly existed where the liberty of selling, a right which belonged to all men, was granted to one. To call the companies monopolies was to support the coast towns and other nations in their criticism of the English state. That state was not to blame if abuses crept in; it was only to blame if the reformation of those abuses by Parliament was denied.

On the other side, it was said that the Merchant Adventurers had a monopolistic advantage. Two-thirds of the clothing industry was managed by less than two hundred men. "By [a] complot among themselves" they would buy at what time, what quantity, and at what price suited them, with the result that clothiers often went home with a loss, "to the utter ruin of their poor workmen, with their wives and children."

On behalf of the companies it was maintained that they had performed a useful service in keeping up the price of English goods abroad; they had prevented glutting the markets where they traded with English commodities. If it were not for the companies, if trade were free, some sellers would "make ware cheap, and of less estimation."

In rebuttal, the free traders alleged that the monopolies kept prices up, that those who controlled the companies kept those prices up "for their own private lucre." They had caused the Holy Roman Empire to issue so many edicts against the Merchant Adventurers, had driven the Adventurers to shift their markets, and had caused the English merchants to be generally hated.

The free traders objected to the high prices enforced by the Merchant Adventurers for their own advantage, but they did not object to good prices for English goods abroad. It was pointed out in Sandys's report that the existence of many buyers at home —under free trade—would make wares dearer at home and hence maintain good prices abroad. It was the store of merchandise and not the multitude of merchants that made goods cheaper. There was no need to worry about good prices abroad; prices had gone up everywhere. In France, where there were no companies, English kerseys sold at an exceedingly good rate. In the Low Countries, where the free traders said that trade was indeed free, traffic flourished, and the Dutch could support the huge charge of long wars by their sales. Further, under free trade natural commodities (raw materials) would be more than trebled in value by the "access of art and industry." Thus the division of wealth would be more equal. The report went on to indicate that free trade led young men to seek out new markets, and that did not hurt the kingdom.

England, with its companies, was not so fortunate as the Low Countries, "for now, by the plotting of the Governor of these companies some few overgrown men devour the wealth and make merry, whilst the rest, even of their own companies, do want and weep."

Those against the bill asserted that it would be possible for men to become merchants without undergoing a lawful apprenticeship, thus wronging those who had served an apprenticeship and handicapping those who had not, for they would venture unskillfully and lose.[13] The answer was that men without an apprenticeship could learn from factors or from their friends. Moreover, wise young men might adventure their stocks with others, as they did in the Low Countries.

Opponents of the bill maintained that it gave access to trade to all and thus, in effect, dissolved the companies.[14] The reply was that it dissolved no company; it merely abrogated those orders that tended toward monopoly. The example of the Low Countries "where are the best merchants in the world" was cited.[15] There provident men consulted and joined together for their common benefit, ease, and safety.

It was said that the bill would interfere with the joint-stock companies, which were necessary in long-range trade, such as that to the East Indies and Muscovy. In answer it was admitted that it was necessary to use joint-stock companies in trade to the East, "and so do the Hollanders." It was pointed out, however, that the bill did not forbid men trading in joint-stock companies; it forbade only the compelling of men to do so against their wills.

As for the Muscovy Company, the supporters of the bill declared that it was really "a strong and shameful monopoly." It was wholly managed by eightscore men and fifteen directors who determined the proportion of goods to be sold by every member. The goods were all consigned into the hands of one agent in Moscow and one agent in London. Those agents bought and sold and rendered accounts as they pleased.

The English sold fewer goods in Muscovy than the Dutch. The Dutch used free trade and had nearly thirty ships in Muscovy as against England's seven. Moreover, the Muscovy Company brought back few goods and sold them at so high a price that they prejudiced the commonwealth.

Opponents of the bill argued from the experience of the companies. In 1588, when all men were at liberty to buy cloth at London, the Merchant Adventurers gave up the trade. Consequently the clothiers could not sell and found themselves with cloth on their hands. They were forced to petition that the former restraints be reimposed.

To the often used argument that, in free trade, small ships took the place of the large, and so great ships would disappear,[16] it was answered that great ships were still used for the main trade into Germany and into the Low Countries, to the East Indies, to the Levant, and to Muscovy.

On behalf of the Merchant Adventurers, it was urged that they were an ancient company that had great credit and could borrow money in the Low Countries and in Germany, an argument of weight.

One of the most telling arguments for the great companies was that there were pirates in the Channel, and many of them in the Mediterranean, where the Levant Company was active; hence ships should sail under protection that only a great company could provide.

On May 31 the bill for free trade was read the third time. A debate ensued and was continued on June 4, 5, and 6. The speakers on the subject were numerous. A few of the King's friends and some Londoners opposed the bill, while members from the outports, from the West Country, and from country constituencies supported it. It is surprising, however, to find Richard Martin, who seldom voted with the Court, opposing the bill. Could he have been retained by the Merchant Adventurers to speak for them? It is not surprising to find Sir Henry Montague on the same side. Sir Christopher Perkins, once a diplomatic agent for the late Queen, who had interested himself in mercantile affairs and who had doubtless been taught in grammar school to define terms, proceeded to define the term "monopoly" and to conclude that the Merchant Adventurers did not constitute a monopoly.

Sir Robert Mansell, Admiral of the Narrow Seas, took another tack. He had sent for the interlopers (those who sold goods on the

Continent independently of the companies), and they had not dared to come for fear of the Merchant Adventurers. The Merchant Adventurers, he maintained, with an emphasis not unknown among naval men, were the monster monopoly of the kingdom. It was time to look into them. As for great ships being necessities of trade, he did not believe it. The strength of the English lay in sailors and in small ships.

Sir Thomas Posthumus Hoby, M.P. for Scarborough, a solemn little squire from Hackness in the North Riding, spoke for the Merchant Adventurers. Sir Richard Bulkeley (Buckley), now in his 71st year, and long a member of Queen Elizabeth's household, argued for the measure. The merchants of London, he asserted, had trade everywhere. One could go round the world with them. None could vote for them save such as willed not to offend; that is, I take it, willed not to offend the Crown. Dudley Carleton, who sat for St. Mawes (Cornwall), as arranged probably by Cecil, and who had been on the staff of the English embassy in Paris, talked of the decay of shipping in the West Country because of the war with Spain. In France, he said, there was no demand for English goods; many of the English traders there were ready to give up. He moved that the bill be postponed till the next session, a motion that would not have displeased the great little Lord who found it troublesome to deal with merchants not "under any orderly constitution, nor never concurring in one mind." [17]

John Tey, who represented Arundel in Sussex and was the second son of an Essex family, opposed the bill.[18] He may have owed his seat to the Sackvilles. Merchants, he believed, should work in corporations. Unless there were order in the export trade,[19] it would decay. It was a mistake, he thought, to call the Merchant Adventurers a monopoly. Sir William Maurice, a tedious orator from Caernarvonshire, discoursed on monopolies in relation to Shrewsbury and the Welsh wool trade.[20] Sir Henry Beaumont, who represented Plympton, supported the bill and had no doubt that the merchants of London constituted a monopoly. He seemed concerned about the liberty of the people and wondered whether anyone would venture to speak against the bill.

John Hoskins, known in his midcareer as a wit and a satirist, had married well and then studied law and entered Parliament in 1604. He quoted a great personage to the effect that merchants caused a stay of buying cloth for a time "for their gain." It was proper, he remarked, for islanders to trade, by which he meant, I assume, to trade without restrictions. He called for a vote, as did Strode from Devon.

Serjeant Snigge, M.P. for Bristol, now in his fourth Parliament and presently to become a baron of the Exchequer, complained that members of the committee on the bill, who reported the bill as full of faults, had never said a word to that effect in the committee. He was perhaps implying that they were speaking up now to gain credit at Court. Sir Thomas Fleming, the Solicitor General, now in his seventh Parliament, believed in the bill, but hoped to see a few amendments inserted. Hyde, probably Lawrence Hyde, spoke for the bill and maintained that its passage did not mean the overthrow of the company. He suggested, however, that the bill continue for twelve years, a proposal at once voted down. Then the bill itself was passed with a large majority, scarcely forty voting against it.

Mr. Theodore Rabb, in a searching article in the *American Historical Review* (April 1964) about Sandys and the Parliament of 1604, takes the view that Sandys, in supporting free trade, "spoke for the gentry." He says that more than one-third of the nonmerchant members of the House of Commons "invested in trading ventures," most of them, I assume, during and after this Parliament. He believes that most of them preferred investment in joint-stock companies rather than in the "regulated" companies. The Members of Parliament did not have the skills required in a regulated company; "they flocked to the ventures that asked for nothing more than an investment." He notes how Sandys condemned the Muscovy Company, which was a regulated company, and that the provincial ports "tolerated the East India Company because it did not encroach on any of their ventures." He observes, too, that Sandys focused his attack on the Merchant Adventurers.

The bill had now to run the gauntlet of the Lords, where any

knowing person could have foretold the outcome. The Lords let
it die by slow degree but with due formality. On June 9 it was
brought from the Commons along with other bills; on June 21
it was allowed a second reading. The governors of the Merchants
Adventurers, of the Eastland Company, of the Spanish Company,
of the East India Company, and of the Turkey Company, that is,
the Levant Company, were to be informed of the bill. Then the
merchants who had brought in the bill were to choose eight men
to represent them, and the companies were to choose eight.

On July 2 the merchants of the several companies opposed to the
bill were heard by learned counsel. At length the Attorney General,
Sir Edward Coke, was heard for the King. He spoke against
the form of the bill, setting forth its many defects and inconveniences,
but characterizing the purpose and intent of the bill
as good.

A conference between the committees of the two Houses must
have followed, although it was not recorded by the Clerk. On July
6, the day before the close of the session, Francis Moore reported
the conference with the Lords concerning two bills, one for free
trade. The bill for free trade was a matter of great consequence,
declared Bacon, and he suggested that commissioners should, between
this and the next session, frame a bill on the subject. It is
a little surprising to find Bacon supporting the bill, even in this
tepid way. Usually he was careful to argue in favor of whatever
he deemed to be royal policy. Perhaps he had hoped to be one of
the commissioners. He may have hoped that the commissioners,
chosen presumably from the two Houses, could be trusted to frame
a measure that would give the merchants from the outports opportunity
to enter the Merchant Adventurers Company and at the
same time to retain for that company the hold of the trade with
the Low Countries and with Germany. He could guess that his
cousin, Salisbury, would not have been opposed to some such
concession.

Would that we had more information about this measure. It
was obviously popular, and yet it was not pushed by many outstanding
members of the Lower House. Sandys, Francis Moore,

Fleming, and Lawrence Hyde were all members who carried weight, but it is hard to think of others of like position who spoke up in favor of the bill. It seems probable that many M.P.'s voted for the measure who were unwilling to speak out. The natural leaders of the House, except for Sandys, did not seem much interested. Were they perhaps more intent on other matters that concerned them more? They may have realized that the Crown was opposed to the bill and that it stood small chance of reaching the statute book.

The bill never found a place in the statute book, but the impressive majority for it was not without effect. Salisbury and some of the Privy Council were sensitive to public opinion as uttered in the Commons. Salisbury was willing to see the trading companies open to all: "For I would have it to be open to all men to trade that would into all places; neither should there be any privilege for sole bringing in of any commodity (as it was before." [21] It was hard for Salisbury to refrain from adherence to certain broad principles.

On May 31, 1605, the Crown renewed a charter of 1577 to the company trading into Spain, but not without changes. There was so much agitation by shopkeepers and retailers in London, says Astrid Friis,[22] that the Crown moved to modify the charter in several ways. There were to be a president and sixty-one assistants, of whom thirty were Londoners, although at least thirty had their homes outside of London. The assistants were to be elected for only one year. On the roll of assistants the ports of Southampton, Hull, Chester, Bristol, and Exeter were well represented. It was significant that the entrance fee was to be from £10 to £20. In other words, the Crown was meeting public opinion even slightly ahead of its expression in the Commons.

As soon as Parliament assembled in November 1605 for its second session, Sir George Somers of Lyme Regis, who had sailed on buccaneering voyages against Spain and whose name is forever connected with the Bermudas, moved for a committee touching the incorporation of merchants since the last Parliament, that is, the granting of a charter to the Spanish Company. That committee was to include the knights of the maritime counties, Secretary Herbert, three Devonshire members, Strode, Ridgeway, and Prowse, and others.[23] As a result, a bill was introduced on February 10, 1606, and committed to the same committee with a few names added.

On February 27 Fuller brought in the bill from the committee. It was to allow His Majesty's subjects to trade freely into Spain, Portugal, and France, which was nothing less than to nullify the recent charter to the Spanish Company, that is, to undo an administrative policy by legislation. Some of the Commons were ready to dare the Council. The committee had put in a proviso to make an exception of Bristol in respect of its charter, given in 1604 (confirming the Elizabethan charters), but the proviso was promptly voted down,[24] and a special proviso proposed by Prowse for Exeter would seem not even to have come to a vote.

On March 12 the bill, having passed the Commons, was sent up to the Lords with a special recommendation.[25] There it was committed to a large committee, the Lord Treasurer, the Lord Admiral, Salisbury, and four other earls, fourteen lesser peers, and eight bishops.[26] A warning was issued on April 1 that the merchants for and against the bill were to attend the committee.[27] In a conference between the two Houses the Lords took exception to certain phrases and declared that, when the bill allowed all men to trade, it was too general and that, when it used the phrase, "notwithstanding anything done or to be done to the contrary," it was too special. The Lords desired further time to consider the bill.[28]

After a second conference Sandys reported on May 2 that one of the merchants proposing to trade with Spain had complained that the merchants had not been allowed to be heard.[29] In the conference it had been asserted that the Commons ought to answer certain statements made by the merchants, but the Commons on the committee had refused to do so, for then "this House plaintiff and the Lords judges." The general resolution of the House was that the "charter was not thought good, the bill well liked of." [30]

The bill was brought back by the archbishop of Canterbury from the Lords committee with amendments, read a third time, and sent down to the Commons where it was "received with great applause." [31] On the same day it was returned to the Upper House with the amendments accepted, and the final bill was retained there for the King's approval.

The reception by the Commons of the Lords bill and amendments "with great applause," would seem to indicate that the Lords had given up some of their objections and had added or inserted only some unimportant amendments. The reading of the statute supports that inference. It states that by the charter "none but themselves and such as they shall think fit, as being meet merchants, shall take benefit of the said charter." This arrangement disabled thereby "all others, his Majesty's . . . subjects . . . who during all the time of her late Majesty's wars, were . . . greatly charged for the defence of their Prince and Country," and also debarred them "from that free enlargement of common traffic into those dominions which others his Majesty's subjects of his realms of Scotland and Ireland do enjoy." This worked to the "manifest impoverishing of all owners of ships, masters, mariners, fishermen, clothiers, tuckers, spinsters and many thousands of all sorts of handicraftsmen, besides the decrease of his Majesty's customs, subsidies and other impositions, and the ruin and decay of navigation." [32]

Then followed the enacting clauses. His Majesty's subjects were to have free liberty to trade into and from Spain, Portugal, and France in as free a manner as was at any time accustomed before the said Charter of Incorporation was granted, "paying to the King's . . . Majesty . . . all such customs and other duties as by the laws . . . ought to be paid . . . the said Charter of Incorporation . . . to the contrary notwithstanding."

One proviso stated that the statute should not afford liberty to persons to go overseas without license, "who by the laws . . . shall be restrained from going beyond the seas without license." [33]

The statute of 1606 was doubtless in part a consequence of the bill of 1604. Salisbury had hardly forgotten the majority for the Free Trade Bill in 1604; that time he could not very well back down. But next time he would be more amenable to parliamentary opinion. When the Lords passed the bill of 1606, they were perhaps listening to Salisbury.

Other consequences of the bill of 1604 are possibly to be found in the wording of the charters that the Crown granted in the years following. Salisbury supported "an incorporation of merchants to which no one who would pay a reasonable fine on entrance should be refused admission." [34]

After the charter for trade into Spain had been granted, Salisbury became interested in a new Levant Company and in a company for trade into France. When opposition over certain points developed, Salisbury consulted Justice Popham as to the legality of the grants. When the charter was finally granted to the Levant Company, it carefully stated that there was no intention to create a monopoly. Moreover, the entrance fee was set at a low rate, £25 for those under 26 years of age and £50 for those of a greater age. When in 1609 the company for trade into France was established, the entrance fee for those under twenty-six was set at £4, and for those older at £10.

It would be hard to prove that Salisbury's policy toward the new companies was an outcome of the agitation over the Free Trade Bill of 1604 but it seems probable that the Minister was not unaffected by what had happened in the Commons. In other words, if the Commons were not yet able to put on the statute book all the bills they passed, they could voice opinion, and their opinions were not wholly disregarded. It is the way things happen. Men strive desperately for certain objectives and fail to attain them. Then administrators carry through in slow motion measures similar to those proposed by reforming legislators.

The Privy Council was becoming in some degree the reluctant servant of Parliament—a reversal of the situation that existed no farther back than the reign of Henry VIII, when the Privy Council made out the program of legislation and waited for the two Houses to put it through item by item. Now the Privy Council was listening, if only with one ear, to what was said in the Commons, and was likely, after a proper interval, to put into effect part of the plan they had resisted.

If those who sought free trade gained less than they had hoped, their efforts were part of a historical movement and had significance. Sandys and those allied with him, a large majority of the Commons, were proposing nothing less than an attack on an old fortress. In spite of the strong language of the statute of 12 Hen. VII, the Tudors had maintained the medieval restrictions on trade abroad. The attack on those medieval restrictions was coincident in time with the great assault, begun in 1604 and continued in the next three sessions of Parliament, 1605/06, 1606/07, and 1610—the assault against the Crown for seeking to abbreviate those rights and privileges that the Commons regarded as theirs by old usage.[35] In her later years Elizabeth had kept a tight rein on Parliament, and James was inclined to the same policy. The resistance was to be headed by Sandys, the same Sandys who led the attack on the Merchant Adventurers.

By the close of 1604 Sandys had gained some influence in the Lower House. His moderation of statement[36] and his quiet manner of bringing forward motions were in part responsible.

He had been supported in the Free Trade Bill of 1604 by Francis Moore; Moore was among the old war-horses of the House to support him on the question of the union and in the many clashes between King and Commons. Sandys and a group of men, most of them older than he, waged skirmish after skirmish for parliamentary rights and privileges; many of the skirmishes were unsuccessful at the moment but, in the long run, not without results.

The struggle over free trade was of course a skirmish on another front, but there was a further difference. The outports and their allies in the House were hoping to do away with old restrictions. They were ready to ring out the old and ring in the new. The "mutineers" or "commonwealthsmen" who took up the constitutional struggle for the rights and privileges of the Lower House were ringing in the old; they were searching among past records to make the case for what they wanted now. Yet whatever reasons they alleged, the skirmishers on both fronts were looking ahead to better conditions for His Majesty's subjects. The parliamentarians in the first decade of the new reign were out, above all else, to free the subject from the wretched burdens of purveyance and wardship, economic burdens imposed by the Crown and thus not unlike the monopolies granted by the Crown to the companies.

The attempt to put through a bill for free trade had possibly another significance. We have seen that country gentlemen in large numbers supported it as well as the burgesses from the towns. To talk of an alliance between gentlemen and burgesses would be premature. Groups were as yet not as well organized as that. Nevertheless, in some instances, landed men and those well-to-do members with trade connections were voting the same way.

Here was nothing strange. During the reign of Henry VIII, and just before and after, a change of great moment had been taking place in the House of Commons, as students of English history well know. Country gentlemen in increasing numbers had been inducing neighboring boroughs to elect them to Parliament. Once in the Commons they were not unwilling to do well by their constituents. Other things being equal, they might find themselves arrayed on the side of the boroughs.

It was natural that they should have become interested in the companies and have sought investments in the joint stock companies. They were not making enough from their rents to keep up with the Thynnes and the Russells. It was in their interest to vote for free trade.

Moreover the gentry were country people, not infrequently sharing the outlook of well-to-do farmers. By instinct they might vote with the country against London. With the passage of time, decades later, they were to make up the backbone of what was to be known as the Country party.

The Apology

IN the long struggle between the Stuarts and their Parliaments the Apology of 1604 is the first noteworthy document. Like Wentworth's speech in 1576, it has found a place in source books. A few sentences deserve insertion here:

What cause we, your poor Commons, have to watch over our privileges is manifest in itself to all men.

The prerogatives of princes may easily and do daily grow. The privileges of the subject are for the most part at an everlasting stand. They may be by good providence and care preserved, but being once lost are not recovered but with much disquiet.[1]

Less memorable but characteristic of some of the leadership is a short paragraph near the end: "We stand not in place to speak or do things pleasing; our care is, and must be, to confirm the love and to tie the hearts of your subjects, the Commons, most firmly to your Majesty. Herein lieth the means of our well-deserving of both." [2]

The Apology interests historians as a summing up by the Commons of their complaints after they had been observing the new regime for more than a year. It is a document prepared largely by Elizabethan Commoners who had long hoped for reforms. The grievances they mentioned had, most of them, been mentioned during the last two decades of the late reign. The summing up was now occasioned by a speech made by His Majesty to the members on May 30, 1604, but some such statement had been in the minds of some members. Of the King's speech we know little save that it caused "grief" to the Commons.[3] It may be that the Privy Council managed to destroy all known copies or notes of the speech. Of the differences that had been accumulating between the Commons and the King the reader cannot be unaware. The session of 1604 had not been one to encourage optimism. If by good fortune the members should succeed in doing away with wardship and purveyance they would have to provide suitable compensation to their sovereign, or "composition." The amount of that composition had been debated in the House, with little indication of any agreement. There was more agreement that it would be hard to find the money.

To make matters worse, the King, who had a way of letting any enthusiasm for reforms evaporate, was beginning to waver about yielding on wardship and purveyance. At the same time the Lords, who had at first shown interest in the plan to buy out the King's right to purveyance, had become lukewarm—indeed, less than that.

More was involved in the struggle than wardship and purveyance. The mind of the King was taken up with the design for the union, a design that was statesmanlike. His Majesty did not anticipate the opposition the design would encounter. He had assumed that Parliament would quickly and gladly put through what legislation was necessary for the consummation. Only as weeks passed did he realize that Parliament was going to take its time and that his pet project would have to be put off until the next session.

He had no conception of the problems involved in implementing the union. The many old laws hostile to the Scots, the complex problems of remanding criminals from each side of the border, the competing trade of the two nations with one another and the Continent, none of these were matters to be simply and quickly solved by legislation. The two kingdoms had different systems of law with the authority of history behind each, and, what made it worse, the English had both statute law and common law. To insert newly quarried stone into old buildings is never easy, and it is less easy when two buildings are of different kinds of stone and the larger has two dissimilar varieties.

About the program of Parliament the Commons were no less disappointed than his Majesty had been about the union. They had passed a measure for free trade and had seen it halted in the Upper House; they had put through a bill to legalize assarted lands,[4] and it was stopped; they had wrestled with the King over the Goodwin-Fortescue election and were not entirely satisfied with the compromise. If hopes were proving dupes, fears were not all liars.

It was about free speech that they at first seemed more concerned. The late Queen had been given to imprisoning for a short time those M.P.'s who spoke out too plainly. James was even more touchy than the Queen. At the beginning of a new reign it seemed best to assert themselves and to reclaim what they professed to believe was an established privilege. It was whispered that there were "many misinformers," who quoted and misquoted to His Majesty what had been said in St. Stephen's. On April 23, 1604, Bacon remarked: "If a man say more than he ought [it is] the hurt of his fortune, if he smother that which he ought to say, the hurt of his conscience." That Bacon could speak up for free speech may be an indication of the way opinion was moving. Bacon liked to go along with the majority if he could do so without offending the bestower of high office. It will be recalled that other men, Wingfield, Percival, Strode, and Thomas Crew had spoken out about free speech. They had in mind those who had been warned about speeches they had made, or might make, or had been asked to furnish His Majesty with notes of what they had said.

The hope for free speech in Parliament was short lived. Such notions were alien to the King's experience. When it was announced that His Majesty would address the House (on May 30, 1604), Martin moved that if the King took exception to what any member had said, the speaker might be directed to answer. Had Martin picked up some gossip that certain members were to be publicly castigated?

The King had been informed again and again of what was being said, and his speech of May 30 was in answer. From the Apology we can hazard a guess at some of his language on that occasion. The Apology reads: "into which course of proceedings we have not been rashly carried by *vain humor of curiosity,* of contradiction, of presumption, or of *love of our own devices,* or doings." [5] The words underlined were words His Majesty was fond of; he had used "curiosity" on May 1. He also scorned "parity," as he called it, in church organization. Kings believed in order and degree. But the particular emphasis in the Apology on free speech suggests that His Majesty had attacked sharply, but not by name, those who had found fault with his government.

Free speech was in theory an old privilege, but more in theory than in fact. Molin, the Venetian ambassador, wrote on May 12, 1604, to the Doge and Senate:

The Parliament is full of seditious subjects, turbulent and bold, who talk freely and loudly about the independence and the authority of Parliament, in virtue of its ancient privileges, which have fallen into disuse, but may be revived, and this will prove a diminution . . . of the royal prerogative.[6]

Molin was a foreigner but knew his way about at Westminster. The Commons were developing a historical philosophy of rights once recognized, as they stoutly believed, then lost, and now to be regained. It was an interpretation of the past and present that was to prove useful in the days to come, but that was hardly as valid history as it was pragmatic philosophy.

The King's speech had brought matters to a head, but the Commons had been moving toward a crisis. On May 1 His Majesty had sent a letter to the Speaker asking the Commons not to be "transported with the curiosity [meddlesomeness?] of a few giddy heads." On May 2 it had been moved that the Speaker ask access to His Majesty to give him satisfaction, and a committee of ten was nominated to prepare the late heads of the Speaker's address to the King. Of those ten only two, Sir Henry Montague and Sir George More, were not among those usually in opposition. Sandys, Strode, Hyde, and Wingfield were of the committee, but Sir Francis Bacon, who had spoken, was apparently left out. On the next day it was decided to forbear to attend His Majesty. What the intent of that decision was the Clerk did not indicate.

On May 18 Sir John Holles had proposed a committee to draw up reasons for the satisfaction of His Majesty touching the purveyors. On May 22 a committee was named to ask the Lords to join with them in a petition to the King for leave to treat of wardship. On May 28 Hastings had raised the question of the book newly brought out by the bishop of Bristol, in which the Commons were censured.

On June 1, the second day after the King's address of May 30, Sandys reported to the Commons the result of the conference of their committee with that of the Upper House. He told his fellow members that the Lords, instead of "acceptation and assent," had indulged in "expostulation," "opposition of reason to reason," "admonition," and "precise caution [intentional delay?] in proceeding." They reminded the Commons that on March 12, 1603, they would have given half of what they had to have what they now enjoyed. They complained of the time wasted on questions of privilege, of purveyance, and of religion.

The attitude of the Lords fitted in, he suggested, with His Majesty's speech "subsequent, advisedly and of purpose made upon that occasion to the whole House . . . on Monday last." [7] In that speech "many particular actions and passages of the House were objected unto them with taxation and blame." Under those cirsumstances Sir Edwin summoned the House to consider what were fittest to be done. Whereupon a Devonshire knight (Ridgeway) declared that since His Majesty had gained such an impression of mislike of the proceedings of the House in general, and since the "grounds conceived touching wardship and matters of that nature seemed to be so weakened and impugned" it was best for the House instantly to advise of such a form of satisfaction as might inform His Majesty of the truth and clearness of the action and intentions of the House "to free it from the scandal of levity and precipitation."

Sandys's report was thus entered in the *Commons Journals:* "This order following was conceived by the Clerk, being so directed." The last three words might imply that the Clerk had put down what Sandys had written.

I have already given the substance of Sandys's report. "Much dispute" followed the report. Holles, Sir Oliver St. John, Croft, Lytton, Strode, Sir Edward Stafford, Sir George More, and Sir Edward Hoby debated as to what ought to be done, and then Ridgeway offered his motion and was supported by the Speaker. A committee was named, the committee of May 22, which was the same committee as the Wroth committee of March 23, plus five other members.

It is conceivable that the begetter of the resolution that led to the naming of a committee, Sir Thomas Ridgeway, was possibly more interested in tranquilizing a certain excitable personage than in making a stand for the privileges of Parliament. Who was Sir Thomas? The heir of Thomas Ridgeway of Devonshire, young Thomas had attended Exeter College, Oxford, frequented by men from the West Country, studied at the Inner Temple, served on the Essex expedition to the Azores in 1597, been Collector of Customs at Exmouth, and Sheriff of Devonshire. He was now in his thirty-eighth year. In an earlier section the letter has been mentioned which Sir John Stanhope wrote to Salisbury at some time before the end of the session of Parliament of 1605/06. He was confident, he wrote, that his nephew Hollyer and his brother-in-law Ridgeway, "who is strong with his Devonshire crew," [8] would do their best to support Salisbury in some matter that was coming up. Ridgeway's subsequent willingness to follow Salisbury and his later career make one suspect that he was not overly zealous for the privileges of Parliament, though some of his associates from the western shires may well have been.

The committee to formulate the statement included many of the more active members of the House. Nearly one-half of them were old Elizabethan hands—Wroth, Henry Neville, Francis Bacon, George More, Edward Hoby, Nathaniel Bacon, Edward Stafford, Croft, Holles, Beeston, Wentworth (of Oxford), Holcroft, Wingfield, Manwood, Edwin Sandys, Doddridge, Hare, Knollys, Tanfield, Lawrence Hyde, Richard Lewknor, John Leveson (Luson), and others. To these, a few of whom had served in one or two Elizabethan Parliaments were added—Mansell, Yelverton, Martin, Lytton, and Francis Barrington.

In the unfinished notes of the Clerk was the sentence: "The former Committee for the Wards, or a select committee for this business out of this to be chosen." [9] In the finished Clerk's Book nothing is said of the select committee, but in the special order set down in that book by the Clerk, possibly as Sandys had given it to him, it was provided for in the Form of Satisfaction, "with this special care that a matter so advisedly and gravely undertaken . . . might not die, or be buried in the hands of those that first bred it." [10] Were some members becoming uneasy lest Ridgeway, dissatisfied with the committee that was to carry out his resolution, might have lost interest in the resolution?

It was late in the session; members were leaving town, and it was unlikely that a large committee would settle down to business, hold one meeting after another, and arrive at conclusions. It is easy to imagine that a small group formally named by the large committee, or possibly acting as that committee, in the absence of many members, might prepare a statement.

Of the proceedings in that committee I have seen neither minutes nor contemporary letters. In the Bath Manuscripts at Longleat is to be found this brief notice: "Appointment to meet on Saturday at the Middle Temple to frame an Apology to the King —And Long Apology by the Commons." [11]

On June 20 Ridgeway brought in the Apology and at some time, probably later, the Clerk started to copy it into the finished *Journal,* set down about thirty or so lines, and left space for more. Fortunately there are today a half dozen or more copies in manuscript and one printed version in Petyt's *Jus Parliamentarium.* The document begins with a pleasant allusion to the wisdom and understanding of their sovereign, but after some unimportant paragraphs comes to the point. The King had been greatly wronged by misinformation that had been the chief cause of the troublesome proceedings so much blamed in this Parliament. The misinformation had been of three kinds:

1. That they held their privileges not of right but of grace only
2. That they were not a Court of Record and could not command view of records
3. That the examination of the returns of writs was outside their compass and belonged to Chancery

The Commons in answer avouched:

1. That their privileges were their right and inheritance
2. That they [the privileges] could not be withheld from them but with wrong to the whole state of the Realm
3. That their making of request to enjoy their privileges was only an act of good manners

4. That their House was a Court of Record and ever so esteemed
5. That no court in the land could enter into competency for dignity or authority with the high Court of Parliament
6. That the House of Commons was the sole proper judge of writs and of the election of its members [12]

They went on to assert that in the first Parliament of His Majesty the privilege of the House and the liberties and stability of the kingdom had been more dangerously impugned than ever (as they supposed) since the beginnings of Parliament.[13]

1. The freedom of persons in elections had been impeached.
2. Freedom of speech had been prejudiced by often reproofs.
3. Particular persons who had spoken their consciences had been noted with taunt and disgrace.

The framers of the Apology had appealed to history, and their critics might well have asked why the rights and privileges asserted had not been pressed upon the late Queen. The answer was given. The rights and privileges of Parliament had not been raised with the late Queen because of her age and sex, "which we had great cause to tender." To have been troublesome to the Queen would have been to imperil the quiet of Her Majesty's succession.

The writers of the Apology turned to the problem of religion. His Majesty, they insisted, had been misinformed when he had been told that the kings of England had absolute power in themselves to alter religion, or to make any law concerning it otherwise than by consent of Parliament.

Having spoken out boldly on that fundamental matter, the writers took a more moderate position. They had not come "in any Puritan or Brownist spirit . . . to work the subversion of the state ecclesiastical," but in another spirit, that of peace. The lasting dissensions among ministers they deplored. It was their hope that in this Parliament laws might be enacted that a few ceremonies "of small importance," might no longer be required, and that a perpetual uniformity might be attained. With a few ceremonies only that had crept in they would like to do away.[14]

As for wardship the writers reminded the King that early in his reign he had advised Members of Parliament that if they knew of unjust burdens to proceed by bill, but if they came upon just burdens they were to approach him with a petition. Hence they had prepared a petition to treat about a perpetual composition for wardship. They had done so the more gladly because the right of the King to control wards seemed a matter of mere profit, and not of any honor or princely dignity. Wardship was a grievance to the subject; it resulted in ill-suited marriages and in the decay of families. In the eyes of foreigners those evils brought contempt upon the English nation.[15]

In a tactful way the Apologists were suggesting that the King had forgotten his promises to them and that he was overestimating the worth of the honor connected with wardship. The honor of a potent monarch, the Apologists declared, was settled on a higher and stronger foundation: "Faithful and loving subjects, valiant soldiers, an honorable nobility, wise Councillors, a learned and religious clergy, a contented and happy people are the true honor of a King." [16]

The writers of the Apology adverted to the "extreme, unjust, and crying oppression" of cart takers and purveyors, who had "rummaged and ransacked" far more since His Majesty's coming than in the time of his royal progenitors. All that the Apologists asked was the execution of the existing laws about purveyors. They alluded to the "demand of a perpetual yearly revenue in lieu of the taking away of those oppressions, unto which composition neither know we well how to yield, being only for justice and due right, which is unsaleable." They continued:

> Neither yet durst we impose it by law upon the people, without first acquainting them, and having their counsel unto it.[17] But if your Majesty might be pleased . . . to treat of composition with us for some grievance, which is by law and just, how ready we should be to take that occasion and color to supply your Majesty's desire concerning these also we hold for unjust, should appear, we nothing doubt, to your Majesty's full satisfaction.[18]

The above passage has to be compared with two long paragraphs near the end of the Apology. In the first of these paragraphs the writers of the Apology dealt with the evils of wardship, ill-suited marriages, and the disposal of children away from their parents. In the second paragraph they asked His Majesty out of

> Your most noble and most gracious disposition and desire to overcome our expectation with your goodness, may be pleased to accept the offer of a perpetual and certain revenue, not only proportionable to the uttermost benefit that any of your progenitors ever reaped thereby, but also with such an overplus and large addition as in great part to supply your Majesty's other occasions, that our ease might breed your plenty.[19]

As I interpret the earlier passage and the paragraphs just quoted in part, the Commons regarded purveyance as having become an abuse and thus an unjust burden, for which they were reluctant to bargain. Wardship was another matter. About that they were well-nigh desperate. To be rid of it, they were ready to give an overplus and large addition. The composition was to be raised "by yearly revenue out of the lands of your subjects, for wardship and other burthens depending upon them, or springing with them";[20] that is, "wardable" lands. They were not bargaining about purveyance, but their overplus and large addition would make it possible for His Majesty to relieve them also of the abuses of purveyance. That is what I think they meant to indicate. Incidentally, it would appear that this perpetual composition upon "wardable" lands would not free the King from the needs of subsidies.

His Majesty never received the Apology, at least officially, but he knew of it. In a parting message to the House on July 7, 1604, he said: "The best Apology-maker of you all, for all his eloquence, cannot make all good. Forsooth a goodly matter to make apologies when no man is by to answer. The King had been nettled by the Apology, but recognized its eloquence.

It was my hope that one of the several manuscripts of the Apology might afford clues as to its authorship. It happens that the manuscript in Trinity College, Dublin, reads: "The Form of an Apology or Satisfaction to be presented to his Majesty by a select Committee, viz. Sir Francis Bacon, Sir Edwin Sandys, Sir

Herbert Crofts, and others. The secretary who wrote that copy might have been right, and he might not.

That Sandys would have a share in preparing any important statement, such as the Apology was intended to be, seems probable. Not only was he a member of the significant committees, but he was a ready and effective writer. That he was used is evident from the statement in the Apology about wardship, part of which is a replica of the report brought in on May 26 by Sandys: "Some Directions for the proceeding of the Committee appointed to confer with the Lords touching the matter of wardship . . . and offered to the House, such as were set down in writing and read yesterday by himself [Sandys]." [21] Further, Sandys in his report of June 1 of the conference with the committee of the Lords quoted the Lords committee. The Lords put them in mind "What we were, in what state we were the 12th of March was twelvemonth: that we would have given half that we had to have that we now enjoy." [22]

These same words (with a difference in the March date) were in the Apology and were the first matter raised in the Protestation that formed the basis of the Apology. It would appear not impossible that the paragraph was lifted from Sandys's report.

Here and there are sentences in the Apology that might have been written by Sandys. The Apology says: "We demand but that justice which our princes are sworn neither to deny, delay nor sell." [23] This was a point that Sandys had stressed in the debates about the kingship.

The "Report on Free Trade," a terse and clear summary of the various opinions presented about that topic to the committee for that bill, reminds us in its balance and rhythm of the best sentences in the Apology, which is far from any proof that the sentences were those of Sandys. The time may come when prose rhythms can be studied metrically so as to make possible the identification of authorship. Not only does the Apology have sentences that seem to bear the mark of Sandys on them, but there are also unusual words to be found in his writings. But this is speculation.

That Bacon had a share in composing the Apology is even less demonstrable. The Apology had something to say about wicked purveyors, and in a report from a committee to the Commons Bacon had more to say. A comparison of Bacon's speech on April 30, 1604,[24] with the passage in the Apology [25] leaves us with little doubt that whoever wrote that passage had Bacon's speech in mind. That Bacon wrote the particular paragraph is much less certain.

The conciliatory statement in the Apology about the Church of England and Puritanism is similar to that of Bacon in intention but not in the words used. In 1603 Sir Francis wrote a long address to the King entitled "Certain Considerations touching the Better Pacification of the Church of England," [26] in which he put the case for moderation and comprehension. In passing, it may be noted that Bacon, in outlining his argument, was fond of the term "consideration," and that the Apology in its outline had one "consideration" after another. However much there was in the Apology of which Bacon would not have approved, he might have assisted in writing it, believing that he could tone it down. The trouble with that supposition is that in the preliminary version, the Protestation, which I shall presently discuss, the case against His Majesty was stated without many qualifications, while the Apology itself had many conciliatory passages obviously designed to make the document more acceptable to the King. But those paragraphs have few sentences of a Baconian quality, while the Protestation has telling sentences that Bacon might have written had he not been a supporter of His Majesty.

The Apology presented an opportunity for a piece of detective work that proved less fruitful than interesting. Among the Petyt Manuscripts in the Inner Temple is a briefer and more pointed version of the Apology, one that would have been less palatable to James I than the Apology itself. It was entitled "Notes out of a Protestation of the House of Commons *I Jacobi*." Its wording led me to assume that it was merely an abbreviated form of the Apology. My supposition was not borne out by a comparison of the Protestation with the Apology. It was clear enough, at least to my eyes, that the writers of the Apology had taken over the

Protestation, used more than nine-tenths of it, changing a few words here and there and adding, especially at the beginning and toward the end, new paragraphs. Those added paragraphs were written in a different and less pointed style and seemed designed to weaken the force of the document as a protest. It is further to be observed that the Protestation always calls itself the Protestation and the Apology is always known as the Apology except once where the words "and desire that this our Protestation" occur in the Apology. The Apology is called the Apology at all times in the *Commons Journals* and is so called in the King's scoffing allusion to it. That the Apology was an amplification of the Protestation will be evident, I believe, to those who will compare the two documents. The Protestation is not at all a breviate of a larger document. It was prepared, if we may judge from its language, by two or three men not unskilled in writing. With the exception of a few sentences here and there, the Protestation was clear, cogent, terse and to the point.

The Protestation deserves close examination. In a considerable degree it was devoted to the Goodwin-Fortescue case, the Shirley case, the blunder of the Yeoman of the Guard, free speech, and other matters that had come up early in the session. Some of the other questions brought up later fit into the Apology almost as if they were later insertions. I have a suspicion, one that I cannot verify, that the Protestation was partially based upon an earlier document. On May 1 His Majesty had written, it will be recalled, a message to the Commons urging them not to be transported with the curiosity of a few giddy heads. That annoyed the Commons who named a committee of ten to frame an answer. On May 3 they decided not to send their answer, possibly because some of them may have had inside information that the King had prepared a friendly message to them, which they would receive the next day, informing them that if they had come to him he would have given them satisfaction. It is conceivable that the committee of ten, who had drafted the reply to His Majesty, when they learned that it was not to be used, put it in storage and that, when a new committee made up of some of the same members were framing the Protestation, they availed themselves of the draft of May 2 and 3 and added to it complaints that had been brought forward more recently. That is no more than a guess.

It would seem that most of the passages worthy of quotation are to be found in the Protestation and that few of the additional passages in the Apology have merit as parliamentary wisdom or even as good prose. The sentences I have quoted at the beginning of the chapter: "What cause we your poor Commons have . . ." were probably the work of a single hand, conceivably that of Sir Edwin Sandys, who could now and then express himself tersely and even vividly; more probably they were the phrasing of some obscure member whose name we shall never learn.

Unfortunately a large part of the Apology was below the standard set by our obscure friend. It was a mishmash, a wordy document put together by a mixed bag of committeemen. There were exceptions. About information the authors of the Apology wrote:

> Let your Majesty be pleased to receive public information from your Commons in Parliament as to the civil estate and government, for private informations pass often by practice [intention]. The voice of the people in things of their knowledge is said to be as the voice of God.[27]

The Apology was not distinguished by that close reasoning by which M.P.'s in late Elizabethan and early Jacobean Parliaments occasionally fortified their orations. The makers of the Protestation were asserting rights and privileges and not offering proof for them.

It has been suggested that the Protestation was put together by two or three men not unpracticed in writing. The only copy known of the Protestation is in a hand so unusual and individual that I have hoped to discover whose hand it was. It is not that of a secretary. My friend, Basil Henning, and I compared the handwriting with that of about sixty M.P.'s of 1604 and failed to discover the penman. I have shown the photostat to a few scholars of the seventeenth century, and no one has been able to identify it.

The final form of the Apology, even with its gracious sentences for His Majesty, failed to win the support it needed for passage. Brought in by Ridgeway on June 20, 1604, it was "much disputed" whether or not it should be delivered to the King. In the debate Bacon, Carleton, Sir Thomas Beaumont, Sir Edwin Sandys, Martin, Bennet, Stafford, Croft, Sir Walter Cope, Fuller, Holles, and Strode took part. Bacon and Carleton were opposed to sending the Apology to the King. We can be reasonably certain that Sir Henry Montague and Sir Walter Cope took the same position. Beaumont and Croft were in favor of forwarding the Apology. It may be suspected that Fuller, Sir Oliver St. John, Wingfield, and Sandys were on the same side, and possibly Martin, who, however, went his own way.

On June 29 the bill on Strode's motion was recommitted, "adding some names." The document was such a mélange that it may have pleased neither those who upheld prerogative nor those who watched over the privileges of Parliament. Moreover, the session was drawing to a close. Members were not following through with the zeal they had shown earlier, when hopes were high, or at least seemed so. If members were not setting out for home, they were perhaps absenting themselves from tedious committees. The Apology never became official.

The failure to make the Apology a Grand Remonstrance was typical of the session. Those who hoped for great things from the new sovereign found themselves disillusioned. Nothing worked as they had hoped. The old leaders had seldom been able to stand up to the late Queen and had ceased trying to do so. The leaders in the new reign, men such as Sir Edwin Sandys, Richard Martin, and Sir Herbert Croft, were attracting attention, and Sir Edwin was by way of becoming a leader. The Commons had not yet discovered that if they protested enough His Majesty was likely to make concessions. It was some time before they were to realize that a compromise might prove, in the long run, a victory, as in the Goodwin-Fortescue case.[28]

Chapter 2

The Second
Session, 1605/06

The Problem of
the Recusants

THE Apology of 1604 hardly mentioned the Catholics. It alluded to the Anglican sermons against Parliament; it appealed for peace and unity in religion and for toleration of differences in small matters. For a body of men, most of whom were somewhat Puritan in their outlook, that was significant. Those members who supported the Apology were intent upon the privileges of Parliament and the rights of the subject and would not allow themselves to be drawn far away from such matters.

Between that June 1604, when the Apology was framed, and the session of Parliament that met in November 1605, the treaty with Spain had been signed, even if not welcomed by the public. The Gunpowder Plot of that November at once made all other topics seem trivial. To understand the consequent proposals in Parliament about recusants that followed the discovery of the plot, it is well to go back and review briefly the Elizabethan legislation concerning Catholics and the actions of James I after he arrived in England.

The laws passed in the reign of the great Queen were directed against the Jesuit missionaries who hoped to win England back to the Roman Church and who worked secretly and ceaselessly toward that end, even risking their lives. The act of 23 Eliz., cap. i, declared that those who persuaded any of Her Majesty's subjects

141

to withdraw from their obedience to their sovereign or to withdraw from the established religion would be regarded as guilty of treason. Furthermore, all subjects over sixteen years of age who failed to attend the English church service were to forfeit £20 a month until such time as they conformed.

Threats from Spain moved Parliament to make the laws more severe. When King Philip assembled ships to invade England and restore the old religion there, Parliament, with the approval of the Privy Council (also nervous about possible uprisings among English Catholics), proceeded to make the laws harsher. The Crown was empowered to take all the goods of those who did not pay their £20 a month and to take two parts of all their lands, leases, etc.; the third part only to be reserved for the maintenance of the offender's wife, children, and family. If the offender submitted and conformed, however, his goods and lands were to be restored.

These laws affected seriously the Catholic gentry, which included many of the well-landed families. With few exceptions, they proved loyal to the Queen, the more so when invasion threatened. Their loyalty was ill rewarded. They found the monthly payments a heavy burden, and they envisaged impoverishment and the loss of that influence in their communities which the holding of magistracies afforded them.

The lot of the poorer Catholics was little better. Those whose incomes amounted to less than 20 marks a year had to report to officials, and, if they finally refused to attend the Church of England, they might in theory be forced to abjure their country, although few except priests were actually driven out of the realm. The laws were indeed so severe that they were enforced intermittently, and, of course, less thoroughly in some shires than in others.

When laws are not thoroughly enforced, there are always those who cry out for more stringent laws, and such men were not wanting in Parliament. They did not understand that too much medicine is often worse than too little.

The Parliaments of Elizabeth's very last years showed little mercy. By the statute of 35 Eliz., cap. ii (passed at a time when another armada was expected), recusants were forbidden to go more than five miles from their homes without special license given by two justices of the peace, with the consent of the bishop of the diocese, or of the lord lieutenant, or of a deputy lieutenant of the county. That law proved little more than an extreme inconvenience to those affected. The recusants could gain the licenses they required from the neighboring justices of the peace, some of whom were old friends or relatives, or at least men disposed to help out fellow gentlefolk, but they could not, when seeking the necessary licenses, escape the annoyances and humiliations of what we call red tape.

Fortunately the recusants, although required to attend church, had in Elizabeth's reign not been required to take Communion.[1] But compulsory attendance at a church in which they had no faith was a blow to their consciences, to their hope of heaven, and to their pride and dignity, and was a continuous drain upon their energies and spirits. Their priests, who flitted on dark nights from a hiding place in one country house to another, urged their brethren of the faith to stand up to the pressures put upon them, and at the same time they wrote to their fellow Catholics abroad, bespeaking an attitude of compassion toward those of their faith who had yielded to the laws and had attended the Church of England services. During this period a great many priests were caught, and a few were hanged and disemboweled before death, enduring their suffering as men unafraid and assured of future felicity.

With a new sovereign the Catholics had hoped for better treatment. James VI of Scotland, in his long quest for the English throne, had promised concessions to many kinds of people. He had encouraged the Catholics to believe that he would come to their aid and grant them toleration, but he was probably too optimistic in estimating what power he would have to help them. As soon as he found himself securely on the English throne, those promises seemed—to the Catholics—to have been forgotten. He was reported to have told Watson, one of the priests later implicated in the Bye Plot, that the papists were no longer necessary to his advancement.[2]

But James was naturally a kindly and merciful man, especially to those of rank and wealth, and was inclined to make it as easy as was feasible for his Catholic subjects, if they would only exhibit loyalty to him. The Bye Plot and the Main Plot rendered him less benevolent. Beaumont, the French ambassador, heard him denounce the Pope as antichrist.[3]

What was more significant, late in February 1604 he had issued a proclamation banishing all Jesuits and seminary priests from England. In June a bill against recusants was introduced into the House of Lords, was passed there, and on July 4 was passed, with various amendments, in the House of Commons. That bill confirmed statutes already on the books and made the lot of Catholics even worse.

But also in July the King received a deputation of loyal Catholics and was believed by them to have promised that he would forbear the collection of £20 a month for nonattendance at the service of the Church of England. The delegation was assured that it was the King's intention "that they should enjoy this grace as long as they kept themselves upright in all civil and true carriage towards his Majesty and the State without contempt." The leader of the delegation, Sir Thomas Tresham of Northamptonshire (father of the Tresham of the Gunpowder Plot), asked if recusancy itself would be regarded as contempt and was assured that His Majesty would not so look upon it. Such is the story to be found in the work of a conscientious Catholic historian.[4] But the King's promise involved the repeal of part of an act of Parliament,[5] no small matter; he already had enough experience with his first Parliament to have realized that a law was not lightly altered or suspended.

James was rash enough to send by a Catholic Scot (Sir James Lindsay) a friendly message to the Pope, and the Scot let the news leak out that in his instructions James had declared that he would never be deterred by his own "preoccupied self-opinion" from receiving anything that might be proved to be "lawful, reasonable, and without corruption." It is hardly surprising that the Pope welcomed Lindsay and appointed twelve cardinals to study the situation and to pray for the conversion of England. That news was soon spread over the Continent and reached England at a time when James was coming under suspicion as having a leaning toward Rome. To prove he had no such leanings James ordered the judges to enforce rigorously the laws against Catholics, in contradiction to the promises he was believed to have made.[6]

The Catholic families were almost desperate. Before the Lindsay episode became known, a group of young hotheads among the Catholics had set in motion the conspiracy known as the Gunpowder Plot. The discovery of that plot made it worse for all Catholics.

The excitement over the plot was shared by the English from St. Michael's Mount to Berwick-on-Tweed. For months men in alehouses and at markets could talk of little else. For the months of November, December, and January, the State Papers were crowded with rackings, confessions, hangings, and disembowelments. The strange narratives that issued from the torture chambers were pieced together and roused resentment against all Catholics, even against the most loyal.

When Parliament met, the question of papistical practices was brought to the fore at once. Sir George More, who made the first speech on the subject, wished the House to consider what would best ensure the safety of the King. The Solicitor General, Sir John Doddridge, spoke of the philosophy of the conspirators: it was lawful, they believed, to equivocate, to lie, to dissemble before a magistrate, and to kill a heretic.

A committee was named (January 21, 1605/06) that included most of the better-known figures of the last session of the House in 1604. It was to meet on that very afternoon to consider timely proceedings against Jesuits, seminarists, and all other popish agents.

As to what happened in committee, we know less than we would. The Speaker asked permission to attend the committee, brought with him "articles ready drawn," and had, so Sir Edward Hoby surmised, "a long labored speech in his breast." [7] His plan was that the Commons should ask the King to issue a proclamation, but the Commons would have none of it. To ask His Majesty to issue a proclamation, they declared not untactfully, was to show distrust of him and draw down more malice upon his person. The spokesmen of the Commons, according to Hoby, were Sir John Holles, Yelverton, Francis Moore, and Sir Francis Bacon.

Sir John Doddridge, the Solicitor, son of a Barnstaple merchant, a graduate of Exeter College, Oxford, a member of the Middle Temple and a learned and judicious lawyer, whose manners and language inspired confidence, seems to have acted as head of the committee. The committee set up a subcommittee, and from that subcommittee the Solicitor reported on January 25 that they had decided to incorporate their ideas in articles and to move the House that the articles might be delivered to the "general committee," who, gathering them together and arranging them, might frame a bill; [8] in other words, the subcommittee was to prepare matters for the large committee, and that committee was to make them ready for the House. The large committee was now called the Committee for Religion,[9] was meeting the afternoon of January 26, and had met before.

On January 29 His Majesty sent word by the Speaker that he approved the intentions of the House touching religion and wished "a speedy proceeding that particulars may not hinder such great causes as are to come in." [10] James was anxious lest the Parliament lose time on other matters when subsidies were sorely needed.

The members of the committee worked rapidly. On February 1, only ten days after the House had met after the long recess following the plot, Nicholas Fuller brought in from the committee sixteen articles that were at once read to the House.

The fifth of those articles was perhaps the most important because it dealt with the new oath to be taken by recusants. This oath had its roots in the late years of Queen Elizabeth and was designed to deepen the quarrel among the English Catholics.[11]

The recusant had to swear that he believed King James was the lawful and rightful King of the realm and that the Pope had neither power nor authority to depose the King, nor to dispose of his kingdom, nor to authorize any foreign prince to invade or annoy him. The recusant had further to swear that, notwithstanding any declaration of excommunication or deprivation made by the Pope against the King, he would bear faith and allegiance to His Majesty and defend him against all conspiracies and attempts whatsoever. He was to swear, also, that he abhorred, detested, and abjured as impious and heretical the damnable doctrine that princes who were excommunicated may be deposed or murdered by their subjects, and that he believed that neither Pope nor any other person had power to absolve him from this oath. He swore to take this oath without any mental evasion or secret reservation.

The oath could be administered by any bishop in his diocese or by any two justices of the peace (one of whom was of the quorum) to any person of the age of eighteen years or above, who was indicted, or to be indicted, convicted, or to be convicted of recusancy (nobles and noblewomen excepted), or of not repairing to church, or not receiving Communion twice within the year. It could also be administered to any other person passing through the country, who, on being examined, should confess or not deny that he was a recusant and that he had not received the sacrament twice within the past year. If any such person should refuse to answer upon the oath to such bishops or justices of the peace, or to take the oath, he was to be jailed until the next assize, and then again required in the open assizes to take the oath, and, if he refused, he was to incur the penalty of praemunire (except for married women, who were to remain in jail until they took the oath).

This law did not compel bishops and justices of the peace to administer the oath, but gave them discretion. What it did do was to put into their hands a powerful weapon not only to use if necessary but to hold over those who would not conform.

So far as we know from our limited records, this oath met with no marked opposition in Parliament, and certainly with no serious attempt to alter or amend it. The archbishop was apparently in favor of as strong an oath as the Puritans could have wished. The King himself had a good deal to say about the oath, after it had been put on the statute book; indeed, he wrote a paper in its defense and understated the effect of the law. James could easily persuade himself of what he wished to believe. He explained that he had hoped to cause a separation between those of his subjects who were popishly affected and yet retained in their hearts "the print of their natural duty" to their sovereign and those carried away with zeal, who thought a diversity of religion a pretext for all kinds of treason. His policy in formulating the oath, he believed, had been successful. "Very many of my subjects that were popishly affected, as well priests as laics, did freely take the same oath." It annoyed the King that the Pope did not cooperate, but sent out two briefs forbidding Catholics to take the oath.[12] The King was convinced that he had been more merciful to the Catholics than his predecessor. Had he not given access to the Catholics, had he not bestowed knighthoods upon them, had he not sent instructions to the judges to spare the execution of priests, had he not released recusants from their ordinary payments?

All very well, but he was nevertheless enforcing the oath. It seems possible that James had qualms, but he had persuaded himself that by the new oath he had put all quiet-minded papists out of despair and had proved to them that he "intended no persecution against them for conscience's cause."[13] As so often, he was inconsistent.

What the form of the oath was when first presented to the Commons we do not know. In its form as presented to the House from the committee it was referred back to the subcommittee "in respect of many exceptions."

So much for the fifth article. To return now to the others. The first article renewed the penalty of £20 a month exacted from every recusant failing to attend church, with the addition that, if the King wished, instead of the £20 a month, he could take two-thirds of the lands, leases, etc. "because 20 *li per mensem* is to the great Recusant a small punishment."[14]

There was another new provision, at least in the final form of the statute. Not only the justices of assize and of gaol delivery were to have power to "inquire, hear, and determine" of all recusants and offenses, but the justices of the peace in quarter sessions were to have the same powers, which meant that the local country gentlemen, most of them (except in a few shires) anti-

Catholic, would have the chance, if they were so inclined—many were not—to discipline their fellow gentlemen.

By the second article a scheme was set forth for detecting absences from church service, so that the Government would not have to depend upon informers. It became the duty of churchwardens to present monthly the names of all recusants, nine years of age and older, who were absent from church. It was suggested in the House of Commons, and accepted, that for this service the churchwardens should receive a fee of 40s. for every absence noted, the sum to be taken out of the income of the said absentee. If the churchwardens failed to give the names of the absentees, they themselves were to pay 20s. for every such failure. But who was to determine the failure of the churchwardens to report, and to whom were they to report? The question of the enforcement of their duty upon the churchwardens was not provided for. In theory, the high constable already had the duty of bearing down upon churchwardens, but he had many other things to do and could hardly keep close tabs on his several parishes.

It was at about this point in the discussion that Sir Thomas Beaumont made a suggestion. He was a Leicestershire Beaumont, representing Tamworth in Warwickshire, and had been educated at Peterhouse, Cambridge. Beaumont proposed that recusants be discouraged from keeping houses and offered "many reasons." The priests would then be unable to resort to them, and their poverty would drive away many followers. The Solicitor was quick to point out that if recusants were deprived of their houses no one would be willing to receive them.[15]

The third article dealt with recusants who conformed by going to church but did not receive Communion. If the recusant refused to take Communion, he was, according to the statute in its final form, to be fined £20 the first year, £40 the second year, and £60 the third year. The Solicitor asked if a man might be compelled by a penal law to a merely spiritual action,[16] a reasonable question.

The fourth article dealt with the problem of whether a man should be compelled to pay for the recusancy of his wife, and was debated at length over parts of two days. Martin asserted that husbands of recusant wives were often good subjects. There was great difference of opinion, and the committee referred the problem to the House, where it was never put to the question.[17] At the end of the session the Lords voted that no one should be impeached for his wife's failure to receive Communion.[18]

By the tenth article recusants were not to practice common or civil law, nor to assume office in any court of justice, nor to hold military posts.

The twelfth article was to the effect that every recusant should be ipso facto regarded as excommunicated and thus subject to all the disabilities of that status.

The thirteenth article provided than any man who should marry other than in some open church or chapel, according to the orders of the Church of England, should be disqualified from having any estate of freehold of his wife's as "tenant by courtesy." Further, it was stated that every woman who should be married otherwise than by the Church of England should be disabled to claim any dower of the inheritance of her husband.[19]

The thirteen articles were voted to be included in the first bill against recusants. The committee brought in a second bill in which five articles were to be considered, the first concerning children of recusants. Those who had been sent to the universities or schools, or into "apprenticeships, service, or other employments . . . under the government . . . of persons well affected . . . to the religion now established in this realm," were in good hands. But sending such children to such institutions was to be done with the allowance of the minister of the parish and of two justices of the peace adjoining, and the parents were to bring to the quarter sessions certificates of the placing of each child. All other children of the age of nine and under twenty-one, residing with their recusant parents, should be taken by these parents to a place of meeting with four justices of the peace and the bishop, or his chancellor, and all such children should be "put forth or bestowed either at the university, school, apprenticehood, or other services or employments under the charge and government of such person or persons as shall there be of the said religion now here established." Moreover, the parents were to pay for the maintenance of their children by those who were well disposed to the established religion. In other words, recusants were to lose control of their children from the age of nine.

That worthy gentlemen could consider such a scheme for the separation of parents and children is hard to understand.

In the second proposed article of the second bill, the matter of wardships was dealt with. The final text stated that convicted recusants were not to control the education of their own children, "much less of the children of any other of the King's subjects." [20] The King could not sell the right of wardship to a recusant; nor could a recusant, under any circumstance, be granted the wardship of any minor. Recusants also lost any claim to choose the mate for a ward.

The third article of the second bill concerned children who were sent overseas in order that they might attend such Catholic seminaries as Douai, or well-known convents. According to the final text of the statute, no child could be sent abroad unless the father obtained a license from the King or from six of the Privy Council, whereof the Principal Secretary was to be one.[21]

The fourth article provided that those eighteen years or older who had gone abroad ("being neither merchants, nor their factors, nor apprentices, soldiers, or mariners") without license should lose the income of all their lands and leases, which would be turned over to the nearest of kin who were not recusants, but if the said offender returned, conformed himself, took the new Oath of Allegiance, and received Communion, he might regain the income of his lands, leases, and so forth. The law was carefully phrased to encourage recusants by economic considerations to return to the Anglican fold.[22]

The articles prepared by the Commons and those by the Lords were brought before the conference held on the afternoon of February 6. That evening Salisbury wrote to Lord Dirleton an account for the eyes of the King of the doings of the afternoon. The two sets of articles, Salisbury wrote, had given great contentment to both Houses.[23] Each House had the same end in view, and it was hoped that the fitting together of the two statements would not take much time. He congratulated them on having a sovereign who was a philosopher, rich in wisdom and in zeal. Salisbury was expressing himself with unusual effusiveness.

Sir Francis Bacon pronounced the articles of the Lords more severe than those of the Commons. He added that Salisbury was afraid that if the Church were not relieved of the problem of recusancy the commonwealth would suffer. He took occasion to read from the King's Meditations. His Majesty hoped that recusants might feel the sting of the law.[24]

Bacon quoted the King, as His Majesty probably intended, who divided recusants into three kinds, the first two being "those old, and rooted, and rotten," and "Novelists the greatest danger." By novelists I assume he meant converts. The third type of recusants were the youth, who were the future tense. The hope of reclaiming them James deemed slight. Papists should be disarmed, he asserted, and should be allowed no places in the magistracy, but they might well be left to the old laws. He hoped that the laws would control marriages and christenings and so nip papistry in the bud. As for priests in their hiding places in private houses, they should be banished "within a time." It would appear that His Majesty was willing to give them time to leave the country and did not propose to execute them, as had sometimes been done in the last reign. Here was a bit of moderation. Was the zeal of the King against the papists lessening as the memory of the Gunpowder Plot faded?

In the conference it was agreed that the articles drawn up by the Lower House should be given to the Lord Chancellor by the following day and that the Lords were to hand over their articles to the Commons. Then a subcommittee was to draw things into form.

On February 8 the Speaker announced that he had received the articles framed by the Lords. He proposed that the articles worked over by the Commons might be perfected, and the Lords' articles were to be ready so that every member might consider them.

About the question of recusancy it was hardly to be expected that the Lords should be as well informed as the Commons. The Commons had the advantage of including within their membership a considerable number of practicing lawyers as well as many members who had been active as justices of the peace, were experienced in local government, and were likely to be useful concerning what was needed in the way of new legislation. Of course the Upper House included bishops who were usually not unfamiliar with the problems of recusancy, but were seldom skilled in the drawing up of statutes. The judges, however, who sat with the Lords, although not members of the Upper House, provided available legal talent. In this particular problem the Lords were probably as well served as the Commons and seem to have taken a larger view.

Meanwhile, another problem was brought before the Commons. Also on February 8 Sir Christopher Perkins, who had been associated with Archbishop Bancroft in framing the Oath of Allegiance, raised a new question: the danger to English soldiers serving under the Archduke in the Low Countries. The Pope, he asserted, had established seminaries of scholars to draw those soldiers away from obedience to the King and was now providing a seminary of martial men to invade and assault the English when the occasion might arise. The Archduke, he believed, did not really aim at the Low Countries but at England.

Sir Christopher's fears [25] seem to have been little justified. Spain and England had just signed a treaty of peace, and it was to the interest of Spain to keep that peace. But Sir Edwin Sandys, who was familiar with the Continent, joined in the warning. Men who came from the Low Countries affirmed that the soldiers serving under the Archduke had no other plan than to alter the state of England.[26]

The House was unduly alarmed about those soldiers. Many were probably not so much recusants as soldiers of fortune, seeking a military career. But the committee, when they were uncertain about their next move, referred the question back to the House, which relayed it in turn to a conference with the Lords.

It was a "tickle" question with which they were dealing, for the King was eager to please the Spanish.

On February 27 Salisbury wrote the English ambassador in Brussels, Sir Thomas Edmondes, that the Spanish were bringing great pressure to be allowed to enroll in England soldiers for the Archduke. He had had to tell the Spanish ambassador that

> it was now a time of Parliament and that the Lower House had conceived such a deep impression that those soldiers which served the Archduke would have been made the sword for England's destruction [which was almost exactly what Christopher Perkins and Sandys had said] as they were now about to make laws for the general restraint of any that should offer to go to serve any Prince or State that is different from them in religion.

His Majesty, Salisbury continued,

> knows well enough how far fit it is for him to yield to any such desires of his subjects and wherein to deny them, yet it is not a fit time now to put him to the exigent of a direct opposition in that point, by which course all other his Majesty's desires that are to be effected by the Parliament might receive interruption.

Salisbury was doubtless speaking for the King, but the phrases have a Cecilian ring. He besought the ambassador to have patience until His Majesty might know the issue of Parliament.[27] In other words, James might be willing to yield to the Spanish request to levy troops in England when Parliament had given him sufficient money and was adjourned. In the meanwhile, he did not wish the House of Commons to come to any resolution for recalling the English troops then with the Archduke, or for preventing the further levying of such troops in England. The King was slowly becoming aware that the body that voted money had to be reckoned with in other matters.

Parliament passed a statute, stating that any person leaving the realm to serve foreign princes, states, or potentates should take the

Oath of Allegiance before his departure. Further, all officers serving foreign princes were bound by oath not to enter into any conspiracy or practice against His Majesty. If an officer should persuade anyone to withdraw his allegiance from the King, or should himself withdraw such allegiance and promise obedience to any foreign potentate, he should be regarded as guilty of high treason.[28]

Between February 13 and February 18 preparations were being made for a conference with the Lords. Doddridge and Bacon had been instructed to prepare for such a conference. Yelverton, Hyde, Shirley, Henry Montague, Winch, and Hare were to be ready and armed with the laws, both for the meeting of committees and for the conference.

There is no more in the *Commons Journals* about recusants until February 27, when Mr. Solicitor Doddridge made a report of the conference. All that we can learn directly is that there had been dispute and "exceptions and alterations to the several Articles." It is curious that we have a fragment of evidence from the next session of Parliament in November of the same year. Sir Robert Harley recorded the debate over the proposed union and had Strode say: "It [the union] is as fit for a bill as that of the Recusancy was, by being in articles, which was the work of our conference." [29] In other words, the conference over recusancy had provoked useful discussion and prepared the way for bills.

On February 28 the larger part of the morning was spent upon the articles. From the brief and unrevealing sentences in the debate set down by the Clerk, it is not easy to make out much of what was happening. It is evident, however, that the article about the education of the children of recusants had given rise to wide differences of opinion and was left "unresolved." Hobart declared that the education of the children of recusants lay at the heart of the problem before the House. Should the articles apply to all the children or only to the eldest, since he was the important one?

It was Hobart, too, who raised the question as to what should be done with the profits of the lands of recusants, when taken from them. Doubtless he was afraid that the friends of the King, and in particular those in the North, would persuade him to allow them the major share of the profits, and that, in consequence, little would accrue to the Crown, which was precisely what happened in many instances to income that ought to have increased the revenue of the Crown. One may well suspect that some of the support for the legislation against the recusants came from those who hoped to buy in at small sums the rights to the fines and forfeitures of the recusants. Probably to prevent such a contingency Hobart proposed that all the profits should be gathered into a bank or storehouse. He was no doubt thinking of the reformed recusants who might be given back their lands and the profits accumulated from them. His sensible idea was not taken up by the House.

On March 1 the baffling question of the recusants' children came again to the fore. The subcommittee of the Commons reported that the difficulties of the problem did overcome them.[30] It was proposed to leave the question of the two bills then being drafted and to pass a separate measure on the subject.

A committee was named on March 5 to draw the bills for recusancy: it included Hobart, the Attorney of the Court of Wards, Sir Henry Montague, Mr. Solicitor Doddridge, and Sir Francis Bacon, all formidable figures. Other members were Thomas Crew, M.P. for Lichfield, sitting in his first Parliament, and Francis Moore.

On March 11 the "Bill for the Better Preservation of the King's Subjects in their due Obedience" was first read, and on March 13 the "Bill for the Better Conforming of Recusants, their Wives, Children, and Servants to the True Religion" had its first reading. The two bills each had their second reading on March 14.

Who wrote them? Bacon, a member of the committee, furnished the answer to that question.[31] In some personal miscellanea, he recorded judgments of men and issues. Several times he alluded to the recusancy bills, the first time characterizing Sir Henry Hobart: "Too full of cases and distinctions. Nibbling solemnly he distinguisheth but apprehends not. The penning of the 2 laws concerning Recusants. No gift with his pen in proclamations and the like." [32] In another part of the half-English, half-Latin abbreviations of his secret thoughts Bacon set forth the pros and cons and wrote: "The Bill of Recusants his [Hobart's]" [33] Such evidence we cannot discount. He said further: "I never knew any of so good a speech with a worse pen." Hobart made good suggestions, but his lawmaking was not precise.

In the committee it was decided that the hard problem of a husband's responsibility for his wife's recusancy should be left to the construction of the law. As I read the final form of the statute 3 Jac. I, cap. iv, art. xxvii, a woman who did not attend the church service would have to pay 12d. for every absence. In the same act, art. xi, it was stated that no husband should have to pay for his wife's refusal to receive Communion.

On April 14 the two bills were passed and sent to the Lords. On April 29 they were referred to a committee headed by the archbishop of Canterbury and including a number of bishops and peers. The question became one of reconciling the differences between the measures of the two Houses.

In a letter to Sir Thomas Lake, Salisbury expressed the opinion that the Commons were emphasizing their differences with the Lords in order to keep Parliament in session and thus gain time for the presentation of their grievances. The Solicitor felt that the differences between the two Houses concerned principally two matters: the receiving of Communion, and the taking of children of recusants away from their parents. On the first the Upper House was inclined to clemency and thus to allow a longer time for recusants to make up their minds to receive Communion. On that point Salisbury had written the Earl of Mar, who was believed to be close to His Majesty, that the Lords were reluctant to set sharp penalties, lest "men should be barred from coming to the place where they might learn to come further; seeing faith comes by hearing." [34]

In the matter of taking children from their recusant parents, the difference between Lords and Commons "consisteth in diverse difficulties": the Lords thought it "unnatural, dangerous, and exceeding difficult and scandalous"; the Commons offered various unconvincing reasons why it should be done. Finally, however, they left the matter to the wisdom of the Lords to deal with the bill as they thought best.

Concerning the oath of allegiance the Lords wished all peers exempted from the statute of 1 Eliz., but the committee of the Commons was unwilling to yield to the Upper House.[35]

The Lords complained that the five-mile restriction upon the movement of recusants made it difficult for the bishops to summon them. The Commons had required that a recusant who had to go farther than five miles from his home was to get the permission of four justices instead of two, and added that all licenses to go farther than five miles should contain the cause of the license and the time limits upon the journey.

In the second bill of the Commons the Lords had objected to the power granted the justices of the peace to search the house of anyone who had been a noncommunicant. Fortunately it was finally agreed to leave these matters "to the Lords parliamental power."

Why did the Commons allow the Lords the last word? We can only guess at the answer. The Commons had seen their bills about ecclesiastical grievances die slowly between readings; they had witnessed all their efforts on behalf of the nonconforming clergy come to nothing. They may well have feared that the two bills against recusants might be lost in the last-minute shuffle. After all the Lords and they were not far apart. The Lords could be trusted to be fairly stiff about recusants; the Gunpowder Plot had not been wholly forgotten. A bill with some modifications made by the Upper House was better than no bill. It is not impossible that some of the Puritan leaders in the Commons had talked things over with one another and concluded not to fight the Lords to the last ditch.

The Lords were conciliatory. They recalled to the Commons the many conferences. "Their Lordships concur in the same zeal and affection with this House." They hoped that the omissions they had made in the bills would not give occasion to make a "sepulchre of the good things."

We understand that message better when we read a letter written by Lake to Salisbury on May 22. His Majesty had heard, wrote Lake, that the archbishop of Canterbury was inclined to hold up the recusancy bills longer. The nervous sovereign was afraid that such a move would cause delay in the adjournment of the Houses, and he hoped that Salisbury would prevent further waste of time.[36]

There was a slight delay, but on the forenoon of May 27 Hobart made a report. The Speaker read parts of the first bill "to satisfy such as were not present at the passing of the bill," and the question passed "with great applause and a general voice of prayer that it may have good success." The second bill was passed "with like applause." [37]

The recusancy articles and bills caused less serious differences between the House of Commons and the King than most of the other measures brought forward; they also caused less trouble between the two Houses. The reasons are not difficult to find. Behind those bills were some of the men in or close to the Government, Doddridge, Hobart, Henry Montague, and Francis Bacon, and with the archbishop of Canterbury and Salisbury in the Lords. Pushing for the bills, and probably for the most severe form of the bills, were some of the Puritans, probably Hyde and Hare, "the tribunes of the people," Nicholas Fuller, Christopher Perkins, and others. To the extreme Puritans the Catholics were tied up with Spain. Did they not represent the fearful danger that England might be drawn back to Catholicism?

It is surprising how little sympathy there was for the Catholics. They had been persecuted throughout the reign of the great Queen and during the second half of her reign driven from pillar to post. Their letters to fellow Catholics and to neighbors and friends exhibit their quiet desperation. Even their Protestant neighbors and friends seldom expressed any personal regret for what the state was doing, though, perhaps, they sometimes said what they were afraid to write in letters. The Catholics did not know where to turn. They tried to be good Englishmen, loyal to their King, but few of their countrymen said a good word for the loyalty that cost them so dear.

It is hard to realize how little notion of toleration there was in a nation known in more recent times for breadth of view and for acceptance of differences of opinion. Yet one must not expect much toleration in the sixteenth and early seventeenth centuries; men were not far away from the wars and hatreds engendered by religious differences.

The details I have related here are not all highly significant. But they are possibly worth setting down, for they reveal, as the history of few other measures, the painstaking labors that went into the framing of every paragraph and, indeed, of every sentence in the recusancy bills. Most of the close work was done in a committee, a subcommittee, or in a small select committee. The men who served on those committees were, from their experience in quarter sessions, versed in the statutes of the last half century. Some were familiar with the ecclesiastical struggles in England and with the Elizabethan policy toward Catholics. Some were still obscure except possibly in the Inns of Court, but were known to their colleagues for intelligence, industry, and dispatch. They proved good committeemen and said sometimes precisely what needed to be said. Amid much foolish and dull talk there were also utterances marked by common sense and clear understanding.

Grievances

NEARLY three weeks after the January meeting of the session of 1605/06 the Commons took up the subject of grievances. On February 10 the question of subsidies had been raised, and a committee named to deal with it. On the following day Wingfield moved that the Great Committee for the Subsidies should consider the grievances offered by any member and that the committee was to make its resolution known to the Lords, a motion well liked by the House.

On February 12 it was voted that the Committee for Grievances should meet that afternoon, as also should the Committee for Purveyance, a provision that suggests an intention on the part of the Lower House to keep the two topics separate. Late in the same morning it was arranged that the Committee on Purveyance was to meet on Friday and that "touching all other grievances" on Saturday.[1]

The proposal of the Commons to vote His Majesty two subsidies and four fifteenths seemed to please him, but the Privy Council, and no doubt the King, continued to hope for more. It soon became evident that the Commons, in return for subsidies, sought concessions. Members could not forget old grievances, and Wingfield called on them to consider new griefs as well.[2]

Lawrence Hyde put forward a program on February 15 not unlike the Petition of Grievances that was to be framed later. He spoke of purveyors, monopolies, patents of privilege, and penal statutes. Meanwhile members were bringing in bills or complaints. Their activities seemed to discredit what the Earl of Northampton told a conference on February 19; he said that letters had been sent out to the country to understand the grievances, and there had been no replies.[3] It is conceivable that the letters had been so phrased that the recipients hesitated to voice their complaints to the Privy Council.

On February 24 it was arranged that on Saturdays committees should deal with the naturalizing of Scots and with grievances in general. On March 4 committees for grievances and for three other topics were assigned to meet on Thursday, March 6. In the House the time was devoted to purveyance. But when on March 11 the Speaker suggested a committee to consider supply and a standing revenue to His Majesty, Nicholas Fuller rose to say: "Grievances to be reported first and then a question." The House voted that at the Committee for Grievances "any other shall have a voice."

On March 15 Fuller brought in a collection of grievances from the committee. The first concerned the ministers deprived of their livings. Various members, including zealous Puritans, spoke in behalf of the ministers. But Sir Richard Spencer, M.P. for Brackley, Northamptonshire, an official in the Common Pleas, warned the House against the "self-weening opinion of some ministers" and maintained that ceremonies agreed upon by a general convocation ought not be subject to the judgment of any private individual. Sir Francis Hastings thought it proper to proceed by petition. If I interpret correctly the brief notes of the Clerk, Hastings declared that the deprived ministers were not asking for innovation in church matters nor for a presbyterian form of government. Sir Francis's reservations suggest that the Puritans were singing low and were ready indeed to be moderate in their demands. Wentworth, an M.P. from the City of Oxford, expressed concern about the poverty of the deprived ministers, some of whom had many children, a luxury not unknown among parsons. Sir Nathaniel Bacon, of an outlook unlike that of his half brother, estimated that 260 ministers had been put out of their livings (an exaggeration, as we now know) and hoped that they might be permitted to preach again.

"He hath a dull spirit," declared Hoskins, "that hath no feeling in this cause"; he urged a conference with the bishops. It was resolved, I infer, to have a conference with the Lords before the first article (about deprived ministers) was put to the question.[4]

On March 17 the second grievance (the Courts of High Commission) was brought forward by Fuller, who probably complained of their unlimited authority, as he did later.[5] He asked that there be only two such courts, those at London and at York. He was answered by the Dean of Arches,[6] Sir Daniel Donne, M.P. for Oxford University, who pronounced Fuller's articles not fit to be presented, and was backed up by another civilian, Sir John Bennet, an M.P. for Ripon. But Wentworth defended the second article. In the end all the articles were recommitted to the Committee for Grievances general. The word "general" may imply also that the committee had been subdivided for the various articles. About the recommitment the Speaker wrote jubilantly to Salisbury: "The grievances pretended were this day so carried that the propounders themselves were driven to desire a recommitment, for that upon my opening of the several parts of them they held them clean out of proportion."[7] The Speaker wished to be sure that his services were not underestimated.

The Puritans had been too eager. Members in general were not so ready to condemn ecclesiastical grievances as those touching their pocketbooks, their families, and their peace of mind. Furthermore, they were doubtless aware that the Upper House would not cooperate with them on the question of religious grievances.

His Majesty could not refrain from urging moderation and judgment. If complaints were heard, members would be filled with untruths. That they should hearken to all complaints was contrary to his expectations. He was willing, of course, where laws fell short, to add his authority by Parliament or by himself, with the advice of his Council.[8] His authority with his Council was precisely what the Commons did not desire.

By April 5 the Committee for Grievances had rearranged the articles and put those about the Church in a separate package.[9] In the following weeks conferences on that subject were held with the Lords but with negative results; the Lords were unwilling to see changes made except by the Church or by the Crown.

On April 7 Fuller brought in from the committee seven grievances agreed upon, and others exhibited to the committee but not yet agreed upon. He spoke of the impositions on currants and of other impositions and said that the imposition raised from 18d. to 5s. 6d. was so heavy that men were no longer building ships and were determined to sell four great ships at a loss.

In the afternoon, Robert Bowyer, whose diary of the House of Commons for this and the next session is indispensable, left another committee meeting to drop in on the Committee for Grievances where John Hoskins was holding forth. Hoskins was having his say about a commission engaged in making men compound for defects in the titles to the lands they held. As usual his words were likely to command attention:

He that rideth on horseback doth prevent the King's subjects of the benefit of his Majesty's grace. . . . His course is, first he sendeth for the party by a letter . . . he telleth him . . . You hold such lands. That title is defective . . . then he delivereth him such cases he thinketh good, and withal he requireth to see the party's evidence, and, upon sight thereof, and notes taken out of it . . . he then seeketh how a quirk may be found in the title, and for this purpose he hath obtained warrants for sight of the King's records in diverse offices, as namely in the Augmentation Records.[10]

Hoskins, commented the sympathetic Bowyer, "used plain words," signifying that the man mentioned by Hoskins had blotted and falsified many records there. By such methods he was said to have gained at least forty or fifty manors. When the tenants came to make complaint they found they were too late. The man promised His Majesty to win him a hundred thousand pounds, but had not so far made a thousand pounds. William Typper had operated in the 1590s under a commission to treat with those to whom Crown lands had been given and who were willing to compound for defects in their titles.[11] In 1600 he had been given a commission for concealed lands. The new King had encouraged him,[12] probably because Sir Robert Cecil had made use of him in his manifold land dealings.

We shall hear again about the man on horseback.

On April 8 a new Committee for Grievances with nineteen members was set up to meet at once. The Committee for the Subsidy, which had been also the Committee for Grievances, was to meet in the afternoon.

The new Committee for Grievances included five men who, as officials or on their own, were likely to support the royal point of view: Sir Henry Hobart, Attorney of the Court of Wards and soon to become Attorney General; Sir Francis Bacon, within sixteen months to grasp a rung on the official ladder; Sir Henry Montague, Recorder of London; Sir John Doddridge, Solicitor General; and Sir George More. Others on the committee were Hastings, Thomas Crew, a freshman in the House, Yelverton, Sandys, Sir Anthony Cope, Sir John Savile, Sir Maurice Berkeley, Sir Nathaniel Bacon, and Sir James Perrot, none of whom could be said to be attached to the royal party. It was a committee of men not given to withholding their opinions.

In the following days, grievances were arranged and rearranged, but I shall speak of them as they fit into the categories mentioned on February 15 by Lawrence Hyde. I shall leave out the purveyors, since the debate over that subject deserves to be dealt with separately. Hyde spoke of dispensing with penal statutes. I shall deal first with that type of grievance, then with the patents of privilege and monopolies, which cannot very well be separated. and lastly with other grievances.

In the final form of the Petition of Grievances presented to his Majesty, it was declared:

> The first kind of grievance doth grow by a general granting or letting out to farm unto several particular persons of divers kinds of penalties due from offenders to your Majesty, whereof your Majesty's loyal subjects conceive two great . . . inconveniences will ensue, the one an impeachment to your Highness justice, and the other to your mercy.[13]

The farmers, it was alleged, "by secret practice dispense or compound in great part with the offenders." [14] An example was the letters patent granted to Lord Danvers and Sir John Gilbert to collect (after the first £2,800 was excluded) three-fourths of the issues, amercements, fines *pro licentia concordandi,* recognizances of good behavior, and appearances for felony, manslaughter, etc. Thus men "not meet to have it" were given the power to "dispense with faults." That power was believed to involve the "oppression and ruin of many thousands of your Highness' poor, faithful subjects." [15]

A patent granted to Sir Roger Aston, Groom of the Chamber to the King, allowed him to farm the fines, amercements, forfeitures and fines *pro licentia concordandi* [16] arising in the Courts of Lancashire (Green Wax) in that part of the Palatinate north of Trent.[17] Sir Roger was to pay an annual rent of £48. Sir Nathaniel Bacon and Sir Robert Hitcham likened it to Bruncard's patent.[18] In defense, Aston explained that the concession was much older than the patent to him and that it was only in reversion, the former patentee still receiving the income from the patent. Aston asserted that he had paid a large sum for the patent and that it would yield the King as much as it did him. Thomas Fanshawe, M.P. for

Lancaster and Auditor for all duchy lands north of Trent, pointed out that the grant to Sir Roger was in force but that the grant for fines south of Trent was still held in reversion.

Apparently the House was perplexed as to what action to take, but finally resolved that the committee should frame such an article as they thought fit.

On April 15 Aston's patent was brought up again, and various members, among them Francis Moore, Richard Martin, Wiseman, Wentworth, Hoskins and Croft, took part in the debate.[19] It was said that the patent, "which is, or may be, of great yearly value," was granted for a small rental. The House voted 109 to 104 that the patent was a grievance.[20]

Sir Henry Bruncard's (Bronchard) patent, already alluded to, was for money coming to the Crown for the nonappearance of jurors at trials.[21] On April 15 Bruncard was defended by Thomas Fanshawe, who said that Sir Henry as Surveyor of Issues was able to punish such jurors as did not appear and, further, that the patent had been given in satisfaction of a great debt (presumably for his services in Ireland). It was resolved that on May 10 his counsel should be heard, but his patent was listed finally in the Petition of Grievances.[22]

I come now to the patents of privilege and the patents involving monopolies. The patent given to the Duke of Lennox was for the searching and sealing of the new draperies and other woolen goods.[23] In the Petition of Grievances the Commons held that patent to be "questionable and in many [parts] unlawful." [24] The farmers and their deputies, it was said, exacted great fees; they pretended to prevent abuses practiced by the artificers, but they really only regarded their own advantage. They sealed such things as stockings which "cannot possibly be sealed without the great impairing of the goodness of the same." The farmers, who were empowered to take 4d. for every sixty-four pounds of weight, exacted sometimes four times as much and occasionally ten times as much. "They threaten and offer violence to the carriers; they strike and beat their horses . . . as many of them have been disabled and some of them have died." The patent led to the diminution, it was alleged, of His Majesty's subsidies and to the "utter undoing of thousands and ten thousands of your most loyal subjects." [25] Sir Edward Greville of Warwickshire, who in late Elizabethan days had looked to Cecil as his patron, moved that the counsel for the Duke be heard, and a day for that purpose was assigned. [26] The Duke was a cousin of the King and was one of those Scots less likely to receive consideration from the Commons.

On April 10 the grievance was taken up again, and counsel appeared for and against the Duke. It was testified that the patent had been abused in its execution, that payment and fees had been exacted for commodities not within the scope of the patent, and that the deputies of the Duke took the goods of men on the highways, opened their packs, and retained the goods opened. In defense of the Duke, it was stated that it had been arranged between the barons of the Exchequer and the complainants, and that everyone was satisfied. It was proposed to refer the validity of the patent to the judges in Westminster. The Speaker did his best to intervene on behalf of the patent, but it was voted a grievance. [27]

Another troublesome patent was that for selling wines. In the last session of Parliament (1604) the statute of 7 Edw. VI, cap. 5 had been repealed; with that move the Commons believed that they had done away with monopolies for taverns and with the sale of wines in them. But "certain persons [the Earl of Nottingham and his son] by color of some grant or warrant" from His Majesty [28] had increased the number of taverns and enhanced the prices of wines. What was worse, the patentees had granted licenses to others to sell wines in villages and towns, where wines had not been sold before, as well as to unruly alehousekeepers, "to the great increase of drunkenness." [29] It was said that the deputies who carried out the licensing were "men of small merit" who managed to "intercept" from the worthy Earl (whose great deserts they acknowledged) the greatest part of the profit of the patent. [30] This patent would hardly have been popular with the justices of the peace, who had the licensing of alehouses in their charge, a power that they usually exercised with discretion. It was possibly not wholly an accident that the Commons, many of whom were justices of the peace, voted the patent a grievance. [31]

The grievance about saltpeter concerned those who collected the substance for the making of gunpowder.[32] It was explained carefully that His Majesty profited in no way from the activities of the saltpeter men. They were a great tribulation to the subjects of the realm. "[They] enter the houses of your subjects, use them continuously, dig up their dove-houses at unseasonable times . . . and the very lodging houses of the poorer sort, take up carriages against the owners' wills." [33] Sir Robert Johnson, who was probably M.P. for the borough of Monmouth, and who was also an official in the Ordnance, told the Commons that since the King's accession neither saltpeter nor powder had come into the store at the Ordnance Office. It was agreed, however, that it was necessary to dig in houses for the service of the state. In the end the transportation of saltpeter, as well as iron ordnance, to foreign nations was put down as a grievance.[34]

A grievance of another type was the patent for the monopoly of making "snare," or "smalt," or "blue starch" granted to Abram le Baker (Le Masser) for twenty-one years.[35] Smalt was a kind of glass, colored deep blue, which was cooled, then pulverized and used as a pigment. It was sold from door to door by peddlers,[36] and that was the trouble. The shopkeepers had been wont to retail it. William Twinehoe, M.P. for Bishops Castle in Shropshire,[37] stood up and admitted to the House that he was a patentee and asked that counsel might be heard on his behalf, which the House agreed to do a week from the following Monday, April 25.[38]

On that day Twinehoe defended the patent; Francis Moore and Nicholas Fuller affirmed that it was a grievance.[39] On May 10 it was included in the list of grievances.[40]

What was called a "patent of toleration" was granted to Sir Arthur Aston; by it he was allowed to import logwood or blockwood (an American wood), out of which was made a poor dye to give false colors to cloth. By three similar statutes the importation of logwood had been prohibited.[41] It "hath wrought deceit and discredit on English cloth vented beyond seas." Those who formulated the grievance declared that the use of logwood, instead of such dyes as woad, indigo, cochineal, argol, and sumac, lost the Crown ten thousand pounds a year in diminished customs from the export of cloth, which was, of course, merely an estimate. Since it cut down the demand for English cloth abroad, it deprived "many poor men of their labor." It had been granted by the King to Aston and others for forty-eight years. The patentees were credited with making ten thousand pounds a year from the log-wood and two thousand pounds from martinwood, to which their patent did not extend. In the final form of the Petition of Grievances it was asserted that the patentees took "violent courses in the execution of their authority . . . to the great enriching of themselves."

There were also grievances that were not based upon patents or royal grants. It was complained that when sheriffs had their accounts passed upon in the Exchequer they had to pay fees amounting to as much as £40, £80, or even £100, and that such fees made gentlemen unwilling to assume the office of sheriff.[42]

Another grievance concerned the exportation of iron ordnance. It was believed in London that England excelled other nations in the manufacturing of iron ordnance as well as cast iron and bullet of iron. They liked to believe further that their success at sea was due in part to the quality of their ordnance. It was therefore a misfortune, so men said, that ordnance was being sold in quantities to continental nations, who were using it to fortify their towns and their ships. The question was put, and the exportation of ordnance was voted a grievance.[43] No one seems to have defended the conduct of the Crown in having allowed such exportation.

Other grievances were the impositions levied at the ports, notable among them the imposition on currants. There had long been a tax of 5s. 6d. on every hundredweight of currants imported either by foreigners or by Englishmen who were not members of the Levant Company. That tax had come about in an odd way. The Levant Company, in order to meet the expense of maintaining agents in Turkey, had been allowed to lay the imposition. All that was changed. In 1600 it was suggested to Elizabeth that she might well collect that imposition for the Crown in return for which she would promise the Levant Company a monopoly of the trade with the Levant. The merchants of the company finally agreed to pay the Queen £4,000 a year in lieu of the imposition, but when the Queen died the company was £2,000 in arrears, and the merchants renounced the patent and dissolved the company.

The new King, James I, went ahead with the plan to enforce the imposition upon all merchants, not merely upon aliens and nonmembers of the company. At length the merchants asked to receive their charter again on the same basis as before, but other merchants aspired to membership in the company. The committee of the Privy Council reported in favor of continuing the company, if new members were admitted on the payment of two hundred ducats, something less than a hundred pounds. This was thought to be too much, and a long controversy ensued. Finally the company agreed to include more members at much lower admission fees, and His Majesty continued to levy the 5s. 6d. It was alleged that the imposition cost the merchants eight or ten thousand pounds a year, thus forcing up the price of currants.[44] Thirty years earlier such a tax had been laid by the Queen on Venetian goods, and the Venetians retaliated by putting an impost upon all English commodities shipped to Venice. Thus royal acquisitiveness had done a disservice to English trade and was likely, it was feared, to do so again. The framers of this imposition, Sir Roger Dallison, M.P. for Malmesbury, and Richard Wright, M.P. for Queenborough, requested that counsel for them should be heard. It was a request unlikely to be denied to members of the House.

On April 11 the grievance was brought up again. The farmers of the customs, who were to be heard on that Friday, failed to put in an appearance. Sir Francis Bacon opened the debate with a defense of the imposition. With his gift for improvising generalizations that gained the attention of members, he asserted that merchants were the guides of princes in the matter of raising impositions. When they devised the rules of trade, all was quiet; when their ideas were abandoned, they "startle and stir." [45]

Sir John Fortescue, who had been a Chancellor of the Exchequer and an Under Treasurer in the last years of Elizabeth's reign, went over the story of the Levant Company and the Queen much as related here. The charter to the company had been renewed, all was quiet, and now the King had a standing revenue, which, in the judgment of Fortescue, was as it should be. Nicholas Fuller was less certain and proposed that counsel for the merchants should be heard. That counsel, Hitchcock,[46] appeared at the bar and pointed out how necessary currants were to the life of men [47] and stated that an imposition ought no more to be put upon that commodity than upon corn (wheat). One of the Masters of Trinity House, perhaps a member of the Commons, asserted that many of the big ships that plied between London Bridge and Woolwich lay idle because the merchants could not supply them with freight; in other words, impositions were hurting trade.[48]

Before Hitchcock left the bar he suggested that some consideration be given to the case of John Bate, who was committed to prison for refusing to pay the imposition on currants.[49] Apparently he blamed Richard Wright for Bate's situation. Wright had, with Sir Roger Dallison, been given on October 27, 1604, a grant of the impost on currants for ten years at a yearly rent of £5,322.[50] He had been associated in a friendly way with the Cecils and may have owed his election for Queenborough either to Salisbury or to Sir Edward Hoby of Queenborough Castle, a first cousin of Cecil. Wright, who had never opened his mouth in the Commons, so far as I can recall, made no proper defense, if we may trust Bowyer, "nor gave any other satisfaction to the House," [51] except to say that Bate was committed by the Lords of the Council.

The merchants had scarcely withdrawn from the House when one of them made a threat "to leave all rather than this shall stand —go beyond seas." Another merchant took a wiser tack; he explained that the imposition which the Levant merchants had levied in the time of the Queen had been spent for the maintenance of ambassadors and consuls and for the provision of presents expected by Oriental rulers.[52]

Shortly after the counsel for the merchants and the merchants themselves had left the House, a merchant, either Hugh Myddleton or his brother Robert, rose and said that the grievance of impositions was that the money went not to the King's use but to "mean men like myself." [53] It was an extraordinary statement for that time, a high-minded comment, not from a country gentleman but from a member engaged in trade. Myddleton added that by the present policy of impositions younger sons of gentlemen who had often risen by merchandise were now left unprovided for.

Sir Robert Hitcham defended the impositions as legal, maintaining that the grievance was that the impositions were so high. Sir John Savile, M.P. for Yorkshire and Chief Justice for the palatinate of Lancaster,[54] answered Bacon's argument that the King could forbid the importing of most foreign commodities and, if so, could set a tax upon those that did come in.[55] It was against policy, he declared, to import more foreign goods than could be sold; if too many were imported, the home commodities sold abroad would not equal in value those bought, and England would lose gold. The King had a right to lay impositions as a means of preventing the loss of gold. But if he put on impositions that were too heavy, the merchants would not be able to sell foreign goods in England, and then foreign traders, receiving less money, would buy fewer exports from England. Savile confessed that he had been much affected by Bacon's argument until he had stopped to think the matter over. When he was a boy, remarked Sir John, he had been told that Mercury was a thief, which he could not understand because he knew that Mercury was a god. Now in his older years, he realized that eloquence, whereof Mercury was the god, was a thief.[56] This classical allusion touched Sir Francis, who seems to have replied, if we may trust the Clerk, that when he did well, no man better, when ill, none worse,[57] a comment upon himself worth remembering.[58]

Bacon was followed by Sir Walter Cope, who declared that the King was binding himself for seven years to lay no further impositions upon commodities. Where Cope, who stood close to Salisbury, or believed he did, gained his information, I do not know; nor can I find any allusion to such a promise. It was in 1610 that the King proposed to lay no further impositions and put no time limit on his proposal.

When the discussion came to a natural conclusion, the House resolved that the article about currants should be included in the Petition of Grievances.

There was also complaint about the duty on tobacco. The duty had been 2d. upon every pound of tobacco and had been raised to 6d.; now it was set at a noble a pound, that is, at 6s.8d.⁵⁹

The petition went briefly into the general question of new impositions. It was asserted that the rates of divers kinds of merchandise had been greatly raised and it was said that merchants, both subjects and strangers, were forced to pay much more than they had in the past. It was feared that the increases would be met by similar increases in the duties laid by foreign nations, which, as a result of English policy, would consider themselves released from their treaties and would proceed to impose duties upon English goods. A more immediate outcome of the new rates was that foreign commodities were made dearer for the English and that merchants were "exceedingly discouraged" and talked wistfully of changing their courses of life.⁶⁰

The grievances about Typper and Sir Edward Hoby, neither of which are found in the Petition of Grievances presented to the King, were unusual and deserve attention.

It will be recalled that on April 7 Robert Bowyer dropped into the Committee for Grievances and found John Hoskins speaking to a case that was not on the agenda, the case of the man on horseback.⁶¹ On April 16 Hoskins delivered in writing to Fuller the complaint about Typper:

> Many cathedral churches, colleges, hospitals, corporations, and foundations erected to charitable uses, infinite numbers of the King's tenants are grieved with unjust vexation and subtle practices of Typper; he pretendeth himself to be an officer authorized to deal with all such as have defective titles and estates derived out of the Crown, and by color thereof carrieth a great port.⁶²

It was charged, also, that he had access to the King's records and induced the Clerks of the Court of Augmentations and of the Exchequer to prevent subjects from using the records to strengthen their titles. It was believed that Typper took bribes and multiplied suits to wear men out.

It was ordered that Typper should appear before a committee with his counsel upon Monday week. On Saturday, May 3, Typper appeared before the House. He appealed to history. From Edward III to Henry IV commissions were set up almost yearly to inquire into defective titles. Such commissions were also granted by Queen Elizabeth. When questioned about the many suits he was said to have started, Typper replied that he had begun only three suits.[63] When Typper had left, it was declared that his commission proceeded from a gracious King (James) and that the commissioners had performed most honorably until Typper began to grieve the people. His case was referred to the Committee for Grievances.

On May 10 Hoskins, as if dissatisfied with the failure of the committee to proceed with Typper's case, raised the issue again. He moved that a committee be appointed to examine the case. Then four less known members of the House—Sir George St. Poll, Sir William Wray, Mr. Tate, and Mr. Bacchus—were named "gentlemen to be present and give evidence." [64]

Typper was not mentioned in the Petition of Grievances. Hoskins's charges against him did not move the committee to action, and it is easy to guess why. The Principal Secretary had been making use of Typper and would continue to do so in 1607. Cecil's influence, even with the opposition, would have been enough.

The case of Sir Edward Hoby is less mystifying. He had a patent to buy wool in sixteen nonclothing counties and to sell it to clothiers. The patent had been given him by the late Queen in 1594 and was confirmed by James I in 1604.[65] Sir Edward had been, in the last decades of Elizabeth's reign, one of the vocal figures in the Commons, and in the first years of James he was still listened to attentively. When his patent was brought up Hoby offered to withdraw from the House for the time being, in accordance with usage, but the Commons willed him to stay, "having lately given that favor to Sir Roger Aston." He remained for a time and then "contrary to expectation" withdrew.

Those who attacked the grant as a grievance maintained that the underlings of Sir Edward bought up all the wool and so enforced the clothiers to buy from them at higher rates. The House resolved that counsel for Sir Edward should be heard.

On May 1 Hoby took his counsel to the bar to show cause why his patent for the "jobbing of wool" was no grievance. It was alleged that his deputies bought more wool in the nonclothing counties than they were allotted and that they mixed the wool with water and sand to increase the weight, a common charge. It was further alleged that Hoby's brokers beat down the price paid to the sellers and enhanced that to the clothiers. The counsel for Hoby pointed out that the patent was not a new one, but had been given to Simon Bowyer before it was granted to Hoby. Even abuses gained respectability with age. When awarded to Hoby, the patent had passed the scrutiny of the council. When James came in, he referred the patent to the Lord Chancellor and the Lord Treasurer, who heard counsel and reported that the patent was fit and necessary. The House resolved that the patent was not a grievance: Hoby had excellent connections and was generally liked, and legislative bodies have often shown themselves reluctant to discipline their own members. My suspicion that Hoby received a most-favored-member treatment may be unwarranted, but I doubt it.

On May 10 the whole statement of grievances was delivered to the House by Fuller. On the day before it had been debated whether the Subsidy Bill should be read before the grievances. Sir Anthony Cope and others had opposed this. It was agreed at length that the Subsidy Bill should be read for the third time but that it should not be sent up to the Lords until the grievances were ready and had been presented to the King.[66]

The grievances, brought in on May 10, were:

1. The letting out of penalties to subjects
2. The letters patent to Danvers and Gilbert. Letters patent of the Green Wax to Sir Roger Aston and Master Grimsditch. Sir Henry Bruncard's patent of Issues, etc. The Lord Admiral's patent of dispensation for selling wines
3. The patent for logwood and blockwood
4. The raising of the rates of customs on merchandise
5. The impositions on currants

6. The new impositions on tobacco
7. The patent of the new drapery
8. The new patent for passing sheriffs' accounts
9. The fees for muster masters
10. The preemption of tin
11. The patent of smalt, (blue starch)
12. The Green Cloth warrants for the maintenance of purveyors and for lessening the price of men's goods by second appraisals,[67] in general the usurped authority of the Board of Green Cloth
13. The transportation abroad of iron ordnance
14. The abuse of digging and transporting saltpeter and gunpowder

It should be noticed that the abuse of purveyance had been slipped in by an inconspicuous side door. The Commons had already been impeded in the matter of purveyance and found themselves dependent upon the King's word. They now set down among grievances several of the abuses practiced by the purveyors. When they listed as a grievance the usurped authority of Green Cloth as a court, they were doing well.

Before the final vote on grievances was taken, the Recorder, Montague, raised again the question of the increased customs duties or impositions and offered reasons why the new impositions should not be regarded as grievances. The officers of the Customs House were brought in to answer questions about the Book of Rates and advanced reasons of their own why the increase was desirable.

At length it was ordered that the grievances should be engrossed, and on May 13 it was determined that Sir Francis Bacon should read them to the King. Fuller moved that the matter of the deprived ministers be orally presented to the King.[68] This I do not fully understand. The grievance concerning deprived ministers had been taken out of the regular list of grievances and put among the ecclesiastical grievances, which had been unacceptable to the Lords. I am not aware that Fuller's motion was actually voted;

nor am I certain about what happened to the motion following, namely that the Speaker, when the grievances were presented, should speak to the King about the execution of the laws against Jesuits and seminarists. The Speaker could be relied upon to do nothing displeasing to his sovereign.

The next day a committee was named to attend the King. This committee was made up of forty-four or so members, both important and obscure. It was near the end of the day and few men were left in the House.

The grievances, in their final form, were phrased with care and tact. It was admitted that even in the most carefully governed states abuses grew up. Some of those abuses indeed had sprung up before His Majesty's time. "By long and laudable custom our ancestors . . . especially in the free and solemn assemblies of Parliament have dutifully presented . . . such informations, complaints, and petitions." They would not be undutiful to His Majesty, who sat "in his seat that delighted in the frequent petitions of his servants." [69] Nor would they be unfaithful to the counties that had sent them there not ignorant of their necessities. Moreover they had received "no small encouragement by former speech and late joyful message from your Majesty." They had restrained themselves to such grievances as were general and weighty in their substance. The dispensing with good and profitable laws caused great public damage and discouraged those in trades and courses of life which had flourished to the great honor and profit of the kingdom. They asked His Majesty not to heed imputations laid upon them that they assumed greater liberties than their ancestors had enjoyed or than rightfully belonged to them. They had no desire to infringe His Majesty's prerogatives nor to enlarge their own rights and liberties; they hoped to live peaceably under those laws and customs of the realm restored to sound strength and vigor.[70] The word "restored" is interesting.

On May 15 Bacon reported on his meeting with the King. His own speech, said Bacon, was but a preamble to a preamble. Though there were grievances, he declared, they were not meant as aspersions or imputations to be laid to His Majesty's government, but were rather the diseases of the time and things that had grown up and been cut down partly by His Majesty and yet sprung up again.[71]

Diseases of the time they certainly were, and yet they were by no means new; nor were they to be quickly cured. Were the diseases as serious as the Petition of Grievances would indicate? I am not prepared to answer that question. About financial corruption, there can be no doubt that it was a generation when men from ministers of state down to country jurors took what we would call bribes. Was violence as rampant? Were the deputies of patentees as rough and violent as they were accused of having been? We know that there was still a good deal of violence in England, especially in the north and along the western border, but I doubt that it was as common as one would infer from the Petition of Grievances.

To Bacon's address His Majesty answered that he could not judge immediately, but such matters as should be presented by a House of Parliament he would not refuse to hear. On four matters the King challenged the Commons. In the first place, they had matters of gratulation as well as grievances. The kingdom now had a King replenished with children instead of a monarch of the weaker sex, a religion established instead of a religion begun, a state conjoined as Scotland instead of a state rent from her bowels as Ireland. James was not reticent about the advantages he had to offer.

He challenged the Commons, secondly, whether these were not grievances of former times, with which they had failed to find fault in the day of the Queen. In that charge there was not a little truth. James asked also whether the grievances came from complaints in the country or had been suggested in London. It may be recalled that Henry Howard, Earl of Northampton, had in the conference between the Lords and Commons thrown out the same idea. Here again James may not have been wholly in error. The opposition probably did not frown on country members who brought forward their grievances.

When the King came to the topic of purveyance, his third

point, he said that he had made an offer concerning it—presumably the offer of a "composition"—and the House had digressed from that grievance to all grievances. As for the officers of Green Cloth, the Commons had not flattered them, and, if he found them at fault, he would flatter them even less. Such promises were soon forgotten.

The book of grievances they had presented was too long, and he was no angel—an allusion to the Book of Revelation, I think. But these grievances should be read again and again both to himself and with his Council. He would put them in their proper forge. For legal matters he would advise with his judges; in matters of state with his council; in matters of traffic with men skillful in that way. Where the grievance was small, and the alteration necessary great and weighty, he hoped the Commons would not urge it, as on the other side he would not give priority to his own profit before a common grievance. Then he indulged in his customary allusion to his own justice; [72] he thought of himself as a kind of divinity who held the keys to the temple of justice. He admonished the House that they should maintain an even mind.

The King's answers, read to the Commons on November 19, 1606, can be stated briefly; in general, they were negative. As to the transportation of ordnance, there had of late been no grants, and His Majesty would be sparing of future grants "except . . . when he shall find it fit in his great judgment."

The problem of the duty on currants had been submitted to the barons of the Exchequer who had rendered a decision in favor of the King.

Concerning the increased duties, the King announced that he had called the merchants together and on their advice had changed the duties according to the prices of the times, abating some customs and enhancing others, "yet with great moderation far under the due in those commodities that are much risen." [73]

Answering the complaint about the license to the Lord Admiral to sell wines at a retail price above that allowed in the law, the judges resolved that the grant was good in law and informers had "abused the Lower House with many untruths."

In the matter of logwood both sides had been heard in the King's council, which had received the opinion of the judges. The judges said that His Majesty's grant was justifiable by law. The King had, however, resumed that grant, and those who lost by that action were to be recompensed.

The patent granted to the Duke of Lennox for search and sealing of new draperies was to be judged by the law.

The judges resolved that the patent granted to Sir Roger Aston of fines, amercements, and forfeitures under the name of the Green Wax, "growing from the tenants of the Duchy of Lancaster," concerned things "grantable" by the King and had been enjoyed by a patent of the late Queen. Since the grant, however, depended upon "some recitals which the Judges have not examined," His Majesty had ordered the patentee to surrender it; he would then grant Aston a new one upon certain specified conditions.

Concerning the complaint about purveyance that was finally inserted among the grievances, His Majesty promised to continue the course he had used "in punishing all that shall abuse the meanest of his subjects." [74]

The New Session Begins

I HAVE been dealing in the last two sections with two preliminary subjects: recusants and grievances. Both of those subjects required a good deal of explanation in order to make clear what follows. Now I am in a position to treat the subject of subsidies in relation to purveyance and other grievances, about which members had much to say.

In August 1605 the Venetian ambassador wrote to his government that deaths had caused vacancies in the House of Commons:

The King desires to order fresh elections in the case of certain turbulent spirits, who are little to his taste. He is well aware how much his neglect of the elections cost him last year. It is thought that he may quite easily affect the bye-elections but that it is difficult, not to say impossible, for him to unseat members already elected.[1]

This statement was probably at second or third hand from the King and may not have been strictly accurate, but it possibly gives some indication of the dissatisfaction of the King's friends with the membership of the Lower House. Three weeks later the ambassador alluded to the King's desire to "weed out certain turbulent and seditious spirits who right willingly thwart all his Majesty's schemes." [2] The King needed as much support as possible: he hoped to obtain enough money to pay off his debts contracted by privy seals; he hoped also to effect the union of the two nations.

The project of the union had to be dropped. On October 12 the ambassador wrote: "His Majesty is now well aware that nothing can be effected, both sides displaying such obstinacy that an accommodation is impossible. . . . The only subject before Parliament will be that of subsidies." [3] So the King hoped. But grievances, and in particular purveyance, became the main topics of discussion, with subsidies popping up now and again, and at length receiving the most attention. On October 10 Henry Howard, now Earl of Northampton and Privy Councillor, had written Sir Thomas Edmondes, ambassador to the Archduke at Brussels, about the coming session of Parliament: "We [the Councillors] sit hard about the preparation of matters for the Parliament" so that the M.P.'s would swallow the pill without nausea and find it to be for their own good. The Earl was given to patronizing the Commons. He continued: "We are about to take away the scandals raised upon purveyors and such proling [prowling?] officers." [4]

Parliament was to meet on November 5, but the Gunpowder Plot changed that. The Commons met, heard some bills read, named a few committees, and were prorogued until January 21.

On that day the House came together, and on January 24 the main issue of the session, that of purveyance, with which the granting of a subsidy was inextricably involved, was brought before the House by John Hare. Hare was in his eighth Parliament and was nearly sixty years of age. In this introductory speech he attacked purveyors sharply.[5] In the last session, purveyors, he commented, had been supported by "such as should specially have suppressed them." [6] He asserted that the Lords had promised to consider the grievances, but they had said nothing about purveyance. He then asked the Speaker to move the House whether they desired a conference with the Lords or whether they wished that the bill now ready should be preferred.[7] The Commons resolved that the bill should be brought in next morning.

On January 30 the abuse of purveyance was taken up on the second reading of the bill. Sir Robert Johnson, who was for the third time representing the borough of Monmouth, started the ball rolling by proposing a "composition" to the King, a given annual sum, if he would surrender the right to purveyance. In 1604 there had been talk of a composition. In that session Nicholas Fuller, it will be recalled, had served on a committee of four to draw a bill about purveyance, and he supported the bill now before the House. The best government, he maintained, was one in which king and subject were ruled by law, thus echoing Bracton. He implied that in respect to purveyance, His Majesty should be limited by the law. As for a composition, he was afraid that within a few years it might become just another tax.[8]

Lawrence Hyde, who had also served on the committee of four in 1604, took exception to certain features of the bill before the House and demanded that there be no carriage ("cartage") without consent of the owners of the carts, a limitation that would have handicapped purveyors, some of whom helped themselves to more carts than were needed. Mr. Brooke [9] hoped that it would be specified in the bill that if anyone were imprisoned by the Board of Green Cloth (the organization of the household that dealt with purveyance) the judges would have the power of habeas corpus to deliver the party and to make certain that he should be tried by the common law courts. The worst feature of purveyance, as Brooke realized, was that the Green Cloth arrogated to itself, with no statute to authorize it, the power of punishing those who would not obey its orders.

The House kept returning to the matter of a composition. Sir Walter Cope spoke for a "contribution," thus using a term more general than "composition." It is possible that he was thinking of an additional subsidy. As for the laws, there were, he said, too many "in the same tune." [10] After the bill had been committed to some fifty members, many of whom had been in Elizabethan Parliaments, Richard Martin spoke for the plan of a contribution or a composition.

The first bill against purveyors, that read on January 29, 1605/06, had been for the "Better Execution of Sundry Statutes against Purveyors and Cart-takers." [11] On February 1 another bill was read; it restrained purveyors from exceeding the limits of their commissions.[12] The introduction of this second bill may have been encouraged by the Speaker after the commitment of the first bill, which might have indicated that Cecil and the Lords would not oppose such a bill. He had proposed that the form of a commission be set down in the text of the statute so that purveyors might have at hand an exact schedule of their rights in taking goods, carts, and so forth. The new measure was introduced by Sir Robert Johnson, who feared that the first bill "so well labored by Mr. Hare and so profitable for the Commonwealth" might not pass. Sir Robert wanted the bill that was moved in the last Parliament (indeed, toward the end of that Parliament) to be brought in "that, if we cannot pass the one bill we may pass the other, which was done." [13]

On May 23, 1604, when that session's struggle over purveyance was ending ingloriously for the reformers, Sir Robert had seen his bill "deferred." [14] Now in 1606 a bill, which bore the same title as that of 1604, was read at once. It was based upon some special knowledge of the purveyance situation. During the session of 1604, Johnson had been asked by Cecil, then Baron Cecil of Essenden, for his private opinion about purveyors, and on February 17, 1605/06, Johnson had sent him a long letter exhibiting the defects in the carrying out of purveyance by the officials of the King and pointing out how laws on the topic might be made more explicit.[15]

Purveyance was obviously much on the minds of the Commons, but they could not come to any agreement as to what should be done about it. That His Majesty would have to be compensated for the loss of purveyance, if it were actually abolished, was beginning to be admitted, but the difficulties about composition or contribution were many and seemed well-nigh insoluble.

His Majesty needed more subsidies, but the talk was all of purveyance. It was not until February 10 that the matter of a subsidy
or subsidies was broached. Then it was brought up by the Sir
Thomas Ridgeway whose name is associated with the Apology,
who had, I suspect, more good connections than talent.[16]

Ridgeway's motion was seconded by Sir Maurice Berkeley of the
Somerset Berkeleys, a frequent speaker and one listened to by the
House. Berkeley regarded the granting of a subsidy as an obligation of duty and discretion. Sir Edward Montague, who had raised
the matter of grievances in 1604, then made a speech. When giving
advice to the King in 1615 Sir Francis Bacon mentioned this very
occasion:

> Those subsidies were never demanded nor moved from the
> King, much less made the business or errand of the Parliament;
> but after the Parliament had sitten a good while, an honest
> gentleman (by name Sir Edward Montague) stood up, and . .
> moved for two subsidies and four fifteenths, concluding with
> these plain words, that so much, he thought, would content, and
> less would not be well accepted.[17]

Bowyer tells the story a bit differently. According to him, Montague said that one subsidy and two fifteenths were too little and
three subsidies and six fifteenths too great for the country to bear.
Therefore he plumped for two subsidies and four fifteenths "to be
yielded voluntarily." [18] Montague was followed by John Bond, the
schoolmaster-physician from Taunton, a passionate man whose
opinions were not always predictable, who had been more or less
assertive in the Parliament of 1601. Wilbraham quotes him as
saying: "Treasure is said to be the sinews of the commonweal; and
the contraction of the sinews in the brain breeds a cramp and con-
vulsion in all the inferior parts." [19] Bond alluded to the benignity,
piety, and bounty of the King, "amplified by many proverbs." He
was given to proverbs. He spoke of the King's mild use of unlimited prerogative and of the mild taxes. Then in a peroration he
waxed grandiloquent, not about England, but about Britain: "of
a weak, feeble, and breathless estate, become the most opulent,
rich, and mighty empire of Christendom." [20]

Sir William Strode, M.P. for Plympton in Devon, who in 1604 had seemed less than eager to please the Crown, urged a vote. Sir Nathaniel Bacon believed the question of fifteenths ought to be considered and called attention to the fact seldom, if ever, mentioned by others that subsidies were not of such value as formerly. Hastings, the quarterback of the Puritan team, wished to give money and to do so quickly. It began to look as if some of those who had hardly been enthusiastic supporters of His Majesty were now inclined to vote him a substantial sum.

John Hoskins, the professional wag of the House, but much more than that, was not in haste to give: he favored no subsidy without a bill and therefore a committee first to prepare it. Wingfield touched on the inequality between subsidies and fifteenths, thinking doubtless of the burden of fifteenths on the poor in towns.[21] Sir John Holles, who was not in favor at Whitehall, followed Hoskins in urging a committee, and so did Fuller. Sandys called a subsidy in time of peace a sign of love, virtue, and thankfulness, and seemed to think the poverty of the country less than it had been. Martin did not believe in buying laws.[22]

The Speaker insisted that a subsidy could not be voted without a bill and put the question for two subsidies and four fifteenths, which was resolved upon, and a committee was named to prepare the bill.

The Commons had been inclined to move slowly and were at this very moment concerned with grievances, yet suddenly they pushed for two subsidies and the fifteenths that would go with them. Had they been talking over the situation with one another and come to realize that the King needed money badly? To refuse him might push him into the arms of those who were no doubt urging him to assume the role of an absolute monarch. Or did they hope, as some certainly did, by showing generosity, to win in return a satisfactory answer about grievances? If they dreamed of reciprocity from James I, they had misread their sovereign. Perhaps at times he really planned to meet the Commons halfway and then was advised otherwise. The tentative proposal to give him two subsidies and four fifteenths seemed to please His Majesty, as noted earlier. He sent for the Speaker and uttered those gracious words that fell easily from his lips: he took more joy, he informed them, in the manner of their giving than if the value were ten times the amount. The grant would bring dismay to "the opposites," [23] that is, those "evilly affected towards him and the State." [24] It had been made more freely than ever before. He declared that he would expose himself to danger "for your good," the last thing he would have done for any man. "His Highness doth yield unto their desire for removing the oppressions by purveyors, which kind of people his Majesty doth so much detest that he wishes both the corruption and name of them to be utterly taken away and abolished." [25] Things looked promising: the Commons were getting ready to make a substantial grant; the King talked as if he meant to curb the purveyors. Was it conceivable that the King and Parliament might work together?

Purveyance and the Lords

THE King's words about purveyance inspired hope. John Hare was soon on his feet and "in a soberly fashion opened the joy which himself in particular from his heart . . . had conceived." He asked the pleasure of the House whether the Bill of Purveyors, which he held in his hand, as perfected by the committee, should be proceeded in, or sleep, or whether the matter should be referred wholly to a conference with the Lords, as His Majesty had suggested. Hare was too optimistic. Was the King, in proposing a conference with the Upper House, counting on that body to stop or emasculate the measure?

The House resolved that the bill should be pushed and that the members of the committee should attend the committee of the Lords. Wingfield urged that all grievances be collected and delivered to the committeemen about the subsidy, "and the committees to acquaint the Lords therewithal." "This motion," wrote Bowyer, "was well liked of by the House," but it was thought fit that the business of the purveyors should not be "intricated with any other matter." [1]

On February 13 Hare brought in the Bill of Purveyors with amendments; the committee had altered a few words in the bill.[2] Remembering His Majesty's message that the Lords might "direct some other course better," they favored a conference with the Upper House, where they might inform the committee from that body of their desires and learn what the Lords proposed. But they did not wish to deal further in the matter—that is, I infer, they were not to argue with the Lords. They would listen to their opinion, but they were wary of accepting it, seemingly wary even of being involved with them.

On the afternoon of February 14 the Commons Committee on Purveyance sat with the committee from the Lords. Hare addressed the joint committee, saying that he could deliver nothing but sorrow and grief. The oppressions by the purveyors were not new to the Lords to whom they had been exhibited during the last session. It had been said that the complaints were untrue and that His Majesty's officers were slandered. He went over the abuses so clearly pictured in the articles drawn up in 1604: the taking of carts, food, wood, etc. The purveyors, it had been declared, collected twice as much as was needed, and they failed to furnish blanks in which the quantities taken, the times, the places, the prices, and other information could be written down, as the law provided. If any withstood the commands of the purveyors they were imprisoned straightaway. Kings had made many good laws against the purveyors in the reigns of Henry I, Henry III, Edward III, and Henry IV, for example. What the Commons now desired, insisted Hare, was the execution of such laws as were in force.

Hare asked that the articles drawn up the last session be read over again lest some of the Lords might not have heard them. "Here the Lords advised privately and softly, as they sat at the table, and then willed him to read them."[3] Hare concluded by saying that the committee had prepared a bill for the reformation of the abuses of purveyance, but, before they pressed forward with it, they wanted to secure the support of the Lords.[4]

Hare's speech was not well received by the Earl of Salisbury. He replied that the Lords had not expected to begin with sorrow and grief. The last speaker had opened wounds and betrayed mistrust. Had not the King graciously willed the Commons to show their grievances, even though he knew how dangerous it was to ask his subjects to complain? He had not expected any of his subjects to take it upon themselves to be tribunes of the people.[5] Salisbury would show the substance of their complaints to His Majesty, but he noted that the manner of the complaints was mixed with vinegar.

Hare replied, asking that what he had said might not be attributed to him alone.

The Lord Chancellor, Thomas Egerton, Lord Ellesmere, regretted the turn events had taken and hoped that the House would remember His Majesty's occasions (needs). The Lord Treasurer, Thomas Sackville, Earl of Dorset, followed, saying that, unlike Hare, he would begin with joy and comfort. He admitted the truth of the articles about purveyance.[6] Then, reading from notes (for which he apologized), he presented in formal fashion the King's expenses and his debts and indicated what was needed in the way of subsidies. Whatever money was granted, he promised, would be used first to repay the loans made to the King, that is, the money exacted from the subjects by privy seals. It was hoped, no doubt, in that way to enlist the support of those members who had been pressed into lending the King money.[7]

The Lord Treasurer said nothing further about purveyance. He may have become aware that the wind was now blowing from the north. The King's recognition of the abuses of purveyance and of the need for reform proved short-lived.

The next morning Hare reported the conference to the House, repeating what Salisbury had said of his speech. Apparently he did not tell the Commons that Salisbury had called him a "tribune of the people."

Neither the report of the conference in the *Commons Journals* nor that in Bowyer leaves the reader with the impression that Hare's utterances were extreme or ill-mannered. Salisbury may have known what he was doing when he spoke of them as he did. He was an old hand who, although removed to a higher form, could guess what the lower form was thinking. He was even more familiar with the mind of the royal personage, and, in order to retain office, he had, in some degree, to assume the moods of his master. He could easily guess that, after the King had sent a conciliatory message in which he deplored purveyors and promised action against them, he would have resented the tone of Hare's speech. To soothe his sovereign it was politic for Salisbury to make Hare seem unduly zealous and even ungracious. If Hare were well spanked in public His Majesty might not press his Councillors to make an issue of the speech.

Lawrence Hyde followed Hare. It is unfortunate that the Clerk's notes contain such a cryptic version of the speech. What I think Hyde said was that the subsidy was not really voted until it was passed in the form of a bill. He suggested that the King receive a profit from the lands of the traitors which accrued to the Crown, capital gains which, as we know, James too readily bestowed upon importunate suitors. Another source of revenue, declared Hyde, would be the penalties imposed upon recusants, and still another, the income derived from the dispensation with penal statutes. He called for a reformation of monopolies and patents of privilege, emphasizing the theme that His Majesty had revenues available with which he was too open-handed. He continued: "No more subsidies. The same hearts that give now will give at another time." Let us wait, he was implying, to vote money until we see reforms accomplished.

Wingfield urged that new griefs as well as old should be considered. Sir Herbert Croft, who had represented Herefordshire in several Parliaments, requested an end to the problem of purveyance.[8]

Hyde, Wingfield, and Croft had all spoken more or less to the same effect. Were they perhaps following the advice given to the opposition to hold the floor with one speaker after another? What they had to fear, however, as Croft possibly meant to imply, was that even the zealous might grow weary of the iteration of grievances.

The Speaker must have surprised members by suggesting an

addition to the list of grievances. Was he taking on this unaccustomed role in order to lead the Commons away from the agitation over purveyance? [9]

That was on Saturday, February 15. On Tuesday Secretary Herbert was sent to inform the Lords that the articles about purveyors would be delivered to them the next day and that the Commons would then be ready to attend them. The Lords asked to have the articles in the morning and the conference in the afternoon. It was determined that the Commons should prepare themselves to answer what might be said in defense of the purveyors and to interpret certain precedents that might be offered.[10]

On Thursday Sir Henry Montague reported the conference held the previous afternoon. Salisbury's speech was relayed to the Commons, many of whom had heard it at the conference. The Earl had gone back again to Hare's message of sorrow. The two Houses, he declared, ought to work together as two hands. He quoted a Latin tag that the grief that was modest and just had a tongue but no teeth. He was grieved on this occasion. Hare had "zealed" the grief of the Commons. His purpose seemed to be the abolition not only of the abuse of purveyance but also of its use. Lord Knollys, of the royal household, declared, doubtless with the laws against purveyance in mind, that laws were made to frighten rather than to be put in execution. He alluded to the two subsidies voted and expressed the thankfulness of the King. His Majesty would lend an ear, he assured his hearers, to the grievances of the people. Knollys went on to picture the present as a golden era.

Salisbury spoke again, dubbing purveyors vexers of the commonwealth; the Lords would join with the Commons in chasing them as hobgoblins. Then the old hand philosophized about his craft: power, strength, and greatness were never free from envy, malice, and conspiracy. He returned to the main theme: the Government had made peace with Spain, not bought it; they had shown the needs of the Crown; the means of satisfying those needs they left to the Commons.

Northampton had reminded the joint committee a few days earlier that if the King had chosen to exercise his prerogative he could be as rich as Croesus,[11] words that gave away Northampton's profound conviction that the state demanded a strong man at the top, able to exercise power and put down opposition.[12] It is not surprising that Salisbury, sensing the serious implications of Northampton's words, assumed "the vein of a pleasant man." He would repeat Stevenson's jest (Stevenson was his servant) that he, Salisbury, was still with child by the purveyors, that is, he had them on his mind. Distribute the money as you like, said the Principal Secretary, only help the King's want. Salisbury was finding it hard to keep in step with his master and yet remain on good terms with the Commons.

After the conference had been reported, Strode expressed the hope that His Majesty should become aware of the grievances of the country.[13] Martin raised another issue: that no committee should be named until Hare's reputation had been righted. Secretary Herbert tried to divert the discussion by suggesting a committee for consideration of the King's wants, another way of hinting that two subsidies were not enough. Sir Edwin Sandys went right back to the question raised by Martin:

> Parliament is no parliament if not free . . . that Mr. Hare might be cleared by this House first, and then a message to the Lords, upon a conference, importing so much. And that their Lordships would not in future time censure any, without the judgment of this House.[14]

Holles called for the question, and the Speaker, however reluctant he may have been, put the question whether Mr. Hare did err in the committee with the Lords. It was resolved that he did not, and the Clerk recorded that they would not send a message to the Lords, but let it be known through members of the committee that Hare had been "justified." This may have been the sense of the House rather than a resolution.[15]

On February 24 and 25 the House returned to the question of purveyance.[16] It was moved that the bill framed should pass and that then there should be a conference with the Lords. It was suggested that the bill should contain a clause "to bind the prerogative," [17] which meant, I assume, to limit the prerogative in respect

of purveyance, and thus forestall any attempt by the judges to declare the proposed law an invasion of the prerogative. By another
it was urged that the jurisdiction of Green Cloth should be taken
away by a law.[18] Neither proposal would have been acceptable to
the Upper House.

The Speaker intervened to say that an answer had to be made to
the Lords about composition. "I drew them," he wrote to Salisbury, "to a committee to advise what was fit in their next conference to your Lordships to be propounded, and till then the bill
to stay." [19] The Speaker prided himself on his crafty manipulation,
but the most crafty conceal their craft.

The next morning Hare reported from the committee. They
were, however, too late, for the King "found the prerogative and
will hardly be drawn to consent to have it taken away." [20] Doubt
had arisen, Hare explained, about composition, as well as about
security, proportion, and distribution. The question of security—
how the Commons could hold the Crown to the bargain—had
been raised before. As for proportion and distribution, I assume
that Hare meant that it would be hard to adjust composition
fairly, since purveyance was likely to be most troublesome to those
counties north of London where the King was accustomed to
hunt.

Hare offered a new suggestion concerning security. Statute law
could be dispensed with, he said, meaning, no doubt, by a *non
obstante,* but common law could not be altered. Would it be
feasible to obtain from the King a charter that would free the
realm of purveyors? Let such a charter be confirmed by Parliament. He was foreshadowing constitutional moves made in the
1620s.

Martin believed that under such a charter purveyors could be
found guilty of felony, but he feared that any bill of the kind proposed would be rejected by the Lords. In that case, however, the
Commons would have the consolation that they had done their
duty, a thin consolation, but a real one to Englishmen, even in the
early seventeenth century.

Hobart said that laws concerning purveyance had never been
executed, implying that what was needed was not more laws but

better enforcement of existing ones. Purveyance, he continued, was an old right of the Crown, recognized in law. Moreover the King was in possession of the right. "We must buy it," asserted Hobart, with a realism not too common among members. It was not possible to deal with the purveyors in the courts "because the contrary power is so great." The contrary power? Was he saying that the Board of Green Cloth would be too strong for the justices of the peace in the shires? Or was he implying more, that the courts at Westminster would be afraid to give a decision against the wishes of the King?

About composition Hoskins made the point that never in the time of their ancestors had an imposition of inheritance been demanded, that is, a special tax to continue from one reign to another.[21] How could such a perpetual composition be established? A pertinent question.

Hyde returned to Hobart's statement that the Commons would have to buy the right of purveyance from the King. He knew of no judicial interpretation stating that the prerogative could not be bought. He plumped for the bill, "and then to think of composition." The question was called for.

The Speaker framed three questions,[22] but the House would have none of them. It was "enflamed," he wrote to Salisbury, to have the Bill of Purveyors proceeded in, and to have the question about that, and about composition, put. He wrote:

> To satisfy their importunity, which I could not avoid, I made the question whether they would proceed with the bill, but took occasion to forbear the second question concerning the composition, for that I found, as the state of the House then stood, it would be rejected.[23]

The House voted that the bill was to be proceeded in and deferred the reading of the amendments till the next morning.

It would seem not improbable that the Privy Council and His Majesty were still hoping for a vote in favor of a composition and that the Speaker avoided the question with the hope that opinion might shift.

Why were the Commons disposed to vote down composition?

Probably for several reasons that they alleged later, but that were, perhaps, in many minds. They could offer persuasive arguments against composition. It was said that it might become a custom for the King to expect to be bought off and that the King might, in the future, make demands for increased rates of composition. How hard it was to deal with one who, as many had come to believe, could not be trusted, and whose weakness in that respect could not be openly asserted. That no one had as yet proposed a feasible method of collecting the composition was another cogent reason why the Commons were unwilling to vote for it. Yet it may be that the Commons opposed the composition for a more impelling reason: they were loath to put up the money. If purveyance were the fearful abuse they said it was, it would have been wise to tax themselves the extra £50,000, or less, to be rid of it once and for all. But country gentlemen, like other men on the land, were thrifty. They were reluctant to reach into their own pockets in order to help an extravagant regime.

What had caused His Majesty to shift his position? Had he not talked hopefully of what he would do to the purveyors? Now he had developed misgivings. As we know, James was easily swayed by the last man with whom he talked. Henry Howard, Earl of Northampton, was ever edging up to the royal chair. It would have been like him to discourse of the high prerogative, and such discourse was not unpleasant to royal ears. Some of the Scots, hovering around the throne, were doubtless equally convinced of the need for the assertion of regal authority. Even a man whose mind was a storehouse of administrative and legislative ideas, that supreme "egghead" of his generation, Francis Bacon, if he had been called upon for his judgment, would probably have given His Majesty the advice he wished to hear. As Salisbury, he aimed to be, one recalls, the shadow of the King's will, and, however much he may have understood the House of Commons point of view, he had to walk warily. The first subject of the realm had enemies behind every curtain, awaiting any misstep he might make.

The Commons were less cheerful than on February 11. Hare's exultant mood then had proved a dream. What had seemed a sunny morning had been obscured by clouds.

The Battle against
Purveyance Lost

THE Speaker in his letter to Salisbury on February 25 had indicated anxiety as to what might happen the next day. On the morning of February 26 he sent word by the Clerk that he had taken pills overnight which had not worked as expected.[1] When at length he appeared and took his chair, Sir Francis Hastings brought in a bill to restore deprived ministers, a measure certain to rouse opposition. The House was waiting, however, to take up purveyance again, and Hare set forth the changes in the Purveyance Bill and offered reasons for the omissions and additions. Sir Henry Montague objected to the inclusive preamble, "confirming all former statutes in their execution."

At this point the Lords sent a message that they were expecting a second conference "to consider what course may be taken not only to reform abuses but to abolish the very name of purveyors."[2] Apparently the Lords were now ready to make use of purveyance as a trading piece; their reason can be conjectured. The King's "occasions," they said, were greater than ever before. Had the word come through that the King and Council were prepared to bargain for a composition? At the conference the judges were to be in attendance to "advise of a course for our security to enjoy what shall be thought fit," that is, presumably, to keep watch lest any limitation of purveyance should endanger the prerogative, possibly, also, to offer suggestions concerning the method of raising the composition. The Commons at once agreed, seemingly with little delay, that the conference requested by the Upper House should be granted. Sandys rose to say that if the rights of the King were not preserved he would refuse his consent, a gesture by which he was endeavoring, I suppose, to assure the King and his friends that they had no need to fear the intentions of the Commons.[3]

The conference was to take place on the afternoon of the next day. It was specified that the committee was not to make any offer about composition; indeed it was, if I interpret correctly the Clerk's notes, "to oppose against it," a policy that could serve only to harden the hearts of King and Council.

On March 1 Bacon reported the conference. It appears that the King, before he made any promise to give up purveyance, wished to know precisely how much he would gain by way of a composition. In the conference it was suggested that the Commons name lawyers who would be prepared to dispute the right of the King to purveyance, while the Lords were to maintain the prerogative, possibly a scheme designed to put the Commons in the wrong. They had not questioned the historical right of the King to purveyance, but had hoped to see the abuses that had grown up in administering it corrected, or, if His Majesty would go so far as to consent, the right itself given up. Meanwhile Bacon added that at the next conference, on the following Monday, the subcommittee was to dispute the King's prerogative and the liberties of the subject. Then he attempted to philosophize: laws positive were never corrective of a king's right, but "directive of a king's will"; that is, I assume, laws were not to limit a king but were, rather, signposts that he might follow.[4] Bacon warned the Commons that at the subcommittee they might be worsted in the debate and that, if they were, there would be a necessity to admit a right.[5]

On March 4 Hyde reported the conference of the previous day. Salisbury was quoted to the effect that if purveyance were removed, the King's estate had nevertheless to subsist. He used phrases more minatory than was his wont, insisting that the King's necessities could not admit that the bill against purveyance should pass. The Lords would see to it, he implied, that the rejection of the bill did not rest upon the King's shoulders. Sadly Hyde remarked: "If neither custom, law, nor love can help us, the Lord help us." [6] The situation seemed desperate.

On March 5 Francis Moore started the discussion. No doubt he had been thinking over the situation and had made up his mind that the Commons should compensate the King. "We [are] making a law," he observed, "that would draw the most princes of Europe into enmity; therefore something to be done by way of composition." He was right in his position, for there was no chance of getting rid of purveyance without a composition, but his reason for it was hardly adequate.

The next morning, when the debate on purveyance was resumed, the excitable Hare announced that he never wanted to hear the name of composition again. If the Commons went home without putting their bill through, the griefs of the country would be doubled, and the abuses of the purveyors ten times trebled. Instead of composition he would offer the King a donation, or "some other requital." Did Hare suppose for one moment that James would give up purveyance forever in return for a donation now and perhaps again? Ridgeway was not in favor of dropping the ball thrown to them by the Lords at the last conference. He supported a composition, "but not," wrote Bowyer, "with much reason." [7]

Sir Maurice Berkeley believed in the bill against purveyors but opposed a composition, lest men be drawn to compound for their lives and lands. He could hardly have shown greater distrust of the Crown. But he wished, nevertheless, some supply of the King's occasions, which might be perpetual, "without charge to the people," "if any such way may be devised," [8] a significant qualification.

Thomas Wilson, who kept notes for Salisbury of what went on in the Commons and who had probably taken Sir John Stanhope's place as a member for Newton in the Isle of Wight, made one of his few speeches. He favored a composition," the same to be temporal, and to continue only for a time, and with condition." [9] This plan he regarded as "the middest way." [10]

Anthony Dyott, M.P. for Lichfield, dealt "in a long learned speech" [11] with technical legal details not recorded for our benefit and "ripped up again the point of prerogative," [12] which in this instance was nothing but the right of purchase ahead of others.

Lawrence Hyde alluded to the King's gracious message and wondered whether it had been followed up.[13] He would be sorry to see the House kill its own measure against purveyance. If it were not thought worthy to pass, the Lords would quash it, and so save the King from being blamed.[14] As yet he had not heard reason enough to make him consent to a composition, even if the House were granted security that purveyance would not be brought back.[15]

Then Hyde went on to make what seems from him a queer suggestion: Let those who had lent the King money on privy seals waive their claims, and let others "of the better sort" lend by privy seals in proportion to their financial ability.[16] With this proposal, which would have undermined parliamentary control of the purse, he added the suggestion that the two subsidies and four fifteenths already resolved upon should not be augmented. Let the gifts made to unworthy persons be resumed by the King.[17]

Hyde was followed by Martin, who lived up to the advice given in *Policies in Parliament* that he who would influence the House should not rise "till all those have spoken whom he feareth will most, and can best oppose it." [18] He took up Hyde's arguments and declared that he was willing to see privy seals forgiven and that he favored an act of resumption, "to resume such lands and annuities and pensions as the King hath given to unworthy persons," the impractical suggestion offered by Hyde. He was himself ready to forgive all the King owed him as well as the woods he had bestowed upon him. He wished other men would do the same, at which there was murmuring in the House,[19] as Martin may well have expected. He was capable of teasing his fellow members. He hoped the House would not grow to a question. Composition had been revived yesterday and strangled today, and he would not revive it. But he had heard no one who would oppose it if there could be security that purveyance would actually be abolished, or narrowly limited. He hoped for further dealings with the Lords: "The Lords are neither such sirens nor we such ill mariners that we need fear to be drawn out." [20] Martin's classical allusion was to the point. The Commons were strangely afraid of being taken in by their betters. Doubtless the members enjoyed, however, the speeches of Martin, even when they disagreed with him. He was lively and "facete," almost a Victorian M.P. Seriously he asserted that the King at his coronation had pardoned £60,000 [21] forfeited to him for want of licenses of alienation or unpaid licenses. Martin was becoming an influential member, but on his own, and not as part of a group. Such speeches as his and that of Hyde indicate how little cooperative planning there seems to have been among those speaking in opposition.

On March 7 purveyance was still in debate. Bacon replied to those who opposed composition: it was neither against the prerogative nor against the public good. To the objection that it would prove a perpetual tax, he proposed that it be a "probationer," until the next Parliament. He was offering the same concession to the opposition as had Thomas Wilson. Compositions, Bacon asserted, had been used already (in several counties, he might have added).

It was evident that members feared that if the King did not live up to his promises, they would have no remedy. If the King found that he could not keep his promises, they would be urged to settle for new compositions.[22]

On March 8 the King sent a message reminding the Commons that the idea of a composition had been his; he had hoped to relieve the grievances of his people and could do it in no better way then by rooting out purveyors. But three things had to be considered: his rights, the security afforded against purveyors, and conveniency. By conveniency he meant, I assume, whether a practical method of levying composition could be worked out. When he talked of leaving the matter of security to the judges, he would not have won over the Commons, for the judges were likely to lend an ear to any word from on high, from Whitehall. His Majesty did not lessen the distrust of the sincerity of his utterances against the purveyors when he wrote the Commons that he had ever exercised care to punish the purveyors, not through the officers of Green Cloth but by means of the Star Chamber.[23] Why should they expect, the Commons might have asked, that he would do more now than what he had done already? But His Majesty said more: "If it be thought inconvenient" [that is, difficult to work out the details], "then his Majesty desireth it may proceed no further" ("farder"). This seemed a command. The matter of his right and of security was to be left to the judges, and, if the details of a composition proved too difficult for the Commons, they were to drop the subject. If necessary, he would take order for reformation by law. His Majesty was fond of the little word "if."

In conclusion he mentioned his wants; he would accept their help as a token of their love for him.[24] In other words, His Majesty was waiting for more than two subsidies and four fifteenths; he had perhaps been told, as the wise biographer of Bacon suspected,[25] that the Commons were now likely to vote him a third subsidy.

Next came a discourse by Sandys, an hour and a half in length. He professed pleasure at the royal message and hoped that the Commons would take a course consonant with it. He warned them against the extreme of flattery—of pleasing the Crown—or of popularity—of joining with the "populars," [26] those who opposed the Crown, the left wing, if we may so call them. Sandys was still affecting a middle position, but was looking to the left. The report that the expenses of the King exceeded his income was the worst news that had ever come to Parliament; the peace with Spain had wormwood in it; now there was a plague that caused more waste than a hundred years of war, and might be a judgment upon them. One of the more liberal-minded men of his time, he was thinking, nevertheless, in terms of Old Testament theology.

He alluded to the poverty of the country. The poor man could not sell his corn nor the grazier his cattle; hence rents were falling off. Thirty gentlemen were behind in the rents due them as against three who were not. He was not speaking to prevent liberality to the King, "because speeches have gone all one way but to lay in a contrary balance."

Boldly Sandys took up the subject of purveyors under three headings. Should the Commons proceed with a bill? Should they turn to the Lords for a proper course? Should they develop some new project? The answers to such questions depended upon the wisdom of the House; they involved the duty of the House to His Majesty and their care for their country.[27] "To leave off now [with purveyance?] were to wrong the King. . . . A just complaint ought ever to have a just audience." [28]

Purveyance was an essential prerogative of the King, but for him to buy at a lower rate than others was not an essential.[29] He laid down three principles: [30]

1. The Commons could not give a supply to the King answerable to his charges.
2. If thirty-six laws have not helped, one more would not.[31]
3. To compound may prove a dangerous precedent.

If the Commons should compound for the encumbrances and oppressions of purveyance, they might have to compound for other grievances. The composition might be levied on land and might make all land tributary to the King. The composition could become a rent charge "for which distress may be taken for the King on all the parties' lands." [32] As for the bill against purveyors, it should not be hurried through nor allowed to sleep.

How were they to find the money for the King? Sandys suggested decreasing the size and numbers of the royal household and the maintenance of the Crown lands, and the resumption of the Crown property that had been given away. How could such a mind as Sandys's conceive of the last suggestion as practicable? The hangers-on of the Court would never allow the King to take from them what they had gained by careful flattery and unremitting importunity.

Sandys seemed more hard-headed when he raised the question of the Fens. Certain persons, he indicated, had undertaken to drain the Fen lands at their own expense. He wanted them drained at the expense of the Crown and predicted that the profit to the King would amount to £40,000 a year. He felt sure that such a public act, from which the King should receive the profit, would be more acceptable to the people than any other. [33]

Sandys's speech was in good part a terse and skillful summing up of the debates that had preceded it and was given with the assurance of one whose words received attention. It was, furthermore, a conciliatory address that would have swayed open-minded hearers, however few there were. His Majesty probably did not relish the reference to the numbers of the royal household, but Sandys seemed not so much to be finding fault as offering ways of ending the financial impasse.

At the conclusion of the debate the Speaker brought a message from the King, which took the House by surprise: it was His Majesty's pleasure, if the Commons liked, that they should not meddle further with composition.

What had happened? Had James been advised by those around him that the Commons were unlikely to vote a composition? Had he decided to move first?

Composition or Not

THE House, ignoring the King's request, went on with the debate over composition. On March 11 John Bond of Taunton opened with a question: were the Commons to make a composition or not, and were they to let composition sleep? "The country expects we should proceed by bill." He was in favor of a short law against the Board of Green Cloth, a principal cause of their distress about purveyors. He turned to Sandys's proposal to raise money from the Fens, which he liked, but this was not time to fish under water. Whether the House would add two subsidies to the two already voted was the question. He did not believe in voting fifteenths, perhaps because that tax would fall upon the poor.

The words of the schoolmaster-physician, interlaced with metaphors and proverbs, may well have entertained the Commons, as they did Sir Roger Wilbraham.[1] It was landed folk, substantial men of their own breed, that carried weight with the Lower House.

Bond was followed by Sir James Perrot, who had the distinction of being the illegitimate son of Sir John Perrot, usually believed to be the illegitimate son of Henry VIII, and thus Sir James was in a way the nephew of Edward VI, Mary, and Elizabeth, from all of whom his father had received favors. Sir James had written pamphlets on political matters and was possibly better informed than most of his fellows in the House. He spoke of Elizabeth's debts as totaling £400,000 and then remarked that those of James were as high. He asserted that among all the projects to help the King he liked best that mentioned by Sandys—that His Majesty might derive a profit from draining the Fens—but he failed to say that it would be years, if not decades, before such a profit could be realized. Then he adverted to the grievances that the Commons were collecting and suggested that the redress of grievances and the relief of the King's needs ought to be reciprocal.

The debate had been confusing. Opinion ran against composition, and yet the very speakers who opposed it were aware of its successful use in the past, both in and out of London. Those speakers realized, too, what a stumbling block purveyance had been between sovereign and people, that, while it lasted, there would be no contentment. Yet to get rid of it without offering a composition was out of the question.

Other proposals were made. Sir John Boys, M.P. for Canterbury, pointed out that if they could rid themselves of the authority of the Court of Green Cloth, they could then bring suits against unjust purveyors and recover damages. Would it not be possible for the judges to devise sufficient assurances and then for the Lords to set down an easy proportion of payments for purveyance? [2]

Not all members were ready to give up on composition. Hedley believed it better, and less dangerous, to compound and relieve the King by bargain than by subsidy.[3]

But the opponents made a case. They feared that His Majesty might not live up to any bargain or that he might discover that he could not give assurance.[4] He could not hope, it was implied, to support his large household without purveyance.[5] There was always the chance that the judges might pronounce purveyance part of the royal prerogative never to be taken from the Crown. It was said, no doubt truly, that there was a "great inconvenience in particular compositions." [6] Yelverton warned the Commons that if a composition were levied upon land, it would prove a "devil's walk." To have it known generally what lands the realm contained, and how much every man had in his possession, would mean purveyance with a vengeance, where now it was but a villainy. New offices would have to be created, and new officials with new fees would abound. Yelverton's warning probably made an impression. The very thought of such a survey would have worried every landholder with titles at all disputable, and there were hundreds of such gentlemen. It was easy to support the argument against composition, and members would have been the more willing to do so as they were beginning to realize that it was a lost cause. Hobart reminded the Commons that there was no law against the requisitioning of carts. "We stand to lose in this point."

If composition were out of the question and the abolition of purveyance would be voted down in the Lords, it was proposed by Sir John Boys that a short bill be enacted taking away the power assumed by Green Cloth of bringing men before that body as a court and of imprisoning them. One law, declared Hedley,[7] against the clerks and officers of Green Cloth would be better than the thirty-six against purveyance already on the books.

At this point the Speaker intervened. He would not put composition to the question because he did not want to see it "disgraced,"[8] that is, formally defeated. He did his best to put a question for a committee to consider a supply for His Majesty and for a standing revenue. For such a move the House was not yet ready. A standing revenue for the King would have been a threat to parliamentary control of the purse. It was more relevant to talk of grievances. The House resolved that the Committee for Grievances should consider grievances and supply and that any member should have a voice.[9] It was a move for delay, lest supply come before grievances.

On the next day, March 12, Hare brought in amendments to the bill against purveyors, and the bill with the amendments was ordered to be engrossed.[10] On March 18 the bill had its third reading and went up to the Lords, who found nineteen objections to it. It was said the bill gave every man power to resist the purveyors and that such resistance might result in tumults dangerous to the state.[11] It was objected, further, that no form of commission could be devised to cover what was called for in the statutes. Moreover, if ready money were to be paid to the purveyors, the King would have to send guards with money up and down the country.

The judges in attendance at the joint conference of committees of the Lords and Commons had assisted in drawing up the nineteen objections. Fuller, who had also been present at the conference, asserted to the Commons that there was a great difference between the opinion of a judge sitting in a court of judgment and in any other place.[12] The Commons were also informed that the Lords feared that the Commons were making a law "to famish the King."[13]

Yelverton answered that the bill was just, reasonable, and fit to pass. It would not famish the King, for his provision would be as ready as it was then. He complained of the inferior officers of Green Cloth, but he dared not hope that the greatness of Green Cloth could be altered by arguments. "If our child," he remarked, "bred with so much pain and travail must needs die, let it appear to the world that it died not of any natural corruption within it but it is crushed." [14] Yelverton could not hold back his bitterness.[15]

The Commons resolved to ask for a second conference; [16] the Lords assented, but said that it was "rare and extraordinary." At that conference the judges were again in evidence, and their opinions did not tally with those of the Commons. They "overruled all on the prerogative side," that the prerogative was not subject to law but that it was "transcendent above the reach of Parliament." [17] The Lords advised the Commons that in kindness the King would do much, but, upon constraint, nothing.

On Wednesday, April 16, an allusion was made to "purveyors' commissions" which were to be considered a week from the following Monday. Attached to the statement were the words: "The bill in Sir Rob. Johnson's hands." [18] Now the purveyance bill which we have been discussing, was already in the House of Lords, where it had been criticized for not containing the form of a commission that purveyors could use. What had happened was that a new bill drafted to remedy the omission of commissions was in the hands of Sir Robert.

A little later on the same day Sir Henry Montague reported the conference of the day before. Apparently the Commons had brought in their answers to the Lords' objections to the bill. Then the Lord Chief Justice cited a precedent used before by the Commons, 36 Edw. III, cap. ii, and asserted that he could make no other interpretation but that the King had prerogative and that he was not bound to make immediate payment, but must make payment in the place where the goods had been taken. Further, he said that acts of Parliament might explain and limit the prerogative, but could not remove it without recompense. The bill proposed to make it impossible for the King to change it by a *non obstante;* any such legislation would be void.[19]

It may have been observed that, while purveyance was threshed over mornings in the House and afternoons in the committee, now and again the need for subsidies would suddenly be thrust forward in the debate. It will be recalled that on February 10 the Commons had named a large committee to draw a bill. In the following week it became evident that the sum decided upon would by no means satisfy the Privy Councillors of the House. More than once His Majesty had hinted at the need for more subsidies and the Lord Treasurer had declared that two subsidies and four fifteenths would not even pay the debts left over from the reign of the Queen. On March 9 Salisbury had written to the Earl of Mar that the King would not put down the purveyors and thus lose £50,000 a year; it was better to push through a law to punish the abuses than to abolish the use. Then came the key phrase: "If possible get somewhat more than two subsidies."

Members of Parliament with long memories could recall how the great Queen had asked for as little as possible and had once returned part of a single subsidy. It was otherwise with the new sovereign. What they failed to take into account was that the cost of living had been going up rapidly; what they could see with their own eyes was the extravagance of the Court. Edward Peake, who represented Sandwich (a Cinque Port) in his seventh Parliament, wished the King's wants to be mentioned no more. William Holt, M.P. for Clitheroe in Lancashire, maintained that a subsidy was a public contribution, not to be used for private purposes, for bounties, ceremonies, etc. It would be better, continued Holt, to try all ways than to "dive into the subject's purse." William Noy, a young lawyer who represented Grampound in Cornwall, said that subsidies went from the poor to the rich,[20] an indirect attack upon the gifts made by the King.

The King had his defenders. Hobart reminded the House of the expenses incurred in the wars in Ireland and of other necessary expenses. Sir George More was no doubt excusing the King's extravagance when he came right out and asserted that a king who wished to retain the love of his subjects had to allow them *panem et circenses*. The member who took that fresh and surprising view had given some thought to monarchy and its functions in past history. The opposition might have suggested that history was the record of changes, even in sacred institutions.

Other speakers quoted precedents about subsidies. Sir Anthony Cope, M.P. for Banbury, declared that many good bills were before the House, and more would come; he believed in dealing first with grievances and then with subsidies.

The Speaker tried to put the question whether two subsidies or one subsidy and two fifteenths, in addition to the two subsidies already granted, should be voted. Sandys remarked that they had given two subsidies without voices opposed, as if to imply that the Commons should go no farther unless by general consent. The Speaker put the question, "whether presently to go to the question," [21] and it was voted that the question should be deferred.

On March 18 the King sent a message concerning both the addition to that which was given and grievances. He complained that his message of February 11 "hath lately produced no other effect but the multiplicity of arguments" [22] and hoped that the Commons would use moderation about grievances. His Majesty required expedition. If the noise of more doubts, debates, and contradictions should continue a few days longer, the value of the additional money granted would be lessened and much of the good esteem that the Commons had won for subsidies granted would be diminished. The presence of Members of Parliament was needed in the country.

His Majesty assumed his magisterial manner: "He is now resolved to understand of you, whether he shall expect any farther addition to that which you have already granted to him." [23] As for grievances, if laws were defective, he would add his authority by Parliament, or by himself with the advice of his Council,[24] the unacceptable offer he had made earlier. He would either give speedy answers or turn the grievances over to the regular course of justice, which meant, if members were to judge from past nonperformance, that grievances would continue as before.

Once more the Speaker tried to force the hand of the House. He asked whether the House would, according to the King's desire, go to the question. Sir Henry Savile moved to defer the question, but the Speaker pressed it, and the Commons resolved to go to the question, "which question prevailed in the affirmative." After debate it was decided, "by the most," that the question should be as near to the King's request as possible. After more debate the Speaker declared there were two questions: one, general, "whether you will give any more"; the other, particular, "whether by way of subsidy and fifteens." [25] Bowyer wrote: "They which studied to please, etc. requiring the general question, and such as continued according to their first opinion, moved only out of conscience, calling for the particular question." Finally the question was put as to whether it would be proper to give any more to His Majesty than had already been given. There were 140 yeas and 139 noes.[26] On the next question—whether it was fit and convenient to add a further help to His Majesty's occasions by way of subsidy and fifteenths—the yeas exceeded the noes by 28. The Speaker proposed another question concerning quantity. Sir William Skipwith, M.P. for Leicester, objected that their vote meant one more subsidy and two fifteenths. The motion to give that amount carried the House with few negative votes. The earlier vote had settled the question. Those on the negative side were not inclined to continue the struggle, and those on the affirmative side were so pleased that they were not ready to press for four subsidies.

It was a narrow squeak for the Crown, but any victory was better than defeat or delay. Salisbury was elated and wrote to Sir Henry Wotton: "They have . . . carried themselves very lovingly and dutifully to his Majesty, having given him three subsidies and six fifteens, [of] which is no other precedent in times of peace." [27]

One would be glad to know more about the events of that critical day. That 139 members could vote against the necessities of the King is surprising when one thinks of all the pressures put upon them and all the fears that prevented them from standing up against the Court. There may have been a prevalent opinion that the King, however extravagant, had to be given supplies, that he needed more money. M. Fontaine of the French embassy in Lon-

don wrote that the three subsidies and six fifteenths were granted
by only one vote. This contribution, he continued, was less liberal
than had been hoped and not freely given. He believed the Crown
would accept the smaller amount as something in hand, and hope
for more from another Parliament with members who were better
chosen.[28]

On March 25 the King sent a message of gratitude,[29] but wished
the Commons so to time the subsidies and fifteenths that he would
be able to make ready payment to those subjects from whom he
had borrowed money. Bacon reported from the Committee for
Subsidies about this matter. The sum of the gift came to £400,000,
and there was a pressing and intractable debt of £500,000.[30] The
question of the dates of payment of each subsidy was discussed,
with Fortescue, Sandys, Sir George More, and others taking part.
Finally a vote of 121 to 113 decided that the second subsidy should
have its first payment a year from November and its second payment two years from May. The third subsidy, if I understand
correctly, was to come from May to May of the third year.

From a letter of Bacon to Salisbury [31] we learn that Bacon was
drawing the preamble to the subsidy bill. Spedding assumes that
he wrote it at some time before April 10 when the bill was brought
in.

It should be noted that the vote on the third subsidy was not
unlike that on the question of whether the House should come to
a vote. In other words, more or less hard-and-fast lines were
slowly forming between those who supported the King and those
who did not. But we may suspect that a good many members who
did not always side with the Court were moved, in this case, to
show their loyalty to the King. It is probable that never again
during this session was so large a vote recorded, and that in spite
of the gradual thinning out of the House.

On April 12 the bill for the granting of three entire subsidies
and six fifteenths was read the first time. It was read the second
time on the afternoon of April 16 and committed to the former
committee, that is, the Committee for Subsidies, with the addition
of William Jones, who had perhaps made some suggestion. On

April 18 the Bill of Subsidy was brought in by the Solicitor and ordered to be engrossed; on May 9 it was offered to be read when Sir Anthony Cope and others opposed the reading until the grievances were read. At last a special order was entered that the subsidy should not pass to the Lords until the grievances were ready and presented to the King. A dispute followed as to whether a question should be made of the third reading, "a very tender question," but the bill was read the third time, and the House was satisfied that no vote should be taken.

On May 13 Bacon was appointed to present the grievances to the King and did so on the next afternoon. The Bill of Subsidy was sent up to the Lords by Mr. Secretary Herbert on May 15, "with the whole House attending him, not one man left, but Mr. Speaker, Clerk, Serjeant. Never seen before." [32]

Chapter 3

The Third Session, 1606/07

The Instrument of Union

IN 1604 the King had hoped to put through his plan for union. In 1605/06 he had again hoped that Parliament would take up the project. In 1606/07 it was understood, both by those favorable to the union and by those less engaged in its support, that it would be the next order of business.

Yet there were reasons, both historic and immediate, why Parliament might be less than enthusiastic about the plans for union. The English had long regarded the Scots as not wholly civilized. They found them, moreover, competitors in trade. "Honest Nick Fuller" told the Commons that the Scots were more like peddlers than merchants,[1] alluding to the Scottish businessmen abroad who made no use of companies but entrusted their goods to salesmen who often undersold the English.

There were more immediate reasons for the English attitude toward their neighbors. As the reader knows, those Scots who came south with the King had not made themselves beloved in London. If Salisbury was Principal Secretary of State, the man seemingly closest to His Majesty was the Scottish Earl of Dunbar, who, when the plums were dropping, saw to it that his northern friends were under the tree. So widespread was the dislike of the Scots that the ambassador from France, Lefevre de la Boderie, in a letter to his government, predicted the failure of the project for the union: "The little sympathy between the two nations, the differences of

their laws, the jealousy of their privileges, the regard of the succession, are the reasons they will never . . . join with another, as
the King wishes." [2]

All that the King will gain, wrote de la Boderie, will be that
the two Crowns will unite in him and his successors. He observed
that the English were taking pains to prevent the Scots from
holding offices. At all the public assemblies the English proceeded
first, even though they came sometimes from new families, while
Scots of the old nobility might follow in second place. From what
one knows of King James, this is hard to believe. The French
ambassador had perhaps been talking to a Scot.[3]

Even before Parliament met, it was evident that troubles were
ahead. The Earl of Northampton told the Lords in a conference
on November 26: "Some have written that distraction would
appear in the handling [of measures for the union]; he wished
that he might be a false prophet." [4]

On December 7, 1606, the Venetian ambassador in London
wrote to Venice: "The King is so eager to see the desired issue that
he employs all his authority and weight to reach it." [5]

However widespread the feeling against the union, the project
was now to be brought forward. Twenty-eight Scottish and thirty-
nine English commissioners had put together, with no little effort,
an Instrument of Union. On November 27 that Instrument was
read to the House of Commons by the Clerk and, from a "brief" in
his hand, "opened" by the Speaker to the members.

The Instrument was no final statement. The articles were to be
propounded to the two Parliaments. So far as Scotland was concerned, the King could manipulate the Parliament of that nation
as he pleased. To persuade the English Parliament to accept the
Instrument was another matter.

The Instrument proposed that all hostile laws and treaties
dealing with the borders should be abolished. It was to be unlawful for Scots to transport to foreign countries such goods and commodities as Englishmen were forbidden to transport. At the same
time, it was to be provided that such goods as were lawful to be
transported by Englishmen could be transported by Scots and

vice versa. This arrangement gave the Scots an advantage because the English transported a great deal more wool and woolen goods than the Scots, and the Scots might buy such commodities from the English, ship them on small boats of their own at lower charges, and then undersell the English in the continental markets. This they could do the more readily because the English, selling their goods by means of companies, had maintained prices at a fairly high level. Those who transported foreign wares from England to Scotland or from Scotland to England were to give bond not to transport the said goods into any foreign country. The value of such a bond was, however, questionable. The man who gave the bond might sell the goods to another Scot under no bond. The goods might indeed be sold again and again and then shipped to a foreign port without much risk.

The Scots were to be allowed membership in the English merchant companies, such as the Merchant Adventurers on the same terms as Englishmen.

It was also agreed by the commissioners that it should be propounded to the Parliaments of England and Scotland that those subjects of each kingdom born since the death of the late Queen should be enabled to obtain, succeed, inherit, and possess all lands, goods, chattels, honors, dignities, offices, and liberties in Parliament and in "all other places of the same Kingdom."

But then came qualification. His Majesty had said that he meant not to confer any office of judicature, place, voice, or office in Parliament upon subjects of the other kingdom "until time and conversation have increased and accomplished an union . . . as well in the hearts of all the people." [6] This promise by the King was occasioned by events that Gardiner has related so well that we need only abbreviate his paragraphs. The commissioners for the union had listened to the legal opinions rendered in 1604 that by the common law of England the *Post-Nati* were not aliens, but were as much subjects as any Englishman. The same was not true of those born before the accession of the King. The commissioners proposed a Declaratory Act pronouncing the *Post-Nati* in either country possessed of the privileges of natives of the other. They also recommended that the same right might be given to the *Ante-Nati* by statute.

This proposal did not please His Majesty. If the statute of naturalization should forbid Scots to hold office, it would limit his right of denization, of conferring English citizenship, since it would exclude those to whom he gave denization from holding office. That right he was unwilling to forego, although ready to promise that he would make no use of it.[7]

At some time in 1607, and probably not long after the Instrument of Union had been formulated, the King wrote this letter to Salisbury:

> Now that . . . this session of the Commissioners hath had so happy a success, to the end that the Commissioners of England and by them the whole people of England may discern the true difference between a crafty tyrant and a just King, I will now . . . open my mind freelier therein than ever I would have done before it had been agreed upon . . . I protest . . . never Scottishman did either directly or indirectly make suit to me for any such preferment as is reserved in your Act, and whether they ever had or not, God is my judge.[8]

It is hard not to assume that the King at that moment of expansiveness believed what he said.

The Instrument had been drawn up with care, if not with economy of words. No doubt the commissioners had aimed to be fair to each nation, but in their desire to please His Majesty seem to have given the Scots the best of it. Certainly English M.P.'s complained of some of the articles. They ought to have realized that it might be wise to give a small and poor nation a few advantages. The English may well have been reluctant to do so because they feared that their own Parliament might reject such recommendations.

The Discussion:
How to Proceed

THE story of the struggle over the union can be pieced together from the running debate carried on in the House of Commons. To understand the attitude of that House we have to follow in some detail the ins and outs of those debates, to observe who spoke for the King, who spoke on the other side, and to mark the several degrees of support and of opposition.

The story includes more than that. Roughly speaking, the House of Lords was arrayed on the side of His Majesty, and that body was ably led by Salisbury. Not all of the Lords could have been ardent supporters of the union with Scotland, but those who opposed it seldom appeared in the few records known. The Lords were active; they asked for conferences and hoped for proper debate in those conferences.

Usually the Commons agreed, not without hesitation and often after some delay, to hold those conferences. But in nearly all cases the Commons refused to engage in debate. In the continuous tug of war the Commons were convinced that they were losers, but that they had really no reason to be discouraged. They were expressing English opinion more effectively than the Lords; they were indeed riding on the wave of the future.

As soon as the Instrument of Union had been read in the Lower House and returned to the Upper, the Lords requested a conference. The Commons named a committee of one hundred to meet with a committee of the Lords "to hear what the Lords will propound, not to give answer but report only."

The limitations set upon the conference were not pleasing to the Lords. At the conference the Lord Chancellor, Lord Ellesmere, declared that silence in consultation effected nothing.[1] He went on to divide the problem of the union into three parts, the repealing of the hostile laws, commerce, and the participation of both countries in the liberties and benefits.[2]

The provisions of the third division would not have seemed

good to many of the English Members of Parliament. The Scots, it was asserted, would derive benefits at the expense of the English. The Lord Chancellor, doubtless aware of that opinion, spoke defensively; he asked the Commons to recall His Majesty's words that they should bring with them "minds of indifferency and equality, to weigh all things and to forbear all terms of bitterness." [3]

Salisbury wished that the Commons had given their committee for conference a wider commission. He adjured the Commons to avoid partiality and fear.

The Earl of Northampton informed the Lower House that he had a part in framing the articles of the Instrument, as if to assure them of the wisdom of the framers. The realm and the world were, he told them, looking to Parliament to bring about the union. [4]

In their own House, the Commons proceeded to discuss the next move. Richard Martin, with his confidence in the meeting of minds, urged every man to speak. The four points he believed ought to be taken into consideration were: the abrogation of hostile laws, commerce, the determination of the differences on the borders, and naturalization. The first two, he thought, should be referred to the Lords, whom he represented "as understanding State better." [5] Conferences, he observed, had never brought advantages to the Commons, yet in this matter they were necessary.

The division of a subject into its parts interested the analytical Bacon, who began, however, on a high moral plane: "If we speak in general, it will be temptation to lead men to ingratiate themselves, sometimes for favor, often for fame, both vices, and to speak as orators only, and not as law-makers."

As an elder statesman, Sir Francis liked to stand above the battle, counseling the contestants to patience and compromise, but he was less impartial than he wished to appear. In this case he was ready with an outline of a program for proceeding. Three topics, hostile laws, commerce, and naturalization were to be treated, not in the two Houses but at a conference between them. Those sitting on higher ground, that is, the Lords, were beings of a wider vision. It was true, of course, that they were likely to have been told more of the inwardness of things. Then Bacon made an adroit suggestion: "If the Lords proceed alone by a bill they will rest more inflexible." [6]

Sir Henry Poole, who had been a knight of the shire for Gloucestershire in 1592/93, and who from 1604 to 1610 was M.P. for Cricklade on the Wiltshire border of Gloucestershire, was regarded by Smyth of Nibley in the 1620s as "our merry soul." In the session of 1604 he was seldom heard or named to committees, and he was obviously not of the inside group left over from Elizabethan days. Toward the end of the session of 1605/1606, when members were leaving town and attendance was slim, Poole was rather suddenly named to one committee after another and made motions and short speeches. He had some knowledge of conditions in the country and was useful. However diligent, he did not add much to the debates. This time he told the Commons that the union was a great work and deserved consideration, but it was an innovation. To call a plan an innovation was not to commend it to the minds of landed gentlemen of that time. The House was ready, he believed, neither for a bill nor for a conference. [7]

The Speaker summarized what had been said, as if to draw the House to a decision. But the Commons arranged to continue the debate on the next day, November 27, when Fuller asked Sir Edward Hoby, one of the commissioners for the union and an old hand who carried weight, why he had refused to subscribe to the Instrument. Sir Edward was not easily pushed into a corner. He refused to comment on the meetings of the commissioners and concluded by saying that he wished he had fellows with him. [8] It was thought fit that he should not yield his reasons. [9]

John Bond, the schoolmaster and physician from Taunton who went his own way, sometimes a contrary one but one that seldom failed to interest the House, said that he had hoped that the problem of the union would have been settled before Christmas; now he despaired of such an outcome. If the Commons would but look back a hundred years, they would find their own House contesting with Henry VII, "our wisest King," who foreordered the union. In the time of Edward VI, "our gravest Council" (Parliament) endeavored to bring about a union; "all things as by his Majesty now desired, were presented to that nation [Scotland], but prevented by the subtlety of our envious neighbors, the French." [10]

At some moment after this speech the Speaker asked the Commons whether they were ready to send an answer to the Lords about a conference. The Serjeant was sent out to round up the lawyers.[11] Two men, Brooke and Edward Alford, M.P. for Colchester, agreed with Martin's proposal of the day before that the House should deal with hostile laws and commerce and leave other matters, the borders [12] and naturalization to the Upper House, who stood near the King.[13]

Fuller said the House needed to consider alternatives and to hear every man speak, rather than a few speak eloquently. "One may see more than another." As for commerce he would have the merchants summoned and consulted. Naturalization he was apparently unwilling to turn over completely to the Upper House; it deserved several days of solemn debate. The crowded condition of England had to be taken into account; neither London nor the trading towns could hold more Scots.[14] "All occupations are so overburthened with artificers." [15]

Near the close of the debate Sandys rose. To him it appeared that the Lower House in its conferences with the Upper usually lost ground. He believed that the matter before them ought to be handled, not in committees, but in the House. He would send word to the Lords that the Commons were not yet ready for conference; they must debate thoroughly. His words were not unheeded. A message was sent to the Lords requesting them to undertake the problems of the borders and of naturalization, while the Commons would deal with hostile laws and commerce.[16]

The Lords answered the next morning, November 28, that they were not satisfied with the message and deemed it "some diminution to the capacity of this House, for whom nothing is too great, nor anything too little." They hoped that the Commons would, upon second thought, yield to a conference, lest there be loss of time. They would welcome a joint committee of the two Houses, or, if the Commons preferred, a conference of all of the two

Houses. Meanwhile they would proceed to such points as seemed fitting to them and leave the Commons to their own course.[17]

It was impossible not to feel the edge of these words. The Commons had been willing, after the preparation of the work involved had been divided between the two Houses, to hold a conference. But now, having thought better of it, as Sir Herbert Croft put it, they would consider the whole matter in the House and by committee, and would then be ready to confer with the Lords. How soon the Commons did not indicate.

On November 29 the Instrument of Union was read for the second time in the Lower House. A motion was made that all members, except the commissioners themselves, should be of the committee. It was finally resolved, however, that to the committee named for meeting with the Lords should be added all the lawyers of the House, all the burgesses of port towns, and all the knights and burgesses of the northern counties, "all the House to be present and have free speech." [18] In other words, this committee was much like a later Committee of the Whole House.

On December 3 the two days' labor of the Committee on the Union and hostile laws was reported by Lawrence Hyde. The committee was ready to consult with the Lords concerning the abrogating of such laws as were set down.

Sir Edward Hoby raised a problem in connection with hostile laws. Certain boroughs in the North had embodied in their "constitutions" laws against the Scots. It was "much disputed whether constitutions were to be repealed." [19] Such laws were private and political.[20] No act of Parliament could take away that which was not established by act of Parliament. The constitutions were best left to the boroughs.[21]

Bacon did not agree. Municipal constitutions hostile to the Scots should be done away with. Local statutes of that type were dead. The Instrument of Union was more for opinion than for effect.[22] He quoted the adage, *Opinio veritate major,* by which he perhaps implied that public opinion was a power that might induce towns to modify their constitutions.

Hobart declared that it ought not to be possible for a single borough to sever the unity of two nations. The problem clearly called for a conference with the Lords.

On December 4 Hyde reported the proceedings of the Committee for Commerce. They had summoned the merchants before them, and the merchants had asked to be given time until the following Monday afternoon (this was Thursday) "to consider and inform themselves." [23]

On December 8 Martin reported the proceedings of the committee on the Saturday before. They had heard from Trinity House [24] and from the merchants. The mariners and the Trinity House were opposed to any equality between the English and the Scots, for that would in time bring all the trade into the hands of the Scots and mean the decay of English shipping. The Scots, it was said, could build and operate ships more cheaply than the English [25] since their sailors lived on oysters and shellfish instead of beef.[26]

Meanwhile the Lords were becoming restive. On December 10 a message from them emphasized the difficulties encountered, especially those in connection with commerce. The Christmas recess was just ahead, and they wanted a conference.[27] The Commons answered that they were interviewing merchants, but would be glad to confer on the following Saturday (this was Wednesday). On Thursday a committee of about twenty-five was named to prepare matters for the conference.

The conference lasted the best part of three days. In the paper the merchants presented to the Commons they asked that all should be left as it was, "without further uniting." [28] For that statement they were rebuked by the Lord Chancellor.

Parliament was put off until February 10 in the coming year. The Commons went home with little to tell their constituents.[29]

Hostile Laws: Commerce and Naturalization

WHEN Parliament reconvened in February 1607 a contretemps between the Speaker and the Commons revealed the tension that had been accumulating. On February 13 Sir Henry Montague brought in his remembrances of what had taken place in the conference in December, "being taken without warrant from the House." [1] Montague delivered the paper to the Clerk of the House and reported that the agreement of the committee was "according to the particulars set down." [2] The Speaker offered to read the said remembrances "but was interrupted by speech and dispute." It was moved and pressed that the remembrances had not been agreed upon by the committee of both Houses,[3] and further resolved to return the document to Montague and that it was not to remain in the House, nor to be accepted as authentic.[4]

It is possible that, in the conference, the members had been maneuvered into a kind of informal agreement that they were now renouncing; it is more likely that in the informal procedure of a committee meeting a difference of opinion might have arisen as to whether a resolution had actually been passed or not. A chairman, with or without intention, might rule that a proposal praised in speech had been accepted. In committee or in conference what seemed the sense of the meeting might be regarded as resolved upon.

There was more to report from the December conference. The Attorney dealt with the matter of hostile laws and asserted that certain old laws against the Scots ought to be repealed. The question of the "constitutions" of some of the northern boroughs was brought up again; it was apparently accepted that they should be left to themselves.

About commerce Hobart reported that it had been agreed that, so long as the Scots had special trading privileges with France, they should pay double customs duties upon goods imported from France.[5] The English merchants, he said, were at special expense; they had to pay charges to the City and to maintain factors and markets abroad. The Scots sent salesmen, as had been noted already. If the English did that, it would cause "disesteem" of English commodities. Already the English were at pains to maintain a certain prestige for their goods as well as what they deemed fitting prices.

The Speaker asked for "further direction," perhaps a move to encourage progress toward a bill. Sir Richard Spencer, M.P. for

Brackley in Northamptonshire, moved that a bill be drawn.[6]
Then he remarked: "That we should not look one upon another;
not fit for so grave a Council." Had members been exchanging
knowing glances, as much as to say we are being hurried by the
Speaker and Sir Richard? Were members in opposition looking
askance on those who supported the Speaker?

The House was not yet ready for a bill, but the next day they
resolved to proceed with the problem of naturalization. That
morning, February 14, Fuller called it a mistake to allow the hostile laws to be abolished without consent of Parliament. Then he
elaborated a general objection to the union that he had mentioned
earlier, the want of room in England for more inhabitants. In the
universities there were so many students that worthy scholars
could not find preferment. Merchants and traders were too many,
especially since the decline in trade. He proceeded to another
topic. That country was miserable where the rich were exceedingly rich and poor very poor. He was apparently alluding to
Scotland when he used an illustration that members would understand: He spoke of two manors where the same rent was charged.
One had commons, woods, estovers, etc.[7] The other manor was
a bare common with a little turf. The owner attempted, by granting some profit from the better manor, to help out the tenants
of the poorer, but it was, nevertheless, "plain wrong" for the
better manor. Near the end he used another figure of speech. It
was not good to bring two swarms of bees under one hive, on a
sudden.[8]

Sir Francis Bacon made one of the better speeches. He asked
members to raise their minds above their own interests and to act
for the dignity and honor of the state. He touched upon the argument advanced by Fuller that there were already too many people
in England. The expectation of large numbers of Scots settling
themselves in England was "rather in conceit than in event." At
first a small number of Scots followed His Majesty south, but that
tide had receded. Few Scottish families had settled in the cities
and towns of England. Was England really crowded? The country
was full of swamplands, commons, and wastes. It was, in fact,

thin-sown with people and many boroughs were decayed. The territories of France, Italy, Flanders, and some parts of Germany contained a far greater number of people within the same space.

Furthermore, Bacon went on, if England needed to send men away, there was the desolate and wasted kingdom of Ireland. He alluded, also, to the room in the colonies and plantations. This was in 1607. But suppose England had a "surcharge of people," what would be the result? An honorable war for the enlargement of borders. For such a war the English ought not to forget considerations of amplitude and greatness, nor to quarrel about profits and reckonings. Such quarrels were unworthy of Parliament.

Bacon dealt with the objection that the Instrument of Union left the laws of the kingdom as they were, which meant that with naturalization the Scots would have rights in England that the English lacked in Scotland. His answer was that naturalization should precede the union of laws since naturalization took away separation; eventually the union would remove the distinction. He had no doubt that English laws and customs would slowly prevail over those of the Scots.

To the third objection, that with the inequality in fortune between the two kingdoms the union would bring advantage to the Scots and loss to the English, he replied that it was true that in external goods the Scots were inferior, but in goods of the mind and body they were the equals of the English. Then he expatiated on the capacity of the Scots, on their understanding, on their ingenuity, industry, and courage. "If they have been noted," he added, "to be a people not so tractable in government, we cannot . . . free ourselves altogether from that fault . . . incident to all martial people." [9] When Sir Francis forgot himself and his ambitions, he could be both wise and generous in his outlook. But in his praise of the Scots he was not endangering his future.

He returned to the topic of naturalization. The *Post-Nati* were already naturalized. Many wished to see the *Ante-Nati*, grown men, no worse off than the younger brothers.

Then he touched upon the degrees of alienship, with precise classifications, and asserted that anyone born under the King's rule was naturalized by that circumstance, as declared in the royal proclamation.

He concluded that unless they proceeded with naturalization the two realms would be in danger of falling apart. Others had dealt with historical examples of union and separation; Bacon's arguments seemed more apposite. To refuse naturalization, he pointed out, would be to create unkindness between the two nations.

In his epilogue he adverted to the greatness of Britain with Scotland united with England, Ireland reduced, "the sea-provinces of the Low Countries contracted, and shipping maintained." That kingdom, he predicted, would be one of the greatest monarchies in forces truly esteemed that hath been in the world." Bacon was an imperialist in intention and not a bad prophet.

One would be glad to learn the impact of this persuasive speech upon members.[10] Like Woodrow Wilson three centuries later, Bacon could hit upon arresting and memorable combinations of words; like Wilson he could lift the debate to what seemed a high level until sometimes, when one thought it over afterward, one asked questions.

The debate of the next three days exhibited the uncertainty of members as to what they should do. Many less well-known figures in the House now ventured to offer their judgments. They recalled instances of the unions of states in ancient and medieval times; they argued from analogy, as debaters of that time often did. The fear that Scotland might gain an advantage over England was seldom absent from their minds. There could be no security for the King and his successors, a member declared, if a regular and formal (well-organized) kingdom fell into the hands of a nation "not so regular." [11] Members were warned against resigning their judgment to other men. They ought not to lean upon the opinions of the judges. They ought to remember that the common law applied only to Englishmen and that men could be naturalized only by the common law. Other speakers were inclined to support naturalization with limitations. They feared that to refuse it would be to throw the Scots back upon the French. It was pointed out that the Scots could not be levied upon by privy seals, that the King had indeed no method of taxing them. Nor was he able to enforce justice on a Scot as against an Englishman.

With so little consensus of opinion, what was the House to do next? Strode was in favor of putting it to the question whether the Scots were naturalized. Sir William Twysden, a man of wide connections in the southeast corner of England, wished the matter determined in the House, but not declared; that is, I take it, he wished a trial vote rather than a final resolution. Wingfield, who was possibly hoping to get back into the good graces of His Majesty, wished to see the Lords and the judges consulted. Sir Robert Cotton, a collector of manuscripts and a purveyor of precedents to his friends, was eager to hear from the civilian lawyers; the question concerned the law of nations. Martin urged a committee, presumably a small committee, since the House had for a time been discussing the matter in committee. Hobart, the realistic Attorney General, told the members that if the House passed merely a resolution they would lose what they were seeking. When they had left Westminster the question would fall into the hands of the judges. As for the Lords it should be recognized that they would not join with the Commons in what was proposed. The Commons could not make law alone. In the confusion of opinion, it was determined that the Great Committee should meet in the House in the afternoon and "collect all the reasons." [12]

On February 23 William Brock, M.P. for St. Ives in Cornwall, reported on the Saturday meeting of the Great Committee. Almost twenty men had participated in the discussion. Francis James, M.P. for Wareham in Dorset, a Cambridge man and a Doctor of Civil Law, seemed to support either an absolute union, perfect in every respect, or a union governed under diverse rules. Whether James was ready to try for a complete union at this time, I am not certain, but I suspect as much. If so, he anticipated Sandys by about two weeks. James asserted that he believed the Scots were not naturalized, which was to say that the proclamation issued was not enough.

The question was put to a vote in the committee, and it was resolved that the Scots were not de jure naturalized. That vote in committee, which reversed the royal proclamation, seemed to be regarded as settling the matter. Had the committee been the House, its right so to resolve might well have been disputed.[13]

As far back as February 14 the Lords had asked for a conference. On Monday, February 23, the Commons agreed to a conference about the point of naturalization to be held on Wednesday, February 25. On February 24 Richard Digges reported from the committee the names of those who were to speak for the Commons at the conference, a formidable array of talent, lawyers, civilians, and "gentlemen of other quality." [14] Bacon was to make the preamble; Sandys and Sir Roger Owen were to offer the precedents. But Hyde, Sandys, and Sir John Bennet excused themselves, and so did Sir Roger, on account of his disability and for fear of distaste,[15] and Brock, because he had never spoken, that is, I assume, in the presence of the Lords. Members were apparently reluctant to speak up in the presence of the Lords. On another occasion Yelverton remarked: "I am against conference; it hath done no good, and if you place some in the fore-front they will not speak, we have found it." [16] This conference proved unusual, however, in that respect. In some degree Lords and Commons answered one another, as men did in committees in the Lower House.

Bacon opened the conference with a speech conciliatory in tone. The Commons, he said, acknowledged the power of proclamations, but proclamations did not explain laws. It was for Parliament to do that.

Sandys repeated what he had said in the House that, where there was neither law nor custom, resort had to be made to reason, which he called the law of nations, or the "mother law." [17] If by the English law the Scots were naturalized, and if the English were not naturalized by their law (as it was said they were not, since the Scottish law was civil law), then there was an inequality. There was a further inequality. The English had to pay taxes and impositions, and the Scots in England had to pay only for defense. He concluded that the Scots were better than aliens but not equal with natural subjects.

Sir John Bennet, a civilian, asserted that when two bodies of law came together in a person, the custom of each body remained distinct. He concluded that the Scots were not naturalized in England but that the King could by civil law naturalize them and confer privileges on them.[18] Here Salisbury interrupted. The argument, he declared, was not to the question. They were discussing the law of England.

The Lord Chancellor alluded to Bacon's speech, and Bacon had maintained, it appears, that the question was not *de bono* but *de vero*. What was the law? The Lords Commissioners had pronounced what it was and had given three reasons—the proclamation of the King, the opinion of the commissioners, and the Act of Recognition—whereby Parliament acknowledged that they lived under one imperial Crown.

Five lawyers, Doddridge, Hyde, Brock, Crew, and Hedley spoke for the Commons, offering reasons why the Scots were not naturalized. Allegiance was tied up to laws and the laws of the two nations were different. The *Post-Nati* were not subject to the laws of England and should not have the benefit of those laws.

The conference continued on the next day at which time the Lords committees desired the judges to deliver their advice and opinion in the point of the law. Lord Chief Justice Sir John Popham, in a long discourse, spoke not only for himself but for Sir Edward Coke, Chief Justice of the Common Pleas, and for Sir Thomas Fleming, Lord Chief Baron. Popham made comments on the laws of England and turned to the question that had been raised of law and allegiance. Allegiance was more spacious than the law. It was before the law and continued after the law. It was what the law was not. It was tied to the body natural of the King, and not to the body politic.[19] From Sir Edward Coke he quoted statutes supporting that opinion.

The judges examined what was to be given the Scots, if they should be naturalized, and answered the question by saying that they were to be protected in their bodies and goods and to be able to bring personal actions. As for voices in Parliament and other dignities, the Scots could not have them "so long as the laws stand distinct."

On February 28 and on March 2 Bacon presented the report of

the conference. One of his comments is worth recording. The question of naturalization was held affirmatively by the judges and negatively by the House of Commons, but there had been concessions on both sides. The Commons admitted the union in the King's person, and the judges conceded the distinction in law between the two nations. "Now whether the one of these do draw on or involve the other, that is the *oculus questionis.*" [20] This effort to bridge the gap in opinion was typical of an earlier Bacon.

When the conference had been fully reported on March 2, a few speeches followed. Fuller reverted to the place of the judges and repeated what had been said before, that a judge in his own court was one thing; his opinion as a counselor and assistant was another. "In this place none between us and God" surely suggestion of the supremacy of Parliament over other courts. The King, continued Fuller, could not naturalize any more than he could give away the ports.

Hyde, seldom a partisan of royalty, differed from Fuller. The Commons themselves, he said, were in doubt about naturalization. For them to make a declaration against the King's right would, if there were any doubt at all, be against their consciences. For them to say no to the King's right, they must have a case as clear as sunlight. To do so otherwise would provoke "just discontent." [21] Even if the *Post-Nati* were naturalized, they were not capable of inheritance from their ancestors and would not be for the next twenty years. He moved that the *Post-Nati* should be disabled in certain respects until there should be a perfect union. He hoped that the Commons would not follow the Instrument of Union in every detail.[22] About that possibility Hyde need not have worried.

At this point a message was brought from the Lords. During the March days and weeks following there were many messages back and forth, and those exchanges reveal more about the changing relations between the two Houses than any other information available. They are worth recounting.

The Lords sent word that they sought to keep step with the Commons. As they understood it, no topic discussed had yet been decided. Only one topic had been in question, and upon that they had delivered no opinion. What they now desired was another conference about naturalization, so that each House might better understand the inclination of the other.[23] That request the Commons promised to consider. But they must have been puzzled as to their next move. Were the Lords rushing them into a decision for His Majesty?

On the next morning, March 3, a select committee met about the request of the Lords, and Hoby reported that, in the judgment of the committee, the Commons should discuss the convenience and limitations of naturalization of the *Post-Nati*, as well as of the *Ante-Nati*.[24] The Lords were then informed that, when the Commons were ready, they would send word. The former committee was named to meet and consider the answer from the Lords; to it were added Martin, Sir Henry Montague, and the Privy Councillors of the House.

The following day Hoby reported that twenty-one (of the twenty-seven) members of the committee had met. It had been moved, probably by a Privy Councillor, that time had been lost and that the Commons should now bring to pass the holy desire of His Majesty's heart. The Commons knew that, although the Lords had heard the pronouncement of the judges, they had not finally committed themselves, hoping presumably to make it easier for the Commons. But the committee resolved to inform the Lords that, if they proposed to treat of the *Post-Nati*, the Lords were already aware of the opinion of the Commons, and that the Commons had heard nothing to alter that opinion. If the Lords wished to confer on the convenience of naturalization they thought it fittest that those best acquainted with state affairs should make a beginning. They hoped the Lords would deal freely with them.[25] Evidently the Privy Councillors added to the committee had not been able to induce that body to shift its position. But the Commons, while maintaining their position, were at pains in their reply to leave out any phrases "which should argue a conceit of a diversity of opinion." It was determined also to speak of their own "inclination" rather than "opinion." Meanwhile the Commons authorized the committee to consider in the afternoon the point of conveniency.

When Hoby delivered the message to the Lords, they asked him to repeat it and then, after a pause, requested his delay for a while. At length they complained of his phraseology in speaking of the Commons; [26] they complained further that the Commons were using "reservation" with them, whereas they had dealt with the Commons in all freedom. If the Commons intended really to meet with them in conference, they hoped it might be with the same committee at the same time on the following Saturday (this was Wednesday). They hoped that when they expected a conference they would not be given merely an audience.[27]

On March 5 Martin reported from the Lords that the committee of the Lords would meet with them on the coming Saturday and join with them "in this great business." [28]

At some time near this date Wingfield wrote to Salisbury:

> Whatsoever is informed by the King, I do freely confess to your Lordship that our House is fully bent to give contentment to the King by taking away the hostile laws; by admitting of commerce, and naturalizing, with reservation of some natural, needful conditions, and these but for a time. . . . For the matter of law whereof we have already conferred, I think the greater opinion of our House is to have it quit of all sides and no more to be spoken on. There is a business also in our House of the King's displeasure towards us, and of the dissolving of the Parliament, but I hope it is not true.[29]

Wingfield's letter, in its optimism about an outcome pleasing to His Majesty, is surprising. As for the threat of a dissolution, this is the first mention of it in the literature of the time.

On March 7 Sandys asked more time for the Grand Committee. They had found that from the multitude of objections the truth emerged. In consequence they had resolved to swerve from the Instrument of Union and to wrap up the *Ante-Nati* and the *Post-Nati* together. If the Lords pressed upon them the opinion of the judges, the committee believed that the Commons should dissent, but modestly. The judges had not heard the reasons of the Commons.

The Perfect
Union Proposed

AT this time Sandys displayed his capacity for decisive action. From the committee he brought in a program that he had no doubt been pondering for some time. As the committee looked at it, two kinds of union were possible: one where the two kingdoms remained distinct; the other where the two kingdoms were merged into one. The committee favored the latter alternative—the perfect union. They proposed that the Scots should be governed by English laws and participate in all benefits along with the English. The committee professed to believe that His Majesty really desired a perfect union. Meanwhile, the less the English yielded to the desire of the Scots for an imperfect union, it was asserted, the easier they would find it to induce the Scots to join in the perfect union.[1] For the most part, the members agreed that some benefits should be offered to all subjects born in Scotland, but that, so long as the two kingdoms stood divided, other benefits to the northerners should be withheld.[2] But such reservations and limitations as they might suggest might easily be annulled, it was pointed out, by a *non obstante* from His Majesty. It was maintained, however, that the King could dispense with the penalties of a statute but not with the statute itself and that, where a law was enacted without a money penalty, the King could not grant a *non obstante*.[3]

It had been asserted in the committee that Scots enjoyed the profits of English lands, but did not share in the burdens and charges involved in ownership. The committee believed that only those who lived within the country should inherit lands and that when Scots inherited English lands they should be subject to all charges and laws.

It was alleged that the Scots carried such treasure as rents from their lands home to Scotland and thus made themselves rich and the English poor. The reporter from the committee became philosophical. He presented an economic interpretation of history. Poverty was the cause of discontent, and discontent was the cause of all innovations. Finally it was decided that the transportation of money into Scotland should be proposed to the Lords for discussion by them.[4]

Wardship had been brought up in the committee. Should Scots be given guardianship over English wards? The committee hoped that the Lords would consider that question.[5] About ecclesiastical preferments it had been agreed that the Scots should receive one in ten and that no Scot should hold two benefices. Nor was a Scot to become a bishop in England.[6]

To hold any ecclesiastical preferment, a Scot would have to be a graduate of an English university; to hold any benefice he would have to be an M.A. To hold any dignity, presumably a canonry or deanery, he would have to be a Bachelor of Divinity. By those provisions nearly all Scots would have been excluded from the good things that the Church might offer.

So far the committee, in the limited time at its disposal, had been able to deal only with questions raised. About secular offices the committee had doubts. At first they had been inclined to allow Scots to be justices of the peace, sheriffs, escheators, etc., but, after deliberation, had decided to put this problem before the Upper House. Was it not possible that the clause in the Instrument of Union that denied offices of judicature to Scots would apply?[7]

On many problems connected with the union there were differences of opinion, and it is interesting how often those difficult questions were referred to the Lords. But the committee had done much. How had Sir Edwin been able to gain the support of the committee for such a program? What had Bacon and others of his outlook to say to all this? It must never be overlooked that Sir Edwin had great skill in presenting a case and in persuading his fellows of its validity. He had to convince both those bearing anti-Scottish prejudice and those at Court who were following His Majesty about the Scots. By some legerdemain he was able to bring from the committee a responsible and moderate set of proposals that would not antagonize either the Scots at Court or the anti-Scots in the Commons too greatly. The report even expressed a certain deference to the Lords.

For the conference the Commons named a series of members to speak on various topics: the laws touching *Ante-Nati* and *Post-Nati;* the holding of lands and of other property by Scots; the problems of Scots and wardships; and so forth. Hedley, who was assigned to speak on "assurance," was "against it, in his opinion." He was excused by resolution of the House [8] and used in another capacity. By assurance was meant security that the King would keep his promise. It was further pointed out that the promise "died with this natural body," and would not bind his successors.[9]

At the conference in the afternoon Salisbury declared that the Lords aimed at a perfect union with restrictions, but with fewer restrictions for *Post-Nati* than for *Ante-Nati*, as provided in the Instrument of Union. Sandys reiterated his stand for the perfect union. He was hopeful that, if the Commons dealt liberally with the Scots, while withholding from them some privileges, the Scots might remove the restrictions against the English.[10]

The Great Committee continued to meet. On Thursday, March 12, Sandys reviewed in the House the preparations for a conference to be held on March 14. The Commons were resolved to listen to the reasons of the Lords about the *Post-Nati* and *Ante-Nati*, but not to yield to them. They were indeed eager to clear themselves from the imputation leveled against the opposition in the Lower House.

It is a fair guess that some peer had implied that Sandys's scheme for a perfect union was a strategem for defeating the whole project of a union. If the imputation was to that effect, historians might indeed wonder if the peer were not right. By calling for a more perfect union, Sandys might raise among those who disliked the Scots an opposition strong enough to kill any kind of union. It was easy to assume that Sandys was playing a smooth game to outwit His Majesty.

Such an imputation would have been unwarranted. Sandys was not acting by himself but in behalf of a committee, and a committee could not easily have been drawn into such a maneuver. If Sandys had been one to sacrifice a pawn in order to open a file for attack, he could not have carried the committee with him. They had wrestled with the difficulties of an imperfect union and had convinced themselves that a perfect union provided them with a simpler and more workable solution. It put them in an easily defensible position.

At the conference on the afternoon of March 14 Salisbury stood by the Instrument, "framed by men whom we trusted . . . with the Commonwealth." As for lands the Lords were willing to grant the Scots the right to purchase inheritances. He did not believe that the Scots would gain by transporting treasure to their country from England; they would still have to pay taxes for their lands in England. But the Lords were willing, nevertheless, to make it a penal offense to transport money out of Scotland, as out of England. As for the Scottish wrongdoers in England who escaped to Scotland, the Lords were willing that means should be devised to overcome that inconvenience. About ecclesiastical preferments, the Lords in some respects agreed with the Commons but would make an exception of those benefices in the gift of the Crown.

The problem of Scotland's ties with France the Lords hoped might be deferred till they could consider it further. To a casual observer, removed in time, it would seem that the Lords were making an effort to meet the Commons halfway.

Sandys stood up to reply. He alluded to the great trust committed to the House of Commons by the whole commonwealth,[11] implying, I assume, that it was committed to them as the elected representatives of the people of England.

The Commons had to balance their care and wariness, Sandys insisted, against the weightiness of the business. Naturalization extended not to one branch of the kingdom but to the whole body; it concerned not one kind of benefits or privileges but all the realm could afford. It was not communicated to a few of the deserving but to a multitude. It was for all time.[12] They had to consider what state of the commonwealth they would transmit to posterity.

The committee, he said, envisaged a perfect union. An imperfect union was a crooked and knotty stick that had to be hewed and pared before it could be used. The Scots had been to blame for the imperfect union proposed when they inserted the clause that their fundamental laws and privileges should not be altered. In the long run two nations with the same liberties, but separate as to laws and customs, might come to hate rather than to love one another. It was not fit, he asserted, to grant privileges of naturalization, unlimited in the event of an imperfect union. That led him directly into the question of the *Post-Nati,* and with that part of his speech and its effect we shall deal in the next section.

The Commons and the Lords Collide

IN the conclusion of his speech Sandys told the Lords that he had been enjoined by the Commons to say that they would not yield to the plan to create a difference between those born since the accession of the King and those born before. Unless the Commons might treat the two together, they would give the Lords audience, but proceed no farther in conference. There was more steel in the seemingly gentle Sandys than his colleagues might have supposed. He had put his faith in reason and would follow where it led.

Why did the Commons insist so stubbornly on making no difference between those born before and after? I am not sure of the answer. It may be that they feared that there would be no restrictions placed upon those born after, since they could not figure in affairs for nearly a score of years and that, in the meantime, His Majesty might, by virtue of his prerogative, give denization to the *Ante-Nati,* and with no more restrictions than had been put on the *Post-Nati.*

In general the Commons were objecting to the imperfect union because it was provided in the Instrument of Union that, while the Scots were to be given rights and privileges in England, the English were not to receive equivalent privileges in Scotland. "We are tied," said Sandys, "to the imperfect Union, not by our own choice, but by the Act of Parliament made by the Scottish nation, and the proceedings of the Commissioners accordingly." [1]

His Majesty and those around him suspected the Commons of a more subtle reason for opposing the imperfect union, one connected with the judges. It will be recalled that in the conference between the two Houses at the end of February the judges had been in attendance and had spoken strongly in support of the naturalization of the Scots. On March 15 Salisbury wrote Lake that the King

> rightly noteth that, to which indeed the House is most inwardly affected, which is to get some such definite sentence passed in the House of the invalidity of the Judges' resolution as may make them dainty hereafter to judge the question, or make the judgment less acceptable.[2]

When Sandys told the Lords that the Commons would not yield on the question of the difference between the *Post-Nati* and the *Ante-Nati* he was presenting the Peers with an ultimatum. It was the boldest refusal to cooperate with the Upper House that the Commons of that generation had ever made. I do not recall any such refusal in Elizabethan days.

No wonder the Lords put "their heads together over the Board," and conferred a while. Then Salisbury explained that it had been intended that more should speak and those "better able than he that had spoken." [3] He went on:

> But now we have resolved to give the Lower House no such conference as shall bear the title of an audience. . . . Wherefore since this day is rather a narrative than a conference . . . we will shut it up without giving reasons, until we may meet on a conference, not an audience, with this, that we may never meet with them who are like to take a dissent for displeasure.[4]

On that sharp note Salisbury broke off the conference.[5] Seldom in his long parliamentary career had he come so close to losing his temper. He was not given to making scenes, but then he had seldom been at the receiving end of an ultimatum.

Of what followed we learn something from Salisbury's letter to Lake, who was in attendance upon His Majesty in the country. He informed Lake that the Speaker had his directions "to remember his provisional order," in case a motion about the judges should be offered in the Commons. What the provisional order was we can only guess. But the Speaker found himself suddenly under the weather and unable to attend the House. Salisbury discouraged him from venturing out until he felt better. When the Speaker learned that members were murmuring about his absence, he thought of resuming his chair in the Commons for an hour, but Salisbury "sufficiently prepared him in that point." [6]

Salisbury was perhaps concerned lest the King should hurry back to London; he was familiar with the King's habit of working himself up into a tantrum. For himself he moved as one calmly confident that, if he waited long enough, the Lower House would come to realize the error of their ways and send messengers to explain themselves. "In the meantime," he wrote, "we will be doing that which we think fittest for his Majesty's princely ends." Within a few days the Speaker felt better, but was encouraged to remain away from the House. "I may not hide it from you," wrote Salisbury to Lake, "that in this point of the difference between *Post-Nati* and *Ante-Nati* there is a great heat of spirit kindled to decide it by a question in the Lower House." [7] Salisbury was not likely to be unaware of the importance of public opinion, though he never, so far as I know, used the phrase, and it was one that had not yet come into general usage. But men often sense a reality before they give it a name. Moreover, it will be recalled that Bacon had talked about the power of opinion only a short while before.

At length, on March 27, the Lords made the first move. They sent a message to the Lower House craving another conference "touching the conveniency of naturalization of the Scottish nation, both *Ante-* and *Post-Nati*." [8] The conference was to be "free and liberal." They hoped to hear the reasons set forth and discussed on both sides, "without dealing with the matter in law." Neither party was to be bound by anything spoken, but each was to endeavor to learn the inclination of the other. The Easter recess was at hand, and the Lords requested an answer as soon as possible.

The astute Martin had urged the Commons to wait,[9] and he had proved right. Salisbury had recognized the excitement of the Lower House but had guessed wrong as to their yielding. In the test of wills between the two bodies the Commons had the better of it. Had Salisbury at length realized that he was rowing upstream against a strong current?

Hyde was soon on his feet to support a meeting with the Lords, but he hoped that the Commons would stick to their resolution to deal with the *Ante-Nati* and the *Post-Nati* together. It was the King's desire and that of the Commons, he believed, that there should be a perfect union. That could be accomplished only by making both peoples subject to the same laws. A year had been spent, and little progress made. The Instrument of Union had proved a hindrance to the Commons. The real difficulty had been the reservations of the Scots. It was an abuse also in Scotland that a few great persons had the power to pardon such crimes as treason, murder, and manslaughter—powers unfit for mere subjects. He suspected that the Scots would gladly yield subjection to English law. He failed to reckon with memories of battles lost long ago: Pinkie Cleuch, Ancrum Moor, Flodden Field, and Homildon Hill.

Then he tried what modern diplomats call a fresh approach. The Commons had hoped for redress of grievances and had been disappointed. Might a bargain be struck? If the English gave the Scots sufficient encouragement, might His Majesty consent to ease the burdens of his suffering subjects in England? In making such a suggestion, he underestimated the pressure that those who stood to gain from wardship and purveyance could bring to bear upon a weak sovereign.

Hyde concluded by saying that, if the Scottish Parliament would renew and enlarge their commission, the English Parliament would in far less time debate and bring about a perfect union, a hopefulness nothing less than touching.

It is possible that Hyde was speaking for a group of members who were profoundly discouraged about grievances unredressed and yet aware that the project for a perfect union had upset the best-laid plans of Crown and Court and rendered those powers conceivably more amenable to compromise. Hyde's particular proposal came to nothing, but the anti-Scot interest was still to be reckoned with.

On March 28 a long discussion as to what to do next was opened by Dudley Carleton. Readers will remember that Carleton had looked back wistfully to those salad days in the Lower House when he had been a "mutineer." Many a man involved in any kind of group activity, as he leaves his youth, likes to picture himself as having been in his twenties a rebel and a pirate.

Nowadays Carleton waved no pirate flag. He had been abroad, had served in a small diplomatic berth, had prepared himself carefully for public service, and, as part of a circle on good terms with Salisbury, had hopes of advancement. If ever he had toyed with mutiny, he was now on the side of the quarterdeck.

At this point he suggested that the Commons treat with the Lords about the *Post-Nati* with such restrictions as they desired, and that then they should treat with them about the *Ante-Nati* in the same way. He was offering what might have been a compromise solution.

Edward Duncombe, M.P. for Tavistock in Devonshire, but a Bedfordshire man who seldom spoke in the Commons, disagreed with Carleton and hoped that the Commons would stand by their guns; they should spend no time in conferences, but await what bills the Lords might send them.

Sir Herbert Croft, a Herefordshire squire who usually had something worth saying, wished the Commons might consider among themselves the matter of convenience, not in committee, but in the House. He had observed that in committees truth was often beaten out; yet he had also observed that in committees, when everyone might reply, some special persons of place prevailed by speaking often and by "countenance" rather than by reason.

As to the Scots he asserted that in their treaty with the English they had managed to give us "merely nothing." To give way to them was to hinder the perfect union.

It had been maintained that such a union would require time. He thought otherwise. If the Scots had as sincere a mind toward the English as the English had toward them, the Commission for the Union could be renewed and enlarged, as Hyde had suggested the day before. He believed that if His Majesty understood how much the Commons desired the perfect union, he would not dislike it. He wished they might think of some way to let the King learn how they felt.[10] He was probably aware that those around the King were out of sympathy with the Commons and that few of the leaders of that House could hope to present their views in conversation with His Majesty. His Majesty, in his liking for complaisant courtiers, had cut himself off from learning public opinion.

Bacon followed Croft and talked first about the union of laws. If England and Scotland had one law, they would never separate.[11] A reconciliation would not be hard to bring about because there was a correspondence between the laws of the two kingdoms.[12] The union of the laws would be the more desirable because the English laws were in confusion and chaos; [13] they needed to be reviewed. Those laws, heaped up rather than digested, proved snares for the people.[14]

But this was not the time, declared Sir Francis, to establish such a union. Never would there be a real unity until the mark of the stranger had been removed from the Scots. "No bird or beast is taught anything before you feed him." As for naturalization the *Ante-Nati* should be treated more liberally than the *Post-Nati*.[15]

Sir Roger Owen returned to the ways of birds mentioned by Bacon. When their feathers molted, they were sick; he noted the want of attendance of members as a sign of the illness of Parliament. As for birds, Owen declared that those in the air could not be enticed by feeding, as if to say that it was of no use to offer favors to the Scots in the hope that they would offer better terms.

Sir Roger believed that the Commons should not confer with

the Lords, but should present to the King their reasons for embracing a perfect union. The Attorney, Hobart, and Sir George More hoped for a conference. Sir George deplored the many protestations and the repetition of arguments. His boredom must have been shared by many.[16]

On Monday, March 30, the Speaker raised the question as to what answer was to be given to the Upper House. Should they confer without binding themselves or touching on points of law?

Sir John Heigham moved to answer the Lords that the Commons would consider the message from the Lords but asked time to deliberate. At their next meeting, after the recess, they would give an answer.

Then up spoke Edward Alford, M.P. for Colchester, who in three sessions had seldom risen to his feet but who in the 1620s was to prove himself a significant figure. He was given to an old English bluntness. The last conference, he observed, had broken up over the matter of *Post-Nati* and *Ante-Nati*. If the Lords were moving for another conference "in the same point and fashion," he knew no reason why the Commons should change their minds. When Alford sat down the Speaker announced that the King wished to address the House at 2:00 p.m. the next day at Whitehall.

The King Intervenes   JAMES'S discourse was long and diffuse.[1] He allowed himself heavy-handed allusions to "delicate speeches," and "precogitate orations," a fling perhaps at Sandys whose speeches were obviously prepared and whose words were often pat ("delicate").

A long time had been spent, declared His Majesty, upon the union.[2] When he first proposed it, he had assumed that there would be no question about it. He had not realized the fears of others or the strange questions that would be asked. Was it because of some jealousy perhaps of him as the propounder that they added delay to delay? James seldom admitted unpopularity; he liked to believe that he was beloved of his subjects. They did not know him, he remarked, as well as they would hereafter. But they all knew that the King's will and intention was the speaking law and ought to be clearer than light. It was as impossible for a King to govern two countries—the one large, the other small, the one poor, the larger one drawing the smaller like a magnet—as for a husband to have two wives. When he had spoken of a perfect union he had not meant the confusion of all things. The English must not take from the Scots their particular privileges that went as well with the union as the customs of the several shires, which were a part of the common law of England.[3] James had a way of passing lightly over the hard questions.

That led him to turn from the question at issue to the common law. It was the best in the world, but was, nevertheless, full of uncertainties and should be looked over and swept clear of rust. There was truth in what the King said, but few of those before him, many of whom had been trained in the Inns of Court, would have applauded.

When Scotland was united with England, there would be occasion to amend and polish the laws. But the uniting of the two bodies of law could not take place without preparation; without decades of effort, he might have added.

Those who advocated a perfect union and allowed no time for preparation had honey in their mouths but gall in their hearts. He continued: "If, after your so long talk of Union . . . ye rise without agreeing upon any particular, what will the neighbour princes judge?"

It was the English rather than the Scots who would profit from the Union. Is not here the seat of justice and the fountain of government?

There was a notion current that the union would lead to the overthrow of England and the setting up of Scotland. "To you shall be left the sweat and labor; to them shall be given the fruit and sweet." As to his policy in such matters, let them judge him by his actions.

He could have disposed, without assent of Parliament, of offices of judicature and of other offices, but he had offered voluntarily to bind his prerogative in that respect. "If hitherto I have done nothing to your prejudice, much less mean I hereafter." True, he had reasonably rewarded his Scottish supporters who might claim any extraordinary merit, but now there were none left for whom he would make a special effort. His first three years, he admitted, had been as Christmas, but "suits go not now so cheap as they were wont." It would be found that former princes had spent far more than he. He was thinking possibly of Henry VIII.

The King turned to his demands about the union. Hostile laws should be done away with. There should be a community of commerce. As for naturalization, they would all agree that the Scots were not aliens, and yet they would not "allow them to be natural." English lawyers and judges had informed him at his first coming that the *Post-Nati* were naturalized, and, in consequence, he had published a proclamation to that effect. He asked them not to discredit ("disgrace") that proclamation or the judges. There must be a difference between *Ante-Nati* and *Post-Nati*. The latter would live age after age. The Union, he continued, would bring peace, plenty, love, free intercourse, and a common society to two great nations.

He reverted to a topic mentioned earlier. The English feared that the Scots would eat their commons bare and make England lean. Could anyone imagine that he would respect the lesser and neglect the greater? Had he not been careful to preserve the English woods and game? His critics might have smiled at that statement. He had his own personal reasons for saving woods and game. If he wished to show partiality to the Scots to the hurt of the English, he went on, it lay within his own hands and power to do so.

As for making aliens citizens, it was part of his prerogative. If there were any doubt about the law, then *rex est lex*. As for community of commerce, it might be that some towns and corporations would suffer. "It may be a merchant or two of Bristol or Yarmouth, may have a hundred pounds less in his pack, but if the Empire gain and become the greater, it is no matter." He was putting it well, but the truth is that he never understood the significance nor the importance of English businessmen. He had used the word "Empire." Would he have been pleased to be its emperor?

He took up the inconveniences arising from the union under three heads: that the Scots had an evil feeling toward the union, that a union was incompatible between two such nations, and that the gain from the union was small or none. In proof of the first point it had been alleged that the Scots had arranged in the Instrument of Union that they were to remain an absolute and free monarchy and retain the fundamental laws of their kingdom. This charge, he said, did not fit in well with the opinion of the Commons of England that the Scots were eager for the union. James had a way of approaching an argument from the side rather than head-on. He had an active and an acute mind, but he was not always logical. He went on to make the boast often quoted: "This I must say for Scotland, and I may truly vaunt it; here I sit and govern it with my pen; I write and it is done; and by a Clerk of the Council I govern Scotland now, which others could not do by the sword." In earlier days he had reduced an unruly nation to subjection, and he was not unaware of this accomplishment. Was he also hinting that strong government by him would be of advantage to England?

James took up the idea put forth in the Commons that the Scots should forsake their arrangements with France before they could expect to be united with England. The league between France and Scotland, he asserted, was only between princes. "In my time when it came to be ratified, because it appeared to be *in odium tertii,* it was by me left unrenewed or confirmed, as a thing incompatible to my person in consideration of my title to this Crown." He admitted that some privileges to merchants had been renewed or confirmed in his time, but it had been a matter left to Councillors, in which he had not meddled.

In conclusion James stressed the advantages to England by the union. Increased territory meant increased greatness. The back doors, Scotland and Ireland, by which England might be attacked, would be forever closed.

He ended with a characteristic assumption of virtue: "For I will not say anything which I will not promise, nor promise anything which I will not swear; what I swear I will sign; and what I sign shall, with God's grace ever perform." James really believed that his word was that of a King, to use a favorite phrase of his. He had the greatest confidence in his own integrity, he relied also upon his "great judgment," and he liked to display his wide knowledge.

But he thought always of himself and, like many egocentrics, acted impulsively and talked recklessly. He could indulge in what is called in the American South "sweet talk" and in the same speech slip into threats. He warned the Commons that when Parliament was adjourned the judges had power over their lands and lives, which was precisely the menace to their property that country gentlemen feared. It is to be said for him that he seldom lived up to his worst threats; he preferred calling men in and badgering them or snubbing them in public view.

Yet in the matter of the Union, he did have a largeness of view, which many of the Commons lacked, and which he failed to show in other matters.

One wonders how such speeches as the one just summarized were received, but there is little information. From isolated bits of evidence one might infer that the middle and upper classes, who had had a chance to appraise their sovereign and had yearned to look up to him, found it hard to do so.

*The Perfect
Union Again*

ON April 20 the Commons returned from the recess, but attendance was slim; the two Houses adjourned again until April 27. On the following day Sir Edwin Sandys addressed the House in a long plea for the perfect union. It was the speech of one who had given thought to English institutions and was not unfamiliar with English history, as it was then understood, and he was more aware of the polity of continental nations than most of those whom he addressed. He set forth propositions that had hardly been worded so definitely before and that may seem to us worn out, but to his hearers were far from that.

With tact he began by quoting the King. His Majesty believed in *unus Rex, unus Grex, una Lex*. It could not have been better put. From Proverbs he quoted: "A divine sentence shall be in the mouth of the King." The King's speech was to him and "may be to us a path to proceed on."

He advanced logically. There could not be one flock until there was one law. That one body of law to be made by one Parliament. The King governed in his person through the laws. The making of laws was communicated to the people "in all just governments," which was not exactly the same as James's *rex est lex*. Sovereignty in the making of laws was in the King and people. It was just and natural that every man be bound by his own act, that is, an act made by his elected representative. For that, one Parliament was necessary, one Great Seal, one Chancellor. He was proceeding logically.

Sandys turned to the imperfect union and pointed out its difficulties. Such a union might be a hindrance to justice. The perfect union could be brought about with less trouble and more benefit. Under the perfect union the various problems, that of the *Post-Nati* and *Ante-Nati*, that of the Scottish alliance with France, and that of naturalization, would disappear.

The uniting of the laws of the two nations would afford an opportunity for reviewing English laws, which were not in as high reputation as formerly. He urged the English to review those laws and to make one code for England and Scotland. The King could more easily govern both kingdoms when they were subject to one law.

As for the nation to be made from joining two, Sandys was far from convinced that the great kingdoms were the happiest. Yet since their neighbors across the Channel had grown so great, it was fit for the British to do the same. Nor did he believe that the back door of England, that is, Scotland and Ireland, had to be closed, as had been asserted. Since the English had given up their claims in France, it was not to be supposed that France would aid Scotland.

He approached the problem of commerce. If the Scots would submit to English laws, he would be glad to see them granted equal rights, at least until the perfect union could be brought about. If, in the meantime, the Scots took advantage of those rights, they might be duly punished.

He offered an immediate program: to abrogate hostile laws, to pass an act to authorize commissioners to prepare a perfect union. If the Commons had to proceed with an imperfect union, he hoped that it might be limited in time while the commissioners made ready a new Instrument.[1]

He protested that he spoke by commandment and from his heart; that is, he was speaking for the committee but was also uttering his own convictions. We can guess that he had been able to dominate the committee.

For four days, April 28–May 1, the debate continued. Sandys's plea for the perfect union was supported by Sir Herbert Croft, Nicholas Fuller, Edward Alford,[2] Sir Roger Owen, William Holt of Lancashire, Lawrence Hyde, and Yelverton. It was opposed by Sir George More, Sir Francis Bacon, the Recorder (Montague), the Attorney General (Hobart), Brooke, Dudley Carleton, and Wingfield, as well as by three members usually arrayed against the King, Wentworth, Martin, and Hakewill.

Those who came to the support of Sandys emphasized the "rubs" encountered in formulating an imperfect union. The committee found itself "stalled." They still had knots and doubts, even in the matter of hostile laws.[3] Might not the judges, who told them that the laws (made upon such good ground) touching purveyance could not bind the prerogative, tell them the same about any restrictions they might put upon the union? [4]

In spite of all the evidence to the contrary a few supporters of Sandys seemed to have convinced themselves that the King was really in favor of the perfect union.[5] Had he not caused to be inscribed on the new golden coins the words: *"Faciamus eos in gentem unam?"* [6]

It was suggested that a committee should draw up the reasons that prompted the Commons, in spite of the opinion of the judges, to take up the cause of the perfect union.[7] They wished that the King could understand their desires and intentions ("minds").[8]

Their fears of the imperfect union were based in some degree, as we have seen, on the conviction that in the framing of the Instrument of Union the Scots had overreached them; they suspected that the Scots would not wish a perfect union lest they lose what they had gained.[9] Already the Scots had at Dieppe all the trade in kerseys.[10] They were advanced in England whereas no Englishman was advanced in Scotland.[11] To give them so many advantages over the English, and then perhaps later on, when a perfect union became feasible, to withdraw those advantages, would create bitterness between the two nations.[12] But if a perfect union were set up at the beginning and if the Scots were to live under English laws, they would become one with the English, and then the English, when they bestowed privileges, would be doing so for their own kind.[13]

Lawrence Hyde was in favor of the perfect union, but wished, nevertheless, to proceed with the abolition of the hostile laws.[14] Yelverton agreed with him in general, believing it would be wrong not to go ahead with the imperfect union.[15]

Sandys's project was opposed by the Speaker,[16] who told the House that the Lords were expecting an answer about a conference and about the *Post-Nati* and *Ante-Nati*. Martin and Bacon asserted that this was not the time for the perfect union. That might come later. To set up new commissioners and to draw up a new Instrument of Union, Bacon declared, was to throw away four years of work and one year of sessions. To form a perfect union was the work of an age.[17] The Attorney warned the members that the Scottish nation, having waited three years for the imperfect union, would not welcome a new project. If in three years the members had been unable to establish an imperfect union they would not set up a perfect union in three times three years. To those who implied that the King himself favored a perfect union, it was replied that he did not think it fit to be brought about yet.[18]

Dudley Carleton made a good debating point against the perfect union. It could hardly prove effective; inconveniences of one kind and another would be revealed, and members would find themselves once more dealing with an imperfect union. Wentworth raised a practical objection. The House of Commons was already so large that the Speaker could hardly moderate; no room could contain the increased membership.[19]

Bacon called the project a "digression." Then he bethought himself and said it had been spoken (by Sandys) *ex candore animi,* that is, in sincerity. That qualification he spoiled at once by adding that the project showed "much art." [20] Was he trying to impeach Sandys's honesty of intention without seeming to do so? The Attorney General was more direct. It was believed abroad, he asserted, that the new project was "but a stratagem to evade and do nothing." [21] Speakers sometimes veiled their own opinions with the phrase: "It was believed abroad."

Another Royal Address:
Conclusion

AT the close of the day on May 1 the Speaker informed the House that His Majesty had heard several constructions of his late speech, and he requested no further dispute before the Commons had attended him the next day at 2.00 p.m. in the Great Chamber at Whitehall.

James told the Commons that as a good gardener he wished to take away the weeds and brambles; that is, to explain himself. "I have not hindered any speech, for it is not my manner." [1] Some had understood him as desiring a perfect union. He proposed an absolute and full union, but not a perfect union.

The commissioners whom they had chosen had brought forth something in a form fit to proceed upon. As for another commission, he would not grant it. He recalled a speech in Henry VIII's Parliament in which the King propounded something. One of the members asserted that the meaning of the King was good, so it were according to law. At the very words uttered in the reign of Henry VIII James grew excited: "I pray you, my Masters, that I may hear no more of such foolish diversions and aversions." [2]

As for the perfect union they had it in him, the head. The accomplished and full union would take time and means. At the outset he had craved a perfect union, but the whole body (did he mean the Parliament?) had drawn back and had said it could not be dispatched at once; they devised what restrictions they could to tie it within bounds.

He alluded to a comment made by a member of the Commons that with the King in London they were more in danger of the royal thunderbolts. He became sarcastic and offered to spend alternate years in London and Scotland. Or he would keep the Court nearer Scotland, say at York, so that both the Commons and the Scots should be far removed from his thunderbolts.[3]

As for the argument that there could be no security for such restrictions as should be agreed on, he could not answer, for he was not well skilled in the English common law. If he could give security, why could not Parliament enter into consideration of it and accept it? If he could not, then they had to leave all to him after the Parliament, to do what he would. "If anything light upon you other than you looked for, you must take and bear that, which your own folly hath brought you unto."

Later in the same speech he threatened again:

> It is no marvel if men of that coat have neither hopes nor fears from me, and fear I shall be well advised, what I do with them . . . I am your King. I am placed to govern you, and shall answer for your errors; I am a man of flesh and blood and have my passions and affections as other men. I pray you, do not too far move me to do that which my power may tempt me unto.

He had started with smooth and conciliatory words, as if he had little to say to them except that they continue in their courses. Speaking seemed to bring out his latent indignation. He began like a lamb, but he did not conclude like one. Nor did he have the dignity or assurance to play the lion. He asked them to proceed with order and diligence, but above all with love for their sovereign. They were to beware of fanatical spirits.

The threat that members should suffer for their unwise speeches and Wingfield's admission that he had reported a speech in the House to the King led members to forget the question before them and to talk of free speech. That was a topic upon which feelings, already exacerbated by the debate over the union, ran high. Freedom was of the essence. Proposals and attitudes were many, and I can touch upon them only as they were an indication of the tension in the House.

It was proposed that when the King wished to learn the truth as to what had been said that he should send for the Speaker of the House or that he should inquire from one of the Privy Council, proposals that would have met with scant support in the House. It was also suggested that members should be allowed to clear themselves to the King,[4] or that they should be cleared by vote of the House. To the last idea Sandys voiced his opposition. It was part of the King's disposition and clemency, he said, that he meant no wrong to members, a statement that had a scintilla of truth in it. Sandys was presumably hoping to appeal to the better nature of His Majesty. He had himself set down, he declared, his own meaning on what he had spoken in the House.

Sir George More, who was never unaware of the case for His Majesty, believed that members should have a free voice in the making of laws. The punishment of those who talked too freely should lie in their own consciences and in the realization that their words were known to the King. He regarded the liberties of the House as never less abridged than in this Parliament.[5] He might have said, than in the last twenty years of the late Queen's reign. Incidentally, he remarked of Sandys's speech: *"Qui in ore laudat, in corde flagellat.* Therefore he would not commend Sir Edwin Sandys."

The Speaker told the House that he had it from His Majesty that he was ready at any time to suspend his judgment until he heard apparent proof of details and that he would be glad to allow any member to explain himself to him. As for the ancient liberty of the House, His Majesty would always be more jealous for the preservation thereof than the members themselves. His Majesty accounted that man not worthy of his place (within the limitation mentioned earlier) who would not freely speak his conscience.[6]

Fine words butter no parsnips. Members, who looked over the

statement carefully and had experienced the impatience of their sovereign with criticism, would not have been reassured. They were dealing with a topic, the union, about which His Majesty was ultra-sensitive and about which many members were emotional. They knew that to speak out about the Scots was to look for trouble. Yet there were those who did speak out and who hoped, perhaps, to arouse a public opinion that might carry weight with the King's Councillors. In the long run they would be successful in their effort to create a historical privilege, even though there was no great body of precedents behind that privilege.

The House did not follow His Majesty's injunction to begin where they had left off.[7] After the discussion of free speech on May 7, William Brock, M.P. for St. Ives in Cornwall, moved that the Bill against Hostile Laws should be committed. That bill was to annul all laws against the Scots that had been passed in England from the reign of Richard II to that of Queen Elizabeth, laws that prevented the exportation of food, armor, and horses into Scotland, that allowed letters of reprisal against the Scots, that prevented the Scots from leasing land in England, and others. At least nine statutes interfered with passages and shipments back and forth.[8]

In the debate against Brock's motion, it was objected that it was customary to debate a bill before it was committed. It was feared that the Commons might be entrapped by the word "continuance," a word that might imply that the union was already in operation. At length the bill was committed to the "whole House committees." [9]

The following afternoon the House sat as a committee, and we have only two accounts of that session: that by Thomas Wilson and that by a less skillful note taker, Sir Robert Harley.[10] Into the details of that debate I shall not go. The House voted statute by statute for the repeal of the hostile laws. They did not repeal customs lest the repeal of customs should affect the validity of such border customs as inheritance and tenant right. It was news to them on the next day that the King favored repeal by particular bills.[11]

Hobart expressed the hope that the preamble to the Bill against

Hostile Laws should include stronger terms than *begun in his Majesty's person,* some such word as "settled" or "grounded" or "inherent." The House regarded the use of the words "grounded" and others as a matter of consequence, one not fit to be debated in so small a committee "as that then was." It was put off to be discussed in the House.[12]

In the discussion it was indicated that, while the Commons had voted against a general statement as to hostile laws, they wished to repeal all hostile laws they could discover. About such matters the Commons aimed to leave as few opportunities as possible to the judges to determine what laws were hostile.[13]

The Commons were afraid of the judges and on the lookout for phrases in the bill they were preparing that might be used by the judges to defeat the purposes of the Commons. They proposed to omit from the bill the words "under one allegiance," lest that phrase be reckoned a judgment in Parliament that the two nations were no longer separate kingdoms and be used to justify free commerce and the naturalization of all Scots.[14]

When the House was awaiting a report about hostile laws from the Committee of the Whole House on May 20, they were taken aback by an announcement from the Speaker that the King had adjourned the House for a week. On May 27, when Parliament came together again, the Speaker proceeded at once to defend himself from rumors in circulation that he had adjourned the Commons in order to prevent matters from coming to a question, that he had hoped to take advantage of the absence of members after the interval to gain the vote he wished. To excuse himself he declared that he had adjourned the House by direction of His Majesty. The King, he added, regarded himself as "much touched in honor" [15] at the rumor; he had no particular end to himself but the good of the land. His Majesty noted the "general absence of the members of this House," [16] but he must have been aware that by adjourning the House for a week he would encourage members to leave for their homes, which was probably what he had hoped for.

The members resolved, after the week's suspension, to deal with that part of the Bill against Hostile Laws concerning offenders flying either from England into Scotland or from Scotland into England. Into this complicated matter of remanding I shall not enter. The two Houses and their committees are involved, the history of the two nations is involved, and the different practices about trial and about jurors are involved. Moreover, the several changes and amendments made by each House in the effort to arrive at a compromise need to be examined closely and in detail. D. H. Willson, of the University of Minnesota, is writing a book on the subject of the union, and I hope that he will cover all the many aspects of remanding. To explain them all here would be to get away from the proper history of the House of Commons and into English and Scottish law. The story needs to be told, but not in this place at the length it deserves.

The compromise arrived at in the Bill about Hostile Laws did not please His Majesty. Indeed, the whole measure was a disappointment to him. The commercial relations between the two countries had been debated now and again, but nothing had been accomplished about them. Nor was anything accomplished about naturalization. That question was to be brought before the courts, and the *Post-Nati* were to be given the rights of Englishmen. The question of Scots holding offices and lands had not been settled either.

The anti-Scots had won a victory. Sandys's proposal for "a more perfect" or complete union in laws and government had been resisted by the Crown and by its supporters. The question of the union was not to be raised again seriously in the near future.

Chapter 4

The Fourth Session, 1610: Before the Recess

The Session Begins

IT was three years before Parliament was summoned to meet again. Meanwhile the situation abroad and at home was changing. After prolonged negotiations, the Dutch had finally made a treaty with Spain for twelve years. The King of England promised at length that if Spain broke the truce, he would send six thousand foot and six hundred horsemen to aid the Dutch, an agreement that was no doubt popular in England, where Spain had within a few decades become the historic enemy.

The Commons had not forgotten the abuses of wardship and purveyance, about which they had been complaining since the session of 1604, and some of them in the last decades of the great Queen. They hoped for other reforms. It will be remembered that a small minority was zealously Puritan and a considerable majority Puritan in some degree. They were to bring up the matter of non-residence of clergymen in many parishes and the holding of pluralities by clergymen. They were uneasy, too, over the tendency of commissary courts to excommunicate men and women for what seemed trivial offenses and over the interference of commissaries in parish affairs.

The lawyers—there were many lawyers in the House as well as

country gentlemen with enough legal training to share the lawyers' point of view—resented the interference of the ecclesiastical courts in matters that belonged, as they maintained, to the common law courts. Sir Edward Coke and other judges were issuing writs of prohibition against the ecclesiastical courts, and the archbishop of Canterbury was protesting to His Majesty against such writs.

When Sir William Maurice, at the beginning of the session of 1610, brought up the question of the union he was greeted by whistling. That subject the Commons were not inclined to revive.

The Commons preferred to listen to Sir Edwin Sandys, who on February 15 moved for a Committee for Grievances to consist of the Privy Councillors of the House, the first knight of every shire, and the first burgess of every borough. It was stipulated, however, that any member of the House might be admitted to the committee. Within a short while the committee became a Committee of the Whole House.

The first conference between the two Houses took place on February 15. Two days later it was reported to the Commons. The event of the conference had been the speech by Salisbury, the Lord Treasurer. Although that speech was a request for money, it was well received. There was nothing redundant in it, said Hobart, and nothing wanting. Bacon praised its brevity [1] and its divisions as well as its "computations and reckonings"; [2] he commended the life, grace, and efficacy of the speaker.[3] Beaulieu,[4] in writing to Trumbull, characterized the arguments as "energetical" and the substance as "persuasive"; [5] he testified that it gave good satisfaction to the minds and judgment of all the House.

The modern reader of the speech must admire its forthright frankness. In every paragraph the personality of Salisbury emerged, a personality it was difficult not to like, although some were able to resist the temptation. The Lord Treasurer set forth the causes of the summoning of Parliament: the creation of the Prince of Wales, and the need for a supply. He sketched the background of the creation of princes, not failing to point out that those princes had been most fortunate whose creation had been ratified by Parliament. In that time many men, even knowing men, looked

to the course of history as a guide to future action, as they sometimes looked to astrology.

Salisbury did not wait long to raise the question of supply,
offering reasons for helping the King.[6] If he were not supplied,
there might be inconveniences and dangers, breaches of treaties
and wars; the subjects might suffer. The King needed money to
support his state, to resist his enemies, to help his friends, and to
make diversions of war, "which is the best policy." [7] He sugared
the appeal to the members: "You are a composition of nobility and
you cannot be true to your own hopes if you suffer him to live in
want." [8] In her last years, continued Salisbury, the Queen had
spent £1,660,000 on her wars in Ireland. The new sovereign could
not quickly bring those wars to an end and had been forced to
expend upon them, in addition to what Elizabeth had expended,
£600,000. Nevertheless, His Majesty had been able to pay off much
of the debt incurred by the Queen, so that now the debt amounted
to only £300,000.[9] He had been able to rid himself of the major
part of the debt by various means: a subsidy voted to Elizabeth of
£300,000; a subsidy to James of £450,000; and aid of £22,000;
£120,000 from privy seals; £400,000 from the sale of lands and
mills; £100,000 from copyholders, freed woods, and assarts; and
£200,000 from old debts due to the Crown. Under the circumstances it would seem to the casual reader, unskilled in interpreting budgets, that, considering the debts accumulated during the
Irish wars, the Government had not done badly.

But the Crown had been recently burdened with heavy expenses: the obsequies of the Queen, the reception of the King, the
entrance of Queen Anne and of the children, the entertainment of
the King of Denmark, and the sending and receiving of ambassadors. To the thrifty predecessor of the King, the size of such
expenses would have needed explanation.

The Crown spent £1,400 a day, said the Lord Treasurer; the
annual outgo was £81,000 more than the income.[10] He appealed
to the House: "Will you now see this ship of Estate so near arrived
to the port, and wherein your own fortunes are imbarked, perish
in sight of the haven?" [11] He asked for a grant of £600,000 for

supply and £200,000 for support, the last to be given annually, "without necessity of new consents and assemblies." [12] The last request would have freed the sovereign from the necessity of calling frequent Parliaments.

Salisbury proceeded to meet the objections that might be put forward. To the possible objection that the precedent (of asking so much) was rare, he replied that in six hundred years the kings had been refused only three times, [13] and elaborated upon the sums given Elizabeth, almost three million pounds.

To the second possible objection, that the King was not at war, he called attention to the still heavy charges in Ireland and the cost of the navy, which, he said, was £40,000 a year. To the third objection, that His Majesty gave away too much money, he admitted that the King's bounty was great, "indeed very great," a wise admission. But the King gave of his own, and bounty was "an essential virtue of the King." "A magnificent mind is inseparable from the majesty of a king." "If he did not give, his subjects and servants would live in a miserable climate." He was born among the Scots and for him not to allow them to share in his good fortune would be to change his virtue with his fortune.

The third part of Salisbury's speech concerned "retribution," that is, concessions the King would offer his subjects in return for subsidies. "To this point he descended by divers degrees." They ought to meet often and exchange thoughts. They ought not to tempt the King to try his power before he had purpose to do so; nor ought they to seek precipitate remedies, whatever the grievance. Salisbury discussed the King's duty, his power and prerogatives, his grace and goodness. Kings, be they never so great, ought not to do what they will nor demand contributions and subsidies at their pleasure; neither ought subjects to deny them out of humor, where there was just cause, *pro bono publico.*

As for the King's prerogative, it was true that the King might "impose upon foreign commodities, yet not so as to destroy commerce." [14] Yet in some things his prerogative was inherent and inseparable, as in impositions. "Secondly, the King's prerogative doth extend to our freeholds, as in tenures and wardships." Thirdly, the King appointed the times and places of courts, and, fourthly, he executed penal laws.[15]

Salisbury spoke of the ease to be offered the subjects. The Crown was ready to hear grievances, "but with cautions." All commonwealths were full of grievances. The subjects must show respect and modesty to the sovereign. Some of the penal laws, he admitted, ought to be repealed. It would be unworthy to deny a King who not only was the wisest of kings, but had the image of an angel, "for he hath brought good tidings." [16] Salisbury concluded that reasonable demands were not to be answered with cold supplies.[17]

Salisbury may have anticipated an unfriendly reception of his appeal. The Commons were apparently not unfriendly, but doubtless disappointed that the chief minister was so vague in his promises and mentioned only a "general redress of all just grievances." [18] High and definite as were the demands of the Crown, the concessions to be offered were not concrete and might prove few.

The English have an old rhyme about the Dutch:

> In matters of business the fault of the Dutch
> Is giving too little and asking too much.

The royal Scot was asking too much and seemed slow to give. For three sessions the Commons had been put off. Had they not been assured that this grievance and that would be done away with? Months had slipped by, and even years, and the abuses seemed as many and as burdensome as ever. The discontent at St. Stephen's was evident to almost all. Men talked of the need to "eradicate the strongest and most inveterate diseases of the State." They feared that His Majesty would, by the assertion of his prerogative, "hereafter resume by little and little unto himself the right and appropriation of the same." [19] So Beaulieu wrote to Trumbull, and his words, "the right and appropriation of the same," seemed to suggest that the King would take over supply and support and possibly legislation. Beaulieu added that the Commons appeared

to be resolved not to proceed with the King in granting his demands (at least in the matter of supply) "but by way of Contract." [20]

Why did His Majesty need so much money? Ill-natured men
said that the whole wealth of the realm would not serve the King's
bounty. Many members of the Lower House believed that the
King was not given to economy. According to the Venetian ambassador, some of the Commons in March 1610 let it be understood that if His Majesty did not regulate the numerous tables he
kept at Court, the cost would prove enormous.[21] Any country
gentleman who looked in at Whitehall—and many did—could see
for himself the English and Scottish favorites faring well on the
royal bounty. His Majesty's impulsive grants of land and pensions
and patents to those around him were so well known that a career
at Court came to be regarded as the short cut to Castle Prosperous.

James was perhaps not more extravagant than other Kings of an
earlier day, but the average man seldom looked back more than
one generation. What he was likely to remember was the thrifty
Elizabeth. The English had long been critical of royal expenditure
and were becoming more so as they took a greater part in affairs
of state.

Beaulieu smelled something in the air: "According to the common opinion and hope [Parliament] is like to bring forth very
great alteration and reformation in the state." [22] As never before,
men were looking to Parliament for better government.

The situation could hardly have escaped the attention of the
watchful Salisbury. So far as I can make out he had the Upper
House in the hollow of his hand. As for the nether body, he had
doubtless been responsible for the election of various of its members; others in the Privy Council had not been laggard in securing
seats for their friends and retainers. The close vote on some
questions before the Commons would have indicated that a considerable minority could be counted upon to follow the lead of the
Privy Council,[23] as the House did in the good old days. That
minority might become a majority if only His Majesty would make

enough concessions. Salisbury was a persuasive speaker and might win for the King the twenty or thirty votes that were needed.

The Monday after the report of the conference, the Commons began the debate. It was February 19, and the Speaker took note of it as a lucky day, the anniversary of the defeat of Hannibal and the birthday of Prince Henry.

Richard Martin,[24] who was seldom afraid to speak out and yet seemed to sidestep the ill will of the throne, suggested that contribution and retribution be considered together. Hobart moved a resolution for supply to be discussed in a Committee of the Whole House. He would make no precedence between supply and grievances; they should be handled together. Sandys[25] hoped that the grievances would not be debated in committee until they had first been brought up in the House. Was he trying to prevent the introduction of a miscellaneous multitude of grievances that might confuse members and obstruct decisions? Brooke was in favor of granting supplies and freeing the King from "fretting charges." Bacon hoped for informal dialogue in committee and agreed with Hobart that grievances and supply should be considered together. Sir Herbert Croft believed that either the Lords should be consulted, or that the Commons should hear from the Privy Councillors what the House should do. He had not forgotten Tudor Parliaments.

In the Committee of the Whole House, opinion was less favorable to the Government. Hyde (probably Nicholas Hyde) believed that great sums could be raised from the lands of those attainted and from the fines and forfeitures derived from the recusants. Fuller developed the ideas of Hyde: the King should resume the patents and grants of customs out of which, as things were managed, the farmers of the customs made an undue profit. He alluded to the book of advice that His Majesty had written in Scotland, in which he had warned the Prince not to impoverish his subjects.[26] Fuller proposed that purveyance should be abolished and the King provided for by a charge at the Court gate. He took up the subject of wardship and declared that the discharge of tenures and wardships would give the subjects ease and contentment, and would be more agreeable to the laws of God (since parents would retain control of their children). By charging a rent on the lands of wards, lands held from the King, His Majesty would derive a yearly income.[27]

Hoskins moved that the whole benefit of wardship might accrue to the King's purse and not to the men to whom wards were committed. His motion met apparently with no support, and one can easily guess why the suggestion was not welcomed by all members. Wentworth made a speech that would have pleased the sovereign as little as that of his father had pleased Queen Elizabeth. All these schemes for increasing revenue, he said, would be of no use unless the King would resume for himself the money he gave courtiers and thus diminish his charges. Of what use was it to "draw a silver stream out of the country into the royal cistern if it shall daily run out by a private cock?" He would never give his consent to take money away from "a poor friese jerkin to trap [adorn] a courtier's horse withal." Few men in the Commons dared speak up in such fashion.[28] Wentworth wished the House would join in a petition to His Majesty to lessen his charges and live off his own, without exacting money from his subjects, especially in a time when there was no war. He recalled an act of Parliament in 10 Rich. II, cap. i, when the King had been wasting his revenues and a Council had been appointed for one year to consider of the gifts, receipts, and expenses.[29] A like law was made in 4 Hen. IV, cap. iv, in which the King promised to refrain from making gifts except to those approved by King and Council.[30]

Sir Julius Caesar answered that the laws of Richard II and Henry IV were not fit for these times. Wardship and purveyance were profitable to the King; wardship was worth sixty thousand pounds and purveyance forty. He offered to give full satisfaction to any member of the House who would consult him.[31]

It was finally resolved that for matters of retribution the House would proceed no further until they had learned whether His Majesty would be willing to discharge his tenures. They would seek a conference with the Lords and find out from them what

His Majesty intended to offer his subjects by way of retribution. It was determined to continue the subject in committee.

The Demands and Concessions of the Crown

THE Commons had decided that the question of contributions and retributions was to be determined in the committee. On February 21 Sandys reported that the committee had agreed that they were to proceed with both contribution and retribution, but that contribution should precede. That decision was a minor success for the friends of the King.

His demands seemed high: to be freed from debt, and to have some annual support to be voted for an indefinite future. As Salisbury put it, there would be no "necessity of new consents and assemblies," presumably during the reign of the King.[1]

The committee asked for another conference to gain further light on particulars. What concessions would the King offer? For themselves, they could pitch upon nothing but tenures and wardship; nothing else seemed as valuable. Of course they hoped to do away with or at least limit purveyance, not because they deemed it a grievance, but because its abolition or limitation would prove a great ease to the subject. They would like also to be rid of old debts to the Crown and not to be in danger from defective titles. Grievances were being brought in to the committee so rapidly, Sandys reported, that a deadline should be fixed beyond which time they should not be received. He named the following Monday, February 27.

The new conference took place on February 24 and was reported on February 27 by the Recorder. The Crown, it appeared, had demanded contribution and had offered retribution, but without particulars. Salisbury had made another speech and had apologized for his earlier one as a "sour declaration."

Then he had turned on the Commons. It was strange and unexpected that when His Majesty had summoned Parliament and told them the cause of calling them together—to supply his wants

—that they should answer with a question—what would the King give his subjects? He had hoped, rather, that there would be a rivalry between Parliament and the King to show their care and love for one another. Salisbury knew better; he had too much experience to have expected such a rivalry. He was aware of the discontent in the kingdom. Was he trying to put the Commons on the defensive? [2] The King, he went on, needed a supply, not for his wantonness, a gibe possibly at Wentworth.

At that point Salisbury deemed it wise to go over the fiscal problem again. His Majesty needed a double supply, to discharge his debts and to maintain his state. Of the £600,000 for supply £300,000 was to pay his debts, £150,000 to furnish the navy (for four ships already built), and another £150,000 to lie in his coffers for war and just occasions. States were maintained, he observed, by reputation. For yearly support the Government asked for £200,000 per annum, little enough. If the King and Prince did not live in plenty, they could not live in safety; nor could the subjects. As for the navy, it was never so great and never worse furnished.[3]

Sir Julius Caesar, Chancellor of the Exchequer, replied for the Commons that, although their willingness was great to do the King service, yet the demand was so great that they could not satisfy it unless there were "an exceeding noble retribution." They wished to know what would be given them. The Recorder, Sir Henry Montague, refused to comment on the sums demanded until a report had been made to the House but he was commanded to put a question: would His Majesty be pleased to treat of tenures, that is, of wardships? [4]

To this query, Salisbury replied that he could give no answer until he had consulted with the rest of the Lords. He had assumed that they would never talk of retribution until they had granted contribution. He would say that their master had been a great spender, but so had Queen Elizabeth in the first twenty-seven years of her reign.

Then Salisbury proceeded boldly to discuss constitutional questions, the powers of the King. It was the King's part to call Parliament, to coin money, to declare war; to deal with matters of justice, the protection of his subjects and the redress of just grievances; to deal with matters that were within the rights of the sovereign, but were burdensome to the subject. As for the first, the King would never part with them for any money. The second, the King would grant without money. As for the third, there was a great number of such rights, and His Majesty might be persuaded, "upon good consideration," to yield them to his subjects. Some of them he named. The King might consent to be bound by the statute of limitations of 32 Hen. VIII, cap. ii, as his subjects were. "What a jewel that were," exclaimed Salisbury, "if the King would part with it." By that act, no person could sue or bring any action for lands, rents, annuities, and pensions, said to have once belonged to their ancestors, if the present possessor or his ancestors had been in possession for sixty years. This provision would have nearly done away with the use of informers, who went snooping around the country searching for "concealed lands" once belonging to the King.

The Lord Treasurer mentioned other burdens that might be relinquished by the King. It might be possible to do away with the name of purveyance and set up a market at the Court gate. The maxim that the King's grants or patents were to be taken strictly could be so altered as to be interpreted in a sense beneficial to the subject. The King's lessees might no longer be subject to forfeiture of their lands for nonpayment of rents, but be subject only to double rent for the year. The subject, upon information of intrusion upon his lands, might be admitted to a general plea, and not be compelled to plead specially.[5] The next concession which Salisbury mentioned was that friends of the ward might have the wardship at reasonable rates so that strangers would not bid for the guardianship of an heir and thus be able to make a considerable profit out of what belonged to the ward. It was proposed by Salisbury that licenses of alienation should be granted at reasonable rates, that is, a man who held land from the King would be required to pay only a reasonable fee for the right to alienate such land to another, or to sell the lease of it.

The tenth concession proposed had to do with the performance of homage. The King charged a fee for excusing tenants from performing homage in person. It had been required that tenants go to London to submit their excuses, but it was now suggested that this fee should be collected by commissioners in the county where the tenant resided, and the tenant could thus take his ease at home and be at less charge. The concessions Salisbury was suggesting—he was not promising them—were of value. The Commons were waiting eagerly for greater reforms, for the abolition of wardship and purveyance. They heard Salisbury mention wardship and throw out the idea that friends of the ward might be allowed to obtain the wardships at reasonable rates, but that was not enough. What would be reasonable rates? Who would determine them? Might friends of the ward prove to be some acquaintance of a Privy Councillor? For purveyance the market at the Court gate might be manipulated by a new kind of purveyor. For the two great abuses long complained of, the Crown seemed to be offering alleviations that might amount to little and might only forestall the complete abolition of the evils.

The Commons had asked if they could discuss tenures and wardship,[6] and Salisbury replied that he did not know what His Majesty would say. The Lords would choose a committee to attend the King and learn his pleasure. Then he warned them that before they could hope to gain all these concessions, they must open their hearts and show love to their sovereign.

James was a sentimentalist who wished to rule from on high over submissive subjects and yet craved their constant professions of personal devotion.

Salisbury concluded by referring to the extraordinary expenses of the Crown and called attention to the absence of any plan for the maintenance of the Prince, of his brother, and of his sister, the Princess Elizabeth.[7] There were other expenses to be considered: the King's house needed to be renewed.

The Commons Consider
Salisbury's Proposals

ON February 28 discussion was continued. It was evident that the ten concessions suggested by Salisbury near the beginning of the session had not been received by the Commons with enthusiasm.

Salisbury's intimation to the Commons that they should not bargain with His Majesty until they had made a gesture of love to him by an offer of money [1] was confirmed by the words of another, Yelverton, who said that the Commons would not gain permission to consider a contract until they had shown a willingness to give. [2] The pride of apparel and the excess in building were commented upon. "Spare of this and give the King." Sir George More did not want the Commons to delay their offer as if holding off for a bargain. [3] The case for the King was supported by general principles. It was important that the sovereign be rich, for, without riches, honor and all were meaningless. His Majesty's revenues were not answerable to the dignity of his position. Let them make an overture to the King that they would give him relief as soon as they had debated.

It was maintained by one who had doubtless heard many precedents advanced in support of Parliament that the King did not govern by precedents but by the rule of right and reason. [4]

Bacon made a speech that was so like that of Salisbury and that of the Chancellor of the Exchequer that one wonders if the three had not discussed together the appeal to be used to the Commons. Sir Francis expressed disappointment that the subjects had passed over contribution in silence and fled to the sweetness of contract; they were exhibiting want of affection or "dryness." For the moment the country was at peace, but who would dare trust the ambitions of princes? The Commons were, he continued, "an abstract of the gentry," but they must not forget that they were representatives of other groups as well. They might be rewarded for granting subsidies; they might build a wall about the possession of the subjects that the royal prerogative could not touch. Bacon was replying to those who feared that, if the King could lay taxes without consent of Parliament, he might, when so inclined, take some of their lands and goods. But he failed to explain, or possibly the Clerk did not record, just how the granting of subsidies would result in the protection of the subjects against the demands of the Crown.

Others were in favor of giving the King support, but in return for concessions. Sir Maurice Berkeley, M. P. for Minehead and seated in Somerset, could see no reasons why the House should not compound for tenures. It was best for the Commons to move slowly and with caution. Fuller and Hyde took much the same view.

Sir Roger Owen sought a compromise solution: that the Commons should not give at once, but "discover an inclination" to give. When abuses had been done away with, the House might give "more largely." An "inclination" was no assurance, it was replied. The demands of the King came first and should have the first answer.

In view of the difference of opinion, there was a demand that the question be put off. It may well be that the friends of the King, realizing that among those present they lacked a majority, hoped to do better another day. The vote in favor of postponement was led by Caesar and Holcroft, the negative vote by Strode and Croft. The noes won by 160 to 148. The Recorder, Montague, was not discouraged and moved a message that the Commons would think in due time of supply and did not doubt to give His Majesty satisfaction. With such a statement Caesar was not wholly satisfied and moved that the Commons should give a plain, open, English answer: that they proposed to give somewhat. Quickly the Speaker seized on that proposal to call for a vote. It was phrased in this way:

> The House hath . . . taken knowledge of the state of his Majesty's wants . . . will in due time take consideration of it, and doubt not but, like dutiful subjects, to give his Majesty good satisfaction.

For the matter of annual support, because they have not heard from your Lordships what course you intend in the point of tenures, lately propounded to your Lordships by them, they have not yet entered into any consideration of it; but when they shall hear from your Lordships, they will be ready to join with your Lordships in conference.[5]

This was read by the Speaker and upon the question resolved.[6]

In the *Lords Journals,* as Spedding points out, the Lord Chancellor reported that the committees of the Lower House had said at the conference the day before: "For the other point of support they hold the same to be a matter most considerable *and proper to be framed by the Lords,* whereof they expect to understand from their Lordships accordingly." [7] In his note, Spedding assumes that the words of the report were "proper to be framed in concert with the Lords." [8] I suspect that the members of the committee felt that the question of support, "in nature transcendent, in precedent very rare," [9] was a new and significant matter that deserved consideration in conference between the two Houses, if and when the Lords agreed with the Commons to petition the King for leave to discuss wardship. If the Lords were to take a part in persuading His Majesty to yield on wardship, they could hardly be excluded from a consideration of the new policy of giving the sovereign a large sum annually, not subject to an annual vote.

By the next morning, March 1, the House was less certain of the wisdom of its message to the Lords of the day before, especially of the word "satisfaction." [10] It was doubtless feared that, by the phrase "they doubted not to give the King good satisfaction," they were promising more than they were as yet prepared to perform. A committee was named to pen a more guarded statement, a committee including Caesar, Hobart, and Henry Montague, all of whom, along with Sir Thomas Lake, could be counted upon to speak up for the Crown. But others on the committee—Edward Montague, Sandys, Croft, Owen, Francis Moore, Fuller, and Berkeley—were often in opposition. The committee returned presently and offered the following message in place of that brought up the day before, which apparently had not been forwarded. The new message read:

> The House . . . hath by your Lordships' relation taken knowledge of the state of his Majesty's wants, the remedy whereof by your Lordships proposed, dividing itself into supply and support:
>
> First for supply, we cannot conceive any other ordinary means than by way of subsidy; which, for that it ever moveth from the House of Commons, we will take consideration thereof in due time, and do therein that which shall become loving and dutiful subjects.[11]

The House had inserted about supply, "for that it ever moveth from the House of Commons," and had also put in after "take consideration" the words "in due time." They had left out the words "doubt not . . . to give his Majesty good satisfaction." Moreover, they had taken more pains than in the earlier statement to separate supply from support.

 In communicating with the Lords on March 1, the Commons had asked for a conference; that conference was set for the afternoon.

Pressure on the King about Wardship   THE conference was held on March 2; the next day Sandys reported it. Northampton had talked of the moral virtues of the King, of his endowments by nature, of his care of religion, of his bounty to the Church,[1] and of his zeal for the happiness of his subjects. His Majesty had reformed abuses in the navy and built four new ships to repress piracy. He gave access to his subjects. He was not given to banqueting or surfeiting; nor was he a prey, as many princes, to the sins of the flesh.[2] He was free from extortion and covetousness; he was at peace with neighboring princes. Now he was demanding supply and support, and he deserved them. His coffers were empty; he had given Parliament an account of his receipts and expenditures. Other princes, such as the King of Spain, were rich. At any time a breach of treaties might lead to war.[3] Other nations would judge England by her strength and by the preservation of the state.

When the Earl touched upon the Prince he became lyrical: the Prince was the child of the Muses.

On Monday, March 5, the Recorder reported the speech of the Lord Treasurer at the same Friday conference. About tenures it appeared that His Majesty craved more time to make up his mind. What was up? Was there possibly some difference of opinion within the Privy Council?

What Salisbury had explained to the conference was that the King had been talking of honor, conscience, and utility. He appealed to Parliament to consider how careful each of them had to be of his honor. How much more careful a King should be! If he gave up the tutelage of the nobility and gentry, an arm of his prerogative, honor might be lost, and honor was more to be prized than money. His Majesty was concerned in his conscience. If he gave up his royal protection he exposed the progeny of the nobility "to the weakness of a common and vulgar protection." [4] He was obviously vacillating about yielding to the desires of the Commons.

Seldom was a more specious case presented to an intelligent body. I wonder that Salisbury could bring himself to make such a statement, even at the King's dictation. As for utility, His Majesty had said that it did not worry him; he was willing to make the subjects partakers with him, but conscience and honor held him back.

To the Commons he gave full liberty to treat of those matters that Salisbury had already proposed to them. If concessions were to be made about wardship and about definite fees for alienations, he asked that the Commons keep in mind not only the present income from those rights but the possible future income. Salisbury ended hopefully: "You may return into your countries [shires] and tell your neighbors that you have made a pretty hedge about them." [5] He was harking back to the speech by Bacon. Crew rose and remarked that he had heard nothing that should dispel the hopes of the Commons; he proposed a committee to prepare for a conference. Bacon agreed and wished a subcommittee to draw up reasons "that may remove obstructions," to which Fuller assented. Sir Edward Montague was thinking possibly of strategy when he said that he did not believe matters of honor and conscience should be disputed. As for the ten concessions put forward by the Lord Treasurer early in the session, he saw in them nothing to bargain about. Did he mean that His Majesty should offer those concessions with no *quid pro quo?* It was suggested that access with the Lords to the King should be asked, so that the King "might grow to a resolution."

To such a move Sir William Strode, who was not given to compromise, was opposed. He advocated a message to the Lords that the Commons could vote neither supply nor support unless the King were pleased to treat. Hobart hoped that the Commons would join with the Lords who were "the aptest" in such matters. It was not wise to use importunity but rather to recognize that the reasons of the King were weighty and that he had a right to take his time. When it came to honor and conscience the Commons should attempt no rebuttal.

Finally, it was voted that Mr. Attorney, Mr. Solicitor, Mr. Recorder, and Mr. Crew were to pen an answer to the Lords concerning tenures. A conference between the Houses was held on March 8 and reported on March 10 by Martin.

Salisbury had addressed the conference at some length on the subject of Dr. Cowell, which we shall deal with in another connection, and that led him to the problem of the prerogative. There he was, he admitted, sailing between dangerous rocks: it was dangerous to submit the power of a king to definition, and he avoided that danger. But he added parenthetically that His Majesty was discontented with certain speeches in Parliament. Though the men who uttered them might lack favor from him, they would be sure of justice. As for subsidies, he would not have been angry if Parliament had refused them. This reservation seems to have pleased the Lord Treasurer, who concluded, "Happy we have a man to our King." [6]

Salisbury was followed in the conference by Bacon, who delivered to the Lords a message from the Commons. That body had no desire to diminish the estate of the King. They hoped that upon the stem of the tree of tenures, when cut down, could be raised a perpetual pillar of support to the Crown. As for the point of honor that His Majesty had mentioned, there were civilians in the House who could tell them that those parts of the law dealing with *De Feodis* were but additions to the first institutions, and not "perpetual." [7] They were not "regal in point of sovereignty." From the common law they learned that wardship was not an incident inseparable from the Crown. As to the point of conscience raised by the King, when he should surrender the protection of his wards, he would transfer that protection to those bound by law and nature to provide for the good of wards.

The last sentence was an unobtrusive and definitive reply from the Commons to His Majesty's scruples about the guardianship of wards. [8] Everyone knew that the Crown sold wardships to those who paid well for them and who hoped to do well from them, at the expense of the ward. Relatives of the ward were more likely to treat him with consideration.

Bacon asked the Lords to join with the Commons in a petition to James to give them an answer as soon as possible. On March 12 the King's answer was given to the Commons by the Lord Privy Seal, Northampton. His Majesty would allow them to treat of the discharge of tenures and of all dependencies thereof. He had been gratified by their humility: they had not presumed to discuss tenures and wardship without asking leave; they had shown dutifulness in deferring to his serious judgment, caution in not calling wardship a grievance, and discretion in recognizing that it was a valuable concession to be paid for; [9] they had shown judgment in joining with the Lords. "They should know that for your Lordships' sakes they shall fare the better." [10]

The Commons had sugared their pill with happy results. But why had the King shifted his ground? Why were his scruples sud-

denly resolved? He was obviously in an oncoming mood. He alluded to the rigor of the penal laws and hoped that in his time [11]
some course might be taken to relieve his subjects of that burden.
As for purveyance, though in itself just and necessary, it was the
occasion of just complaint.[12] He would part with it willingly to
his subjects "for their good." He was of the opinion of Agesilaus,[13]
who declared the greatest happiness he could enjoy was to have
the affection of his peoples.

The King had paused in his speech and then continued, as
Northampton related, on what one would call a note of self-pity.
He had to taste the world's ingratitude and the evil construction
put upon his benignity. Day by day he grew more wary of importunate suitors with their infinite desires. His means were finite.
He realized that this would be the last extraordinary help he
could expect. It would be easier for his subjects to repair his
estates while he still had some means of his own. If those means
should be exhausted, the burden of maintaining the sovereign
might prove serious. But as long as there was a monarchy, the
subjects must maintain the monarch—a telling premise with men
who believed with religious fervor in the institution of monarchy.
They were only a few generations away from the Wars of the
Roses, and the memory of those struggles over kingship, as it was
passed down, made thoughtful men fear the danger of a weak
sovereign.

Northampton, in reporting to the conference what the King
had said, mixed the utterances of His Majesty with his own comments so that it is hard to disentangle King and Lord Privy Seal.
It was possibly James who urged speed. If things were carried
with the "former relaxations," he would despair of any happy
issue. From his lofty position Northampton bestowed kindly
advice. In private families the members deemed it best to leave
a stock in the hands of the steward for use in emergencies. Thus
his hearers ought to rely on the caution and wise consideration of
the High Steward, the steward of all stewards. The King had
before him weighty causes, secret issues, into which his subjects
ought not to search.[14]

He returned to the topic of subsidies. The King was smarting for want of money, but would not venture to importune the House. The royal vessel leaked, and the leak must be stopped.

The King's
Offer Discussed
O N March 14 the Commons began consideration of His Majesty's offer that they might treat of wardship. This was the fair Helen they all wooed. The King was offering them flowers, declared the Attorney General, Sir Henry Hobart, but not without conditions. What he would concede depended upon what they voted him by way of subsidy.[1]

They were, of course, pleased, but felt by no means out of the woods. The King, wrote Sir Thomas Edmondes to Trumbull, had asked for a great sum of money. How much were they prepared to give in return for his possible concession? To find as large a sum as he asked would be a difficult undertaking.[2] Further, the abolition of wardship would affect unfavorably many private interests and thus meet with opposition. Edmondes, a diplomat and a servant of the Crown, wrote as if he were not unsympathetic with the aims of the Commons, but were aware that it would require zeal ("affection") on the part of the leaders to overcome the opposition. He foresaw that Parliament would be drawn out to great length.

Wentworth made a surprising speech: the Court of Wards, he declared, had been managed with justice, sincerity, and impartiality. Was he tossing a bouquet—he was not given to bouquets—to Salisbury, who possibly had been helpful to the Commons?[3] Was he trying to say that it was not because of Salisbury's mastership that the Commons wished to do away with wardship?

The House wandered off into a discussion of how to convey their thanks to His Majesty.[4] In the meantime the Attorney urged the members not to seek what compensation they would be given, but to make an offer and trust the King's judgment. Hobart was taking advantage of the good feeling of the moment and of the natural loyalty of members, in order to persuade them to leave all the cards in the hands of the King. Had the members not learned that His Majesty was likely to play his hand as did Bret Harte's "heathen Chinee"?

On March 15 the House began planning for the full discussion of tenures and wardships and of other grievances. The Committee of the Whole House was to meet at 7:00 or 8:00 and to sit until 9:30 a.m. Then the House itself was to meet for general business until 11:30 a.m. At 3:00 p.m. the Committee of the Whole House was again to hold its session. Up to that time the House would deal with private bills. This was a heavy program for the ordinary member, and one to which he was not accustomed. From the beginning many failed to appear. The Committee of the Whole House dwindled in attendance. It divided itself up into subcommittees to deal with this grievance and that, but the subcommittees also were slimly attended.

The King's decision to allow the Commons to treat wardship and tenures in return for a "composition" had not been easily secured. It is an old story that James was likely to hesitate. Beaulieu wrote Winwood on March 15 that, although the King was "by the whisperings and dissuasions of some of those which are about him," made "more averse than he had been before from yielding to this composition and making away the wardships from the Crown, yet in the end he hath been brought unto it." [5]

It has been suggested in the "Introduction" that Salisbury may have pressed the King for concessions to the Commons.[6] The Venetian ambassador reported that Prince Henry was opposed to the abolition of wardship.[7] It was the same ambassador who reported that the Commons were standing firm in the determination that, if they were not granted the abolition of wardship, they would vote no more than an ordinary subsidy.[8] No such resolution is set down in any other account, but the determination expressed may well have been that of members who had been talking to the ambassador.[9]

It was a strange situation. The Commons were planning to work over the tenures involved in wardship and were proposing also to deal with the problems of purveyance. They were looking forward to making a contract with the King. An obstacle, however, lay across the road. The King had made his conditional concessions but, as usual, was wavering afterward, and the Commons were beginning to fear as much. They were willing to pay for the abolition of wardship and purveyance but less than the King was asking, and now it was whispered that he was about to raise the price.

Early in March the Commons had been considering what they were to do. Heavy pressure would be put upon them to grant what seemed to be an enormous sum, far beyond any precedent of Elizabeth's time. They did not propose to "engage" themselves till His Majesty would consent to yield equivalent benefits.[10]

It will be remembered that at the beginning of the session Salisbury had suggested ten possible concessions that the King would consider, concessions of "great ease and advantage to the subject," but the Commons desired "to redeem a greater burden and thraldom," that is, relief from wardship and purveyance. For six years they had been asking relief from those thralldoms. If it were true that His Majesty desperately needed money at once, now was the time to bargain.

The position of "the great little minister," Salisbury, was hardly a comfortable one. He had been brought up by Queen Elizabeth and his father to be careful with money and to ask for as little as possible. If he should offer to surrender his highly profitable position as Master of the Wards in order to smooth the way for the Great Contract, he would be making a gesture of goodwill to a body to which he probably felt a lingering loyalty.[11]

For a month and a half after this time, we hear little of what was going on in the House of Commons. The significant debates were taking place in the Committee of the Whole House. On March 19 Sandys, who, more than anyone else, was calling the turns, proposed that the Committee of Grievances should meet all day for six days a week and added: "The subcommittees to attend more diligently." On that same day it was announced that the House was to meet the King the next day in the Banqueting Hall.

From then until July the emphasis was to be on grievances. When I have dealt with grievances until July, I shall return to March and follow the debates about what money and how much would be voted to the King. Before taking up grievances, I shall summarize and comment upon the King's speech of March 21.

The King's Speech

THE King gave his speech on March 21. There had been speculation, he declared, within and outside Parliament as to whether he intended to continue the Government according to the ancient form of the state and the laws of the kingdom, or whether he planned to alter them and rule as an absolute King.[1] Some indeed feared that he wished to replace the common law by the civil law. Such criticism led him to consider the position of the monarch and to render an account of his actions to his subjects.

Once again he wished to remind the Commons of his need for money, but he also wanted to answer his critics.

The state of monarchy he pronounced the supreme thing on earth. By God himself kings were called gods; he likened them also to fathers of families and to the heads of the body. Then he proceeded to draw implications from those similes, as if they were fundamental premises. Kings had power to exalt low things and to make high things low. The king could move his subjects as a chess player moves pawns and knights. Those subjects owed him affection of the soul and service of the body, and they were bound to relieve their king according to the form and order established in this kingdom.

James introduced a fragment of his own philosophy of history. Historians and political philosophers have long speculated about the origins of government. King James had the answers. He knew exactly how kings had their beginning, that is, either by conquest or by election by the people, "their wills at that time served for law." As soon as kings found their nations settled, they put down their thoughts ("minds") in the form of laws,[2] which were properly made by the king only, but at the request ("rogation") of the people, "the king's grant being obtained thereunto." Thus the king became *lex loquens.*[3] In consequence, every king was bound to observe "that paction made to his people by his laws" and to frame his government thereby.

As for the common law, he of all kings had least cause to dislike it. For a king of England to despise the common law was to neglect his own Crown. He did wish, however, that the common law were written in the vulgar language and not in a mixed tongue understood only by lawyers; he wished, moreover, that there were in all cases a settled text. The contrarieties in the decisions ought to be scraped out of books, and penal laws no longer in use should be repealed.

He had been looked upon as an enemy of prohibitions.[4] He would like to see every court kept within its own limits, as every river within its banks: "I see every court will take and engross as many causes unto them as they can."[5] His function was to make every court remain within its own limits. Writs of prohibition should not be granted upon every slight surmise; it was for archbishops, rather than bishops, to deal with such writs.

As for grievances, the people should show them in such an assembly as this, "because the King doth not know the particular and several wrongs done unto his people."[6] They were for Parliament as "the representatives of people, the highest Court of Justice." Grievances concerned "the Lower House properly."[7] But grievances should not be eagerly sought out or taken up in the streets. He hoped that they would not exhibit as grievances matters established by settled law. "All novelties were dangerous." It was not for them to meddle with the main points of government: that was his craft; to meddle with them was to lessen him. For thirty-six years he had been a king, and he had accomplished seven years' apprenticeship in England. Complaint had been made of the Court of High Commission. That Court was of so high a nature that there was no appeal from it. He had restricted such appeal to the two archbishops.[8]

James finally arrived at his main point: supply. He had requested his Lord Treasurer to give a true account of all income and expenditure, a favor seldom bestowed upon subjects. To him they had a duty: to give him a supply of money. The members would bear him witness that he had not asked for any particular subsidies or sums; nor had he requested Privy Councillors to gain voices from him in Parliament. He detested hunting for votes.[9] He hoped that members would not cloak their own humor by alleging the poverty of the people. Then he went on: "For, although I will be no less just as a King, to such persons . . . yet ye must think I have no reason to thank them or gratify them with any suits or matters of grace, when their errand shall come in my way." He carried the threat a bit further: "For him that denies a good law, I will not spare to quarrel." [10]

His personality emerged now and then; when talking about the money he needed, he said: "I am a very ill orator to speak for myself, being against my nature to beg." [11] His needs were not long out of his mind.

> If I should have come into the Kingdom, my wife and children, poorly in a mean fashion, not have sent ambassadors to return thanks to foreign princes, [not] entertained the King, my brother, [not] performed my coronation with state, and [not] buried the late Queen, your mistress, you would have thought much, and the not performing of these things would have been as much to your dishonor as to the dishonor of your King.[12]

He understood, he said, that the members of the Lower House, "being but a representative body," gave not for themselves but for the towns and shires who paid the taxes. He feared they might be too eager for the affection of the people and consider too little their King's necessity.[13] He admitted that he had been liberal in his gifts. If he had failed to reward those who had long given him honest and faithful service, he would have been deemed ungrateful to his countrymen with whom he had been raised.[14] Then he made a shrewd thrust:

> What I have given hath been given amongst you and so what comes in from you goes out again amongst you. . . . I hope

you will never mislike me for my liberality, since I can look very few of you this day in the face that have not made suits to me at least for something either of honor or profit.[15]

James again took up the old refrain that if Parliament failed to vote him the supplies needed, he would lose standing abroad. Princes would take advantage of his weakness to make war upon him. It was an argument that would not have weighed heavily with all those listening, some of whom would have replied that England was never so well off as when at war.

The King adverted to religion. Papists had waxed as proud as they had ever been. Catholicism was on the increase, especially among the upper classes and their women. Yet he did not want Parliament to pass severer laws against recusants; instead, let the statutes already on the books be well enforced. He had never found that severity and the shedding of blood aided in the cause of religion. Gallant men should not be forced to die and be reputed martyrs.[16]

He recommended that a new statute be passed for the preservation of woods. A bill offered in the last session had been cast out, possibly because it had been warmly supported by the King. The decay of woods would bring about the decay of shipping and thus injure commerce, which "is a main pillar of this Kingdom."[17] They all knew, he remarked, conceivably with a knowing smile, of his delight in hunting and hawking. He was distressed about those who stole game in the night, "the looser sort of people," "clowns." Such sports as hunting should be reserved for gentlemen. "Whether you love sport or no . . . none of you but will be glad of a pasty of venison."[18]

James failed to make the most of his best talking point. He had asked gentlemen to vote him as much money as each of them might throw away in one night, implying that they were not impoverished and that they were quite able to help him. He was right about that; he should have emphasized their wealth. The landed classes and the merchants in London and the larger towns could well have afforded to grant their sovereign much more than they ever thought of giving him. The England of 1610 was by no means a poor country and might have allowed its sovereign even a touch of "magnificence." But country gentlemen were in some degree farmers and reluctant to part with silver and gold pieces.

The King's speech was not in the best taste. It was unnecessary to talk of the divinity of kings. John Moore, writing to Winwood, said that even the most religious could have wished that His Highness would have been more sparing in using the name of God and in comparing the Prince's sovereignty with that of the Deity. Moore did add that the speech had the plausible conclusion that "howsoever the sovereignty of kings was absolute in general, yet in particular the kings of England were restrained by their oath and the privileges of the people." [19] Moreover, James had not overlooked the position of the Commons as a representative body, as has been seen. His seven years in England had taught him at least a little of English political usages.

His inclination to grant some toleration in religious matters must be set down to his everlasting credit.

He expressed himself well. He had skill in hitting upon idioms and figures of speech to drive home the points he made, though the points were not always pleasing. It was sedition, he asserted, to dispute what a king may do in the height of his power. "I will not be content that my power be disputed upon," he exclaimed, but I shall ever be willing to make the reason appear of all my doings and rule my actions, according to my laws."

He was extraordinarily sensitive to what was said in Parliament.

It has been observed that he never understood the English. Except for Salisbury, none of the English whom he gathered about him were of the better type. Neither Northampton nor his nephew, Suffolk, were, aside from their rank, men looked up to in their day. James did not know a good man, a competent or disinterested man, when he saw him, and of course there were few of the latter in the Court. With the kind of men whom the great Queen delighted to honor, he would have felt ill at ease. Indeed he never felt at home with Salisbury.

Ecclesiastical Grievances IT will be recalled that during the last part of March and in early April the members of the Lower House had been spending their afternoons in the Committee of the Whole House dealing with grievances. Grievances were brought in so fast by members with unhappy constituents that Sandys found it necessary to warn members that no more grievances should be introduced after a certain date. On March 11 the Venetian ambassador reported that thirty-two grievances had been brought in; on March 18 he estimated the number at sixty. Sandys no doubt feared that the accumulation of many grievances would make it harder for the committee to examine thoroughly the more serious ones.

He was the floor leader, even if not so named, but it was beyond his power to keep the House working toward a single end. It was natural for an M.P. to believe that the grievance of his shire was the most significant; it was natural for zealous Puritans to assume that nonresidence and pluralities, the high-handed methods of Church officials and of commissary courts, and depriving nonconforming clergy of their livings were the crying evils of the time.

But the Puritans must have realized that they could not hope for much ecclesiastical legislation of the kind they desired. They had made a serious effort in 1604 to deal with ecclesiastical grievances and had been held up by the Upper House, where the influence of the archbishop of Canterbury was potent. They knew, too, that except on the question of excommunication for trivial reasons, the King was opposed to them. In the opposition of the Lords to ecclesiastical changes, it was implicit that they believed such matters were best left to the Privy Council, as in the days of the great Queen. It is little wonder that with Crown and Lords against them the Puritans became discouraged, but they continued, nevertheless, to bring in bills.

To many members, the most pressing grievance was the failure to enforce adequately the stringent laws against recusancy. The committee for the consideration of that matter was the only one scheduled to meet during the recess of April 3–16. Not, however, until April 27 was "An Explanation of the Statute of 23 Elizabeth, cap. i, To Retain the Queen's Subjects in their due Obedience" read for the first time.[1] The bill was committed on May 8 to a small committee of the King's learned counsel and seventeen others, including a half dozen of the more zealous Puritans in the House. On May 18 the problem of the recusants was discussed, in particular the opportunities afforded priests in prison to visit and converse with one another. Sir Francis Hastings told the House on May 25 that there were not so many recusants these seven years as now, that the Recorder had declared that one hundred citizens had been indicted at the sessions, presumably at the Middlesex Sessions,[2] and that the houses of the ambassadors were crowded with English people attending Mass. It was proposed that a proclamation should require all recusants to leave London; apparently the Government was not opposing such a measure.

On the next day (May 19) Sandys reported from the subcommittee the articles they had drawn up. A conference with the Lords showed that they were prepared to cooperate. The Recorder presented to the Lords the articles: [3]

1. That a proclamation should be made that all recusants were before June 2 to leave London or the Court and not to remain within ten miles of London or the Court
2. That all recusants be disarmed
3. That no English subject resort to the houses of foreign ambassadors
4. That all priests and Jesuits imprisoned be straitly restrained
5. That the Oath of Allegiance be tendered in the Court by the Lords of his Majesty's Privy Council and others [4]

In the same conference the Lords agreed with the Commons to petition the king concerning his safety. His answer to them expressed his gratitude for their pains to uphold the religion that he had always professed and would maintain. The religion of the papists was, as in times past, the butchery of saints and now of princes. He thanked them for their care of his person. Now the papists would realize that the moves against them were endorsed by his subjects and were not the mere result of his own humor. That the petition against them had its origin in the House of Commons gratified him. As for the execution of the laws against recusants, he would advise with his Council. No further forbearance should be shown them.[5]

The proclamation which the King issued on June 2 called for the due execution of all such laws. The recusants should be given a day to return to their dwellings and not to the Court, and they should not remain within ten miles of London. They were also to be disarmed, and Jesuits and other priests were to leave the country.[6] The Oath of Allegiance was to be administered "according to the law." Nothing was said in the proclamation, however, about the English hearing Mass at the houses of ambassadors nor about the freedom allowed Jesuits in prison to visit one another.

One may suspect that the King was only too glad that the Commons had requested a proclamation, particularly at a time when the House was becoming increasingly critical of the use of proclamations. As a matter of fact, there were quite enough statutes about recusancy already on the books.[7]

The grievance of pluralities and nonresidence, which was before the Commons in 1604, had been mentioned again and again in the reign of the great Queen. Indeed, as far back as the first year of Henry VIII, a statute (cap. xiii) had been passed forbidding ministers to hold more than one benefice where the value of the living was more than £8 a year. That statute contained provisos that were said to frustrate the intention of the measure. In 1604 the Commons passed a bill repealing much of the act of 21 Hen. VIII that enabled ministers to take a license or dispensation to hold more than one cure of souls.[8] It was further set down in the bill that if one minister had several benefices more than three miles apart, he should elect which to serve and should supply the others with preaching ministers to whom he would allow £20 a year or the better half of the profits of the said benefice. That bill was passed in the Commons and was read once in the Lords.

In March 1606 a bill similar to that in 1604 had been introduced into the Lower House. But in the new bill a minister who held more than one living above four miles apart was to supply a preaching minister in the same way as in the earlier measure. This bill, too, passed the Commons and was read once in the Lords.[9]

The session of 1610 had barely gotten under way when Sir Edward Montague, who had been deprived of his lieutenancy and justiceship of the peace in Northamptonshire for joining in a petition on behalf of the silenced ministers, preferred a bill against nonresidence and pluralities.[10] The bill went quickly through the Commons and was sent up to the Lords with a special recommendation. The text was probably not very different from that brought forward in 1604 and 1606. This 1610 version the Lords debated at considerable length before they committed it, and then it was debated in committee. The archbishop of Canterbury wished it committed to the uttermost pit of hell. He offered various arguments, the strongest being that clergymen were so poorly paid that the only immediate way to help their situation was to allow them extra livings and nonresidence. The archbishop insisted that the Commons should not meddle with Church matters, and the bishop of Lincoln supported that view. Such questions belonged to Convocation. A half dozen or so peers spoke for the bill, including Lord Saye and Sele and Lord Russell. The bill had been deliberated on in the Commons and commended to the Upper House. The Lower House as a representative body, said Lord Knyvet, spoke for thousands of people. Salisbury was inclined to look at things historically. The Church did not have one-fourth of its former income from tithes and other sources. In conclusion, he offered to give a tenth part of his "impropriations." [11]

The bill was never passed by the Lords. Meanwhile the leaders of the Commons, no doubt aware of the probable fate of the bill, inserted in their petitions (submitted at the end of April) one concerning pluralities and nonresidence, implying that there was "toleration of non-residency," and that in consequence many people were without religious instruction. It was further declared that pluralists, "heaping up many benefices into one hand," kept learned men from maintenance, "to the discouragement of students and hindrance of learning."[12]

The King's answer on July 23 expressed his detestation of the covetous and immoderate heaping up of many benefices together. He promised to lay a strict charge on all bishops to teach and instruct the people. If they failed to do so, he would make it appear how much he disliked their neglect.[13]

The "Bill for Restraining the Execution of Ecclesiastical Canons not Confirmed by Parliament" had a history like that of the "Bill for Non-Residence and Pluralities." It will be recalled that in May 1604 the Commons passed a bill to restrain the execution of ecclesiastical canons not confirmed by Parliament. A measure of the same kind also passed in 1606[14] and was read twice in the Lords. In 1607 a similar bill went as far as commitment in the Upper House. The significant part of the text of the bill of 1610 can be found in footnotes in Mrs. Foster's masterly edition of *Proceedings of 1610*.[15] It was to be that "no canon, constitution, or ordinance ecclesiastical heretofore made or ordained within the space of ten years last or hereafter to be made . . . shall be of any force or effect . . . until the same be first confirmed by act of Parliament."

Such an Erastian measure was, of course, opposed by the bishops, but read twice in the Lords and committed, strangely enough, at the suggestion of the archbishop. He opposed it as both scandalous and injurious to the state. Bishop Neile of Rochester spoke against the bill as bringing the prerogative into question. The bishop of London supported the bill and said the Pope had usurped in England the making of canons.[16] William Barlow, bishop of Lincoln, said the Church only, and not laymen, had the power to make canons because the Church had the keys, and those things it bound should be bound.[17] The Lords St. John, Knollys, and Saye and Sele favored the bill. Salisbury was afraid that it encroached upon the power of the King; he had observed that in this Parliament the Lower House had called the prerogative in question.[18]

Before the conference on July 6 the archbishop had in the morning issued a warning to the Lords that they owed their authority and power to His Majesty, and it was from him that the canons received their life.[19] In the afternoon at the conference Sir Roger Owen pointed out that in France the canons were made by the laity as well as the clergy and that before Henry VIII's time in England canons never required royal assent. Hyde called attention to the danger of excommunication faced by every man who did not consent to the canons. The archbishop interrupted to say that he had not expected to hear the canons "ripped up with such bitterness." [20] William Brock, M.P. for St. Ives, Cornwall, objected to various canons on various grounds but especially to those canons which prevented conscientious and honest men from doing good in the ministry. They lose their livings to which they have as good a right "as any of us to that we hold." Wentworth maintained that by the canons the bishops could declare a man a heretic and that such a declaration touched the goods, the liberties, and the lives of men. Northampton queried whether the bishops had power to judge heresy, and Crew offered an argument for the affirmative. But nothing, he continued, ought to be called heresy except by act of Parliament. Another conference was proposed by the Lords, but the end of Parliament was at hand, and nothing came of it.[21]

It will be recalled that the grievance of excommunication for trivial reasons was brought up in 1604 and that the Government seemed willing to have something done about it, by the Privy Council. In 1610 the grievance was not formulated as a bill, but was put among the articles in the petition of grievances and voted on April 25 to be laid before His Majesty. That part of the petition is worth quoting in part:

And forasmuch as excommunication is the heaviest censure which the church can inflict for the most grievous offenses and yet is oftentimes exercised and inflicted upon the common people by sundry subordinate officers of the jurisdiction ecclesiastical, for very small causes, in which case the parties, before they can be discharged, are driven to great expense for matters of very small moment to . . . the unspeakable grievance of your Majesty's poor subjects. We therefore . . . beseech . . . your . . . Majesty, that some due and fit reformation therein may be had.[22]

The petition declared that the rich escaped censure by paying for commutation of penance, "to the great scandal of the Church government."

The King's answer on July 23 admitted the abuse about which he had tried to do something, he said, "where the original cause was of no great weight." A bill had been drawn and exhibited in the Lower House and had found no passage there.[23] But he promised that when a bill should be agreed upon that would enable ecclesiastical judges to punish contempts in causes before them otherwise than by excommunication he would give his consent thereto.[24] This answer left things much as they had been.

The grievance of the silenced ministers that had been raised in 1604 was brought up in 1610 from the Committee of the Whole House by Sandys. It became a question whether the matter should be dealt with as a grievance or by a petition. Sir Francis Hastings, the spokesman of the zealous Puritans, was in favor of a petition. A petition was at length framed and passed by the Commons. His majesty was asked to license the said clergymen to

instruct and preach unto the people in such parishes and places where they may be employed, so long as they apply themselves . . . to wholesome doctrine and exhortation and live quietly and peaceably in their callings, and shall not by writing or preaching impugn things established by public authority.[25]

To this moderate statement the King answered that he would take such order as in his princely wisdom he found fit. But he seems to have added that if any gentleman of the Commons would come to him in behalf "of such a particular minister as hath been long in the ministry, or is learned and hath been peaceable I will give him a reasonable answer." [26]

One of the last ecclesiastical grievances mentioned by the Committee of the Whole House was that of the power of the Court of High Commission, which was included in the petition to His Majesty. In 1606 complaint had been made of the multitude of commissions whereby bishops arrogated to themselves the powers belonging to the two High Commissions of Canterbury and York.[27] It was complained in 1610 that under the statute of I Eliz. cap. i, which bestowed upon the Crown the jurisdiction over the state ecclesiastical, the members of the High Commission had exceeded their powers by fining and imprisoning men and exercising other authority not conferred upon them by the statute. The commissioners, it was asserted, directed their commissions into all the counties of England and for any petty offense used powers not belonging to them, compelling offenders for small matters to come to London. The committee declared that the commissioners exercised both spiritual and temporal power, that there was no appeal from their decisions, and that no writs for the review of their decisions could be issued in any other courts. Furthermore, men were punished for speaking of the misdemeanors of clergymen, and sometimes houses were broken into and rooms rifled, as if those sought were accused of treason. In other words, the protection of the subject guaranteed by the common law was imperiled by the continuous intrusion of the ecclesiastical courts.

In his answer the King alluded to "needless and imaginary fears" of his subjects and assured them that his commissions should be directed not to persons but to a number of selected commissioners sitting in court. The commission would allow no more punishment than a reasonable fine or imprisonment. His Majesty would see that his subjects be not drawn to London or York for small offenses. He assured his subjects that no canons were in force that were contrary to the laws, statutes, and customs of the realm.[28] To the complaint of the committee about the power of the High Commission the King said:

Complaints have been made of that Commission before now. To prevent which hereafter I have set down certain directions. If they be transgressed and complaint thereupon made, I will so redress. And whereas I have commissions but to the two archbishops, I have likewise ordered that none shall be cited from remote places, but for exorbitant causes.[29]

Other Grievances

OF nonecclesiastical grievances I shall deal only with those most talked about: writs of prohibition, of habeas corpus, and *de homine replegiando;* [1] the conciliar control imposed upon the four western counties adjacent to Wales; proclamations; and the impositions on alehouses.

The writs mentioned were deemed a "chief means of relief to the poor and distressed." The Committee of the Whole House asked that the people should have speedy relief and the benefit of those writs. To this His Majesty answered that he wished to uphold all courts of justice, temporal and ecclesiastical. Concerning writs of prohibition he said: "I will yet take more pains that every jurisdiction shall know her own." [2] He felt, further, that the writs of habeas corpus and *de homine replegiando* should be granted according to law.

The grievance of the four western counties—Gloucestershire, Worcestershire, Herefordshire, and Shropshire—was that the Council for the Marches of Wales had availed itself of the pretext of the statute of 34 Hen. VIII to usurp authority over them.[3] In the 1605/06 session of Parliament, the Commons had passed a bill declaring that the intent of the Henrician statute was not to subject those counties to government by instruction. The bill had gone no further, and the inhabitants of the four counties were said to be "utterly discouraged."

The Council for the Marches of Wales was an appendage to and servant of the Privy Council, which could reverse its decisions and give orders to it, as it pleased. In consequence, the Four Shires, as they came to be called, found themselves under conciliar government and given less local self-government than the other English counties. Sir Herbert Croft was pushing the claims of the Four Shires and had met with support in the Lower House.

To this grievance the King's answer was a decided negative. To change the government of the Four Shires would tend, he asserted, "to the alteration of a settled state of government continued by the space of many years." [4]

The abuse of proclamations received no little attention from the Committee of the Whole House for Grievances. Hakewill, Nathaniel Bacon, Hoskins, and Owen discussed the proposed Article VIII on the subject, an article that had been committed and recommitted. On the recommittal it was resolved that a catalog of proclamations complained of [5] should accompany the formal complaint. The statement came to nearly four folio pages.[6] The happiness and freedom, the document read, that had been enjoyed by His Majesty's subjects existed in part because they were governed by "the certain rule of law." [7] Out of that principle had grown up the right of the people not to be punished in their lands, bodies, or goods, except as ordained by the common law of the land or by the statutes.

Proclamations had become, it was asserted, more frequent, some of them tending to alter points of law, even to make new laws; [8] some had been issued after the session of Parliament "for matter directly rejected in the same session"; others had prescribed punishments to be inflicted before any lawful trial, naming penalties as if the proclamations were penal statutes.[9] It was said also that proclamations were severely executed by sentence in the Star Chamber, "with punishment greater than penal statutes." [10]

The King answered that he thought it was his duty to "restrain and prevent such mischiefs and inconveniences . . . growing in the Commonweal, against which no certain law is extant," which prerogative his progenitors had enjoyed. But since proclamations had, in his reign, become more frequent, he wished to be informed thereof. Therefore he would confer with his Privy Councillors, his learned counsel, and his judges, and cause such proclamations as were passed to be reformed. For the future he would provide that none should be made but such as should stand with the laws and the statutes, and such as, in cases of necessity, his progenitors had used.

The grievance of impositions on victualing houses and alehouses was a serious one, since the impositions were authorized by letters of instructions and not by assent of Parliament. Such houses were said to be often "harbors of idleness, drunkenness, whoredom, and all manner of felonies, the licenses are now . . . rented and taken by the looser and baser sort." [11]

It had been a custom of long standing, justified by statutes, that the justices of the peace in the local community regulated alehouses, licensed them, and took away their licenses. Such control was one of the main functions of the justices of the peace. But now, declared the statement of the Committee for Grievances, the justices of the peace found themselves unable to put an end to evil alehouses, for the persons upon whom the impositions were levied affirmed with clamor that they had toleration for a year. In consequence, many justices of the peace were perplexed as to their duty. The committee recommended that the former letters and instructions for impositions upon alehouses "be countermanded or stayed." It was not the last time that the government of James I would attempt to take away control of alehouses from the local authorities in order to develop a new source of income or to give the friend of a favorite the opportunity to make a substantial profit. On July 10 the King promised the Commons that the payment upon alehouses should cease.[12]

Dr. Cowell and
The Interpreter

AMONG the grievances never marshaled in the formal petitions, nor embodied in bills, was that of Dr. Cowell's book *The Interpreter* (1607). The Commons had been in session only a few days when John Hoskins quoted John Cowell, then professor of civil law at Cambridge, as saying under the head of "Subsidy:" "Whereas the Prince of his absolute power might make laws of himself, he doth of favor admit the consent of his subjects therein, that all things in their own confession may be done with indifferency." [1] Hoskins urged his hearers to glance through the headings in *The Interpreter* under "Subsidy," "Parliament," and "King," suggesting that some members might be named to censure books that dealt with the common law. It was resolved to refer the question to the Committee for Grievances.

On the next day, February 24, Sandys was reporting from the Committee for Grievances, which had already been looking into Cowell's publication. Sandys pronounced it "a book very unadvised and undiscreet, tending to the disreputation of the honor and power of the common laws." Sandys was, however, no bigot nor one inclined to jump to conclusions. He added to what he had said that it was hard to censure a book or a sentence in a book "without the contexture." Therefore he moved for a subcommittee.

When Martin reported from that subcommittee, he asserted that certain headings in the book were rash, dangerous, and pernicious. Cowell quoted from Adam Blackwood, who in 1581 had published a work called *Adversus Georgii Buchanani Dialogum de Jure Regni apud Scotos pro Regibus Apologia*. Martin added: "concludes we are all slaves by reason of the Conquest." [2]

Martin declared that the Commons should not call their own rights in question, but should call Dr. Cowell in question. Fuller wished to see the matter looked into.

Martin was distressed because the common law referred to (by Cowell, I take it) was false; he called for consultation with civilians, with Privy Councillors, and with judges. Bacon characterized the license of the pen as a disease of the time; he would have been no friend of freedom of the press. But he was ready to speak up for the common law. Cowell had been putting his sickle into another man's harvest, that is, as a civilian, he was meddling with the common law. He had been inducing misunderstanding between the sovereign and his people. Hoskins mentioned other treatises of the same nature as that of Cowell. At the instance of the Speaker, who for once was running with the hounds, it was resolved that the subcommittee should consider with what to charge Cowell. Sir Anthony Cope, a Banbury Puritan, and one ready to believe the worst, suspected that confederates from abroad might have had a hand in Cowell's work. Cope may have been glancing over *The Interpreter* and have caught references to continental authorities, a suspicious circumstance to the zealous.

The subcommittee to deal with the Cowell matter was made up of members of the Government, of three civilians, and of several protagonists of the rights of Parliament. Two conferences were held with members of the Lords.[3] That House was ready to join in the examination of Cowell as well as in his censure and punishment, as the cause should deserve.

A formal conference was held on March 2, at which the Attorney told the Lords that the committee of the Commons found parts of the book dangerous and offensive. Cowell was not disputing, as in universities, for the sake of discussion, but was talking of kingdoms and states and their powers. It appeared that he had written, not from ignorance, but from presumption. Martin followed and dealt with Cowell's use of "subsidy," of "kingship," and of "prerogative." Whether Cowell had overshot himself in speaking of the King's power they left to the Lords.[4]

On March 5 the Upper House considered what they would say to the Commons about Cowell. Salisbury was doubtful about punishing a man for what had been written outside of Parliament, but he was in favor of dealing with the Commons about it.[5] "The book is brought to our hands by those with whom we have promised to hold all good correspondency. How they should seek it better or in better fashion I see not." [6]

Another conference was held with the Lords on March 8. When, on March 10, Martin reported Salisbury's speech at the conference, he told the Commons (quoting Salisbury) that the King had taken notice of the book and had called Cowell in to examine him.[7] He liked to examine men and regarded himself as a professional in ferreting out the truth. This man "hath been too bold in some things with the common laws of the Realm," [8] he pronounced. It was presumptuous in any subject to deal with such matters. To submit the King to a certain definition was a delicate matter.[9] Martin told the Commons that the King would suppress the book; indeed, he hated everyone who defended it.

Then James used the occasion, in talking to some Lord who must have quoted him in the conference, to draw attention to a matter nearer his heart. Cowell discussed supply without consent of the people. The King, reported Martin, was many times pleased and could be passionately displeased. He would not be angry with those who denied him supply. Such members of the House might want favor, but they would be sure of justice. "Happy we have a man to our King," said Martin.[10]

Dr. Cowell proved a unifying element between the Lords, the King, and the Commons. The Lords had seemed to the Commons to move a trifle slowly about Cowell, waiting, perhaps, to learn what the King would say. Possibly the Commons were a bit surprised to find the Lords in substantial agreement with them; they were delighted to learn that the King was on their side. Beaulieu wrote Trumbull about the Cowell episode and said that it was thought the Commons, if the King gave them leave, would go very near to hanging Cowell.[11] On March 15 Beaulieu wrote that the King promised that the book should be suppressed, but he wished the author not to be troubled nor to incur any danger. At that point the Commons dropped the pursuit.[12]

The King was right; the House of Commons had been too quick on the trigger. Anyone who will take the trouble to read here and there in *The Interpreter* will discover that it is a useful book, a dictionary of legal and constitutional terms, worthy to be shelved near the desk of any student of the English past. Dr. Cowell wrote a modest foreword to his readers and seemed genuinely anxious for criticism. To judge from his language he was an unassuming, devoted scholar; he was also a learned man who read widely and quoted from Bracton, Fortescue, and Sir Thomas Smith, and from many obscurer English political works, as well as from countless continental treatises. Deeply versed in medieval law and custom, he was undoubtedly under their influence. The medieval works tended to exalt the imperial power. Those fair Latin tomes with their vellum bindings and their clear lettering carried more weight with the closet scholar than the news of the last decades from St. Stephen's. Dr. Cowell was, I suspect, hardly a man of sharp and probing mind. He culled quotations where he could find them, quotations that often disagreed with one another, and he found it hard to choose between different opinions. He was too willing to set diverging views against one another and let it go at that. About legislation he had written:

> Only by the custom of this Kingdom, he [the King] maketh no laws without the consent of the 3 estates, though he may quash any law concluded of by them. And whether his power of making laws be restrained . . . or of a godly and commendable policy, not to be altered without great peril, I leave to the judgment of wiser men, but I hold it incontrowlable that the King of England is an absolute King, and all learned politicians do range the power of making laws *inter insignia summae et absolutae potestatis*.[13]

Spedding says that the trouble with Dr. Cowell was that he had no friends. Certainly he had one old Cambridge friend—Archbishop Bancroft—but by this time Bancroft was an ill man.[14] However, he may have sent word to the King to order the book put down and to allow its author to go scot-free.

Wardship to the Fore   I HAVE been following the struggle between the Commons and the King in the session of early 1610 (February to July) over the question of grievances and subsidies, with emphasis on the more significant grievances. Now we must return to March 8 and examine week by week and almost day by day the ups and downs of negotiations between the Commons and the Lords and between the Commons and the King over "supply" and "support." Those questions concerning the granting of money are inextricably involved with grievances, and it is impossible wholly to disentangle them. It will not be forgotten that in February Salisbury had, in addressing a conference, laid before the conferees and thus before the Commons as well as the Lords, the demands of the King. On March 8 Edmondes wrote Trumbull in Paris that in the ears of M.P.s the demands sounded high. Salisbury had asked £600,000 for supply and £200,000 for support, sums that seemed enormous to those who could remember the modest requests of the late Queen.

The Commons, declared Edmondes, were proceeding carefully; they did not propose to commit themselves to so great a sum until His Majesty should consent to grant equivalent benefits to the subjects.[1] It was true that in the conference Salisbury had offered tentatively ten concessions. Of those Edmondes wrote: "Though . . . they are such as will be of great ease and advantage unto the subject, yet we desire to redeem a greater burden and thralldom." In other words, the Commons were insisting that the system of wardship be dissolved and were little disposed to consider other benefits until they had gained that object.

When on March 14 they were granted permission by the King to treat of wardships and tenures as well as purveyance, they were gratified, although they realized that they would have to contract for the favors proposed by offering a considerable contribution in money. "The King," the Attorney General told them, in reporting from the Lords, "offers this [sic] flowers," yet the King's judgment depended upon the offer they would make.[2]

The necessity of haste had been stressed by the Solicitor and his warning did not go unheeded. Six days a week the Committee on Tenures was to meet. Before them lay four problems calling for solution:

1. What obligations of wardship ought to be done away with
2. How to secure themselves so that they would be forever free from the burdens of wardship
3. What offers were to be made to the King in return for the abolition of wardships

4. What course should be taken for the levying of the payment in the country.[3]

Edmondes wrote Trumbull on March 15 that the Commons were wrestling with the problem of how much money they should offer and how they should raise it. To find the money was difficult, and whatever method was adopted would encounter opposition from private interests.[4] The same was true of any attempt to abolish purveyance: the purveyors could quickly assemble what would appear weighty reasons to prove that without their ministrations the King would be badly off.

It soon appeared that the Commons were in a sea of troubles in formulating a contract. Tenures, they discovered, were entangled with the prerogative and could hardly be separated.[5]

The Commons proposed to abolish tenures *in capite* and in knight service, to reduce all tenures to socage tenures.[6] That would have been a simplification of a complex problem, for there were tenures and tenures, fees and duties and honors tied up with them. It seems probable that early in the proceedings of the committee, or conceivably in earlier sessions, members had been quietly informed by Privy Councillors (and possibly by others in the King's entourage) what tenures, fees, and honors His Majesty deemed indispensable for the maintenance of his exalted station. The committee went ahead to work out in detail the tenures to be done away with or to be limited in scope, reserving to His Majesty those symbols of sovereignty with which he was unwilling to part. To the Crown they reserved such rights as "the rents, personal services, suits in court, escheats, and reliefs." The tenure of grand serjeanty was abolished, but the service of honor connected with it was retained. Homage, both ancestral and ordinary, was taken away, but "coronation homage" reserved, that is, the ceremony of homage performed at the King's coronation.[7] Many rights were, for the time being, left undetermined, presumably to be settled later. Nothing in history is duller than feudal rights, yet the Lords seemed to enjoy lingering over them. Were not their titles among the remnants of feudalism? [8]

It was hoped to make "wardable lands" supply the large sum

the Commons would have to provide for the King in lieu of wardship; that sum had to be definite and not dependent upon the income of a particular year. To find the sum necessary the Commons planned to rate not only those lands of wards held from the King but also those held from lesser overlords. Out of the "wardable lands" had also to be found the money to furnish the Prince of Wales, the Duke of York, and the Princess Elizabeth with £25,000 a year. Of those who were drafting the scheme Beaulieu wrote: "It is presumed that . . . these jealous and circumspect spirits will not a little belabor their brains, so that a man may guess that this only point of the wardships is not yet near its perfect conclusion." [9]

The "Memorial," containing among several reforms the proposals concerning tenures and incidents connected with them, was presented to the Lords on March 26. To that same body was submitted the plan to give the King £100,000 a year. The Commons hoped that the Lords would join with them in the Great Contract now under consideration.

The Lords took time to deliberate. When the Commons offered £100,000 a year [10] they believed that they were giving the King more than he had received from wardship and purveyance.[11] Some letters imply that the £100,000 was granted for the abolition of wardship and its appurtenances, but from what goes before and after it appears reasonably certain that the £100,000 was for wardships and its appurtenances and for purveyance as well. These letters estimated the income from wardship as about £40,000 a year, that from purveyance at something less, and assumed that £100,000 was an ample compensation, not only for what the King received, but for what he might hope to receive in the future. The Commons believed that they were being generous with the King.

Meanwhile there was a contretemps. It was whispered that Salisbury had hinted that he intended to surrender his position as the Master of the Wards in return for a considerable sum (£5,000) per year. Could it be true that the King's first minister was ready to give up his second office (the most profitable of all high offices) in order to facilitate the abolition of a burden on the subjects? It seemed improbable, but his willingness had been indicated in such a way that "the whole House took it [for] granted." "Yet now they find him nothing inclined unto, nor can challenge any such offer of him." [12]

The rumor was picked up by the usually well-informed ambassador from Venice, who wrote that Prince Henry was said to have aspired to the position of Master of the Wards but that Salisbury hoped by abolishing wardships to increase the royal revenue, to give satisfaction to the Commons, to recoup his loss of income by accepting an annual pension, and to avoid the possibility of falling out of favor with the King.

It is not impossible that Salisbury, in conversation with one or more leaders of the Commons when in one of his moods of depression, may have toyed with the notion of giving up his position as Master of the Wards. When he began to realize that the King was drawing back from the proposed bargain with the Commons and increasing his demands, Salisbury may have concluded that a generous gesture to help the Crown would win him little credit where he needed most, with His Majesty.

The changeable sovereign was raising his sights as to the "composition" to be demanded. On April 5 Edmondes wrote: "Our Parliament is broken up till the week after Easter, and till then we are put off for receiving the King's answer how he liketh of our offer for the suppressing of the tenures. It is said that he desires to raise us to 300,000*li.*" [13] At a conference on April 20 the Lords presented the King's views on tenures.[14]

On April 26 Beaulieu wrote Trumbull that the King would not yield to the cutting off of the tenures *in capite,* as the House demanded in their scheme to extinguish wardships; he considered it a matter too prejudicial and dishonorable to himself and to the gentility of England to abolish the noblest tenures of his kingdom and to reduce his subjects, base and noble, rich and poor, to one tenure of lands. Otherwise he was content to put down wardships utterly and to give the House such assurance in the Great Contract as they should desire.[15] He was still haggling for further concessions. It soon appeared that, while beating down the Commons on the concessions to be granted them, he proposed to ask for a great deal more money.[16] From Salisbury's speech later we learn that James had determined to refuse the offer of the Commons unless they would satisfy him in the matter of honor. He awaited their answer, but meanwhile he was off to the country and left provisional authority with the Lords to answer the Commons.[17]

At a conference on the afternoon of April 26 the Attorney General told the Lords that the Commons were willing to meet the King's demands about the honors connected with tenures and that they wished to know the price, that is, what the King expected them to give, in return for the concessions he was asking of them.[18]

The King Raises
His Demand

ON the afternoon of April 26 Salisbury made a long speech,[1] which Sandys relayed to the Commons that same day. Salisbury expressed gratitude to the Lords for laboring to advance the cause of monarchy and for the flexibility (not his word) they had shown in their dealings.

He was aware that the Commons expected an answer that day as to how far their offer of £100,000 "did work in the King's mind to join with us in contract." But he had bad news for them and used many sentences in leading up to it. The nub of it was that when His Majesty had demanded £200,000 a year there had been no thought of parting with wardships. Unless the Commons offered his complete satisfaction, that is, £200,000 a year "above whatsoever we defalked from him by our Contract, the wards will not be had." [2] The King was adding another £100,000 to his demand. When the £200,000 had been proposed, it had been assumed that in return for that sum His Majesty would make great concessions. The Commons had possibly jumped to the conclusion that they could purchase the abolition of wardships and purveyance and various other minor grievances for that price. Now the King was insisting that, in addition to the £200,000, he had to have whatever more should be necessary to recoup his loss for having given up wardships and purveyance.[3] He had pared down the concessions concerning wardships, and now he was asking for more money, for £100,000 more.

Salisbury encouraged the House to hope that for that total sum they might have wardships, purveyance, "and those other incidents with what else the Parliament shall think fit." They must not, he warned them, think of other concessions, lest they might dwell in error, by his error, if he encouraged them to do so.

He volunteered eight items of advice. In the first place, he took for granted that the King's just necessity must be relieved by his people, and, in the second, that the King was not to depend absolutely, in the matter of subsistence, upon the will of the people. Thirdly, he warned the Commons that the King's prerogative by the law of nations was as great as that of any Christian king, if it were not restrained by the municipal laws of the kingdom. But the scale of the prerogative in any matter of charge was limited by the public weal, words that must have been observed in St. Stephen's with satisfaction. He went on to his fifth point in the same vein. When princes extended their prerogative too far, it worked not the good but the grief of their subjects, and the princes limited their own greatness. If in the time, in the frequency, in the proportion, there be excess, the session of Parliament is a fit time to complain, and subjects may be bold there to dispute against the prerogative, and to desire moderation, yet so as not to strike at the root. Such roots were not to be pulled up. He advised the Commons, in the sixth place, not to put forward their own private opinions against decisions rendered in courts; that was to bay at the moon. Seventh, he declared that when princes asked more taxes than the subjects could bear, the Sovereign must hear with benignity, and may be refused. In the eighth place Salisbury warned them that if the subjects asked for peace in their time and that of their successors, they must pay for it— words of warning that sound as if they came from the royal mouth.

Salisbury was speaking for his master, but not wholly. Some of his sentences came from one who had long breathed the air of St. Stephen's and might have been quoted against him to His Majesty. He was taking the chance of losing that slender hold he still had on a fickle and ungrateful master.

On May 2 Beaulieu wrote Trumbull that the Commons were considering the King's reasons against extinguishing the tenures *in capite* and were willing to yield to him. What they meant, Beaulieu indicated, was that they would cut off the stock and leave the root. Had not the King promised that the root would never spring up again?

But with his excessive demands they were "very much distasted and stricken dumb." They would give him no answer, but would remain silent until His Majesty would be pleased to make some more reasonable proposition "or break absolutely the bargain wherefrom they do not seem now much averse, thinking to have done enough, and to have dealt very liberally with the King." His Majesty, Beaulieu added, had planned to stay two or three weeks longer in the country but was now going to return to London. Until he did so, nothing would be done in the matter.[4]

Was His Majesty mad? His first demands had shocked the Commons, and now he was preparing to increase them by a half. What had led to this change?

His Majesty tried another tack. In April he negotiated a loan of £100,000 from the Corporation of London.[5] By May 2 the matter was known to Edmondes and to John Chamberlain, and by May 6 to the Venetian ambassador. With £100,000 in hand he could, with the aid of wardship, purveyance, etc., manage to remain solvent for the time being. He did not look far ahead.

But he needed a great deal more than the loan would furnish him. Why under those circumstances had he asked so much of Parliament, more than he could hope to get? Who prompted him to raise his demands? Hardly Salisbury, who was a cautious man, not given to gambles. Moreover, Salisbury's star was declining and, after this Parliament, was to sink almost to the horizon.

The King was perhaps looking to other Councillors, to insinuating advisers, such as Northampton,[6] who were eager to see James rule as a monarch should. Why should he not free himself from the unpleasant task of begging subsidies from disagreeable and disloyal subjects? Was it not evident, those near His Majesty may have whispered to him, that the Commons seemed unwilling to give £200,000 in annual support for relief from wardship and purveyance? Let His Majesty raise his demand to £300,000, and, if he got it, he would no longer have to call upon ungrateful knights and closefisted burgesses. If not, let him dismiss Parliament in royal rage, borrow the money, or take it from his subjects without benefit of the Commons.[7] All this is hypothesis, and yet it is not impossible.

On May 1 the House resumed the debate over tenures and wardships. Martin,[8] who kept an eye on the program of the Commons, reminded them that an answer was due to the Lords. Bacon proposed "a decent, modest, respective message." Sir Robert Johnson, a member from Monmouth for the third time, an officer of the ordnance, a man on good terms with Salisbury, but an enemy of purveyance and a plainspoken Commoner, remarked: "That seeing 300,000*li* for all our offer for part, not to sit down thus." What he meant, I think, was that since the King wanted more and conceded less the Commons ought not to sit down but speak up. Sir Roger Owen believed silence best, "or else to send a message that we can go no higher, and leave it to their Lordships." Sir George More, by long habit a moderate supporter of the Crown, hoped the House would deliver the reasons why they could go no higher.

The question arose whether to debate the matter in the House or in committee. The long silence that ensued, presumably a kind of protest or gesture of unhappiness by the House, led Sandys to say, "No dull silence in anything that is between the King and the House." He was calling, I think, for moderate counsels in dealing with His Majesty. The discussion was put off till the next day.

On that day, May 2, Sir Maurice Berkeley brought in the draft of an answer to the Lords, which was read by the Clerk and then by the Speaker.[9] Sir William Twysden cited a precedent of 13 Edw. III [10] in which the Commons requested that they might consult their constituents. About Berkeley's draft there were various comments, and a subcommittee was named to amend the answer. The amended version, which Sandys brought in from the subcommittee,[11] was read to the House. There was still criticism of the wording, but a motion to recommit was lost by 135 to 125.

The Commons declared that they had offered for tenures and wardships and other incidents £100,000 of yearly revenue whereas the King had demanded £200,000 above his present profits from various sources. They had proposed to contract with him about wardship and tenures connected therewith, and he had asked to contract for all those things together ("in gross") and not for tenures and wardships alone. The Commons had intended that the sum for wardship should be raised from those who were partners of the benefits, that is, the owners of the lands that bore the burden of wardship "and not the generality or meaner sort of his Majesty's subjects." They found no cause to change their decision. As for the £200,000 "in gross" that His Majesty was demanding, they could not consent to it. They could not forget the trust that thousands reposed in them and the extreme "discontenting of his . . . loving . . . subjects by pressing them with a burthen in former ages never heard of, and in their present known poverty impossible." [12]

The next morning the Commons asked for a conference with the Lords, and Sir Julius Caesar was sent up to the Lords. The conference was set for the afternoon of the following day. The Lords requested that since the conference was weighty each House should confer authority on its committees to debate and answer questions. That authority the Commons failed to give.[13]

On May 3 Salisbury commented to the Lords about the reluctance of the Commons to debate with them. He feared that the Commons would stress the impossibility of yielding to the King's last demand, which they found "peremptory." They had observed the steps by which the King had risen in his demands. He hoped that when the Commons committee joined in the conference they would come so warranted that they could answer at once what the Lords might say to them. Neither side should feel bound by what was said. It seemed that the Commons had concluded peremptorily to give £200,000 and no more. Perhaps the Lords could reason with them, and the two Houses might decide to give more or less.[14] The old hand in Parliament was showing all his skill and tact, but he had to deal with a Lower House that was weary of the shifts of the sovereign.

At the conference on the next day (May 4) Sir Julius Caesar, Chancellor of the Exchequer, spoke in behalf of the Commons to the Lords. The Commons, he said, did not know how to raise so great a sum as the King asked, "without giving discontentment unto the subjects, which we know would be much displeasing unto his Majesty." [15]

Salisbury reminded the Commons in the conference that, although the two Houses were divided in place, they constituted but one "law-maker." [16] He took note of their "glance" that they spoke for thousands, and the Lords but for themselves, and went on: "Those that you bind, are they not . . . our followers, servants, and kinsmen? . . . You cannot coöperate without us." Never had the Lords, he asserted, dealt more lovingly with the Lower House than now; he did not add that he had been in some degree responsible for that attitude. He continued: "If you do not agree with his Majesty, if I make not more of the wards than you have offered, without either any noise, or that the subject find fault at, I will leave my place." [17] In some notes by Dudley Carleton the statement by Salisbury is put in this way: "To these and others [the offers made by the Commons] we [the Commons] have made bare replies, as if it were not worth thinking of. The wards may be more worth to the King than what we offer." [18] In other words, if the Commons would not accept the concessions Salisbury dangled before them, the King could make more than the Commons were offering him by raising the price of wardships.

The same suggestion had been made two months earlier (March 2) and was perhaps not sufficiently taken into account by the Commons: "For, said he [Salisbury], if we compound with the

King we must not only consider what the present profit is of the wardships and of fines for alienations, but what may be made of them." [19] This, wrote Hurstfield, was

> a promise and a threat. . . . Having given a clear warning that their position was not impregnable and that the initiative did not lie with them, he offered them sweeter words: "Let your resolutions sort with these considerations . . . and then you may . . . tell your neighbors that you have made a pretty hedge about them." [20]

The answer of the Lord Treasurer to the Commons' statement of May 2 did not please the members of the Lower House, who were fully aware of His Majesty's repeated attempts to overreach them. Now he was saying, through Salisbury, that he could make more money by increasing the burden of wardship than by a grant from them. He was threatening to make their most serious grievance more grievous than ever.

One may ask if the Commons had been quite fair with the King. It has been pointed out earlier that the landed classes and the bourgeoisie in many country towns were not impoverished. They were, however, so accustomed to paying taxes based upon old and low valuations that they could not imagine themselves paying a good deal more, even if it were but a small fraction of their incomes. That conditions at the moment were not propitious was, of course, to be taken into account.

The Recorder, in reporting (May 5) the conference,[21] indicated that the Lords had hoped for an exchange of arguments. The ten points of retribution put forward early in the session by the Lord Treasurer had been met by bare replies, as if hardly worthy of consideration.[22] Then Montague suddenly professed to wonder "what tempest had fallen that it was become a danger to ask a question." [23] Such an inquiry tells us something of the state of the House. Were those in opposition showing themselves unwilling to listen to the King's friends? [24]

Montague's speech was ill received. He had failed to tell the whole story. Strong language had been used in the conference and by a great ecclesiastic, and word of it had been passed from member to member. Sir Francis Barrington, a landed gentleman from Essex, suggested that all the speeches in the conference should be reported. It was then proposed that what had occurred should be set down in writing by all the gentlemen who had been present.

It was Hoskins, never afraid to speak out, who reported that the archbishop of Canterbury had expressed sorrow that things had not been carried, that is, I assume, that subsidies had not been voted. As things stood the King would have to help himself. In speculative divinity, he took it that the kingdom must support its king. Some fine wits were in the Commons, but their orations, when analyzed, amounted to nothing but froth.[25] Bancroft was an ill man but even when well he was not likely to be conciliatory.

This was the cat that had not been let out of the bag by Montague. The Commons were annoyed, of course, but they did not protest. One could not expect that Archbishop Bancroft would have good words for the Commoners; it was he who stood between them and legislation about silenced ministers.

At this point, on May 8, Salisbury addressed the messengers from the Commons and other members of the Lower House who had been invited to come up to the Lords.[26] He broke the news that the King of France had been assassinated. That King had always stood like a "rampier" [rampart] against all conspiracies and dangers that were "hatched and threatened against them here," that is, against James and his family. He urged them to keep watch for the safety and good of their Prince and to assist him with such means as were requisite. Salisbury seemed to insinuate, wrote Beaulieu, that this accident meant that they would have to give their King greater assistance.[27] Salisbury went further than insinuation. He told the Commons: "We must now give occasion for foreign dispatches to advertise how careful we are of our King, and how we provide for him, and money is the only antidote for future mischief."[28] The state needed to have money in hand, he insisted, lest they had to seek it suddenly.[29]

Salisbury no doubt realized that the Commons had cooled about the possibility of a bargain with His Majesty. If he failed to win the Commons he was aware that his standing with his master would be endangered. The time had come for a concession. He explained that the sums put before them had been tendered by way of estimation rather than as a demand, and he urged his listeners not to let such an opportunity slip away.

Beaulieu commented:

> "They are not like to trouble themselves much further in the matter, until the King shall have modified and reformed his propositions." [30]

Salisbury would possibly have been better advised to have allowed the Commons to discover for themselves that their country faced new dangers and needed to strengthen its position. Some would doubtless have argued that to vote money for defense and alliance was a wasted gesture since the money was likely to fall into the hands of favorites. Members may well have whispered to one another that James had not the least notion of being drawn into war, and Salisbury must have known as much. Yet he knew that England should be in a strong position, and for that money in hand was necessary.

The King Clamps Down on Debating Impositions

ON May 11 the Speaker had a surprise for the Commons: a message from the King forbade them to dispute his power and prerogative to impose upon merchandises imported or exported. On that a judgment had been rendered.[1] His majesty was taking the offensive.

The Commons were startled and perplexed. It was known that the King was off to the country, some distance to the north of London, engaged in hunting.

Wentworth was the first to speak.[2] Judgments given in the King's courts were not reversible, he said, except by error or attaint. About the proceedings in the Commons, His Majesty was misinformed; no one attempted to reverse the proceedings in the Bate case. But no other man in England was bound by the judgment in that case. Anyone might try the law in a new action. Should all other courts be at liberty to dispute the law, and should this court be barred from disputing it? Was not the King's prerogative disputable? "Do not our books in 20 cases argue what the King may do, and what not do, by his prerogative? . . . Nay, if we shall once say that we may not dispute the prerogative let us be sold for slaves." [3]

He concluded by moving a Committee of the Whole House to frame an answer. Seven or eight speakers followed Wentworth, "all to the same conclusion," [4] among them Hoskins, Fuller, and Richard James, probably the M.P. for Newport in the Isle of Wight. James made a long discourse and alluded to "restrained by Council's letters." [5] Sir Francis Hastings recommended a committee, as Wentworth had done.

Sir William Twysden put questions to the Speaker: how had he received the message, whether by letter, and in what manner? Those queries were pressed upon the Speaker, who excused himself. Sir Edward Montague remarked that since the King was out of town the message must have come by letter, or from some great person.

The Speaker was "troubled." [6] He told the Commons that they had received fifty-six or fifty-eight messages from the King and never before had he been pressed into saying how he got them. [7]

> You have had experience of my fidelity and I hope there's none of you thinks I dare deliver this without I had authority to do it, for that were more than I am able to bear. But to make me a precedent without precedent and offer that to me which you never did to Speaker, I hope you will not. [8]

Croft replied that it had become too much the custom that the Speaker should bring messages from the King; he should not do it, except when he had been sent by the House itself to the King. Twysden declared that the Speaker was not to go to the King but by leave. [9] Since Sir Edward had been constantly writing to the King, or sending word to him, Twysden's words must have sounded strange to him.

Sir George More rose to the defense of the Speaker. One of the petitions at the beginning of Parliament was that the Speaker should have access to the King "at convenient times and with a convenient number." [10] Sir George believed that the Commons ought not to call in question the proceedings of the King.

The Speaker evidently implored the Commons to wait until the next day, but the members were not to be put off. "Whereupon, after he had in the middle of some men's speeches spoken with Mr. Chancellor of the Exchequer, Mr. Secretary Herbert, and Sir Walter Cope who sat near the Chair,[11] he made answer that he received it from the body of the Council." [12]

The admission did not seem to mollify members. Hoskins asked what questions should be referred to the committee: how far were the Commons to treat impositions; how far might the Speaker deliver messages from the King to the Commons and from the Commons to the King?

Sir Edward Montague did not wish any Lords to mediate between the House and the King, but hoped that the Commons would stay proceedings until His Majesty returned. He moved that since the message came not immediately from the King,[13] but from the body of the Council, it was not fit that the House should receive it. The receiving of a message by the Speaker from the Council, he insisted, should not be regarded as a precedent for the future.[14] On the same afternoon records were searched in the Tower touching the business.[15]

The next morning (May 12) Fuller reported from the Committee for Privileges the order penned by them about messages from His Majesty. The order was to be set down in the Clerk's Book, but was not entered there. It is found in the *Parliamentary Debates 1610* as follows: "That the same message coming not immediately from his Majesty, should not be received as a message, and that in all messages from his Majesty the Speaker, before he delivered them, should first ask leave of the House, according as had anciently been accustomed." [16] What the Clerk did write in his book was: "Mr. Speaker, with license of the House, delivereth a message—every part of the message delivered from the Lords to be by two several writings—sent from his Majesty—to be true in all." [17] This somewhat mysterious phrasing may be partly explained by a passage in Add. 48119, where the Speaker is quoted as saying:

> Upon his Majesty's coming to town I was required to attend him, it pleased his Majesty to take notice that the message delivered yesterday by me from the Lords was his own and by 2 several directions to the Lords by letter given them in charge to deliver [to] me. Then it pleased him that I should again as from his own mouth deliver the same, wherein I shall desire your leave to use the help of my paper. [18]

In the Record Office of the House of Lords is a fragment of the "Draft Journal of House of Commons," which contains a statement that the Speaker read to the Commons:

> The King gave express commandment. . . . He esteemeth all those proceedings by which there may be any doubt or question made of his authority in that kind [i.e. impositions] to be so much to the derogation of that prerogative which he deriveth from his royal progenitors (not only in point of law but by use and practice of the same) as when he considereth to how little purpose any such disputations among you can be. . . . He can no longer forbear to command you by my mouth to give over all such arguments or directions as may in any way tend to the examination of his power and prerogative in the general or the reason of that judgment which hath been given . . . as a matter out of your power to examine or determine. [19]

His Majesty, who was not far away, was supporting his Council and the Speaker. It is not surprising that the Speaker read the document over twice.

Martin moved that a committee should consider what course to take touching imposition and what answer to give. This was Saturday; it was determined that the committee meet on Monday afternoon, [20] probably a Committee of the Whole House. All the lawyers were to be present. On that same Monday the Speaker received another message from the King, requiring an answer from the House. His Majesty commanded them with all possible expedition to return him a clear and direct answer whether they would at any time refuse to receive any message if the declaration was made to them that it came from His Majesty himself in word or writing, or from the Privy Council "by his direction and in his name [my italics]." [21]

For the Speaker it must have been an agreeable morning—his sovereign was standing by him against the Commons. The episode would not, however, have reduced the tension between House and Speaker. How were the Commons to reply to offended Majesty?

On Monday, May 14, it was determined to refer the matter to a committee in the afternoon, "together with the other message," that is, the message from the Privy Council. The Speaker was asked to leave his papers containing his versions of the two messages with the Clerk, who was to attend the committee.[22]

It was a crowded Committee of the Whole House that afternoon, "more than ever I saw at any time in the House before," wrote the author of Add. 48119. For some obscure reason the committee "appointed" John Hare, M.P. for Horsham, the "unconsiderate firebrand," as chairman. Hare asked to be excused on account of his "insufficiency," but was commanded to take his place, conceivably because it was assumed that he would not be given to compromise. The Clerk read the order of May 12, and the paper "which Mr. Speaker used for the help of his memory." Then Martin proposed that the Commons should answer first concerning the message sent by the King, and then concerning the message sent by the Privy Council, "which order was not misliked." A general silence, now almost routine in crises, ensued in the committee, and then Sir Henry Montague said: "it seemeth by this great silence men do not think it safe to speak." The Speaker, he continued, had a double capacity: as Speaker he might not bring a message from the King, but as a private man he might, as any other servant of the King.

It was not a convincing distinction. Hoskins declared the King a god upon earth; they should pray him that it was not in their thoughts to refuse any message. Is it possible that Hoskins, in his known role as a jester, was poking a little fun at the King's habit of comparing himself with the Deity? For speaking of His Majesty as a god upon earth he could hardly be punished.

Dudley Carleton called the question one of good manners. The Speaker would never deliver a message from the King without first asking the House whether they wanted to hear it. Carleton's notion was "liked" and was seconded. But the House resolved to answer the King that they had no purpose to, and would not at any time, refuse to receive any message from the King if the Speaker asked permission from the House. When the chairman read the resolution to the committee, a general aye was given.

Edward Alford of the Inner Temple, M.P. for Colchester, objected to the proviso in the statement, "so as the Speaker first asked the license of the House." The motion contained a "negative pregnant," by which he meant something conceived in the future but not delivered,[23] that is, the House should not commit itself for the future but stick to the present.

It is hard from a single, even if a detailed and interesting, source for the proceedings of the committee, to make out what happened. When Hare, an insufficient chairman, as he had warned the committee, asked whether Carleton's motion should pass without the addition of the "so as" clause, the members cried "No." When he put the question that it should pass with the addition, again they cried "No." It appears that the majority did not like Carleton's motion. In neither form did it meet the King's demand. It seems probable that members, in their differences, were becoming excited and even perhaps confused.

Wentworth, who was not given to assisting royal programs, suggested an answer: "that we have neither will nor purpose to refuse to receive any message." That would seem to have included any message from the Privy Council, but the wording was applauded by the committee, "notwithstanding that other projects were offered."

Then Sir Robert Harley, a zealous and fussy Puritan from

Herefordshire, who seldom took the floor, but was not without intelligence, proposed an answer: "We have neither purpose nor will to refuse at any time to receive any message which our Speaker shall have in commandment immediately from your Majesty, by word or writing, to deliver to the House, according to the usual and continued custom of the House." [24] The important words here were "immediately from your Majesty." It will be observed that messages from the Privy Council had been carefully excluded. The writer of Add. 48119 noted that Harley's draft was received with a "great and general liking, but impugned by Mr. Chancellor of the Chequer, Mr. Secretary Herbert, and the King's Learned Counsel, and Sir George More."

Hobart, the Attorney General, reminded the House that the proposed draft was not "clear and direct to the King's question," "with word weighed, and warily couched," and required a more considered answer than was possible for any one man on his own at once to set down on paper. Six or seven projects had been offered, and others might be offered. Let a committee be chosen to consider the answer, taking with them Harley's paper and one on the other side, and then referring it to the House to decide which they liked better.

The committee, a subcommittee of the sitting Committee of the Whole House, which included the King's Privy Council and learned counsel, Sir George More, and "2 or 3 other gentlemen," brought in almost at once the following wording: "We neither have had, nor have any purpose to refuse, nor will at any time refuse to receive any message committed to our Speaker, or any other that shall be our Speaker hereafter, upon declaration made unto us that the message comes immediately from your Majesty." [25]

Why this statement displeased the House is hard to discover. Was it because the subcommittee consisted largely of the King's friends? Who had chosen the subcommittee? Had it been done by nomination from the floor, and had the "insufficient" chairman been responsible by allowing the first few men named to constitute the subcommittee? Or was it that members with their sharp differences concerning policy were getting out of hand?

Unless more diaries are discovered, we shall never know, and perhaps not even then. The inside story of what happened in the House is too often a secret reserved for the gods, or possibly for some new Maitland.

What we do know is that the House cried, "Away with it, away with it," and even at the first reading of these words, "nor will at any time refuse to. . . ," cried, "No, no," [26] though they then expected to have had Sir Robert Harley's draft read after it, which they immediately called for.

It was answered for the subcommittee that they thought the first form only fit and had rejected the second. Bacon attempted to defend the subcommittee of which he had apparently been a member, pointing out that an answer had to be made "and that clear and direct, and digress or balk the question we may not." In the answer drafted by the subcommittee, there was, he asserted, no peril, since orders were not like acts of Parliament and did not bind future sessions.[27] Bacon's persuasive words, though uttered "with all advantage that wit, words, or eloquence could add to them moved the House no whit." [28] They were in no mood to be entertained even by the best of entertainers. The members called for Harley's draft

> which Mr. Hare, being not forward to come unto, and the King's Privy Council and Learned Counsel (seeing no hope to stir the constant resolution of the House, not so much as to defer the question till the next morning, though they had then sat from 2 o'clock till 'twas almost 7, but said expressly there was no cause nor need to defer it at all, but cried To the Question, To the Question) rose abruptly and suddenly, a good part of the House following them, but not near the half part, they that remained debating whether they should proceed to the question, but in the end contented (because it was late and they would not determine it against them behind their backs), to let it alone.[29]

Next morning, May 15, the King sent word that he would press no further answer from the House until he should signify his further pleasure.[30] The Commons, probably because they were not prepared to arrive at a decision, resolved on May 16 not to sit on the following day, but that committees might sit at their pleasure.[31]

On Friday, May 18, it was resolved on Croft's motion that the Committee of the Whole House should meet in the afternoon "to treat of a message to his Majesty to give him satisfaction" and to send the message by the Speaker.[32]

At the afternoon committee meeting Martin was called to the chair. William Noy, a Cornishman and an M.P. for Grampound, who had attended Exeter College, Oxford, and Lincoln's Inn, raised the question of whether there was a negative power to prevent the Commons from disputing. He admitted that it had been a "practiced power in former Parliaments to send messages not to dispute of this or that"; [33] he was thinking, doubtless, of Elizabeth's sharp injunctions to Parliament. But, continued Noy, if Parliament could not dispute, it was a Parliament "but to one intent," by which he meant, I assume, to vote money and do no more. If they did not stand up now, he implied, they would have little chance to do so later.

Wentworth, by now almost the watchdog of those in opposition, added that to ask moderation in impositions was to admit the King's right to lay them. They must dispute impositions, and he hoped there were none present who would accept the prerogative as a reason why they should not. When the councillors of King Cambyses declared that they had a law that the king might do as he wished, they were "branded with that note of infamy to all posterity." [34] As for the legal judgment cited, that had been given on a point of pleading and was not conclusive for Parliament. Parliament was a high court and should render its own decisions.

The Solicitor, Sir Francis, would not remove established boundaries: the wall between the King and his subjects must stand. Then he became vaguely optimistic about the liberty of Parliament: for them to stand upon their rights was not necessary; they had full latitude to obtain their ends, but just how he did not explain. Bacon could become indefinite and even verbose about the hard questions.

A motion was made for a subcommittee to consider an answer to the King. Sandys favored such a committee, "if the matter of the answer were agreed upon" first. Crew believed that if the Commons could not debate impositions, their case was hard. If they did not bring to their constituents some ease in those matters and in respect to subsidies and support, they would not be welcome at home.[35] Sir Edwin reverted to the proposal for a subcommittee to frame the answer, citing the instance in 1604 when the Commons, in choosing the commissioners for the union, had arranged that every name be voted on separately. He wished to see the names of this subcommittee voted on in the same way. Sandys perhaps had in mind a recent case when a subcommittee had been made up of friends of the King; he may have been trying to prevent such an outcome in this instance. Old usage was too strong for him. It was asserted that everyone who had spoken should be on the committee, and Sir Edwin withdrew his motion, although it was not without support. It was also customary to add other names from the floor. Whether that was done in this case we are not told.

The King's Message: His Speech and Its Reception

NEXT morning (May 19), at the meeting of the subcommittee to frame answers to His Majesty, a message was received from the King, which was relayed to the Committee of the Whole House and then to the House itself.[1]

His Majesty was extremely disquieted by the delay in giving him satisfaction touching the message sent them, and he was unhappy that they had entered into other questions. He would have nothing meddled with till he was satisfied about the other message. If they failed to answer him, they would eventually receive a message from the Speaker (dissolving Parliament?). If they would, however, answer him, he would not restrain them afterward in the other messages, and they would receive a gracious proceeding. In other words, His Majesty threatened them, but if they would give him a favorable answer concerning the receipt of messages sent them, then he would be kind in the matter of disputing impositions. A bargain was possible.

Wentworth was sorry that their proceedings troubled His Majesty. He moved that the order made by the House be not entered. Whether the order was Wentworth's motion—that they would not at any time refuse to receive any message from the King to the Speaker—it is hard to determine from our only source (Add. 48119, with a few unenlightening sentences in *CJ*). It is possible that it was Wentworth's own motion that he now proposed should not be entered in the Clerk's Book, a motion "misliked by the greater part of the House." [2]

It was believed by some that the order had never been voted by the House, since the Privy Council and a considerable minority had walked out of the House and since those remaining had hesitated to put the question to a vote. Sir Maurice Berkeley suggested that the Clerk be asked whether the order had been entered, and, if not, that it should not be. [3] Bacon wished to see affairs returned to the state they were in before the order was made. It had long been his opinion that questions concerning the power of the King and the liberty of the subject should not be textual, positive, and scholastic, but "slide in practice silently," a Baconian aphorism. The sovereignty of the King and the liberty of the Parliament were two elements of state. Take away Parliament, and the wounds of the realm would bleed inwardly; touch the power of the King, a monarch by long continuance and succession, and " 'twould be dangerous." He regarded it as the finger of God that the order had not been entered. [4] It may have been the finger of the Clerk, on the suggestion of the Speaker.

Fuller commented that Bacon's speech was full of art and rhetoric and yet had "some good substance in it." [5]

Sir Walter Cope, Salisbury's henchman, read a form of a message to be sent to the King:

We had no intention to vary from that duty which our predecessors have, and ought to have performed to your royal progenitors, and are humbly desirous that nothing by us done may be taken in any contrary sense, neither had we any other meaning in any order conceived by us than to retain those due respects from our Speaker, which appertain unto us during the time he possesses that place.[6]

This phrasing, which evaded the main question, was "exceedingly well liked by the House in general." [7] Minor alterations were made, but the phrase "in any order conceived by us" became the subject of debate. It was asserted that the order had never been passed, but replied that an order brought in by the subcommittee and read in the House might be termed an "order conceived." Finally, "in any order conceived" was replaced by "in any our proceedings."

Cope's motion was agreed to by the committee and then reported to and accepted by the House.

On Monday morning, May 21, Caesar related that His Majesty was fully satisfied with the message, but wished to address the House that afternoon at Whitehall. (The royal discourse is found among the State Papers.[8]) His Majesty had a grievance: fourteen weeks had elapsed since Parliament met, and nothing had been done in the "principal errand"; not half as many days had been spent on supply as on other matters. He was almost gracious: "God is my judge I would not trouble the state, nor make a contestation with you. You can bear me witness how I have fled all such occasions." As for impositions, he recalled having told them earlier that it was not lawful to dispute what a king may do, but good kings always make known what they will do. Doubtless James had in mind an example of such a king. To complain of any just grievance, he admitted, was the right of the Commons, but they must not dispute his power of imposing in general, which he had both by judgment and the law. "Leave to the King [that] which is his in power, and do you take into your consideration the inconveniences." [9]

The theories James was setting forth would have taken away from Parliament significant functions. To expect country gentlemen who had exercised authority in their own communities to come to London only to learn what the King intended to do, to point out inconveniences, and to vote money was to put a low estimate upon their talents and the value of their time and efforts. The best of the members were reading men who knew about the Roman Republic and of the government of Venice in a later time. From their experience as justices of the peace many knew something of what laws needed to be made or revised.

James, too, looked to history, to the power that kings had always possessed and that two queens had exercised.[10] In alluding to the examples of Mary and Elizabeth he was on firm ground, as he was in another matter. Admit, I think he meant to say, that "customs in England are part of your freehold." They were also part of his. In 1604 the Commons had passed the Bill of Assarts, which was intended to take from him what had been his or his predecessors' for hundreds of years. They had "encroached and crept in upon the King," and then they complained that what they had long possessed should be called in question.[11]

The King's point was well made. It must never be forgotten that the power of the King interested James profoundly, not only because of his craving for power, but because government was a topic upon which he had examined old works of theory and had cogitated not a little.

Three arguments about why impositions could not be laid except in Parliament, he observed in his speech, were being tossed about in some men's minds. The first was precedents, when kings, having laid impositions, recalled them; the second was acts of Parliament to restrain impositions; the third was that if he could take impositions he could also seize his subjects' lands and goods and would not have to ask for subsidies.

To the first argument he answered that it was false logic to assume that because kings had done such a thing they had no power to do otherwise. No doubt many impositions had been laid hastily and perhaps rashly. When the subject complained of such an abuse, the matter was set right and compensation was given.[12] Such satisfaction, explained His Majesty, he would never refuse.

"What a King will do upon bargain, is one thing and what his prerogative is, is another." James had in vexation spoken of the Commons as "merchant-like," but he, too, was a trader.[13]

He left the second argument to the men who studied laws, but would affirm that no act of Parliament denuded [14] the King of power to impose. Penal statutes, he remarked, were acts of Parliament, and yet the King might decide not to enforce such a statute, if he felt it would be cruel to do so.[15]

He answered the third argument by saying that it involved poor reasoning in implying that if a King had once done something in excess, he could not do it at all.

Beware of such arguments, he admonished the members. Do not pass laws that make shadows of kings, or dukes of Venice. Such opinions of kingship were not those of true Christians, but of papists and Puritans. If you have a good king, you are to thank God for him, but a bad king is a curse to the people, and prayers and tears are your arms. But may you bridle him? No more than you can deprive a heady and ill-disposed man of the privileges he abuses. "Deal with me," he implored,

> as you would be dealt with. You cannot so clip the wings of greatness. If a king be resolute to be a tyrant all you can do will not hinder him. . . . Put not me to precedents unless you will let me reckon precedents too for my prerogative. I would not willingly press you neither would I have you to press me. Kings must be trusted, and if you have no trust in my person, why would you propound that to me which was never asked of any king? [16]

He was the first king who ever descended so far as to allow them to treat of wardships. That he did in his capacity as a great landlord. As a monarch he had a great power, if he chose to use it, that could not be taken away. They were not to question what a king may do. But if they suffered inconveniences, one or two impositions, that they would have taken away, let them consider what they would offer in return.[17]

When the last impositions were laid he vowed that the money

accruing should not be thrown away upon particular people; he would bestow it as a legacy for the better maintenance of the state. His second vow was that unless there arose an extraordinary necessity, he would lay no more impositions except in Parliament.[18]

In laying impositions he might err, he admitted. He might happen to consult twenty or thirty merchants who had their own ends in view. But he would try to gain full knowledge and acquaint Parliament with the situation and hear what both the Lower and Upper House had to say. They might think it fit and see reason for it; they might discover some better way of raising money and supply it. He even mentioned the "consent of the people." He would, however, reserve the final judgment to himself. Many things he could do without Parliament that he would do with Parliament. Good kings were helped by Parliament, not for power, but for convenience, that the works might seem the more glorious.[19]

He would be careful that the people knew whatever concerned the commonwealth.

> But be not misled . . . the more wayward you shall be, I shall be the more unwilling to call you to Parliament. For such behavior will make me call you the seldomer to counsel. If a great action [?] of war were in hand, would I not be glad of your advice in it? Yet you know I can do it without you. As a good king should ever be ready to declare to his people his intent, so are they peevish and undutiful subjects that will petition to the King for that wherein they know his mind already; it is both superfluous and a piece of contempt.

The Lord Treasurer had shown them what the King needed. Because the need was so great, they were not to give up and do nothing.

> I was born to be begged of, not to beg. . . . I ask what I need; you are to give what you are able. . . . If I claim more than

you can well spare me, you may humbly answer me so. Touching the security offered you for the wards, as you were contented with that which I propounded, so God grant it never do me, nor my posterity good to resume that which I once bargain for. And for the sum which I have demanded I will never so scorn you as to make a high demand to drive you on to a lesser sum.

As for religion, he reminded them that he had foretold the plots of the papists.[20] They aimed not only at the French King but at himself.[21]

The speech was a careful argument based on premises that were his own deepest convictions. No one had written it for him. I doubt if Salisbury had much to do with it. It was in James's own language. There was common sense in his argument about precedents. As much as any of his addresses, however, it exhibited his assurance of his own right to absolute power.[22] His direct statements and their implications indicate that.

The speech was said to be "distasteful in some parts thereof to the House." [23] Of it John Chamberlain wrote:

> The 21st of this present he [James] made another speech to both the Houses, but so little to their satisfaction that I hear it bred generally much discomfort, to see our monarchical power and regal prerogative strained so high and made so transcendent every way, that if the practice should follow the positions, we are not like to leave to our successors that freedom we received from our forefathers, nor make account of anything we have longer than they list that govern.[24]

Chamberlain was a typical middle-of-the-road, middlebrow Englishman who was critical of parliamentary agitators but not enthusiastic about the King. His judgments were probably not different from much informed public opinion.

The debate that ensued was not wholly characterized by sweetness and light. Hastings proposed a committee to consider some satisfaction between the King and his subjects. Sir Thomas Beaumont, M.P. for Tamworth in Warwickshire, feared lest the whole liberty of the subjects be swallowed up.[25] Wentworth had listened to the King's speech with great desire and hope, but had come away "exceeding sad and heavy." He alluded to the Sir John Fortescue of the fifteenth century (1394 [?]–1476) who had taught the Lancastrian heir to the throne and might have been inclined to favor royal power, but had told the Prince that the difference between England and France was that by the law of England no imposition could be laid without the assent of Parliament. He reminded his audience that there was a speech of James in print in which he called it seditious to dispute what a king might do.[26] If that were true, Wentworth remarked, then all their law books were seditious. He believed they ought in all humbleness and reverence to make some answer to the King, showing him that they had discharged their consciences in dutifully advising him and had proved their fidelity to their country in preserving the liberties that they had lost.[27] Wentworth's words might well have landed him in narrow quarters.[28]

Caesar came back at Wentworth. Out of the same garden, he observed, came bees and wasps, and from the same flowers the one sucks honey, the other sharpness and tartness. He asserted that there was never any thought in the minds of the King nor of his ministers that he might lay impositions upon lands and commodities. He frowned on the plan of a Committee of the Whole House, which Hastings had proposed that morning. If the Commons would wait they might receive some more pleasing message from the King.[29]

Fuller answered that the King was very wise and yet a stranger to the government. He had spoken of what was done in the time of the two Queens. "I remember not any such thing." [30]

James Whitelocke, the newly elected member for Woodstock in Oxfordshire,[31] asserted that the King had now made claim before both Houses to a right of levying impositions. If they passed over that claim in silence, all posterity would be bound by it. If they did nothing, the ancient frame of the commonwealth would be much altered in the very way in which it now differed from other commonwealths in fortune and blessedness. He laid down three principles as characteristic of the English nation: [32]

1. That what the subjects owned could not be taken from them without their consent but by due course of law
2. That the laws could not be made without the consent of the three Estates (The edict of a prince was not a law.)
3. That Parliament was the storehouse of the liberties and rights of the subjects [33]

Whitelocke had a way of setting forth constitutional principles as if uttering the last word. He closed his speech by moving that a committee be appointed.

After various motions as to what to do next and efforts by the Speaker to prevent the House from choosing a committee to consider the course to be taken, he finally recalled a motion of the preceding Saturday for a committee, and Sandys, whose unobtrusive leadership had often been timely, approved the motion for a committee. Further, he observed that when there had been misunderstandings between the King and the Commons the differences had been straightened out by messages. His Majesty was suspicious that the Commons intended to impugn his prerogative.[34] He need not have feared, for all members had taken an oath to assist and defend all privileges, preeminences, and authorities belonging to the Crown.[35] Further, the King had taken an oath to protect all just laws and customs.[36] With his usual tact, Sandys had incidentally called attention to the King's oath.

Without more ado, the House settled for a committee that afternoon.

The Petition of Right

OF that gloomy afternoon session of the Committee of the Whole House we have only two accounts, each of them brief. Sandys was chosen to take the chair. The debate was temperate, we are told. After each speech was a long silence.[1] Croft moved for a Petition of Right to the King showing how in all Parliaments they had freely disputed of everything concerning themselves and requesting His Majesty to relax his restraint upon them. All agreed that until the Petition was sent they should refrain from disputing.

Here Bacon made one of his most effective speeches. Croft's conclusion was sound, asserted Sir Francis, if he could maintain the premises, that is, if the Commons had really been denied the liberties allowed to their predecessors. He wanted to say it often enough that he might be believed: they should learn from the old prophet to stand upon the ancient ways and to find the right way and to walk in it.[2] If the Commons examined the precedents, they would find them inconclusive. He was a Parliament man when he was seventeen,[3] and he could remember the inhibitions they had received from the Queen. In 23 Eliz. a fast was proposed, and the greater voice approved it. The Queen commanded them to forbear; it was a matter that belonged to the bishops and was under the authority of the Queen. The House did forbear. In Queen Mary's day, when the House wished the Queen to look strictly to her officers of revenue, she forbade them to discuss the matter.

These inhibitions had been in matters that concerned the Queen. But if an inhibition were sent in anything concerning *meum et tuum* [4] he would advise them to obey de facto, but to ask the King for freedom of debate, according to the use of Parliament, in which freedom was granted at the beginning as a matter of form, and not elective to be granted or denied.[5] Bacon cited good Marian and Elizabethan precedents for the Crown's right to levy impositions, thus adding validity to His Majesty's allusion to the practice of the two Queens. He concluded by urging the Commons not to question the King's prerogative to impose, but to present the impositions as a grievance to the commonwealth, which the King had given them leave to do.[6]

It was answered that his precedents did not match the case in question. The Marian and Elizabethan inhibitions were personal [7] and therefore justified. But if it were true that Parliament could not be inhibited from discussing the right of the particular subject, as the Solicitor had admitted, much less could they be inhibited from discussing the matter of impositions, which concerned all subjects.

It was arranged that a subcommittee should draw into form the Petition of Right. Among those named to the subcommittee were the Privy Councillors, the Chancellors of the Exchequer and of the Duchy, Mr. Secretary Herbert, and the learned counsel, Mr. Attorney and Mr. Solicitor. The writer of Add. 48119, says: "They all went away. But there were 5 or 6 and 20 of the subcommittees that stayed and agreed upon the course of the Petition and upon the reasons that they meant to offer in the Petition." [8] Why did Privy Councillors and the King's officials go away? Was it because they feared to be connected in any way with a Petition of Right to the King? Those who stayed and argued finally asked Sandys to draw the words of the petition into form and submit it to them the next morning. At that time they made minor alterations, and then the Speaker brought the petition before the House. It was moved that it be entered in the Clerk's Book, which, in spite of vehement opposition, was done.

The petition alluded to the King's commandment restraining debate about impositions. His Majesty had no intent, they felt sure, to infringe upon the ancient and fundamental right of the liberty of Parliament to discuss all matters concerning them and their possessions and rights. If freedom of debate were once foreclosed, the essence of the liberty of Parliament would be dissolved. The right of the subject on the one hand and His Majesty's prerogative on the other were dealt with daily in this and in all former Parliaments. The Commons had no desire to impugn but to inform themselves of His Majesty's right on this point, in order to satisfy the subjects, who had been grieved by these new impositions and languished in sorrow and discomfort. [9]

They did not propose to reverse the judgment in the Exchequer [10] but to learn the reasons upon which it was grounded, because there was a general notion that the reasons of the judgment might be extended much further, "even to the utter ruin of the ancient liberties of this Kingdom." Further, that judgment was given in one case and against one man; it could bind in law no other and was reversible by a writ of error. The Commons felt sure that, had not the restraint been put upon them, they would have carried themselves in so orderly and moderate a fashion, and would have given His Majesty so true a view of the right of his subjects, as to have satisfied him. Otherwise they could not proceed without giving up forever the full examination of these new impositions, "that so we may cheerfully pass on to your Majesty's business, from which this stop hath by diversion so long withheld us." If the King had a way of concluding a speech with a threat, the Commons could end with a courteous hint that his message to them was delaying the vote of subsidies. The petition was a tactful statement written by old hands and with moderation.

On Friday morning the Chancellor of the Exchequer brought His Majesty's answer, which had been delivered to twenty members the day before. It was characteristic of the variety of the attitudes taken by the personage at Whitehall.

They had mistaken, he informed them, and made a jealous interpretation of his speech. His message did not absolutely forbid them to treat impositions, but only until they heard his further pleasure.[11] He had no intent to restrain them, but, being seventy miles away, he wished to understand their intentions. In his speech he had meant only to stake out his claim as King of England *in abstracto*.[12] He did not plan to meddle with property, nor to impose upon lands and goods of his subjects, but only upon merchandise, and to do that in Parliament.

As to their petition, he granted it as they had set it down. He asked them not to impugn his prerogative, but to seek his content and satisfaction and to endeavor to confirm the hearts of his subjects.[13] Never had he meant to abridge their liberties.[14] He could not believe, he said, looking at the members, that any of them disliked his person, or that they would deny him support. He was sure none of them failed to realize his wants and hoped they would not take from him with one hand what they gave him with the other. His fame and fortune were involved. Other princes were active. Did they want him to stand at gaze?

He was as gracious as it was possible for him to be. In their petition he discovered more "duty" than he had heard of before. But when he talked of action and not standing at gaze, he was deceiving himself, if not the Commons. He made an unusual gesture: he would be content to see ten or twelve members, not in a solemn way of Parliament, but "homely," to come and acquaint him with their intentions. His last words were to urge upon them speed in granting him subsidies.[15]

To see His Majesty stepping down from his throne moved the writer of Add. 48119, who wrote: "One thing I may not forget which I cannot but with joy remember, to see in what fashion a noble, great, and wise Prince did vouchsafe to speak to his people."

The subcommittee to deal with recusants, impositions, and support—the two subcommittees must have become one—decided that they could proceed no further with the matter of support until the Lords sent them a message or answer. "The business, as we conceived, stuck with them." [16] Yet if the Lords should not, on the next day, answer them, it was thought the Commons ought to send a message to quicken them.

Conferences with the Lords

THE next morning the Lords sent a message for a conference concerning tenures.[1] Salisbury hoped that a conference could be held as soon as possible, not to deal with supply, but to prepare for a free conference in which the necessity for it might be "better spread and infused" into the House. He was aware that many of the Commons had gone home and that those still in attendance hesitated to conclude anything until the absentees returned. Yet he hoped that they might agree to a free conference.

At 3:00 p.m. the Commons and the Lords in conference were addressed by the Lord Treasurer, who urged upon them a free conference. He had confidence in the uses of debate: the *calor generativa*, the heat of debate, bred ideas. "Interlocution," he explained, "would bring forth free replies." [2] No man knew all, every man knew something, and what some member knew might prove of advantage. For such a conference there were precedents, as in the Francis Goodwin case, the union, the hostile laws, and exchequer fees, and "in diverse others." [3] In all those matters men had not hesitated to answer one another.[4] Thus spoke an old House of Commons man, who had long realized the uses of debate.

Salisbury held out hopes to the Commons but with a condition. The King, he said, was determined to fall in his demands. If he fell, the Commons would rise. How much the Lords would fall was not for him to tell them now, but they would never find out unless in a free conference. The Lords asked them to change dry messages for an ingenious conference.[5] It was time to proceed to something now, "or that we took a resolution to part." [6]

At the close of the afternoon the Commons in their chamber returned to the question of the proposed conference. Those who hoped for reform knew well enough what the Lords would say and were in no hurry to hear them or to move about subsidies. Time was on the side of the Commons.

Of course, the Chancellor of the Exechequer, Sir Julius Caesar, looked at matters in another way. He was eager to see the Commons negotiate with the Lords. But Sandys was not in favor of a free conference unless the case to be presented to the Lords were carefully considered and the heads set down, so that the Commons could make propositions. On Saturday it was decided that such propositions should begin on the following Wednesday.[7]

While everyone in London was awaiting the festal event—the creation of Prince Henry as Prince of Wales—the Lower House, on Friday, June 1, went into committee with Martin in the chair to consider the ten concessions. A subcommittee was named of all the lawyers in the House and of others, who were to draw seven of the ten concessions into "such forms as they may be most beneficial to the subject." It was understood that the Grand Committee was to consider whether the ten concessions were valuable and whether they should bargain for them, as also for wardship. The subcommittee was not to value the concessions.[8]

Sir John Savile, a knight of the shire for Yorkshire, of a notable family and one not given to modesty; Sir Roger Owen, a man of convictions that he did not keep to himself; and others took an unusual step in the Grand Committee on June 2: they refused to serve on the subcommittee. The concessions, declared Savile, were not fit to be bargained for as against supply and support. A hundred thousand pounds, he insisted, was the most the subjects could yield. He wished the words "support" and "supportation" had never been heard of. If the Commons bargained for the seven concessions as grievances, grievances that were either the straining of the prerogative against the liberties of the subject or the abuses of inferior officials, every Parliament from that time on would be faced with new grievances and have to grant new support to be relieved from them. Sir John was from the North Country and possibly was not eager to pay more taxes.

John Tey, M.P. for Arundel in Sussex,[9] was opposed to bargaining for purveyance, the abuses of which lay, in his opinion, with subordinate officials. He put forward the suggestion that if the Commons were to give more than a hundred thousand pounds they might "buy out" a general statute of explanation of the King's prerogative insofar as it concerned the liberties of the subject. Tey was proposing nothing less than a constitution purchased to order.

James Whitelocke, who was now making what I assume was his second speech, said that the matter of support was a thing strange and unheard-of before this Parliament, save once in the eleventh year of Henry VI's reign.[10] As for purveyance, it was of no use to compound for it; the abuses and charge would grow up again. Tonnage and poundage had been granted in order to get rid of impositions, and now they saw that impositions were continued and increased daily.

The Upper House was fast losing patience with the Lower. On Friday, June 8, Salisbury reminded the Lords that an invitation had been given the Commons to join in another conference and that they had not heard from the Commons. "If the Parliament take no care hereof," Salisbury told the Lords, "I think there may be a record entered, there was never such a Parliament." [11] The Lord Treasurer's remarks led to a message from the Lords to the Commons expressing regret that they had to spend so much labor persuading the Commons to hold proper conferences with them instead of "meetings." They regretted "all protraction in this so great and necessary a business." [12]

To this message the Commons took exception. The writer of the *Parliamentary Debates in 1610* noted that no answer was returned. But the Clerk of the Commons sent word that, when the Commons were prepared, they would answer.[13]

On June 11 a message came from the Lords; it asked for a conference "to impart such things as by his Majesty's commandment they are to impart to this House." That phraseology nettled the Commons. Sir Edward Montague hoped that no precedent was being established whereby the Commons would receive messages from the King by way of the Lords.[14] Others rushed to the support of Sir Edward.

A committee including Sandys, Owen, Martin, Sir Edward Montague, Hastings, Savile, Croft, and Berkeley was nominated to consider what was fittest to be done. The Solicitor, the Recorder, and Sir George More were indeed the only members named who might fairly be labeled as regular supporters of the Crown. Almost at once the committee brought in a report that the Chancellor of the Exchequer should be a petitioner from the House in order that the ancient forms be observed in the sending of messages, that is, that either the Speaker or some members of the House should be the means of communication between the King and Commons. This plan was deemed "unseasonable."

It was decided that the Solicitor should deliver a message to the Lords that if they desired a meeting only to communicate their own "conceits," or anything they had received from His Majesty, they would be glad to receive it, but if the Lords were employed in this matter only as messengers to the Commons from His Majesty, they wished to signify to the Lords that this order was contrary to the ancient orders and liberties of the House.[15]

Bacon conveyed to the Lords the feeling of the Commons. He was followed by Salisbury, in his best dove-like mood. The Lords did not want to contend upon formality, but craved correspondence and union. He hoped that by a courteous and civil answer the Commons might receive satisfaction. The Lords sat nearer the stern of government and thus were acquainted first with the *arcana imperii*.[16] They had a message from the King and were willing to communicate it. Whether the Commons intended to hear them was the question. The committee answered, "Yes, Yes." [17]

After a pause Salisbury resumed his speech. His Majesty was worried about ending this Parliament, which had lasted long. He wished them to think of what had been done and to prepare themselves for what was to be done. If they had doubts about the necessities of the King, "this is not the day, nor I the man that can better imprint it." The King's necessities had grown so great that if the cure did not come soon it would come too late. Then Salisbury turned to using ingratiating words: the Lords looked upon the Commons as "upon men of extraordinary quality," and would speak with them, not of corn and grain, but of statecraft and foreign policy, of things worthy of them.[18]

The Lord Treasurer alluded to the murder of the King of France, who had sent ambassadors to the English to quicken them in the intended campaign. All that was now changed. The new King was under a lady regent, and irresolution in French policy was possible. What would come of it? On the previous Friday they had sent over £6,000, and £30,000 must follow.[19] "If we do not take another course we may end with this Parliament." [20]

Shall a King be murthered? Shall Europe change? And shall England lie in a lethargy? Shall a Parliament be called, the King's wants told the first day and 120 [21] days spent and no way found to help them? . . . This is the longest day of the year [June 11, that is 21 by modern time]. . . . It is St. Barnaby's Day. As the sun changeth the course, I wish we looked back and changed ours. . . . The Judges must away, the Court must part, the King goes his progress, he may not stay, the nobility and gentry, I think, are all weary. What can be the end of this session, if you entertain things in no other sort than yet you have done? We have had many meetings; never yet a conference. And a better device to keep men in differences can never be found out than never to have conference.[22]

Salisbury appealed to what he called the second power of their minds—their wills [23]—to choose between the good and ill.

When the King began to think of his needs . . . he made his resort to you . . . measuring your affections to him by his own to you. . . . He knew he made a great and strange demand. . . . He offered you some branches, nay, some fruits such as were never gathered, as fair as any in Britain. You spied a red apple; he did not cast a net upon it. These things you had liberty to debate. The King asked too much; you offered too little and yet a fair, an honorable . . . offer. The distance is great, the time is short, the difficulty infinite.[24]

To reconcile the distance a middle ground had to be sought, but in another day and season. Had the Commons at the conference heard correctly? Was Salisbury promising another session? Now he repeated the promise of May 26, that the King would make a great fall from his great demand.[25] Bitter reports had come to him that some of the Commons spoke as if their constituents at home were discontented that their representatives had made any offer at all. He suggested that they let the matter of the Great Contract be suspended for a while.[26] His Majesty was willing to postpone support until the next session.

But supply was another matter. He asked them to think with some compassion of the strange state of England. Let it never be said that there was no surplus on hand for the defense of the realm. There might be a revolt in Ireland,[27] and they might have to take the sword in hand. Let there be no dispute at that point.

However the former demands may seem exorbitant, I conclude, if this be not done, England stands in a miserable case. The King shall have cause to complain of this great Senate. And I think no honest servant, no faithful subject, nor no good patriot can appear to deny the King supply in this necessity. Bear with me I pray, if I speak in passion and impute it to zeal. I move not for relief for a vain war of ostentation, nor to succor any pretended title. . . . I see a cloud of further change and I think it fit to take a cloak before the storm come. The sum of all is this, that we forbear all other things till supply be provided, that the Parliament be prorogued, that we keep afoot the Contract, that some surplusage be deposited.

Salisbury reverted to the problem of impositions. Some allowance had to be made to the merchants of the outports. A good many impositions had been taken away; those upon manufactures, with two exceptions, had been remitted. Moreover the King had made an offer not to lay any impositions except in Parliament. He was aware that the increased cost of goods was blamed on impositions, but members should be able to see for themselves that it was not true; no man paid more for his button or for his shirt. He was authorized to tell them that till they met again in Parliament the King would lay no more impositions, "which is worth thanks, coming after your liberty to dispute of the power to do it." [28]

This address was one of Salisbury's most appealing performances. The speech had order, logic, and a hint of humor; it was given in the best Cecilian manner—personal, conversational, and engaging.

On June 13 Bacon reported Salisbury's speech at length. The Clerk of the Commons called it "a long persuasive speech." Moreover it had been marked by "passion," as Salisbury admitted, and with many audiences passion is strangely persuasive.

The Debate: One Subsidy Rejected and Later Voted NATURALLY Salisbury's speech led the House to the question of subsidies. Thomas Dammet (or Dannet), a fish merchant from Great Yarmouth, who had been active in the affairs of his borough and had represented it in Parliament four times,[1] was a member who seldom took the floor or served on committees, but who, when he did venture to rise, had something to say, and said it racily.[2] He now declared that if a private gentleman told his friend that he was in debt and had to sell his land, the friend would answer that some other course must be found. Such a suggestion would have stuck in the minds of members. The Commons, concluded Dammet, must supply the King's wants.[3]

Humphrey May, a royal official, urged the Commons to give two subsidies and two fifteenths—a grant of much less than the King was hoping for, but probably quite as much as the Commons could have been persuaded to vote. May was later to prove himself something of a realist.

Sir Thomas Beaumont, who had in his last speech feared for the liberties of the Commons, thought the King ought to be supplied and that two subsidies were not enough. But he believed, also, that, for the King's safety and honor, for their own credit, and for the satisfaction of the country, the Commons ought to defer voting until they had an answer to their grievances and had concluded the contract for tenures.[4] Beaumont's judgment was probably that of many members.

Sir Thomas Lowe, a figure in the Merchant Adventurers and the Levant Companies, hoped that the Commons would not be mercenary or sparing; he spoke for two subsidies and four fifteenths.[5] Lowe no doubt knew of the loan already negotiated by the King.

Hastings agreed with Beaumont in delaying the vote for subsidies.[6] Tey was thinking of grievances when he remarked that, if members returned home with nothing for the good of the commonwealth, their constituents would say that they had been all this while like children catching butterflies.

Sir William Maurice, M.P. for Caernarvonshire, who was not always listened to attentively but was not easily discouraged from talking, suggested three subsidies. Sir William Cope, replying to Lowe, suggested that Sir Thomas should persuade his brethren (the city merchants) to lend the King money at 5 percent or even gratis. That would be better than if the Commons should now grant a subsidy in order that His Majesty might be able to pay interest to the merchants till Michaelmas (September 29).[7] This proposal was applauded.

The King's supporters, who could hardly have been pleased at the course of the debate, would not have been comforted when the Recorder, who usually stood with the King's men, but who may have had a finger up to feel the way the wind was blowing, spoke for one subsidy now and one a year later. He may have reasoned that such a sum was as much as the King could hope for.

Croft declared the question before the House was whether to give now or to wait until they had received satisfaction for grievances; he left little doubt as to which alternative he preferred. Sir George More suggested a subsidy or two now and not to vote the money until the grievances were in the hands of the King. He felt certain that His Majesty would give them satisfaction.[8]

Hoskins urged the House to show an inclination to give.[9] The word was chosen with care. It was a "weasel word," to use the idiom of Theodore Roosevelt. Doubtless Hoskins meant that the Commons should really vote the King money when he had answered their grievances, and that in the meantime they would placate him by showing themselves favorably disposed.[10]

Martin realized perhaps that the King's friends were singing low and wished to see the debate put off. He added a pointed sentence that, as many of his sentences, deserved amplification: "we shall give more hereafter than any great subject dare in reason demand." Was he implying that when wardship and purveyance were abolished, the Commons would be ready to grant more than any Privy Councillor might reasonably hope for?

Sir Robert Mansell, M.P. for Carmarthenshire and treasurer of the navy, feared that the state could not get along until October. The navy, he said, was to get £30,000 by Michaelmas. Mansell mentioned one subsidy now, and then he hoped the House would go forward with grievances. Here was another civil servant who was talking of one subsidy for the time being.

Sir Julius Caesar, Chancellor of the Exchequer, rose and, "finding the House bent against subsidies," announced that he bore glad tidings from the King.[11] His Majesty was as anxious to satisfy the House about their griefs as he was to be relieved of his wants and to move for their safety—a hint that if he were left without money, the realm might prove defenseless. Some might fear, continued Caesar, that, as soon as money was voted, His Majesty would dissolve Parliament and the Commons might discover that the matter of tenures was "offered and not meant." Caesar answered that the King expressly intended that Parliament should meet again. To those who feared that there would be no answer to their grievances came the reply that the King would make haste to relieve their grievances with a present answer. Grievances would go with the vote of supply and would not wait for the vote of support.[12] Meanwhile, Caesar hoped that the Commons would at once vote two subsidies and four fifteenths, "that his Majesty might be the better encouraged to extend his grace and favor towards us." [13] They might even have a larger pardon than they expected.[14]

Caesar was not unaware of the Commons' suspicions that when they had voted the subsidies the King would forget his part of the bargain. The Commons were not without experience of their sovereign's promises. Was Caesar trying to rush a vote for two subsidies on the basis of the King's expansive, if not explicit, promises about grievances?

Why was James so expansive? Had his ministers been alarmed at the way the debate was going? Had they advised him to make promises about grievances? His Majesty's supporters had been urging the Commons to grant subsidies and await his gracious favor. When the Commons were reluctant to do so, the King fell back again on promises, vague and general promises.

Such promises were becoming an old story. The King needed much money. Why did he not proceed boldly to abolish abuses on a large scale? I am inclined to believe that the Commons might have outdone themselves, might even have voted both supply and support. What a popular sovereign he might have become!

For such a move he was not prepared. James was surrounded

by men who profited from the abuses of which the Commons complained. To put an end of such abuses—they had been long accumulating—would have meant almost a revolution at Court. If Salisbury had supported such a revolution, he might have lost his place. Privy Councillors and the hangers-on at Court may have warned His Majesty that to offer the reforms proposed would make him dependent upon Parliament, a dependence that would have been contrary to his profound convictions and a blow to his pride. The courtiers had the advantage of being able to talk to the King. It was a misfortune of the Commons that few of their leaders, except Bacon, had any chance personally to present their case to His Majesty, and even the entertaining Bacon was not a favorite.

The greatest part of the House, "distasting Caesar's motion," seemed not yet inclined to give any subsidy. When a move was made to put the matter of subsidies to a question, those in favor of a subsidy cried out to put it off till the next day, realizing possibly that on the present day the motion was likely to be defeated.[15]

On the next morning, June 14, Caesar brought another message from the King. His Majesty insisted that he would answer their grievances before the recess, but that he could not name a price until he knew what they would take from him, that is, how much he would lose by clearing grievances. He hoped they would first show him their love by voting a supply.[16]

Debate followed from 9:00 a.m. until 1:00 p.m.[17] Alford, M.P. for Colchester, replied to the plea for a show of love by maintaining that never had there been more show of love for any king. "Many spake one way and many t'other." Nearly everyone, it appeared, was willing to grant one or more subsidies at some time in the near future, but most of those who spoke hoped to see grievances redressed before subsidies were voted. It was said that no more burdens should be laid on the subject until he had been relieved; that the King ought to be informed of the poor condition of his subjects; that if their petitions were not answered they could not give "with preservation of the hearts of the people to the King"; that no more privy seals should be sent out; that after a patent was taken away from Lord Danvers, one of the same kind but worse was given to Sir Stephen Proctor, "of which we complain now." The clearest way was to hear the answer to their grievances, and then perhaps they could give double.[18]

On the other side it was asserted that they had not formerly received such messages as the Chancellor brought, nor like promises of good answers to their grievances. Another, who was usually in opposition, pleaded with the House to make England again a happy state, alluding to Salisbury's characterization of its miserable condition. To demand much and give little would be a great discredit.

The forthright Nathaniel Bacon spoke for delay. "Stay and pause, till grievances be proceeded in." Then would be the time, he implied, to be generous. His half brother, Sir Francis, rose. He would not blast the affections of the House with elaborate speech, he declared, as if aware of his failure to carry the House with him at other times. He had hope in his heart; they ought to proceed upon hope. It was becoming a habit on his part to be optimistic.

Others were less hopeful. Sir John Savile quoted the Scottish warning to the English that in James they had a good King if they did not spoil him. The more a subsidy was importuned, said another, the more reason there was to defer it. Yelverton suggested that His Majesty would gain much by deferring.

An immediate grant was pressed for by the Attorney General, who urged one subsidy and two fifteenths, as if he realized that the friends of the King could not hope for more. Sir Henry Poole, Sir William Paddy, Sir William Strode, and Mr. Duncombe supported him. So did Sir Edward Montague, surprisingly enough. He proposed one subsidy and two fifteenths now, and that Parliament should meet again at Candlemas (February 2) and then vote more to the King.

The unknown writer of Add. 48119 set forth what was happening. Those who favored giving differed among themselves as to how much to vote: some were for one subsidy and two fifteenths; others for two subsidies and four fifteenths. In support of two subsidies, it was maintained that one subsidy and two fifteenths would imply a "coldness of affection." Two would be a Parliament gift, and three desirable. Another pressed the point that the gift ought to be made freely and without division, or not at all.[19]

The policy of giving two subsidies had been backed on the day before, but on the second day of the discussion, there were few to uphold that policy.

Those who sought an immediate grant believed that the House ought not to bargain with His Majesty, but to give first and hope for retribution later. Had not the King promised a good and gracious answer?

Upon the message from the King on the second day of the debate, divers Members admitted that they had changed their minds and were ready to give presently. It was argued that the gift of the Commons would be but an "earnest penny." [20] The King must know that he would have to resort to Parliament for much more and would take pains to heed their petitions. The old argument was brought forward again that the eyes of the other kingdoms were upon Parliament. The heads of those nations, before they ventured to attack, would consider how well provided with revenues the English ruler was and how much support he could expect from others. Thus argued the Attorney General, who hoped that the House would not rise without giving something as a token of their love. Sir Robert Cotton [21] cited a precedent of 5 Hen. IV where it was decided by the Commons that the proper course was to give the King money before they received answers to their petitions.[22] Those who were against giving, says our best chronicler, asserted that their grievances were "large and [of] many kinds"—some that were characterized by want of justice, as purveyance, impositions upon alehouses and upon commodities carried from port to port within the land; some that were characterized by overextension of the prerogative, and these too common. Those who reasoned thus maintained that they had been sent by their countries to gain ease of their griefs.[23]

The news from the Chancellor of the Exchequer that they

could expect good answers to their grievances did not convince many members. "Messages may be disavowed or not well understood." The relief from grievances promised before had come to little. Those who argued in this way believed it "more fit to stay a while, that by deferring the gift the gift may [be] double." How could the delay of twenty or thirty days, it was argued, be dangerous or prejudicial to the King? Nor did they believe that the death of the French King was an omen to make them afraid.[24] " 'Twas not for want of ships or money, but God withdrew his protection from him." It was easy, at that time, to explain the unusual as an interposition of the Divinity.

Toward the end of the debate Sandys rose and said that he did not think it fit to put the matter to a question. If it were carried by three or four votes it would be a disreputation of the King; if it were defeated, it would be worse. The question was whether to proceed to the question, and the Commons resolved in the negative. Gleefully Martin hailed that day as the fairest he had ever known in Parliament. Sandys, too wise to betray elation, moved a message to His Majesty that they would lay aside all other business and endeavor within a short time to give him satisfaction.[25] The motion as passed was:

> We have received this day a most gracious message and do return his Majesty most humble thanks, and though this supply be deferred for a time, yet the purpose of the House is to set all other business aside and principally to intend his supply and the subjects' grievances, and they hope in due time to give his Majesty satisfaction to his good contentment.[26]

On June 16 the King sent a message to the Commons.[27] He was surprised that so mean a matter as one subsidy and two fifteenths should be so much controverted, especially in view of his promise to answer their grievances. He had intended to satisfy any reasonable man, as soon as they had shown their affection.

He brought up another matter: he had a right to be justly offended with those who made bold with his Government,[28] "fetching arguments from former times not to be compared to these." Now he professed to be indifferent as to whether or not any motion for supply were made before they received the full answer to their grievances.[29] His sudden indifference seems strangely out of character, but may have been due to his assurance that he would get a loan from London.

Three matters were now before the Commons. First, impositions were to be threshed over in the Committee of the Whole House on many afternoons (meetings that will be dealt with in later sections). Second, the Commons were also interested in obtaining from His Majesty the price they would be expected to pay for the hoped-for retributions. Third, they had to formulate as soon as possible their list of grievances.

Also on June 16 Croft reported from the Grand Committee, which had considered seven of the ten heads put forward by Salisbury on February 24, and the question of annual "support." They wished a conference with the Lords about what was to be included in the Great Contract.

On June 18 the Commons resolved to ask the Lords to think of some other heads of retribution to be proposed to His Majesty, to inform them what price the King would demand,[30] and to ask what projects for raising the money, other than upon the land, were to be entertained.

The message to the Lords was not ignored by that assembly. On June 19 Salisbury addressed the Upper House, telling them that in some points the Lords attending the conference could decide for themselves, but that in others they needed the direction of the King. With this view the Lords concurred. Twelve members of that House, four of them bishops, were named to interview His Majesty that afternoon. On Thursday the group was told that the King would fix the price by Tuesday afternoon. The Lords then, in answer to the request of the Commons, said that they would confer with them on Tuesday afternoon.[31]

The decision took more time than His Majesty had forecast. On Tuesday, June 26, he sent word that he would leave the first and third points to the Lords, in whom he had implicit trust. As for the second point, the price to be asked, he wished a further night to sleep on it.[32] Before the conference that afternoon Salisbury addressed the Lords. His Majesty hoped that they would deal freely with the Lower House. He himself intended to look into both sides. If he moved anything unfit for the people but fit for the King, and thus caused a separation between them, he would be unworthy to sit in this House. If he did not, on the other hand, set forth the King's necessity, he would be unworthy of the staff.[33] Then he spoke with great freedom:

> If the King do not abate of his price, then his Majesty performeth not that he gave me in charge, being his instrument. . . . If your offers be not better than they have been yet . . . I know not what to offer. For the price you shall know it as soon as I.

He could not but betray doubts concerning the conference. Nothing much would happen there, he predicted, but that they should learn the King's price.

He added that the object of the Lords was a free conference. Then he gave them the substance of the King's letter as to the price: His Majesty demanded seven score thousand pounds more by the year than he had already of clear value, besides his present sources of revenue.[34]

Salisbury's pessimism about the conference was justified. As soon as it opened, Caesar explained for the Commons that they had come to confer and had no commission to treat until they had reported to their own House. Martin qualified that statement by saying that they were prepared to treat about the ten heads but nothing else. Those heads, declared the Lord Treasurer, were worth more than what the Commons had offered.[35]

The joint committee of the two Houses went over the ten heads, the Lord Treasurer emphasizing to them the losses the King would sustain by the various concessions. He informed the committee that it would be impossible to maintain the royal household without purveyance. If the Commons wished His Majesty to give up the income derived from assarts, they would have to pay heavily. In a general way Salisbury suggested that the

House ask for more retribution rather than for a reduction of the price they would have to pay. "In this price you shall have whatsoever else you can think of that toucheth not the King either in honor or profit, and our best furtherance besides in your counsels for the levy of the money." In his desire to mollify the Commons, Salisbury had gone rather far. They would take full advantage of his words.

Salisbury ended with a plea that in the conference the Commons should deal with the Lords in a free and loving fashion. Such conferences as this one he liked, "wherein neither party hath distaste." [36]

In the *Parliamentary Debates in 1610* are notes of this conference and notes of what appear to be the conclusions arrived at. At the end we have these sentences:

> The sum demanded is too high.
> Not unwilling to rise if the fall be such as we may effect.
> We do not think it fit to lay a greater burthen upon land than 100,000*li* per annum.[37]

Some progress had been made. When Sandys, on June 27, reported the conference he seemed optimistic. The seven heads had been accepted for consideration, and eight more concessions had been added by the Commons to be considered by the Crown.[38] As for wardships, the wards were reckoned to be worth £40,000 and purveyance the same amount. When the £80,000 was added to the £140,000 asked by the King it came to £220,000.

Those seven heads in their final form, as set down in the Memorial of the Great Contract,[39] presented by the Commons, were much the same as the first seven of the ten concessions proposed by Salisbury on February 24. They were mostly concessions designed to favor landholders as against their feudal overlord, the King. To the concession, however, about the statute of limitations, it was added that those who held assart lands and had paid the rents for sixty years should continue to hold them and at the same rent. The arrangements about penal laws and informers were less precise; they were to be ordered for the "ease and benefit of the subject." Purveyors were to be abolished, as in the February proposals. Nothing was said about fees for alienations of lands nor about reducing the trouble and expense of homage. But the country gentlemen who made up the bulk of the House of Commons would have reason to welcome the provisions that were now to become part of the Great Contract.

In Sandys's report of the conference eight other heads brought forward by the Commons were "accepted into consideration." The first of these dealt with the new impositions, the second with the ecclesiastical commissions, the third with proclamations, the fourth with the Four Shires on the border of Wales, the fifth with the new drapery (from which the Duke of Lennox profited by his patent), the sixth with the license upon wines (from which the Lord Admiral had an income), the seventh with the imposition upon alehouses, the eighth with the imposition on coals at Blyth and Sunderland.[40]

Meanwhile Salisbury had failed to get the kind of conference with the Commons for which he had hoped. He had aimed by an interchange of views to come to an understanding about the sum to be offered for the concessions proposed.

On July 7 a committee was named to present these matters to the King and on July 10 His Majesty called upon the Lord Treasurer to give an account of how the Government came to take up impositions as a means of raising money.

Salisbury replied that the cause of impositions was the wars in Ireland. There had been no time to call a Parliament, and therefore it was resolved by the Council to lay impositions. That was in the time of his predecessor as Lord Treasurer (Thomas Sackville, Earl of Dorset). A hundred merchants had been brought together in the Guildhall, and it had been thought fit by them, by the Chancellor of the Exchequer, by the barons of that court, and by Salisbury himself to lay impositions upon certain imported goods. The statement bruited about that the cost of the merchandise was raised and the traffic in it overthrown was not true. His Majesty's customs did not decay, and, if there had been a loss of £20,000 that year, it was because of the wars in the Low Countries.

When a member of the Lower House maintained that impositions were contrary to law, Salisbury answered that the King had the law to justify him, thinking of the decision in Bate's case. Though it was reported there were 1,100 new impositions, 300 were worth nothing and 500 were worth no more than £300 per annum. Twenty of the 1,100 were worth more than all the rest together, those upon wines, spices, satins, velvets, gold lace, and the like, which were worth £50,000 per annum. When necessity came upon them, like an armed man, His Majesty decided not to trouble his subjects but to borrow money, and he took every other course until the tide of poverty almost overflowed the banks of the Exchequer. "I assure myself that I shall be freed from being either an Empson or a Dudley." He hoped that impositions might end with this Parliament.[41] "Yet would to God I might quickly end if they [impositions] and I might end together." [42]

When Salisbury had concluded, the King called on the Clerk of Parliament to read the answers to the Commons' petitions, which IIis Majesty had ordered to be put in writing. The King, it was explained, had not had the time to examine all the petitions. Those to which he now gave answers all concerned profit rather than government.[48]

His Majesty gave up the imposition of one shilling a chaldron on the coal from Blyth and Sunderland. In regard to the grant for the sealing of the new drapery made to the Duke of Lennox,[44] he answered: "I will confer with my judges and what they say is against law shall be redressed." [45] He hoped the courts would proceed expeditiously. To the elimination of the imposition for licensing alehouses and to the abolition of the license of wines, given to the Lord Admiral, the King consented. The King did not wish, Salisbury reported, to use too severe a hand with his people. But he knew well enough that the Lower House was not the place to determine the law in the case of a private man, "much less concerning a Prince's right." Yet His Majesty was pleased to assure them (besides the great abatement he had made in this session of divers imposts, to his great loss) that he would be willing to assent to an act by which his power should be suspended from imposing any more upon merchandise without consent of Parliament.[46] "If I have done wrong," he added, "blame the Lord Treasurer, who told me that I might impose." [47] As for which impositions were to be suspended, that remained to be seen in a book then in press, but in general many imposts were to be taken away or abated; the remaining ones were largely those that produced the most revenue and hence were likely to raise prices.

Spedding, in his *Life of Bacon,* took the view that the King, having the law on his side (by the decision of Bate's case), had made a considerable concession and that the Commons should have accepted the concession "with . . . gratitude and joy." He believed, also, that it would have been wiser if His Majesty had left the assertion of the right to Salisbury (who repeatedly asserted it) and had himself said no more than that he was willing to divest himself of the right by act of Parliament.[48] But James could never resist maintaining his position, even when he was holding out his hand for subsidies.

Carleton wrote to Edmondes of the satisfaction of the House, except about the new impositions already laid,

> in which, though he promised to give way to a bill that never any hereafter should be laid but with the grant of Parliament, yet, because he did not as freely take away all which were last imposed, they went away ill satisfied, which they testified in their next day's meeting.[49]

The next day (July 11) Caesar praised the King's speech and his concessions and then pointed out that time was threatening and the House had done nothing except in the matter of grievances. To those concerning government the King would give an answer before the end of the season.

The debate that followed was lively, and members who were seldom heard took part. It was suggested that something should be given the King "in hope of a good answer" about grievances. There were various proposals. It was pointed out that neither subsidies nor fifteenths brought in as much actual money as in the time of the late Queen, and the moral of that was obvious.

Strangely enough, no one called attention, so far as I know, to the fact that money was buying less. There was opposition to fifteenths. Sir William Maynard, who had just been elected for Penryn in Cornwall, spoke for two subsidies and no fifteenths, because the fifteenths pinched the poor; five others also opposed the fifteenths. Sandys thought that a fifteenth might be granted in time of war, but not for "magnificence." [50] Opinion seemed to support the giving of one subsidy.

But at length it was voted by 149 to 129 to add a fifteenth to one subsidy. The giving of two fifteenths was voted down by 145 to 130. The decision in favor of one subsidy and one fifteenth, an unusual vote, was followed by a dispute as to the time of payment.[51]

Why did the Commons at this time vote a subsidy and a fifteenth? Only a month before, after a spirited debate on June 13 and 14, they had voted not to proceed to a vote. On the earlier occasion the friends of the King had been divided as to the number of subsidies to be requested. If those friends had stood together for one subsidy and one fifteenth, they might have won. By now, however, the situation had changed. The King had met the House partway as to grievances, but a small part of the way. Members might have been somewhat encouraged to hope that he would make more concessions.

Bargaining with the King

ON the following day, July 12, the Speaker proposed that the week and one day that the King had allotted to Parliament before the recess should be devoted to the discussion of tenures, that is, of wardship. The question involved, as was indicated, what further grievances should be brought to the King's attention, how much the Commons were prepared to give for the abolition of wardship, and how the money was to be found. That the Speaker raised the question of wardship would seem to suggest that the Crown had not lost all interest in the Great Contract.

A Great Committee [1] (or Grand Committee) sat in the afternoon, and Sandys reported next morning that it had been there proposed that 2d. in the pound, something less than 1 percent, should be raised by taxation on the land. It had been agreed to offer the King £180,000 and "no penny . . . more." His Majesty had come down from £240,000 to £220,000. There was talk in the Commons of delay so that constituents could be consulted. Hoskins observed that the Commons were declaimed against in the universities and in the pulpits,[2] but the groans of the people under their burdens seemed to him more significant. He believed that no decisions should be arrived at until they heard from the country and until there was a larger attendance in the House. William Noy also wished that members should talk with their constituents.

As to the form of taxation, Sandys opposed a special tax on the land and preferred an absolute sum.

Sir George More thought the King ought to have liberty to seek other means for his support. Was he suggesting some new move not initiated by Parliament? He was willing to see land taxes imposed, but not for more than £100,000, thus agreeing with the King.

At length a question was put as to whether the Commons would give £180,000 in return for tenures, the "incidents" connected with wardship, and "all other matters of ease," and it was so voted.

That was Friday, July 13. In a conference on Monday afternoon, Sir Henry Montague explained that the Commons were prepared as to what to offer and what to ask, but they had not given thought to the security to be given or the levying of the money.[3]

In the same conference Sandys discussed wardship and purveyance. He estimated the value of wardship to His Majesty at £30,000, but said that the Commons were willing to pay £40,000 to cover the sum to be awarded as pensions to the officers of the Wards who would be displaced.

He asserted that the Commons in their debates did not see how

His Majesty could manage without purveyance, unless he reduced the expense of his household. Then he made a startling statement about that expense, a statement to which Salisbury, usually quick to correct mistakes, never alluded. France and Spain were large in "their dominions, men and coin." Yet they did not spend in the whole year in their Courts as much as the English King "in the little and poor island" spent in one quarter.[4] Sandys estimated that purveyance was not worth more than £27,000 a year and the cart-taking £30,000.

In answering Sandys Salisbury quoted the King as saying: "unless you marry his virgin, you shall have her no longer in your hands." That is, unless the Commons accepted the King's terms, they might as well give up. Salisbury was quick to correct Martin's figures of the income from wardship: it was not £27,000 but £26,000 brought into the Exchequer, and that did not include those wardships that came in through other channels.

Salisbury turned to purveyance: "I pray you, do you think the King may live without purveyance? Yes, I think he may, having money. The commission shall cease and composition. But I do not see how fowls and wood and carts can cease." A few minutes later he remarked that unless the two Houses could agree on security, then "do we but beat the air."[5] He might have meant security from His Majesty that he would carry out the agreements proposed, but it seems, rather, that he meant security from the Commons that they would find the necessary money.

Sandys replied that in any contract there must be security on both sides.

Salisbury answered that for his part he wished that he and his might perish if he did not mean that they should have those things, "if it pleased the King, so he had a worthy satisfaction for them. For, although his Majesty, as you say, hath some things other kings want, so wanteth he some things they have."[6]

On July 16 Martin brought in certain propositions, which, I suppose, came from the subcommittee of the Committee for Grievances.

1 and 2. In outlawries and attainders the debts of the delin-
quents should be paid before His Majesty took the rest of
the property by forfeiture.

3. It should be lawful to arrest the King's servants who were
in fault.

4. No man should be forced to lend money to the King.

5. In criminal cases the accused should be allowed to produce
witnesses (on oath).

6. The clause of 34 Henry VIII giving the King power to make
arbitrary law for Wales should be repealed.[7]

Such were the proposals as John Pory stated them in a letter to
Winwood.[8] In the Huntingdon notes, Martin is made to include a
seventh: that no man be troubled for land gained by the sea, by
defect of title, or by inquiry of wardship.

It seems probable that in the conference it was agreed to
submit the six new propositions to the King and that the four
Peers were to be sent to interview him, "not as Parliament men,
but as persons otherwise interested in the King's service." [9] Those
Lords were Salisbury, Northampton, Suffolk, and Worcester, all
Privy Councillors. His Majesty granted the first two requests at
once; he refused the third and the fourth; the fifth he could not
grant because it meant that men would perjure themselves for
their friends; the sixth he granted.[10] The four Lords had gained
for the Commons the less important of the six requests. His
Majesty found it hard to yield any right or symbol of power. The
King's mood had evidently changed during his interview with the
four Lords; it had begun with dark clouds and ended with "sunny
intervals," to use an English weather idiom.

On Tuesday morning, July 17, Salisbury had something to say
to the Upper House about that interview. His Majesty had asked
the four Lords at once about the conference and had marveled
that the Lower House should call in question things never spoken
of in the days of other kings.[11] The Commons had not added to
their former offer, but were asking more in return. Of course
Salisbury had invited them to do so, a fact to which the Lord

Treasurer did not allude. In a letter that the King commanded Salisbury to read to the Lords but that was intended for the ears of the Commons, His Majesty emphasized again his dislike of being pressed into doing things that had usually been left to the grace of princes.[12] In the same letter he asserted that no king was more anxious to derive strength from the love of his subjects. That was the mood he had shown at the end of the interview with the four Lords the evening before when, with a certain graciousness, he had made a considerable financial concession to the Commons. It is little wonder that the Commons hesitated again and again as to how to deal with this mercurial monarch.

On that same day Salisbury told the conference of the two Houses of the concession the King had made in asking £200,000 rather than £220,000. Then Salisbury alluded to his own self-denying act: he was giving up his "right arm," the greatest strength he had with which "to merit the love of many." [13] He should have the loss of so fair an office as any subject in Christendom.[14]

Then he appealed to the Commons: "What should hinder us from so eminent a good? If poverty, it is but *paupertas imaginaria* . . . if this be refused, *inter peritura vivimus.*" He concluded on a personal note:

> And now for a close, to have all sourness and all jealousies removed and buried at our parting, I must crave excuse and pardon of you gentlemen of the Lower House, if any of you have conceived any mistaking to proceed out of these lips this session; and the like loving opinion I treasure up concerning the generality of your House, and of every particular person thereof.[15]

In the same letter Pory wrote that, as the Commons were parting, Salisbury called them back and told them that he had delivered His Majesty's final and peremptory resolution, that the distance between the sums proposed was little and the bargain advantageous. If they refused, His Majesty would instantly dissolve Parliament and never renew the offer,[16] a threat that he had probably been commanded to make. The Commons returned to their own chamber. Salisbury had exhibited tact, and it must have come hard to threaten. Sir Julius Caesar talked of the divine and sacred offer. "Let not our posterity," he pleaded, "curse us that we have refused."

The House divided, and the noes yielded. According to Harl. 777, the yeas won by sixty votes or thereabouts.[17] It seems that a considerable minority was still reluctant to accept the Great Contract until they knew more about the concessions to be offered, and about the form of the levy.

According to Pory, the King in reducing his demand from £220,000 to £200,000 sent word that he had granted them sundry demands of importance never dreamed of when he made his last concession from twelve score to eleven score.

The Committee for Grievances was still going over the multitude of grievances that were being handed in by members. So pressed were they that when they finally exhibited their grievances to the Lords, they gave them a mixed bag of ill-digested, ill-arranged items.[18] Those items had been set down at various committee meetings, as, for example, on March 26, June 26, July 16, July 18, and July 20.

On July 18 the Commons made an extraordinary reservation. In the final contract they wished "a former liberty to propound anything else." [19] The following day Sir George More reported from the committee that, in view of the extra £20,000 they had offered, they hoped the King would admit any other project, during this contract, not concerning the King in honor in point of sovereignty.[20] That request implied the possibility of more and more requests about grievances. There was continuous pressure by men who believed they held face cards. "The Lower House," wrote Samuel Calvert to Trumbull, "hath kept the King at the staff's end." [21]

On July 19 the Lord Treasurer discussed the situation with the Lords. The Commons now knew, he said, what they should have, and the King did not know what he would receive.

The tenures are sinews of this bargain, for which 100,000*li* upon land. The purveyance, why should it not lie upon the land as now it doth, for if the King be left upon uncertain profits, the revenue may decay. Now the number of the Lower House are but a maniple [handful]. We are more like to pass things than when they are all here.[22]

The Earl of Exeter, Salisbury's elder brother, added that the Lords must pursue the same course as do men in bargaining, for the Commons would not bind themselves until they saw how they could levy it. Was the Earl suggesting that the Lords offer counsel to the Commons as to how the levy should be made? Lord Zouche believed that the Commons would do nothing about the levy until they met again. Lord Sheffield feared that if the Lords held back on account of the levy, the bargain might terminate. He confessed himself to be much "enamored" of the bargain. Bishop Abbot of London believed in setting down the bargain in definite words, so that gentlemen could talk over the terms with their constituents. The Lord Treasurer favored caution about the contract; he was as "enamored" of it as any, but he did not wish the Crown to accept silver for gold and, with the bishop of London, wished to see the contract drawn in definite terms.[23]

That same day there was a conference between the two Houses. Sir Edwin Sandys referred to the "happy resolution of this Contract, which is not a private contract, but with the whole Kingdom." He alluded to the £20,000 addition to which the Commons had consented and hoped that the Lords would be willing that the Commons should add anything else to the contract bounded "within the lists of [the King's] honor and profit." The lawyers had gone their circuits, and the Commons were tired.[24] It was not to be expected that the Commons would make a final end of the business now. They asked the Lords' assistance in the petition to His Majesty that the Four Shires might be exempted from trial, but, if not, that the trials should be held in Westminster Hall, and not in Wales. "No one thing will bring a greater generality of contentment to the people." [25] They asked that His Majesty should be bound in demurrers, "as in the 27th of Queen Elizabeth"; [26] that all fees of courts might be made certain; that a survey might be taken of all penal statutes and all of one nature set together; that nothing was more requisite than to yield justice to all good subjects.[27] These were new requests, except that about penal laws and that concerning Wales, which had been part of the petition of temporal grievances.

Sandys turned to the question of the officers of the Court of Wards. He hoped the Lords would join with the Commons in petitioning the King to consider their losses. Sandys alluded to the person who held the "prime office," the Lord Treasurer, who "shall lose most by this bargain." "He hath dealt very honorably with us." [28]

As for purveyance, Sandys thought more of it might be laid on the land. But there was no longer time to think of the levy. The Lord Treasurer responded:

> I cannot see any cause to break this Contract, but the rumor of the world, if we part before we express our own meaning by some act. There are some of the ancientist blood of this kingdom, noblemen that shall lose someone as much as forty of your House . . . Do not think I compare with your House, for I owe as much to it as yourselves.[29]

The Lord Treasurer was receiving the praise given him as due to the Lords in general, or so it would appear, but he had in the last sentence become personal. He continued, saying that he owed to the Lower House "as much to it as to yourselves." It had not been in his power to hinder the contract, "yet I must confess in my affection I have furthered it." He himself would have to pay. "I owe more unto my country than this, yea, my life." [30]

When, on July 21, the Lords were dealing with the petition to the King about the officials of the Court of Wards, he asked the Lords to leave him out for he was sure His Majesty would be pleased to reward him. Then he remarked that the sum given had to be tied to the Crown, for the navy and other things. "If the

King do spend out of magnificence anything more than he hath he must look to have it out of other means." [31]

On that afternoon there was a conference. Sandys spoke and alluded to the £200,000 per annum. He said that the sum was in return for purveyance of all kinds and natures, for tenures, and all things incident to them such as wardship of body and lands, "and what things else soever we shall insert at our next meeting that toucheth not his Majesty either in point of honor or profit." [32]

"As for th'assurance it was resolved to be by Act of Parliament in such sort as by the advice of my Lords, the Judges, shall be thought sufficient, both for his Majesty's annual revenue by the Contract and also for the people's security." [33]

Sandys referred to the four elements that now brought a curse on the kingdom during the years of the Parliament. There had been great fires in many towns. The air had been infected with the plague. The waters had raged and burst forth

> that never in our times, nay long before we were, hath there been heard of the like inundation. The earth by reason of the unseasonableness of the weather made so barren that it yields nothing near her former increase. The seasons so unseasonable that our winters have been like our usual springs, springs summer, summer autumn, and autumn winter . . . . These things, my Lords, have been the cause why we have levied so little upon the poorer sort and accompanied this one subsidy only with one fifteen, abating one contrary to the former manner, knowing . . . that some poor souls have been driven for payments of this kind to sell their pot, pan, nay clothes of[f] their bed.[34]

Sandys proceeded to speak of four comforts the people might receive. The first would benefit the poor: no impositions might be laid upon victuals. The other three would aid the "better part": first, they might carry down copies of the contract to the country; second, they might have His Majesty's gracious answer to their grievances; third, they might be suitors for other benefits that they could not now arrange, the House being empty and the large number of members gone to the country.[35]

Among things they would mention to the Lords were:

1. That penal laws may be preserved as may be best for the subject [that is, I take it, that those less good for the subject should be taken off the statute books].
2. That all purveyance be taken away. . . .
3. That the composition of purveyance be dissolved [that is, the payments made in place of purveyance].
4. That his Majesty would give no protections contrary to law [that is, royal documents granting immunity from arrest].
5. That all exposition of the Contract should be left to the Commons House.
6. That any additions to the Contract that toucheth not his Majesty in point of sovereignty or matter of profit may be added at the next meeting.[36]

Then Sandys presented four points "principally considerable in this Contract":

1. That the sum be stable and firm.
2. That the assurance should be the best they could have on the best advice.
3. The levy to be made with the greatest ease to the people.
4. The grievances to be satisfied and the Contract perfected.[37]

It appears, as already suggested, that the Commons were expecting a great deal.

Salisbury's answer did not indicate agreement with Sandys. "It stands against the rule of State, of safety, of greatness, to receive words and no money. Nothing is more ordinary than that a King never makes a bargain with the subject but he is a loser, though the people will not think so." [38] Salisbury added that for concessions about assarts, defective titles, and inundated grounds, a treble subsidy would not be too much.

In a second speech he alluded to the request about Wales and said that the King kept the Four Shires under his control, yet left the problem of their future undecided. Demurrers were a matter that touched the King in honor, and yet the Lord would join with the Commons in a petition. His Majesty was willing that a search be made of lawyers' fees and the penal laws to see how many there were, and of what nature. The Lords would join in a petition to the King for satisfaction to the officials of the Court of Wards, except the principal officer, who had satisfaction enough in their love. He warned the Commons that their demands must be bounded; yet if in the next session they dealt in supply more bountifully, the King would deal with a more open hand.[39]

On that afternoon the Lord Treasurer addressed the Lords: "We grant nothing nor deny nothing, but keep ourselves upon the same reservations. I have set down some things under my hand, which . . . I will offer unto you, whereupon they were read, which were in effect the other memorials." [40]

Parliament adjourned with the Great Contract so much at the fore that it was sure to be discussed by members as they returned to their constituencies.

In all the discussions of the past weeks impositions had not been forgotten. On June 27 it was arranged that the Great Committee was to meet that afternoon and that all other committees were to cease. From June 27 to July 2 debate over the question of impositions went on so continuously in the Grand or Great Committee that the meetings of the House of Commons were brief and largely devoted to routine business. The Lower House was giving its attention to a full-dress debate on the fundamental problem of impositions. That debate was important in English history and must be covered at some length.

The Great Debate

THE debate on impositions began on June 23 in the Committee of the Whole House and continued until July 2. The question before the committee was clearly put: did the King have the right to lay impositions upon merchandise without the assent of Parliament?

Nicholas Fuller, M.P. for the City of London, recently imprisoned for questioning the authority of the Court of High

Commission, a man of convictions and nevertheless of some breadth of view, opened the discussion.[1] He asserted that the common law of England had its foundation in the laws of God and in approved reason. It was of such a nature that neither the King without his subjects nor the subjects without their King could alter them. By that law the subject held property in lands and goods, and without their consent His Majesty could take no part of that property from them. He cited cases from his experience in the courts to prove that actions based on the prerogative could be censured and annulled by the rules of law and by the authority of the judges.

For the same reasons the King could not take from any subject his lawful trade nor the profit from it without his consent. Therefore, he could not restrain the merchants, in whom lay the reserve power of England, by putting impositions upon their goods. He cited five cases from the reign of Edward III where the King had recalled impositions because they had not been granted by Parliament. He went further and said that if a judgment should be rendered in court against the principle of parliamentary control of impositions, it was reversible in Parliament. After his speech a great silence ensued.[2]

Dudley Carleton asserted that when a foreign prince levied taxes upon English goods it was best for the English to impose in turn upon the commodities of that prince, and that the English, if they had to wait for Parliament to enact the impositions, would suffer much wrong. To this Fuller answered that in Henry VI's time, when the Duke of Burgundy set impositions on English goods, the English Parliament forbade the importation of Burgundian products. James Whitelocke [3] supported Fuller's argument by referring to a similar case in the time of Henry VII when the Venetians imposed a tax on English goods.

Sir Henry Montague maintained that in certain cases where impositions were unreasonable or immoderate they were unlawful, but, with these limitations, the King had a right to impose. Impositions were but an increase of customs, and customs were an inheritance of the Crown, just as the right to fees upon writs, murage, and pontage. When the subject received protection in his trade, the King could lawfully impose; it was his due as the defender of commerce. Montague admitted that upon the three staple commodities (wool, woolfells, leather) the King could not impose.

William Jones, M.P. for Beaumaris and a member of Lincoln's Inn, who was later to have a judicial career, addressed the committee at some length, maintaining that, although the sea was open, the King could restrain commerce for the good of the commonwealth but that he could not make money out of such a restraint. He presented the arguments for and against impositions with citations but concluded that, in cases where the merchants had granted impositions to the King, the law took away the right to levy them; it also removed the right of the King to increase customs.

Jones was followed by Sir Francis Bacon, Solicitor General.[4] The importance of the subject under discussion, he announced, called for the greatest strength of argument. Several questions about imposing were raised, among them the question, not whether the King might alter the law in the matter of imposing, but whether he had not such a prerogative by law. Here Bacon was, of course, answering Fuller. He began by making admissions. The King could not lay taxes within the land nor on coastal commerce between one English port and another. The question of duties on wool, woolfells, and leather had to be ruled out of consideration; there the King's hands were tied by the *antiqua customa*.

But the King had, nevertheless, a right to lay export and import duties on goods to and from foreign countries. In support of that proposition he was ready to put forward a universal negative; there was not a single record in which an imposition laid at the ports had been overthrown by the courts. Since the question of impositions had never been brought before the courts until Bate's case, "but still brought to Parliament," it was fair to conclude that they were legal. If they were not illegal but too extreme there was a remedy: let the subjects bring them up in Parliament. Bacon talked about the courts and Parliament as if he had never thought of Parliament in terms of the High Court.

He alluded to the impositions set by merchants as arranged with the King. The power of the King, he said, gave force to those impositions. This argument had been advanced by Jones, and it was not easy to refute.[5] Sir Francis looked back to the beginning of customs, which were obscure. He quoted Dyer as having given the opinion in his *Reports* [6] that the customs on wool, woolfells, and leather were by the common law. Dyer had been wrong, Bacon argued, for those customs were called the *nouvel coutume;* thus there were more ancient customs. To assume, however, that the earlier customs were made by Parliament was, he insisted, no more than a conjecture. Acts of Parliament had not been "much stirring" before the Great Charter of 9 Hen. III, a startling understatement. He was quoting, of course, the reissue of the Charter in that year. Sir Francis believed, however, with Dyer, that whatever the ancient customs were, they were by the common law, and, if so, must have had their beginnings from the King.

Bacon made another good point. The defenders of parliamentary rights had insisted that the King himself, in answer to petitions against impositions, had always given way. Not so, declared Bacon, and he was quite right. The King had answered in various ways, now assenting to a petition, now assenting in part, or for a limited period, and now disputing the petition and doing nothing. Indeed, the King had never disclaimed impositions as unlawful.[7]

Bacon then took up some of the precedents quoted by the opponents of impositions. He asserted that the many petitions by Parliament to abolish impositions were made promiscuously, as much as for giving up impositions established by Parliament as those set by the King. "So then to infer that impositions were against law, because they are taken away by succeeding Parliaments, it is no argument at all, because the impositions set by the Parliaments themselves . . . were . . . afterwards pulled down by Parliament." [8] Here was something new and persuasive, if it had been the whole truth.

Bacon declared that the impositions set by Parliament had been annulled by that body. Such impositions—he was alluding to the maltote which had been voted by the merchants and accepted by Parliament—were later objected to by Parliament. Parliament had embodied in a statute of 1340 an agreement by the King not to continue the maltote, and, when the King in 1342 levied the customs without consent of Parliament, the next Parliament in 1343 asked him to enforce the statute made by them in 1340 against the maltolte.[9]

Thus Bacon's argument was farfetched and seems disingenuous. Was he possibly taking a chance that the opponents of royal impositions would never find out that he was misusing the Rolls of Parliament? It is more charitable to assume that he had not read them with sufficient attention or had used an assistant to read them.

He met the statement that from Richard II's time to that of Queen Mary, a space of almost two hundred years, there had been an intermission of impositions by asserting that for an equal number of years impositions had been levied, through the first three Edwards and during the last sixty years (that is, during the reigns of Mary and Elizabeth).

Bacon stopped at this point in his draft of his speech.[10] But according to the writer of *Parliamentary Debates in 1610* he had more to say. Later laws, he maintained, abrogated earlier ones. Records were reverend things, but were like scarecrows.[11] The right to levy impositions was based upon the government of the kingdom in relation to foreign parts. "The law hath reposed a special confidence in the King," as in the pardoning of offenders, dispensing with laws, coining money, and making wars.

Thomas Hedley, M.P. for the borough of Huntingdon and later a well-known judge, dealt first with those who maintained that the decision of learned judges settled matters, and that the Court of Parliament did not have jurisdiction to examine the issues decided by them.[12] He was thinking of the decision in the case of John Bate who had refused to pay the imposition laid upon currants and had lost his case in the Court of the Exchequer. His Majesty interpreted that decision as giving him the right to levy impositions. According to Hedley, other juries and other judges might come to a different decision. Then he affirmed that Parliament had power over all parts, sciences, mysteries, and professions and could make laws for the reformation of all abuses. It was the *regnum representantium* and "so compact of the best and ablest of all professions whatsoever." It was recognized by the lawyers, Hedley asserted, that judgments in the King's Bench and in the Exchequer were examinable and reversible.

Hedley asked whether impositions were warrantable by the common law of the land, without the assent of Parliament. To answer that it was necessary to determine what the common law was. It was not merely what the judges willed; nor was it merely common reason. The statute laws were both reasonable and good. But the common law was of more force and strength than Parliament and its statutes. With statute law the King could dispense, but not with the common law. Parliament might indeed amend faults in the common law, but it could not abrogate it, nor could it establish new common law. Hedley quoted Bacon as having said that the statute laws were grounded upon reason and the wisdom of Parliament, but the common law was tried reason, indeed the quintessence of reason. Hedley had asked himself what could try reason better than Parliament. It was not the judges, nor the King and his nobles, nor the clergy, nor the Commons, but the essential form of the common law, "in a word . . . time, which is the trier of truth, author of all human wisdom, learning and knowledge. . . . Time is wiser than the Judges, wiser than the Parliament, nay, wiser than the wit of man." The common law Hedley defined as reasonable usage throughout the entire realm, approved time out of mind in the King's courts of record and profitable for the commonwealth. In the common law he included custom, but with qualifications. Whatever endangers the good of the commonwealth, any general mischiefs or inconveniences, the common law would reject. It would indeed be subject to changes as new conditions arose.[13]

The new impositions were against the common law. The precedents alleged for them had been only the acts of kings in time of war or in their urgent necessities and never had allowance by any decisions of judges till now. Hedley went into the various cases of impositions brought up by previous speakers and to be taken up by others.

At length he pointed out how new impositions had discouraged and even undone many merchants. Within the last four or five years there had been a general decay of trade.[14]

Lastly he adverted to the courage of English soldiers and their superiority over the peasant soldiers of other nations (he had Crecy and Agincourt no doubt in mind), because they were accustomed to freedom.[15] If this ancient liberty were taken from them and their lands and goods fell into the hands of another, they would have lost their care for the commonwealth and their courage.

John Hoskins denied that customs duties were the inheritance of the King and that he had the right to increase them. The regal power was from God, but "actuating" it was from the people. The King could do nothing against the common peace or common profit. Hoskins seemed to be feeling his way toward a political theory that the King would have regarded as "popular," and hence dangerous. One wishes that Hoskins had elaborated his thinking further; it is just possible that he did and that the notes taken of his speech have not escaped the wastebasket or fire. In the House of Commons and out of it Hoskins was looked upon as an amusing man who could be satirical. Yet he could be deadly serious, as serious as Wentworth.

Sir Robert Hitcham took a middle course. As a regular practice, he believed that the King could not impose, but in special circumstances he could do so: if it were for the good of the commonwealth, if the commonwealth received no prejudice and the King no benefit, or if the merchants gained thereby. In time of war, impositions were beneficial.

Hakewill Speaks

THE next speaker put the case against impositions so cogently that he deserves a chapter. William Hakewill,[1] the son of an Exeter merchant, a member of Lincoln's Inn, an M.P. for St. Michael's, Cornwall, was an indefatigable searcher among records and, more than that, a scholar who would weigh the language of a document, examine the occasion of its formulation, and try to discover the probable intention of its begetters. Moreover, he was an antiquarian who could look backward over the decades and centuries and fasten together old resolutions, petitions, and decisions into a chain of meaning.

We have two accounts of his speech. *Parliamentary Debates in 1610,* edited by S. R. Gardiner, is a report by an anonymous writer who had skill in getting down many of the words spoken, although he failed at times to make sense of them. Thirty years later Hakewill himself drew up an extended version of his speech based upon the notes he had made. Of that version he wrote: "It hath now extended itself beyond the probable proportion of a speech or argument, by the insertion of many records and acts of Parliament more at large, which at the delivery of it were merely quoted."

I have used Hakewill's extended version so far as the account in *Parliamentary Debates in 1610* goes, comparing it at every point with the contemporary account. When that concludes in the middle of the argument (as if the reporter had been called out), I have ventured to continue the argument in brief form from Hakewill's later version, since it was an expansion of the notes made by him at the time. I have tried to stick to the main lines of the argument that would have been in the original notes.

He entered upon his discourse with tact. He had been persuaded, he admitted, that the King's right to impose was clear and indisputable, and he had been sorry when Parliament began to call impositions in question, especially since His Majesty had promised never to lay any impositions except by the advice and free consent of his subjects.[2] He had listened to the arguments advanced in the Bate case concerning duty levied on currants and had been much affected by "the weighty and unanswerable reasons (as I then conceived them) of those grave and reverend Judges." It was a conciliatory prologue and one that must have made his listeners intent upon what was to follow.

He had been asked by the Commons, he continued, to search the records and had discovered that some of the records brought forward in that case were "untruly vouched and many misapplied." [3] He had, therefore, been forced to the conclusion that His Majesty had no right to impose. The customs levied on exports and imports were due by common law and were not to be increased at the King's pleasure, nor by way of impositions.[4] The common law gave the King no perpetual revenue nor matter of profit from the subject but it either limited a certainty therein at the first or provided that a certainty should be arrived at by a legal course. Hakewill proceeded to canvass the other revenues due to the King in order to show that the common law gave them to him but always with a certainty attached; thus King and subject knew exactly what was due. In cases where the Commons gave the King a revenue not certain at first, it was always reducible to a certainty by a legal course, as by act of Parliament, by judges, or by a jury, and not at the King's pleasure.[5]

Hakewill's next argument was that, as the subjects owed the King loyalty and obedience, so the King owed his subjects protection and defense. But protection and defense cost money. Therefore, the Commons allowed the sovereign great prerogatives and favors, such as wardship, forfeitures upon treason and outlawry, fines and amercements upon penal laws, profits from courts, from treasure trove, from prisage,[6] butlerage,[7] wrecks, and other incidental dues.

> To what other end hath the common law thus provided for the maintenance of the King's charge . . . but only to this end, that, after these duties paid, the poor subject might hold and enjoy the rest of his estate to his own use, free and clear from all other burdens whatsoever.

Sir Robert Hitcham said that in special circumstances, such as an unexpected war, the King might not only levy impositions but levy a tax within the realm without the assent of Parliament.

That the King could by his absolute power levy subsidies or impositions was a dangerous doctrine and might bring his subjects into bondage. "Who shall be judge between the King and his people of the occasion?" [8] For unexpected contingencies such as war the common law made provision. In the case of an offensive war against the Welsh or the Scots, the King could ask the military service of his subjects at their own charge (escuage). To allow the King to charge impositions, tallages, or taxes without consent of Parliament would lead to "the utter dissolution and destruction of that politic frame and constitution of this Commonwealth." [9]

Hakewell turned aside from the main thread of his discourse to offer an argument of inference, as he called it. All kings of England since Henry III had sought or obtained an increase of customs by the gift of their subjects. Edward III, for example, on undertaking a just and honorable war, asked the three estates to give him a relief and was well content to have the fact entered of record.[10] Other kings suffered the same sort of records to be enrolled and printed. If they could have laid impositions at their own pleasure, would they not rather have done so at once rather than have awaited the action of Parliament? If they were unaware of their prerogatives, had they not wise counselors to put them in mind of what they could not do? Kings had the right to make war and coin money. Did they ever ask the consent of Parliament to perform such functions? Edward II and Edward III borrowed money from the merchants and bound themselves to repay it. Would any wise man in the world who thought he had but a shade of right prejudice himself so much as to borrow that which he might take without leave? Edward III had been indeed so pressed for money that he had pawned his jewels,[11] yet he did not resort to any absolute power of imposing but asked an increase of customs.

Another argument from inference concerned the *Carta Mercatoria* of Edward I (anno 31). By that document, continued Hakewill, the foreign merchants in return for certain liberties and immunities granted by the King and also for relief from prisage, allowed the King an increase of customs. In the same year the King sent word to his customers that the English merchants were willing to pay him a like increase of customs,[12] if they were granted the same liberties as the foreign merchants; but the customers told him not to compel the English merchants to pay it. Hakewill suggested, on what evidence is not apparent, that Edward I did not expect the English merchants to pay an imposition.

Hakewill pursued the question of grants by merchants further. When the merchants granted the King an increase of customs the King in drawing up the commission to the collectors of the customs would justify himself by reciting his great necessity and add that the grant had been made by the merchants. And yet, declared Hakewill, these impositions "by grant of the merchants" were always complained of by the Commons when they met in Parliament.[13]

Hakewill developed the case against impositions from the forbearance of the sovereigns to put their pretended power in practice. He asserted that from the Conquest to the reign of Queen Mary, a space of 480 years, the kings had been so sparing of impositions that only six, if that many, proper impositions had been laid by twenty-two kings, and those moderate, in times of great necessity, and almost all but for a short time. Yet every one of those impositions was complained of and "upon complaint taken away." [14] It was a sweeping statement, a "universal affirmative," to which exceptions could have been offered. The impositions laid today, said Hakewill, were to endure forever.

There were, indeed, other impositions besides those six, impositions "relied upon as so many precedents to prove the lawfulness of the impositions now complained of." [15] But such impositions were of a different nature from those used in Hakewill's day. He proceeded to examine a series of cases in the reigns of Edward I, Edward II, and Edward III. Three cases mentioned in the reign of Edward I seemed to give the sovereign the right to lay impositions—16, 21, and 31 Edw. I, the last being an instance brought up by the Solicitor in his argument for the King. Those cases, Hakewill declared, were all very different from the present impositions, being laid under special circumstances, two of them at least for a short time. The third was given up in the next reign at the request of the Commons.[16]

In the reign of Edward II there was not a single imposition laid; there were, on the contrary, four examples of actions by the King, sometimes under pressure, made against his right to levy.[17]

Edward III did everything possible, Hakewill insisted, to bring his people under the yoke of impositions. He asked the merchants to grant him on their own an imposition on exports and imports, but this device was resisted as unlawful. In 17 Edw. III the Commons pronounced such a grant by the merchants "a great mischief." In 25 Edw. III the merchants had offered His Majesty an increase of customs, but the Commons prayed that the commission to collect the increase should not be awarded.[18]

From the end of the reign of Edward III until that of Queen Mary, some 170 years, no large impositions were laid.[19] Hakewill surveyed that long interval and showed the serious situations when the sovereigns between Edward II and Mary badly needed money and did not resort to impositions.[20]

From here on we have only Hakewill's version of his speech as uttered long before and now extended with extracts from laws and other documents.

Mary revived impositions, and under unusual circumstances. It was pointed out that the customs on wool carried out of the realm were larger than that on cloth. When the Queen increased the duty on cloth, the merchants of London complained that the increased rate had not been granted by Parliament,[21] but the complaints were unheeded. The profits to the Crown were so desirable that the new customs were continued.

In the fifth year of her reign the Queen also imposed a tax of 40s. upon every tun of French wine imported, but a judgment given in the Exchequer against that imposition put an end to it. At about the same time Her Majesty laid an imposition upon all French goods brought into her realm; it was continued until the first year of Queen Elizabeth and then dropped,[22] because, as Hakewill believed, it was illegal.

Hakewill turned his attention to what he called statute law. He quoted from Magna Carta cap. xxx (1215, cap. xli) and dealt with the words "tolls," "impositions," and "custom" or *consuetudo.* He went on to the second statute against impositions, *De Tallagio non Concedendo,* which was not really a statute but only a proposal for one. Whatever the date, the occasion was the laying of a great imposition upon wool, and Hakewill proceeded to answer the objections to its validity.[23] The third statute against impositions, that of 25 Edw. I, cap. vii, released the subjects, said Hakewill, from the maltote upon wool and promised that there should be no more such things without common consent except for the customs on wools, skins, and leather.[24] The fourth statute was that of 14 Edw. III, cap. xxi, in which the King promised that his subjects should not be charged or grieved to make any aid, or sustain charge, if it be not by the common assent of the Lords and Commons, and that in Parliament.[25]

Hakewill concluded with answers to some arguments advanced in support of impositions. Into the intricacies of these disputations it is unnecessary to follow him. If occasionally he pushed an argument rather far, if he did not always admit the force of the case presented by the friends of prerogative, he was still more scrupulous than many antiquarians. On fundamentals he was usually right. He constructed an argument, the strength of which was impressive.[26]

Speeches by Yelverton,
Hobart, Crew, and
Doddridge

THE two important speakers who followed spoke for the King. The first was Henry Yelverton, son of Sir Christopher Yelverton, an Elizabethan judge. Yelverton had attended Christ's College, Cambridge, and Gray's Inn, and represented the borough of Northampton. He had been inclined to lean toward the opposition, but was not to be counted in that camp. In the Goodwin-Fortescue issue he had at first urged that Goodwin be allowed to take his seat but later, when the King's anger blazed forth, Yelverton surprised the House by declaring that the King's command was like a thunderbolt or the roaring of a lion.

That speech was not nearly enough to win royal favor for him.

He had offended Sir George Home (or Hume), earl of Dunbar, by a Latin pun upon Home's name. He had offended other Scots by supporting the bill to naturalize Lord Kinloss and had offered as a reason that Lord Kinloss was half English. He had offended James by criticizing certain features of the proposed Act of Union.[1] When Sir Francis Bacon was attempting to influence the voting in the House by quoting the King's opinion, Yelverton was said to have remarked that he would weigh His Majesty's reasons as he did his coin. Such statements were quickly carried to the King who soon indicated, without the least subtlety, that Yelverton was out of favor.

Yelverton finally appealed to Lady Arabella Stuart to recommend his suit for a reconciliation with the King to the Lord Chancellor of Scotland (Sir Alexander Seton, Earl of Dunfermline). Dunfermline offered little encouragement, telling Yelverton that the King was incensed at him, but promising nevertheless to carry a letter from Yelverton to the King. Yelverton wrote Dunfermline an exceedingly submissive letter and gave an even more submissive one to be delivered to His Majesty.

James sent word that Yelverton was to ask access to Lord Dunbar and that "the King's Majesty will understand your own further purgation in these matters." James was going to see to it that Yelverton moved slowly through the vale of humiliation, and Yelverton was ready to tread that lowland way. He wrote another letter to the King saying that he groveled under the weight of the King's indignation; he also groveled before Dunbar. All this suited the King who found pleasure in seeing men kiss the rod. Dunbar received Yelverton and told him that of all men living he had hated him most because of his enmity to the Scots. Yelverton denied that he had ever been anti-Scottish; he added that he had always assumed it was the King's pleasure that "we should use liberty of speech, and the experience of the place teacheth us so much." It was a remark wasted on a Scots nobleman who was probably not versed in English parliamentary privileges.

Yelverton was at length granted an audience by His Majesty,

but on his knees and with three Councillors present to witness his abasement. James gave him a lecture on his sins. He explained that, unlike Henry VIII, he (James) believed in free speech.[2] More than once the King had informed Parliament that he supported free speech. He went on to give reasons for his anger at Yelverton. Had not Yelverton spoken up in the Commons against the granting of a subsidy? [3] "There is neither equity nor justice to deny so small help as I required; it being the duty of every workman to keep the head and foundation whole," said His Majesty. Yelverton was not without readiness and subtlety in putting the best interpretation on his speeches and actions, so much so that the King reluctantly relented. Yelverton promised to serve His Majesty faithfully in the future. James warned him to be careful.

Yelverton took an early opportunity to prove himself a reconditioned member. He began a speech in the committee by saying at once that the King could impose. The House, he continued, should judge the King in cold blood. "Let him impose upon what cause he will, the reason and cause thereof will never come in question." He could impose in order to maintain equality among the merchants themselves or in order to keep the balance between himself and foreign princes. Customs were due by common law, he declared, but the King could not impose new customs. Neither the common law nor statute was against impositions, however, if they were set by way of penalty. The imposition upon John Bate was upon a restraint. "You shall bring in no currants. If you do, you shall pay so much."

Yelverton closed his plea by saying that, even if impositions were excessive, yet none could judge that but the King, "no more than the restraint." He seemed to be steering a middle course: he accepted in part the parliamentary doctrine concerning what the King could not do, but left a loophole by which the King could levy as he pleased.

No doubt many in the House knew of Yelverton's ordeal and realized why he spoke so decisively in favor of the right of the King to levy impositions. But those who had taken a stand in the

Commons against the King's policies were not likely to forgive him.

Martin, who followed, remarked: "Mr. Yelverton hath concluded that this matter is not determinable by law, but Bate's case was adjudged by the Judges of the law, and so he hath brought himself into a praemunire already." Martin's words were, I suspect, intended as humorous; but like much seventeenth-century humor, it was heavy-handed and not in his best vein. Martin continued: "Mr. Yelverton's position, an arbitrary, irregular, unlimited, and transcendent power of the King in imposing." [4] To Yelverton's assertion that the sovereign had the right of imposing, not by common law, but by the law of nations, Martin retorted: "the question is, whether the King of England by the law of England have any such power." Then he enunciated a constitutional principle, one that was often to be heard of later: "The King of England the most absolute King in Parliament, but of himself, his power is limited by law." As usual Martin was content with a few sentences.

Sir Henry Hobart, Attorney General, M.P. for Norwich, who had served in four Parliaments and whose later career proved him no unswerving follower of the Crown, declared that the principle that the King could not make laws without the assent of Parliament was recognized in the common law and in statute law. By the statute of 25 Edw. III, the King was bound to redress all mischiefs by means of Parliament,[5] But the right of laying impositions seemed to belong to the King, unless it could be proved otherwise. If the King could prohibit subjects from leaving the realm or from doing harm to the state, then he could impose. There were two ways to impose: by the power of the King, and by Parliament. "But," asserted Hobart, "if you confess my precedents, the question is at an end." [6] The first customs, until the time of Edward I, were laid by the King's power, not by Parliament. The imposition in 21 Edw. I of 40s. per pack of wool was not made by Parliament but by a grant of merchants. That grant, stated Hobart, repeating what Bacon had said, was really by the power of the King.[7]

So far the Attorney General was in a strong position. His next statement was less convincing. The petitions by the people to be relieved of impositions implied that such impositions had been justly made. There was indeed no act of Parliament declaring impositions wrong. Here he was playing with words. Again and again Parliament had sought to nullify impositions. The intermitting of impositions, he continued, did not take away the right to make them. In conclusion he said that monarchy was the best form of government (a statement few of that generation would have disputed), and, if so, the King must be trusted in some things.[8]

Hobart was followed by Thomas Crew, M.P. for Lichfield and a member of Gray's Inn. Eight years after this Parliament James, when asked if there were any reason why Crew should not be made Recorder of London, "confessed but one, and that was Sir Thomas Crew." The quip was in the Jamesian manner; the King did not forget those who had opposed him. In his speech Crew quoted precedents to prove that the King could not impose except in time of war.

Mr. Serjeant Doddridge, M.P. for Horsham (Sussex), lately Solicitor General and destined to become a justice of the King's Bench, maintained that customs were an ancient inheritance of the Crown by the common law, a right as old as the Crown itself.[9] Further, the King could restrain traffic at his pleasure; if he could restrain, he could also impose. It would be, he said, a miserable situation for the state if the King could not impose when dealing with foreign powers who set tariffs against England. Doddridge quoted the statute of 25 Edw. I, cap. vii, where the commonalty had been grieved at the maltolte of wool and the Crown had released the merchants from that toll and "granted for us and our heirs that we shall not take such things without their common assent and goodwill, saving to us and our heirs the custom of wools, woolskins, and leather, granted before by the commonalty aforesaid." He seized upon the words "take such things without their common assent" and explained that "such things" meant excessive burdens or impositions. He took a similar case from 14 Edw. III, cap. ii, where the King promised that all merchants, denizens, and foreigners, "except those which be of our enmity," should come and go, paying the customs, subsidies, and reasonable profits. Reasonable profits could mean nothing else, he insisted, than reasonable impositions. He dealt with the statement, by the fifteenth-century Sir John Fortescue, that the King could lay impositions only by Parliament. The words, he declared, were "strange impositions"; and "strange" at that time meant unreasonable. Other arguments he mustered from a wide range of sources, not confining himself to the *Rotuli Parliamentorum* and the Year Books, but drawing on medieval materials seldom used. To my mind, he made a rather strong case for the King's right to lay impositions, especially in his reinterpretations of well-known passages constantly cited against the King's right. That the same words might have different meanings in medieval days from those in the seventeenth century is more easily understood by historians than by country gentlemen in the reign of James I. I am not enough of a medievalist to judge Doddridge's interpretations of words, but they sound reasonable. His long disquisition lacked the philosophical sweep of Hakewill and was less likely to convince his listeners.

Whitelocke's Argument

THE next speaker was James Whitelocke, a new M.P. who had succeeded Richard Lea as member, on his death in 1609, for Woodstock. Whitelocke was to become a justice of the King's Bench and was a remarkable character, if we may read between the lines of his *Liber Famelicus*.[1] One of four sons of a London merchant, he was brought up by a wise and extraordinary mother. Young James studied at the Merchant Taylors' School under the famous teacher Richard Mulcaster, then proceeded to St. John's College, Oxford, and from there to the New Inn and the Middle Temple.

At Oxford his studies had included logic, classics, Hebrew, and the civil law (under the celebrated Gentili). But he had labored, often until midnight, above all in history, "in which he took great delight." He was elected a fellow of St. John's, and that fellowship, I infer, made it possible for him to pursue the common law along with the civil law, the experience of his mother with her property having induced him "to draw that way." He married a gentleman's daughter who brought with her "a competent portion." He accumulated friends easily, men who seemed devoted to him, among them Sir Henry Neville, Humphrey May, and Richard Martin, all three of whom sat in the Commons with him. He was on good terms with John Donne, Sir Robert Cotton the antiquary, Sir Edward Coke, and with many lawyers.

It is unwise to appraise a man's character by his diary, but one cannot read Whitelocke's brief memoranda about his life without observing that recorderships and positions of trust were thrust upon him as soon as he began practice, as if his fellows quickly recognized his integrity and legal learning.

It was probably his knowledge of parliamentary history that soon won him influence in the House of Commons. He began his speech on impositions in the Committee of the Whole House, which had been sitting (with brief interruptions) for several days. He declared at once that the King's letters patent for impositions without the assent of Parliament were illegal.[2] He promised to develop four arguments and to avoid repetition of what had already been said. In this résumé of his utterances, I shall deal only with the first and fourth part of his case. His first reason for denying the validity of impositions by the Crown was that the levying of them was against the natural frame and constitution of the kingdom, which was *jus publicum regni*. The levying of impositions would subvert the fundamental laws of the realm and bring about a new form of state.[3]

What was Whitelocke talking about if not the unwritten constitution of England? To levy impositions would bring on a "new form of state." He outlined the present state as he conceived it. The King had a twofold power: the one in Parliament, and the other out of Parliament. The first power was the greater and controlled the second. If the King made a grant out of Parliament, it bound him and his successors, but a grant with the assent of Parliament could be changed. Moreover, by writs of error it was possible to appeal from the King out of Parliament to the King in Parliament. The King in Parliament could make laws, could naturalize foreigners, could erect an arbitrary government, could judge without appeal, and could legitimate. The King out of Parliament had the right of coinage, of denization, and of making peace and war,[4] opinions Whitelocke scarcely held in line with those of his sovereign.

He put the question: can anyone give a reason why the King can make laws only in Parliament? He answered: it was the original right of the kingdom and "the very natural constitution of our State and policy [polity?]."[5] Whitelocke was thinking of a constitution that had been long coming into existence and that was indeed being slowly won by the very claims that he, Hakewill, and the leaders of the 1620s, and of the Long Parliament put forward. He was really appealing to what he believed to be the opinion of intelligent people (not in the King's employ) concerning the rights of Parliament.

If the King might levy impositions, continued Whitelocke, he may alter the laws of England in one of two fundamental ways: he must either take his subjects' goods without their assent,[6] which was against law; or give his own letters patent the force of law, which was also against law. That the King could not take those goods without the assent of the owners did not need to be proved; it was *"jus indigena,* an old homeborne right."

Kings have not dared, he continued, to go directly against the right, but instead have devised colors and shadows for their wrongdoing: commissions, loans on "privy seals" ("apprests"), and "benevolences." Cardinal Wolsey, he asserted, in the reign of Henry VIII, attempted to raise money for a proposed war by sending out commissioners to value property and then demanding a fraction of those valuations. By that device he stirred discontent and in some places actual rebellion.[7] When called to account he put the blame on the judges, quite falsely, saying that they had advised him to raise money in that way.

Long before that, in the reign of Edward III (25 Edw. III, cap. xvi) loans called privy seals were complained of in Parliament as against reason and the franchises of the land, and the King yielded with these words: "It pleaseth our lord, the King, it be so." [8] By a statute (I Rich. III, cap. ii) "benevolences" were ruled out: "The subjects and Commons of this land from henceforth shall in no wise be charged by any such charges or impositions called a benevolence." [9]

I am omitting some twenty pages of Whitelocke devoted in part to a rebuttal of arguments put forward by the supporters of the Crown that would involve repetition of what had been already said by others.

Whitelocke's fourth point was that the imposing of customs without assent of Parliament was contrary to the custom of the forefathers (*contra morem majorum*). Impositions had been set for a short and certain time, and upon a few commodities (he was repeating Hakewill). The impositions that the King was now going to lay upon hundreds of commodities were to be continued perpetually. No example could be cited, he continued, where the sovereign had ever asserted that imposing was part of his prerogative. Either he discharged the impositions he had laid, entreated his subjects to tolerate them for the time being, or waived his present possession and took that as a gift of Parliament which had been set by his absolute power.

Whitelocke next observed that the kings had acknowledged that it was not their right to lay impositions, and he produced interesting evidence. Furthermore, he alleged that those advisers of the sovereign who had urged him to lay impositions had been accused of their sins in Parliament, notably Wiliam Latimer and Richard Lyons in the time of the Good Parliament.[10]

If Whitelocke was less skillful than Hakewill in presenting legal and historical data to country gentlemen and less persuasive in manner, his learning nevertheless commanded their respect.

Other Speakers
on Impositions

SIR Walter Cope, member for Westminster and Chamberlain of the Exchequer, offered a compromise solution of the debate. There should be a petition to the King to refer the present impositions to a parliamentary committee for reform, "where need is," and a further petition that it might please the King that Parliament should pass an act that no imposition should hereafter be set but by Parliament. We may follow Gardiner in assuming that Cope would hardly have sprung this proposal without the assent of the King and that he was acting at the instance of Salisbury, whom he delighted to serve.

Lawrence Hyde thought that the King could not impose in time of peace upon goods transported or imported. He summed up the debate:

> One said he [the King] may impose by law of nations. Another said, it shall be by way of penalty, another, by imposition, by increase of custom. Another says that the first custom was by limitation [initiation?] of the King, because it appears not that it was given by Act of Parliament.[1]

Finally Hyde moved that a law of explanation should be made that these (the recent) impositions were unlawful. He proposed, further, that Parliament should lay some impositions on superfluities.

Dudley Carleton, who described himself as "one of the loose shot that drew on the skirmish, which hath been entertained with great strength on both sides for many days together," seemed to imply that Hyde had broken some agreement arrived at "before dinner," presumably to call an end to the discussion. Perhaps Carleton hoped that Cope's solution would be accepted and the long debate brought to an end. At any rate, it is evident that Carleton was doing his best to mollify contentious members by asserting that the quarrel was not mortal. They were making love, not to Socrates and Plato but to *amica veritas*. Truth was to be found, moreover, on high and not down a well. I assume that, by those who looked down a well for truth, Carleton meant men who referred to fourteenth-century precedents.

Carleton reviewed the debate, alluding to what the Solicitor and the Attorney had said. Twice he referred to Yelverton, not without an edge to his words. Carleton wished to see the question of right waived and rather to hear the grievance dealt with. There were diseases of which the physicians knew little, and yet the empirics found the cures within their practice.

He examined the customary usages in France and Spain and came back to his own country. "In our laws, though prerogative be not so hemmed in but that it may break out upon extraordinary occasions, as *tempore guerrae* . . . yet is it so entangled as it cannot go at pleasure." [2] Petitions and statutes, at which Yelverton had taken a fling (thus discounting the sources upon which his own profession depended), do, in a mannerly style, "tell the King how far he may stretch his prerogative and the subject claim his liberty." [3]

Obviously Carleton was trying desperately to win over both sides to an agreed policy, even making thrusts at Yelverton, thrusts that would not harm Carleton with those who regarded Yelverton as a turncoat. Carleton asserted that the Commons had promised not to reverse the judgment in the Exchequer (the Bate case),[4] but he hoped that judgment would not be drawn into other matters, and that it should not be held as a determination of right. Let the question of right be passed over, he urged; let the Commons frame a petition to His Majesty about their grievances, showing how they languished. The kings of England have been accustomed of old to ease their subjects' grievances. Carleton was making a plausible case.

But some would ask, he went on, if we omit the question of right, what have we gained by all this dispute? We have regained the liberty of disputing "without controlment." How shall we use this liberty? he asked the members, answering that we may now make impositions a matter of grievance. We promised the King that we would use moderation. Let us do so; the King will be contented, and grievances may be eased. Carleton, seldom optimistic about his own affairs, was overly hopeful about his sovereign and those around him.

His speech was conciliatory and must have seemed a breath of fresh air in St. Stephen's Chapel. It may well be that Carleton had been given an inkling that Whitehall was ready for a compromise such as that arrived at in 1604 over the Goodwin-Fortescue episode. Carleton's suggestion was not far from that put forth by Cope.

The House seemed, however, hardly ready to close the debate. Sir Roger Owen, an M.P. for Shropshire, who had been in the Parliaments of 1597 and 1601, declared that impositions were not agreeable to the law of nations, nor to the practice of modern nations, nor to the law of England. He went back to Augustine to prove that men had property in their goods by the law of nations. He alluded to the Grecian state, to that of Rome, to that of France, to those of Portugal and Spain, and arrived at length at the government of England. His speech revealed learning, as possibly he intended. As was once said of another, he beat about the bush but he did not start the hare. Once in a while he did.

Richard Gore, an M.P. for the City of London and a well-known merchant,[5] pointed out that impositions particularly concerned the English because they lived on an island.

Heneage Finch of the Inner Temple had been elected to Parliament in 1607 as a member for Rye. In a carefully prepared speech he declared that the question was whether, according to common law, the King had power to lay impositions; if he did not, the question was at an end. If he had such a power by common law, did any act of Parliament restrain or abridge that power? He asserted that common law did not give the King the power to make impositions and that such power as he did have had been clearly and expressly taken away as far as Parliament could take it away.[6]

Finch alluded to Doddridge's and Yelverton's question: if the King could not use impositions, how was he to take action against foreign princes who put impositions upon English goods? He answered his question by maintaining that the English were well stored with commodities and had little need of foreign goods. To Bacon's comment that in the early days Parliaments were not "much stirring," he answered that Parliaments were as ancient as the laws, a statement easily disproved. He spent time in answering Yelverton, Hobart, and Bacon, with precedents from the Tower, from chronicles and Year Books; he used arguments too involved to be summarized here and in many cases repetitious of what had been said earlier. The reader who wishes to follow up the cases he presented should consult Mrs. Foster's *Proceedings in Parliament, 1610.*

The next day (July 3) Sir Edwin Sandys made a report of the great debate, and then a subcommittee, presumably of the Committee of the Whole House, was assigned to consider the frame of a petition to be offered to the King.[7] The committee included most of those who had participated in the debate and a few others whose speeches escaped record or who were put on the subcommittee for other reasons. The following day Martin reported the Petition of Impositions, which was then twice read and voted.[8] But on July 7 the grievances as a whole, now engrossed, were read to the House. The article about impositions assumed that

> though the law of propriety be original and carefully preserved by the common laws of this Realm . . . yet those famous kings . . . agreed that this old fundamental right should be further declared . . . by act of Parliament. . . . We therefore, your Majesty's most humble Commons . . . finding that your Majesty, without advice and consent of your Lords and Commons, hath lately in time of peace, set both greater impositions and far more in number than any your noble ancestors did ever in times of war, do . . . present this most just and necessary petition unto your Majesty, that all impositions set without assent of Parliament may be quite abolished and taken away.[9]

It was a statement carefully drawn by men less timorous than in earlier sessions about speaking up to the sovereign.

On the morning of July 10 Sandys reported the grievances from the Committee of the Whole House. Along with them were nine bills ready to be introduced and sponsored presumably by the same committee. The second bill, that against impositions, was probably in some degree a recasting of the bill of 1606.[10]

As Mrs. Foster points out, Nicholas Fuller had earlier in the session suggested such a bill, and on July 2 Sir Walter Cope had made a similar suggestion.[11] Sir William Twysden, Sir Robert Cotton, Sir Roger Owen, Mr. Hakewill, and Mr. Tate were to consider the registering and recording of the grievances now to be delivered to the King. They were also to collect the arguments made about impositions and reduce them to writing. They, four of the King's learned counsel, and Sandys, Fuller, Whitelocke, Crew, Hoskins, Wentworth, William Jones, Hakewill, Brock, and Finch were to assist in the work.[12] It was a committee somewhat the same as that named to draw up from the debate the petition on the same subject.

On the afternoon of July 10 the Parliament met the King in Whitehall. If we may trust the French ambassador, the King received them with ill looks and had little to say. No doubt he had read the petition about impositions and had probably been told about the bill. His speech was hardly gracious:

> First I say that some of these impositions were laid before my time. Secondly I promise that hereafter none shall be laid but by Parliament. In the meantime I scorn that you should stay to give me an answer to the point of supplying my present wants, which was the errand for which I called you together at this time.[13]

He then called upon Salisbury to explain why the impositions had been laid. That tax, answered Salisbury,[14] was rendered necessary by the wars in Ireland where there was cause to fear "some new defection," "the Kingdom being in great fear." Dorset, whose memory Salisbury cherished, had been at that time Lord Treasurer. The Council had met and debated what course to pursue "to preserve the state of the Kingdom." It was resolved to lay impositions. "What should be the reason to lay so many I know not, but I am to judge the best of him that's gone." A hundred merchants from London and other places were called in. They agreed with the Chancellor of the Exchequer in favoring impositions on imported goods. That seemed the "best temporary remedy . . . rather than to make choice of extending the King's prerogative for raising of money any other way." [15] It was thought unwise to fall back upon penal laws, monopolies, or "other vain projects devised by bankrupts and hatched in prisons." Salisbury defended himself: he had done what befitted an honest man and an official of His Majesty. The impositions had been set by a lawful power after a judgment in court. He maintained that the impositions had not raised the price of commodities. If the King's customs had lost £20,000 within the year, it was a result of the peace with Spain and its many effects on commerce.[16] The Crown had borrowed money until the tide of povery had almost overflowed the banks of the Exchequer. Those who opposed impositions were of three types: those who did not know of the right to impose, those who were in error as to that right, and those who envied the Lord Treasurer.[17] Those who had criticized, had they known the King's necessities, would, he believed, have done as he did. "Let them think of me as they please." He would not attempt to answer one of the Lower House who had asserted that impositions were contrary to law. For three hundred of the new impositions His Majesty received nothing, for five hundred not above £300. Thirty of the other impositions upon wines, spices, satins, velvets, gold lace, and the like, the use of which had "grown to great excess," would raise £50,000.[18] "It was thought a good policy of State to impose upon such commodities as (being brought in unwrought in their simple materials) would increase manufactures at home." [19] Salisbury did not precisely say as much, but it must have been apparent to all that the impositions were laid upon imports required by those who were fairly well-to-do. Impositions, he concluded, were ancient. Queen Mary laid them and her sister, the late Queen, laid even more. As he finished, he knelt before the King and asserted that he had not abused His

Majesty's trust, "nor deserved the censure of Empson and Dudley." [20]

It was a closely reasoned speech and exhibited a knowledge of English commerce and an understanding of economic considerations, considerations that had hardly been alluded to in the great debate over impositions.

A Scottish manuscript used by Mrs. Foster makes the King say: "If I have done wrong, blame the Lord Treasurer, who told me that I might impose. But these shall continue, and I am content that ye make a law against impositions to be set hereafter." [21]

When Salisbury had concluded, the King called on the Clerk of Parliament to read the answers to the petition of the Commons. The King, it was explained, had not had time to examine the petitions. Those to which he now gave answers all concerned profit rather than government.[22] It seemed a neat device to put off the Commons; the concessions concerning profit were not considerable.

His Majesty gave up the imposition of 1s. per chaldron on coal from Blyth and Sunderland. As for the grant for sealing of the new drapery to the Duke of Lennox,[23] he answered: "I will confer with my Judges and what they say is against the law shall be redressed." [24] He hoped that the courts would proceed expeditiously. To the abolition of the impositions for licensing alehouses and for licensing of wines, a patent given to the Lord Admiral, the King consented. He did not wish, however, to use too severe a hand with his people. He knew well enough that the Lower House was not the place to determine the law in the case of private men, "much less concerning a Prince's right." Yet His Majesty was pleased to assure them (besides the great abatement he had made in this session of divers imposts, to his great loss) that he would be willing to assent to an act by which his power should be suspended from imposing any more upon merchandise without consent of Parliament. As to which impositions were to be suspended, that would appear in a book then in press, but in general many imposts were taken away or abated; those that were left were mostly upon "silk, lawn, spice, fruit, and such like." [25] These, it may be added, were the impositions that produced a large share of the revenue and hence were those likely to raise prices.[26]

Spedding, in his masterly *Life of Bacon,* gave it as his judgment that the King, having the law on his side (by the decision in the Bate's case), had made a considerable concession and that the Commons should have accepted the concession with gratitude. He believed, also, that it would have been wiser if His Majesty had left the assertion of the right to Salisbury and had himself said no more than that he was willing to divest himself of the right by act of Parliament.[27]

Neither the King's answer to the grievances nor Salisbury's speech had been well received by the Commons. They "went away ill satisfied," [28] and the next day voted one subsidy and one fifteenth.

The following day (July 11) Sandys alluded to the priority of the bills that were to accompany the Petition of Grievances, one of which was a bill against impositions. No doubt Sandys was looking out for it, but Thomas James, M.P. for Bristol, who had been an alderman and mayor of that city, and who had long opposed impositions, was active in promoting a bill that was given to a subcommittee of the Committee for Grievances on July 14. That subcommittee consisted of Thomas James, Fuller, Whitelocke, Sandys, Nicholas Hyde, "and all that will come." It was to meet at seven on Monday morning, July 16.[29] All the members named, except perhaps Myddleton, were opposed to impositions. Robert Myddleton, M.P. for a Dorset borough and a merchant, was unlikely to have different views. On the afternoon of July 16 the bill was reported from the subcommittee by Hakewill and ordered to be engrossed.

The bill touched on the history of impositions and alluded to the several statutes whereby the propriety of any man's goods could not be altered or changed or charged by the absolute authority of the king without the assent of Parliament. It referred to the recent impositions and then provided that

all impositions, taxes, payments, charges, or exactions whatsoever, by what name soever they now are, or hereafter shall be

called, imposed, or set at any time heretofore by the King's
. . . Majesty, or any of his ancestors, or predecessors, or to be
hereafter imposed . . . by the King's Majesty, his heirs or successors, by color or pretext of any restraint, dispensation, license,
grant or assent of merchants, or otherwise . . . shall be adjudged in the law void and to none effect.[30]

The bill was passed on July 17 and sent up to the Lords, where it
received but one reading.

The controversy that ended with a whimper—a single reading
in the Lords—had been a less orderly performance than one
might infer from the account set forth here. It is true that now
and again a member answered the last speaker with a rebuttal
point by point, and was in turn answered by another. But the
debate had seldom been as sequential as that. Not uncommonly a
member gave a long and dull discourse, as if he were the only one
dealing with the subject in hand.

The reader loses interest as the same arguments keep recurring.
He runs into foggy statements, for clarity of exposition was exceptional even among lawyers. Yet he cannot read Salisbury's concluding speech without admitting that there was a good deal to be
said for impositions at that time. Why did so few members speak
up for His Majesty, or speak so unconvincingly? With the exceptions of Bacon, Doddridge, Hobart, Henry Montague, and Carleton, the defenders of impositions were wordy and not always easy
to follow. Were they perhaps intimidated by the strong case put
forward by Hakewill and those on his side? Were they counting
upon Salisbury's precise knowledge of facts and skill in presenting
them to win the debate for impositions?

The opponents of impositions put their money upon history.
They went back into the fourteenth century and found precedents
in Rolls and Year Books from the reigns of the first three Edwards,
especially from the reign of Edward III. To one who reads their
speeches it appears that the fourteenth century (and to a lesser
degree the fifteenth) was a period of constitutional progress, when
one Parliament after another was asserting itself, as if to win the

power of the purse, and thus other power. It is easy, if dangerous, to assume planning and forethought by members of those Parliaments, because we know so little about them. But surely these members showed continuous ability to meet situations. They were intent upon correcting abuses. They took note of waste in Court and Exchequer and moved to do something about it. Occasionally they ventured to refuse subsidies unless reforms were promised and passed. They were at times not without some simple notion that "what touched all should be approved by all." They discovered that a condition attached to a grant of money was a potent means of persuasion.

When Sir Robert Cecil, later the earl of Salisbury, had fourteenth-century precedents tossed at him during the last decade of the Queen's reign, he answered that the precedents were "likely enough to be true in that time when the King was afraid of the subject." [31] Sir Robert had read history to his advantage, but he had not read quite enough. Edward III may have been worried by his subjects but he was not afraid of them.

Nor did the Tudors greatly fear their subjects. Henry VIII found in his later years a highly profitable source of revenue—the lands of the Church and had no need to worry Parliament. Elizabeth would not have hesitated to take money without consent, had circumstances been different and had she not been born thrifty. On other matters she took a high line with Parliament. The members were not allowed to deal with various problems, and they submitted tamely. Was she not so honored a figure that she might be allowed to have her own way for the time that was left for her? The English have always been deferential to age.

Thus, during the reign of James I, those who would maintain the rights of Parliament found it prudent to go back and recall the fourteenth century. In so doing they made a rather telling case, one more philosophical than that put forward by the friends of the King. They made it over and over again through the early seventeenth century. Moreover their speeches found their way into print during the years of the Long Parliament and became at length part of the Whig lore of English history. The speeches of

Hakewill, of Whitelocke, and of others became the mines worked by the defenders of parliamentary rights and privileges in the centuries following. The precedents the speakers quoted were laid down in legal and constitutional texts, without too much historical criticism, and became almost as sacrosanct as the common law. It was the lawyers perhaps more than the Whig historians who built up the Whig tradition.

The speeches of those seventeenth-century legal antiquaries served another purpose: they initiated the concept of the unwritten constitution, which Hakewill and Whitelocke had really been talking about. Other men in the eighteenth and nineteenth centuries went on talking about the unwritten constitution and making use of it until it was heard of in the far parts of the world, and became part of the glory of England, more lasting perhaps than empire, something finer than *la gloire*. The Great Debate was a pre-Civil War battle, fought with words but nonetheless memorable.

Chapter 5

The Fourth Session, 1610: After the Recess

Country Opinion   WE know little of what happened during the intermission of Parliament from July 23 to October 18. During that interval Sir John Holles did his best to gather the opinions of his fellows in Nottinghamshire. He had not forgotten, he wrote to Salisbury, that the Members of Parliament were supposed, during the interval, to sound out the disposition of their constituents as to the Great Contract.[1] He had hoped to furnish the Lord Treasurer with a full account. He had expected to meet some of his constituents when the commissioners for the subsidy came together at Southwell, but, unfortunately, Sir Henry Pierpoint had set the meeting in a remote corner of the county, at Wansfield. Nevertheless, Sir John did undertake a journey over the county and reported that "the better sort" had a "very sharp appetite" to assist their King, but that the "plebs"—he meant perhaps the smaller gentry, the yeomen, and the townsmen—were of "a very uncertain temper," and grasped eagerly at the idea that purveyance should be abolished. They disliked, also, the troubles connected with their tenures from the King, the escheators, and the prowling agents for the Crown.

Sir Thomas Beaumont of Leicestershire told the Commons in November that he had acquainted his constituents with what had been done and had requested their advice, "telling them the sum offered and withal that some gratuity must come." They answered that they were glad that His Majesty's favor reached as far as to them, but they pressed Beaumont as to whether the King were going to give up the impositions, which the Parliament had declared to be illegal. As for the levy to be determined upon to meet the wants of the King, the constituents, he explained, favored it if it were not all upon land. If they got the contract they were willing to vote £200,000 a year and also "some present supply." [2]

Unfortunately, we have no further direct information as to constituents and what they were thinking.[3] We are able to pick up bits of comment about the constituencies from what developed in the years immediately following, however. An anonymous writer, probably Sir Henry Neville,[4] in discussing whether a Parliament should be summoned in 1614, alluded to "men's perversion to the last Parliament, which is still retained in people's hearts, by what we see in the election of knights and burgesses now to be chosen, where there is exceptions to all those that have any way a dependence of his Majesty." [5] That same point of view was mentioned by Lake who, in writing to Salisbury in 1611, spoke of the reluctance of the shires to compound, that is, to loan money on privy seals, and believed that that reluctance showed the King that the Lower House had taken away all the respect for him and his Council felt by the people.[6] It was the opinion of the anonymous writer that the apprehensions of the members of the Lower House had, during the summer recess of 1610, been given wide circulation over the country.[7]

The King may have been not far off the mark in suspecting that the Commons, by their speeches, had been awakening latent public opinion. When men who had been vaguely but quietly discontented were informed of what others had said openly at Westminster, they were likely to become vocal. Those who set out to create public opinion sometimes find themselves swayed by the opinions they have helped to set going and are occasionally led by their zealous followers into more extreme action than they had intended. However much or little the members had been influenced by the country or the country by them, those members, when they came together again in late October, carried themselves as if they had received some reinforcement of conviction from their fellows at home; they were more outspoken and decisive in resolution. Not only so, but the friends of the King seemed more on the defensive.

The change of attitude was recognized by ambassadors. The Venetian ambassador, Marc Antonio Correr, had in the spring been fairly confident that the King in his struggle with the Commons would get his way.[8] By autumn Correr was less certain of the outcome and took the opposition of the Commons more seriously. De la Boderic, the French ambassador, was pessimistic as to what might happen. "The most wise," he wrote to Villeroy, "are astonished, and prophesy nothing but evil." [9]

In various letters de la Boderic made much of the bitterness of the people against the Scots. It was dangerous to exhibit that feeling within St. Stephen's, or outside, but it was to be detected in letters,[10] and between the lines of speeches.

Something else was happening that may have affected such of the Commons as were aware of it. In the King's answer to the grievance of proclamations he had promised that he would confer with his judges and would cause such proclamations as had been passed to be "reformed," "where cause shall be found." He had promised, further, that for the future he would see that none were made but "such as shall stand with the former laws or statutes," or "such as, in cases of necessity, our progenitors have by their prerogative royal used in times of the best and happiest government of this Kingdom." That the promises seemed to the Commons evasive is evident from the debates in the autumn session. From the speeches it might be supposed that the King had turned down their grievance, which he had not done. One can explain their attitude only by assuming that they had lost what little trust they had in him.

Spedding wrote that on September 20 Sir Edward Coke was sent for to attend the Privy Council concerning the legality of two proclamations that had been complained of. One was about new buildings; the other, about the restriction on the making of starch from wheat. The question, according to Spedding, was whether the restriction and regulations could be enforced by the Crown alone, without Parliament. From Coke's own account, it appears that the Lord Chancellor believed the King had, or ought to have, such power. If necessary, a precedent should be made at once. Coke explained that the problem was new to him and asked for time to consider. Bacon reminded him, no doubt with quiet amusement, that the question was not a wholly new one. "Divers sentences had been given in the Star Chamber upon the proclamation against building; and he had himself (Coke) given sentence in divers cases for the said proclamation." If he (Coke) had given such sentences, it was significant. Nevertheless, Coke continued to ask for time. Meanwhile, a resolution was passed by the two Chief Justices, the Chief Baron Tanfield, and Baron Altham, in conference with the Lords of the Privy Council,

> that the King by his proclamation cannot create any offence, which was not an offence before . . . that he has no prerogative but that which the law of the land allows him . . . and that if the offence be not punishable in the Star Chamber, the prohibition of it by proclamation cannot make it punishable there.[11]

As a result of this opinion, Spedding tells us that a proclamation was put forth on September 24 touching some former proclamations and that a considerable number were withdrawn. Coke wrote that after this resolution no proclamation imposing fine and imprisonment was made.

The Commons were not satisfied. On November 17 Sir Nathaniel Bacon brought up, among other grievances unreformed by the King, that of proclamations.[12] When "The Thirty" of whom we shall hear later, were called before His Majesty, it appears that prohibitions, proclamations, the Four Shires, and impositions were all threshed over. Furthermore, when the King wrote the

Commons a letter from Royston he referred the Commons on the question of prohibitions and proclamations to "the report of the thirty doges." [13] What he had promised "The Thirty" we do not know; nor do we know of any report they made to the House.

The Lord Treasurer Speaks: The King Pleads THE autumn session opened on Tuesday, October 16, when an old bill left over from the last session was read. On the next day the Speaker was unwell and asked leave for the following day. The House did not meet on Saturday, October 20. The House was called at 2:00 p.m. the next Monday, but when less than a hundred members turned up, it was decided not to call the roll of the House. Some moved that the next meeting should be on Wednesday; others moved that it should be on the following Saturday or Sunday. Imprisonment or fines were proposed for those who failed to come. When the Speaker put the question the following Wednesday, the noes prevailed, an outcome that seemed to annoy him, and he told the Clerk to call the House, according to a former resolution. When the Clerk began doing so, Croft rose and made "a discreet, stout, and well-tempered speech" [1] affirming that the Commons had power to put off the calling of the House. It was agreed, however, that the House should rise and not appoint another time for the calling of the members, but should allow that matter to be disputed in the House the next day. On Tuesday, October 23, a message came from the Lords calling for a meeting that Thursday, with fifty members from the Upper House and an appropriate number from the Commons, to which the Commons gave assent.

That conference was addressed by the Lord Treasurer. He was not going to deliver his conscience of all he should hold fit to be spoken. "It is not material to you what presseth me and my opinion (though strong to myself, haply delivered to you, may seem weak)." Salisbury had a habit of giving his inmost thoughts half away in parenthetical phrases.[2] He was in a hard position. He was holding on to his great office against the wishes of powerful enemies eager to rush in and throw him out; and at the same time, he was trying loyally to serve a hard master, who expected him to bring Parliament round, and who—if he did not—might give heed to the enemies of the minister. At the same time he was risking the continuance of that favor he had long received from the House of Commons.

He had no agreeable task—to break the news to Parliament that the need for money was greater than ever,[3] "which is an argument that slow counsels do better serve to preserve than to help a state" [4] (that is, I assume, counsels to move slowly). Everything now depended, he told the conference, upon the Commons; the Lords were waiting to learn what the Commons would do, "because all now to be done riseth from your own great desires, not from the King." In other words, the Great Contract was being held up because the Commons were asking so much in the way of reforms. Salisbury was complaining of their high demands, which had been accepted *sub modo* (tentatively), when he must have been aware that His Majesty was about to demand £500,000 more than was provided for in the Great Contract. It is little wonder that he had told the Commons that he was not going to deliver all his conscience.

He proceeded to remind them of the "Ten Heads" offered them back in February, "valued at nothing and perhaps not well remembered." [5] Six of them were, he suggested, "worth thinking of." But men were always wanting more than they were offered, and the Commons had asked the release of tenures. A worthy member of the House had ventured to say that, if the Commons were given that, there was nothing that the King wanted that they would not furnish.

It had been agreed, he continued, that tenures should be a matter of deliberation, and that subject had been so worked over in detail that "men might known by that general what the particular might amount unto." Matters had at length fallen into shape, and men had looked forward to the repose that would come with the next session, and so Lords and Commons had parted upon fair terms. The Memorial presented by the Commons had been accepted *sub modo,* as a contract and no contract, for power was left to add, diminish, and explain. They had made an entrance to a bargain, but no binding bargain. The Lords had gone along with it only in so far as it should make for "the public good," and the King was not enamored of it.

Salisbury warned the Commons that if they proposed to add or subtract from the Memorial they must do it at once and finally.[6] He returned to the monetary position of his master and used a metaphor about seafaring men in danger of drowning, then suddenly abandoned his metaphor and added, as in afterthought, "his case is so miserable and desperate that without the Parliament relieve he cannot subsist." He would say that the consequence of not relieving His Majesty would be dangerous both to King and people. The King's yearly income, he explained, was £60,000 less than it had been; that was due in part to the complaints of the Commons about impositions and the resultant dropping of some impositions. The debts of His Majesty had risen, Salisbury estimated, from £300,000 to £500,000. Does this mean that a closer examination of the financial situation of the Government revealed that debts were £200,000 more than had been earlier assumed? Or does it reflect the recent loan from the aldermen of London?

Salisbury returned to the Memorial. The King had two maxims about it: first, that it should never pass unless it were "digested"—that is, I assume, put in a more orderly and precise form; second, that it should not be accepted if it left him poorer than he had been. The longer the Commons delayed, the more would the King's indignation kindle against the Great Contract. Salisbury hoped that the Commons would not think that, because the King's wants multiplied, the demands of the Commons should multiply. "You are wise," he said to them, "and able to consider what it is to leave a King in want," that is, you are aware, I think he meant, of your advantage. Take heed, he warned them, not to lose the hold they had. "I speak not by way of menace, for when it comes to that, I shall be miserable." [7] "I do not say the King shall send you an Empson and Dudley, but this I say, the King must not want." Then he broke out impatiently: "If you resolve all within your own doors; if all our conferences come under the style of meetings . . . if we have not yet spent days enough, but must spend more," he was afraid that the end would be worse than the beginning. Nowadays, he observed, Parliament met for four or five months. In former times it was not so. If this session did not end this business, they would never have another for the Great Contract. He would not threaten them. But if they did not hear from the Commons they (that is, the Crown) must think of "some other way." If the Commons used their time thinking of security and of how they might create commissions to placate the country before they had made their bargain perfect, they might lose their advantage.

Some scheme was evidently under consideration in the Lower House to send commissions down to the country to evaluate estates, with reference to some special tax, in order to find the £200,000 for support.[8] "It is," confessed Salisbury, "an injurious thing that a Commission should go down to know my estate, except my estate be made happy by it, and to have Commissions go down and be returned this session, these no man, I think, expects." [9]

On the morning of October 27 Sir Maurice Berkeley rose and remarked that it was either the absence of members or something else that made the Commons backward in the business before them. He believed it was something else. He urged the Commons to call for the King's answers to their complaints. If those answers were satisfactory, they could proceed with the Great Contract; if not, the Commons could have a law made for their security. If they could not find a way to be sure of the King's promises, how could they have the courage to go on with the bargain? [10] Berkeley's motion was seconded by Fuller.[11] Sir George More spoke on the other side. No grievance was as great as the want suffered by the King. But the House followed Berkeley and Fuller and resolved to hear the King's answers to their grievances. They could not get a copy at once since the Lords were not sitting.

On Wednesday, October 31, the Clerk had begun to read the answers when the Chancellor of the Exchequer delivered a message from the King that at 2:00 p.m. His Majesty would address them in the Banqueting Hall at Whitehall.

The King began by saying that never had a King of England so often spoken publicly to his people (a statement that historians would hardly dispute), and yet the Commons delayed, consuming time in nothing but "Good Morning and I Thank You."

"His estate lay a-bleeding, so his honor lay a-bleeding; for to require help of his people and be denied [were] a disgrace both to him and his people." He had asked for supply and support. They had chosen to deal first with support, giving him assurance that afterward they would consider supply. The Commons had promised him that, if they were given leave to treat of the wards, they would deal more freely with him. In return for grants of money he had offered "retribution," "which was without example of any King before," a statement that proved how little some of those who advised him knew of English history.

"After all delays, in the last 8 or 10 days of the Parliament," a "posting conclusion" had been made, a kind of agreement in the nature of a "Memorial," which was to be further dealt with in the autumn, so he hoped they would "begin to make a conclusion." It was possible that they doubted his "intention of performance," or feared for their security. He tried to reassure them of his sincerity, but uttered a doubt whether "it were lawful for subjects to have such reputes of their sovereigns." [12]

The House had taken on a thousand errands and put off help to him. His charges exceeded his revenues. He could not abate his expenses, nor cut his coat according to his cloth, because he could not know his cloth until the Parliament was done. By their grievances and delays they had left him deeper in debt.

If you have any feeling, if God hath not taken away all, and sent a plague upon the King and people, look upon my fortunes overtaken by my necessities, and they increased by your delays. Alas, I am your King. When your cloths were arrested in

France, if I should have delayed you but 3 or 4 months, the merchants might have been undone. Ye that are merchants know this, ye lawyers know, and ye that are gentlemen know that 'twere better for you to lose your actions than plead seven years. . . . You have a King, not only one whom I suppose ye have all cause to love, but a King whom God requires you to obey. The Parliament is called by the King to treat of such things as he shall propound; your writs tell you so.

You may say, he continued, that you wish an answer to your grievances. He had given them an answer. To require it again was *actum agere.* "Have you," he demanded, "any grievance so great as the want of the King? I would know what good subject can say it." He desired a speedy answer whether they would proceed with the Great Contract, yea or no. If they refused to proceed, he might resolve upon some other course to supply his wants.[13] He was concluding, as so often, with an implied threat. He had made a good case for himself—if an emotional one—but he had evaded the fundamental complaints, about which he had offered few and unimportant concessions, and he was asking a great deal of money in order to make up for his extravagance.

The House met on Friday and Saturday, November 2 and 3, first as a House, and then, for the best part of two days, as a committee.[14] They had listened to the King's speech and were perplexed as to their next move. Were they to give an immediate answer, or should they move slowly? Were they to raise again the question of grievances (which some called "aggrievances")? They could not but recognize that the King was putting something over on them, and they were not happy.

After a short debate it was resolved that the Memorial presented in July should be read. One of the active members of the House then moved that the House "might be less forward because some things in the Grievances were doubtful," and should be cleared in the answer.[15]

When the House had gone into committee, Sir Maurice Berkeley called for an immediate answer to the King before they proceeded further, and offered a draft for that purpose. The Commons were to excuse their delay "by want of [a] competent number" of members in attendance. If their demands were granted, they would go forward to undertake the Great Contract. Berkeley's proposal was rejected as "too ceremonious and complimentical, and not real and actual." [16] Yet "all thought 'twas fit an answer should be made." [17]

Others who rose to speak were more cautious. It was said that His Majesty wanted an immediate and "resolute answer," but it could be given only after consideration. "We must be careful to him [the King]," continued the same speaker, and "faithful to the Commonwealth" (Fuller). Did he mean careful in dealing with the King, or careful of his interests? Equally obligatory was their duty to the commonwealth. It was urged by another that the Commons could not reply to the King until they had examined the grievances and the answers to them. But Croft, who held much the same view as the two men who had spoken, pointed out that an answer was first to be thought of, since the King might not wait for them to conclude of the Great Contract.

One of the most outspoken members of the House seemed to insist that if they wished to advise for the kingdom they must avoid discord. Their doubts, he continued, were about security. "If the King have a power over the laws we cannot have security, therefore we must see if the law can bind the King" (Wentworth). The answer to the King must be conditional, said a Midland member, "first if we may obtain the things, next if we can be assured, lastly if we can be told how to raise it" (the necessary money).[18] He put the problems tersely; they were problems not easily solved.

The King had told them, declared another, that his wants must be relieved. If the King demanded, as did the "horny Minotaur," "no reason that such wants and the like should be relieved" (Brooke).[19] Such daring words would not have been uttered in 1604.

A few were ready to speak up for His Majesty: "The King's needs bleeds, the Commonwealth bleeds, let's us [*sic*] take reality, not *verba*. If we proceed to consider the Contract, it is a just and plain answer. If we mean it not, then not to proceed by a new delay" [Caesar].

It was proposed that a subcommittee should draft an answer, but the Committee of the Whole House itself wished to deal with the question before them. It was said by one close to Salisbury (Sir Walter Cope) that the King's jealousy fanned the fear of the Commons, that is, I assume, his jealousy of the Commons' itch for power. But Cope also urged the members as a committee to proceed both with grievances and the Great Contract.

We have two brief accounts of what Bacon said, and they are not easy to interpret. He wished the answer to the King to be not ceremonial but actual. He had been glad to hear the King say that he would not give another answer about grievances.[20] "But let us not by securing our hopes too swiftly cut them off." I think he meant, do not push the King too hard about many grievances, lest you get none redressed. He hoped the Commons would clear the clouds from His Majesty's face. He was so good a King who sought the content of his subjects; he was virtuous and religious.

The Chairman, Martin, summed up the debate: the members wished the Memorial perfected, the grievances considered, and an answer to the King prepared. He found no man of opinion that they should not answer.

It was presumably on the next day, November 3, that Fuller again addressed the committee. He alluded to the things that caused grief between the people and the Prince, although the people were willing to give "double and treble money." [21] He was afraid that now the King might make a hard bargain. What the Commons meant by law was being challenged. He would like to see it put into a statute that impositions were against the law. He brought up two other abuses. The Court of High Commission, he asserted, inverted fundamental law. To right it, they must not put their trust in "verbal strength," that is, I think, promises by word of mouth. He was admitting that distrust of His Majesty which many felt but dared not mention. He touched also upon the Council of Wales and its control over the four counties on the Welsh border. The three abuses should be the occasion of a charter. He hoped, also, that the committee would take up the whole matter of security.

Sir Dudley Digges, whose father and grandfather had been mathematicians and Kentish gentlemen and who had recently been elected to the House for Tewkesbury, ventured to suggest that the Commons had received satisfaction in part and should take what they had been offered. Hyde (probably Nicholas) called the bargain good but the price high. If they could but find the money, the House ought to proceed, but in such a way as to gain what they had bargained for. The control of impositions by Parliament he regarded as fundamental. The Solicitor, Bacon, uttered a warning. If they wished to break off the Great Contract now was the time to talk about it. If there were knots (difficulties) that might cause its overthrow, they should be handled first. Alford, who seldom rose, but, when he did, chose his few words carefully, looked upon impositions and proclamations as the main problems before them. "The King knoweth whether he will yield or no, and so we can grow to a conclusion."

Sir Julius Caesar declared:

> Wants reduced to support and supply. We must have both together, for if we relieve the one and leave the debts he [the King] is undone; if we pay the debts and not relieve his supply, the debt must again increase. . . . Let us proceed to know whether we will or no. . . . Let the King know what we will him both in supply and support, yet so reserved as we be no bounden, but by demonstration. So shall we see what the King will do, what he may do, and so we shall know [what to] put in for the aggrievances.

Sir Julius put things well; he was clearheaded and confident, as always. He was doing his best to placate the opposition.

Sir Roger Owen promised to speak openly and plainly. He did not agree with those who thought the King was insincere in the bargain proposed. "The very value speaketh it." That is, the enormous sum asked meant that he was in earnest. But the Commons had given more than any King had in a similar length of time while at peace. The King was asking more than Henry VIII had received from the fall of the abbeys. As others, he made no allowance for the change in the value of money.

> Tenures and purveyance are goodly things [to be rid of] yet not to give too much. Helen a goodly creature but not worth the destruction of Troy. Lesser sum will make it up. . . . Colossal sum. Aid all upon land, it cannot be, and therefore to give a conditional answer.

He desired a full answer to grievances, with no way left open for the King to impose new burdens and tolls. He hoped the tax would be least burdensome to the poor. Care should be taken that the King did not enhance the coin and so make £2,000 into £6,000. He would like to be sure that, though the wants of the King were supplied, there should be Parliaments hereafter, and there might not be if they gave too much. He believed provision should be made that the £200,000 should not be alienated; that is, I assume, thrown away on courtiers. He hoped the Crown lands would not be given away. His distrust of the King appeared in almost every sentence.

Hoskins urged the House to take up the Memorial and answer the King that they were dealing with it. *Submittatur legibus principatus.* Let the Government yield to the laws. If the King would do that, they would believe that they had good security.

The Recorder, Montague, spoke up: "Sir Roger Owen's pure, plain speech hath resolved me. . . . The King's direction was to examine the Memorial, and then to give the King an answer. Clear first the security, and all things will follow the better." [22]

At that point Martin, as Chairman, announced: "As many as do think thus upon the next motion say Aye." Apparently the House resolved that, when they met again on the following Tuesday, November 6, they should go on perfecting the Memorial.[23]

In the two-day debate most of the speakers had come to grips with the main issues, and, if one can judge from the limited records, there had been more plain speaking than ever before in this Parliament.

*The King Demands
£500,000 Supply*

ON Tuesday, November 6, Martin, as Chairman, moved that, since the Committee of the Whole House was coming to the point of passing the Memorial, the Recorder, Montague, who best understood the business, should take the Chair. Differences about that proposal were arising when the Speaker took over the chair and announced that he had a message from His Majesty.[1]

His Majesty required their resolution and expedition concerning the Great Contract. He had expressed himself so clearly and kept his form (the framework of his demands?) so constantly that "neither obscurity nor variety hath had place in any part of his course towards you." He appealed to their memories whether his first demand had not been for the repair of his wants and the establishing of his estate. They would recall that the distinction between "support" and "supply" had come from them. His Majesty had never yielded to have that first point of support handled until, by a general promise,[2] he had received satisfaction (for his debts as well as for annual support). If he should proceed to the bargain, he expected £500,000 in supply. Although it was far below his necessities, he was content to take a sum not answerable to the value of the retribution offered them. It will be seen that he had drawn the amount of the supply lower than at his first demand in February. But his demands were over and above the subsidy and fifteenth last given. All who wished him well would wonder what might have moved him to entertain—much less to conclude—any bargain in respect to anything that the Commons had offered him. Their offers would not come near to preserving his estate from present and future difficulties.

After the hard and close bargaining in the Great Contract over annual support, His Majesty ought to have realized that it was now out of the question for the Commons to give £500,000 more to cover his debts and contingencies. Such a sum might indeed have been amortized so that the Commons would pay so much a year toward the King's debts. It was not, however, an opportune moment to propose a larger sum. The Commons were wrestling with the problem of how to find £200,000 for annual support, a sum larger than they had at first intended to give. How were they to devise new taxes to bring in £200,000? Some extraordinary method of taxation had to be initiated, and members were at sixes and sevens as to where to look. To many members it seemed that the King was raising his demands beyond the possible. Like Old Testament characters, they hardened their hearts.

The King, who was usually well informed of the debates in the House, implied that members did not speak out in such a way as to give him clues as to what they intended.[3] He did not mean to make the offer for supply so obligatory that they could not recede from it if he did not grant them such favors as could be expected from a good and wise king. His Majesty was astute enough to know that, once the Commons had made an offer toward supply, it would prove difficult to withdraw it. But he did not seem to realize how far they were from making any offer.

He wished to be informed about the proposed levy. He would not accept any levy that was not firm and stable, that burdened the poor [4] or that diminished in any way the profits he now received. Further, he asked the Commons to take pains that those officials who administered wardships, tenures, and purveyance should be compensated for the loss of their posts.[5]

Had some adviser been urging him to take the offensive and raise his sights? Gardiner suggests that he had been reading the document prepared by Caesar as Chancellor of the Exchequer.[6] There was a case for the King. Salisbury had been explicit back in February about the £600,000 needed for debts and contingencies, such as war. Not all members had forgotten Salisbury's budget statement early in the session. It will be recalled that Sir Thomas Beaumont was to say, on November 7, that he had consulted his constituents and that, in addition to support, they expressed willingness to give "some present supply." [7]

Beaumont's testimony was reinforced by that of Croft, who in the debate two days later indicated that it had been agreed that nothing should be spoken of "supply" until the House had concluded with "support." [8] Thus two men of some weight in the House offered evidence that the matter of supply had been merely postponed.

The money the King asked from Parliament was four or five times as much as the late Queen had ever asked in any one Parliament. To the members of that body it seemed an unbelievably large sum, and the sovereign who was asking for it was expressing his dislike of the Great Contract. He loathed it, he had told them. Yet he was the man who had exhibited his willingness to bargain about grievances. Now he appeared to hate the bargain. Was it not conceivable that he might accept a large sum and then wriggle out of the bargain?

The M.P.'s may have noticed what the reader can hardly fail to see: that in all his speeches and messages His Majesty had little to say about grievances, the mention of which he seemed to regard as casting aspersions on his government. Again and again he would repeat the simple theme, his need for money, with little variety of utterance. Did not subjects love their King? Would they not respond to his pleading? [9]

The next morning, November 7,[10] Sir Jerome Horsey,[11] who represented Bossiney in Cornwall and lived in Buckinghamshire, pointed out that when the King said there must be no diminution in his revenue, he meant that no part of the levy could be taken out of impositions, now part of the regular income. Horsey hoped that the Commons would confer with the Lords and learn whether they would join with the Commons in an answer to the King. Horsey's proposal received some support, but not generally. A long silence was broken when Brook [12] expressed dislike of Horsey's motion. As for supply, he refused to be worried about it; the matter of supply was the easiest to [be] resolved; [13] it might be met by three subsidies and six fifteenths. He did not wish to see the bargain break down. If the King did not get the money with his right hand, he would take it with the left, a possibility that had doubtless occurred to others. Brook regarded the levy as impossible and inconvenient. He felt sure that it would not be feasible to raise £200,000 out of land, and he appears to have suggested that part of the £200,000 should be found by a tax on merchandise and a running subsidy from moneyed men only.[14] What he intended, I am not sure. Brook did not believe that the Commons could bargain unless the King were restrained from further impositions. "Better it were the King should impose alone than we and the King too." [15] He did not wish the subject to be doubly burdened.

To Sir Thomas Beaumont, who spoke next, the situation appeared ominous. The Commons were undone; either the wants of the King could not be supplied, or the people would be driven into great want. "Want and beggary is too base for freeborn men, and therefore to agree to the bargain upon these terms we may not." On the other hand, if the Commons broke with the King, what would become of them, "when even as things now stand, our liberties are infringed in such sort as we see they be"? He recalled the Great Charter which, in his words, "our ancestors got with much sweat and blood." In spite of many laws that impositions could not be set without assent of Parliament, impositions were not only put upon them, they were also justified. Beaumont alluded also to the thirty-six statutes against the abuses of purveyors, which seemed to be of little avail. He cited the Elizabethan statutes that had been passed "only for the repression of Papists," and were now used to check other men for other reasons. If things went on in this way, what might the Commons expect in the future? The walls between the King and his people were the laws. If ministers of state leaped over them and broke them down, what security was there for the subject? Contempt for the law was as dangerous to the Commonwealth as a tormented spirit to the body. Beaumont's words suggest a desperation that may have been affecting many members of the House.

Richard James, M.P. for Newport, Isle of Wight, declared that so long as an arbitrary power of Government used impositions without number, as well as proclamations, the Commons could have no heart for business.[16] For all their debate, "which was never so much in point of right," they had been given an answer (to their grievances) "such as, I think, was never made in the like case." He was reinforcing what Nathaniel Bacon had said: that the King was really offering little to alleviate their grievances. They ought to deliberate and press for a better answer. He feared that the great Lord Salisbury had been misled by a single judgment in the Exchequer, whereas he ought to have been guided by the judgment of the House.

Nicholas Hyde, M.P. for Christchurch, Hampshire, pressed for the question, remarking that "supply" was not now in question. The question was whether, upon the terms now propounded by His Majesty, they would accept the Great Contract or not.[17]

Sir John Holles hoped that before they gave an answer they would acquaint the Lords. He was supporting the motion made by Horsey. Hoskins countered that supply came from the Commons, and he wanted the question put, as did others.[18]

The Speaker, "after much varying of the question and somewhat perplexing it," put it at last, "and the whole House (I think not five voices excepted) answered No." They were not accepting the Great Contract on the conditions laid down by the King.

At this point the Speaker warned them that they might think of that on the morrow if they did not hear further from the King, "who must of necessity take notice of this day's resolution." [19]

The Contract Abandoned   THE next day the Speaker proposed that a few committeemen should be chosen to draft an answer to the King. But Sandys, fearing perhaps that Francis Bacon and a Privy Councillor or two might be named to the committee and frame an answer softening the resolution of the House, declared that the matter in hand was too weighty for a few men to determine without direction from the House. He proposed a debate by a Committee of the Whole House, and then that a subcommittee might be chosen, if the Committee of the Whole House so wished, to draw the opinions of the large committee into form.[1]

Sandys was then named Chairman of the committee, as he may

have foreseen, and it was moved that the Speaker should deliver the text of the King's letter to the House. The Speaker said he had no warrant to do so, but would sit by and answer possible queries.

Sandys then repeated the essentials of the King's message: that he must have £500,000 supply, that the levy for support must be firm and stable, that it must not cut into the King's profits, and that the officials who would lose their places should be compensated.

Edward Duncombe, who represented Tavistock in Devon and who was likely to be in opposition to the Crown,[2] expressed the discouragement felt by the House at the King's answers to grievances, especially concerning the deprived ministers, the Four Shires, proclamations, and impositions, to none of which had they received satisfactory answers.

Croft maintained that the Commons had gone so high that they could go no further. To make supply a part of the bargain was to draw in the Lords who were involved in the bargain, but the initiation of subsidies properly belonged to the Commons.

Fuller must have startled members when he informed them that he was ready to give something out of his estate, but only if he were assured that he could retain the rest.[3] In other words, he was expressing the fear that was in the minds of members of the landed classes. It was conceivable that the King might call in leases and bestow them on his friends, that he might do so on a wide scale and then frighten the judges into pronouncing such steps legal. The propertied classes held many of their acres on long leases from the Crown and might lose them if His Majesty found himself thwarted and was persuaded to act arbitrarily. Fuller did not say as much. He did urge the Commons to abide by their decision not to accept the contract on the terms laid down by the King, and to give no reason.

His motion was seconded by Sir Edward Montague and approved by the Committee of the Whole House. They sent a subcommittee up to the committee chamber to frame the headings of an answer. These were reported to the Committee of the Whole

House and by them to the House. The House agreed that the answer should be put in form by Sandys and Bacon by the next morning.[4]

The address they proposed to forward to the King was conciliatory. They expressed their gratitude for the leave given them to consider the problem; they thanked him for dealing so clearly with them that they were able quickly to arrive at a decision. The decision was that they would not proceed with the contract, and they asked him to accept it graciously. They concluded tactfully by alluding to their affection for him.[5]

Not all the members were satisfied with this statement. It was said that something should be added to show that they had not lost interest in the contract, that is, the contract as it was before the King had raised the question of £500,000 for supply.

After debate the subcommittee formerly named was again sent out to reword the statement. They added the words, "To take in gracious part our proceedings, wherein we hope to have shewed no coldness of affection to the Contract and to the advancement of your Majesty's service thereby, in which our desires we still continue." [6]

It came to this, I suspect: that members were not willing to accuse the King of going back on his bargain ("contrariety"); nor had they lost all hope that he might reconsider and accept the contract. They had known him to shift his course suddenly.

Yet on a fundamental issue he had proved unyielding. At one time and another the Commons had done what they could to discourage the extravagance of their sovereign, but with little success. They had every reason to fear that much of the money they might vote him would be bestowed upon those who gave him the good words he craved. To them he was the kindly Scot.

Members were, however, doubtless aware of the case for the King: the debts inherited from the last reign and the expense of putting down rebellion in Ireland. Nor could they have forgotten Salisbury's plea that it was becoming in a great and rich nation to display a certain "magnificence." To make a show was to enhance the King's reputation on the Continent, a matter of consequence to one who had not enjoyed much pomp and circumstance in his northern realm.

On Wednesday, November 14, His Majesty sent a message that he accepted the answer of the Commons and recognized that the bargain was at an end. Since they had now come back to the place where they had begun, His Majesty asked them to consider how they would supply him, "and doubteth not but you will deal therein like loving subjects." [7]

It was a strange move on the part of James. The Commons would not vote him money in return for favors hoped for, and now he was asking it without any "retribution." It was not the act of a proud man, nor even of the wise King he called himself. He believed that his subjects were morally bound to supply his wants.[8]

On November 13, the day before the King's message to the Commons, Salisbury had urged the Lords to send to the Lower House about the weighty business for which Parliament had been called. There was a "cessation" in the Commons that "made him at a stand," as he put it, and worried him. He did not understand why the Commons had not answered his message. Salisbury suggested that the Lords ask not for a conference but for a meeting. A message was sent, and the Commons, after due hesitation, agreed to a meeting the next afternoon.[9]

On the morning of November 14 the Lord Chancellor addressed the Upper House. The Commons, he told them, had brought forth nothing but a Memorial. Back in the early spring the Commons had promised in the matter of supply "to do . . . that which shall become loving and dutiful subjects." [10] He made an allusion to that promise.

The Lord Treasurer rose and said the Commons were "but the representation of the Kingdom," and therefore it was the more strange that they refused to grant the King a supply. He held out the hope that the King would bestow further favors, which he believed the Commons would not refuse. "Seeing we cannot have what we would . . . let us see what the King will give us." [11]

The Lord Treasurer met with some opposition in the Lords.

His elder brother, the Earl of Exeter, said that the Commons were "much distasted" that their grievances were not dealt with. Lord Knollys believed the time too short this session for them to do much.[12]

Salisbury spoke again and mentioned favors already discussed, naming five, all of which were, he maintained, of great benefit and ease to the subject. He mentioned impositions and complained that, when the mercers of Cheapside were charged an imposition of threepence, they made the subjects pay eighteen pence.[13]

That afternoon a meeting of a hundred Commoners and fifty Lords was addressed by Salisbury, Northampton, and Ellesmere, the Lord Chancellor. The Lord Treasurer made it clear that he was speaking, not for the King, but for the Lords, between whom and the Commons there was such unity of interest as ought to make for uniformity of proceeding. The Lords were of the opinion that it was unsafe to leave the King without supplies. As for the Commons he had always been conscious of their goodwill toward him, and he asked them to put the best interpretation on what he would say.

His Majesty, he said, had caused his wants to be made known to them.[14] Those wants had been delivered in more detail than wisdom would have dictated. Experience had shown that it was not safe for Parliament to know as much as the King, nor for others to know as much as Parliament.[15]

The King had been content to deprive himself of power and profit in the hope that his subjects would relieve his wants. Now he learned that those wants were greater than were likely to be relieved by his people.[16] He realized that his subjects were acting as they did, not from ill will but from diffidence and distracting opinions.[17] It was a pleasant but misleading interpretation of the King's attitude toward the Commons, for his indignation at the activity in the Lower House was by no means a secret. Salisbury was trying desperately to induce the Commons to provide money, and he was exhibiting a fanciful picture of his master as a tolerant and understanding father of his people. The portrait was not a convincing one. Alas, Salisbury was a weary man, and he had to do what was against his nature.

The King, he informed his members, was now £50,000 worse off than at the beginning of the Parliament.[18] He did not doubt that the difficulties His Majesty had experienced would have led him to be careful how he pressed his subjects hereafter.[19]

God was punishing them all, he suggested, for their sins; otherwise they might have proceeded to such a contract as would have brought felicity both to King and subject. Salisbury was exonerating his master and those who found fault with him, and putting the blame on an evil generation.

He now proposed that the two Houses should ask for eight concessions, not quite the same as seven of the original ten mentioned on February 24.

1. Sixty years possession a bar against the King
2. No lease to be avoided for defect of security, or conditions broken
3. Upon outlawries the creditors to be first satisfied before the King
4. Respite of homage to be taken away
5. Penal laws to be reformed
6. All obsolete laws to be taken away
7. Power to make laws in Wales to be repealed [20]
8. No imposition to be hereafter set but by Parliament, and those that are to be taken as confirmed by Parliament [21]

The last clause (no. 8) was far from a concession. The impositions set by the King were to be regarded as passed by Parliament.

Northampton made the point that as long as the government was a monarchy it was the duty of Parliament to maintain it. He admitted that the King had "flowed too much in his gifts." [22]

On November 15 all the speeches were reported by the Solicitor, the Recorder, and Sir Dudley Digges. One utterance by Salisbury had not, according to Sir William Twysden, been reported, and this gave Twysden comfort. The Lords, Salisbury had remarked, agreed with the Commons in not wishing to change the laws of England,[23] "which is . . . as much as we desired in all our great parchment of grievances." Twysden hoped, therefore, that the Lords would join with the Commons in taking up grievances and supply.

Martin was quick to take up Twysden. Upon a good foundation Twysden was building a hasty structure. Martin had not been impressed by the reasons offered by the Lords. All those reasons were to be found in his table book,[24] that is, I take it, in the notes he had made of daily events in the Commons. He was stating that the reasons were those advanced on behalf of the last three subsidies granted. They might be printed and serve as an almanac for the next sixty years. If the reason were good, that the Commons must give because the King was in want, then he might be in want next year and every year. Was it better that the King or the kingdom should be in want?

Friday, November 16, was marked by the speech given by Samuel Lewknor of Shropshire.[25] It was a hard choice, he began, when a man must either speak with danger to himself, or against his conscience. A word ill taken might blot out the memory of many well-deserving actions. "The fury of the King, saith the wise man, is the messenger of death." Nevertheless, when the country required his aid a man must speak his mind. From the outset he had been afraid that the contract was never intended for anything more than to please the Commons for the time being.[26] "We did but please ourselves with a vain imagination." His fears had been justified. The members had lost time and labor and now they were being blamed for breach of the contract. They courted the mistress, he remarked, with an honest desire to wed her. Their forwardness had caused her to be set at a higher rate. The winds that have blown these clouds together are invisible, "we cannot guess from what quarter they blow." He made another allusion to unknown pressures, possibly with Privy Councillors in mind.

He believed there were none present who did not sympathize with him in being sorry for the King's wants and who did not wish they were in a position to relieve him. From three sorts of

people help for the King might fairly be expected: from the commonalty, the merchants, and the nobility. As for the commonalty,
if the King was poor, certainly the commonalty was not rich. He
would speak plainly and let the King hear the voice of his Commons. They were fallen into a gulf of misery and poverty. They
had given him more in time of peace than had been voted to any
of his predecessors in time of war. It had been their hope not only
to have paid his debts but to have stored his coffers. The common
people would say: "Where are the hopes you fed us with? You
began well: why did you not continue so? What bring you home
but your own shame and our undoing? Alas, what gain is this,
when the benefit that the King has by a subsidy comes out of
the tears of the people?"

As for the merchants, they complained of delays in shipments.
Many of their companies were broken or bankrupt. They viewed
impositions as one of the causes of their trouble. They would be
unable and unwilling to yield supply.

As for the nobility, His Majesty had shown them his bounty
with an expansive hand. Let them show their gratitude. When the
Persian King, Cyrus, exhausted his treasure by reason of his
gifts and could not be supplied by his people, he called upon his
friends, and they brought great sums.[27] If such a plan would
not serve the turn, he could think of only one other. Julius Cap-
itolinus wrote of the Emperor Antoninus that, finding his treasury
empty, he freed himself from his idle and needless followers, who
consumed the riches of the commonwealth and did nothing to
help it.[28] He was urged to take away their pensions and salaries.
By such methods the King might gain a great treasure and not
estrange the hearts of his people, to whom contributions were a
bitter pill. Lewknor could hardly be called to account. Was he
not talking in the main about the ancient world and its ways? [29]

The Commons had been warned, he continued, that "extremity
of law" might be used. A good king, he remarked, would do what
is becoming, not what is allowed. If God disposed otherwise, he
added, with perhaps a hint of quiet desperation, they must arm
themselves to endure it patiently. He concluded by asking that
no evil exposition should be made of anything he had said.

Sir George More praised the speech as "excellently delivered by a gentleman dutifully affected to the King and the Commonwealth." "If silence should fall upon us all," continued Sir George—there had been a long silence after Lewknor sat down—"I know not how we shall proceed or how the King will receive courage to call us hither again, or our countries have comfort to send us hither."

Lewknor's classical allusion and his carefully considered words were evidently uttered with a good deal of feeling, and the House may have shown itself not unsympathetic. It would seem that he had so carried the House with him that even the ranks of royal adherents could scarce forbear to praise.

Sir George indeed did not disguise his own feeling. The Commons, he insisted, must keep the bond of love between the King and his people. So long as the great, the fair contract was in hope, he never set his feet within the doors of the House but his heart said, *hoc age*. "But that hath an end. I am sorry for it." [30] He professed himself ignorant of why the end had come, but was probably not as unaware of those forces in the Court arrayed against Parliament as he pretended to be.

The Commons, he believed, must answer the demands of the Lords. Want in a king is a thorn that pricks and festers. Yet he hesitated to see the Commons give without receiving any encouragement. They were not rich; many of the Lords were decayed; trade was in a slump; the numbers of the poor were increased. He hoped the Commons would not disable the state by admitting that they were unable to give, nor allow their adversaries to say: see the affection of those that are religiously affected.[31] The Commons should join with the Lords; they should consider what was fit to give to, and fit to ask of His Majesty.

Sir Nathaniel Bacon said that since the Commons had given the last subsidy they had been granted little ease of grievances. The King had given up licensing of alehouses, a matter of only £4,000 a year; he had dropped impositions on coal at Blyth and Sunderland, a saving of only £200 a year. The Commons had complained of the Lord Admiral's patent on wines, but that was to stand during the lifetime of the Admiral and that of his son. By the end of those two lives, the promise of the King to end the patent might be forgotten, or a new patent might be issued. The exactions upon the new drapery were still in force, and no decision had been rendered by the judges. In other words, the concessions made so far amounted to little. The Commons should proceed no further in the matter of supply unless the contract were set on foot again. He saw no reason why the Commons should do anything.[32]

Wentworth moved that the House adjourn until the next day so that they might have time to think of some things of moment to be requested. Hyde called for the question and so did Sir Samuel Sandys, who went on to say that, since they could not win the fair Helen, the Lords would have them settle for her foul apron.[33] He was alluding to the speech by Northampton at a conference on March 13.[34] Others were ready to speak, but it was growing late, and the Speaker, who could not have liked the turn the discussion was taking and whose natural impulse was to put off the unpleasant, entreated the House to postpone the debate until the next day.

The Conference with "The Thirty"

THE day was not over. His Majesty had a surprise in store. As members were hurrying through the doors, the Serjeant approached thirty of them and showed them their names on a warrant, warning them to come to the King at 2:00 p.m. The Serjeant had waited until the Speaker was out of the chair, and thus members had no chance to protest or to dispute the move of the King in the House.

"The Thirty" met the King in his Council Chamber at Whitehall. His Majesty put the question at once: Did they not believe it true that he was in want? A silence followed. Then the King pointed at Sir Nathaniel Bacon,[1] who that morning in the Commons had shown how much they had given and how little had been done for them about grievances. At that the King made it clear that he would take no exception to anything said and would indeed love him the better who spoke his mind freely.[2] He had sent for them, not as Parliament men, but as private men with whom he would confer. Was it not true, he asked again, that he was in want?

Sir Nathaniel answered that he believed His Majesty's debts were such as had been reported to them. Contribution depended, however, upon retribution from him, that is, concessions about grievances. He feared the time was unseasonable for relieving the King.[3]

Sir Nathaniel's half brother, Sir Francis, began to speak "in a more extravagant style than his Majesty did delight to hear,"[4] when the King put the question—the same question—to Sir Henry Neville; he enjoined him to answer according to his conscience. Neville replied that the King was indeed in want. His Majesty moved the next question: "Tell me, whether it belongeth to you that are my subjects to relieve me or not." Neville parried: "Where your Majesty's expense groweth by the Commonwealth we are bound to maintain it, otherwise not." Then Neville went straight to the main point. In this one Parliament, he added, they had already given four subsidies and seven fifteenths, "which is more than ever was given by any Parliament at any time upon any occasion; and yet withal they had no relief of their grievances." He was emphasizing what Sir Nathaniel Bacon had said in the House that morning. His Majesty may well have been nonplussed. There was really no answer to be made. The King had possibly hoped to overawe the members by his presence, or he may have fancied that a gesture of friendliness toward his inferiors would win a more obliging attitude from them. He allowed Neville to set forth, one after another, the grievances of the Commons, a topic that had seldom enlisted His Majesty's passionate interest.[5] Sir Henry had not been overawed; he was not even diffident or apologetic, "and so began to say that in matters of justice they could not have any indifferent proceeding (aiming perhaps at His Majesty's prerogative, *nullum tempus occurrit Regi*)."[6]

At this point Croft, who had on his mind, as usual, the wrongs of the Four Shires on the border of Wales, broke into the discussion. If we may trust Moore, Neville would have given his judgment on all the grievances had Croft not interrupted to talk about his pet grievance, "and so spent a great time in debate thereof." [7]

"The King discoursed long with these gentlemen hereabout and with some others of the Lower House." [8] If we may trust one account, the King himself raised ("descended to") the question of impositions.[9] According to another narrative, Sir Thomas Beaumont, Sr., "shewed the greatness of impositions." [10] The Rutland Manuscript includes what no other account mentions: a set-to between Salisbury and Thomas James of Bristol about impositions.[11] Thomas James had long been an opponent of impositions, as already indicated.[12] But it was Sir Edwin Sandys who proceeded to justify to the King the proceedings of the Lower House in respect to impositions,[13] and he seems to have stressed the poverty of the people.[14]

It would appear that the King stood his ground about impositions. That the members "received good satisfaction" about prohibitions, proclamations, and the Four Shires was reported by a member who in all probability was not one of "The Thirty" members present and whose account is somewhat confused.[15] It is conceivable that His Majesty made concessions in conversation that he conveniently forgot later, but I think it more probable that, except about proclamations, he listened to the members with such attention and friendliness that they went away with more hope than proved to be justified. His Majesty was acting a part that he had probably been importuned to perform; it was new and not in his repertoire. "The Thirty" were said to have left the royal presence feeling that they had been well treated.[16]

Nathaniel Bacon, Neville, Croft, the elder Beaumont, and Edwin Sandys had dared to speak plainly to their sovereign. True they had been promised that they should not be punished for what they said, but the pledges of James I were not always honored. The Crown had less than subtle ways of making it unpleasant for those who were censorious.

John Moore, in a letter to Trumbull, commented:

Some of that body have very freely discovered their grievances, both in the House and at Whitehall before his Majesty, whereupon it was rumored that Parliament should be quite dissolved *re infecta,* but I never believed that so great a Prince and so loyal subjects should make so unwholesome a conclusion.[17]

The subjects were loyal, but they were dealing with a majesty who possessed no magic of greatness. High position in his case had not wrought that miracle of transformation with which it is sometimes credited.[18]

The Finale

THE following morning (November 17) the Speaker called on Lake to read the message from the King (in his own hand) to the Speaker. He had compared the answer of the Commons with his own declaration and as a result could discern no ground to expect from the Commons any such help as would justify him in binding himself and his posterity to any absolute bargain. He could not part with so many flowers of his Crown without receiving in return such a contribution as would establish his estate so that neither he nor his posterity (except in case of war or similar violence) should be driven to press upon his subjects. That the contribution he now asked would press upon them did not seem to occur to him.

He had been anxious that nothing should be misunderstood either in or out of Parliament concerning the late episode. The particulars of the late meeting he left to the report of those who had been present. He was going out of town and intended to entertain no further discussion of the Great Contract; it was now at an end. He required them to forbear discussing supply until they heard from him. He commanded them to adjourn until Wednesday, November 21.[1] His technique of adjourning the sessions at intervals was possibly designed to wear down the Commons, although any such motive would have been hotly denied.

It is tempting to speculate what went on in his mind after he talked with "The Thirty," with Neville, Nathaniel Bacon, and others. May he have realized that there were a few fundamental grievances, such as wardship, purveyance, and impositions, about which the Commons would prove unyielding? He was not prepared to make real concessions as to those matters and some others.

What course should he take? Could his subjects be induced to put their trust in his princely judgment? Was it not almost treason to question that judgment? He could not shake himself free from those around him, the Scots, the Howards, and hopeful courtiers, who were doubtless urging him to show his mastery in his own house, advice that fitted in with his experience in Scotland.

He found it hard to give up. He had called off the Great Contract, but by November 21 he was dealing again with the Commons. As for impositions, the House must not take away those already in force, but he was willing (as already indicated) that the House should pass an act restraining him from laying further impositions. He suspended judgment about the Four Shires until midsummer, but would leave that problem to the course of law. He wished that the use of proclamations be reviewed, and those that were contrary to law (if there were any), taken away. He had another proposal: if the Commons would give him the money needed he might accept a composition for giving up his right to the "custody of the body" of his wards, that is, to the marriage of his wards (male or female under certain circumstances).[2] That right he could sell, often for a considerable sum. Sir Robert Harley seems to have mentioned the sale of the marriage of wards in the Commons, and the King authorized four Lords to see what could be done about it.

The King's proposal came to nothing. It seems likely that it received only a short discussion in the Lower House. The King declared that he would not press the Commons to give more than they thought fit to offer, but His Majesty was probably still hoping for a considerable grant and was not ready to offer much in return. The King's own feeling was described by Lake: "His Majesty said therefore in conclusion that no man must blame him for dealing warily with a multitude from whom he hath received so little comfort." [3]

It is time to turn from the words of a disappointed sovereign to the discussion in St. Stephen's of the late meeting of "The Thirty" with the King. Hakewill said that the precedent might prove dangerous. The King might summon thirty, twenty, or "as he pleased" to know the opinions of the whole House, which would be a great infringement of their privileges.[4] On the other hand, he pointed out that "The Thirty" were the King's subjects and hence were bound to come when summoned. His Majesty had conferred with them as a private man. He hoped that good would come of it. "We live in a happy State," he remarked, "but that commonwealth is best which is framed for all times." Things were not so bad, he was saying, but what they desired was a state that would withstand all weather. For that they needed all possible advice and opinion. The King might send for thirty more and so on ad infinitum and thus uncover the several shades of opinion. Hakewill evidently had that Puritan confidence (as in the interpretation of the Bible) that out of full discussion useful ideas might emerge.

That was well and good except in one respect. The members who met with the King were not all equipped with the wisdom of the House and might offer the weakest reasons and overlook the best. Hakewill moved an order that in the future none should do what "The Thirty" had done, without first acquainting the House therewith.[5] They had not kept their rank, as good soldiers should do. But then with Hakewillian honesty and learning he recalled that there had once been a soldier who left the ranks and won the victory.[6]

Finally it was resolved that no report should be made of the meeting of "The Thirty." But it was agreed that a committee should meet "for drawing of an order to this purpose," that is, to meet with the King.[7] The order seems to have been (if we may trust the author of Cottonian MSS., Titus F IV) that

no member of this House do hereafter presume or take upon him as a private man or otherwise to deliver his opinion or the reason of his opinion by way of conference or otherwise, touching any matter depending in consultation in this House, either to the King's Majesty, or any of the Lords, without the assent, direction, or special order of the House in that behalf.[8]

It will be recalled that on November 21 the King had sent word that he would not press them about money. He made it clear, however, that he hoped they would make him a grant. In consequence, the Commons took up the question of a subsidy or subsidies.

Whitelocke, who on the preceding July 2 had made a carefully reasoned argument against impositions, at this time took a pragmatic view. Impositions might be endured for a few years, he suggested, if the judgment in the Exchequer were reversed and if a law were passed to restrain His Majesty from imposing thereafter. Whitelocke was looking to the future of what we would call constitutional principles.

Anthony Dyott, M.P. for Lichfield, who usually took a middle position, believed that if they had a law about impositions, if they had some ease of purveyance, if wardships of the body were discharged, and if there were a limitation of time on debts due to the King, that the Commons might find reason to give a supply. Dyott was ready to settle for what had been more or less offered the Commons (ease in purveyance had not been offered) but for a great deal less than the Commons were holding out for.

Sir Thomas Beaumont, M.P. for Tamworth, Warwickshire, pointed out that impositions would reduce the prices offered for wool by one-fourth and increase the cost of food and apparel by one-sixth, the first M.P., so far as I know, to offer statistics.[9]

Mr. Solicitor Bacon declared that if it were a question of the proportion of supply to be given he would be as moderate as others, as if to suggest that the Commons did not have to vote a supply of £500,000, and certainly not all at once. But the King had laid his wants open to them and he would be sorry to hear them sing so sad a countertenor. About the poverty of the country he did not seem as certain as other speakers, though he admitted that he did not know the country well. In the region where he lived there were signs of wealth, even of riot and excess. He did not believe the want of the people was so great that they could not give the King some supply toward his "greater necessities." [10]

Fuller alluded to the general discouragement at the failure of the Great Contract. The Lord Treasurer at the last conference had recognized the desire of the Commons for it and had declared that the King would willingly have given his consent.

Fuller was inclined to agree with Salisbury that God had not bestowed his blessing.[11] There were signs of that lack on all sides. The merchants, who constituted a calling of great use in the realm, the very legs of the commonwealth, had received no blessing of late,[12] nor had the clothiers,[13] nor the mariners, nor the shipwrights. Shipping itself had been weakened. God had not blessed the treasure of the realm,[14] with the result that Prince and people were in want. The lawyers, except for a few, had not received the increase of their labors, as in the past.[15]

For what we would call a depression, Fuller had a less rational explanation: the people were being punished for their sins. The Jeremiah of the House, the Old Testament Puritan, lamented the crying sin of swearing, the silencing of good ministers, and the gross evil of pluralities and nonresidence. Concerning that evil a bill had been passed at the last session, and another was now ready.[16]

If only the Commons had been able to do away with abuses, "what would we not give to supply the King's wants and to support him in a most royal and princely state?" As it was, they could not supply the King's wants because they could feel no certainty as to what would remain after the gift,[17] that is, what would remain after His Majesty had showered more favors on his friends.[18]

The question was called for, presumably on a motion to give the King some supply, but Wentworth was not ready for the question. He wished to signify to His Majesty the causes of their doubts. What about the late Mrs. Venables, who left her property for the Puritan ministers who had lost their livings and whose will had been disallowed? He agreed with Fuller in fearing the

Deity was angry. He would be glad, he concluded, to hear that the King of Spain spent his all upon favorites and wanton courtiers.[19]

Hoskins asserted that the question of giving was tied up with another: how could things be altered for the better? There had been sovereigns who had been able to amass treasure without heavily taxing their subjects. "Well governing of revenue hath been a means used by princes to supply revenue." He blamed those who begged so much from the King that Parliament had to sit seven years to find ways of supplying him. The Irish were not to blame.[20] The water leaked out of the cistern as fast as the Commons filled it.

On November 24 His Majesty sent a letter to the Speaker ordering the House to adjourn until November 29. He asserted that he had offered various things of grace for the good of his subjects, but "the more he was desirous to give them contentment . . . the less it was regarded and that new grievances and complaints were raised in his dishonor." [21]

The King was in no happier mood when he wrote to Lake—who quoted him to Salisbury—that he had been patient with the assembly for seven years and had received from them "more disgraces, censures, and ignominies than ever prince did endure." He reminded Salisbury that he had followed his advice to have patience and to hope for a better issue. "He cannot have asinine patience; he is not made of that metal." Obviously he was vexed with Salisbury, as well as with the Commons, and there were those who would not have dissuaded the captain from dropping the pilot.

He was beginning to consider the problem of how to dissolve Parliament "with fairest shew." But there were details to be ironed out. He asked for a particular account of what had taken place on Friday, November 23, for he understood that some of the speeches were treasonable, or "at least so scandalous . . . that he thinketh he shall have just ground to call the speakers to account." [22]

On November 29 when the House was assembling, although

less than a dozen were present, the Speaker read a letter from the King adjourning the House until December 9. The purpose of the precipitate adjournment, writes Mrs. Foster, was, "members believed, to forestall the reading of the order forbidding members of the House of Commons without special direction to express opinions to the King or Lords on business pending." [23] That resolution had been fathered by Hakewill.[24]

There may have been other reasons for the King's move. He had been shown a paper (probably by Sir Roger Aston, Master of the Great Wardrobe, who had received many valuable grants from the King) setting forth reasons why the Commons should yield no supply, that they were to examine the answers to the grievances and to indicate wherein they were not satisfactory, and that they were to consider what "immunities and easements" were to be demanded for the people.[25]

The King was also told, probably by Lake, that it was proposed to petition the King to send all Scots home. Salisbury was apparently not told of this proposed petition, but Lake informed His Majesty that he himself had been told of it by Salisbury.[26] On December 4 Lake questioned Neville, Strode, and others of the Lower House about the petition, who declared that such a petition was the notion of "an intemperate brain" and would have been rejected by the House. When His Majesty first heard the story, he took it lightly, but presently became excited and then indignant to think that Salisbury had known of it and had not told him. Also on December 4 Lake wrote Salisbury that all the trouble had been stirred up by Sir Robert Carr who was trying to sow discord between the King and the Lord Treasurer.[27] If that was his object he was highly successful. Aston's paper and the story about the petition were probably both fabrications and should have been recognized as such.

The King wrote to Salisbury: "It is true that I have found by the perturbations of your mind that you have broken forth in more passionate and strange discourses these two last sessions of Parliament than ever you were wont to do, wherein for pity of your great burthen I forbear to admonish you." He also made it clear to Salisbury that he knew Lake had made a mountain out of a molehill.

> The worst of it is that he spread this mistaking of his to three or four of the Lower House. . . . It is now time for you to cast your care upon the next best means how to help my state, since ye see there is no more trust in this rotten reed of Egypt, for your greatest error hath been, that ye ever expected to draw honey out of gall, being a little blind with the self-love of your own counsel in holding together of this Parliament, whereof all men were despaired, as I have oft told you.[28]

His Majesty should have apologized to Salisbury for having ever been taken in by the document and for having been angry at him. It must be said, to the King's credit, however, that he had some compassion for his overburdened Lord Treasurer.

The King assumed that there never had been a chance of obtaining subsidies from the Commons. By this time there was not much chance. About the attitude of the Commons John Moore wrote to Winwood:

> It is true that since his Majesty hath spoken of the Great Contract the Lower House hath been very *farouche* and untractable, flatly refusing to yield any contribution without an equivalent retribution. Which troubles my Lord's [Salisbury's] spirits the more because on him the world will call for money; and further, because, (as some suppose) his Lordship may have given the King hope of some real assistance . . . without any great material retribution from his Majesty's part.[29]

That His Majesty had really hoped to procure the money he needed with a minimum of concessions is a possible conjecture from his actions, from what Salisbury said to the Commons, and from what Moore, who was usually well informed, wrote Winwood. It is hard to imagine that Salisbury was so unaware of opinion in the Commons as to believe that they would vote the King both supply and support with few or no concessions. Was His Majesty the only one who had remained an optimist about that?

The King found it hard to accept defeat. He tried to win a
lost battle. The same letter of December 1 from Moore to Winwood reported that some more plausible propositions were being
considered and that the King's party would deal with his friends
in the House "to work some better reason." Moore added his own
judgment: "I conceive by the common discourse that the Parliament could be content to replenish the royal cistern (as they
call it) of his Majesty's treasury, were they assured that his Majesty's largesse to the Scot's prodigality would not cause a continual
and remediless leak therein."

It will be recalled that on November 29 Parliament was adjourned until February 9 (1610/11). On that date it was finally
dissolved.

Meanwhile the Government's financial situation was deteriorat-
ing. John Moore had persuaded a Mr. Levinius, who seems to
have had some connection with Winwood, to call on the Lord
Treasurer to find money for his friend, Winwood, whose salary
as ambassador at The Hague was badly in arrears. Salisbury promised some money on privy seals and then decided to put off the
payment, saying: "Sir Ralph Winwood is no poor man." Then,
presently, Salisbury "fell into a great passion about the great
penury of the Exchequer and the exceeding difficulty that would
be found in the replenishing the same." [30]

It was less than two weeks after Salisbury's "passion" that the
King, as desperate as Salisbury, made another move. Again we
must depend on Moore, writing to Winwood (December 15). His
Majesty summoned to Whitehall thirteen of the "best moneyed
men of this City," men to whom he was already in debt. They
were told by the Lord Treasurer that the interest on the debt
owed them would be paid, but he prayed them to forbear pressing
for the principal a little while longer, and, in the meantime, to
lend the King what money they could upon good security. But
the moneyed men, according to Moore, could not be induced to
lend any more; they were, indeed, not happy about what they
had already advanced. Since then, he added, officials of the Exchequer had been negotiating with various citizens, asking them
to lend on private security. Their requests brought in little

money. Moreover, £4,000 worth of Crown lands were said to have been offered for sale, but no financial entrepreneurs were prepared to entertain the bargain.[31] Moore was afraid that Salisbury would find it hard "even to furnish the expenses of the approaching feast." Mrs. Foster has rummaged among the masses of Caesar manuscripts in the British Museum—writings hard to decipher—and has come upon an interesting statement made by the Chancellor of the Exchequer on December 29. He suggested that Parliament be prorogued rather than dissolved, "because the company present have most experience and have already debated the things." But if a dissolution were determined upon, he believed it should be carried through without attempting any justification. There was nothing politic that could be said. If reference were made to the last Parliament, then jealousies would develop between the Commons and the Lords, or between the Commons and the people, who already thought themselves abused. To give notice of another Parliament would likewise be poor policy; it would indicate a dislike of those Parliament men "who are held amongst the common people the best patriots that ever were," and looked up to for "their greatest contempts to the King." [32]

In his proclamation of December 31, James seemed unaware of his own weak position and unprepared to face realities. He said that he had continued Parliament longer than usual, longer than stood with the important affairs of state, "or with the public business of three whole terms spent in the last two sessions, or with the occasions of the country." As a result of the long sessions, hospitality had been missing in the country, and shires, cities, and boroughs had been burdened with allowances for their representatives. The nobility had had to bear expenses. Some weighty causes had been in deliberation for the supply of His Majesty's estate and for the ease and freedom of the subjects.[33] Many of them were proposed by His Majesty, far differing from and surpassing the favor and graces of former kings. His Majesty did not admit that his expectations had come to nothing, but one could read that between the lines of the proclamation.[34]

The preface to *A Record of Some Worthy Proceedings*, issued ostensibly by some Englishman living abroad (but possibly written in England and not published until 1641), professed to be an answer to the King's proclamation dissolving Parliament. The author wrote that in the proclamation "the worthiest House that ever was, was covertly traduced." He aimed to prevent the "heartburning" that he feared the proclamation would occasion between the King and his Commons. Further, he asserted that no House of Commons had ever shown "greater zeal for the ease and freedom of the subjects than the late House had." [35] He professed to believe that "the overlarge preamble" was the writer's and not the King's, and that only the body of the text was under the King's direction.

Part of the King's indignation fell upon Salisbury. So far as I can determine from a cursory examination of the calendars of the Cecil Papers for December 1610 to May 12, 1612, Salisbury was allowed little share in the counsels of the Crown. The King did not force his resignation, but merely gave him less to do. James might easily have made his minister's illness an excuse for excluding him from significant decisions. By this time His Majesty was leaning more and more on the handsome young Robert Carr, but probably listening also to Henry Howard, Earl of Northampton, and to Thomas Howard, Earl of Suffolk.

It has already been suggested that the Commons had from 1604 to 1610 been strengthening their position, in contrast to the Lords; they had also been standing up more frequently and more successfully to the Crown, as the unhappy and exaggerated complaints of His Majesty testified. One cannot read the political literature of the time without discovering that the King was losing much of the goodwill that usually adhered to the Crown.

The writer of that interpretative narrative of the Lower House of 1610 (Add. 48119) realized the power of the opposition and its increasing influence with the public. The men who wrote letters to their associates and friends were aware of the lessening respect for the sovereign, and of the growing confidence in the Commons.

The opposition, still to be spelled without a capital, did not lack leadership. Sir Edwin Sandys was easily its best but moderate spokesman; yet such men as Richard Martin and half a dozen others were involved in the leadership.

Would that we had more information about the inner councils of Sandys and his friends. It is hardly to be doubted that they held quiet conferences, decided on lines of argument, arranged who would present them, and weighed with one another possible motions and resolutions. We come upon details and asides that point in that direction. The reader of that extraordinary document, for its time, "Policies in Parliament," will suspect that it was put out as a handbook for members in opposition. The more strident Puritans, as has been earlier indicated, wrote advice for those who were to start skirmishes about nonresidence, pluralities, and other ecclesiastical abuses.

There is still much to learn about what went on in the Lower House. Perhaps we shall have to be content with fragments of information. Yet new diaries may be turned up. It is not over three decades ago that I first in a Hampshire house looked upon what is now Add. 48119. As the manuscripts in country houses are finding their way into county archives and the British Museum, are being catalogued, and eventually will be printed, diaries and letters never yet pored over by historians may offer answers to many questions. Important members of the Commons may have written to their friends and told them what we would be glad to know. We know so little.

Chapter 6

The Development
of Committees

Prelude:
*Committees before 1603*TO learn about committees, when they began and how, what was the nature of their membership and procedures in their early days, is to search for the mention of such bodies in a haystack of rolls and chronicles, where mention may be rare or nonexistent. It may be that scholars will come upon bits of parliamentary diaries or notes of speeches in Parliament that prove more rewarding than the account of a House of Commons in Henry VII's reign found in the Red Book of Colchester. It is conceivable that a closer examination of the evidence to be gleaned from the *Lords Journals* and the *Commons Journals* and other records by scholars accustomed to interpreting, in Maitland fashion, scattered fragments hitherto unrelated, may prove useful. We have the Clerk's brief notation of bills in the *Commons Journals* from the reign of Edward VI; at that time there were committees of one or more men, usually experts about the bills offered. By the first years of Queen Elizabeth more light was shed on committees, and we come upon usages that may be relics of earlier practice. It is evident, however, that during the reign of the great Queen an impressive evolution was taking place in the use of committees. If one should plot that evolution by a line it would be a zigzag one.

During the first decade of the new reign committees were fairly small, though larger than they had been in the time of Edward

VI and Mary. A committee of twenty-four meant that the subject to be considered was of some importance. Procedure was less fixed. A bill was read three times and committed, usually on the second reading. But there had been occasional examples of four or five readings, which may mean that the use of three readings was a rather recent development. The size of the committees would seem to have been determined by the Speaker, who, as members called out names for the committee from the floor, indicated when a sufficient number had been proposed. It may be that, earlier, nominations had not always been made by the members. In 1571 we read of a case (April 11) when Mr. Seckford, Master of Requests, "prayed for a longer time to consider of a bill . . . and that the committee may be. . . ." Then he named ten men, including himself, for the committee. It is not impossible that some early committees, where legal knowledge was necessary, were nominated not from the floor but chosen in some other way, by the man who initiated the bill, by a member of the Privy Council who was also an M.P., or—conceivably—by the Speaker.

The committees were increasing in size. In 1558/59 the Committee for the Subsidy was composed of twenty-four members; in 1563 it included the Queen's Council—that is, the Councillors in the Lower House—twenty-four men from the shires, and six from Wales. In October 1566 a committee to make suit to the Lords to join with them in pushing for the marriage of the Queen included the Queen's Council and forty others. The Committee for the Subsidy was in that year made up of the Privy Councillors of the House, the Master of the Rolls, and forty others.

In 1571 two committees interest us, a committee of over thirty members to consider the subsidy and one of thirteen members (later expanded) "for motions of grief and petitions." Here it is best to quote Neale. He bases his statement on an anonymous diary, on that of John Hooker, and on the *Commons Journals.* Puritan speakers had been complaining, and a committee of twelve men was named to draft the necessary bills. Those who had made the motions were to collect notes and hand them to the committee. "Here," says Neale, was the first committee for grievances, a procedure which was to develop in later Elizabethan and early Stuart Parliaments, and, as one of the Commons standing committees, was to be a prime factor in winning the initiative in public as distinct from private bill legislation.

Neale goes on to point out that Parliament had always been an organ for the expression of grievances and that the notion of pressing grievances was not a novelty. "The new device of a committee for grievances was calculated to appropriate a share in that role for the House of Commons, to provide the House, as it were, with a Privy Council of its own." [1] It is not to be assumed that the Privy Councillors had ceased to prepare legislation. They learned from the judges returned from their circuits which laws ought to be enacted or amended. The Councillors made use of their positions on committees—they were the first named on almost every committee—to advance what they regarded as needed legislation and to halt legislation that the Crown disliked. They could bring pressure to bear on timid committeemen and induce them to vote as the King wished. Their influence on committees is hard to trace, but when we find a committee where zealous religious reformers abounded taking actions that would satisfy a conservative archbishop and Her Majesty, we are led to suspect that Privy Councillors had ways of manipulating committees.

Yet that was not the whole story. The Commons were not only considering measures brought in by members unconnected with the Government, but they were also using committees to formulate legislation or to establish preferences in bills to be pushed. At least twice in the reign of Edward VI and once in that of Mary a committee had been used to prepare laws. In 1571 a committee of fifteen men was named to appoint such bills for the commonwealth as shall be "first proceeded in and preferred before the residue, but not to reject any," a Ways and Means Committee.[2]

During the years from 1572 to 1584 committees were doing more and more of the work of the Lower House. The committees were larger than ever before, and there were more of them. The

Committee on the Subsidy increased in numbers from Parliament to Parliament. Some of the more significant debates were those in committee, and an official such as Mildmay, Chancellor of the Exchequer, might lead the discussion there. Other committees were slowly growing larger.

There were small committees that dealt with the less important measures. Such measures and others sometimes went through a kind of assembly line. A bill might be referred to say four men who would examine it and recommend a new bill. The *billa nova* might be turned over to six or seven men, none of whom had perhaps served on the original committee, and the new committee might decide on a third form of the bill.

The decisions of committees were seldom reversed by the House. It will be recalled that when Sir Walter Ralegh tried to have the judgment of a committee on which he had served reversed by the House itself, "the House cried No."

From 1586 to 1601 the evolution of the large committee is the significant fact.[3] In 1586 the committee about Mary Queen of Scots ("the great Cause") included "every other member of the House that would." When the House met in February 1588/89, the threat from Spain was still in most minds, and a committee was quickly named to consider a subsidy; it was composed of the first knight of every shire (if the first were missing, the second) and about forty-one others, a committee of nearly one hundred members.

In 1593 the Committee on the Subsidy included all the knights of the shire and more than fifty-six other members, a total of nearly 150 members. That committee met once, argued all afternoon until 7:00 p.m., and met again next morning. Finally the proposal for three subsidies and six fifteenths was put to the question and voted. Then the committee returned to the House, and their judgment was accepted without debate.

In 1597 the Committee on Monopolies had all the knights of the shire, all the burgesses of port towns, the knights and citizens of London, and about fifty-four others, that is, something more than two hundred members, or nearly one-half of the House.

A few days later, with the danger from Spain not forgotten, the House named to the Committee on the Subsidy all the knights of the shire and all of the citizens of the cities. That committee and the Committee on Monopolies had obviously not been chosen by calling out names. It is possible that some member of the Privy Council, perhaps Cecil or Fortescue, suggested the several sets of members.

In 1601 the question of monopolies was again pressed, and a committee was chosen of all the knights of the shire, ten named men, and "divers others," together with the knights and citizens of London, the barons of the Cinque Ports, and Dr. Caesar. The committee met on two afternoons in the House itself, and carried on debate much as if in the House.

Another committee was equally important. The Lord Keeper had suggested that the greatest matters should be handled at the beginning of the session, and a committee was chosen to meet on November 7, 1601, to certify to the House what those matters were. Its members were the knights of the shire, the barons of the Cinque Ports, the knights and citizens of London, and about forty-four others, that is, at least one hundred and sixty men. Except for the forty-four others, almost the same names were included as those on the Committee on Monopolies.

That the committee resembled the House in session came out in an utterance of Wiseman, a well-known figure in the Commons and a London merchant of consequence: "Let us therefore draw to some head and save our orations and speeches fitter for a Parliament than a committee."

When Sir Walter Ralegh was discussing in a large committee the incidence of the subsidy, Sir Edward Hoby demanded that he speak out: "You should speak standing so the House might the better hear you." Sir Walter answered that "being a committee [man] he might speak either sitting or standing." The next man to address the House was Sir Robert Cecil, who began tactfully: "Because it is an argument of more reverence I choose to speak standing."

Two days later Cecil, early in his address to the House, remarked: "I need not recite the form of the committee, by reason of so good attendance, being little inferior to our assembly at this present." On November 21 Heyward Townshend made a speech at the Committee for Monopolies and wrote: "The House parted and agreed to meet on Monday in the afternoon." Townshend was speaking of the meeting of the committee as if it were the House.

Not only were large committees meeting in the afternoon, but there were smaller committees of, say twenty or thirty members. The result of so many committees and such important large committees with a considerable duplication of membership was confusion. The same man might find himself on five committees, with several meeting at 2:00 p.m. Privy Councillors were on many committees and could not possibly be present at all of the meetings they were expected to attend. Nor could active private members.

Confusion increased because several bills would be assigned to a single committee originally set up to deal with one bill. Sometimes the committee had such varied duties that the bill for which it was first established was overlooked. It seemed as if the House were less interested in choosing competent experts than in making sure that some committeemen, it did not seem to matter much who, would look over bills. In one instance the Commons collected a whole group of committees into one omnium-gatherum.

It did not eliminate confusion that select committees and subcommittees grew out of the Great or the Grand Committees or of "general" committees. If it is hard for the historian to follow the ins and outs of committees, it must also have been hard for the members of the House.

The average member must have found the permanent standing committee something regular, in a shifting world of committees. By 1592 the Committee for Elections and the Committee for Privileges had been merged into one body, although as late as 1601 the House itself might deal with those topics. By December 11, 1601, the Committee for Continuance and the Committee for Repeal of Statutes had been merged.

The development of Great, Grand, General Committees was

to lead to something significant—the Committee of the Whole House. Meanwhile the many new large committees seemed to render parliamentary business more interesting and to give the diffident member a better chance. In committee a member was able to take up what the last speaker had said and either reinforce his point or undercut his argument. That made an interesting occasion and also encouraged the quiet member to slip a sentence or so into the debate.

Of course we know much less than we would like about what happened in committee, especially in the small committees. They did not go back to the House for authority to act, and they seem to have been allowed a good deal of latitude. There was often disagreement in committee. Men might hold differing opinions, and they were not always tactful or skillful in finding common ground. In general, however, they were too prone to compromise. To gain agreements they would put forward amendments and provisos until the final form of the measure was burdened with exceptions and qualifying clauses that are hard for us to interpret and must have worried the justices of the peace who had to make decisions based on the wording.

Cecil complained of the inefficiency of committees and used the bill for the relief of poor soldiers as an example. The members of the committee talked "to contrary effects" and arrived at no decision. Bacon did not mention committees, but marked the divisions in the House and the resulting inability to push legislation through. The weaknesses of which he spoke were due in some degree to the failure of committees to meet and, when they did meet, to arrive at clear-cut conclusions.

They wanted leadership, and that is not surprising. The chairman or moderator might be the first man named, one possibly nominated by a Privy Councillor, or one chosen by the members out of two proposed; he might venerate old custom and view reforms with misgiving. Such men were not unknown.

The records of committees in Elizabethan Parliaments provide an introduction to their use in the first years of James I. One is impressed with what appears to be rapid development in the first half of the Queen's reign and with the comparatively slow rate of change during the last two decades of her reign. It took a score of years for the Committee for Continuance and Repeal to become a fixture of the Commons and almost as long for the Committee for Privileges and Elections. The interval between the first Grand Committee, where all who wished could attend, and the Committee of the Whole House is much longer than might have been anticipated. The House moved slowly in taking up new forms of procedure.

The evolution of new and large committees may in part have resulted from the new kind of membership in the Commons. It is now an old story that a new and more enlightened membership was appearing on the scene. Those members were taking things into their own hands, as we know. It is not surprising that some of the measures they drafted required reworking and put a burden on committees. But if the new men made more committees necessary, the new committees also required a membership more skillful in law and procedure, more imaginative in bending old custom into new and usable forms.

As committees gained significance and did more of the everyday work of the Commons, the members naturally craved places on them and took pride—now and then the pride creeps through in a sentence from a diary—in being assigned to a certain committee.

All that is true, I believe, and yet, until the last decade of Elizabeth's reign, service on committees—excepting of course the Grand or Great Committees—was restricted in practice, doubtless without intention, to a small minority of the House. The speeches, at least those of which we know, were made by an even smaller minority.

At the same time that minority was steadily, if not rapidly, increasing. More hitherto unknown men from Herefordshire, Shropshire, Staffordshire, and other far-away shires were venturing to utter opinions and thus to gain places on committees. Into those committees they brought the complaints of their communities, and thus more and more grievances were aired. To set forth grievances was not to remedy them, but grievances publicized at

Westminster over the years were not lost sight of, indeed, they were likely to be remedied within a generation, more or less (as in the Parliaments of 1601 and of 1624).

Is it too much to imagine, then, that committeemen were doing their part to democratize a nation still, in its social structure, emerging from the shell of the feudal world? The new large committees carried weight. One hundred and fifty men gathered as a committee in the afternoon were likely, when they heard the story of abuses set forth in plain language, to grow restive and to break out in indignation. Sir Robert Cecil was alarmed at the confusion in the Grand Committee on Monopolies and had to speak softly to members; the Queen eventually had to do more.

Committees in the Session of 1603/04

THE Parliament summoned less than a year after the accession of James I to the English throne was marked by the expansion of committees. Committees that met in the afternoon and that included from one-third to one-half of the House were becoming common. Subcommittees of those large committees were not only used, but were occasionally transformed into large and significant committees. Small committees for minor matters did not disappear; they were likely now to include about twelve or fifteen members. Such committees, when they dealt with technical legal questions, were often made up almost entirely of lawyers.[1]

Two committees already established in earlier Parliaments as standing committees were nominated at the beginning of the session. The Committee for Returns and Privileges, now composed of about seventy members, was a larger committee than it had been in 1597 or in 1601. This was probably because everyone in the Commons knew that the Goodwin-Fortescue issue was to be decided. Among its seventy members the committee included about forty of the most active and best-known members of the lower House.[2] Sir Edward Montague, in his notes concerning this session of the Commons, set down the motion for the committee and then added: "Some stick there was at the first, but put to the question it was agreed there should be a committee.[3] Perhaps the "stick" was because friends of the King feared that the Commons might have too much to say about the Crown's move to put in Sir John Fortescue as a knight of the shire for Buckinghamshire and to displace Sir Francis Goodwin.

The other permanent committee, the Committee for Repeal, Continuance, and Revival of Statutes, had become larger than in the two Parliaments before, and now included almost fifty members. On April 19 it was resolved by the House that no bill for continuance should be brought in by any but the Committee for Continuance, doubtless an attempt to regularize committee procedure.

Two grand committees were set up almost as soon as the session began, both for grievances. It will be recalled that Sir Robert Wroth and Sir Edward Montague, who sat side by side, set the ball rolling about grievances on March 23. Wroth mentioned seven grievances, of which the two most important were wardship and purveyance, but monopolies and the dispensation of penal laws by the Crown had been named as abuses. It will be remembered that the Clerk wrote of Wroth's speech that it "passed in silence." The Commons were waiting for the next speaker. Montague got to his feet and with little felicity of speech or manner mentioned three grievances of his county: the burdensome charges of the commissary courts, the suspension of ministers for failure to use all the ceremonies prescribed, and depopulation by enclosures.

As a result, it should be recalled, a committee of forty-seven members was named to consider the grievances brought forward by Wroth, and a committee of about sixty-one to investigate the grievances enumerated by Montague. Nearly a score of the same names appeared on the two lists of committees. Between them the committees included a considerable number of those surviving who had been active in the last Parliaments of the Queen.

Other large committees deserve paragraphs. On March 26 a committee was named to deal with the wants and miseries of the officers who had served in Ireland against the threat of Spain; it was made up of the knights of the shire, one citizen from every city, and about thirty-two others, altogether around 150.

An even larger committee was that for the bill against the "Transportation of Woollen Cloths Undressed and for Setting the Poor Commons on Work." This committee included all the Privy Councillors of the House, all the knights of the shire, the first burgess of every borough, all the citizens of London and two others, a total of possibly 240 members, more than one-half of the membership of the House.[4]

The Committee for the Union with Scotland had its inception on April 14, when a body of one hundred was named to meet with forty of the Lords in conference.[5] That conference was followed by a debate that lasted for a few days. On April 20 the committee of one hundred was appointed to attend His Majesty, and thirty-nine members were added.[6] It was set down by the Clerk that "any member of the House, being no committee, hath liberty to accompany them to the King."[7]

After the meeting with the King and a conference with the Lords, the debate over the union continued in the committee and "all gentlemen of sufficiency or learning" were expected to "yield their opinion."[8] No man's opinion was to be forestalled by threats. What did that phrase suggest? Had men in committee been talking freely? For some reason His Majesty sent a message allowing "freedom and liberty of speech to all." He professed to hope that they would speak freely "the depth and innermost conceit of their hearts."[9]

Strange words from a sovereign who was no friend of free speech, and the more significant because he was taking notice of what happened in committee. He was doubtless unaccustomed to committees, probably unaware of the importance of this one, and perhaps did not realize that the House, by naming a committee of its best members, was taking time to think things over.

Someone may have told him, however, that this committee was to be important and should be encouraged. He had been so unused to opposition, so unaware of the difficulties in fusing two very different kingdoms, that he had not awakened to the necessity of preparing the case. In discussion the members of the Lower House had come to realize that the problem of the union had manifold ramifications, and they could not refrain from canvassing them in committee and in the House. They met as a committee on the afternoons of April 24, 25, and 26, and the meetings on April 24 and April 26 were reported in the House. The House itself did not forego consideration of the problems involved; indeed, it seems to have continued in the morning the debate of the afternoon before in the committee; if so, members were assuming that the committee was not essentially different from the House.

The two committees set up on March 23 as a result of the motions by Wroth and Montague were at a disadvantage because so many other committees were established at about the same time, and with much the same membership, and because the Goodwin-Fortescue election issue drew the attention of members away from other topics.

On March 29 Wingfield complained of the failure of members to attend the committee named to deal with the grievances mentioned by Wroth.[10] With truth Sandys remarked, in April, of committees: "Too few taketh away reputation, too many, action," [11] that is, too few limit the influence of a committee, too many prevent clearly defined conclusions.

The committee that resulted from Montague's motion did not get down to business quickly. The committee for Wroth's motion met at once, that very afternoon, and resolved that the House should be moved for a conference with the Lords about framing a petition to the King that they might treat of wardship and "offer him a project." [12] About purveyance it was, I infer, the same committee that ordered a few lawyers to draw a bill and bring it in for further consideration.[13]

Slowly Wroth's large committee branched out into a number of subcommittees, which took things pretty much into their own hands and framed bills.

The story of Montague's committee is not very different. To be sure, it took much longer to get under way. The emphasis of

Montague's speech had been on religion, and it was weeks before Sir Francis Hastings proposed on April 16, a select committee to consider the confirmation and reestablishing of the religion now in use, and also the settling, increasing, maintaining, and continuing of a learned ministry and "whatsoever else may incidentally bring furtherance thereunto." [14] A committee of thirty-one was eventually named, and those thirty-one included eighteen or nineteen members of the committee on Montague's motion.

To follow the ins and outs of Montague's committee and the committees on religion is to become entangled in a maze of committees related in various ways to one another. Suffice it to say that Montague's committee was enlarged and that subcommittees proliferated from it. In committees and subcommittees various bills were put together—no doubt with the help of Hastings and his Puritan friends—some of which passed the Commons and were sent up to the Lords. It becomes evident that those subcommittees or select committees, which were a kind of subcommittee, were usually made up of thirty or forty members, possibly with the idea that in rather large groups Privy Councillors would be unable to exercise much influence. Meanwhile the pressures for religious measures would seem to have come from Hastings and his limited circle of zealous ultra-Protestants, who may well have cooperated in calling out the names for committees—it was part of their program—and thus filling committees with their allies.

A few usages, new or seemingly new, in respect to committees deserve to be noted. In late May the Lords suggested a meeting of nine Lords and twenty Commoners to name a subcommittee of the two Houses to consider matters of religion. A subcommittee of the two Houses was set up, the first of its kind, so far as I know.[15] On June 8 Hastings explained that, in a conference between the subcommittees of the two Houses over religion, a bishop had expressed dissatisfaction "that the House of Commons should deal in any matters of religion." That was to interfere, the bishop suggested, with the liberty of the Church. He wished to maintain the freedom of the Church from state control. He was carrying the war into the enemy's camp.

Alarmed by this bold assault upon Erastianism, the Commons resolved to select a subcommittee of their own to "search, view, and consider of all such precedents as have warranted or may warrant this House to intermeddle with matters ecclesiastical." [16] On June 13 Hastings reported the travail of the subcommittee.[17] Whether that subcommittee had reported to the Great Committee, and the Great Committee to the House, I do not know. In such matters there might have been a certain carelessness and informality.

On June 9 it was ordered that such as desired to be heard by counsel should be heard at committee.[18] This order became a regular practice.

The session of the Commons in 1604 had witnessed some slight expansion of the committee system, but no further development of the Great or Grand Committee, which met in the afternoon and which all members could attend. Such committees had been used earlier and would be used again. In May 1607 they would flower into the Committee of the Whole House.

Committees in the Session of 1605/06

THE session of the Commons for 1605/06 does not offer much that is new in the use of committees. The large committees, for purveyance, recusants, grievances, and subsidy, met on different afternoons, but they were enough alike in personnel to seem the same committee meeting for different purposes. The large committee, which included a considerable proportion of the Lower House, was not unlike the later Committee of the Whole House.

Of the four large committees, the proceedings of two were constantly reported to the House; they met for long afternoon sessions. The Committee for Recusants included nearly one hundred members; the Committee for Subsidies, which also became the Committee for Grievances, had thirty-eight named members, plus all the knights of the shire. If we allow for duplication, we may guess that it had about 120 members.

The committees met in the House itself, in the Court of the

Exchequer, or elsewhere.[1] It was not uncommon for two of the committees to meet at the same time. On March 19, the Committee for Grievances sat in the Commons House, while the Committee for Recusants sat in the Court of Wards.[2] On April 24 the Committee for Grievances, "or so many of them as were present and such as offered," left the House and "went up into the Committee Chamber to marshall these grievances." During that period, a full hour, "the House did sit idle." At length the committee sent down word that "they would come down into the House, if it so pleased the House, and confer with the company, not as in the House, but by way of committee."[3] The Speaker explained that in this case he was to depart, and so he did; and "most of the company departed with him." A few stayed until eleven, "expecting the coming down of the committees," and then gave up. Apparently the committee returned after those with the Speaker had left the House.

That many members left with the Speaker shows that the large committee was not yet a Committee of the Whole House. Bowyer's diary concurs with this. On April 7 Robert Bowyer had been in the Exchequer, it will be remembered, attending with his patron, Lord Buckhurst (the son of the Lord Treasurer, the Earl of Dorset), the committee concerning the "Bill for the Preservation of the Spawn of Fish." Along with Buckhurst, Bowyer strolled over into the Chamber of the Commons, "where the committees were handling the matter of grievances."[4]

There was no Committee of the Whole House, but the large committee sometimes included everyone who cared to come. On March 11 it was ordered that

> the former committees appointed to consider of grievances should consider further thereof, and likewise what is fit to be done for supply of the King's occasions, and at this committee any of the House to be present and every man present to have a voice.[5]

The schedule of committees set down in the *Commons Journals* on February 12 reveals something of the arrangement of committees:

The same committee (Wednesday) on Friday, for matters of Purveyors, and other things incident of the King's charge, supply etc.

Tomorrow, the meeting of the Great Committee, touching the Lords' Articles (Recusants).

Friday, the conference touching the Purveyors and other matters incident, etc.

Saturday, committee touching all other grievances of the Commonwealth.

Monday, a further conference touching the Articles.

On that same day it was set down by the Clerk: "Committee for Grievances this afternoon and that of the Purveyors." [6]

Committees were increasing in numbers and size at least partly because of a wider realization that Parliament was a body where abuses would be heard and might be remedied. In earlier days boroughs and companies looked to someone in the Privy Council, and they still did so. But now they sometimes told their troubles also to their representatives in Parliament and hoped for action in the form of bills.

So many bills about abuses were brought forward that the average member must have been confused with the multiplicity of measures and proposals and by the variety of opinions on those proposals. Not all bills were welcomed. It was always possible on the first or second reading of a bill to shout, "Away with it." Seldom did members do so.[7] More often they were ready to commit bills. In many cases the member was not quite sure what attitude to take toward a proposed measure: he would be better able to make up his mind when he heard the report from the committee. When a bill touching fees for copies (of legal documents) was read the first time, it was "much excepted against because it did not pursue the agreement of the committee." [8] It was probably a new bill presented by some member of the committee who had not supported the majority report about an earlier bill.

Not only did the average member await the report of the

committee, he was also glad to have the bill discussed again after the report, in the light of the findings of the committee. Nine times out of ten, indeed more, the member would vote to sustain the committee.

Not only the casual member welcomed more committees. The Speaker or the Privy Councillor who was holding a watching brief for the King might wish to see a bill committed. The Speaker found it a way of evading what he conceived as his responsibility to Salisbury to see that certain bills were rejected. He could blame the nonrejection of the bill on the committee. So could Privy Councillors; sometimes, indeed, they could manage to hold back or put to sleep bills in committee. The bill might be put on ice until the session of Parliament was nearly over and it was too late for its supporters to warm it up.

About the relation of the Grand or Great Committees to sub-committees, it is not easy to generalize. Grand Committees were likely in many instances to make use of subcommittees to prepare material in outline for their consideration. On January 25, 1605/06 the Solicitor reported to the House from the subcommittee, of which he had been a member, that the subcommittee had drawn their ideas about the limitation of the activities of recusants into articles. Now they wished the Grand Committee to confer with them.[9] Hence the Solicitor moved the House that the articles should be delivered to the General Committee, so that a bill might be framed.[10]

The House was not always so regular or consistent in its procedure. On February 3 the articles devised by the General Committee were offered to the House and debated. After long discussion Article 4 was referred back, not to the General Committee, but directly, it would appear, to the subcommittee.[11] When disagreement arose in the House as to how far the Lords should be informed of what the Commons were doing, Hastings urged that the Commons should confer with the Upper House only about what the Commons had referred to the subcommittee touching the laws then in force against recusants but that they should not reveal to them the articles "now in hand." It was concluded that the subcommittee should meet that afternoon, but the committee members assigned to confer with the Lords were to meet the following afternoon. Apparently the policy was to be determined by the subcommittee.[12]

On the other hand, on March 1, 1605/06 Sir William Strode proposed that bills about recusants should be drawn in the House and then gone over by a subcommittee.[13] I am inclined to asssume that there was no fixed relation of subcommittees to the general committees and that sometimes the House, sometimes the General Committee, and sometimes the subcommittee initiated policy, or revised drafts presented to them. We shall never be able to speak certainly about the relation of these several bodies to one another unless more parliamentary diaries containing more details are discovered.

What seems evident, however, is that the system of committees and subcommittees meant that measures, bills, and policy were discussed in one place, then in another, and finally in the House itself. Out of repeated debates in the House, in committee, and in subcommittee, measures ought to have been put into sharply defined form. That was not always the outcome, as we have observed in another connection. Much debate on various occasions and at intervals led to unfortunate compromises and, now and again, to ambiguous language.

There is a strange case relating to subcommittees, and I am unsure of its meaning. On January 22, 1605/06 a committee was formed to consider of a learned ministry and about nonresidence of ministers already placed.[14] On February 15 it was recorded by the Clerk: "Learned Ministry, Bill for Establishment of True Religion: Sir James Perrot, Mr. Fuller, Sir Anthony Cope." [15] Were these three men, at least two of them Puritans, a subcommittee of the committee of about thirty named January 22? None were among the thirty then named. Were they perhaps additional members? They are not recorded as such, but listed, rather, as if they were members of a committee. Were they possibly named to see that the committee met and acted? Or were they another committee?

How were the members of a subcommittee chosen? From stray bits of evidence from earlier and later Parliaments it seems probable that they were named by the committee and not by the House. We note that these subcommittees were often made up of a few practiced draftsmen,[16] and it is hard to believe that a large general committee would call out appropriate names. It is conceivable that an important member of the committee, when he moved to refer a matter to a subcommittee, would name in his motion the members of that subcommittee. We have a few instances in the 1620s where an M.P., in moving for a subcommittee, did suggest its personnel.

The use of committees by the two Houses in their dealings with one another deserves mention. On February 7, 1605/06 we come upon a proposal for a joint committee of the two Houses regarding recusants. The articles drawn up by the Commons on that matter were to be shown to the Lords, and those formulated by the Lords shown to the Commons.[17] It will be recalled that between the two sets of articles, the Commons were assured, there was much agreement. On February 10 Sir Edward Hoby wrote Sir Thomas Edmondes, recounting events in the Commons on February 7 and later, and adding:

It was agreed upon, in the end, that our House might be moved to deliver their articles unto the Lord Chancellor, and the Lords would do the like of theirs unto our Speaker; that a subcommittee might thereby be appointed from both Houses to draw a bill; which was assented unto by the House.[18]

That assent is not recorded by the Clerk of the Lower House. On February 10 the *Lords Journals* reported that the articles drawn by the committee of the Lower House were read to the Lords, and afterward the articles which the committee of the Lords delivered to the committee of the Lower House were also read. Then

Moved by the Lord Chancellor that the Lords committees may have authority from the House to meet with the committees of the Lower House, at times convenient; which was assented unto, but thought necessary that, before such meeting with the Lower House, the Lords committees . . . should meet to consider among themselves of the said articles, so as they might be the better prepared for the next conference.[19]

Apparently Hoby was wrong in saying that the Commons assented to a joint subcommittee about recusants. On March 1 Bowyer tells us:

Some moved that we should join with the Lords in appointing a committee to draw a bill wherein the articles conceived by both Houses touching Recusants might be inserted; but after sundry motions both ways the rule of the House was that we should not join with the Lords in appointing any committees, *ut supra,* but that we should of ourselves draw our bill; and their Lordships one other, if they shall think fit and convenient. For it was affirmed to be contrary to the custom and usage of this House to join in drawing any bill, but that every bill ought to be drawn and passed in one of the Houses and sent to the other. Only it was said that the last session a committee was appointed by both Houses to draw a bill for the Union, which being the most extraordinary case that ever was, ought to be no precedent to direct any other.[20]

Some dissatisfaction arose over the calling out of names for a committee. On January 28, 1605/06, Nicholas Fuller had moved that no man should name more than two members to a single committee. Fuller seems to have been persuaded that there was an old precedent for such a limitation in naming members, but others did not agree, and the motion was set down by Bowyer as "frivolous." [21] Fuller may have been right, but I have never found in the Journals an instance earlier than this date, nor later, when members were limited in their right of nomination.[22] That there was not more complaint of the way in which the membership of a committee might be managed in favor of special interests is surprising.

We do come upon a statement in connection with the membership of a committee that awakens suspicion about another aspect of naming committee members. On April 10 the Bill for Free Trade, a controversial measure in which the West Country and many small ports were arrayed against the London merchants was in the works. Sir Robert Mansell, Treasurer of the Navy, who represented Carmarthenshire, told the House that he had found divers men set down as members of the Committee for Free Trade whom he had not heard named in the House. Some of those names were those of men interested in the corporations "desired by the House to be dissolved." The names had been inserted between the lines, as if the Clerk had added them later. In other words, Mansell was accusing the Clerk, and possibly the Speaker, of sharp practice.

The Speaker's answer was that when any man's case was in question he was to have no voice but to withdraw himself, "but if the bill be general, in that case a party specially interested hath a voice, and is fit and able to be a committee." [23] It will be observed that the Speaker evaded the really serious charge that the names of interested persons had been inserted by the Clerk. The episode is not mentioned in the Clerk's Book. It is hazardous, however, to draw inferences from what may be merely lacunae in the Clerk's Book.

Committees in the Session of 1606/07

IT will be recalled that in the last Parliaments of Elizabeth two Committees—that for Privileges and Returns and that for Continuance and Repeal of Statutes—were becoming a regular feature. The second committee was in evidence at the beginning of the new reign in 1604, but not in the session of 1605/06 nor in that of 1606/07.

In all three sessions, however, the Committee for Privileges and Returns was active. The new committee named on November 19, 1606 was said by the Clerk to consist of the members who had sat on the same committee in the last session, "with some added."

To be exact, ten members were common to the Committee for Privileges and Returns in 1605/06 and 1606/07. The new committee of 1606/07 was almost entirely made up of well-known figures at Westminster, as the former committee had been.

In 1606/07 there were two large committees. The Committee for the Union consisted of well over two hundred members. The only other large committee, that Committee for the True Making of Woollen Cloths, included all the burgesses of the clothing towns, all the knights of the clothing counties, and nine other members. It is doubtful if the clothing boroughs or the clothing counties were strictly definable terms.

The Committee for the Union met on many afternoons. In Elizabethan Parliaments one committee had usually held the stage, the Committee for the Great Cause, the Committee for Grievances, or the Committee for Subsidy, or the Committee for Monopolies. In 1607 the union of the two kingdoms by parliamentary enactment was in the mind of the Sovereign and was the immediate question before the two Houses. However much they may have wished to dodge the issue, the Commons could not avoid dealing with it.

The Committee for the Union was not yet a Committee of the Whole House; we find instances where one or two small committees were meeting at the same time as the Committee for the Union. But more often small meetings were postponed so that everyone could attend the larger gathering.

That committee offered a better chance,[1] as we have seen, to the "back-bencher" (to use a nineteenth-century term) to put in his word. The few sentences he volunteered from his seat in the committee, he may have hoped, were less likely to be remembered and reported to Whitehall.

The back-bencher, not as yet quite accustomed to the large committee, may have been less regular in attending it and at first slow to participate. In the lengthy debates over the union and the endless details involved, it seemed sometimes a nice question with members whether or not the House should go into committee.

There was little doubt in Sandys's   mind. On November 27, 1606, he took up before the House the question of whether they should confer with the Lords and moved for such a conference, but not before the members had debated it "by points." As to whether that preliminary debate should be in the House or in committee Sandys was explicit: "I think, by a committee, because there a reply is admitted, which is not here."[2] What Sandys meant, no doubt, was that members who had once spoken in the House could not answer the arguments advanced against their cases, whereas in committee they could argue back and forth as long as they pleased. Sandys may also have had in mind the fact that in the House men were occasionally inclined to make long and formal speeches without much reference to what had been said just before. In committee such speeches were more easily interrupted.

The issue of committee versus House came up again two days later when the Instrument of Union had been read and motions were being offered as to how the discussion should be carried on. It was moved:

1. That a committee should be named
2. That it should be first debated and then committed
3. That the whole House (except the Commissions) should be of the committee
4. That a particular and select committee should be named
5. That it be questioned whether or not to have a committee

The reader should not overlook the possibility mentioned here of a Committee of the Whole House, with the exception of the commissioners for the union.[3] It was finally decided that the hundred chosen to meet the Lords in conference, all the lawyers of the House, the burgesses of all the port towns, the knights and burgesses of the northern counties,[4] and some forty-two others, (named)—more than two hundred in all—should make up the committee to debate the Instrument of Union.[5]

In other words, the House seemed to decide against a Committee of the Whole House (though they did consider it) in favor of a committee that included more than half the membership. In his notes Sir Edward Montague wrote: "We fell into debate what course to take in the proceeding of the Union. A committee of most [of] the House was chosen and appointed to meet in the House on Monday in th'afternoon." [6] Bowyer added an important sentence: "All the House to be present and have free speech." [7]

The *Commons Journals* bear out Bowyer's words: "The Court arose at ten a clock and departed, being put in mind to meet at one a clock upon the Grand Committee for the Union, in the Parliament House." [8]

That afternoon the Grand Committee for the Union met, the session being reported to the House of Commons the next morning by Lawrence Hyde and Richard Martin. For practical purposes, this afternoon session lasting several days was a Committee of the Whole House.

On December 11 a select committee of about twenty-nine was named "to consider of and prepare such matters as were to be propounded and handled in the conference." This committee was to meet at 7:00 a.m. the next day.[9] It amounted to a subcommittee of the Grand Committee and included most of those who had been making speeches: the Attorney General, the Solicitor, Hastings, Bacon, Sir Henry Montague, Sandys, Sir Edward Montague, Croft, Hoby, Nathaniel Bacon, Francis Moore, Henry Yelverton, Richard Digges,[10] and Thomas Wentworth.

According to a manuscript of extracts about procedure in this Parliament compiled by an unknown member, there was, on December 17, a development in the use of committees:

> A committee touching the Union being appointed in the House and adjourned from the afternoon before to the morning following [Dec. 17] in the House, the Speaker the next day being sat, it was moved that the House would give leave the committee, which was done, the Speaker arising out of his chair, and sitting by, and one appointed by the committee taking the place of the Clerk.[11]

Here is an arresting statement. One asks eagerly: Was it written down at the time? Or was the writer relying upon his memory and putting a later practice back half a year? We can only say that the writer was deeply interested in procedure.[12]

His story is in some degree borne out by the words of the *Commons Journals:*

> Moved by one of the Great Committee [Martin] named for the conference that where the conference was yesterday in the afternoon adjourned till this morning, that the House, now sitting, would be pleased to give leave for the committee to attend. Which was yielded unto.

> Mr. Speaker stayed in the House till half an hour after eleven a clock, at which time the conference ended, and [the committee] was continued until the afternoon.[13]

The man whom I have been quoting added: "This course was held inconvenient and the motion denied 27 June 1607." [14]

What had happened at that time was that at 10:00 a.m. Strode had proposed that the Speaker depart and the House proceed by committee. Opposition arose at once. It was said that in the forenoon there was never a committee in this place and that the Speaker never left them all sitting.[15] The House voted against Strode's proposal and voted to meet as a committee in the afternoon.[16]

No one objected to a committee of all who wished to come in the afternoon; in fact, there had, before June 26, 1607, been Committees of the Whole House in the afternoon. But it seemed a different thing to conservative Members of Parliament to turn the House sitting in the morning into a committee and put the Speaker aside; it was an innovation the Commons were not yet prepared to accept. The time would come, and shortly, when the House would turn itself at any time into a committee.

Apparently the author of the procedure MS. I have been quoting believed that the House did, on December 17, 1606, move into committee in the morning. He was a careful student of procedure, and he may have been right. The House, or a large part of it, had been meeting in the afternoon in committee, and it might well have done so in the morning and still, at a later date, have refused to do so.

When the House, after the long Christmas recess, came together on February 10, 1607, the problem of the form of the union was still uppermost in the minds of members, but much of the debate on the subject was carried on, not in committee but in the House. That good results had come from the earlier committee meetings in November and December was testified by Sir Richard Spencer (M.P. for Brackley in Northamptonshire), who, in addressing the House about the union on February 13, remarked: "This intended Union hath some good in it, because it passed censure of so many matchless committees." [17]

The Commons, although carrying on much of their discussion in the House, were always on the point of referring the question in hand to the Grand Committee. Fuller, always active and ready with a suggestion, moved that the House consider every particular and "then refer it to committee." [18]

The evolution of the Grand or the Great Committee into the Committee of the Whole House was not retarded by the discussion over the union. It will be recalled that in the debate about the union the problem of naturalization demanded solution. Martin called for a "speedy committee," with instructions to take time to "ripen" the union.[19] But the Grand Committee, meeting in consequence, resolved on February 21 that the Scots were not naturalized by the laws of the realm.[20] That significant vote was ratified by the House.[21] On March 16 the Speaker conveniently (but perhaps actually) became ill, and the question arose about what to do. Two committees were due to meet, and, if so, why not the Grand Committee? Fuller talked about the pressure of business and proposed a Committee of the Whole House. To Sir George More, it will be recalled, that was an innovation. But the Committee for Privileges was instructed to consider the situation. On March 16 the Speaker was himself again, and the debate on the union was resumed.

Croft declared that it was as easy to make a "perfect Union" as to do what they were proposing to do. He continued:

I think that before conference . . . we consider of the matter of convenience, and this to be in the House, not by committees. For as I do confess that in committees by short arguments many times truth is beaten out, yet I have observed that in committees, when every man many reply, some special persons of place by speaking often, and countenance, do prevail more than by their reasons.[22]

On March 31, it will be recalled, the King made a long speech to the Parliament and then adjourned it for three weeks.

When they met again, the question of a "perfect Union" was under consideration. On May 7 Sir George More introduced the debate on hostile laws by alluding to "speeches carried or miscarried to his Majesty." Then he flung out at Sandys: "he would not commend Sir Edwin Sandys." [23] It was Sandys's grievous transgression, I assume, that he was proposing the perfect union.

Yelverton rose and discussed at first the "carriers of words," those who had been reporting speeches of the Commons and, not impossibly, those of Yelverton to the King.[24] Finally he said: "If the Speaker be not here, all the House may be a committee. This bill committed, tomorrow at two o'clock in the afternoon to the Whole House, the Speaker excepted." It was the Clerk who wrote: "Affirmed that if Mr. Speaker were absent the whole House might be a committee, and thought fit to commit this bill to the whole House, Mr. Speaker only excepted." [25]

Thus it came about that on May 7, 1607, the Committee of the Whole House was accepted as a parliamentary device; it is still used today over the English-speaking world. The date is to be remembered; it is more significant than that of a battle in the Wars of the Roses so elaborately recorded in the old textbooks. Like other events, it was only the culmination of a process that had been developing for a generation.

The next morning in the House some committees were adjourned so that everything might be clear for a full House at the committee in the afternoon. Sir Robert Harley set down a detailed account of the meetings of the committee on May 8 and 9.[26]

Hardly less detailed were the notes of Thomas Wilson, probably for the use of Salisbury.[27] Did Harley and Wilson realize that something momentous was taking place? I doubt it. The M.P.'s of that day were hardly aware that they were making history. Yet they did take pains about precedents.

The meetings of the committee were far from dull. The question of the repeal of the hostile laws was to be dealt with and, first, the preamble. The committee argued at length about phrases in that preamble and finally reached agreement, but by a formal vote. The committee was voting.

Then the committee fell upon the problem of whether they should repeal the hostile laws in general, or by the mention of particular laws. At first they voted on that question, but they decided at length (as nearly as I can make out from Wilson's somewhat cryptic narrative) to come to no decision until they had referred the question to the House.

That move is interesting. Again and again the House, when in a quandary, had turned a problem over to a committee; now the Committee of the Whole House, uncertain what to do in this instance, was tossing the question back into the hands of the House.

But the Committee of the Whole House was not yet established as a regular committee for afternoon sessions. The problem of the criminals at the border and whether they should be remanded to the country of their origin to be tried was a hard nut to crack. A Grand Committee would often meet in the afternoon and carry on the debate. That in several cases it was not, however, the Committee of the Whole House became evident because other committees were meeting at the same time, or the Speaker and a remnant of the House itself were sitting in St. Stephen's and awaiting the return of the Grand Committee.

Sometimes that Grand Committee was used to determine policy, sometimes to deal with details.

A nice point about committee procedure arose. The Grand Committee was meeting on the morning of June 4, but with few present. Bacon was presiding and set forth to the members present, as we have seen in another connection, the objections of the King to the decision arrived at by that committee about the use of sworn witnesses by Englishmen in border trials. Bacon explained that he could not deliver to the House the King's message because it was directed to the committee. It was pointed out that the committee, once it had made a decision, could do no more than the House to change that decision. The small attendance at the committee worried those present, and one of their number was sent to the House itself to ask members to join them. The committee, now enlarged, resolved to report its decision to the House. Bacon, as Chairman, reported to the House. The Speaker was awaiting the decision of the committee, which raised two questions. One concerned the decision to which His Majesty had objected: that prisoners should be allowed sworn witnesses. About that the House was not ready to vote, but seemed hesitant to follow the Crown. What interests us here is that formalities of procedure between the committee and the House were being carefully observed.[28]

Earlier we noted the proposal that the House meeting in the morning should become a committee. It would seem probable that on June 26, 1607, it was again proposed that the House in the forenoon should become a Committee of the Whole House. In the *Commons Journals* (the more finished version) it is stated that the amendments and provisos to the Bill of Hostile Laws sent down from the Lords were "secondly read and committed to the Great Committee named upon the second reading of the bill itself." It was then moved that the Speaker might depart, and the committee, "being compounded of the whole House, and now together," might "enter into consideration of their charge." It was disputed whether it were fit or not, "being without precedent," and resolved that the committee should meet in the afternoon.

The Committee of the Whole House was established, but the Grand or Great Committees were, nevertheless, still doing much of the work that would later be done by the Committee of the Whole House.

*Committees in the
Session of 1610*

DURING the last two months of their sitting, the Commons in 1607 had begun to make more than a little use of the new device, the Committee of the Whole House. But they had not yet learned to avail themselves of all of its potentialities.

The course of events served to awaken them to its possibilities. In the two and a half years between July 1607 and February 1610 the leaders of the Lower House had leisure to reflect on what had happened and to talk over the issues between Crown and Commons with fellow members and with their constituents. In those conversations they may well have alluded to the Speaker and to his transparent maneuvers to thwart them. Was it not possible, they may have asked themselves and others, to bypass the Speaker with the new Committee of the Whole House?

Whether they planned to do so or not, they did in 1610 make use of the committee on many occasions. The author of the brief procedure notebook about Parliament described what was happening:

> The Committee for this great business was the whole House sitting in the Parliament House, Mr. Speaker sitting by upon the lower seats next on the right hand of the chair. And when anything resolved by the Committee was to have the approbation of the House, Mr. Speaker came presently up into his chair and then a short report being made by the Moderator [1] of the Committee, who, during the Committee, sat in the Clerk's chair, but when he made his report, came and took place upon one of the seats, the matter was resolved by a question put by the Speaker, and then Mr. Speaker, as occasion was, left his chair again, and the Moderator took his place in the Clerk's chair. And so by several changes the same company was sometimes the Parliament House and sometimes a committee divers times in one day, which had not been seen in former Parliaments. 19 May, 1610. The like during the dispute of impositions, 28 June, 2 and 3 July, 1610. [2]

At some later date the Speaker, as a member of the Committee of the Whole House, occasionally participated in discussion.

The changeover from House to committee and from committee to House had an advantage, which was soon discovered and made use of. On a motion by Sir Francis Barrington [3] it was ruled that a committee, once having come to a decision, could not reverse itself.[4] But the committee could, it will be recalled, become the House, and then reverse the decision of the committee.

There were other rulings about the committee and the House. It was ruled by the House, and probably assented to by the Speaker, that not everything spoken in a committee was to be reported to the House, but all and only such things as the committee should direct.[5] It was further ruled by the Speaker that a committee might create a subcommittee, but that the subcommittee could not deal in any business before the House was acquainted with it.[6] I am not sure that this ruling was always followed.

The Committee of the Whole House was, however, slowly edging out the Great or Grand Committees. Both those members who might have been called the "opposition" (a word that comes into use much later) and those "near the Chair" were likely to propose that the House turn itself into a committee. The Committee of the Whole House needed no mandate or commission. Once organized as a committee, with the Speaker out of the chair and a chairman or moderator sitting in the Clerk's chair, the members could wander at will from topic to topic, as the spirit moved them. The committee sitting in the morning to deal with a certain problem might prove less inclined than the House to limit its discussion to one theme.

Yet on July 5 and 6, 1610, when the Grand Committee had been debating "support" for the King, Martin, in his report from the committee, requested an "enlargment of their commission." [7] The northern and remote parts, he explained, "desired to bargain for the wards singly, the rest for wards and purveyance together." A fundamental difference of policy had arisen, and the committee asked for a ruling from the House.[8]

This is the only instance in the Parliaments of 1604–1610 that

I have found where a Great or Grand Committee or of a Committee of the Whole House asked for a given power. In this case the request was quickly granted. The House ordered that the Grand Committee should have "free liberty, warrant, and power to debate and treat of any proposition offered touching support for the King, or ease of the subject, or any other circumstance considerable in the general bargain or composition intended with his Majesty." [9] When members of the House were perplexed as to the next move, it was natural to refer the problem to the Grand Committee or to a Committee of the Whole House. In May 1610, when the sovereign suddenly forbade the Commons to debate impositions, the Commons moved the very next morning that the Great Committee meet that same afternoon "to consider what answer to make to the King concerning the matter of Impositions." [10]

On November 6 the Commons faced another crisis. They had hoped that they might make a Great Contract with His Majesty, but just then the King insisted, it will be recalled, that "supply" as well as the "support" they had been planning to offer him be given. The "supply" meant £500,000 more. The Great Contract, upon which hopes had been centered, seemed to be going by the board. On November 7 some members pressed for a vote on it, and the Commons resolved that they could not go ahead with it.[11]

At once the question of what they were to say to the King arose. The next morning the Speaker proposed that "some few committees might be chosen to make this answer, which was in a manner agreed unto, and some committees named." But Sandys stood up, as the reader will remember, and declared that "it was a matter of too great weight for a few to take upon them at the first without the direction of the House. For either they should prejudice the House in declaring the reasons, or might omit many of the reasons," and therefore he wished that it might first be debated by a Committee of the Whole House, and then that that body, after they had agreed, might choose a subcommittee to put the conclusion into form.[12]

The motion was "yielded unto" and Sandys called to the chair.

It is not improbable that the Speaker had hoped by his suggestion to see a small committee named in which Privy Councillors might oversway the others. Such a body might have taken the negative answer to be given and phrased it so graciously that negotiations might have been resumed. The Speaker might have been able to maneuver the Commons into conceding more than they had intended. In the stubbornness with which he pursued his ends, he was almost a Molotov. No doubt Sandys intervened because he was familiar with the ways of the Speaker. That he could intervene after nominations were in progress would seem to indicate that the Speaker recognized Sandys's influence and dared not rule him out of order.

This Committee of the Whole House, so important in modern English history, is still so much a part of parliamentary procedure that every detail of its workings in its early years should be set down.

One asks, first, who was the "Moderator" or Chairman of the committee? How was he chosen? We know that Sandys was often Chairman, and, in the earlier sessions, Bacon. Martin was sometimes Chairman. What happened? There had been Chairmen of Grand or Great Committees for a long time, and we may assume that the Committee of the Whole House, when it was definitely set up in May 1607, chose Chairman as they had been chosen before. At the first formal session of that committee, on May 8, there was a struggle over the chairmanship. But Sir John Doddridge (Solicitor General) and Sir Francis Bacon were "reclaimed," that is, rejected by the "populars," "it being secretly alleged amongst them that their hands were in penning the bill [about hostile laws between England and Scotland]." [13] The "populars" named Nicholas Fuller. "Yet in some doubtfulness of the voices of the callers-out of either side, Sir Fr. B took the Chair." Evidently members called out names for Chairman in committee as they did in the House for members of a committee. But there was no one to take the floor and count the votes. Sir Francis was used to presiding and assumed the chairmanship, perhaps at a quiet nod from a Privy Councillor. Sir Francis was not shy; he really knew his own worth.

On June 26 of the same year there was again a choice to be made of a chairman of the Committee of the Whole House: "After dinner members assembled in the House. The voice, as I and others conceived, was for Mr. Fuller to take the Chair, and some on Mr. Attorney. Mr. Fuller modestly refusing (*ut est moris*), Mr. Attorney offered himself to it." [14]

In 1610, when the King had forbidden the House to discuss impositions and when that worried body was making up its mind how to answer His Majesty, they named John Hare to the chair. Hare, who was far from a popular figure with the friends of the King, tried to excuse himself, it will be recalled, on the ground of his "insufficiency"; he could not direct discussion nor sum it up. Yet he was compelled against his will to take the chair.[15]

On November 3 of that year Martin was chosen to the chair, "Mr. Speaker having leave to depart." Three days later, Martin, who was in the chair, explained that the committee was now ready to pass the Memorial and that the document had been "drawn to head . . . whilst Mr. Recorder kept the Chair, who best understood it," and hence the Recorder should take his place and preside. Many yielded, we are told, to Martin's suggestion. Others, however, called upon Martin to keep the chair "and made the question whether Mr. Recorder should be sent for, to take the Chair or no, and decided that he should, . . . and so Mr. Martin left the Chair." [16]

The word "decided" would imply that a vote was taken, but we cannot be sure. Just at this point, the Speaker, who had taken the chair as Martin left, informed the House that he had a message from His Majesty.

It would appear that when the Committee of the Whole House assembled for its first meeting that a member would propose some well-known figure for Chairman. If there were no opposition the man so nominated would take the chair. But if another name were suggested, a vote was likely to be taken as to which of the two should be Chairman.

In an earlier chapter it has been noticed that when the Speaker proposed a small committee for a certain purpose, Sandys countered with a suggestion that it should be the Committee of the Whole House. His motion was carried, and he was then named Chairman, as he perhaps foresaw. It was not unusual that the man who moved a Committee of the Whole House was called to be Chairman.

The matter of the chairmanship of the Committee of the Whole House was apparently still in a fluid state. In 1621, if we may trust Henry Elsynge, when two men had been nominated to the chair, the Speaker was called to the chair, the Committee of the Whole House became the House and voted as to who should preside over the committee.[17] Whether the method was used earlier I do not know.

Other questions suggest themselves. Did the Chairman of the Committee of the Whole House keep the debate to the point? Did he make rulings as to procedure? Did he tell a member that his speech was not related to the issue before the Committee? Did he declare a motion irrelevant?

We do know that early in November (probably the third) Martin was in the chair. The debate was about three matters, and Sir Maurice Berkeley had insisted twice that the Commons must answer the message from the King. The Chairman alluded to the three matters under discussion and replied to Sir Maurice that the answer to the King had been "much stood upon." He added: "I find no man of an opinion to have no answer, though divers motions. To proceed according to his Majesty's mind." (The word "mind" is almost illegible and uncertain.) In making this interruption the Chairman was apparently—if I read correctly— trying to keep the debate in one channel.[18]

How far the Chairman would go in rulings as to men and motions in what was presumably an informal meeting, I am not sure.

What was the relation of a subcommittee to the Committee of the Whole House or to the Grand or Great Committee? The subcommittee was chosen by the Great Committee or by the Committee of the Whole House, and was sometimes large but more often a small committee of from three or four to ten or fifteen.

Did the Great Committee or the Committee of the Whole House choose the subcommittee by calling out names from the floor, as committees were usually chosen in the House itself? I suspect that it sometimes did so.

Did the subcommittee so chosen need the confirmation of the House before it could carry on with business? On July 1, 1607, the Speaker had ruled that a committee might make a subcommittee but that the subcommittee could not do business before the House was acquainted with it, "which most of the House then present claimed to be. *Quod mirandum,*" wrote Bowyer.[19] Little wonder that Bowyer exclaimed in Latin. The Clerk did not record this ruling by the Speaker, and I find no evidence that any such practice was used in the session of 1610.

Did the subcommittee report decisions to the Committee of the Whole House, and were they then passed by that committee and presently reported by it to the House? Did a subcommittee occasionally report directly to the House, thus bypassing its superior body? These questions cannot be answered simply.

It is best to look over a few cases. On November 8, in the Committee of the Whole House over which Sandys was presiding, Fuller's motion that they should not offer His Majesty reasons for giving up the Great Contract but that they should simply declare their resolution to do so was "embraced by the whole Committee (which was the whole House)." [20] Then a subcommittee was presently chosen, "who went up to the committee chamber to frame this answer."

After debate the subcommittee agreed "only upon the heads of our answer, and thought fit they should be reported to the Great Committee and by the Great Committee to the House." [21] It was their hope that if the body of the statement were "well liked" it might be reduced into form by the next morning. The Solicitor reported to the Committee of the Whole House, and then the Speaker took the chair and Sandys reported to the House itself. The House agreed that the statement should be put in form by the Solicitor and Sir Edwin Sandys before the next morning, and then shown to the subcommittee and presented by them to the House.

The next morning, November 9, the brief resolution was read to the House. Some words were added to the resolution by agreement of the House, but not without opposition from four royal officials, "and some others." After a "large debate" on both sides the subcommittee, "formerly appointed" went up into the committee chamber and formulated words different and slightly more gracious than those at first presented in the morning. Those words were carried to the House and "liked by all." [22]

The story of that May crisis when the King forbade the House to debate impositions deserves attention again, even though once narrated. The Committee of the Whole House was meeting on the afternoon of November 22, and Sandys was presiding. It was agreed after some debate in the committee that a subcommittee should be chosen to draw "this matter of Petition of Right into form," and then to present it to the House the next morning.[23] The Privy Council, the Chancellor of the Exchequer, the Chancellor of the Duchy, the Secretary, and the learned counsel, the Attorney and the Solicitor, were appointed subcommittees, "but they all went away." There were left, however, "25 or 26 of the subcommittee that stayed and agreed upon the course of the petition and the reasons they meant to offer in the petition." They called upon Sandys "to draw the same into such form as he should like." [24]

They arranged to meet the next morning, "which they did, and made some small amendments in it." Then "t'was presented to the House as soon as the Speaker came and was read there." [25]

Did the subcommittee go through all the formalities? When they had inserted the small amendments to the version handed them next morning by Sandys and Bacon, did they submit it to the Committee of the Whole House, and then did Sandys as Chairman of that committee present it to the House? Or did the subcommittee bypass the Committee of the Whole House and present their version directly to the House? It is hard to say. The first alternative, that the document went from subcommittee to the Committee of the Whole House and then to the House seems more probable. The Calthorpe Manuscript (Add. MSS., 48119) says the petition was presented to the House "as soon as the

Speaker came," which suggests that the House had been in session before as a committee.

These cases, and others that I shall not go into,[26] lead me to believe that the subcommittee as a general rule reported to the Committee of the Whole House and that body in turn to the House itself. But in other cases, perhaps when the House happened to be sitting at a time when the subcommittee was ready to report, or in cases of amendments and of alterations, the subcommittee may have reported directly to the House. A certain informality, not unknown in the annals of the English, might still be practiced in the use of committees, and few were likely to protest against such irregularities. Was it not all between friends?

The cases I have been mentioning as illustrations have a certain similarity. The House used the Committee of the Whole House to discuss this subject and that, to consider conversationally, so to speak, the bearings of a problem before moving toward a decision. The assignment of a problem to the Committee of the Whole House was in many cases a delaying tactic by those who hoped, by drawing out a wide range of opinion, to come upon the best solution. It was more than that. In a crisis—and 1610 was a series of crises—when a policy had to be determined upon, and not deliberately, the Grand Committee was the natural resort of men who did not know precisely what to do next. Members might listen to their leaders, but they never ceased to hope that someone in committee might bring forward some new scheme, better than any so far suggested. In a way they had a certain confidence in democracy, that is, in a democracy of landed gentlemen (with a few townsmen) who might, by going over a measure in subcommittee, again in the Committee of the Whole House, and finally in the House itself, eventually arrive at the best answer.

The subcommittee had various uses, but the most common one was to put the conclusions of the Committee of the Whole House into form to be brought again before the committee for further consideration and perhaps verbal revision. Not uncommonly the subcommittee called on one or two lawyers skilled in draftsmanship to draw up statements for them. They did not speak of such men as subcommittees.

Occasionally the distinction between the Grand Committee and the subcommittee was set forth in the House. The Grand Committee, now usually the Committee of the Whole House, was to "consider whether they [the ten concessions offered by the King through Salisbury] be valuable, and whether they [the members of the House] will bargain for them or no, together with the wardships." The subcommittee was not to value the concessions but to draw them "into such forms as they may be most beneficial to the subject." [27] In this instance the subcommittee was no small group, but was to consist of all the lawyers of the House and others named.[28]

Grand committees and subcommittees had enough to do. At times the Committee of the Whole House was meeting almost every weekday afternoon, occasionally late into the afternoon, and not infrequently in the morning as well.[29]

Subcommittees were many and much occupied with business. On March 12 Sandys asked that all subcommittees concerned with grievances should sit from 1:00 until 3:00 p.m. and then come in—"All committees to sit at Westminster that they may be sent for." We may assume that his suggestion was acted upon by the House though the Clerk did not so record.

Committees and subcommittees must have become a burden to members, most of whom had their temporary abiding places in the City, had errands to do there for their wives and friends, and found long sittings at St. Stephen's tedious. They would absent themselves in such numbers that committees had to be postponed again and again.[30] The Clerk noted the times and places of committees to refresh the memories of members, but often in vain.

If the relation of committees to subcommittees seems ill defined, we must remember that committees had developed in numbers and functions more rapidly than any recognized procedure about them. The manuals of procedure were at least a decade, but more often two decades, behind the actual ways of carrying on in the House.

It has been pointed out earlier that debates were not the same in the Committee of the Whole House as in the House itself.[31] In committee, men did not have to stand up; from their seats they could have their say in a sentence or two, or more. Men could speak as often as they pleased and answer one another back and forth.[32] They did not have to address the presiding official, and usually they did not; later, in the 1640s, they did. Everything was informal. All that had been true of Grand and Great and General Committees in late Elizabethan Parliaments and true in early Jacobean sessions. I am afraid that I find little to support that difference between committee and House in 1610. It would appear that men spoke much less formally, but they did make long speeches and deal with more than one topic. They spoke sometimes with great freedom in committee, but such men as Wentworth, Sir John Savile, Sir Thomas Beaumont, Sir Roger Owen, and others spoke their minds in the House as well as in committee. The leaders of the opposition, Sandys, Martin, and others, chose their words carefully both in the House and in committee and made it hard for their enemies to make a case against them. To some degree the Committee of the Whole House, now a great deal in use, was losing its special character.

It was, in fact, used constantly, possibly more often by those who could not be regarded as of the King's party. It would appear from the results rather than from an examination of details (which we lack) that Sandys, Martin, and their friends manipulated committees with skill and must have understood the uses of those bodies as well as their limitations.

Chapter 7

The Role of the Speaker, 1604–1610

The Speaker's Election and Qualifications

THE story of the Speaker in the parliamentary sessions of 1604 to 1610 is necessarily centered on Sir Edward Phelips. Not one of the distinguished Speakers, nor one of the more popular, his personality had, nevertheless, to be reckoned with.

He was chosen Speaker in 1604 and was to hold the position until 1610. His nomination came as a surprise to the Commons. It is doubtful if anyone outside of the Privy Council had thought of him as a possible presiding official. When the Second Secretary, Sir John Herbert, proposed his name as a fit man, the motion was followed by silence, "the House not naming any."

> At last he being named again, some few cried, "A Phelips," some cried, "No, no," but then an ancient Parliament man, directing the House, said it was not sufficient to say "No," but they must propound some other. So some cry, "Phelips" again, some one or two cry, "Sir Edward Hoby"; some one, some another. But it being put to the question, "as many as will have a Phelips, say 'I,' " most cried "I," and the rest "No"; some five [?] cried, "No." [1]

Phelips was deemed elected and made the speech expected in the circumstances, disabling himself and pointing out his unfitness. After he had performed that established ritual, "no man rising up to speak and enable him, or to commend him to the allowance and choice of the House," a silence ensued that the Clerk noted. The House seemed less than enthusiastic about the nomination.

Yet something was to be said for Phelips. He had sat in five Elizabethan parliaments since 1584 and had made occasional short speeches. He had also had some judicial experience.[2] But for this post he had better qualifications. On matters of procedure in the Commons he was at least competent. Robert Bowyer, whose parliamentary diary avails us much, could with a terse biting phrase characterize performances in the House and would have been the first to pounce on blunders made by Phelips. So far as I can recall he did not do so.

Phelips was unimpressive. He was timid and could not conceal that weakness. It may be added, on the basis of later performance, that he had not the least trace of personal magnetism. One wonders how the Privy Council came to choose him and can only conjecture that he was selected as one who would follow instructions from the Crown.

His task was no easy one: to preside over some 460 men, most of whom were used to being personages in their own communities, and to enforce upon these men rules of procedure that were still somewhat fluid and might not be accepted. To a considerable degree he had to depend upon tradition. True, there were the *Commons Journals* in the hands of the Clerk (extending from 1547 to 1601), and the older Rolls of Parliament. Those Rolls were, however, not in good shape for immediate and rapid use. Nor were there as yet published manuals of procedure to which the Speaker might turn. That the Clerk of the House of Commons had some kind of precedent book, or at least a kind of index to the Journals, seems likely from the promptness with which precedents were produced for the Speaker.

Much of the information called for was to be found, however, in the minds of "ancient Parliament men" and, like many old men, they were willing to share their memories with younger men. Fortunately, memories were more dependable then than they are today. Men read fewer books and remembered them longer and more exactly, since they had less to keep in mind. Phelips himself could sometimes, on the spur of the moment, cite relevant precedents drawn from the reign of the great Queen. Neither medieval precedents nor those connected with the reigns of Henry VIII, Edward VI, and Mary seem to have been well known to him.

Moreover, the precedents he quoted seldom involved constitutional questions such as the right to levy impositions or the privilege of free speech. Phelips had little notion, if any, of the cases of constitutional significance from Edward III to Richard III, cases that were always being quoted by parliamentary antiquaries.

He was interested in motions, in the readings of bills, in amendments and engrossings, in the granting of permission to members to go home for reasons of health, or for pressing affairs, and in the sending out of writs for elections to replace those who had resigned or died. He was no less interested in the relation of the Lower House to the Upper—in the forms connected with the messages back and forth, in the conference between the two Houses, and in preparations for such conferences. Like many men of his own and other generations he was concerned with forms and did not inquire into the philosophy behind them.[3] He was not a victim of intellectual curiosity.

But he had useful facts at his command: he knew exactly what had been done the last session, what bills had been passed, what bills had been left in the hands of committees, what bills had been once read. When Bacon was reporting from a conference and had to omit some arguments and answers because his "tables" failed him, the Speaker was able at once to fill out the story.[4] On an earlier occasion he had offered to give a report of part of the King's message, but asked for time since he was not prepared. Promptly next morning he made the report.[5]

He was able to sum up a debate, presenting the pros and cons. Once in 1604 he was designated to do it, and at least twice in

1606–1607 he did so.[6] He kept track of committees. Moreover, at the close of the session of 1604 he asked all members to bring in such bills as they had, doubtless the bills left in the hands of committeemen.[7] Those bills might be useful at another session.

The Speaker and the House

ABOUT the relation of the Speaker to the House, various questions suggest themselves. How far could the Speaker determine what bills should be read, and in what order? To what degree was he responsible for the form of the questions put to a vote at the end of a debate? When could he interrupt a speech?

As to what bills should be read and in what order, the Speaker probably arranged that with the Clerk when he planned the order of the day's proceedings. It was customary for a member who wished to bring in a measure, if he did not ask help in the drafting of the bill,[1] to frame it, with or without the help of others. Once the bill was phrased in proper legal terms, the member would turn it over to the Speaker so that he could make a breviate of it for his memory when he set forth the bill to the House. I assume that when the Speaker returned the bill to the member concerned he gave him some rather definite indication of the day and the hour when the bill was first to be read.[2] It would appear that, at least in some cases, the member knew when he was to make his motion for the reading of his bill.

Of course the order of the day might be disarranged. The Speaker might recognize someone who differed sharply from those who had just spoken, and a debate back and forth might ensue. Such debate the Speaker might encourage.[3] Or an alert young lawyer might take the floor unexpectedly and make a point no one had considered, and those who followed might pounce upon him or support him with examples from their own communities. Thus the program for the morning might go by the board. A talkative old member was likely to make a diversion. He might go far afield and wander from the issue before the House, but he was revered for his age and flowing courtesy. Because he had been a good fellow in his day and had cousins all over the House, the Speaker would hesitate to put him down. When he had finally concluded, half a dozen men might be eager to gain the floor,[4] and the Speaker had to choose which one to recognize; he might put it to the question which of two men should be heard. About the order of the day, the Speaker usually seemed to have his way, and yet certain men in the House could win the members to overrule him. William Hakewill, in his account of how laws were passed, wrote:

> The Speaker is not precisely bound to any of these rules for the preferring of bills to be read or passed, but is left to his own good discretion (except he shall be especially directed by the House to the contrary), and howsoever he be earnestly pressed by the House for the reading of some one bill.[5]

As early as 1601 the Speaker was about to have the Bill for the Continuance of Statutes read, when members of the House suddenly cried out for the Ordnance Bill (forbidding the export of iron ordnance). Carew (or Carey), M.P. for St. Germans, Cornwall, asserted in defense of the Speaker that he had the right to determine what business should be handled. "If he err or do not his duty . . . we may remove him," said Carew.[6] Hakewill demanded that a question be put, whether or not the Bill of Ordnance should be read, and he prevailed. Sir Charles Howard, in his minutes of the Commons for 1621, wrote: "Tis at the discretion of the Speaker to read what bills he will, if the House call not for any in particular, but if the House do so, then those must be read."[7] We may guess that the principle, which had been in use in 1601 and was recognized in 1621, was known in the years 1604 to 1610.

Hakewill tells us that sometimes members would move to defer the question to the next day or to some later date, "especially if it be a matter which they desire should either pass with unanimous consent, or not at all." In such a case, wrote Hakewill, the Speaker ought to make the question, "whether they will have it then put to the question or defer the putting thereof till some other time; or whether they will have any question at all to be put, as he findeth the inclination of the House either to the one or to the other." [8]

A closely related question was how far the Speaker could determine the form of the question to put to the House at the end of the debate. The debate was usually occasioned by a motion, but not always. The whole form of the debate could be changed, as we have noted, by what someone who was getting at the root of the matter had said [9] or by a new suggestion. Phelips was not the Speaker to formulate the question. He was more likely to pick up a phrase from someone's speech and use it as the basis of the question, but in such a way as to blunt or evade the main issue. He was not unpracticed in thwarting the aims of the House and in making glad the hearts of Privy Councillors. The reader of Sir Edward's letters to Salisbury in the footnotes to Bowyer's diary will discover for himself the exultation of Sir Edward when he believed that he had circumvented the majority by the form in which he had put the question.[10] He prided himself on his subtlety; his opponents might have thought of him as not at all subtle but, rather, adept at confusing members as to the issue before them.[11] It was hard, nevertheless, to stand up to the man in the chair, who had usage on his side. It was a principle, "not to gainsay the Speaker in making the question." [12]

How far could he stop men from speaking? [13] Bores were not unknown, and they would hold the floor until young members would "hem and haw." The Speaker might deem it the part of kindness to cut off an orator.[14] He might offer the excuse that it was time for such and such a committee to meet, but he hardly needed excuses. When the House was jammed with motions and bills it became necessary to turn away new business, and the Speaker would refuse motions that called "for committees, of multiplicity, or infinite business." [15] He could exercise discretion.

Occasionally he was blamed for exercising it unfairly. In 1581, the Speaker (John Popham) was accused by Anthony Cope of putting the question in order to "prejudice the speeches of the

members of this House." [16] I do not recall that Phelips was ever
censured for putting the question in order to choke off a speech,
though from what we know of him it is hard to believe that he
did not. On the last of June, 1607, in a debate on the sale of
copyhold lands, Sir Robert Johnson, an M.P. for the borough of
Monmouth and an officer of the ordnance, rose to address the
House and, when he saw the Speaker's frown, resumed his seat.
Perhaps the House disapproved of the frown, for they called Sir
Robert up, and he was allowed his say. [17]

On at least one occasion the House approved Sir Edward's interruption of a speech. On May 28, 1607, the House was dealing
with the vexing problem of remanding—that is, whether an
Englishman or a Scot who had been accused of crimes in the
other nation and had fled to his own native country, should be
remanded to the other country for trial. It was a complicated
problem, and Sir Daniel Donne was discussing it when the
Speaker interrupted him. Phelips had asked for and been given
leave by the House to interrupt. The Speaker went on to ask all
members to forbear discussing the subject, since it concerned the
King, who had given royal commissions for remanding. [18]

The Speaker had to remind the House of this matter and that.
The Commons were likely to postpone a topic until a future day
and then to forget it on that day and have to be reminded the
next morning. Again and again the Speaker had to tell a member,
who would bring up what he deemed an important subject, that
the matter was already under discussion in a committee. To keep
the House on the rails and to make certain that it followed
through on matters that had been raised required watchfulness.
In that respect Phelips was not wanting.

The duty of maintaining the privileges of the House devolved
on the Speaker. Members of the House were arrested for debt;
more frequently their servants were arrested for one reason or
another. Such arrests were quickly brought to the attention of
the Speaker. He would raise the question of privilege, and as
soon as possible the House would take action to set the member
or his servant free.

Freedom of speech was another privilege where the Speaker might have played a useful part. Such members as Fuller, Hoskins, and Wentworth were likely to make speeches that would be quickly reported to the King and would rouse his anger. Fuller might allude unpleasantly to the Scots, and Wentworth might cite precedents against the right of the Crown to levy impositions. Occasionally the Commons might absolve such members by a resolution, in order to head off action by the King against the outspoken member. More often the watchful Salisbury would somehow fail to move against offending members until His Majesty's attention was turned to something else. On at least one occasion Salisbury called in four members, including the three mentioned above, and conceivably may have told them how difficult they made it for him with his master. I do not find that the Speaker tried to cut off such men from speaking, but this may be because we have so few records. It is possible that the Clerk, perhaps with the connivance of the Speaker, left out of his minutes some speeches that would provoke royal recrimination. One runs across stray allusions to plainspoken speeches that are not mentioned in the *Commons Journals*.

In general the Speaker failed to express the will of the House. At the very beginning of his regime, when the Goodwin-Fortescue election controversy had reached an impasse, he must have been aware that the Commons were deeply interested that they, and they only, should decide upon the validity of elections to their membership. This was the time when the Speaker might have upheld the will of the House, or at least have been neutral. Instead he did what he could to assist the King and the Privy Council in what was a rather shady maneuver. Finally, on April 2, 1604, he made an effort to draw the House into a reconsideration of its decision not to confer with the judges about the case. The Commons resolved that "a question being once made . . . cannot be questioned again." [19]

Now and then the House did overrule the Speaker. On February 13, 1606/07, after the holiday recess, the Speaker offered to read to the Commons the notes delivered to him by the Recorder,

Montague, of the conference between the committees of the two Houses. The reader will recall the episode. Those notes, affirmed Phelips, were the objections and answers made in that conference.[20] The conference had been a stormy one, and the Lords had pressed the Commons hard. The Commons rejected Montague's notes and resolved that the Commoners who had taken part in the conference should report orally to them.[21] They could hardly have indicated more clearly their want of confidence in their presiding officer.

In small matters Phelips was useful.[22] When the Commons resolved to send thanks to the King for allowing them to treat of tenures, but were proposing to convey their gratitude on their own by their Speaker, Phelips urged them to inform the Lords, a proposal that the Commons readily accepted.[23] When Fuller brought in from the committee a series of grievances, the Speaker suggested that the grievances ought to be divided into two kinds, those against the law and those not against the law, but nevertheless grievances.[24]

When the Cowell case was before the Commons in 1610 the Speaker proposed that the Committee for Grievances (from which Sandys was reporting) should consider again with what to charge Dr. Cowell, implying, possibly, that a precise charge might be hard to formulate.[25] But Phelips was at his best in pointing out small corrections, additions, and subtractions that would improve the text of a bill or statement. A proposed addition to a bill was unnecessary, he might indicate, because the matter was really covered in an existing statute.

The Effect of the Speaker on Bills and Committees IT was the business of the Speaker to keep the House moving. Frequent consultations with the Clerk were necessary. None knew better than he the various kinds of pressure for this or that measure, or the dissatisfaction that accumulated when certain bills did not move forward.

The bringing in of bills had its proper times. Important measures were not to be introduced until eight or nine in the morning. The time before that was allotted to private bills, over which the Speaker (with the aid of the Clerk) had special oversight.[1] Bills were not generally read in the afternoon, but once in a while an afternoon session had to be given over in part to bills. In that case the Speaker was likely to run over those bills the next morning for the benefit of those who had been absent the preceding afternoon.[2]

The routine of keeping bills moving was well established. All bills were read twice; the second reading usually followed within two or three days of the first. After the second reading the bill was committed, engrossed (if there were no debate or opposition), rejected, or, in rare instances, recommitted.[3] If it became evident to the Speaker after hearing debate that the bill had a good deal of support, he would await a motion for committing it [4] and then would hear nominations from the floor for membership on the committee; when he deemed that enough had been nominated, he would shut off further nominations. Thus he was the judge of the size of the committee, assisted, no doubt, by the Clerk.

Meanwhile the Clerk had been setting down the names as fast as they were called out, not always with complete accuracy. It would have been possible for the Clerk to add or subtract names; it is conceivable that the Speaker might have gone over the list with the Clerk, after he had written them down, and, by way of correction, have inserted or subtracted names. The choice of names was not accidental. It was believed that the members of the Privy Council made more than their share of the nominations. The author of "Policies in Parliament" tells us that "fault hath been found and motion made against it that they above the Chair [Privy Councillors] have named all the committees." [5]

In a general way, all those who had spoken in favor of a bill or who had made suggestions for its improvement in phraseology, or for its clarification, were at once put on the committee. But the Speaker had to be careful that no one who had opposed the bill be given a place on the committee.[6] In this matter it was rather easy to overreach the Speaker. A member who wished to undermine a bill might speak for it, making, however, a plea for certain amendments. Almost automatically he would be named to the committee and then, in committee, he could press for amendments nullifying the intentions of those who drew up the measure. The author of "Policies in Parliament" wrote: "Tis a common policy . . . if any man be against a bill, but would not seem to be so, to speak for it and by way of objection to shew such matter against it, as may not be answered, which notwithstanding he must seem to answer himself."[7] Against such maneuvers the Speaker seems to have devised no remedy. Nor was he in a position to prevent the packing of a committee either by Privy Councillors or by zealous Puritans who urged their supporters to do just that.

It was the duty of the Speaker to see that the committee system functioned, that committees were set up, and that they reported.

When a bill was committed, the paper draft of the bill with the names of the committee and place of the meeting inscribed on one side of the folded paper was sometimes handed to the one who was to take charge of the bill. Did the Speaker name the man to take charge, or did the Clerk do it? Or did someone from the floor nominate him? We can eliminate the last possibility. In the last years of Elizabeth it would appear from D'Ewes that the man to take charge of a bill was not uncommonly a Privy Councillor or some leading official. But in the reign of James I the man to take charge was often the one who had originally proposed it, and who was "following" it.[8] He was to see that the bill came into the hands of the committee. I do not find that he presided over that committee.

The reports from the committee constituted a problem for the Speaker. It is hard to discover just how the Speaker brought pressure upon the committee to bring in its report. Possibly he left that to the Clerk. If he had not exerted himself to push committees into action, many committees would never have brought in their reports, a failure he did not always regret. When the report was finally made, the troubles of the Speaker were not ended. Deletions from and additions to the bill would bring forth new arguments, and the upshot might be a bill interlined with amendment. Such bills were not always approved by the Lords, who might return the bill to the Commons, meaning more delay.[9]

The development of the committee system eventually affected the importance of the Speaker. Whether Phelips realized that the constant use of the committee was limiting his activities, we do not know. He made no public comment, as far as I know, upon the committee and its relation to himself. I am not certain that any of those members who had to do with the expanding use of the new parliamentary mechanism foresaw its consequences. The Speaker might well have pointed out to the members of the House that to thresh everything over twice, once in the Committee of the Whole House and then in the House, was to waste time and energy. Sometimes, as has been noted in an earlier chapter, a bill was discussed in the House and then in the Committee of the Whole House and then in the House again. Had there been serious complaint about such double or triple scrutiny of bills, members might have replied that it ensured adequate consideration of complicated measures.

The Speaker's Function in Debates

THE Speaker's main function was to preside over debate. The debate on a bill followed the second reading, and the Speaker had to keep it within bounds. If there were tilts between members and the exchange of sharp words, it was the Speaker's duty to see that the discussion ran smoothly and made progress. At the same time he aimed to give every member, even the tedious, a chance to relieve their minds.

When the subject under discussion involved the interests of certain members, the Speaker would ask the members concerned to leave the House during the debate. However, this request was seldom made.

The Speaker had to deal with long silences. When the House was distressed by a message from the King and did not know what to do next the members were likely to lapse into silence, as we have seen. There was little for the Speaker to do but to wait until the House was ready to resume discussion. In one instance, the Speaker, to fill in the time and occupy the attention of the House, read the new proclamation sent out by the King about purveyance. Perhaps he hoped in that way to indicate to members that the Crown was doing something to ameliorate the evils of purveyance.

The role of the Speaker as a participant in the debates of the House was somewhat ill defined. In Elizabethan days the Speaker had now and again been accused of interfering in the debate, of supporting a measure, of bringing up again and again a bill that had been rejected, of moving for a committee to frame a bill, or of rising and leaving the House in order to prevent a vote on a measure.[1] Such charges were not, however, common. In some cases the Elizabethan Speaker cooperated with the Commons and was not looked upon as an agent of the Queen; but it was not always so.[2] Phelips regarded himself as a servant of the Crown, and he found it hard not to speak up for his master. It will be recalled that he opposed the Bill of Assarts. Twice in the debate on remanding in 1607 he had taken part in the argument.[3] When on June 25, 1604, the Bill against Simony was reported from the committee and some defects were pointed out (presumably by the Speaker), it was moved by the Speaker that some of the committees meet with him in the afternoon to confer about the bill before it was brought in the next morning.[4] In 1604 the role of the Speaker in the debate was summarized: "If any doubt arise upon a bill the Speaker to explain; sometimes to argue—always fit and he ought. Not to sway the House with any reasons or disputations."[5] The statement was nearly as vague as the actual practice of the time.

Whatever his rights historically, it is clear, I think, that the first Speaker in a Stuart Parliament—perhaps because there was so much opposition to the King and because Phelips was so obviously trying to check that opposition—had less actual influence on debates than most of his predecessors.

The question of the union drew the Speaker into the debates. On May 24, 1604, the Lower House was debating the Commission for the Union when the opinions of the lawyers were mentioned. That brought Sandys to his feet. He declared that, by the cunning of the lawyers, matters had been carried in the last three Parliaments "clean contrary to the meaning of the House in matters ecclesiastical." Sandys was not unacquainted with ecclesiastical problems. The Speaker tried to defend the lawyers but was "interrupted and not suffered to speak," [6] so the Clerk recorded.

On November 27, 1606, the Speaker was summarizing the debate on hostile laws and over commerce between England and Scotland, and "descending to the question," when he was interrupted by a speech of Sir Edwin Sandys.[7]

It will be remembered that on April 28, 1607, Sandys did not please the Speaker when he pleaded for a "perfect Union." For months, as the reader will recall, the House had been wrestling with details of the union and had become increasingly discouraged with the complexity of the problems involved. Sandys suddenly offered a cure-all—the "perfect Union." [8] This was too much for the Speaker, who rose and said that the project now offered was new [9] and had not been moved either in the House or in the committee, "which," he continued, "I take to be the cause of the present silence." Would the House, he inquired, deliberate on this subject until tomorrow, "or now to dispute of those matters which have already been dealt in?" [10]

When Sir Thomas Holcroft, M.P. for Cheshire, urged the Commons to discuss the matters in hand where they had been left, the Speaker jumped at the suggestion. At that point Croft rose and accused the Speaker of disingenuousness. The Speaker, he declared, had asked the House to forbear any further move until they heard from His Majesty. Now he was telling them that the project of Sir Edwin was new and not to be dealt with, but that they should dispute of the matter already discussed which he had asked them to put off until they had heard further from His Majesty. Whether Croft's charge was just or not—we can hardly judge without more knowledge of the details—an important member of the House had openly charged the Speaker with playing fast and loose, and no one, so far as we have information, made any move to defend him.

The Speaker and the Lords

THE Speaker was at pains to see that negotiations between the Upper and the Lower Houses proceeded smoothly and that conferences between committees of the two Houses were held. He would remind the Commons that this and that subject made a conference necessary and that preparations for a conference should be made.[1] When, in March of 1607, the Commons complained that their elderly members suffered from having to stand up during long conferences, and it was suggested that Bacon be sent to the Lords to ask that the Commons be granted "more ease" on such occasions, Phelips broke in to say that he believed the matter was known to the Lords and that they would provide ease for the Commons.[2] The Speaker did not wish the Commons to forget or to neglect their betters. The Elizabethan House of Commons had often conferred with the Lords and sought their opinions. The early Jacobean House was still willing to have the Lords seem to lead, if they led in the right direction. But by 1607 and 1610 their deference to the Lords was less evident.

It has already been mentioned that the Speaker was interested in conferences. He was familiar with the use of them in Elizabethan times. When, on June 9, 1607, Sir Anthony Cope moved that, at the first meeting of a committee with a committee of the Lords on the subject of hostile laws, the Commons should only listen and not argue but at the second meeting the spokesmen of the two Houses might confer about doubtful points, the Speaker agreed that such a policy was proper when new matters had been brought before the Commons from the Lords. He maintained that, when the Commons had brought up a matter with which they were familiar and were prepared at once to argue the case, they ought to do so.

An examination of sources from 1572 to 1601,[3] from such incomplete records as are known, makes one suspect that about the matter of debating in conference there was as yet no fixed policy but that in many conferences the two Houses did discuss matters with one another. In the early years of the reign of James there was a marked change in this respect, a change that David Willson brought out in his masterly study of *The Privy Councillors and the House of Commons.*[4] Many of the conferences, he wrote, became meetings between committees of the Houses and the Privy Councillors and others from the Lords. The committee members from the Commons, addressed by one Councillor after another, found it hard not to yield to their authority. Francis Tate, M.P. for Shrewsbury, in writing of Elizabethan Parliaments declared that nothing shook the liberty of the House of Commons so much as "often conferences." He spoke of the "terrifying" of members by the Lords, merely by their presence and perhaps by their opinions. In 1604 Sir Edward Hoby, an influential figure from Elizabethan days, objected to a conference because he thought the Lords had made up their minds, and "being resolved they were over-weighty for us."[5] On November 26, 1606, Sandys commented: "In the conference with Lords we have rather lost ground commonly than gained."[6] Again and again Salisbury sought to persuade the Commons that the conferences should consist of proper debates back and forth. But the Commons would have none of it. The Speaker's opinion had no weight with them. It seldom had.

*The Speaker and
the King*

IT has been more than hinted that the Speaker and the Commons did not see eye to eye, and that the Speaker was more interested in pleasing His Majesty than in making smooth the way for the Commons.

In the eyes of James, Parliament had one significant function: to grant him money. Laws were useful of course, he would have admitted, but enough of them were already on the books. If abuses needed attention, he could take care of them by proclamation and administration. He knew how to keep the state on an even keel, but it required money.

The Speaker collaborated. With a touching, if timeserving, loyalty, he did what he could to lead the House toward the consideration of subsidies and away from the less agreeable theme of grievances. He was persevering. When at long length the Commons voted one or two subsidies, he would suggest that something might be added. When he proved unable to persuade them of that, he would propose that the first subsidy be paid at an earlier date than that set down.

He displayed equal zeal in forwarding the union. He knew the importance the King attached to that; it was to be James's monument in the ages to come. In raising that monument the Speaker was a persistent collaborator. From 1605 to the end of 1607 he strove to encourage discussion and to lead the House to a vote and a conclusion. When some aspect of the proposed legislation displeased those in Whitehall, the Speaker was quick to point out to the Commons that this and that clause touched the King's honor. He had lit upon a magic phrase that put the Commons on the defensive, but their leaders were seldom better than when in that position. It had required only a few months for the Commons to take the measure of their Speaker and their attitude toward him hardened.

An episode of May 1607 (dealt with in the last section on the union) put the Speaker and then His Majesty on the defensive. It will be recalled that the King, through the Speaker, adjourned the House for a week. Bowyer commented: "So the expectation of the House to have had a report of the proceedings of the committees in the Bill for Abolishing Hostile Laws and of the newly-added proviso against the remanding of prisoners was frustrate. . . . So in this some doubted art." [1] That is, the King was suspected of adjourning the House in order to wear down members and thus induce them to accept his clause as to remanding. The Speaker was also blamed by many, and he was at pains to indicate that he had acted under orders. He was not content, as a subordinate, to take the blame and thus help out His Majesty.

In the spring session of 1610 the Speaker and the Commons disagreed sharply, it will be recalled, over the supposed message from the King forbidding the Commons to discuss impositions. It was a startling message, the most serious attack on their privileges that they had experienced. If they could not debate the King's right to levy impositions, they would lose control over the purse, and the King might find Parliament unnecessary. They were in hard case, to use the idiom of the time. But they could not fail to notice a revealing circumstance, that the message had come as a direct result of what had happened the day before and that the King was, as everyone knew, out of town. They pressed the Speaker, it will be recalled, as to how he received the message, and from whom; they worried him into letting the cat out of the bag, that the message had come from the Privy Council.

Had the King been responsible for the message (we now know that he was), the Speaker could have cited precedents for his action from the reign of the great Queen. Many of those who sat in the House could have remembered the sharp injunctions from the Queen to cease discussing certain subjects, and they would have been glad to forget how tamely they had accepted her commands and had not even said a word about old privileges.

There was this difference between Phelips and those Elizabethan Speakers. Their sympathies, we have seen, had sometimes been with the Commons. Phelips was intent at all times to serve His Majesty, hoping, no doubt, for the good things that came with royal favor. This time, too, the House had caught the Speaker out. His hand had been forced, and, they may have whispered, could be forced again.

Phelips was, however, often successful. He could hold up or put off measures that he knew the King did not like. It was easy to suggest that, before such and such a bill were passed, precedents bearing upon it should be looked up. When the Duke of Lennox's patent for the new draperies was brought forward as a grievance, the Speaker proposed that former statutes and patents be examined. The bills to do away with ecclesiastical abuses, pluralities, nonresidence, etc., which were continually being introduced, moved slowly from stage to stage, as the Speaker probably intended. On May 11, 1604, Richard James from Newport on the Isle of Wight called for a second reading of a bill against pluralities, but the Speaker interrupted him and cut him off.[2] This he could do by the ruling he had made that Members should not speak when introducing bills.

Phelips was able to push certain measures. On May 26 he brought in a bill against shooting with guns and the destroying of hares and for the preservation of pheasants and partridges. This measure had been drawn by the King's command, and the Clerk believed that it had been drawn by His Majesty himself. On its second reading it was sent to a committee of about thirty-two members. It was a revamping of an earlier bill introduced on April 19 that was "dashed" on May 19. The new bill from His Majesty passed the Commons and the Lords.

Phelips did much else in support of the King. He was able to put off the consideration of grievances; he sought to limit the number of them presented and to have the evils connected with them minimized. He tried to circumvent those who were pushing for a law against purveyors. He talked of the "inconvenience"[3] of the purveyance bill and suggested, with what seemed almost defiance, that the King could issue a *non obstante* and thus dispense with such a law.

His way of taking matters into his own hands in order to help the King did not please all members. A minister named Arbury had drawn up a petition, had it printed by a Mr. Jones, and a copy handed to the Speaker. The Speaker informed the Commons briefly of the petition but refused to have it read. He forwarded it to His Majesty, who promptly ordered Jones imprisoned. Martin declared that it was injurious that any Speaker should deliver any bill to the King without the privity of the House, and Berkeley concurred.[4] Strode mentioned another cause of dissatisfaction. The Speaker had received a message from the King through some of the Lords. It was growing upon the

Speaker, declared Berkeley, to receive messages from some of the Lords. Yelverton remarked of the Speaker: "not [to] believe him as he is Speaker."

At times the Speaker had a good case. The Bill of Assarts (1604) was brought into the House by some obscure person; it was proposed to regularize the holdings of country gentlemen who had helped themselves to Crown lands, some of them on the margin of their own lands. Phelips told the House that he could point out thirty-two absurdities in the measure, and he put in a paper on the subject which was indeed a forceful argument. It did little good. Country gentlemen were eager to establish their titles to lands that had belonged to the Crown and voted for the bill.[5]

In June and July 1607 the Commons and the Speaker collided. A committee had framed a petition for the better execution of the laws against recusants, and the Speaker was pressed to read it. He explained carefully to the House that His Majesty had taken notice of the petition and would be careful to enforce the laws. It was a matter, declared the Speaker, belonging to the King.[6] When members asserted that to deny the petition was to wound the dignity and gravity of the House, the Speaker reminded them of Elizabethan precedents where the Queen had restrained the House from meddling. As to those precedents he was right, but the members of the House, who were accustomed to seeing precedents quoted only against the Crown, seemed ill satisfied. His Majesty, ever quick on the pen, sent a long message on the subject, but concluded with a concession, or at least with what seemed a concession. His Majesty would not be offended if the petition were read in the House.[7]

On the day following it was moved that no entry should be made in the Clerk's Book (the *Commons Journal*) of any matter concerning privileges, or of any message or letter from His Majesty, unless the same were allowed by the Committee for Privileges. This course the Speaker "much dissuaded," and with good reason. The Clerk, he explained, made at first only short notes and then perfected them after the Parliament had ceased—

too late for a committee to act.[8] But Alford and Sandys opposed the Speaker, and the motion was carried. Why were the Commons so cautious about allowing the Clerk to record the messages of the King? Was it sheer antagonism to His Majesty? Was it to prevent the arguments set forth by the King from being used by the supporters of the Crown in later Parliaments? Were they afraid of precedents for prerogative? Or were they merely voting against a presiding officer whom they had come to dislike?

The Speaker's role as a protagonist of royal policy had been a difficult one. In the Queen's time there had usually been enough Privy Councillors in the Lower House to speak for the Crown, and there were other members competent to present its case. In her day Privy Councillors had more influence with the House, not only because they were abler men but because they were at times sympathetic with the Commons and even receptive to complaints about grievances, especially if they were not ecclesiastical.

The Jacobean government had at first one Privy Councillor in the House of Commons, and that was Sir John Herbert, a man of little influence. Sir John Fortescue, who had been a Privy Councillor in the last years of Elizabeth's reign and who continued to be one until his death in 1614, became in 1606 an M.P. for Middlesex. He was, however, old and tired and had little to say. Sir Thomas Parry, earlier an ambassador to France and a Privy Councillor, became an M.P. for St. Albans in 1610.

It was Sir Robert Cecil, Earl of Salisbury, a former House of Commons man, who, by the conferences arranged between the two Houses and by his connections with the leaders in the Lower House, was able to do much for the cause of His Majesty.

Nevertheless the new sovereign had no such hold on the Commons as his predecessor had easily maintained throughout a long reign. Elizabeth had been something of a tyrant, no doubt, but she had a way with her, and success was written on her banner. The new sovereign was an "intellectual," to use a modern word, but he had an uncanny talent for making himself disliked, and within one short year. Hence it was that Phelips's aggressive support of the

Crown did not make his task as a presiding official an agreeable one. His concluding days in office were far from happy. The long struggle in 1607 over the union, and the May 1610 cross-questioning of him by unfriendly members of the House about the message concerning impositions, must have left their mark upon him. Last of all, an episode at the close of the 1610 session seemed to be the undignified anticlimax to his career as Speaker. With almost incredible simplicity he complained to the House that Sir Edward Herbert had challenged him on the street and "popped his mouth with his finger in scorn." The very next morning he had done it again, "put off his hat, put out his tongue, and plopt with his mouth." [9]

Rashly the Speaker demanded satisfaction. Herbert rose and declared that he had meant no offense to the House, a lame apology and regarded as such by the Speaker, who was "worse satisfied than before."

Whether the House laughed the Clerk does not inform us. Certainly the members took no steps, so far as the records show, to punish Herbert, or to condemn his childish gesture. They remarked that the Speaker should not have asserted that he would complain to the King. Such a complaint would no doubt have been regarded by some as an interference with the privileges of the House. The position of the Speaker must have become almost unendurable.

Yet he had all the appurtenances of dignity attached to his office. At the close of the day's proceeding he rose first, and members awaited his progress toward the door before they ventured to rise and depart. When members went out early, they bowed to him. All speeches were addressed to him. When a member violated any rule, he had to apologize to the Speaker.

Phelips could not measure up to the dignity imposed upon him. His methods of attaining his ends were less than becoming. His continuous effort to serve the Crown by small delays and petty excuses did not become his office, and exposed him to the indignity of being overruled. He lacked that confidence and poise which sometimes command success.

Epilogue

I WISH to add a few pages of comment on topics already mentioned, comments which, if inserted in the debates, might render the narrative less easy to follow. I shall offer a few observations on the relations of the Privy Council to the Commons. I shall go on to say something about the committee system and the changes taking place in it. In their struggles with the Crown the Commons were meeting with some success, especially as to freedom of speech. Rashly perhaps, I have gone out of my way to deal briefly with a few might-have-beens; they afford footnotes to history and are not wholly irrelevant. I cannot conclude without further remarks about the character of James I.

First, as to the Privy Council and the Commons, it will be recalled that Sir Edward Hoby in a letter to Edmondes in 1606 had noted the want of able Councillors in the Commons.[1] This weakness was brought out in a long essay (1924) and in a book (1940).[2] Since I wrote the first draft of this book, I have gone over the sources for the Commons in its relation to the Privy Council from the beginning of the *Commons Journals* (1547) to 1610 and have not found a great deal to restate. But I have ventured to say it again in brief for the sake of the layman, and to add a few details.

The role of an Elizabethan Councillor in the Commons was a responsible one. In an earlier time the Councillors had looked upon Parliament as a ratifying body that added a sanction to policies or measures already determined upon, and also as the bestower of subsidies. If in the Queen's last years the Privy Councillors were possibly less dominant than before, they were still the recognized leaders of the Commons. The Queen had a group of about three to seven in the Commons, smoothing the way for certain bills and putting the brakes on those distasteful to Her Majesty. Some of those Councillors, such as Cecil and a few others, were at times not unwilling to go along with the Commons, so far as feasible; one of them might even mention a grievance that called for consideration. Councillors served on many committees, a task they dared not shirk, for decisions made in committees were seldom reversed in the House.

In the first decade of the following reign the role of Privy Councillors was less significant. When the Commons met in March 1604 two Sir Johns were Councillors and M.P.'s: Sir John Herbert, M.P. for Monmouthshire, Second Secretary; and Sir John Stanhope, M.P. for Newtown in the Isle of Wight and Vice-Chamberlain. Neither seems to have been a leader in the Jacobean House. Herbert appears rarely in the *Commons Journals,* and Stanhope, so far as is known, never spoke for or against any bills, but was useful in relaying messages between the King and the Commons and between the Lords and the Commons.

Three other men (possibly four)[3] served between 1606 and 1610, the last two only in 1610, as both Privy Councillors and M.P.'s. In February of 1605/06, Sir John Fortescue, a Privy Councillor since 1589, was found a seat as M.P. for Middlesex; but he was old, seldom spoke in the Commons, and died in December 1607. Sir Thomas Parry became a Privy Councillor in December 1607 and an M.P. for St. Albans in 1610. He served on two committees; if he made a speech, I have not found it. In 1610 Sir Julius Caesar, a Privy Councillor since 1608, appeared in the Commons as M.P. for Westminster and proved a Councillor somewhat on the Elizabethan model.

If the new sovereign had no impressive core of Councillors in the sessions of the Commons from 1604 to 1610, he had other means of getting his case before them. The persuasive Cecil, who had been lost to the Commons, was able in conferences between the two Houses—probably by personal connections—to look out for the interests of the King. Further, His Majesty often addressed the Parliament, not always to his advantage. It has to be added that the royal cause was not advanced by the King's obvious preferences for his Scottish cronies. He would have been wise to cultivate those M.P.'s in the Commons who took the lead in upholding his policies: Sir Francis Bacon, Sir George More, and others. He was quick to snub those who worked or spoke against what he deemed his aims, but not shrewd enough to play up to those on his side.[4]

I have alluded earlier to the significance of committees. It will be recalled that in the later years of the Queen a few committees were being overburdened with bills to consider. But a more serious problem was that the active and well-known figures were nominated to one committee after another, occasionally to as many as five, and, since many committees met at 2:00 p.m., those members found it impossible to attend all the committees on which they had been placed. Hence committees with useful measures before them had sometimes to be put off for want of attendance, and important bills failed to be reported out from committee. It was also unfortunate that the less well-known M.P.'s were put on minor committees, or on none.[5]

In the 1604 session and later ones, the piling up of bills on a few committees became less common, and obscure members were more often—though not often enough—named to committees. It seems not unlikely that those who talked over the coming session in advance may have taken steps to see that bills were distributed to more committees and that the important committees were not so largely made up of the same old group of prominent figures but included able men not yet in the public eye. For some reason committees were functioning better, though there was still dissatisfaction.

It has been observed already, but is relevant here, that committees usually met in the early afternoon and that by that hour the more easygoing and less concerned members might well have found their way back to their lodgings or offices, while those intent on change and better government may have stayed on to attend committees. Thus the zealous might gain their ends.[6]

It was not only in respect to committees that the new House of Commons was doing better. In the old days the Upper House had among their members a majority of the Privy Council and had in general been an ally of the Crown. The Lords were still likely to support the King, but the changes ahead were to lessen the influence of the Lords and to increase that of the Commons. When we look back as far as the reign of Henry VIII, we do not find much precise information about the relative position of the two Houses, but we do discover that things were stirring in the Commons and that the sovereign, in his conflict with the papacy, welcomed the help of the Commons. In the latter days of the Queen, the Commons, despite her authoritative interferences, were gaining in assurance and, I suspect, in public interest and estimation. Occasionally they were venturing to differ sharply from the Lords, and that august body was at times assuming an almost defensive attitude.

About the fundamental privilege of free speech, the Commons in the reign of James were moving ahead more rapidly than in the preceding reign, perhaps more rapidly than ever before. From an early date the Speaker had been accustomed to ask that the Commons, among their old privileges, should enjoy free speech. It was a request regularly granted, occasionally with reservations, and sometimes as if it were of slight consequence. But in 1593 the Queen spoke out in unequivocal language:

> Privilege of speech is granted, but you must know what privilege you have, not to speak every one what he listeth, or what comes in his brain to utter that; but your privilege is I or No. Wherefore, Mr. Speaker, her Majesty's pleasure is that if you perceive any idle heads which will not stick to hazard their estates, which will meddle with reforming the Church and transforming the Commonwealth, and do exhibit any bills to such purpose, that you receive them not until they be viewed and considered by those who, it is fitter, should consider of such things and can better judge of them.[7]

Elizabeth's threat to confiscate the lands of those whose speeches displeased her was no more high-handed than her command to the Commons to drop certain measures before them, or her sending to prison for a vacation (usually short) those whose utterances dealt with matters that she believed to be her prerogative.

James was even more intolerant of speeches in opposition. In one instance he came near to identifying criticism of royal policy with treason. He urged upon the Privy Council immediate punishment for such speakers as Wentworth of Oxford, but found Councillors in no hurry to carry out his wishes. It has been suggested earlier that Cecil may have been to blame for the failure to imprison the offenders, and he may have been supported by other Councillors, such as Lord Knollys and Julius Caesar.

In their skirmishes with His Majesty, in their differences with the Lords, and in their gradual assumption of an initiating role, the Commons were gaining a new status. It was most apparent in their dealings with the sovereign. More than at any time in the preceding reign the members were taking issue with the Crown, and not wholly in vain. In 1607 the King had failed to gain approval for his design of the union. In 1610 he had struck boldly at the right of the Commons to discuss impositions and had been maneuvered into retreat. That great power of which he boasted was slowly proving a mirage. In time the Commons discovered that, when opposed, James would wobble (he had been timid from childhood) and then explain that he had been misunderstood, or cover his retreat by some other device.[8] The Commons did not forget that discovery.

The opposition moved as if they felt things coming their way. Opinion in that time is hard to gauge because men were wary of putting on paper what they thought of the King. But there can be little doubt that public opinion had turned against the King, not only in general but on the issues between King and Commons. Even such intelligent upholders of the Crown as Sir George More and Sir Henry Montague were affected, I infer, by the shift of opinion, and were trimming their sails. It seems probable that Cecil, whose ear was always to the ground, was aware of the trend of opinion and may have tried to inform His Majesty, who still cherished the pleasant illusion that he was beloved of his people.

If the King had pursued a more moderate policy, if he had listened more to Cecil or to Francis Bacon, who had ideas about "comprehension" and might have led James along a middle path, and listened less to Northampton or to those of his ilk, the opposition in the Commons might have seen its majority of twenty to thirty slipping away. The King might have been voted the subsidies he sorely needed. To continue the might-have-beens—a practice historians should indulge sparingly—the Civil War might have been avoided and the Revolution proved unnecessary. Parliament might have shared power with the King, and the Cabinet system —the greatest of the several English political gifts to the world— might possibly have evolved earlier than it actually did. The long but steady growth of English popular government may be regarded as a constitutional romance with a happy ending. From the first Henrys the juries of appraisal suggest some faint approaches to local government. From the first Edwards, men in the county court and in the boroughs were choosing other men to speak and act for them at the center. In the long run—the very long run—Parliament was to prove too much for kings.

Or, to look at it from another angle, take the tour of Windsor Castle, gaze at the portrait of Hanoverian kings of England, and consider whether those rather dull men were likely to retain real power in an enlightened era.

The might-have-beens are many, and it is easy but nevertheless tempting to speculate further and along another line. It would seem to be labeling insincerity as a virtue to suggest that the Commons did not flatter His Majesty enough. But should not the leaders in opposition have been willing to stretch the truth as brazenly as Cecil did when pleading with the Commons to come to the help of their sovereign? [9] At the very time when James was indignant—indeed angry—with the Commons, Cecil was informing them that the King had confidence in them and that he recognized they had dutifully and discreetly entertained his request for subsidies. Had the leaders in opposition masked their distrust of James and poured forth honeyed words, they might conceivably have won real concessions.[10] Those leaders were too downright, too earnest, in well-doing, too old English, to indulge in the emollient phrases that might possibly have proved effective. His Majesty fished for adulation; [11] he required it for his health, as he required hunting. The opposition might have followed the example of Sandys, who now and then let fall words of praise for His Majesty. As for his insincerity, Sandys did not in all cases say exactly what we can be reasonably sure he believed.[12] Had he been as forthright as Hoskins or Wentworth of Oxford, he might have found it hard to maintain the majority for the opposition. To keep running in the same light harness Puritan extremists, those who disliked the Scots, and those intent on doing away with wardship, required a cool and flexible driver, and that Sandys was. But again I am playing with ifs.

A comparison of the debates in the Lower House during the last decade of Elizabeth's reign with those in the first decade of the next reign must be impressionistic, since we command much less than the whole story. But it seems fairly evident that the Elizabethan speakers were dealing at one time or another with a wide range of topics in which they happened to be interested, a miscellany in which the opinions uttered were in some degree individual and personal. In the first decade of James, the M.P.'s devoted themselves mainly to wardship, purveyance, the union with Scotland, ecclesiastical abuses, and trade topics upon which they were informed and able to speak, not only for themselves but for those with whom they had talked, a body of opinion. About a few serious grievances they felt deeply, and thus the debates were, I am inclined to believe, on a higher level than in late Elizabethan days.[13] Certainly the speeches were more pungent.

That is hardly surprising, for in session after session the Commons were gaining a more enlightened membership. The best of the reading country gentlemen and the abler lawyers were coveting seats at St. Stephen's and were pulling strings to get them. I suspect that the membership continued to gain in quality in the following decades, but that remains to be proved. In 1610, when the debates afford good reading for those interested in constitutional trends, we come upon the speeches of Hakewill, Whitelocke, and others with pleasure and even excitement. They had been pondering on the annals of the English, on the *Rotuli Parliamentorum,* on Bracton, and on various chronicles, and were feeling their way toward a philosophy of English history—a lawyer-like philosophy, but a philosophy that was long to engage thinkers and theorists.

It is not possible to prove it beyond question, but I have little doubt that the leaders in opposition were getting together in 1607 and 1610,[14] and that a few of them, perhaps around a table in a committee room or in one of the Inns of Court, were arranging the course of the next day's debate. That may also have been happening in 1605/06 when the list of grievances had to be trimmed down to the most serious. It was not yet happening in 1604, for the opposition had not found itself.

The reader will hardly have forgotten the amazing egoism James displayed in his conversations with ambassadors and others, conversations that were gleefully relayed to Paris and that no doubt occasioned amusement among Londoners in the know. To the ambassadors from France he must have seemed naïve and unsophisticated. He told listeners that during the last years of the Queen he had really ruled England. He regarded himself as a great monarch, one of the two greatest in the last hundred years. That he was a kind of god on earth and in touch with a Higher Power was implied more than once. As one reads over his seemingly confident but utterly inaccurate statements about his dealings with the Commons, one asks if this strange personage did not in some mystical fashion assume that what he said was the truth, or became the truth.[15] Yet in another mood he could declare himself a man with a man's passions. The Scots could be both mystics and realists. To one who has had to read his conversations, it would seem that he deceived himself and lived much of the time in a dream world. He did not intend to lie, nor was he adept in that ancient art, though he had practiced it from childhood.

A foolish man, look you, like Shakespeare's parson, but without that character's benevolence. That he was wanting in common sense Elizabeth and her diplomats in Edinburgh soon discovered. Yet he was learned—at least for royalty—and had been brought up on the writings of the learned. He was also familiar with logic and was not inept at reasoning from his own premises. Seldom, however, did he make those nice distinctions which become the careful thinker.

He was not, as we have seen, the best judge of men. To be sure, in his service there were a few competent administrators, most of them inherited from the last reign. We may grant him one or two good appointments, which he may have been pushed into making. He failed not only to understand English personalities but also to adjust himself to English codes and traditions. In James's England there were already occasional examples of that broad-mindedness which we like to observe in the best of the English today, who are able to appraise men and situations.

Broad-mindedness was beyond James's ken, nor did he recognize and treasure it in others. To him, Francis Bacon was just another ambitious courtier, or so he treated him—and he had not the least notion of Bacon's breadth of outlook and of his other stigmata of greatness. Cecil he valued but tired at length of his advice. He preferred and pushed good-looking young men who were not overly gifted except in looking out for themselves, their relatives, and their friends. To them he would increasingly entrust the affairs of state. By 1614 he was a weary old potentate, disinclined to effort, and still happiest in the field, where the deer were said to have been driven before him.

Notes

Introduction

1 About 462 men were in theory elected to Parliament. I would guess that the average daily attendance was less than 200. Occasionally as many as 300 were present; now and then, toward the end of a session, there might be fewer than 100.

2 The Committee on Tenures in 1610 met from 7:00 to 9:00 a.m.

3 See the excellent article by Theodore K. Rabb, "Sir Edwin Sandys and the Parliament of 1604," *AHR*, 69 (1963):646–70. In the section on free trade in Chapter 1, I have made use of Mr. Rabb's conclusions.

4 Edward Grevill and the two Beaumonts ought to be remembered as three early English Liberals, who stood for the individual (not as members of a party).

5 *CSP Ven.*, 1603–07, p. 150.

6 In 1606 he had written Lord Dirleton: "Only this I will say that whilst my worn body holds my mind, it shall serve him, till by serving him I shall trouble him" (*HMC Salisbury*, 18:45).

7 More than once he alluded to the fate of Empson and Dudley—servants of the Crown who were finally executed—as if it came often to his mind.

8 In the last decade of Elizabeth's reign, Edward Coke (later Sir Edward) had, on behalf of the Crown, started action against men who had been taking over Crown lands.

9 Joel Hurstfield, *The Queen's Wards* (London, 1958), pp. 303 ff.

10 "Considering how the Lord's actions do appear every day more and more to tend to honor and reputation than to profit" (Beaulieu to Trumbull, March 1, 1609/10 [Winwood, 3:126]).

11 It is strange that his enemies did not make more of his financial operations, probably because he only did what they would have liked to do. It is true that one writer of the time did make a strong case against him. Even when he ceased to make such a large income from wardship, he did well by other means. See Lawrence Stone's *The Crisis of the Aristocracy* (Oxford, 1965), a book that deserves reading and rereading.

12 Observations for the Tyme (Add. 38492, ff. 42–42v, 62).

13 *SP*, 14/1/68, ff. 1–2.

14 Moreover, those who had been leaders in Elizabeth's time were growing old.

15 S. B. Babbage, *Puritanism and Richard Bancroft* (London, 1962), p. 217.

16 For the passage of this statute, see J. E. Neale, *Elizabeth and her Parliaments 1559–1581* (London, 1952), pp. 203–07.

17 See the Six Articles of the Commons Committee (*CJ*, 1:199–200); also the bill of 1610 (Foster, 1:124–25 n. 2).

18 Foster, 1:101.
19 *CJ*, 1:172–73.
20 June 30 (*CJ*, 1:1000).
21 Adv. 31.7.2, ff. 14–21v; see also *LJ*, 2:658–60.
22 See Holdsworth, 3:292–93.
23 See W. K. Jordan, *Philanthropy in England, 1481–1660* (London, 1954).
24 But see Sir Edward Hoby to Edmondes, March 7, 1606 (Birch, 1:61–63).

Chapter 1

JAMES I, KING OF ENGLAND

1 *CJ*, 1:142.
2 Cecil and others must have known how little confidence Elizabeth had in her cousin of Scotland.
3 *HMC Salisbury*, 15:31.
4 It is strange that so little information about the character of James I percolated through from Scotland to the English court. But these were matters not to be written down on paper, and more than a few people may have had inklings of the weaknesses of James. Elizabeth had had much experience of his want of worldly wisdom, and it is no wonder that she had hesitated to support him for the succession.
5 N. E. McClure, ed., *The Letters of John Chamberlain* (Philadelphia, 1939), 1:192.
6 The English of that day expected the great to maintain a high dignity and reserve. That expectation comes out in books of advice and in plays.
7 Rosny to the French King, July 10, 1603 (Maximilien de Béthune, Duc de Sully, *Memoires des Sage et Royalles Oeconomies d'Estat, Domestique et Militaires de Henry le Grand* . . . [Amsterdam, 1638], 2:142). Rosny makes the King out to be a good listener. De Beaumont had found him one who always interrupted. He could stop long enough to listen to praise.
8 On April 8, 1603, de Beaumont had predicted the troubles of James I: "For I maintain that it will be necessary for him to have as much good fortune as prudence if he is to adjust himself to this nation, and even more, if he is to succeed in bringing together the English and the Scots" (*SP*, 33/3/35, f. 21v). De Beaumont again and again made shrewd analyses of James as well as of the English situation.
9 Reports of the French ambassador from London, June 13, July 10, 17 (F. L. G. von Raumer, *History of the Sixteenth and Seventeenth Centuries* [London, 1835], 1:199).
10 Rosny to Villeroy, July 6, 1603 (Sully, 2:132).
11 De Beaumont to Villeroy, May 17, 1603 (*SP* 33/3/35, f. 75).
12 Charles H. McIlwain, *The Political Works of James I* (Cambridge, Mass., 1918), p. 270.
13 De Beaumont to Villeroy, May 12, 1603 (*SP* 33/3/35, f. 69).
14 Royal, 123, f. 168.
15 Report by the ambassador to the French King, May 24, 28, 1603 (von Raumer, 2:197). Cf. Scaramelli to the Doge, June 26, 1603: "The King is absolute now and declares that there are no ministers and no law of which he is not the master" (*CSP Ven.*, 1603–07, p. 56).
16 Carte, 82, f. 152v; Sully, 2:122.
17 Sully, 2:124.

18 Scaramelli to the Doge, May 22, 1603 (*CSP Ven.*, 1603–07, pp. 32–34).

19 Rosny to the French King, June 25, 1603 (Sully, 2:124–25). Northumberland's secretary, Ralegh, and Lord Cobham told Rosny that, if the Spanish could not persuade the King of England to go to war for his territories in France, then the two Kings of Spain and England might make overtures to the provinces named, offering them very great freedom under the respective flags of Spain and England to govern themselves. It was a strange story, and Rosny was right in doubting its authenticity. What could Cobham and Ralegh have wished? Did they hope that France would support them in unseating James or in compelling him to take other advisers? At this point in 1603 Northumberland had much the same mistrust of the King as did Cobham and Ralegh—Northumberland probably because of the favor shown the Scots; Ralegh and Cobham because they had been snubbed by the new sovereign. All three men doubtless knew of the increasing unpopularity of James, and such a fool as Cobham may have convinced himself that a movement against the King would succeed. The story makes one really wonder if Ralegh were involved in the Cobham plot later. I find it hard to suppose that Ralegh would have abetted such a wild scheme and cooperated with Spain.

20 Even Queen Anne, who had of course her own troubles with the Scots, predicted evil times for her husband, due to the violence of the Scots and the misunderstanding of him by the English. Her husband was too good—by which she meant, I think, too kind and too ready to give things away; she also characterized him as too negligent. These remarks were made to the French ambassador. The Queen was less loyal than she was discerning (Carte, 82:f. 154v).

21 Rosny to the French King, June 20, 1603 (Sully, 2:108–09). Cf. Rosny's letter of July 10, 1603 (Sully, 2:150, or Royal, 123, ff. 217–18).

22 It was observed that James would spring from one subject to another, never taking time to discuss any of them thoroughly: "He moves in this or that direction suggested to him by those about him, but ascertains neither the foundations nor the merit of the subject, so that, as I foresee, he will let himself be surprised in all things" (Henry IV to de Beaumont, March 13, 1604 [von Raumer, 2:191]). In this judgment Henry IV was no doubt relying to a considerable degree on what de Beaumont had written to him. But the French King was quite capable of forming his own judgments and arriving at his own decisions. Rosny gives many details of his long conversations with James. He tried to woo James away from his pro-Spanish advisers and for a while thought that he was succeeding. James fished for compliments with the eagerness of a teenage girl, and Rosny supplied them (Rosny to Villeroy, July 10, 1603). His flattery worked for the time being: "Et comme je recognus par quelque mutation en son visage, gestes extraordinaires, et paroles entre-jettrées . . . que mes raisons, les louanges que je lui avois données, et les vertus que je lui avois attribuées l'avoient fort ebranlé à suivre absolument premières resolutions entre nous prises, sans aucun esgard des contestations et oppositions de ses Ministres, encor qu'en effet ce Prince no soit pas d'humeur guerriere, qu'il ne se plaist pas en entrer en propos des executions et factions militaires" (Sully, 2:142).

In the same interview Rosny praised the two Kings (of France and Britain) together: "Ausquelles paroles qu'il tenoit pour des louanges exceedans toute mesure, puisqu'elles le comparoient à votre Majesté il tesmoigna une indicible ioye et une espèce de courroux contre ceux qui l'avoient voulu dissuader de conclurre les ounestures qui avoient este faites comme un resultat de conseils

entre nous tenus, sommairement escrit de ma main, puis corrigez de la sienne"
(Sully 2:145).
23 Molin to the Doge, December 1, 1604 (*CSP Ven.*, 1603–07, pp. 195–96).
24 Winwood, 2:40.
25 Royal, 123, ff. 168–168v. That James had lost the good opinion of his intelligent subjects within a year of his accession can be shown from more than the
reports of the French and Venetian ambassadors. It is to be found in the
State Papers and in the memoirs and letters of the time by those who read
between the lines. Men feared to say openly what they thought, but they
often gave themselves away. The speeches in Parliament show, from the beginning, how little real respect his better-informed subjects had for the King.
26 Worcester to Cranborne, May 3, 1604 (Edmund Lodge, *Illustrations of British
History* [London, 1838], 3:137–38).

PARLIAMENT BEGINS: THE GOODWIN-FORTESCUE CASE

1 For the finished version of the King's speech, see McIlwain, pp. 269–80.
2 That is, they opposed an ecclesiastical hierarchy, "which maketh their sect
unable to be suffered in any well-governed Commonwealth" (ibid., p. 274).
3 *CJ*, 1:148, 934.
4 See Notestein, Simpson, and Relf, *Commons Debates 1621*, 4:200, 5:323, 6:85–
86. Apparently officials of the Treasurer's Remembrancer of the Exchequer
had developed a new writ *De Quo Titulo Ingressus* to be used against the
heir of a King's tenant, which involved him in heavy charges. The grievance
of the writs had come up as early as in 1601. See D'Ewes, pp. 433, 434, 435,
436, 624.
5 Montague had arranged to run with Sir Robert Spencer of the well-known
sheep-raising family when Sir Richard Knightley wrote to him about the candidacy of his son, Valentine. Montague felt too tied to Spencer to help Knightley, but the messenger from Knightley assured Montague of Spencer's approval of Knightley's candidacy, and so Montague resolved "to move gentlemen
and freeholders . . . for him." Spencer became a Peer in July 1603 (*HMC
Buccleuch*, 3:75, 77–78).
6 Ibid., 3:91.
7 *CJ*, 1:151.
8 One of the debaters cited a precedent of 27 Eliz. in which the Commons refused to commit a bill (against fraudulent conveyances) sent them from the
Lords and informed the other House that they intended to bring in a new
bill. That they refused to give the Lords a reason for their rejection of the
bill, as the debaters asserted, does not appear in D'Ewes's narrative, which
seems, however, to be incomplete. See D'Ewes, pp. 338, 369, 370, 371, 372,
373.
9 Rutland, 14:204.
10 Ibid.
11 Ibid.
12 Ibid.; also *CJ*, 1:937.
13 *CJ*, 1:937.
14 Ibid.
15 *CJ*, 1:156.
16 Titus F IV, ff. 7–7v.

17 Ibid.
18 Ibid.
19 *CJ*, 1:158, 938.
20 *CJ*, 1:158. This is a characteristic statement by James. The whole plan of
    raising the issue of outlawry had been concocted in the Privy Council. Cecil
    wrote to Winwood: "It was advised by the King's learned Counsel and Judges
    whether there were not some means by the laws to avoid it [making void
    Goodwin's election], whereupon it being found that he [Goodwin] was out-
    lawed and so certified by the sheriff, and consequently a new writ sent forth"
    (*SP*, 84/64, ff. 135v–136, April 12, 1604). Cecil had been involved in the plan
    to put Goodwin out. At the conference on March 26 the Lords withdrew and
    asked the Commons to wait. "When they came out again the Lord Cecil de-
    livered a very fine speech, but in th'end propounded unto us the matter of
    Sir Francis Goodwin's, concerning his election, and that if we had any authority,
    he would show us their reasons of their dislike" (*HMC Buccleuch*, 3:83). That
    Cecil, who was deeply involved, should not have consulted James is hard
    to believe.
21 *CJ*, 1:158; Rutland, 14:205.
22 See Holdsworth, 1:214, 452.
23 Rutland, 14:206.
24 Sir David Williams (ibid.).
25 *CJ*, 1:158. Montague added a detail: "If we did resolve, that we should make
    repair to his Council, by whom we should know his Majesty's pleasure"
    (*HMC Buccleuch*, 3:83).
26 *CJ*, 1:159, 939; Titus F IV, ff. 8–8v.
27 Titus F IV, ff. 8–8v.
28 Rutland, 14:206.
29 Ibid.
30 *CJ*, 1:939.
31 Ibid.
32 *CJ*, 1:159.
33 *SP* 14/7/2.
34 *CJ*, 1:939; Rutland 14:206.
35 *CJ*, 1:159.
36 *CJ*, 1:939. James's only legion was the prestige of the sovereign. The men
    mustered by the Lord Lieutenant would have been of little use.
37 Ibid.
38 Rutland, 14:206.
39 D'Ewes, p. 645.
40 Rutland, 14:206v.
41 Ibid.
42 Titus F IV, f. 8v. See Yelverton's own copy of this speech in Add. 48116, ff.
    214–15; I have drawn largely on it.
43 "Cowardness . . . which yielded unto were the way to have a *quo warranto*
    brought for the rest" (Rutland, 14:206v). "This may be called a *quo warranto*
    to seize our liberties" (*CJ*, 1:939).
44 Yelverton suggested that the Commons ought to consider how far the over-
    throw of all their authority as a court might "extend to the undoing of all
    their estates" (Titus F IV, f. 9).
45 "For by that means the Lord Chancellor and his under officers might make
    the knights and the burgesses for the Parliaments" (Titus F IV, f. 9).
46 Ibid.

47 *CJ,* 1:159.

48 Add. 48116, ff. 214–15. All that follows of Yelverton's speech is from the same MS.

48 Rutland, 14:206v. Cf. *CJ,* 1:940.

50 *CJ,* 1:940, 160.

51 Rutland, 14:207.

52 Ibid.; also *CJ,* 1:940.

53 James could hardly refrain from condescending.

54 April 1, 1604 (*SP* 14/7/1).

55 *CJ,* 1:161.

56 *CJ,* 1:163; *Statutes at Large* (London, 1769), 1:469–70.

57 The reader may look at D'Ewes, pp. 392–93, 398–99, 344–45, 337, 332, 156, 80, 39. It has to be admitted that there are many gaps in D'Ewes, that the *CJ* add little, and that the *Rotuli Parliamentorum* seem to give us no clues as to how the returns of elections were handled. Nor do the chroniclers, so far as I can determine.

58 A writ commanding the sheriff to summon the defendant to appear and deliver himself upon pain of outlawry.

59 His Majesty commanded a conference with the judges before the Council "that so he may judge and lay the fault where it is" (*HMC Buccleuch,* 3:85). The King was arrogating to himself the final decision.

60 *CJ,* 1:943.

61 *HMC Buccleuch,* 3:85; *CJ,* 1:943.

62 *HMC Buccleuch,* 3:85. This expression of the King has a familiar ring. Such graciousness did not mean much. His Majesty was later to hold Yelverton in marked distaste. The Frere MS (*HMC 7th Rep.,* p. 526) tells us a little of this meeting: "Sir Francis Bacon was appointed to speak and so he did wonderfully well. The King afterwards spake more than excellently well. He was somewhat angry at first but afterwards the matter was pacified and the King and the House agreed both together to put them out both." This addition suggests how much of the story may be missing for want of adequate sources.

63 We know that earlier he had resolved not to press for a subsidy unless he had a good chance of getting it.

64 *CJ,* 1:944. Did Bacon mean that Chancery was a [confidentiary] court for Parliament for the time before Parliament met?

65 *HMC Buccleuch,* 3:85.

66 Molin to the Doge and Senate, April 8, 1604 (*CSP Ven.,* 1604–07, pp. 141–42).

67 Molin to the Doge and Senate, April 15, 1604 (ibid., p. 143).

68 *CJ,* 1:168.

69 *HMC Buccleuch,* 3:85. This was probably Christopher Brooke, whom Montague calls an "outward barrister."

70 *CJ,* 1:168.

71 The compromise solution seemed to leave the government well pleased. But Henry Howard, Earl of Northampton, was far from satisfied. He wrote to some of the justices of the peace for Buckinghamshire, to Sir T.D., Sir J.K., Sir A.T., Sir W.B., and Sir E.T. The justices addressed were probably Sir Thomas Denton, Sir Anthony Tirringham, Sir William Borlace, and Sir Edward Tyrell; who Sir J.K. was I do not know. In his letter, Northampton wrote that the King had expressly given him charge to find "some further notion and overture of the ground of that so high and hot opposition." Goodwin, when called before the Council, had suggested some "practice or indirect attempt against him for second place." These justices were directed to study

the conduct of Goodwin and, if necessary, find witnesses. Whether this investigation was pursued further I do not know. Northampton was the kind of man to rush in officiously and fail to follow through. See Rawl., 918, f. 35.

PRELIMINARY DISCUSSIONS OF THE UNION

1 *CJ*, 1:171, 946. The text throughout this chapter is based upon the two versions of the *CJ*, and reference to them will be omitted.
2 My friend and colleague, Professor S. F. Bemis, has called my attention to the use of *Gran Bretagna* in *Don Quixote* (1604).
3 Was this perhaps the first time that the comparison was made in a record still available? It would seem possible that Samuel Daniel or one of the playwrights made these same suggestions.
4 I have put this speech together from two versions which differ, one from notes rapidly compiled by the Clerk's assistant and a more formal one given by the Clerk as from the King. It is noticeable that the formal version leaves out much that was probably said in the speech. The informal version gives us a better speech than the formal.
5 On May 3 the discussion of the union was put off, and the Clerk wrote in the margin: "The latter the case."
6 June 1 (*CJ*, 1:230).
7 *SP*, 14/8/93.

WARDSHIP

1 About this whole question, consult Hurstfield's *The Queen's Wards*, a thorough and careful book and a contribution to the history of the time.
2 Ibid., p. 121.
3 John Bruce, ed., *Correspondence of James VI of Scotland with Sir Robert Cecil* (London, 1861), p. 59. Some time before the death of the great Queen a Catholic wrote "A Discourse of the Providence necessary to be had for the Setting Up the Catholic Faith When God shall call the Queen." He proposed that the English should be conciliated by confirming church lands to their present owners, by abolishing the Court of Wards, by restoring freedom of speech in Parliament, and by reforming the law courts (*CSP Dom.*, 1601–03, pp. 281–82). See also T. F. Knox, *Letters and Memorials of Cardinal Allen*, p. 107.
4 H. S. Scott, ed., *The Journal of Sir Roger Wilbraham* (London, 1902), p. 63.
5 Edmund Buriche, Feodary of Cornwall, to Cecil, October 20, 1603 (*HMC Salisbury*, 15:264–65). See also Cecil to Sir John Savile and others, October 3, 1603 (Lodge, *Illustrations of British History*, 3:41–46).
6 *HMC Salisbury*, 15:276.
7 It tells of the conservatism of the English gentry, and that they had suffered so long the abuses of wardship without much complaint.
8 Rutland, 14:202v.
9 *CJ*, 1:153.
10 Sir Thomas Hesketh, Attorney of the Court of Wards, asserted that fees for alienations ("alien tenures") "were of the King by his grant to keep the castle

of Dover and divers other castles, which were not given as the former [by knight service]." Hesketh asked what should become of those and was answered that the House might make provision for them, as for the other (Rutland, 14:202v).

11   Ibid.

12   *CJ*, 1:153.

13   Rutland, 14:202v.

14   Respite of homage is mentioned often in the debates on wardship, and eventually a separate committee was set up to deal with it. The duty of homage was becoming a "ceremony of constantly diminishing importance" (Holdsworth, 3:56). Indeed, homage itself was not normally used. In the statute of 33 Hen. VIII, cap. xxii, dealing with the Court of Wards, the fees for respite of homage in the case of smaller fiefs were put down. In Thomas Blount, *Glossographia*, 2nd ed. (London, 1661), respite of homage was thus defined: "The forbearing of homage, which respite [i.e., fees for respite] was paid upon divers good reasons, but most frequently by such as held by knight service (*in capite*) who, because their Prince could not be at leisure to take their homage, did pay into the Exchequer every fifth term some small sum for respite of homage till the Prince might be at leisure to take it in person."

15   By the law of 1 Edw. III, cap. xii (*Statutes at Large* [1759], 1:194), lands held of the King *in capite* could be alienated by a "reasonable fine taken in Chancery by a due process." More and more the right to alienate lands had been recognized, but the King continued to make a little money out of it.

16   The author of the Rutland MS (f. 203)—possibly Sir George Manners, M.P. for Lincolnshire—wrote that the conference was to be the next morning at 9:00; however, an examination of the *CJ* convinces me that the writer was wrong.

17   Montague's minutes (*HMC Buccleuch*, 3:82). The crowding in of those who had not been nominated was doubtless the result of the growing custom that such persons could attend afternoon committee meetings if they so wished.

18   It is to be noted that on April 16 a bill "for the due receiving of homage and fealty by the Lord Great Chamberlain for and in the behalf of the King's Majesty" received its first reading. On April 26 that measure had its second reading and was committed to twenty-four or so members, most of them lawyers. On May 8 the committee on respite of homage was appointed to meet the next afternoon.

19   *Primer seizin* was the right of the grantor, in this case the King, to take possession of a fief when the tenant died. He would retain it until the heir had performed homage and paid his relief; then the heir could take possession.

20   *CJ*, 1:227.

21   *HMC Buccleuch*, 3:89.

22   *CJ*, 1:230.

23   Sir John Stanhope to Cecil, before August 20, 1604 (*HMC Salisbury*, 16:264).

24   William Petyt, *Jus Parliamentarum* (London, 1739), 241–42.

THE PURVEYORS IN 1604

1   *HMC Salisbury*, 16:425–26.

2   Rutland, 14:201.

3   Ibid.

4 D'Ewes, pp. 657, 664, 555, 581, 668, 623; Hayward Townshend, *Historical Collections* (London, 1680), pp. 258, 277. Hyde claimed credit for framing the monopolies bill of 1601 (Townshend, pp. 232–33).

5 Bowyer, p. 326.

6 Birch, 1:60.

7 D'Ewes, pp. 432–33; about Hare's activities in Parliament, see pp. 353, 372, 478, 481. See also Townshend on the Parliament of 1601.

8 Bowyer, pp. 38–39 n. 3.

9 *HMC Salisbury*, 16:128. He had been a "client" of Burghley's, according to Neale (*Elizabeth and Her Parliaments 1584–1601*, p. 209).

10 D'Ewes, pp. 481–82, 335, 431, 471, 477, 622.

11 See *DNB*. In the Bodleian Library there is a manuscript diary (recently acquired) of a Berkshire parson who made Tanfield out to be notorious for his corruption. Tanfield was appointed a Puisne Judge in the King's Bench in 1606 and Chief Baron of the Exchequer in 1607.

12 *CJ*, 1:176.

13 *CJ*, 1:950.

14 Composition had been going on for some time; indeed, as early as in the reign of Edward VI there had been composition in Northamptonshire for sheep and cattle. The great period for composition in the shires was the 1590s. As a result of agitation in Parliament in 1589 by John Hare and others, agitation which the Queen bitterly resented, Lord Burghley had with great effort secured economies in the royal household and compelled counties to sign composition agreements about certain commodities called for by the royal household. Thus composition was an established practice, even if purveyors were still on the rampage. Of course the system did not work perfectly. About the subject, see L. B. Sears, "Purveyance and the Royal Household in the Reign of Queen Elizabeth," *Journal of Political Economy*, 24 (1916):755–74. See also the more recent, more thorough studies: Allegra Woodworth, "Purveyance for the Royal Household in the Reign of Queen Elizabeth," *Trans. Am. Phil. Soc.*, 35 (Philadelphia, 1945):1–89; G. E. Aylmer, "The Last Years of Purveyance, 1610–1660," *Econ. Hist. Rev.*, 2nd ser., 10:81–93. For the various types of composition as set forth by Aylmer, see p. 516 n. 24 below.

15 Allegra Woodworth (p. 18) says that between Magna Carta and the opening of the reign of Elizabeth the royal assent was given to more than forty statutes dealing with purveyance.

16 The case against the purveyors was probably not as bad as appears in this statement, which was a collection of abuses reported from various counties, probably including some of the worst cases. No doubt there were honest purveyors, but the post was regarded as one of the highroads to fortune. Both business and government were honeycombed with corruption.

17 Bacon spoke with his usual emphasis: "There is no grievance in your kingdom so general, so continual, so sensible, and so bitter unto the common subject as this whereof we now speak." He said that the purveyors took for timber trees "which are the beauty, countenance, and shelter of men's houses, that men have long spared from their own purse and profit; that men esteem (for their use and delight) above ten times the value." He made another charge: "They use a strange and most unjust exaction in causing the subjects to pay poundage of their own debts, due from your Majesty unto them; so as a poor man when he hath had his hay, or his wood, or his poultry . . . taken from him, and that not at a just price but under the value, and

cometh to receive his money, he shall have after the rate of twelve pence in the pound abated for poundage of his due payment, growing upon so hard conditions." For Bacon's whole speech, see Spedding, 3:181–87.

18 Justices of the peace may well have been afraid to interfere with the royal officials.

19 The record of Elizabeth's officials was not too good. When they took advantage of her for their own profit, she did not always discharge them but turned over their duties to other men. But both Green Cloth and its agents, the purveyors, had bad records over a long period.

20 *CJ*, 1:961.

21 *CJ*, 1:200.

22 *CJ*, 1:202.

23 *CJ*, 1:204. This statement by Bacon is puzzling. Even if the King had greater means, it would have been unwise of Bacon to say so. Did Bacon possibly mean that His Majesty had more ways to curb purveyors? The context does not bear out such an interpretation.

24 Aylmer describes the three kinds of purveyance. Miss Woodworth describes the machinery for levying composition used in Northamptonshire in late Elizabethan days: in the last years of the Queen, "the Lords in Commission for Household Causes" suggested that the counties employ "purveyors as undertakers for the composition" (Woodworth, p. 50). The suggestion, she says, was accepted by many counties, especially for "acatry" products (meat, fish, and salt). When the plan of using former purveyors failed to work well, the undertakers were often a group of justices of the peace (Aylmer, p. 83).

25 The towns of Brill and Flushing and the Castle of Ramakens had been turned over to Elizabeth as security for the money advanced by England to help the Dutch in their war with Spain.

26 *CJ*, 1:204, 967.

27 By supplies *in specie* he must have meant supplies in kind; that is, part of the composition would be in commodities.

28 *CJ*, 1:204, 967. Perhaps this suggestion was put forth by someone who wished to kill the whole program for a composition. It was a suggestion not likely to be welcomed by the Upper House.

29 *CJ*, 1:969.

30 Sir Richard Browne was added to the committee, no doubt because he had made a speech that ensured him a place. He was Clerk of Green Cloth and would uphold the interest of the purveyors. On April 26 Thomas James, a newly elected member from Bristol, had informed the Commons of the struggle between the Board of Green Cloth and the Mayor of Bristol. The Mayor, John Whitson, had resisted the King's Customer, who, by order of the Board of Green Cloth, had demanded a composition for groceries. The Board then sent an arrogant letter to the Mayor, which James read to the House. The signers of the letter, among them Sir Richard Browne, rebuked the Mayor for his contempt of the royal prerogative and warned him that he would hear more about his audacious proceedings unless he gave good satisfaction to the King's Customer (John Latimer, *Annals of Bristol in the Seventeenth Century* [Bristol, 1900], p. 20; cf. *CJ*, 1:185). James reported that, when he showed the letter to the committee, Sir Richard Browne said: "It were good he [James] were sent for after the end of Parliament." Years before Browne had got into trouble with Queen Elizabeth about his misdoings as Clerk Comptroller of Green Cloth (Woodworth, pp. 16–17). Thomas James offered to bring witnesses in to confirm his testimony as to Browne's words. But nothing is re-

corded in the *CJ* to indicate that the witnesses were summoned or appeared. It is surprising that the Commons did nothing about this threat to free speech in Parliament.

Earlier in the session the Commons had been more sensitive. When Griffith Payne, M.P. and Mayor of Wallingford and himself a purveyor, had in a speech in the Commons said that the House sought "to dishonor the King, disgrace the Council, discredit the opinion of the Judges, and did now by this bill go about to hang some of his servants" (*CJ*, 1:162), he was called to the bar and suspended for the time being. Why did the Commons act with such severity in one case and name to a committee a man who was at least accused on a more serious charge? One suspects that those supporting the King had things more their own way in the early days of the 1604 session than later.

31 On his way down from Scotland James was welcomed by large numbers of the northern nobility and gentry who doubtless found it not inconvenient to live on his bounty. Moreover, there were Scots in his train who were no less inclined than others to refuse a good thing.

32 *CJ*, 1:223.

33 *CJ*, 1:978.

34 Ibid.

35 *CJ*, 1:984.

FREE TRADE

1 Astrid Friis, *Alderman Cockayne's Project and the Cloth Trade* (London, 1927), p. 149, from *LJ*, 2:334. See also the exaggerated report of the Venetian ambassador: "The Lower House, on a petition complaining of monopolies signed by many merchants, has dissolved all companies" (Molin to the Doge, June 23, 1604 [*CSP Ven.*, 1603–07, pp. 161–63]).

2 Lansd., 487, ff. 179–82.

3 *CJ*, 1:221.

4 Lansd., 487, ff. 179–82.

5 That is, the customs officials who would not allow such goods entrance or suit (ibid.).

6 *CJ*, 1:219.

7 E. Lipson, *Economic History of England* (London, 1931), 2:252–53.

8 John Latimer, *History of the Merchant Venturers of . . . Bristol* (Bristol, 1903), pp. 60–62.

9 Friis, pp. 150–51. A writer for the Merchant Adventurers offered two reasons for the decline of the outports: "It is the wars with Spain which hath been the means thereof, and not going afishing, which trade of late years hath been in a manner given over" (Some Reasons in the behalf of the Merchants Adventurers, in Lansd., 487, ff. 288–92).

10 *CJ*, 1:218.

11 "And where it is said that there are not any companies in foreign countries, it is not so. For they of the United Provinces very lately were forced to follow the example of England, for the trade to the East Indies, otherwise they found by experience that they should have traded without gain. Besides the Hansa Towns have been a society of long continuance. And in Italy, Germany, Spain, and Portugal there are divers companies very ancient" (Lansd., 487, ff. 288–92).

12 *The Constitution and Finance of English . . . Joint-Stock Companies to 1720*
(Cambridge, 1912), 1:121–22.

13 The case for experience was neatly put by John Wheeler: "One day still being
a schoolmaster unto the other, and men by experience, use, and knowledge
of foreign people, and their fashions, orders, and kind of dealing, growing
daily and from time to time to an exacter course and greater perfection of
matters, and understanding of their own estate" (G. B. Hotchkiss, ed., *A Treatise of Commerce* [Middleburg, 1601; New York, 1931], p. 338).

14 "But to this will be said that it is not meant to dissolve the Company of
Merchant Adventurers, nor any of th'other societies, notwithstanding, seeing
that men are at liberty by this Act to trade at their own wills and pleasure,
whensoever and whithersoever, it is not possible that the Company can stand"
(Lansd., 487, ff. 288–92).

15 The English, in making comparisons of themselves with people of other nations, have long been self-critical.

16 "For when we shall go straggling for Holland and Germany, every man to
what town he will, we must of force freight vessels of much less burden . . .
because every man in this time of peace will desire to send his cloths etc.
as soon as he can to the market, which will set small ships a-work, and the
great ships will soon decay, which may be dangerous for our state in time
of war" (Lansd., 487, ff. 286–92).

17 *SP*, 14/15/54, quoted in Friis, p. 156.

18 Tey was a merchant tailor who, with another, farmed the alnage for woolen
cloths and for the new draperies in London.

19 By "order" Tey meant what Ulysses in Shakespeare's *Troilus and Cressida*
meant by "degree, priority, and place."

20 T. C. Mendenhall, *The Shrewsbury Drapers and the Welsh Wool Trade* (London, 1953), p. 169.

21 *SP*, 14/15/54, quoted in S.R. Gardiner, *History of England from the Accession
of James I to the Outbreak of the Civil Wars* (London, 1883), 2:5.

22 Friis, pp. 156–57.

23 *CJ*, 1:256.

24 *CJ*, 1:275.

25 *LJ*, 2:393.

26 *LJ*, 2:399.

27 *LJ*, 2:405. On April 10 Sir Robert Mansell made a charge against the Clerk
of the Commons. Mansell had found names set down in the Clerk's book of
members of the Committee on the Bill for Free Trade which he had not heard
called out in the House, and these same members were those interested in the
bill.

   The Speaker in his answer did not deal with the question of whether the
names had been inserted by the Clerk; he answered that if any man's special
case were in question, he could not serve on the committee, but if the case
were general, a man "specially interested hath a voice and is fit and able to
be a committee" (Bowyer, pp. 115–16). The main charge that the names had
been inserted the Speaker did not refute, so far as the records show. Nor was
the matter discussed further.

28 Bowyer, p. 124.

29 *CJ*, 1:304.

30 *CJ*, 1:304.

31 *LJ*, 2:424.

32 Friis, p. 162. See also *Statutes at Large* (1770), 3 Jac. I, cap. vi, 3:51–52. On

April 3, 1606, a bill for the Liberty of Free Trade into all Countries had its second reading (*CJ*, 1:292). A large committee included many leaders of the House as well as Privy Councilors, the King's learned counsel, and burgesses of the port towns. About this measure, which may have been a revamped version of the bill of 1604, I can find nothing more.

33 *Statutes at Large* (1770), 3 Jac. I, cap. vi, 3:51–52.

34 *SP*, 14/15/54, quoted in Cecil T. Carr, *Select Charters of Trading Companies, A.D. 1530 to 1707* (London, 1913), pp. 40–43.

35 The leaders of the Commons would have denied that they were attempting to curb the powers of the sovereign; they would have asserted rather that they were seeking to preserve those privileges and rights that had belonged to Parliament in the fourteenth and fifteenth centuries.

36 His moderation proved more effective because there were many members of the House who had strong convictions and did not hesitate to utter them.

THE APOLOGY

1   Petyt, *Jus Parliamentarium* pp. 232–33; *SP*, 14/8/70, f. 5.
2   Petyt, p. 242; *SP*, 14/8/70, f. 12.
3   Would that some historian searching among the many parliamentary manuscripts in the British Museum might happen upon it.
4   *CJ*, 1:182.
5   *SP*, 14/8/70, f. 1; Petyt, p. 227.
6   *CSP Ven.*, 1603–07, p. 150. The upholders of prerogative, had they understood history as well as it is understood today, could have made a wonderful case for royal government. It was strong royal government that organized Europe out of her feudalism; it was royal government that gave England her judicial system, her local government, and the ties between central and local government.
7   *CJ*, 1:230.
8   *HMC Salisbury*, 16:264.
9   *CJ*, 1:984.
10 *CJ*, 1:230–31.
11 *HMC 3rd Rep.*, p. 185.
12 This passage is a summary rather than a precise quotation (Petyt, 230–31; *SP*, 14/8/70, f. 3).
13 A statement put in by someone who knew little of English history.
14 Petyt, pp. 238–39; *SP*, 14/8/70, f. 9.
15 Petyt, pp. 241–42; *SP*, 14/8/70, ff. 10–11.
16 *SP*, 14/8/70, f. 11; Petyt, p. 241.
17 Petyt (p. 240) reads "consents unto" instead of "counsel unto."
18 *SP*, 14/8/70, f. 10; Petyt, pp. 240–41.
19 *SP*, 14/8/70, f. 11; Petyt, p. 242.
20 *SP*, 14/8/70, ff. 10–11; Petyt, p. 241.
21 *CJ*, 1:227.
22 *CJ*, 1:230.
23 Petyt, p. 240; *SP*, 14/8/70, f. 10.
24 *CJ*, 1:192–93; Spedding, 3:181–87.
25 Petyt, p. 240.
26 Spedding, 3:103–27.
27 Petyt, p. 243.

28 Since writing the above account of the Apology my attention has been drawn to Dr. Elton's article in the volume in honor of Mattingly (Charles Carter, ed., *From the Renaissance to the Counter-Reformation* [New York, 1965], pp. 331–47). That the Apology was less important in the history of the growth of the English constitution than it has been made out to be is, I think, true. Elton is right too about the many slips and one significant omission in Petyt's version of the Apology. I wish he might edit the Apology from the various MS copies and the Protestation.

Chapter 2

THE PROBLEM OF THE RECUSANTS

1   35 Eliz., cap. ii, art. vii; 23 Eliz., cap. i; 29 Eliz., cap. vi.
2   "Na, na, gud fayth, wee's a not neede the papists now" (Confessions of Anthony Copley, *SP*, 14/2/51, quoted in C. Dodd, *The Church History of England*, ed. M. A. Tierney [London, 1839–43], 4:App. I, p. 1).
3   D. Jardine, *A Narrative of the Gunpowder Plot* (London, 1857), p. 20. Jardine was quoting from French transcripts, but the information is also to be found in Sully's *Memoires*.
4   Dodd, 4:38 n. 1. According to Chamberlain (Chamberlain to Winwood, February 16, 1605, quoted in McClure, *Letters of John Chamberlain*, 1:202–05), James told his Council that he never had any intention to give toleration to the Catholics, that the mitigation of their payments was in consideration that none of them had lifted a hand against his coming in, and that in consequence he had given them a year of probation to conform themselves. Seeing that this probationary period had no effect, he had fortified all laws against Catholics except those calling for blood, from which he had a natural aversion. It will be noted that in some degree James's statement supported the claims of the Catholics. His denials should always be taken with several grains of salt.
5   23 Eliz., cap. i, art. iv.
6   S. R. Gardiner, *History of England from the Accession of James I to the Disgrace of Chief Justice Coke* (London, 1863), 1:223–26.
7   Birch, 1:45.
8   Bowyer, p. 7.
9   *CJ*, 1:260.
10 *CJ*, 1:261. "With all speed convenient to proceed in the bills for service of God and preservation of his royal person" (Bowyer, p. 12).
11 It was hoped that many Catholics, especially those known as Appelants, who were at odds with the Jesuits, while maintaining spiritual loyalty to the Pontiff would forswear political allegiance to him and render such allegiance to their King. About that quarrel, see Joel Hurstfield, "The Succession Struggle in Late Elizabethan England," in *Elizabethan Government and Society*, ed. S. T. Bindoff et al. (London, 1961).
12 Bacon wrote in 1608: "My Lord of Salisbury at that time opined that this violent proceeding of the Pope in condemning the Oath of Allegiance was to draw the King to blood, and so the people to greater despair and alienation, and foreigners to malice and quarrel, the better to expose this Realm to a prey." To this the archbishop replied that by "that reason with the more fury Rome proceeded, the more remiss we should be—*Quod nota*" (Spedding, 4:91).

13 McIlwain, *Political Works of James I*, p. 72. "For Recusants the new oath, the refusal whereof bringeth praemunire, not to be tendred but to the Apostatans [those who had renounced their Catholic orders but without legal dispensation] and practicers: this was generally spoken by the King. The new oath limited to be tendred to three persons, the indicated Recusant, the non-communicant, the vagrant person. And question came incidentally whether the oath should be tendred to the non-communicant. And it was probably inferred that if some of the indicted by the King's speech were to be spared, *a fortiore* those which are no Recusants" (Spedding, 4:91).

14 By 23 Eliz., cap. i, all forfeitures were to be divided into three parts, of which one part was to go to the King, a second part to the poor (via the King), and a third to anyone who sued for it under certain conditions.

15 *CJ*, 1:263.

16 Ibid.

17 Ibid. Cf. *CJ*, 1:291, 298; *LJ*, 2:414. See also *Statutes at Large*.

18 Bowyer, p. 183.

19 From the memory of Lecky's history, I should guess that the men who drafted the terrible eighteenth-century legislation against the Catholics in Ireland had examined the English legislation of the reigns of Elizabeth and James I.

20 3 Jac. I, cap. v, art. xxii.

21 Ibid., art. xvi.

22 Ibid., art. xvii.

23 *HMC Salisbury*, 18:44–46.

24 *CJ*, 1:265. Cf. Birch, 1:51.

25 Sir Christopher had been a Jesuit and may have had the zeal of one who had changed his faith.

26 It was useless, he said, to require recusants to swear to an oath of allegiance because they could be absolved by their confessors.

27 *HMC Salisbury*, 18:61–63.

28 3 Jac. I, cap. iv, art. xviii–xxiii.

29 Harl., 6850, ff. 55v, Harl., 6842, f. 5v., quoted in Bowyer, pp. 193–94.

30 *CJ*, 1:276.

31 Bacon probably favored a mild measure. In 1606 he set down in his memoranda: "My Lord of Salisbury is to be remembered . . . that he will deal moderately with Recusants" (Spedding, 4:46). Bacon's whole philosophy in religious matters favored moderation. But he would have had little sympathy for recusant parents who were to give up their children. On December 4, 1606, he said: "The wisest and best lawgivers had in the best-governed commonwealths ordained that children should be brought up by commissioners' appointment and not according to the humorous education of the parents" (*SP*, 14/24/13; Bowyer, p. 201 n. 2).

32 *Commentarius Solutus sive Pandecta, sive Ancilla Memoria* (Spedding, 4:46–95).

33 Ibid., 4:91.

34 Bowyer, p. 161 n. 1.

35 See 5 Eliz., cap. i: An Act for the Assurance of the Queen's Majesty's royal power over all estates and subjects within her Dominions. Section xvi requires the "Oath of M.P.'s . . . provided always that forasmuch as the Queen's Majesty is otherwise sufficiently assured of the faith and loyalty of the temporal Lords of her Highness's Court of Parliament . . . this Act shall not extend to compel any temporal person of, or above the degree of Baron of this Realm to take the oath aforesaid."

36 *HMC Salisbury,* 18:142.
37 *CJ,* 1:313.

GRIEVANCES

1   *CJ,* 1:267.
2   *CJ,* 1:269; cf. Bowyer, p. 33.
3   *CJ,* 1:269, 271.
4   *CJ,* 1:285.
5   April 5 (Bowyer, pp. 102–03).
6   The Dean of Arches is the Judge of the Court of Arches, which is the court of appeals for the province of Canterbury.
7   *SP,* 14/19/51, quoted in Bowyer, p. 82 n. 1.
8   Bowyer, pp. 83–84.
9   Ibid., pp. 102–03.
10 Ibid., pp. 106–07.
11 Ibid., pp. 106–07 n. 1.
12 James was an easy mark for the smooth talker, as many discovered to their profit or loss.
13 Petition of Grievances, 1606 (PRO, Sackville MS, f. 16). See also Petyt MS (Inner Temple), ff. 234v–239, and Harl., 6258A, ff. 2–8. In both places the Petition is misdated. See Foster, 2:269 n. 16.
14 Sackville, f. 17.
15 Ibid., f. 18; Bowyer, pp. 112–13.
16 The *licentia concordandi* was a royal license for the levying of the fine, for which the Crown paid a sum of money called the King's silver.
17 Sackville, ff. 18–19.
18 *CJ,* 1:295.
19 Ibid.
20 Bowyer, p. 127.
21 *CJ,* 1:295; see also Bowyer, p. 127.
22 Bowyer, p. 154. About Bruncard, see *HMS Salisbury,* 16:55, 465.
23 *CSP Dom.,* 1603–10, p. 233.
24 Sackville, ff. 20–27.
25 Ibid., ff. 28–29.
26 Bowyer, p. 112.
27 *CJ,* 1:299.
28 *CSP Dom.,* 1603–10, p. 174.
29 Bowyer, p. 110.
30 Sackville, f. 19.
31 *CJ,* 1:295; Bowyer, p. 110.
32 Bowyer, pp. 131–32.
33 Sackville, f. 38.
34 Bowyer, pp. 132, 156.
35 *CSP Dom.,* 1603–10, p. 501.
36 Bowyer, p. 132.
37 Twinehoe owed his seat in the Commons to the Earl of Northampton (*Shropshire Arch. Soc. Trans.,* 10 [2nd ser.]: 110).
38 Bowyer, p. 132.
39 *CJ,* 1:301.

40 Bowyer, p. 156.

41 For these statutes see Bowyer, p. 111 n. 3; Sackville, f. 21.

42 Bowyer, p. 154; Sackville, f. 29.

43 *CJ*, 1:295; Bowyer, p. 109; Sackville, ff. 37–38.

44 See Alfred C. Wood, *A History of the Levant Company* (Oxford, 1935); S. R. Gardiner, *History of England, 1603–1642* (London, 1899), 2:1–6.

45 It is worth notice that several of those who received patents from the Crown happened to be M.P.'s.

46 Probably Thomas Hitchcock of Lincoln's Inn, who became an M.P. for Bishops Castle in 1614.

47 Bowyer, p. 118. About the demand in England for currants, see Wood, p. 78. See also *CSP Ven.*, 1640–42, pp. 234–35.

48 Even in that day the English hoped that exports would equal imports.

49 Bowyer, pp. 118–19.

50 *CSP Dom.*, 1603–10, p. 161.

51 Bowyer, p. 119.

52 *CJ*, 1:297.

53 Bowyer, p. 119. I suspect that this was Hugh Myddleton, who represented Denbigh in this Parliament, although his name is not down in the official list of members. It might have been Robert. There were four brothers, all distinguished enough to find places in the *DNB*. Sir Thomas became Lord Mayor of London, William was a poet and a seaman. Hugh is best known as the man who projected and put through the New River, but he was also a goldsmith—that is, a banker—and a cloth merchant. He was eventually made a baronet.

54 A few months later Sir John, as a Baron of the Exchequer (since 1598), ruled that the King by his prerogative could levy impositions upon imports and exports. He was a Yorkshireman, a brother of Sir Henry, the scholar, and from his comments in the Commons upon Bacon one would guess that he was an amusing speaker, a type not too common. Incidentally, Sir John owed his post in the Exchequer to Burghley, and probably in reality to Sir Robert Cecil.

55 Bacon spoke on April 11, and I have quoted above what he said. But he said more than is reported by the Clerk or by Bowyer. Savile gives the main point of Bacon's argument.

56 Bowyer, pp. 119–20.

57 *CJ*, 1:297.

58 Now and again Bacon saw through himself. As a speaker he could command his audience, even when he slyly evaded the main point.

59 Sackville, ff. 25–26.

60 Ibid., f. 26.

61 Bowyer, pp. 106–07.

62 Ibid., pp. 132–33.

63 Ibid., pp. 147–48.

64 *CJ*, 1:307–08.

65 *CSP Dom.*, 1603–10, p. 134.

66 *CJ*, 1:307.

67 I think this means revising the price by a second and lower valuation.

68 *CJ*, 1:308.

69 That His Majesty so delighted was a "terminological inexactitude."

70 Sackville, ff. 12–16.

71 Bowyer, p. 165.

72 Ibid., pp. 165–67.
73 *CJ*, 1:317.
74 *CJ*, 1:316–17.

THE NEW SESSION BEGINS

1 Molin to the Doge and Senate, August 25, 1605 (*CSP Ven.,* 1603–07, pp. 267–68).
2 Molin to the Doge and Senate, September 14, 1605 (ibid., p. 270).
3 Molin to the Doge and Senate, October 12, 1605 (ibid., pp. 280–81).
4 October 10, 1605 (Stowe, 168, ff. 169–70).
5 Hoby to Edmondes, February 10, 1605/06 (Birch, 1:45; cf. Bowyer, pp. 6–7).
6 The debates in the *CJ* do not enlighten us as to whom he meant. He might have meant Salisbury.
7 Bowyer, p. 6.
8 Supposing it proved just another tax, was it not better than purveyance as that was said to be practiced?
9 This might have been Giles Brook, M.P. for Liverpool, or Christopher Brooke, M.P. for York. It was probably not William Brock, M.P. for St. Ives, Cornwall, for the Clerk of the House of Commons always spelled his name with a "ck" at the end. I doubt that it was Giles Brook, who never opened his mouth in five sessions, so far as I know, and who went home on April 16, 1605 and probably did not return during that session—while a "Mr. Brook" continued to be named to committees and to report from them. We need to examine all the occasions in 1604 and 1605/06 when "Mr. Brook" either made a speech or was named to a committee. On April 18, 1604, "Mr. Brook of York" made a speech on the union, and on the next day "Mr. Brook, a lawyer" spoke on the union. It has to be taken into account that Christopher Brooke was a member of Lincoln's Inn and that Giles Brook was not connected with Lincoln's Inn, Gray's Inn, the Middle Temple, nor the Inner Temple. Giles Brook was an alderman of Liverpool and probably associated earlier with his father in mercantile and shipping affairs. After these two references to a "Mr. Brook," throughout the sessions of 1604, 1605/06, 1606/07, and 1610, the Clerk simply mentioned the name as if he assumed that there was only one Brook who mattered. In the session of 1605/06, "Mr. Brook" was mentioned on February 18 as being named to the committee about York, Hull, and Newcastle merchants; on March 5 he reported from that committee. On March 15 he was named to the committee formed to draft a bill to prevent extortion by customs officials in ports, etc. On April 10 "Mr. Brook" was added to the committee for free trade. On May 22 he reported from a committee dealing with two bills, and on that same day he seems to have taken part in a debate on a bill for the restraint of excommunication in ecclesiastical courts. I may add that it is evident in several speeches that "Mr. Brook" was on the Puritan side. The *CJ* for 1606/07 mention "Mr. Brook" several times, once on April 30 when he alludes to the Nicene Council and to other matters that only a scholarly person would know about. Christopher Brooke was a poet and a friend of John Donne and of other reading and learned men. In the session of 1610 "Mr. Brook" appears again and again, serving on many committees and making speeches. He remained in the House when attendance was falling off, and he became a man worthy of being named to various committees.

10 Sir Walter Cope was not taken seriously either by Dudley Carleton or John Chamberlain, but he was a handyman for Salisbury and was not wanting in common sense. He was a cousin of Sir Anthony Cope of Hanwell and Banbury, but he had a very different outlook.

11 Bowyer, p. 10; *CJ*, 1:261.

12 Bowyer, pp. 16–17; *CJ*, 1:262.

13 Bowyer, pp. 16–17. A purveyance bill is to be found in *SP*, 46/61, ff. 345–47, but I am not convinced that it was the bill presented to the committee.

14 *CJ*, 1:223.

15 *HMC Salisbury*, 18:55–57.

16 *CJ*, 1:266. Sir Edward Hoby, who knew his way about in the House, had no high opinion of Ridgeway: "Whereby it seemed, that the former day's work, first propounded by Sir Thomas Ridgeway, and seconded by such like (for I must tell you that I think the State scorneth to have any Privy Councillors of any understanding in that House), came short to expectation and necessity" (Hoby to Edmondes, March 7, 1605/06, in Birch, 1:59–60).

17 Spedding, 5:178.

18 Bowyer, p. 31.

19 Scott, *Journal of Sir Roger Wilbraham*, p. 77.

20 *CJ*, 1:266.

21 *CJ*, 1:266. "It was further moved by the Commons to increase the subsidy (for 15ths lay upon the poor towns very heavy)" (Scott, p. 277).

22 "If we buy our laws of justice it were dishonorable to so gracious a King" (ibid.).

23 *CJ*, 1:266–67.

24 Bowyer, p. 32. Wilbraham discussed the early weeks of this session: "For 7 weeks nothing done for any public bill . . . the time most while spent in invectives against purveyors . . . which were termed vultures, harpies, cormorants, and caterpillars and vermin" (Scott, pp. 75–76).

25 Bowyer, p. 32.

PURVEYANCE AND THE LORDS

1 Bowyer, p. 33.

2 Ibid., p. 34.

3 Ibid., p. 40.

4 Ibid., p. 41. Hare was outspoken; it is noticeable that later important members rallied to prevent royal reprisals against him.

5 Ibid., p. 42.

6 *CJ*, 1:269. Dorset's words would have carried weight.

7 "The virginity of the King's promises for repayment of privy seals like to be lost, to his great dishonor" (Scott, p. 76).

8 Croft was an uneasy soul.

9 The strategy of the lapwing in leading intruders away from the nest was imitated as good politics in the early seventeenth century.

10 Bowyer, pp. 46–47.

11 *CJ*, 1:271.

12 For some patronizing remarks by Northampton about the House of Commons, see *HMC Salisbury*, 18:92.

13 Strode was reverting to an old English constitutional device: the King was not well informed. If told the truth, he would do right to his subjects.

14 *CJ*, 1:272.

15 On February 22 Sir Maurice Berkeley moved that a message be sent to the Lords that Hare was cleared, with an expression of hope that there might be no reprehension in conferences. Sir Henry Montague mentioned the conference with the Lords scheduled for the coming Wednesday (this was Monday) as a time when the message might be delivered. It was pointed out, however, that the episode had taken place in committee and that the message should be given to the committees (joint) of the two Houses. On February 24 Yelverton reported from that committee that the message about Hare might be delivered to the Lords at the conference about purveyance, that it should be "mildly tempered" and "only a preservation of the privilege" (*CJ*, 1:273). If the Lords required their reasons, they were to answer with silence, but if they were pressed for an answer, the answer should be given mildly (Bowyer, p. 53). There were wise heads in the House when it came to what we call "public relations."

16 Bowyer, p. 53.

17 Sir Rowland Lytton of Knebworth, M.P. for Hertfordshire, speaking (*CJ*, 1:273). He was a spirited gentleman, an old King Cole, who was on good terms with Salisbury but who followed his own independent line. Frequently a host to John Chamberlain and Dudley Carleton, he was part of a pleasant circle.

18 Hedley speaking (ibid.).

19 *SP*, 14/18/115, quoted in Bowyer, p. 54 n. 1. Of the Speaker it may be said that procrastination was his policy.

20 Hare speaking (*CJ*, 1:274).

21 He mentioned tonnage and poundage, voted regularly by Parliament, as exceptional.

22 *CJ*, 1:274.

23 Cf. the Speaker's letter to Salisbury (*SP*, 14/18/115, quoted in Bowyer, p. 54 n. 1).

THE BATTLE AGAINST PURVEYANCE LOST

1 Bowyer, p. 54.

2 Ibid., p. 55.

3 *CJ*, 1:275.

4 Bacon was quoting from Theodosius: "*Princeps quamvis sit solutus legibus, legibus tamen dirigitur.*" This phrase was later used by Martin on March 6 (*CJ*, 1:279). If I may judge from bits of advice to his sovereign, Sir Francis assumed that every man had his price (in honors, offices, etc.), and if the King wished the support of the Commons he should meet the prices expected.

5 In the same report, Bacon alluded to an "apology touching the speech of Croesus riches." Had Northampton offered an apology, or had some peer apologized for him? His careless but characteristic words in February had no doubt provoked censure; they implied that the King, if he chose, could raise as much money as he liked without the consent of Parliament.

6 Meanwhile the question of free speech was brought up again. At the conference mentioned, the judges had taken exception to words uttered by Yelverton. It was consequently resolved by the Commons that the Speaker should

inform the judges how "tenderly" the Commons regarded the slander of Yelverton, that is, that they were sensitive to slanders upon him.

7   In the midst of the discussion over "composition," members broke away from the subject to bring up the question of subsidies. Sir William Maurice "in a long discourse to little effect" proposed to offer the King four subsidies and six fifteenths. John Bond urged three subsidies and six fifteenths and felt that to enter into the question of a composition was to fall from the frying pan into the fire. Two subsidies and four fifteenths would yield only £250,000 and the King's debt amounted to £750,000. The state had a burning fever, said the physician, and the Commons had to cure it. To wait for another Parliament would cost a subsidy. Whatever the Commons decided to do they should do quickly, so that the King would be able "to fight the Lord's battles [presumably, battles for the Dutch against Spain]" (*CJ*, 1:278; Bowyer, p. 62; *HMC Salisbury*, 18:69).

8   Bowyer, p. 62.

9   Ibid.

10   *CJ*, 1:278.

11   Bowyer, p. 62.

12   *HMC Salisbury*, 18:69.

13   *CJ*, 1:278.

14   Bowyer, p. 63.

15   *HMC Salisbury*, 18:69.

16   Bowyer, p. 63; *CJ*, 1:278.

17   Bowyer, p. 63 n. 1; *HMC Salisbury*, 18:69; *CJ*, 1:279.

18   Catherine S. Sims, "Policies in Parliament," *Huntington Library Quarterly*, 15 (1951):48.

19   "And wished that other men would do the like, which some murmuring against, he said, 'I cry you mercy. I will not pursuing [*sic*] so, for then I should do the King['s] honor wrong, who hath provided for repayment of the loans.' Then said he would speak in earnest" (Bowyer, pp. 63, 64).

20   I have combined Bowyer's account of Martin's speech (pp. 63, 64) with that in *HMC Salisbury* (18:69) and that in Harl., 6850 (quoted in Bowyer, pp. 63–64 n. 2).

21   *CJ*, 1:279. Bowyer (p. 64) records Fortescue as saying "fourscore thousand."

22   Sir Roger Wilbraham's judgement about composition is worth quoting: "The great objection against composition was that King or Parliament could not secure the composition . . . for if 36 acts of Parliament cannot restore the people to their right of inheritance against purveyors, one act now is not available." He seemed to favor the abolition of the name and use of purveyance altogether (Scott, *Journal of Sir Roger Wilbraham*, p. 76).

23   To punish those purveyors who refused to obey the law by the use of the Star Chamber was to sidestep the common law courts.

24. Bowyer, p. 69; *CJ*, 1:280. Cf. the letter from the King to the Commons as published in *HMC Salisbury*, 18:88–89. That letter was largely corrected by Salisbury and in several ways was different from the letter which the Speaker quoted to the Commons. The letter in the Salisbury MS was possibly a draft prepared by Salisbury, much of which was not used by his Majesty.

25   Spedding, 3:270–71.

26   Sandys was philosophical about careers: "Popularity is won with a trifle and lost in an instant. Great men can only be populars, for from hence we return to our private." Did he mean that only great men, if they became "populars," could avoid the loss of their posts?

27 Sir Robert Harley's notes (Harl., 6846, ff. 197–197v, quoted in Bowyer, p. 70 n. 1). Cf. *CJ*, 1:280–81.

28 *CJ*, 1:280.

29 Wilbraham wrote in his notes that it was supposed by the lawyers of the Commons "that the King's Majesty had by prerogative only a preemption, but no prerogative in prices" (Scott, p. 76).

30 Bowyer, p. 70 n. 1; cf. *CJ*, 1:280–81.

31 "If thirty-seven laws produced no effect, then thirty-eight none" (*CJ*, 1:281).

32 Bowyer, p. 71; cf. Wilbraham's point of view (Scott, p. 87).

33 In early May the idea of the King developing an income out of the Fen lands was presented by the Speaker to the King, but in Lake's opinion the King was so hurried that he had given little attention to the plan. Lake assumed that the Speaker would not have written to the King without the approval of Salisbury (Lake to Salisbury, May 8, 1606, in *HMC Salisbury*, 18:131).

COMPOSITION OR NOT

1 "The benignity, bounty, and piety of our King and his necessity amplified by many proverbs" (Scott, p. 77).

2 Bowyer, pp. 74–75.

3 *CJ*, 1:282.

4 Bowyer, p. 72 n. 1.

5 Yelverton speaking (*CJ*, 1:283; Bowyer, p. 75).

6 *CJ*, 1:282.

7 *CJ*, 1:282.

8 Ibid.

9 At that Great Committee the afternoon of the next day, Bowyer came in late and found the members considering supply to the King. Various people spoke, and then Mr. Gawyn (Walter Gawen from Heytesbury, Wiltshire), "a plain fellow who remembered that the King's debts were delivered by an honorable personage to be seven hundred seventy thousand pounds, but quoth he, here is no mention of any deduction in respect of 2 subsidies and a half and 4 fifteens granted to the late Queen, and since her death paid to his Majesty whereby the debt ought to be so much the less" (Bowyer, p. 77). To this charge I have not seen an answer, but that is far from saying that no answer was made.

10 *CJ*, 1:283.

11 An argument that could have been made against many useful laws.

12 *CJ*, 1:297; Bowyer, p. 121. Fuller introduced his speech and concluded on a personal note. When in the joint session with the Lords he had asked time to answer the objection of the Lords, he had been told by a "great one" that he had better leave that unsaid. He wanted witnesses to confirm that he had spoken nothing offensively. "All the House with a general acclamation and approbation of his speech did clear him of all fault." This episode in the history of free speech in Parliament the Clerk did not record.

13 Sir John Savile speaking (Bowyer, pp. 121–22).

14 Yelverton was given to metaphors but not to understatement. He had not as yet been put through the wringer by his Majesty.

15 I have combined Carleton's phrasing of Yelverton's metaphor in his letter to

Chamberlain (*SP*, 14/20/36, quoted in Bowyer, p. 134) with Bowyer's wording of the metaphor (Bowyer, p. 123). In the conference Sir John Popham, the Lord Chief Justice, had insisted, contrary to statements made repeatedly in the Commons, that the King had in some things a prerogative of prices to be taken. Sir John, who was seventy-four, was trusting to his memory of what he believed he had once seen in a book. Yelverton, in reply, declared that there was no such thing as a prerogative of prices to be taken. Cf. *CJ*, 1:297; Bowyer, pp. 120–22.

16 *CJ*, 1:298.
17 Carleton to Chamberlain (*SP*, 14/20/36).
18 *CJ*, 1:299.
19 Bowyer, pp. 134–35. About the *non obstante*, see p. 533 n. 3.
20 On March 11 Myddleton had remarked: "The peace and fruits of the peace in a few men's hands." Myddleton (whether Hugh or Robert I am not sure) was himself a member of a wealthy family.
21 A clear example of what was later to be called the previous question.
22 *SP*, 14/19/57, quoted in Bowyer, p. 83 n. 2.
23 Bowyer, p. 83 and nn.
24 Ibid., p. 84.
25 Ibid.
26 Ibid.; *CJ*, 1:286. Sir Robert Drury, in a letter to Salisbury (*HMC Salisbury*, 18:94), asserted that he came into the House at the right instant to sway the House by a single vote. On March 14 he had declared there was a necessity to grant more (*CJ*, 1:284). He had evidently consulted Salisbury about one speech, but he felt compelled to apologize to him for another speech.
27 *SP*, 14/19/59; *Bowyer*, pp. 84–85 n. 1.
28 Bowyer, pp. 84–85 n. 1.
29 See the form of the message in *HMC Salisbury*, 18:89–90, which is somewhat different from that recorded by Bowyer. It has corrections by Salisbury and was probably Salisbury's draft of what he proposed that the King should say.
30 *CJ*, 1:289.
31 Spedding, 3:277.
32 *CJ*, 1:309.

Chapter 3

THE INSTRUMENT OF UNION

1 Carleton to Chamberlain (*SP*, 14/24/23, quoted in Bowyer, p. 208 n. 1).
2 Antoine Lefevre de la Boderie, *Ambassades de la Boderie en Angleterre . . . depuis les Annees 1601 jusqu'en 1611* (Paris, 1750), 1:433–34.
3 The Scots regarded their nobility as of longer lineage than their English counterparts.
4 *CJ*, 1:1004.
5 *CSP Ven.*, 1603–07, pp. 438–39. For a very unfriendly account of the Scots in London, see Godfrey Goodman, *The Court of King James the First* (London, 1839), 1:320–21. Goodman was writing from memory of the past generation and is not to be taken too seriously.
6 *CJ*, 1:323.
7 S. R. Gardiner, *History of England*, 1:325–27.
8 *HMC 3rd Rep.*, pp. 11–12.

THE DISCUSSION: HOW TO PROCEED

1   *CJ*, 1:1004.
2   Bowyer, p. 191.
3   Ibid., pp. 191–92.
4   *CJ*, 1:1004.
5   Ibid.
6   Spedding, 3:303–04.
7   Bowyer, pp. 193–94.
8   Ibid.; *CJ*, 1:325.
9   Titus F IV, f. 94, quoted in Bowyer, p. 194 n. 1. Did his fellow members suspect that Hoby believed the English commissioners had yielded too much?
10 Harl., 6850, ff. 61–62, Harl., 6842, ff. 6–7v, quoted in Bowyer, p. 195 n. 1.
11 Bowyer, p. 195.
12 It is little wonder that the Commons were willing to leave the problem of the border to the Upper House. About conditions on the border, see G. H. Powell, ed., *Memoirs of Robert Cary* (London, 1905), pp. 37–50, and many references in the State Papers Domestic from 1603 to 1610.
13 Harl., 6850, ff. 61–62, Harl., 6842, ff. 6–7v, quoted in Bowyer, pp. 195–96 n. 1, 195–98.
14 It was at this point that the question of escuage was raised in the House. It will be recalled that escuage was the feudal obligation to accompany the King for forty days (in some small tenures for fewer days) on warlike expeditions into Scotland. It was said in the House that the King's proclamation meant that escuage came to an end. The question was raised by Fuller, first on November 27 and then on December 3; it was argued on the next day. In the debate Fuller maintained that the union took escuage away, and Francis Moore agreed with him (Wilson to Salisbury, in *SP*, 14/24/13, quoted in Bowyer, p. 201 n. 2; *CJ*, 1:107). Wilson, the notetaker for Salisbury, wrote: "The arguments of both sides were many. . . . The most and best that spake, was for the remaining of escuage. But the generalist applause was upon them that would have it taken away." Evidently some eager beavers in the House hoped that the end of escuage might bring with it the end of wardship (de la Boderie, 1:475–65). The matter came up again on December 15, and the arguments for and against it were then rehearsed. It was finally determined to request the opinion of the Lords, as Richard Martin had suggested. On December 18 Carleton wrote Chamberlain: "The matter of escuage which you left so hot in dispute was concluded by the Chief Justices in one word, that though the service ceaseth, the King's profit must continue" (*SJ*, 14/24/23).
15 He was right about artificers. The English villages, at least in the eastern counties, were crowded with them.
16 Harl., 6850, ff. 55v, 61–62, Harl., 6842, ff. 6–7v, quoted in Bowyer, pp. 195–98, p. 198 n. 1; *CJ*, 1:1005.
17 *CJ*, 1:1005. Were the Lords beginning to be a little on the defensive?
18 Bowyer, p. 199; *CJ*, 1:326.
19 *CJ*, 1:1006.
20 Could "political" here mean "of local policy"?
21 Fuller speaking (*CJ*, 1:1006). The ultimate supremacy of Parliament had not yet been established.

22 *CJ*, 1:1006.
23 Bowyer, p. 201; cf. *CJ*, 1:1007.
24 The guild or fraternity dealing with lighthouses, pilots, buoys, etc.
25 *SP*, 14/24/16, quoted in Bowyer, p. 203 n. 2.
26 *CJ*, 1:1008.
27 *CJ*, 1:1009.
28 *SP*, 14/24/23, quoted in Bowyer, pp. 208–09 n. 1.
29 On December 18 Wilson wrote to Salisbury: "At my coming forth Mr. Naunton told me privately that it was voiced in the House that my Lord of Salisbury is a furtherer of the matter and would be willing for the glory of your name that in your time of being Master of the Wards, the wards might be taken away." It is conceivable that Salisbury was toying with such a step (*SP*, 14/24/13, quoted in Bowyer, pp. 201–02 n. 2).

HOSTILE LAWS: COMMERCE AND NATURALIZATION

1   *CJ*, 1:1012.
2   See Titus F IV, f. 77–78.
3   *CJ*, 1:333–34; Bowyer, p. 207. Cf. Carleton to Chamberlain, *SP*, 14/24/23, quoted in Bowyer, pp. 208–09 n. 1.
4   *CJ*, 1:333–34.
5   *CJ*, 1:1012–13. The Scots had eight several privileges allowed them by the French.
6   Presumably about hostile laws (*CJ*, 1:1013; cf. Bowyer, p. 209).
7   The right of a tenant to take necessary wood from his landlord.
8   *CJ*, 1:335, 1013; W. Cobbett, *Parliamentary History* (London, 1806), 1:1082–83.
9   Spedding, 3:307–25.
10 Arthur Wilson (*History of England* [London, 1653], p. 37) said of Bacon's speech: "'These arguments pressed with gilded oratory by the Solicitor and his partakers, could not prevail, though urged with all the power wit could invent, or hope aim at. For being new-budded in Court, he was one of those that smoothed his way to a full ripeness by liquorish and pleasing passages. . . . But such sweets, though delightful at present, breed rottenness in the end." Bacon was not yet Solicitor but was soon to be so. Wilson had just been summarizing Bacon's speech and did not remember that he did not become Solicitor until the following June. Wilson's last comment shows that not uncommon distrust of facility.
11 Holt speaking (*CJ*, 1:1017).
12 *CJ*, 1:1019.
13 *CJ*, 1:339. "The opinion of the House touching the point of naturalization was contrary to that which had been delivered by the Judges. Whereupon much dispute grew how they might have their opinion of force against that of the Judges, and to remain to posterity. It was thought that a memorial made thereof by the Clerk in his Book would little avail in another age, and they were assured they should never pass a bill thereof. So as, whatsoever had been said therein, and the reasons delivered were nowhere recorded" (Titus F IV, f. 99).
14 *CJ*, 1:1020–21, 340.
15 *CJ*, 1:1021.
16 Bowyer, p. 283.

17   *CJ,* 1:345, 1022.

18   The best report of this conference is in Somers Tracts, 2:133–43. Cf. Sir Francis Moore's *Reports* (*English Reports* [Edinburgh and London, 1907]), 72:908–17.

19   Spedding, 3:329–32, from *SP,* 14/26/66; Somers Tracts, 1:139; *CJ,* 1:1024.

20   Spedding, 3:329–31.

21   *CJ,* 1:1024.

22   Ibid. I have ventured to enlarge and interpret the brief notations of Hyde's words by the Clerk.

23   *CJ,* 1:1025.

24   Ibid.

25   Bowyer, p. 211; *CJ,* 1:1025–26. See also *SP,* 14/26/70, quoted in Bowyer, pp. 211–12 and n. 2. When the committee reported to the House there was debate. The Recorder, Montague, asserted that the Scots were neither naturalized nor aliens. If a Scot, being in the King's allegiance, purchased land in England, "the law cannot deny him." But while in England he could not be a juror, an officer of the Crown, nor anything else. If he departed from England and left his land, he was no longer bound to the subjection of England.

26   The Lords complained that Hoby had spoken of the "Knights, Citizens, Burgesses and Barons of the Commons Court of Parliament." Hoby told the Commons that he had said, "Barons of the Commons House of Parliament." In any case, the Lords, displeased with the Commons, saw a chance to score a point against them.

27   *LJ,* 2:483.

28   *CJ,* 1:1027, 349; Bowyer, p. 217.

29   Bowyer, p. 214 n. 1. Since it comes out that Wingfield had talked to the King about speeches in the House, he was probably not in the inner councils of Sandys and his associates.

THE PERFECT UNION PROPOSED

1   In committee Sandys was reported to have said: "The fault or defect why the Union cannot be so perfect as were to be desired, is on the part of the Scots, by reason of a restriction or reservation made in their Act for preservation and continuance of their fundamental laws, and not in our Act.

"While they continue a distinct body from us, it is no reason to communicate all the benefits of our estate to them. It may be better to grant a measure only of the benefits at this time than to yield all at the first, lest they, having a complacence [*sic*] and acquiescence therein, shall not care, or be unwilling hereafter to proceed to the more perfect Union of the laws. And therefore good to keep them in appetite, hoping that, when they shall find their own fault, why there is no more granted at this time, they will be readier to reform hereafter, and this is to be taken for a great sign of our love" (Rawl., A. 123, f. 9v).

2   The relation of Scotland to France after the union with England was the topic of much discussion in the committee and of difference of opinion. "It was thought good by the Committees that they shall renounce their incorporation with France, but not so resolved to be, but to be proposed to the Lords to receive further light from their Lordships" (Bowyer, p. 220).

3 About *non obstante* see Sir Edward Coke, *The Third Part of the Institutes* (London, 1660), pp. 154, 236. Coke says: "It hath been conceived (which we will not question) that the King may dispense with these laws by a *non obstante,* be it general or special (albeit we find not any such clauses of *non obstante* to dispense with any of those statutes, but of late times)." Cf. Edward Coke, *Reports* (London, 1826), 12:f. 18. See also *The Reports of . . . Sir Henry Hobart* (London, 1671), pp. 75, 148, 214, 230–31; and *Un Continuation des Reports de Henry Rolle* (London, 1676), p. 115. And, in particular, see *The Fourth Part of the Institutes of the Laws of England Compiled . . . By Sir Edward Cooke,* Published and Reprinted . . . since his death by William Prynne (London, 1667), pp. 129–31. Prynne deals at length with *non obstante.* For Plucknett's view, see T. P. Taswell-Langmead, *English Constitutional History,* rev. T. F. T. Plucknett (Boston, 1946). Plucknett speaks of "this obscure legal situation." It would appear that there was still a question as to just how far the King could make use of a *non obstante.*

4 "Sir Roger Owen. That it was to be lawful for them to purchase and inherit. But order to be taken that they shall not convey away the treasure of this Kingdom, since by possibility of their great possessions, this Kingdom may be impoverished and the greater become the less." The source of this quotation has not been discovered, but see Bowyer, p. 227, for a similar account of Owen's remarks.

5 Francis Moore dealt in committee with the question of wards: "Education of the ward to be in England, if the ward be bestowed on a Scottishman, because it is inconvenient; since they shall not be trained in our laws and customs, the school and seminary of this Kingdom to those that shall have offices in the Commonwealth" (Rawl., A. 123, f. 11). Francis Moore talked like a nineteenth-century man about the relation of the "public schools" to the Civil Service.

6 Sir John Bennet's detailed statement (Rawl., A. 123, f. 11), is practically the same as that in Bowyer, p. 227 n. 3, and in *CJ,* 1:1028.

7 In the Instrument of Union it had been proposed that Scots be allowed to acquire lands, inheritances, offices, dignities, liberties, privileges, immunities, benefices, and preferments "other than to acquire, possess, succeed, or inherit any office of the Crown, office of judicature, or any voice, place or office in Parliament" (*CJ,* 1:323).

8 *CJ,* 1:350, 1028. Cf. Bowyer, pp. 226–27; *SP,* 14/26/78.

9 Bowyer, p. 231.

10 Ibid., pp. 224–25.

11 *SP,* 14/26/85, quoted in Bowyer, pp. 237–39 and n. 1.

12 Ibid.

THE COMMONS AND THE LORDS COLLIDE

1 Bowyer, p. 238.

2 Salisbury to Lake (*SP,* 14/26/91, quoted in Bowyer, p. 240 n. 1).

3 Bowyer, pp. 239–40.

4 This was an allusion to a sentence in Sandys's speech: "I am sorry that it is my fortune to deliver anything displeasing to your Lordships, and dissent is always displeasing" (Ibid., p. 238).

5 "We conferred with the Lords but brake off upon the difference of *Post* and

Ante natos" (*HMC Buccleuch*, 3:114). Sir Edward Montague was intent upon having his Latin accusative.

6 Salisbury to Lake (*SP*, 14/26/91, quoted in Bowyer, p. 241 n. 1).
7 Ibid.
8 Ibid., p. 243.
9 *CJ*, 1:1032.
10 Bowyer, pp. 246–47.
11 Spedding, 3:335.
12 Bowyer, p. 247.
13 Spedding, 3:336.
14 *CJ*, 1:1034.
15 Bowyer, p. 248.
16 These two paragraphs are based upon *CJ*, 1:1034, and Bowyer, pp. 248–50.

THE KING INTERVENES

1 Alford had proposed that Bacon and Montague, the Recorder, should take notes of the proceedings before the King (Bowyer, p. 251), but others thought that the Speaker was the proper person to inform the House, "If occasion be." See Foster, 2:376.
2 McIlwain, *Political Works of James I*, pp. 290–305; *CJ*, 1:357–63.
3 Was he thinking of the anti-Scottish provisions in the "constitutions" of some northern boroughs?

THE PERFECT UNION AGAIN

1 This account of Sandys's speech is based upon the Harley Papers quoted in Bowyer's footnotes, upon Bowyer's account, and upon the account in the *CJ*.
2 In *CJ*, 1:1037, Alford is put down as John Alford. There was a John Alford who served in Parliament for Hedon in 1588 and for Shoreham in 1625–26, but I doubt if he (or they) were in this Parliament. The speech was probably by Edward Alford, M.P. for Colchester.
3 Croft speaking (Bowyer, p. 262; *CJ*, 1:1036).
4 Fuller speaking (Bowyer, pp. 263–66).
5 E.g., Owen (Bowyer, pp. 269–70; *CJ*, 1:1037); also Holt (Bowyer, p. 277; *CJ*, 1:1038).
6 Owen speaking (Bowyer, p. 270. Cf. Hobart's answer, ibid., p. 273; *CJ*, 1:1037).
7 Croft and Fuller (Bowyer, pp. 262, 266; *CJ*, 1:1036, 1037).
8 Croft speaking (Bowyer, p. 262).
9 Fuller speaking: "Then having both they will never come nearer to us" (ibid., pp. 264–65).
10 Fuller speaking (ibid., p. 265; *CJ*, 1:1037).
11 Ibid.
12 Alford speaking (Bowyer, p. 267 n. 1); Yelverton speaking (ibid., p. 283; *CJ*, 1:1038).
13 Alford speaking (Bowyer, p. 267).
14 Ibid., p. 280.
15 Ibid., pp. 282–83.

16 Ibid., pp. 261, 274.
17 Ibid., p. 268; *CJ*, 1:1037.
18 Bowyer, pp. 272 n. 1, 273.
19 Ibid., pp. 278–80.
20 Ibid., p. 269.
21 *CJ*, 1:1037.

ANOTHER ROYAL ADDRESS: CONCLUSION

1 *CJ*, 1:366–68.
2 By which he would seem to have meant that the opinion that the King was under the law was a foolish diversion. The Henrician member had perhaps been quoting Bracton.
3 The suggestion of the thunderbolts he might hurl may not have displeased him.
4 *CJ*, 1:370, 1041.
5 Bowyer, pp. 376–78.
6 Ibid.
7 Ibid., pp. 378–81.
8 Ibid., pp. 289–90.
9 Ibid., pp. 376–81.
10 Ibid.
11 Ibid., pp. 382–83; Cf. *SP*, 14/21/17, quoted in Spedding, 3:343–45.
12 Bowyer, pp. 382–83.
13 Ibid., pp. 383–86.
14 Ibid., pp. 384–85.
15 When James talked of his "honor" it was best for the Commons to be wary.
16 Bowyer, pp. 298–99; *CJ*, 1:1046.

Chapter 4

THE SESSION BEGINS

1 It took two hours to deliver (Harl., 777, ff. 2v–14; Add. 48119, ff. 143–59).
2 *CJ*, 1:395.
3 Add. 48119, f. 150.
4 An elderly friend and regular correspondent of Trumbull's (*HMC Downshire*, 2:217).
5 Winwood, 3:123–24.
6 For Salisbury's introduction to his financial statement, see Harl., 777, ff. 5–5v.
7 *Parl. Debates 1610*, 4. Cf. de la Boderie to M. de Puiseux, April 20, 1610 (*Ambassades*, v: 187): "La verite est que tous les peuple crient apres la guerre."
8 Add. 48119, f. 146v.
9 Beaulieu, writing to Trumbull, made the sum £400,000 (Winwood, 3:123). The *CJ* (1:395) made it £300,000, as did Harl., 777, f. 7. See also Spedding, 4:157 (quoting from Titus C. x, f. 125v, and *Parl. Debates 1610*, p. 5).
10 Beaulieu (to Trumbull) made it £81,000 (Winwood, 3:123). The writer of the account in Add. 48119 (f. 147) made it £81,000. The author of *Parl. Debates 1610* (p. 5) made it £46,000 per annum. But Harl., 777, f. 7, made Salisbury say that the inequality had risen to £140,000 by Michaelmas 1609. Brooke, in

a speech on February 19, spoke of £81,000 (*CJ*, 1:397). Gardiner, in a foot-note to *Parl. Debates 1610* (p. 5), says that this difference is explained by one report which took account of the extraordinary expenses neglected by the others. Salisbury later made a comment on his figures: "I am the worst reckoner in the world. My papers will yield you a better reckoning than my brain" (Lansd., 486, f. 129).

11   Add. 48119, f. 147v.
12   Beaulieu to Trumbull, February 23 (Winwood, 3:123–24).
13   " 'Tis without precedent in 600 years that the Parliament was ever so close-fisted . . . as to deny to give aid when 'twas demanded" (Salisbury speaking, quoted in Add. 48119, f. 147).
14   Harl., 777, f. 13.
15   *Parl. Debates 1610*, p. 8.
16   The last five paragraphs beginning with Salisbury's answers to objections are based on five sources: *CJ*, 1:395–96; Harl., 777, ff. 11–15; *Parl. Debates 1610*, pp. 7–9; Wilson, *History of England*, pp. 44–45; Add. 48119, ff. 146–49. Wilson's account is not to be ignored; it was evidently made from notes taken at the time. About the King's influence in the speech, see Foster, 2:10. Salisbury had started by saying that he did not expect to use elaborate phrases, as orators might. If the speech were made at the "appointment and direction of the King," it contained statements that were characteristic of an old House-of-Commons man.
17   Add. 48119, f. 148v. "His first three years were his Christmas," so Salisbury is made to say in the Folger MS. "As for the King's bounty it cannot be blamed . . . being unknown to the people, and they most importunate and unman-nerly in asking, [he] could not deny them" (Fogler, V, a. 277, f. 3v).
18   *Parl. Debates 1610*, p. 8.
19   Beaulieu to Trumbull, March 1 (Winwood, 3:124–26).
20   The first reference that I know of to a Contract was on February 21 and was made by Sir Edwin Sandys (*CJ*, 1:398).
21   Correr to Doge and Senate, March 18 (*CSP Ven.*, 1607–10, pp. 446–47).
22   Beaulieu to Trumbull, March 1 (Winwood, 3:124–26).
23   "His Majesty's party will deal everyone with his friend and acquaintance of the House to work them to some better reason" (ibid., 3:235–36).
24   Surely this is Richard Martin, who had taken a large part in debates. The other Martin, M.P. for Wootton Bassett, so far as I know never said a word.
25   When I mention Sandys I mean Sir Edwin, who was much to the fore. When I mean Sir Samuel Sandys, I shall so call him.
26   *Basilikon Doron* (1596).
27   "Without charging the poorer sort who have no lands" (*Parl. Debates 1610*, p. 11).
28   Occasionally in the Elizabethan House of Commons a voice was raised in be-half of the common man, usually in the matter of taxation.
29   *Statutes of the Realm* (London, 1767–77), 2:39–43.
30   Ibid., 2:133.
31   *Parl. Debates 1610*, p. 12. Caesar probably prepared many of the figures and estimates Salisbury had presented to the House. He was a competent man of business and, for his time, as disinterested an official as was likely to hold office.

THE DEMANDS AND CONCESSIONS OF THE CROWN

1 Winwood, 3:123. Why did Salisbury assume that the Commons would be pleased with a plan that made their assemblies unnecessary?

2 "Now to talk with the Lower House about the retribution before we receive contribution, I think is altogether unfit" (Salisbury to the Committee of the Whole House of the Lords, February 24, in Folger V, a. 277, f. 7v). Ellesmere, in his speech on the same occasion, was less hopeful: "Here is nothing but *quid vultis mihi dare,* and, unless the King will retribute he is likely to have no contribution. . . . which seemed to him as strange as might be." He added that, in all the Parliaments of which he had read, after the King's ends were satisfied he would give way to the petitions of the Commons (ibid., f. 8).

3 The Braye MS, 61, f. 1, gives some account of Salisbury's speech. He asked £146,000 for His Majesty's ordinary expenses and provision for the Prince, the Duke of York, and the Princess Elizabeth. For the King's extraordinary expenses he asked £600,000 ("which falleth within men's guess"), and he wanted £180,000 as well to be *in deposito* for emergencies. He wished some offer from them, not necessarily final. The speech is clearer in Harl., 777, ff. 15v–17v. The Folger MS (V, a. 277, f. 8v) records Salisbury as saying: "If our demands be too great, offer what you will, and then will we show you our reasons without prevarication." Salisbury was obviously worried about the size of the demands. Earlier in the same conference he had asked for money "that we of his Council may not be driven to stand as we have of late with our caps in our hands to the usurers."

4 Folger, V, a. 277, f. 9.

5 "That it may be lawful for the subject to plead, Not Guilty, to an information of intrusion exibited by the King's Attorney, and in the meantime, till the matter be tried, to keep possession. This can no way prejudice the King's just title, for if he have right it must take place for all his pleading, and for the possession chiefly it relieveth the subjects in suits commenced against them in the King's name upon a surmise, when it stands with great justice to help them until the surmise be proved" ("A Collection of Such Things as have been by Several Men Desired to be Obtained of his Majesty for the Good of his People," in Carte, 77, ff. 131–32). "The subject upon an information of Intrusion shall be admitted to his general plea of Not Guilty, and not be forced to plead specially, neither stand in fear of any injunction to turn him out of possession, when he hath continued a certain time, etc. which now rests merely in the discretion of the judge" (Harl., 777, f. 17, in *Parl. Debates 1610,* p. 16, n. *c*). "At Common Law in an information of Intrusion the defendant might plead *Non Intrusit* generally . . . or Not Guilty. . . . But the King in virtue of his prerogative could compel him by a *scire facias* to show his title specially" (Coke, *Reports,* p. 42, n. *g*). It was in 1624 that the benefit of pleading the General Issue of Not Guilty was finally granted to those in possession twenty years. See 21 Jac. I, cap. xvi; also *Commons Debates, 1621,* 3:284, 5:142, 175, 7:263–64 (the proposed statute of 1621), 301; E. Nicholas, *Proceedings and Debates of the House of Commons* (Oxford, 1766), 2:23; John Cowell, *The Interpreter* (1607), "Issue," "Intrusion," "Entry."

6 "The Lower House did move us to move the King that they and we might

treat touching the wards, not that we should now dispute whether we would advise the King to depart with the wards, but to understand his pleasure whether that matter shall be disputed" (Salisbury speaking in the Lords, in Braye, 61, f. 2).

7 "A great many members here call for £10,000, £30,000, etc. The Navy lies unfurnished, the staff in the King's house must be renewed. The vessel is defective. All the forts need present reparation. The Realm not in safety without these. These will require £150,000, in all £450,000" (Harl., 777, f. 18). Cf. *CJ*, 1:401.

THE COMMONS CONSIDER SALISBURY'S PROPOSALS

1 On February 26 Salisbury, in speaking to the Lords, had remarked: "Yet seeing we had promised to inform the King of the Lower House desire, it were fit we should be as good as our words. Although he had little heart to speak of retribution before contribution" (Folger, V, a. 277, f. 10v).
2 Harl., 777, f. 19; cf. *CJ*, 1:402.
3 *CJ*, 1:402.
4 Ibid.
5 *CJ*, 1:403.
6 Ibid.
7 *LJ*, 2:560; my italics.
8 Spedding, 4:163 n. 1. On March 1, at the conference in the afternoon, the Commons raised with the Lords the question of supply and support: "For support, it being a thing most strange unto us and unusual, we depend upon your Lordships' answer." In answer, Northampton said: "Your willingness to enter into consideration of the King's wants with us shews the like desire unto ours, being both of us but one body unto our Master, the golden head thereof" (Folger, V, a. 277, f. 13). Further on he remarked: "It seems there is a fear that the King will continue his great expense but . . . you may assure yourselves . . . he will limit himself within the bounds of judgment and moderation" (ibid., f. 14).
9 *CJ*, 1:401.
10 Harl., 777, f. 20.
11 *CJ*, 1:403.

PRESSURE ON THE KING ABOUT WARDSHIP

1 "No Church in distress but the King had salved it out of his bounty" (Harl., 777, f. 22v).
2 There was something amusing in the old reprobate's praise of the King's morals.
3 "Neither may we strike up a drum and then gather cockles" (Harl., 777, f. 24v).
4 *Parl. Debates 1610*, p. 21.
5 Ibid., p. 22.
6 *CJ*, 1:408–09; cf. *Parl. Debates 1610*, pp. 24–25. Salisbury was praising, I think, the largeness of the soul of the King in promising not to be angry if he

were refused subsidies. If so, he was possibly praising a quality in the sovereign which he hoped James would exhibit.

7 In *Parl. Debates 1610* (p. 26) the word is 'imperial," which I have changed to "perpetual," as in the Folger MS. Probably "imperial" was a copyist's error, though the word is possible.

8 James's defense of wardship was typical of the kind of unreal argument in which he liked to indulge. On March 8 Beaulieu wrote Trumbull of the King's scruples and ventured the judgment that they were artificial, "pour encherir d'avantage le Marche" (Winwood, 3:129–30).

9 *Parl. Debates 1610*, p. 27.

10 Folger, V a. 277, f. 21.

11 'He was confined [confident] in God that he should effect it in his reign. He would be glad to bind the hands of his heirs that they, though they might have minds, they should not have means to give [grieve] the people" (Harl., 777, f. 29). Northampton's version from the Braye MS (61, f. 12) is clearer: "His Majesty spake of the businesses in hand among us, first of grievances, which he was willing to ease, so as if any of his successors should have will to grieve the people again, they should have no power." Cf. *CJ*, 1:410.

12 "Purveyance, etc, he is willing should be taken away, if you can devise him any course how to maintain his honor and the necessaries for his house" (from the account of Northampton's speech in which he reported the King's address, in Folger, V, a. 277, f. 22).

13 Thus *CJ*, 1:410. The Folger MS (f. 21v) has Northampton say "Astyages."

14 Titus C VI, f. 451v, in *Parl. Debates 1610*, p. 28 n. *a*.

THE KING'S OFFER DISCUSSED

1 "It pleased him [the King] to marshall other things that for corruption of ministers and palpable abuses in their execution of trust, as purveyance, etc., have been oftentimes complained of, but ever . . . acknowledged to be so necessary for the maintenance of regality, as without the same it could not possibly subsist. But yet his Majesty is pleased . . . to depart with it upon such valuable consideration as might give ease to the subject, without his own prejudice" (Titus C VI, ff. 450–51).

2 March 15. *HMC Downshire*, 2:262–63. Cf. Edmondes to Trumbull, March 17, 1609/10 (Winwood, 3:137).

3 Perhaps after the members heard a résumé of Northampton's speech they realized that they had best put their hopes on Salisbury (*CJ*, 1:411; Harl., 777, f. 30).

4 There seems to have been a difference of opinion as to how the thanks should be conveyed to the King. On March 14 a committee was named to confer with the Speaker on the matter. Finally it was determined that the House should not cooperate with the Lords in sending their thanks but should send their Speaker to the King and inform the Lords that they had done so (*CJ*, 1:411; *LJ*, 2:568–69; Titus F IV, f. 112v). In all this Salisbury played an interesting role, according to the Braye MS (61, ff. 13v–14v). When it was proposed in the Upper House that the Lords send thanks to the King, the "Lord Treasurer thought it fit that the Lower House is to have priority in presenting their thanks, they having held so good correspondency with us, and for that they first moved this course." In a second speech, the Lord Treasurer urged that

the Lords' message to the King be short, since "far too many orations are used" (ibid.). Compare the Braye version of Salisbury's speech with the Folger version (V, a. 277, f. 24).

5 Winwood, 3:131; cf. Taverner to Trumbull, March 30 (*HMC Devonshire*, 2:85–87).

6 Beaulieu to Trumbull, March 1 (Winwood, 3:124–26.) Cf. Correr to the Doge and Senate, March 11 (*CSP Ven.*, 1607–10, pp. 443–45).

7 Correr to the Doge and Senate, April 1 (ibid., pp. 450–51).

8 Correr to the Doge and Senate, March 18 (ibid., pp. 446–47).

9 Or it is possible that the Venetian ambassador misunderstood what was said to him?

10 Edmondes to Trumbull, March 8 (*HMC Downshire*, 2:257–58). I am depending here on the analysis of the situation by Edmondes, who was a member of the House and whose information was often correct. There is much in the later conduct of the Commons to confirm the opinion of Edmondes as to the feeling of the Lower House. See also the letters of the ambassadors—Contarini and Correr—to the Doge and Senate on March 4 (*CSP Ven.*, 1607–10, pp. 438–40).

11 Cf. Correr to Doge and Senate, ibid., pp. 443–45, 446–47, 450–51, 474–76. See also Taverner to Trumbull, March 30 (*HMC Downshire*, 2:85–87).

THE KING'S SPEECH

1 If James were reporting accurately the rumors he had picked up, it would appear that some members were talking rather desperately of the intentions of His Majesty. It is possible, of course, that those Councillors who hoped to see the King take a stronger course were passing him such reports in order to encourage him to asesrt himself.

2 The speech is to be found in McIlwain's *Political Works of James I* (pp. 306–25) and was reprinted from a pamphlet edition of 1647. Both Arthur Wilson and Sir William Sanderson gave brief accounts of the speech based upon contemporary notes.

3 Cf. Adam Blackwood, *Adversus Georgii Buchani Dialogum de Jure Regni apud Scotus pro Regibus Apologia* (1581), p. 61. From a hurried skimming of this book, I am inclined to believe that James was familiar with it.

4 About prohibitions, see Gardiner, *History of England, 1603–1642*, 2:35–42, 122–23.

5 Folger, V a. 277, f. 29.

6 Ibid.

7 Sir William Sanderson, *A Compleat History* (London, 1656), p. 355.

8 McIlwain, pp. 315–16.

9 It is conceivable that James had not asked Privy Councillors to look out for elections to the House of Commons, but he must have known that some of them had long been busy asking boroughs to elect certain men whom they nominated. The King had not named the number of subsidies he desired, but his Councillors had been definite about the sums of money needed by the Crown, and it is hard to believe that Salisbury's speeches concerning the financial needs of the government had not been uttered after careful consultation with His Majesty.

10 McIlwain, p. 318.

11 Folger, V a. 277, f. 30.
12 Ibid.
13 Ibid. He added something more, to be found in the official version: "For though it was vainly said by one of your House, that ye had need to beware that by giving me too much, your throats were not in danger of cutting at your coming home" (McIlwain, p. 317).
14 Folger, V a. 277, f. 30v.
15 McIlwain, p. 320.
16 Sanderson, p. 358.
17 An interesting statement from James, who gave little thought to the world of commerce.
18 Folger, V a. 277, f. 32.
19 John Moore was a secretary and general factotum to Winwood and later became Clerk of the Signet (Winwood, 3:141–42).

ECCLESIASTICAL GRIEVANCES

1 *Statutes at Large,* 2:624–25.
2 C. J. C. Jeaffreson, *Middlesex Co. Records* (London, 1888–92), 2:212–15.
3 The formulation of those articles was, of course, influenced by the news of the assassination of the King of France, attributed by many at the time to the Jesuits.
4 Add. 48119, ff. 171–171v.
5 On June 10 Samuel Calvert (a cousin of George Calvert but apparently not of the Catholic faith) wrote to Trumbull that Parliament was attempting to "secure the State." They had gained a proclamation by the King against recusants "which, if it take effect, will be happy for us." He said, further that the Lords, or some of the Privy Councillors, were keeping the King in a cloud and that he could not distinguish between judgment and affections. Calvert believed that the populace thought there had never been a House so honest to the State; he seemed to believe that the King was adjusting himself to the desires of the Lower House. Yet he ended on a somber note (Winwood, 3:181–82).
6 Robert Steele, ed., *Bibliotheca Lindesiana* (Oxford, 1910), 1:129.
7 For example, 23 Eliz., cap. i; 27 Eliz., cap. ii; 35 Eliz., cap. i; 3 Jac. I, cap. iv.
8 By a proviso every clergyman, who under the old law could have taken a second living of the value of £8 or above, should be allowed to accept a dignity or living in collegiate or cathedral churches. Presumably such a living involved little labor and less residence.
9 A similar bill passed the House in 1607 and was read once in the Lords.
10 It will be recalled that Montague, at the opening of the session of 1604, had set the ball rolling by bringing up three main grievances of his country, two of which were religious.
11 Cf. Braye, 61, ff. 31–34v, 37–39v; Folger, V, a. 277, ff. 45–46v, 47–50v. The Cecil family had not done badly during the Reformation.
12 *SP,* 14/20/57.
13 *LJ,* 2:658a–b.
14 This bill is to be found in the Record Office of the House of Lords.
15 Foster, 1:125 n.
16 Folger, V a. 277, ff. 66–66v.

17 *HMC Hastings,* 4:222.
18 Folger, V a. 277, ff. 66v–67v.
19 Ibid., f. 83.
20 Ibid., ff. 83v–84v; *LJ,* 2:636, 637–38. See also *SP,* 14/56/9.
21 *LJ,* 2:638.
22 *SP,* 14/20/57.
23 The King was doubtless alluding to the bill rejected on May 22, 1606 (*CJ,* 1:311). On April 1, 1606 the archbishop of Canterbury had told the Lords that his Majesty had informed him of great complaints about excommunications upon matters of small importance. His Majesty believed that excommunication should be used only in matters of great importance and wished some course to be considered for framing a bill. The Lords named five lawyers, including the Lord Chief Baron and the Attorney General, to attend the archbishop with such others as the archbishop should call to him to plan a bill. The bill that resulted was read on May 19 (*LJ,* 2:436) and referred to a committee of four bishops, including the archbishop and twelve peers (*LJ,* 2:437). On May 22 it was passed in the Lords; on that same day it was rejected in the Commons "with much distaste," apparently upon the motion of Richard Martin: "That the King's grace should be illuded in this bill. That the King might see it, and see that it is 'mere spleen.'" One can only guess what happened. For weeks the Lords had been dealing with a petition sent up from the Commons for endorsement by the Upper House. The fourth article of that petition concerned excommunication for slight causes. One can imagine that the Commons threw the bill out because it had been so watered down as to have little significance. The phrase "mere spleen" would seem to point at Bancroft, who had the bill in charge and was possibly trying to push through a bill that would leave his opponents in the lurch.
24 *LJ,* 2:658.
25 *SP,* 14/20/57.
26 Adv. 31.7.2, ff. 14–21v. See also *LJ,* 2:656.
27 Bowyer, pp. 102–03.
28 *LJ,* 2:658–59.
29 Adv. 31.7.2.

OTHER GRIEVANCES

1 A writ by which the sheriff could be compelled to release a prisoner on bail or mainprize. Holdsworth, 4:526. "Mainprize" was where the surety for the accused gave merely security; the *NED.* says that in the sixteenth century it meant as well receiving into friendly custody someone who would otherwise be imprisoned.
2 Adv. 31.7.2, ff. 14–21.
3 34 Hen. VIII, cap. xxvi, provided for the government of the twelve Welsh shires "and divers other dominions, lordships and manors in the Marches of Wales, united and annexed to the shires of Salop, Hereford, and Gloucester, as by the said late Act [27 Hen. VIII, cap. xxvi] more plainly appears." In that Act certain lordships, towns, parishes, etc. on the borders of Shropshire and Wales were annexed to Shropshire, and other lordships to Wales. The same was done about Herefordshire and Gloucestershire. It would seem that Worcestershire was drawn into the jurisdiction of the Council of Wales in the first

part of Elizabeth's reign. See C. A. J. Skeel, *The Council on the Marches of Wales* (London, 1904), p. 32 ff.

4 *LJ*, 2:659–60.

5 The Clerk's report of the debate is somewhat cryptic. But Hakewill's words, "the reason of printing light," seem to make sense. The Commons were apparently objecting to the fact that the proclamations issued by James I were published in book form and thus given a kind of special validity. Hakewill was saying, I think, that there was no good excuse for publishing the proclamations in a book. Bacon and Hakewill were also apparently discussing the proclamation of Richard II, "touching going beyond seas," and they differed as to its legality. Salisbury's words in his speech of February 15 seem to confirm this interpretation. See Harl., 777, f. 10v.

6 The proclamation of 5 Rich. II was omitted from the list because the King was said to have had just cause to prohibit travel abroad.

7 *SP*, 14/56, part 2; see Foster, 2:257–71. This was Hakewill's favorite phrase. Hakewill was one of the early constitutionalists.

8 Richard James, speaking in November, remarked: "So long as an arbitrary power of the government [impositions, proclamations] shall remain, what heart can we have to go on to the business?" (Add. 48119, f. 199).

9 *SP*, 14/56, part 2.

10 *SP*, 14/53/121.

11 *SP*, 14/56, part 2.

12 *Parl. Debates 1610*, p. 153. The King also promised that the impost upon coal shipped from the River Blyth (near Newcastle) would be taken away. About the patent for the new drapery granted to the Duke of Lennox, the Commons characterized it as "in all, or the most part of it, to be questionable, and in many [parts] apparently unlawful, and the execution thereof . . . stretched by the farmers and deputies beyond the extent of the said letters patents" (*SP*, 14/56, part 2). Salisbury declared that it would be referred absolutely to the law (*Parl. Debates 1610*, p. 153; *HMC Downshire*, 2:331).

DR. COWELL AND *THE INTERPRETER*

1 Cowell, *The Interpreter*, "Subsidie."

2 I cannot find the statement in Blackwood, but I have only skimmed it.

3 On February 27 the Commons asked the Lords to appoint a committee to meet with their committee about Cowell. When the Lords were discussing the coming conference, the archbishop of Canterbury spoke up and called Cowell a very honest man and a sufficient scholar, which was probably an accurate characterization. He hoped the Lords would not deal sharply with him but would suffer words written without evil intent to be drawn to a worthy sense. Saye and Sele hoped that the Lords would deal lovingly with the Commons, "for else it might much hinder matters of greater consequence which we had now in hand." Salisbury urged the Lords to do what was fitting for their honors (Folger, V, a. 277, ff. 11–11v). The two conferences were held on March 1 and 2.

4 Folger, V a. 277, ff. 14v–15v.

5 Ibid., ff. 16–16v.

6 Braye, 61, f. 7v.

7 *CJ*, 1:408–09. For Salisbury's speech at the conference which Martin reported,

see also Folger, V a. 277, ff. 18–19. For another important version see Petyt (Inner Temple), 537/14, ff. 163–67.

8 Petyt, 537/14, f. 164v; See also *CJ*, 1:409.
9 *CJ*, 1:408–09.
10 Repeating Salisbury's remark at the conference.
11 Winwood, 3:124–26.
12 Ibid., pp. 131–32.

> He thinketh the book in some things too bold with the common law. Likewise, that he doth in some sort mistake the fundamental constitution of the Parliament. . . . If he had seen the book afore the Parliament he would have taken order, as well for the suppression of the book, as to prevent the writing of the like. . . . There was never a King more unwilling to give the least shadow that the world should think he holdeth not and knoweth not himself to be as absolute a monarch as ever was here, yet in such a case where a man hath drawn things into dispute, matters so tender as this, where the matter is not, what is the truth, but what is the apprehension. Knowing that he is upon the stage and hath a great enemy, the Pope. To calumniate, equivocate, to deprave [*sic*] his writing, and that nothing will be to them more welcome than to find the difference between his respect and his subjects' affections, and to limit a King who never had a thought to impeach the fundamental constitutions of this Christian marriage. . . . He resolveth to suppress this book . . . and with his own pen declare his mind not to have any purpose to violate the least of the fundamental law of England [Braye, 61, ff. 9–9v].

See also Winwood, 3:129–30, as an indication of the administrative point of view. After speeches by Canterbury and others, Salisbury more or less apologized for having suggested the search for precedents. One thing he said deserves to be quoted: "If a lawyer think the jurisdiction ecclesiastical too great, or the civilian mislike the common law, he is not to write against it, for this is to stir strife" (Braye, 61, f. 10). On other occasions Salisbury had shown some faith in the value of free speech.

13 *The Interpreter,* under *Prerogative of the King.*
14 The Archbishop, speaking to the Lords, said it had been assumed that, because the book was dedicated to him, he had a finger in it. He observed on February 27 that Commons, in their care to preserve their privilege, had been "contented to hear a set discourse against the civil and ecclesiastical laws." "I hope," he concluded, "your Lordships will [not] in your wisdoms suffer thoughts and words in conscience written without evil intent to be drawn to a wrong sense" (Braye, 61, f. 3). In another speech on March 8, the Archbishop said: "He never read or saw any line of it before it was and had been printed 6 weeks. . . . I think he wrote with as much humility and as loath to offend as any man that wrote a long time. . . . Many book[s] as *De Jure Regni apud Scotos* hath been written against the King's prerogative, and that Kings have their power from the people, and the people to judge their actions and to bridle them. The divines of this time which were. . . Jewell, Nowell, etc. ever have written against it. I conceive your Lordships' direction was first to understand what precedents have been of punishing things of like nature in Parliament; and if no precedents be, then I think if it shall be thought to appertain to the Parliament to examine all books written amiss, there will be work enough, though they set 7 years together" (Braye, 61, f. 9).

WARDSHIP TO THE FORE

1 March 8 (*HMC Downshire*, 2:257–58). Cf. Edmondes to Trumbull, March 17 (Winwood, 3:137).
2 *CJ*, 1:411.
3 Edmondes to Trumbull, March 22 (*HMC Downshire*, 2:267–68).
4 Edmondes to Trumbull, March 15 (ibid., 2:262–63).
5 Beaulieu to Trumbull, March 29 (Winwood, 3:144–46).
6 A tenure of land by other than knightly service.
7 "Only coronation homage to remain in respect of honor" (Braye, 61, f. 20).
8 For a discussion by the Lords and judges of these various tenures, see Folger, V a. 277, ff. 34–36v, 40v–41v. On April 20 Coke declared to the Lords that "wardships and alienations are no sovereign but common prerogatives which subjects have" (ibid., f. 41).
9 Beaulieu to Trumbull, March 19 (Winwood, 3:144–46).
10 Winwood, 3:144–46. The Lords discussed the proposal of the Commons in detail, going into the several types of tenures, the duties and obligations connected with them, and the sums of money involved. When the Commons asked for a conference about wardship and tenures, the Lords hesitated; the Commons had considered this among themselves and gone ahead without consulting them. On March 29 Salisbury remarked to the Lords: "Whether to join or no in any farther conference is one of the questions" (Braye, 61, f. 18). In legal matters he feared the Lords would not be able to meet with the Lower House, but in matters of government and state he felt otherwise. He resented the conduct of the Commons, who took twelve or fourteen days to advise, and expected the Lords to answer them within two days.

The Lords met on Saturday, March 31, in a Committee of the Whole House and went over the proposed offer by the Commons, examining the details of the tenures involved (ibid., ff. 18v–22v).

On Monday, April 2, the Lords met, and the Lord Chancellor reminded them that the Commons expected a conference and that in his opinion the Lords were not yet ready for it. Salisbury complained that it was said abroad that "4 or 5 speak all and others set [*sic*] still." Some of the Lords who were learned and experienced in public affairs had said nothing. He urged the Lords to send word to the Commons that the matter in hand was of great weight and concerned tenures, and that they would be unable to meet with them until after the recess (ibid., f. 22v).
11 Edmondes to Trumbull, March 29 (*HMC Downshire*, 2:269).
12 M. Taverner to Trumbull, March 30 (*HMC Downshire*, 2:85–87); Correr to Doge and Senate, March 15 (*CSP Ven.*, 1607–10, pp. 450–51). As early as March 1 Beaulieu had written Trumbull: "I have heard for a certain truth that my Lord Treasurer himself is he that in good earnest doth most effectually put it forward; knowing how great a service he shall thereby do to his Prince, how much good he shall procure to his country, and what an eternal commendation and love he shall get to himself and his posterity by such a worthy deed. And this reason for my part I hold very probably, considering how the said Lord's actions do appear every day more and more to tend rather to honor and reputation than to profit" (Winwood, 3:124–26).
13 *HMC Downshire*, 2:271.

14 On April 18 the Lord Treasurer reminded the Lords that there was a uniform resolution not to proceed without the King's permission: "For us to confer with them now were to go upon crude arguments. To argue it now among ourselves were to reckon without our host" (Braye, 61, f. 24). He did not think they should go ahead until they understood the King's mind. About tenures it would be necessary to consult with the King; about the money to be given he did not believe it appropriate to confer with the Commons: "For if we shall ask more they will reply. But if we offer more shall we have it?" He urged them to name a committee to know the King's pleasure (ibid.; *LJ*, 2:578).

The next day Salisbury reported to the King that the committee depended wholly upon his pleasure. The Lords, he said, were afraid to meet with the Lower House since they were not sure that the desires of that body stood with the honor of His Majesty. The Commons wished to change all tenures into common and free socage. "We find that in no case he will compound for the matter of tenures in this condition." The House would learn his price when he saw that he could safely part with wardship.

The Lords resolved to confer with the Commons on the following day, April 20 (Braye, 61, ff. 25–25v).

15 Winwood, 3:152–53.

16 On April 26 Salisbury told the Lords that the King had asked for supply and support. When the King demanded them he expected satisfaction; at that time the wards had not been thought of. "He knoweth no cause to ask less now than at the first, viz., six hundred thousand pounds in a year for supply, and two hundred thousand pounds a year support above all that which he now hath . . . if they take liking of that which the King offereth, so as they deal not with matter of honor, he licenseth them to dispute of anything. . . . Towards sovereign power and authority, as power to impose upon foreign commodities either homewards or outward, I think not fit to dispute" (Braye, 61, ff. 29–29v). There is a mistake here. The King asked for £600,000 supply, not in a year, as is said, but in this year, to pay his debts, etc. The writer of the Braye MS (Bowyer) actually wrote £6000,000 and £2000,000; he sometimes made mistakes with his zeros.

Later in the discussion Salisbury added: "When I shall carry to the Lower House a demand of £600,000 supply and £200,000 support, I must go furnished with good reason. I think this reason is necessity, which must be relieved. If they answer, 'not able,' we may then farther consider. If the war of Cleve go on, it must of necessity draw on war with Spain. . . . Then have we reason to insist upon our demands" (ibid., 61, f. 30).

The Folger MS (V a. 277, f. 43v) gives more details of Salisbury's speech: "True necessity must be satisfied and not disputed. The necessity of Cleve go forward, Spain and we must go to wars. France, the Low Countries, and the King, my Master, must support them, and we must not seek for money when the drum soundeth. If one ask me whether without the wards we expect £200,000 per annum, though I could bring arguments for it, yet could I bring more against it, for as every day teacheth all wise men, much more myself. If the King for his profit take away the office he bestowed upon me, it is but his own which he gave me. I am contented, for besides my duty to his Majesty, I owe my country more than to prefer my own particular before the public good."

17 *Parl. Debates 1610*, pp. 147–52; *CJ*, 1:422.

18 Hobart was an old House of Commons man, as was Salisbury. Moreover, he

was a friend of Salisbury and had reason to regard the great little man as his patron. See Goodman, *Court of King James the First*, 1:42–43.

THE KING RAISES HIS DEMAND

1   *Parl. Debates 1610*, pp. 147–52.

2   Ibid., p. 151.

3   The Earl of Huntingdon made notes of Salisbury's speech: "I take it *pro concessu* the King's just necessities must be relieved by his subjects; the King by the law of nations, if not tied by the municipal laws, may relieve himself. . . . Of the excess and abuse you may dispute. . . . The King is contented you shall have these things that have been offered you, but will not abate of his first demands" (Folger V. a. 277, ff. 44v–5).

4   Winwood, 3:153–54. On the same day Edmondes wrote to Trumbull that it was now doubtful whether the Commons would proceed with the Contract for dissolution of wardship. "This high demand hath very much disturbed the House and they have this day resolved to return their answer to the Lords that they cannot proceed to treat further upon these terms" (*HMC Downshire*, 2:284–85). On the same day Chamberlain wrote to Winwood: "Our Parliament is at a stand and knows not (as they say) *de quel bois faire fleches*. Their offer of £100,000 yearly for wards and tenures is neither refused nor accepted, but withal they were given to understand by the Lord Treasurer, that the King, besides that, must have two hundred thousand pounds more of yearly support, which makes them pull in their horns, and know not what to say, for the Realm grows poor and traffic decays apace, insomuch that the customs of London are fallen this year £14,000 and fewer ships arrived by 360, so that this proposition breeds much discontentment already, and I am sorry to see us in this as in all the rest to grow so fast into the French fashion of loud speaking and base suffering" (McClure, *Letters of John Chamberlain*, 1:297–99).

5   Robert Ashton, *The Crown and the Money Market, 1603–1642* (Oxford, 1960); *HMC Downshire*, 2:284–86; *CSP Ven.*, 1607–10, pp. 479–81. See also Repertories of the Court of Aldermen, 29: ff. 207–08v.

6   Henry Howard, Earl of Northampton, left behind him a mass of letters, speeches, intended speeches, aphorisms, etc. They were written in a difficult hand to decipher. The reader of them cannot but conclude that here was an unnatural and warped personality worthy of study by a reputable psychiatrist. Northampton hated Salisbury and put that hatred on paper. He was jealous of Salisbury's influence over the King; that power he craved for himself. Convinced of the necessity of royal power, he regarded the Commons as children dealing with matters beyond their reach. He was a nobleman left over from the high Renaissance days with the outlook—and morals—of one of the least pleasant Italian dukes. But he had an active and knowledgeable mind and spoke often in the House of Lords, sometimes very sensibly. That James should have been on good terms with him is significant of the King's desperate need for flattery, to reassure himself. Godfrey Goodman (*Court of James the First*, 1:50) denied that Northampton was a flatterer, but he had not read the letters of Northampton to the King, now available in the British Museum. It was an age of flattery, but in that art Northampton was *facile princeps*. Arthur

Wilson (*History of England*, p. 3) speaks of Northampton as "famous for . . . cunning flattery."

7 In 1614 it was believed by some that the King was being urged to take a high hand with the Commons so that they would find themselves sent back to the country. Northampton was thought to be one of the prime movers in this scheme.

8 Richard Martin. So far as I know, Henry Martin, M.P. for Wootton Bassett (Wilts.), never spoke; but Richard had become one of the leaders of the House. Had Henry Martin ever spoken, the Clerk would have made some distinction, as he usually did when there were two members of the same surname.

9 At that point John Bond, M.P. for Taunton, made a speech which provoked "much hissing and spitting." I infer from the Clerk's notes that he was "stayed" by the Speaker. In 1601 a speech of his against compelling people to go to church had raised the temperature of the House.

10 *Rotuli Parliamentarium*, 2:104.

11 Sandys, Croft, Owen, and Berkeley were the subcommittee.

12 Harl., 777, ff. 40–40v.

13 *CJ*, 1:424.

14 Braye, 61, ff. 34v–35v.

15 Folger, V a. 277, f. 50v.

16 Folger, V a. 277, f. 51.

17 Ibid., 1:81.

18 *SP*, 14/55/58.

19 *Parl. Debates 1610*, pp. 21–22.

20 *Parl. Debates 1610*, p. 22, quoted in Hurstfield, *The Queen's Wards*, p. 319.

21 Salisbury reported the conference to the Peers. When the Lords asked to be given in writing the message the Commons had sent them, they were refused. At that point Salisbury told the Commons that their "straitness" might "cause the King to take more benefit of his own in things in point whereof no man could find a grievance, and yet may be burdened . . . yet out of their purses it would go to clerks, to officers, etc." That threat came from His Majesty, I suspect, and one wonders what he had in mind. Salisbury went on to tell the Commons "that they did a little look upon their own greatness and power and too little into other men's." The last sentence also sounds as if it came out of the King's mouth (Braye, 61, f. 40v). Cf. the report on May 7 in *LJ*, 2:589.

22 *CJ*, 1:425. "If we discard them [the ten points of retribution proposed on February 24] we did not truly value tenures alone. That and alienations were more worth than all we offered" (Harl., 777, f. 42v). The Recorder was reporting Salisbury's speech at the conference. See *SP*, 14/55/58.

23 Harl., 777, f. 42v; *CJ*, 1:425.

24 The left wing, as so often in history, demanded freedom of speech and was unwilling to give it to others.

25 "I know I am suspected without cause to incline too much to contribution and to the King's authority. God doth know my mind. I esteem my country as well as any man, and if I were a young man and so I would not give my place to any he that should say he did more affect his country than I. Therefore these objections become not grave men. Young humors may have them. . . . If I should insist upon my place, and my place had that power it hath had, and ought to have still, my words should bear some weight with you, and then I would persuade you" (from Canterbury's speech, in Add. 48119, ff. 183–183v). The Earl of Huntingdon reported the close of Canter-

bury's speech as follows: "Although I must confess there be some wise and grave men amongst you, yet many speeches are both of spleen and from such green and young heads, as being judicially weighed, will prove to be nothing else but froth" (Folger, V a. 277, f. 52). Bancroft's words and incidental words of others suggest that a good deal of heat was being engendered in the House of Commons.

26 Beaulieu, in his letter to Trumbull of May 9, speaks of the Lord Treasurer as "having called yesterday both House together" (Winwood, 3:159–61). According to *CJ* (1:426) the messengers from the Commons were in the Lords when the Lords told them that they had an important matter to discuss and asked some to come up. It was debated by the Commons whether the Speaker should go or not, but resolved in the negative. It would seem that others, probably most of those in attendance, did go. The Chancellor made a report to the Commons of the speech.

27 Winwood, 3:159–61.

28 *SP,* 14/54/29.

29 Salisbury said to the Lords: "By how much we see things as they are, by so much the more need we to have money to be employed and not to seek for upon any occasion" (Folger, V a. 277, f. 54).

30 Winwood, 3:160.

THE KING CLAMPS DOWN ON DEBATING IMPOSITIONS

1 *Parl. Debates 1610,* p. 32; *CJ,* 1:427. "And could not be undone but by error, but if there were any cause for us to complain, in regard of the time, the nature of the merchandise, or the unproportionableness of the imposition, his Majesty would be as ready to afford grace as we should be to petition him for grace" (Add. 48119, f. 151). "That for the burden, the time, the quality, or other circumstance, he liked well they should enter into dispute, but for [the] right of his prerogative, or the judgment already given, he required them to forbear, etc. If in a judicial course by writ of error they wished it might be handled he would give leave. But in this place they were no judges to determine it, therefore commanded they should not dispute it" (*HMC House of Lords,* new ser., 11:119).

2 If we follow the Clerk of the Commons, but he left out speeches.

3 Add. 48119, ff. 151–151v. Wentworth took up other matters, historical matters: "Was it not resolved in 4 Hen. 6, in the Chequer Chamber, by all the Judges, that the [blank] should have the wardship of the issue in tail, and not the King; and yet the experience is at this day contrary in the Court of Wards."

4 Add. 48119, f. 151v; *CJ,* 1:427.

5 Possibly members in opposition had been warned by Privy Councillors against speaking.

6 Add. 48119, ff. 151v–52.

7 *CJ,* 1:427.

8 Add. 48119, ff. 151v–52.

9 *CJ,* 1:427.

10 Ibid.; cf. Henry Elsynge, *The Ancient Method and Manner of Holding Parliaments in England* (London, 1679), p. 166. This citation seems hardly to the point. I doubt if good precedents can be found for the Speaker to be accompanied by members of the House when seeing the King.

11 The phrase "who sat near the Chair" had come to mean a Privy Councillor. But Sir Walter, it happens, was not a Privy Councillor. Probably in the want of Privy Councillors Sir Walter, who was an understudy for Salisbury, was allowed to sit near the Chair.

12 Add. 48119, f. 152.

13 The King had really been responsible for the message, though it was drawn up by Salisbury. Salisbury wrote to Aston: "I pray you tell his Majesty that I have received his commandment by Sir Thomas Lake concerning the restraint disputing the King's right in the matter [page torn] impositions in which the House is so violent (especially town burgesses, all that merchants can procure) that we will rather follow his Majesty's commandment o[n] his authority to forbid it than to have that [page torn] done which may so justly offend the King. . . . Between this and Monday we shall discover more, but the Speaker shall have a provisional order to use his Majesty's name in that point, as soon as any man offer [page torn] such an argument. If any exception be urged by any man to any proportions or to any nature of commodity. . . it may have his passage and is usual" (Cecil Papers, Hatfield, 128/92). Mrs. Foster dates this significant document as May 3, basing her opinion upon Braye, 61, ff. 35–35v, and *CJ*, 1:423. (Foster, 2:82 n. 2).

14 *CJ*, 1:427; cf. Add. 48119, f. 152v.

15 Add. 48119, f. 152v.

16 *Parl. Debates 1610*, p. 32; Add. 48119, f. 152v.

17 *CJ*, 1:427–28.

18 Add. 48119, f. 153.

19 *HMC House of Lords*, new ser., 11:121.

20 *CJ*, 1:428.

21 Add. 48119, f. 154. Cf. the version in *Parl. Debates 1610* (p. 33), which leaves out the important words "by his direction and in his name."

22 Add. 48119, f. 154v.

23 *Parl. Debates 1610*, p. 33; cf. Add. 48119, f. 155v.

24 Add. 48119, f. 156.

25 Ibid., f. 156v.

26 Ibid.

27 Ibid., ff. 156v–57. This speech is not recorded in *CJ* because it was given in committee. Spedding (4:177–79) includes a speech by Bacon on May 14, but that speech belongs on another day or possibly was never delivered. See *CJ*, 1:430; Add. 48119, f. 158v.

28 Add. 48119, f. 157.

29 Ibid., f. 157; cf. *Parl. Debates 1610*, p. 33. This gesture by the Privy Councillors had never been used before, so far as I can recall.

30 *CJ*, 1:428; Add. 48119, f. 157.

31 *CJ*, 1:429.

32 On May 16, Beaulieu wrote Trumbull: "Great crosses are risen in Parliament by the King's high demands and the stiffness of the Lower House. The King doth endeavour to reconcile all matters and bring them again to the former terms" (*HMC Downshire*, 2:295–96). The Commons had given up talking about subsidies and gone back to the formulation of grievances; they were considering among others those of the impositions recently ordained by the King.

33 Add. 48119, f. 157v.

34 Herodotus, Bk. 3, 31.

35 In the 1610 sessions we get more allusions to what the constituents would think or say.

THE KING'S MESSAGE: HIS SPEECH AND ITS RECEPTION

1 *CJ*, 1:429; Add. 48119, ff. 159–159v. See also *HMC House of Lords*, new ser., 11:124.
2 Add. 48119, f. 160.
3 Ibid.; *CJ*, 1:430. The Clerk made a few notes of the proceedings of the committee.
4 Add. 48119, ff. 160–160v.
5 Ibid., f. 160v. Bacon was regarded by some in his own profession as rather a lightweight, and Fuller's comment may imply as much. Lawyers were not given to rhetorical flourishes.
6 Ibid.
7 Ibid.
8 *SP*, 14/54/65, summarized and with some quotations from *Parl. Debates 1610*, pp. 34–36 and n. *a*.
9 Add. 48119, f. 162v.
10 "Two women before him had it" is the way the phrase reads in the State Papers (*SP*, 14/54/65; *Parl. Debates 1610*, pp. 34–36 and n. *a*).
11 Add. 48119, f. 162v.
12 Ibid., f. 163.
13 Ibid.
14 It is "deludes' 'in Add. 48119, f. 163, but "denudes" in *SP*, 14/54/65.
15 Add. 48119, f. 163.
16 Ibid.
17 Ibid.
18 *Parl. Debates 1610*, p. 36.
19 Add. 48119, f. 164v.
20 Ibid., ff. 165–165v.
21 The comments of the Venetian ambassador on the speech deserve mention: "The King's ill humor with Parliament still continues. He has this week addressed to them vigorous remarks complaining that his message, sent through the speaker, was not read: he threatens them, if they continue to treat of royal prerogative, but promises to take into consideration any representations that may be made to him about the abolition of certain imposts levied by him. It seems, however, that Parliament insists that this shall be done of right and not of grace" (Correr to Doge and Senate, June 2, *CSP Ven.*, 1607–10, pp. 499–501).
22 We have only two accounts.
23 *Parl. Debates 1610*, p. 36.
24 McClure, *Letters of John Chamberlain*, 1:301.
25 *CJ*, 1:430.
26 McIlwain, *Political Works of James I*, p. 310.
27 Add. 48119, f. 166. I do not think Wentworth meant to say that the Commons had now lost their liberties, but rather that they had been lost. Was he possibly thinking that the Commons had gained such liberties in an earlier time (such as that of Edward III) and lost them later (as in the time of Mary and of Elizabeth)?
28 It was this speech to which de la Boderie was alluding: "Qu'un d'eux eut la hardiesse do demander en vertu de quoi il les pouvoit mettre, et d'alleguer

un de leur vieux auteurs, qui faisant la différence du pouvoir de nos Rois a ceux e'Angleterre, disoit que Le royaume de France etoit un Royaume absolu, mais celui d'Angleterre etoit un Royaume politique, c'est-a-dire, compose du peuple et du Roi et que par consequent il no pouvoit aussi disposer des affaires qu'il avoit enterprises jusqu'ici sans leur participation et consentement" (de la Boderie to Villeroy, May 24, 1610 [*Les Ambassades*, 5:271–72]).

29   Add. 48119, f. 166; *CJ*, 1:430.

30   Add. 48119, f. 166v.

31   Whitelocke may have owed his election to the running fight he carried on in the courts against Sir William Pope, who had intruded on his farm near Witney (about six miles northwest of Oxford) and cut down 1,200 trees. Whitelocke was successful against him in the courts and won reclame in the county. See John Bruce, ed., *Liber Famelicus of Sir James Whitelocke* (London, 1858), pp. 21–24.

32   *Parl. Debates 1610*, p. 37. Cf. *CJ*, 1:430; Add. 48119, f. 116v. The last sentence of item 2 is from this last source.

33   *Parl. Debates 1610* records Fuller as quoting these three principles from an earlier speech by Whitelocke, but a reading of Whitelocke's speech as cited by the Clerk of the Commons and by Add. 48119 convinces me that the writer of *Parl. Debates 1610* either made a mistake or was copying someone else and misunderstood Whitelocke.

34   Add. 48119, ff. 166v–167. Sir Edwin occasionally leaned backward as if to give an appearance of impartiality, or perhaps because he was genuinely anxious to be fair. He was a man of subtlety, and it is not always easy to pass judgment on his words and deeds. As a floor leader he was unsurpassed in his generation.

35   The Oath of Supremacy required of all M.P.'s.

36   Add. 48119, f. 167.

THE PETITION OF RIGHT

1   Add. 48119, f. 167.

2   Jer. 6:16.

3   Bacon was twenty when he entered Parliament. See Foster, 2:111 n. 3.

4   He meant, I infer, the rights of the subjects as against one another. But cf. *Parl. Debates 1610*, p. 38.

5   Compare versions of this speech in Add. 48119, ff. 167–68; *Parl. Debates 1610*, pp. 38–39.

6   Spedding, 4:182–83.

7   The Queen's inhibitions to Parliament might concern marriage, the state of her body, and what was fit for her to do; or they might concern her politic capacity and her ecclesiastical powers (*Parl. Debates 1610*, p. 39).

8   Add. 48119, ff. 168–168v.

9   *CJ*, 1:431–32. The language of this statement reminds one somewhat of that of the Apology of 1604.

10   For Bate's case, see Gardiner, *History of England, 1603–1642*, 2:5–11.

11   A rereading of the King's message does not bear out his contention that he meant to forbid them to consider impositions only until they heard his further pleasure.

12   James had a Scottish liking for abstract principles.

13   Was James possibly concerned lest public opinion be running against him?

The moderate statements by the Commons as opposed to his sweeping claims may have affected public opinion.
14 *Parl. Debates 1610*, p. 42.
15 I have used two accounts of this speech, that in *Parl. Debates 1610*, pp. 41–42, and in Add. 48119, ff. 169–70v.
16 Add. 48119, f. 171v.

CONFERENCES WITH THE LORDS

1 *LJ*, 2:601.
2 Harl., 777, f. 43v.
3 I have put together this speech from the accounts in Add. 48119, ff. 172–74; Harl., 777, ff. 43v–44; and Montague's partial report in *CJ*, 1:433. What Salisbury said was in the Cecilian manner, but it had been prepared at least in part by the Lords.
4 Salisbury was persuasive in arguing for a conference: "No form is so proper and certain as . . . dialogue, in which kind this Parliament hath had a strange misfortune; that we had never any trusted to make a reply. . . . Divers of us have been beholding to you and none so much as myself, for reporting tedious and unpleasing narrations, wherein you have mended much that which I have expressed." He asked: "If any of you conceive you shall receive [dis]advantage by it, what is it? 'Tis not to bind. If we chance to [treat] of any point in law you are two to one, if in eloquence there be anything you know your advantage. If in point of greatness you fear we have the odds you know that doth nothing in a cause where reason is the judge and the best argument must decide the question," continuing: "Never subjects could give a King better satisfaction than you have done, nor a King been more ready to hearken to his subjects than the King to us" (Add. 48119, ff. 173–74).
5 Ibid., f. 174.
6 Salisbury had talked in a conciliatory way: to threaten at the end seemed ill-timed, but possibly it was a result of directions from the King. On the morning of May 26, before the conference, Salisbury talked to the Lords, explaining that the monarchy was "declining in respect of money and revenue." He went on: "The whole traffic of this Parliament hath been only in messages where there is no reply there, though a man may receive something yet understand not all things. I wish that we may send back unto the Lower House to desire a conference, though it is like this time will cause a recess both in respect of the time and men's wearisomeness in business. Say the Lower House have determined to say nothing till after the holidays, yet they may prepare things ready against that time, and I assure myself they will hear what we say because faith cometh by hearing, although they will not reply, and then a mean capacity may deliver very sufficient reasons to persuade them. What this will work I know not, for I cannot judge of contingences [contingencies]. If my notion be liked of, then may it please your Lordships to send unto them" (Folger, V a. 277, ff. 57v–58).
7 *CJ*, 1:434.
8 *Parl. Debates 1610*, p. 46.
9 Tey owed his seat to Robert Sackville, who, like Lord Buckhurst, had long served in the Commons (indeed, until the death of his father, the Earl of Dorset). See Titus F IV, f. 121.

10   *Parl. Debates 1610*, p. 47.
11   Folger, V a. 277, f. 64v.
12   *CJ*, 1:436. Their Lordships referred to the absence of so many members of the House of Commons at the time of year when the King was in progress, the judges on circuit, and gentlemen were needed in their shires (Harl., 777, f. 44v). The writer of *Parl. Debates 1610* emphasized the bluntness of the message from the Peers, "wishing us to go roundly about our business and to use no more delays than of necessity we must" (p. 50; cf. *LJ*, 2:609). It has to be said that the writer was not the most exact recorder of words used; it is possible that he made his contemporaries speak more bluntly than they really did.
13   In the *LJ* (2:609) it was reported that the Commons answered that they had not slacked and that as soon as they were prepared the Lords would hear from them.
14   *CJ*, 1:436.
15   *Parl. Debates 1610*, p. 51. Salisbury had perhaps imparted to the Upper House the wishes of the King—a natural thing to do—and that House assumed that the Commons ought to hear these wishes.
16   *Parl. Debates 1610*, p. 52; cf. Add. 48119, ff. 175–175v.
17   Add. 48119, f. 175v.
18   Ibid., f. 176. Salisbury seldom resorted to flattery; he was trying to soothe ruffled feelings.
19   Ibid., f. 177.
20   Folger, V a. 277, f. 69.
21   Ibid. Add. 48119, f. 177, says twenty days, which is obviously a blunder by a copyist. The author of *Parl. Debates 1610* (p. 53) records Salisbury as saying "having now spent almost 5 months in matters impertinent and extravagant discourses."
22   Add. 48119, ff. 177–177v.
23   Earlier in his speech Salisbury had said that the mind had understanding and will. The understanding weighed whether that which was spoken was *verum* or *falsum;* the will searched whether it were *bonum* or *malum*. It was his object, Salisbury asserted, to move the second faculty of the mind, which had power over the affections (*Parl. Debates 1610*, p. 52).
24   Add. 48119, f. 177v.
25   Ibid., ff. 177v–178.
26   Ibid., f. 178; *CJ*, 1:437.
27   Add. 48119, f. 178v.
28   Ibid., ff. 179–80. That Salisbury should claim credit for His Majesty because he promised to lay no more impositions during the intermission of Parliament and because he had given them liberty to dispute impositions was asking them to be grateful to the Sovereign for not doing what the Commons believed he had no right to do.

THE DEBATE: ONE SUBSIDY REJECTED AND LATER VOTED

1   In 1601 Dammet had made an interesting and vigorous speech about the two base towns of Dunkirk and Nieuwport which raided the eastern coast of England.

2 The successful merchants from country towns were sometimes more original and wiser from experience than country gentlemen of more education.

3 *CJ*, 1:438.

4 *Parl. Debates 1610,* p. 55.

5 *CJ*, 1:438.

6 Ibid. Hastings complained of May's sharp words against those not of his opinion (*Parl. Debates 1610,* p. 55). The Clerk of the Commons was inclined to leave out the ill words men used to one another. They are interesting as indicative of the tension in the House.

7 *CJ*, 1:438.

8 *CJ; Parl. Debates 1610,* p. 55. More's defensive attitude suggests that some of the King's supporters were not too certain that his Majesty would give satisfaction.

9 On February 28 Sir Roger Owen had moved that the Commons "discover an inclination" to give (*CJ*, 1:402).

10 *CJ*, 1:438.

11 *Parl. Debates 1610,* p. 56. His Majesty was being informed quickly of the debates in the Commons.

12 *CJ*, 1:438; *Parl. Debates 1610,* p. 56; Add. 48119, f. 180. Caesar represented the King as promising that "we might dispute of his power to impose." Add. 48119 (f. 180) reports that the King allowed them to present all their grievances including impositions.

13 *Parl. Debates 1610,* p. 50.

14 Add. 48119, f. 180v.

15 Ibid.; *Parl. Debates 1610,* p. 56.

16 Add. 48119, f. 180v.; *Parl. Debates 1610,* p. 56; Harl., 777, f. 46v.

17 Carleton wrote Edmondes that they lost their dinners both days, June 13 and 14 (Birch, 1:114–17).

18 This summary of the debate is based on the *CJ*, Add. 48119, and *Parl. Debates 1610.*

19 Add. 48119, f. 181. Who the speaker was we are not told, but perhaps it was Sandys. See *CJ*, 1:439.

20 By Sir William Strode, M.P. for Plympton, Devonshire. Judging from two speeches and his role as a teller (*CJ*, 1:397, 963, 403), Strode was by no means a supporter of the Crown. Cf. *CJ*, 1:406. For Strode's speech, see *Parl. Debates 1610,* pp. 56–57.

21 Add. 48119, f. 181v.

22 *Parl. Debates 1610,* pp. 57–58; *CJ*, 1:439.

23 Add. 48119, ff. 181v–183.

24 Ibid., ff. 182–83. Wentworth had remarked that it was a little error in the Lords and Commons to make an argument out of the death of the King of France (*CJ*, 1:439), an obvious thrust at Salisbury and possibly at M.P.'s who had repeated the argument.

25 *CJ*, 1:439.

26 Petyt (Inner Temple), 537/14, f. 78. Mrs. Foster believes that the passage may come from the supplementary papers of the Clerk (2:148 n. 22).

27 *Parl. Debates 1610,* p. 58.

28 He must be alluding to speeches on June 14 (*CJ*, 1:438–39; Birch, 1:114–17).

29 *Parl. Debates 1610,* p. 58.

30 Cf. *LJ*, 2:616; Folger, V a. 277, ff. 71v–72. Salisbury said to the Lords: "I take it unseasonable to ask what we will give. They may ask the King's land in fee farm and *non quantum.* We are come now unto the crisis." Did Salisbury

mean that the Lords might find that the Commons were getting out of hand and might demand anything, or whot did he mean? He urged the Lords to defer the dispute until the next day (Folger, f. 72).

31 *LJ*, 2:619.
32 *LJ*, 2:624.
33 Folger, V a. 277, f. 76.
34 Ibid. ff. 77v–78. "Besides the nature of those things I have unto my purse."
35 Ibid., f. 78.
36 Folger, V a. 277, ff. 78–80v.
37 *Parl. Debates 1610*, pp. 121–23.
38 *CJ*, 1:444.
39 *LJ*, 2:660–62.
40 *SP*, 14/56, part 2.
41 Folger, V a. 277, ff. 86–88.
42 *Parl. Debates 1610*, p. 162.
43 Spedding points this out (4:203–04).
44 September 16, 1605 (*CSP Dom.*, 1603–10, p. 233).
45 Adv. 31.7.2, ff. 14–21v.
46 Harl., 354, ff. 2–8; *Parl. Debates 1610*, pp. 153–54.
47 Adv. 31.7.2, f. 15v.
48 Spedding, 4:205–06. S. R. Gardiner, in his account of Bacon in the *DNB*, says that the King offered to compromise by giving up about one-third of the impositions recently set and agreeing to set no additional impositions if the Commons would accept the remaining two-thirds. Gardiner bases this, I assume, on G. D.'s statement in *Parl. Debates 1610* (pp. 153–54), but the one-third and two-thirds are not to be found in the latter. The King had withdrawn a good many impositions. Gardiner may have had some MS source for his statement; he was seldom wrong.
49 Birch, 1:122.
50 The shrewd politician was perhaps courting the favor of up-country members.
51 *CJ*, 1:448.

BARGAINING WITH THE KING

1 The Clerk, in putting down the meeting for the committee chamber, set down also the names of Crew, Sandys, Berkeley, Croft, Owen, and Neville. Why?
2 See, for example, D. Carleton to Edmondes, July 17 (Birch, 1:128–30).
3 Folger, V a. 277, f. 92v.
4 Ibid., 277, f. 93v.
5 Ibid., ff. 94–94v.
6 Ibid., f. 94v.
7 34 Hen. VIII, cap. xxvi, item 119. The version of the requests in the Folger MS, as given by Martin at the conference, is somewhat different: "First, when a man is outlawed, out of those goods to pay the parties at whose suit it is. Second, in felony and treason, the debts of the creditors to be satisfied before the King have any benefit. Third, that none be forced to lend unto the King. Fourth, that the flaws in the Statute of 28 H. 8 for Wales may be taken away. Fifth, that the Judges may take [administer] oath in criminal actions against the King. Sixth, that no servant of the King's may be freed from arrest. Seventh, that no man be troubled for land gained by the sea, by no defect of title, nor by inquiry of wardships" (Folger, V a. 277, ff. 92v–93). It will be

observed that in article iv the Earl has cited the statute about Wales incorrectly. See the beginning of this footnote.

8 Winwood, 3:193–95.
9 *LJ*, 2:646. See also Folger, V a. 277, ff. 95–95v.
10 Winwood, 3:193–95.
11 Folger, V a. 277, ff. 94v–95.
12 *LJ*, 2:648.
13 John Pory, M.P. for Bridgewater, Somerset, to Winwood, July 17 (Winwood, 3:193–95). Pory appears often in John Chamberlain's letters. He was secretary to various men. He was not the most reliable of men, too often "whittled," but I suspect a fairly good reporter.
14 *CJ*, 1:451.
15 Winwood, 3:193–95.
16 Ibid., 3:193–95. The Huntingdon Notes are almost the same. Salisbury had already told the Lords that the King, "finding their [the Commons'] resolution, and not liking their offers, will dissolve the Parliament and carry them on no longer with hopes" (Folger, V a. 277, f. 95).
17 Harl., 777, f. 54. The Clerk wrote "iii xx."
18 *LJ*, 2:660–62.
19 *CJ*, 1:450.
20 *CJ*, 1:452.
21 July 25 (*HMC Downshire*, 2:328).
22 Folger, V a. 277, f. 100.
23 Ibid., ff. 100–01.
24 "Our bodies much wasted" (Sandys speaking [Ibid., f. 101v]).
25 Ibid.
26 Cap. v; see also Holdsworth, 3:614–15, 629.
27 Folger, V a. 277, f. 101v.
28 Ibid.
29 Ibid., ff. 101–101v. By "yourselves" he meant his fellow Peers. What a worthy thing it was to be of ancient blood!
30 Ibid., f. 102v. The exchange of courtesies between the Prime Office and the leader of the opposition was in the best tradition of a later day, of the nineteenth and twentieth centuries.
31 Ibid., f. 104.
32 Ibid., f. 104v.
33 Ibid.
34 Ibid., ff. 104v–105.
35 Ibid., f. 105.
36 Ibid., f. 105v.
37 Ibid.
38 Ibid., f. 106v.
39 Ibid., ff. 107–107v.
40 Ibid., f. 108. The Lords' reservation (*LJ*, 2:662) was basically the same as that of the Commons.

THE GREAT DEBATE

1 Of Fuller's speech Dudley Carleton wrote: "Who speaks . . . always honestly, but that time very sufficiently," *Parl. Debates 1610*, p. 85 n. *b*. About Fuller, see R. J. Usher, "Nicholas Fuller, a Forgotten Exponent of English Liberty,"

AHR, 12:742–60. This article includes some information, but a better account ought to be written. Fuller is not included in the *DNB*.

2 *CJ*, 1:443; *Parl. Debates 1610*, pp. 58–61; Add. 48119, ff. 51–65.

3 About Whitelocke, see pp. 326–27, 378–79, 552 n. 31.

4 For this speech there are three sources: *Parl. Debates 1610*, pp. 66–72; Spedding, 4:191–98 (from Harl., 6797, f. 147), 200–01 (Carleton's notes, *SP*, 14/56/3).

5 Eileen Power's *The Wool Trade in English Medieval History* (Oxford, 1942) shows how merchants had been brought together to speak for the merchant class. The merchants might conceivably have become a regular body consulted about taxation. Eileen Power makes the mid-fourteenth-century struggle less constitutional and more economic than do such writers as Stubbs. Yet Stubbs, despite his preoccupation with the growth of the constitution, recognized in some degree the role of the merchants in taxation. Stubbs was seldom far wrong.

6 Sir James Dyer, *Les Reports des Divers select Matters et Resolutions des Reverends Judges et Sages del Ley* (London, 1666), ff. 43, 92.

7 Bacon seems to have had little conception of the slow but steady accretion of influence and power by Parliament, a strange want of insight on the part of a man of his philosophic outlook. It is the more strange because he had long experience in the House of Commons. In 1593 he had stood stubbornly for the rights of the Commons against the Lords in initiating money grants and had lost for the time being the favor of the Queen. At that stage in his life he seems to have valued the historic rights of the Commons and to have been willing to throw his cap over the wall for them. But although he wrote a brilliant biography of Henry VII, he had not the historian's interest in orderly change. At this time he was eighteen years older and had lost some of the zeal of his early thirties. Now he was examining precedents largely to make a case for his King. His ambitions had been thwarted time and again; the position he deserved he would win soon or never. He had come to believe that the power of the gentry (as shown in the Commons) was a menace to the good subject (as Gardiner has pointed out) and thus that royal power hand in hand with wise Councillors such as himself was best. He knew how the Commons might be manipulated. The leaders of the Commons had their price, in offices and honors, which they should be given. His advice to the King, more often proffered than accepted, was judicious and often farseeing. He was the English Machiavelli with a difference.

8 Spedding, 4:195.

9 In 1336 the King had called together a select list of merchants (Power, pp. 81–82; Stubbs, *Constitutional History of England* [Oxford, 1875], 2:379–80), and they had agreed to a tax of 40s. on every sack of wool exported by denizens. That agreement by the merchants was ratified by Parliament, no doubt because of the exigencies of war. In October 1339 a new Parliament admitted that a grant to the King was necessary (Stubbs, 2:381), but the magnates complained of various abuses and expressed a wish that the maltolte of '36 and '37 might cease. The Commons asked for a new election and set out six points upon which they desired redress, one of which was the maltolte (Stubbs, 2:381; *Rot. Parl.*, 2:104; J. R. Lumby, ed., *Chronicon Henrici Knighton, Monachi Leycestrensis* [London, 1895], p. 15).

In the newly elected Parliament of 1340 it was proposed to give the King the ninth sheaf, the ninth fleece, and the ninth lamb, but on the condition that he agreed to certain petitions which Parliament put forward. Those petitions were drawn up in the form of articles and embodied in a statute to which the King gave his assent (Stubbs, 2:382–83). The first of these articles promised a cessation of the maltolte. That is the basis of Bacon's assertion that the Commons repealed an imposition they had made. They had in a war emergency passed a maltolte for a year on the condition that it be not renewed, and they were still trying to do away with it. In 1343 the Commons brought in thirty-five articles in which, among other things, they remonstrated against the maltolte as "a great exaction and grievous charge" (*Rot. Parl.*, 2:140) and asked that the statutes they had passed in 1340 be put in force (Stubbs, 2:392–93). The King in 1343 revoked the statute of 1341 (B. Wilkinson, *Constitutional History of England, 1216–1399* [London, 1948–58], 2:203). In the long run, the Commons won the battle of the maltolte. See B. Wilkinson, *Studies in the Constitutional History of the Thirteenth and Fourteenth Centuries* (Manchester, 1937), pp. 73–77.

10 Possibly Bacon, in writing the draft of his speech, was interrupted at this point and never resumed writing it. Gardiner suggested that Sir Francis may have felt ashamed of the last part of his speech, after Hakewill's "masterly refutation" (*Parl. Debates 1610*, p. 69 n. *b*), but Bacon was too sure of himself ever to have felt ashamed.

11 Did he mean that they were warnings to be observed but not taken too seriously?

12 For Hedley's speech, see Foster, 2:170–97, from Exeter MS, 128, ff. 154–68.

13 Hedley remarked that the price of things was "improving" and the value of coin abating, an obvious fact seldom mentioned by the men of the time.

14 It might have been replied that many of the impositions had been laid in the last three years.

15 One would like to know how old the idea was that the English were a superior people because they were accustomed to freedom.

HAKEWILL SPEAKS

1 Hakewill came first to the attention of the Commons probably at the time when monopolies were being discussed in the Parliament of 1601. When the several monopolies were being recapitulated, Hakewill quietly asked: "Is not bread there?" A whisper of "bread?" went around the House, and Hakewill spoke up again: "If order be not taken for these, bread will be there before the next Parliament" (D'Ewes, p. 648).

2 He was alluding, I assume, to the King's promise to make no more impositions without consent of Parliament.

3 William Hakewill, *The Libertie of the Subject against the pretended Power of Impositions* (London, 1641), p. 3.

4 Ibid., pp. 6–10.

5 Ibid., pp. 10–21; cf. *Parl. Debates 1610*, p. 80.

6 An ancient customs duty upon imported wine.

7 A duty paid to the King's butler on wine imported by aliens.

8 Hakewill, p. 22.

9 Ibid., p. 24.

10 Ibid., p. 25.

11 Ibid., p. 29.

12 Ibid., pp. 30–32. Actually the merchants refused to do this. Cf. Stubbs, *Constitutional History of England* (Oxford, 1896), 2:165.

13 Hakewill, pp. 32–34. Those increases of customs duties were complained of less for constitutional reasons than because the country sellers of wool soon found out that the merchants who had agreed to the King's tax consequently paid them less for their wool. See Power, *The Wool Trade,* p. 77. Professor Wilkinson comments here that the problem of the incidence of the tax cannot be entirely diverted from that of consent.

14 Hakewill, pp. 34–35.

15 Ibid., p. 37.

16 Ibid., pp. 38–48.

17 Ibid., p. 51.

18 Ibid., pp. 51–52.

19 Hakewill, pp. 72–79.

20 Ibid., pp. 79–93.

21 Ibid., pp. 93–95.

22 Ibid., pp. 96–98.

23 Ibid., pp. 112–115. The *De Tallagio* was not, Wilkinson says, a statute, but only a proposal for one, made by the barons in 1297. It forbade further imposition of the maltolte.

24 Ibid., pp. 116–18. The *Confirmatio Cartarum* of 1297, Wilkinson says, was the first statute against the imposition, unless we count *Magna Carta.* The consent to the maltolte, if it was to be levied again, was to be that of "the greater part of the community."

25 Ibid., pp. 188 ff.

26 Hakewill was followed by Francis Tate, M.P. for Northamptonshire and one of the original members of the Society of Antiquaries. He began by citing instances from Anglo-Saxon times, talked about port duties in the time of the Roman rule of Britain, and came down to earth at length by asserting that impositions were never levied in time of peace. He concluded: "He delivers his opinion, for one of his feet stands in the clouds of antiquity and the other upon the water; for this imposition hath no ground upon the land."

SPEECHES BY YELVERTON, HOBART, CREW, AND DODDRIDGE

1 *Archaeologia,* 15 (1806): 27–52.

2 In rebuking Yelverton James remarked: "For if a king should force to bind all to his opinion, when usage consonant to reason hath given the subject free consent of denial and rejection, it were the part of a fool or a tyrant; and therefore I commend Bacon [Sir Nicholas] who, when Henry VIII sought by Parliament to make his proclamation a law, and this with such violence thrust on your house or none durst stir his finger. Then did Bacon, as reason would, stand up and speak with boldness against it, for the King's seeking in that point was tyrannical" (*Archaeologia,* 15:43).

3 Yelverton maintained that he had merely asked for a delay in collecting the subsidy.

4 "This Henry the Hardy had the honor to do absolutely the worst, and for tyrannical positions that he was bold to bluster out, was so well convassed by all that followed him, that he hath scarce shewed his head ever since" (Dudley Carleton to Edmondes, July 13 [Birch 1:120–22]).

5 "By the statute 25 Edward 3 where it is said the King can make no law but

by consent in Parliament" (*Harl.*, 6846, f. 169); Cf. *Parl. Debates 1610*, pp. 89–90.

6 *Parl. Debates 1610*, p. 91.
7 Harl., 6846, f. 169.
8 "After by law in the 22th of Edward I an imposition was laid by the assent of merchants, not in Parliament, but by the mere power of the King, for 2 or 3 years, if the war continued so long" (ibid.).
9 Harl., 5176, ff. 14–24.

WHITELOCKE'S ARGUMENT

1 Bruce, ed., *Liber Famelicus*.
2 Sir James Whitelocke, *A Learned and Necessary Argument to Prove each Subject hath a Propriety in his Goods, Showing also the Extent of the King's Prerogative in Impositions* (London, 1641), pp. 6–8. For part of the speech in a slightly different version, see Rawl., D. 155, ff. 40 ff.
3 Ibid., f. 8.
4 Ibid., pp. 9–11.
5 Ibid., p. 11.
6 "The question how we have . . . is a question of our very essence . . . whether we shall have anything or nothing, for if there be a right in the King to alter the propriety of that which is ours without our consent we are but tenants at his will of that which we have. If it be in the King and Parliament then have we proprieties and are tenants at our own wills, for that which is done by Parliament is done by all our wills and consents, and this the very state of the question which is proposed" (Rawl., D. 155, f. 40v).
7 Whitelocke, pp. 11–12. See A. F. Pollard, *Wolsey* (New York, 1929), pp. 132–48.
8 See *Rot. Parl.*, 2:239.
9 Whitelocke, pp. 13–14; cf. *Statutes at Large*, 2:54.
10 Whitelocke, pp. 37–46; cf. *Rot. Parl.*, 2:325.

OTHER SPEAKERS ON IMPOSITIONS

1 *Parl. Debates 1610*, p. 109.
2 Seldom has the problem of the prerogative been better phrased.
3 For Carleton's speech (*SP*, 14/55/55), see Foster, 2:224–25, and *Parl. Debates 1610*, pp. 110–12. Carleton was one of the few parliamentarians of that day who could give his sentences a slightly humorous note, more characteristic of late nineteenth-century English oratory than of the early seventeenth century
4 Just when the Commons made any such promise I do not know, but our information about those late June and early July days is exceedingly limited.
5 Gore, or Gower, is not in the official list of members, but see *CJ*, 1:257, 963, 967, 968, 971.
6 *Parl. Debates 1610*, p. 116; cf. Add. 48119, ff. 66–85.
7 *CJ*, 1:445; *Parl. Debates 1610*, p. 120.
8 *CJ*, 1:445.
9 *SP*, 14/56/part 2.
10 *Parl. Debates 1610*, pp. 162–63.

11 Foster, 2:272; *CJ*, 1:439; *Parl. Debates 1610*, p. 109.
12 *SP*, 14/56/21.
13 Collections of Sir Francis Fane, Add. 34218, f. 112.
14 For this speech, see Foster, 1:130–33, 2:274; also Harl., 354, ff. 218, in *Parl. Debates 1610*, pp. 154–62.
15 *Parl. Debates 1610*, p. 156.
16 Add. 34218, f. 112v.
17 True enough but better left unsaid by Salisbury.
18 "Of the muster of eleven hundred commodities . . . some thirty natives bear nine parts [out of ten] of the burden" (*HMC Downshire*, 2:336). "Twenty of the other 300 raiseth . . . £50,000 *per annum*" (Add. 34218, f. 112v).
19 *Parl. Debates 1610*, p. 160.
20 Folger, V 2. 277, f. 88. Salisbury had read enough history to know that he might find himself "shorter by the head." Economic historians will all be interested in the version of the speech to be found in *HMC Downshire*, 2:330–339.
21 Adv. 31.7.2, ff. 14–21v.
22 Spedding points this out (4:203–04).
23 September 16, 1605. *CSP Dom.*, 1603–10, p. 233.
24 Adv. 31.7.2, ff. 14–21.
25 Harl., 354, ff. 2–8, in *Parl. Debates 1610*, pp. 153–54.
26 On the evening of that day Salisbury arranged a meeting with a "select number of the Lower House, Sir Henry Neville, Sir Maurice Berkeley, Sandys, Croft, Sir John Scott, Sir Francis Goodwin, Mr. Alford and one other." What took place we do not know, but we can suspect that impositions were discussed.
27 Spedding, 4:205–06.
28 Birch, 1:122.
29 *CJ*, 1:438, 448, 449, 450.
30 Folger, V a. 121, f. 13.
31 D'Ewes, p. 649.

Chapter 5

COUNTRY OPINION

1 *SP*, 14/57/32.
2 Add. 48119, f. 198v.
3 It is not imposssible that, with so many manuscripts moved out of country houses and into county archives, much more will be learned about the feeling of local communities as to events in this and other Parliaments.
4 Sir Henry Neville of Berkshire and Sussex, an M.P. for Lewes, was a man of moderate but somewhat "popular" opinions, who was discreetly critical of royal policies. About himself in the Parliament of 1610, he wrote in 1614 that he had been "one that lived and conversed inwardly with the chief of them that were noted to be the most backward, and know their inwardest thoughts on that business" (Gardiner, *James I to Coke*, 2:391).
5 Titus F IV, f. 351.
6 *CSP Dom.*, 1611–18, p. 23.
7 Gardiner, *James I to Coke*, 2:389–94.

8 Contarini and Correr to Doge and Senate, March 4, 1610 (*CSP Ven.*, 1607–10, pp. 438–40). Correr to Doge and Senate, April 15 (*CSP Ven.*, 1607–10, pp. 464–65).

9 December 9, 1610 (de la Boderie, *Les Ambassades*, 5:506–13.) De la Boderie wrote that if only there were a leader, there might be great revolts. In general, neither James nor his Councillors worried a great deal about the possibility of an uprising, though Elizabeth and her Councillors had often been fearful of rebellion. It is true that the Gunpowder Plot gave James and his entourage much to think about, and the enclosure riots of 1607–08 called for action. But Salisbury had an excellent information service; he knew the English and did not lie awake nights thinking about possible popular movements.

10 See, for example, the paper telling of Yelverton's troubles with the King (*Archaeologia*, 15 [1806]:27–52); "Advertisement of a loyal Subject to his gracious Sovereign, drawn from the Observations of the People's Speeches" (*Somers Tracts*, 2:144–48); Moore to Winwood (Winwood, 3:235–36). It would be possible to fill pages with references to the anti-Scottish feeling of the time.

11 Spedding, 4:220–21.

12 *Parl. Debates 1610*, pp. 135–36.

13 *HMC Rutland*, 1:424–45. Dubbing "The Thirty" he had summoned to discuss matters with him the "thirty doges" was no doubt royal and somewhat heavy-handed humor. He and his Councillors had chosen the particular men to summon, and several of them were his "servants." He had asked those men to speak freely and told them that he would pardon what they said to him (*HMC Hastings*, 4:227). Cf. Add. 48119, f. 209v.

THE LORD TREASURER SPEAKS: THE KING PLEADS

1 Add. 48119, f. 184v.

2 In the latter part of the speech he said that he had to speak somewhat largely, that is, at length, "lest my darkness make you mistake" (ibid., f. 187).

3 On November 1 John Moore had written to Trumbull: "The Great Contract sticks like the great ship in the launching. The sum is too great for the subject to pay, and too little for his Majesty to receive" (*HMC Downshire*, 2:388–89).

4 This may be a quotation from some ancient or medieval writer, but whom?

5 *Parl. Debates 1610*, pp. 15–16.

6 "If in interpretation you do anything it must be final" (Add. 48119, f. 186).

7 Did Salisbury mean that if the King were not supplied by Parliament he would extort the money in some other way? In that case he (Salisbury) would be "miserable." In the speech he was assuming, I think, that he was dealing with a body friendly to himself personally.

8 Add. 48119, f. 188; cf. Scott, *Journal of Sir Roger Wilbraham*, p. 104.

9 It would seem that the Commons, as a result of the King's demands, were devising some complicated scheme for breaking the bad news to the country of what they would have to pay and possibly of estimating how much certain taxes would bring in and what modes of taxation would meet with the most approval. Salisbury had gotten wind of the scheme and was warning them that there was not time to carry it out. A good deal was going on behind the scenes that was hardly mentioned in the debates.

10 Perhaps some members had learned from friends in the country—whispering

the news before it broke—that His Majesty was wobbling about the Contract and was going to ask for £500,000 over and above it. This was a renewal (with a lessened figure) of the demand for £600,000 for supply made at the beginning of the fourth session.

11 Add. 48119, f. 190v.

12 Ibid., ff. 192–194v.

13 *Parl. Debates 1610*, p. 126.

14 The account of the debate on November 2 and 3 is based largely on the almost indecipherable notes of Sir Robert Harley (Portland, 29/702, ff. 75–83v). This MS is deposited in the B.M. I made a transcription of it and Mrs. Foster made important additions and emendations to be found in her *Proceedings in Parliament, 1610*, 2:392–400.

15 Portland 29/702, f. 75. Croft speaking. Does he mean that some grievances in the Memorial needed clearing up (the obvious interpretation), or possibly some of the King's answers to them?

16 *Parl. Debates 1610*, p. 127.

17 Add. 48119, f. 194v.

18 The last two paragraphs are based largely upon Portland (29/702) but also upon Add. 48119 and *Parl. Debates 1610*, all under the date November 3.

19 There were three Brooks in the House (if we include Brock from Cornwall). We may suspect that this was Christopher Brooke, son of a York merchant and himself a poet. Christopher would have been the Brooke to speak of the "horny Minotaur." See p. 524 n. 9.

20 This was the boldest riposte Bacon had made to the opposition.

21 Fuller was not in the inner circle of those in opposition, but when he suggested that the Commons would be willing to give "double and treble money," he was probably not making an overstatement.

22 Portland, 29/702, ff. 84–84v.

23 Add. 48119, f. 195.

THE KING DEMANDS £500,000 SUPPLY

1 Add. 48119, ff. 195–195v.

2 The few documents available do not bear out such a promise, but it is possible that certain members of the House made an informal bargain with the King. Also, some Privy Councillors in the Commons may have had dealings with what seemed to be the opposition.

3 Add. 48119, f. 197. In fact, members such as Owen, Hoskins, and Montague had been pretty outspoken, and one wonders if the King had been told of their speeches. Of course there were members who were afraid to be definite, and there were also those who tried to please both sides and seldom succeeded in pleasing either.

4 James's concern for the poor reveals an unsuspected aspect of his character.

5 Add. 48119, f. 197. The Commons seemed in their Petition of Grace to have left that burden upon the King.

6 Lansd., 151, f. 128a, in *Parl. Debates 1610*, pp. 163–79.

7 Add. 48119, f. 198v; cf. *Parl. Debates 1610*, p. 130.

8 Add. 48119, f. 200v.

9 "This answer I expect, no dutiful subject can refuse. I plead" (ibid., f. 194v).

The King seemed well aware that the show of emotion was useful in persuasion.

10 In *Parl. Debates 1610* (p. 129) this is put down as of November 6, but it is evident from Add. 48119 (f. 197v) that it was the seventh: "This being read twice [the King's message] the Speaker moved (it being now late and the matter of weight) that we might defer till the next day. At which day [in margin: Wednesday, November 7] it was read again." Presently, after Caesar's speech, Horsey, Brooke, and Beaumont spoke.

11 Add. 48119, f. 197v. Horsey traveled several times to Russia and served the Muscovy Company and the Russian government in many errands. By the Muscovy Company he was charged at length with a whole series of frauds, to some of which he had to admit guilt. That did not prevent his appointment in 1604 as Receiver General for Crown lands in Bucks. He had been in the Parliaments of 1592/93, 1597, and 1601.

12 It is hard to distinguish the Brooks. See p. 524 n. 9.

13 Add. 48119, f. 197v.

14 A "running subsidy from the monied men" sounds strangely like privy seals through which the King had been collecting money. What the tax on merchandise would have been is hard to say.

15 The speeches of Horsey and Brook I have put together from Add. 48119, ff. 197v–198, and from *Parl. Debates 1610*, p. 129.

16 Richard James wished they might never hear the new Parliament phrase "We must give supply, we must give support."

17 Hyde anticipated the possible effect of his speech: "He would deliver his opinion and he knew not what should make him fear to do it, for he was in a free Council" (Add. 48119, f. 199).

18 This account of Hoskins's speech is based upon *Parl. Debates 1610*, pp. 130–31.

19 Add. 48119, f. 199v.

THE CONTRACT ABANDONED

1 Add. 48119, f. 199v.

2 Duncombe may have owed his election at Tavistock to William Russell, Lord Thornhaugh, the father of Francis Russell, who became the fourth Earl of Bedford. The Russells were actively Puritan and controlled seats in the west country.

3 Add. 48119, f. 200.

4 The writer of the narrative in Add. 48119 was evidently a member of the subcommittee and presumably an active member of the House. See f. 200v.

5 Ibid.

6 Ibid., f. 201. "This was done [rewritten] with great caution, lest from thence might be inferred that we did impute to his Majesty any contrariety between the Memorial and his last Declaration. Neither was it thought fit to say plainly that we would willingly proceed according [to] the Memorial, lest thereby we should tie ourselves too strictly to any inconveniences which might be drawn from thence" (*Parl. Debates 1610*, p. 131). It is to be remembered that the writer of *Parl. Debates 1610* was not in the inner councils of those who were formulating policy.

7 Add. 48119, ff. 203–203v.

8 Before the King's message was brought in, Martin—presumably Richard Mar-

tin, a level-headed man—made a speech that seemed out of character. He feared that the King's need for money might drive him to extreme measures and that the prerogative might be extended. He was not afraid, he said, of Privy Councillors, who were noble and honorable men. They would not support a policy which would make them and their posterity servile. The men to be feared were those who preached in the pulpits and wrote in corners exalting the royal prerogative. Such clergymen would tread on the neck of the common law to get a double benefice or a high ecclesiastical dignity. They denounced "prohibitions" as against the law of God. Did not a clergyman (Harsnett, Bishop of Chichester) declare that subsidies were not gifts but duties? Had not a hedge priest said that trial by common law was by ten fools and two knaves? Martin proposed a law "somewhat sharp"; he would hang those who would sell the liberty of the people. His friends advised him to spare that. He then offered a less drastic plan: that such clergymen should lose their dignities and, for the second offense, undergo the penalties attached to praemunire (16 Rich. II, cap. v). How would it have been feasible to formulate such legislation, to define legally the crime of selling the liberties of the people? That the writer of Add. 48119 attributed the proposal to Martin would seem to mean that he attributed it to Richard Martin, one of the leaders of the opposition in the Commons and as such almost second man to Sandys, a careful man who usually acted with discretion. Could the writer of Add. 48119 have meant Henry Martin, M.P. for Wootton Bassett in Wiltshire? Henry Martin never spoke in Parliament, so far as I know, and I do not remember him as a committee man. It seems probable that the writer would have indicated if a Martin other than the one constantly mentioned developed this bizarre idea about the clergy. The speech seems unlike Richard Martin, yet discreet men may be unwise about some one question on which they have strong feelings.

9 Folger, V a. 277, ff. 113v–114.
10 See *CJ*, 1:403.
11 Folger, V a. 277, ff. 114v–115.
12 Ibid., ff. 115–115v.
13 Ibid., ff. 116–117v.
14 "This experience of want hath so taught his Majesty what it is to want as he will never come unto the like again" (*HMC Hastings*, 4:223).
15 "It is impossible to have secrecy kept, for 3 may keep counsel if 2 be away, so as neither the vulgar people, nor foreign states, whose ambassadors are legiers in this City can be ignorant thereof" (ibid.).
16 Add. 48119, f. 205v. "You offer so slowly as neither his Majesty nor we know whether you mean to bring anything" (ibid.).
17 Salisbury's comments were interesting: "None that spoke against it meant ill." In the same speech he is quoted as saying: "I conceive we have lost our contract *per motum trepidationis*" (ibid.).
18 *Parl. Debates 1610*, pp. 131–33.
19 Add. 48119, ff. 205v–206. Salisbury's assumption that the fault was on both sides and that the King would be more careful hereafter would hardly have pleased His Majesty.
    One suspects that Salisbury was a gardener. He spoke of the tree of tenures as possibly rooted out, and in whose place it had been hoped to plant a "fine vineyard of sweet grapes and pleasant wine" (*HMC Hastings*, 4:223). Such asides would have been well received by country gentlemen.
20 34–35 Hen. VIII, cap. xxvi, no. cxix.

21 *Parl. Debates 1610*, p. 133. "Though you may say he had no just right unto them, that was more than he knew, for those impositions were not *de novo*, but came to him in the right of his Crown" (*HMC Hastings*, 4:223).
22 Ibid., 4:224–25.
23 Twysden quoted the historic medieval Latin lines *nolumus mutare leges Angliae*.
24 Add. 48119, f. 206.
25 Samuel Lewknor represented Bishops Castle in the Parliament of 1604–10. His name does not appear on the official list, but Bishops Castle was taxed for payment of his expenses as an M.P. (Stanley T. Weyman, "The Members of Parliament for Bishops Castle," *Shrop. Arch. Soc.*, 2nd ser., 10:40). He was again an M.P. for Bishops Castle in 1614 (*HMC 10th Rep.*, p. 401). His uncle was Sir Richard Lewknor, who was a member of the Council of Wales and Chief Justice of Chester, and who wrote letters to Salisbury. Weyman says that Samuel Lewknor attended Cambridge University, but his name has not been found among its records. In 1600 he published *A Description of all those Cities where do flourish privileged Universities* and dedicated it to his uncle, Richard Lewknor, Serjeant. The book reveals a considerable reading of Latin and continental authors and was probably written by a man with some university training. On May 6, 1607, he made a speech in the Commons about freedom of speech in Parliament (*HMC Buccleuch*, 3:116), which, from the brief notes we have, suggests that he was not wanting in clearness or frankness. In his introduction to the book, he tells us that he was more acquainted with the warlike sounds of martial drums than with the schools and lectures of philosophy. One might guess that he had spent a year or two at the university and then gone soldiering in the Low Countries.
26 "The Great Contract *pend au croc*. His Majesty's intent was not it should ever proceed as the Lower House understands it. Yet a large supply is pressed, which the Commons will not grant without reciprocal retribution" (John Moore to Trumbull, November 22, 1610. [*HMC Downshire*, 2:396–97]).
27 Lewknor garbled the story. See Xenophon, *Cyropaedia*, VIII, 2:13–16.
28 *Scriptores Historiae Augustae. Vita Antoninii Pii*, 8:5 12. The text of Add 48119 reads *Ausonius*, but that must be a copyist's mistake of *Antoninus*. Cf. the version of the speech in Harl., 4228, f. 16.
29 I have used Add. 48119, ff. 206v–208, and Harl., 4228, ff. 16–17v.
30 Add. 48119, ff. 208–208v.
31 Ibid., f. 208v; *Parl. Debates 1610*, p. 135.
32 Add. 48119, ff. 208–09; *HMC Rutland*, 1:424.
33 Ibid.
34 *CJ*, 1:410; *Parl. Debates 1610*, pp. 27–28.

THE CONFERENCE WITH "THE THIRTY"

1 Add. 48119, f. 209v.
2 Titus F IV, f. 131v.
3 *HMC Hastings*, 4:226. The time was unseasonable, "having delivered unto the country what they should have, being now otherwise." Does this mean that it was too late, because members had promised the country that the King would make concessions which he did not make?
4 John Moore to Winwood, December 1 (Winwood, 3:235–36). The King was

snubbing Sir Francis, possibly because he thought Sir Francis had not supported him zealously enough in the Commons but more probably because his language did not please the King, who wished to hear the other side. Moreover, James was not unwilling to humiliate people in public.

5 That he was not moved by Neville's recital of grievances is evident from what he did the next day.
6 John Moore to Winwood, December 1 (Winwood 3:235–36).
7 Ibid.
8 *HMC Hastings*, 4:227.
9 Add. 48119, f. 209v.
10 *HMC Hastings*, 4:226.
11 *HMC Rutland*, 1:425.
12 Latimer, *Annals of Bristol*, pp. 20–21.
13 Add. 48119, f. 209v.
14 *HMC Hastings*, 4:227.
15 *HMC Rutland* 1:425.
16 Add. 48119, f. 209v.
17 *HMC Downshire*, 2:396.
18 It was probably about earlier events in this autumn session that Sir William Cecil wrote to Sir John Holles. Sir William, Lord Burghley, was the son of Salisbury's elder brother, the Earl of Exeter, and had in June 1610 been elected M.P. for Weymouth. He wrote: "I do see that stout honesty in all your companions of this Parliament, except some sycophants, who are in my calendar, that one of their words shall be of more regard hereafter with me than another's bond" (*HMC Portland*, 9:153). This statement is hard to understand, but I think "one of their words" is an allusion to "your companions of this Parliament," not to the sycophants. Lord Burghley meant, I think, that he would keep in his calendar the words of those of stout honesty. The men in the early seventeenth century often wrote ambiguous sentences.

Sir John Holles, although apparently on good terms with Salisbury, could not be called friendly to James I, and no doubt Lord Burghley knew this. Cf. Holles's comment on James in *HMC Portland*, 9:113.

The letter in which Holles expressed himself about the King is undated but was written in the autumn of 1610, as "this seven years brand" and the allusion to "supply and support" would suggest.

THE FINALE

1 Add. 48119, ff. 210–210v.
2 Hurstfield, *The Queen's Wards*, pp. 130–56.
3 *SP*, 14/58/35.
4 *HMC Rutland*, 1:425.
5 *Parl. Debates 1610*, p. 139. Hakewill believed that "The Thirty" should have answered the King "as Judge Fineux did Henry VIII upon a question touching the high constable or his office, which was to entreat leave to confer with his brethren before he gave an answer" (*HMC Rutland*, 1:425).
6 Epaminondas of Thebes (Diodorus Siculus, 15:71, 6–72, 2).
7 Add. 48119, f. 211v; cf. *Parl. Debates 1610*, p. 140.
8 Titus F IV, f. 132v.
9 Salisbury dealt with figures in the financial picture but not with statistics.

10 *Parl. Debates 1610,* pp. 142–43; Add. 48119, f. 212.
11 *Somers Tracts,* 2:151. "God hath not looked upon our merchants of late with that eye of wealth . . . that in times past he did, and yet they labor as much as ever and adventure further" (Rawl., B 151, f. 8).
12 It was in the House of Commons and in the theatre that the merchants received their due as the backbone of the Commonwealth.
13 "Clothing is also much down the wind . . . that maintaineth many thousand subjects" (Rawl., B 151, f. 8).
14 "The treasure . . . of the Realm, is it in the warm sun or is it not in the cold shadow?" (ibid.).
15 "And for lawyers there is more increase of their numbers lately than of their wealth, save for some favorites and some few wits among them" (ibid.).
16 "Which hath been twice read and agreed upon by the committees" (ibid.).
17 *Somers Tracts,* 2:154.
18 At this point Sir Henry Montague put in a word for impositions as necessary to prevent the importation of foreign superfluities and to hinder the exportation of food, silver, and gold.
19 *Parl. Debates 1610,* p. 144. The King was eager to punish Wentworth for this speech, but his Councillors, or some of them, dissuaded him. Cf. Lake to Salisbury, December 2 or 6 (*SP,* 14/58/54 and 62). In the sentence quoted above, Wentworth may have been alluding slyly to the unsavory reputation of Northampton and possibly to that of young Sir Robert Carr, soon to become Earl of Somerset. It would have been hard to make a case against Wentworth from his words.
20 He was discreet not to mention the Scots. The French ambassador in London wrote to Paris that the Council begged the King to cut his expenses, a reform which would affect the Scots. The Scots, according to the ambassador, retaliated by attacking Salisbury (French Transcripts, Public Record Office, London, 31/3/41, January 6, 1610/11).
21 *Parl. Debates 1610,* p. 145. I suspect the King believed what he was saying. He had a gift for self-deception.
22 *SP,* 14/58/35.
23 Foster, 2:346. See Titus F IV, f. 132; *HMC Rutland,* 1:425.
24 *Parl. Debates 1610,* p. 139.
25 Ibid.
26 "It is true that the first night of Lake's coming to Royston, he did broadly and roundly inform me that you had told him that there was a worse thing in head than anything whereof you had advertised me, which was that he had intelligence that, if the Lower House had met again, one had a motion for a petition to be made unto me that I would be pleased to send home the Scots, if I looked for any supply from them. The next morning when I urged him [Lake] to repeat the words again, he minced it in those terms ye now have it under his hand, which is yet directly contrary to that which ye affirm in your letter" (James to Salisbury [Cecil Papers, Hatfield, 134/65, quoted in Foster, 2:346]).
27 Foster, 2:346. Mrs. Foster, by using the Hatfield MS, has added to the story of Lake's duplicity. I wrote an appendix dealing with it, but I am glad that Mrs. Foster has covered it so fully in her long and important footnote that my appendix is unnecessary. Lake played an ignoble role and got Salisbury into hot water. Salisbury was deeply shaken but was generous enough to see that Lake did not lose his post. Those familiar with the Northampton MSS in the British Museum will recall that Carr and Northampton were on good

terms. It is easy to suspect that Northampton was involved in these shady transactions.
28 Cecil Papers, Hatfield, 134/65, quoted in Foster, 2:346.
29 Winwood, 3:235.
30 Ibid., pp. 235–36.
31 Ibid., 3:239–40.
32 Add. 34324, ff. 61–61v.
33 The King's general attitude is fairly well shown by a proclamation issued on March 26, 1610. This proclamation calls for the delivery of John Cowell's *Interpreter* to the mayors or to the sheriffs of counties. But the proclamation continues: "His Majesty declared how grievously the people of this latter age . . . are fallen into verbal profession, as well of religion, as of all commendable moral virtues, but wanting the actions and deeds of so specious a profession, and the unsatiable and unmeasurable itching boldness of the spirits, tongues, and pens of most men: so as nothing was now left untouched from the top to the bottom, neither in talking, nor writing of the highest mysteries of the Godhead and the inscrutable counsels of the Trinity, nor of the confused actions of the devils in the lowest pit of hell, such is the misery of this age that most men in their extreme niceness and curiosity spare not to aspire [to] God's secrets and audaciously to invade the deepest mysteries that belong to kings and princes, and to all regal government" (J. Stow and E. Howes, *Annales* [London, 1631], pp. 896–99). The language is almost hysterical, but it indicates something of the King's belief in his relationship to the Supreme Being.
34 Foster, 2:348–49.
35 *Somers Tracts* 2:150–51.

Chapter 6

PRELUDE: COMMITTEES BEFORE 1603

1 Neale, *Elizabeth and her Parliaments 1559–1581*, p. 220.
2 At some time around 1590 Francis Tate, then probably an M.P., proposed that committees of the House consider the bills offered, put forward the most necessary ones first, but in no way make motions rejecting any ("although indeed it amounteth to a rejecting of those that be of small importance") (A Discourse Importing the Assembly of a Parliament [Harl., 253, f. 34]).
3 Yet there was an effort to reduce the size of committees. On February 20, 1588/89, the Vice-Chamberlain proposed that the Commons "would henceforth in their commitments use to name a fewer number than they have hitherto in this session" (D'Ewes, pp. 435–36). Nothing seems to have come of his suggestion.

COMMITTEES IN THE SESSION OF 1603/04

1 Lawyers were needed to frame laws but were often so busy that the committee had trouble commanding their services. Some of those who gained

great influence in committees were lawyers who had small practices, such as
Hakewill and, I suspect, Francis Moore.

2 To be a figure in the Commons of that time meant to be known not only
for speeches and committee activity but as a landowner and a justice of the
peace and of the quorum.

3 *HMC Buccleuch*, 3:80.

4 *CJ*, 1:165, 942.

5 *CJ*, 1:172, 946, 947.

6 *CJ*, 1:179–80.

7 *CJ*, 1:180.

8 *CJ*, 1:183.

9 *CJ*, 1:183–84.

10 *CJ*, 1:938. On April 12 complaint was made of the failure of a sufficient
number to attend committee meetings (*CJ*, 1:169).

11 *CJ*, 1:184.

12 *HMC Buccleuch*, 3:81. Bacon, in his report of the proceedings of the Committee for Wardship, had said on March 26 that the Commons wished to confer with the Lords and to offer the King "the matter plotted, or first to ask
leave to treat" (*CJ*, 1:935).

13 *HMC Buccleuch*, 3:81.

14 *CJ*, 1:172.

15 See *CJ*, 1:215; *LJ*, 2:300, 305.

16 *CJ*, 1:235, 988–89.

17 *CJ*, 1:238, 991.

18 *CJ*, 1:235.

COMMITTEES IN THE SESSION OF 1605/06

1 Of some of these committee meetings we have accounts in Bowyer; for other
sessions we have to rely upon reports from committees in the *CJ* and *LJ*.

2 *CJ*, 1:287.

3 Bowyer, p. 136.

4 Ibid., p. 106.

5 Ibid., pp. 76–77.

6 *CJ*, 1:267.

7 A bill might not be welcomed, but it was voted just the same that any member had the right to put in a bill (*CJ*, 1:288).

8 *CJ*, 1:288.

9 *CJ*, 1:260.

10 Bowyer, p. 7.

11 Ibid., p. 22. Of course Bowyer may have omitted details, but he was not
likely to do so. He was interested in details of procedure (*CJ*, 1:263).

12 Bowyer, p. 25; *CJ*, 1:263.

13 *CJ*, 1:276.

14 *CJ*, 1:258.

15 *CJ*, 1:268.

16 On February 3 the House was dealing with the fourth article about recusants
and resolved that it should be considered "this afternoon in the Parliament
House, in respect of sundry exceptions" (*CJ*, 1:263). A little later the Clerk
added: "Mr. Yelverton, Mr. Lawrence Hyde, Mr. Winch, Mr. Tate, Sir John

Boys, these to attend the General Committee this afternoon." To attend it—
what does that mean? Were they to be a subcommittee, if necessary? Or were
they appointed for their legal expertise as advisers?

17 *CJ*, 1:265.
18 Birch, 1:51. Here a joint committee of the two Houses was apparently proposed, but, as in 1604, not much came of it.
19 *LJ*, 2:371; cf. *LJ*, 2:373, 381. See also *CJ*, 1:267, 269, 270, 275, 276, 277, 283,
284, 288, 295, 298, 300.
20 Bowyer, p. 57 and n. 1.
21 Ibid., p. 9.
22 Henry Elsynge, in his *Memorials of the Method and Manner of Proceedings
in Parliament in Passing Bills* (London, 1670), says of the nominating to committees: "Any members that please may name one a piece, but not more to
the committee" (p. 47). Whether any such principle that one man could make
only one nomination developed in the 1620s or earlier I do not know; I
doubt it.
23 Bowyer, pp. 115–16.

COMMITTEES IN THE SESSION OF 1606/07

1 Of course we know less about what went on in committee than in the House.
But we are not left wholly in the dark. Robert Bowyer, Sir Robert Harley,
Thomas Wilson, and Dudley Carleton all at one time or another kept notes
of committee sessions. Indeed, Carleton summarized the utterances of members in analytical form and probably rendered them more orderly in sequence
of thought than they had been when spoken.
2 Bowyer, p. 197; *CJ*, 1:1005.
3 *CJ*, 1:326.
4 Northumberland, Cumberland, and Westmorland. Cf. Bowyer, p. 199 .
5 *CJ*, 1:326.
6 *HMC Buccleuch*, 3:109.
7 Bowyer, p. 199.
8 *CJ*, 1:1006.
9 *CJ*, 1:329, 1009.
10 M.P. for Marlborough (1597, 1601, 1604–10, etc.), a resident of Marlborough,
and a member of Lincoln's Inn.
11 December 17, 1601 (Titus F IV, ff. 94–94v).
12 It would seem likely that the Commons used a Committee of the Whole House
on December 17, 1606. On December 1 of that year the House of Lords made
use of such a committee. Whether the Lords took over the idea from the
earlier practice by the Commons of using a committee that was practically
a Committee of the Whole House or whether the Commons in taking the final
step were influenced by the Lords we shall hardly find out unless more diaries
turn up. See E. R. Foster, "Procedure in the House of Lords During the Early
Stuart Period," *Journal of British Studies*, 5 (1966): 67–69.
13 *CJ*, 1:331, 1011. The writer may have been Sir Robert Cotton.
14 Titus F IV, f. 94v. This was June 26, not 27. The writer adds: "But in the last
session of this Parliament it was a common practice."
15 Bowyer, p. 351; *CJ*, 1:1054.
16 *CJ*, 1:1054.

17 *CJ*, 1:1013.
18 Ibid.
19 *CJ*, 1:1017.
20 *HMC Buccleuch*, 3:112.
21 *CJ*, 1:1020.
22 Bowyer, p. 246.
23 *CJ*, 1:1042. Probably he suspected, as did others, that the proposal by Sandys for a complete Union was a trick to upset any plan for Union.
24 "After the bill was committed Mr. Hare rose up and had much ado to be heard, and it had been better he had not been heard, for he renewed only the frivolous motion of clearing Mr. Yelverton by voices" (Bowyer, p. 377).
25 *CJ*, 1:371, 1042.
26 Bowyer, pp. 381–82, 383–85.
27 Spedding, 3:343–45; Bowyer, pp. 376–78.
28 Bowyer, pp. 310–14.

COMMITTEES IN THE SESSION OF 1610

1 The author calls the man in the chair at the committee the "Moderator." He tells us that the Speaker, when he came in at nine o'clock, sat in the Clerk's chair, "where before his coming Mr. Recorder, Moderator of the Committee, sat. The Clerk stood at the Speaker's back and Mr. Recorder sat at the table by Mr. Speaker upon a stool, and did moderate as before" (March 23, 1609/10).
2 Titus F IV, f. 121v.
3 Bowyer, pp. 313–14.
4 *CJ*, 1:979, 1048; cf. Elsynge, *Proceedings in Parliament in Passing Bills*, p. 50.
5 Bowyer, p. 314. Possibly this ruling initiated new procedure.
6 Ibid., p. 364.
7 Harl., 777, f. 51; cf. *CJ*, 1:447.
8 Later, in the 1620s and in the Long Parliament, committees asked for and were granted special powers. Sometimes, too, limits were set upon their power.
9 Harl., 777, f. 51–51v; cf. *CJ*, 1:447.
10 Add. 48119, f. 165v.
11 Ibid., ff. 199–199v. "I think not 5 voices excepted answered No." Cf. *Parl. Debates 1610*, p. 131.
12 Add. 48119, f. 199v.
13 *SP*, 14/2/17, quoted in Spedding, 3:343–45.
14 Bowyer, p. 351.
15 Add. 48119, f. 154v.
16 Ibid., f. 195.
17 Elsynge, *Proceedings of Parliament in Passing Bills*, p. 37.
18 Portland, 29/202, f. 78v. Berkeley had spoken twice (f. 75v, 78v). Later "Sir R. Phillips," as the writer calls him, desired to put the project of Sir M. Berkeley to the question, i.e., to draft an answer to the King (f. 79v). R. Phelips was, of course, the son of the Speaker.
19 Bowyer, p. 364.
20 Add. 48119, ff. 200–200v.
21 Ibid. "A Grand Committee of the Whole House was appointed to sit in the House (the Speaker sitting by). After some debate they appointed a sub-

committee presently to make a draft of a writing (which is never conveniently done but by few), who go into the committee chamber and consider of it. In the meantime Mr. Speaker goeth up into his Chair. As soon as the subcommittee returneth Mr. Speaker leaving his Chair, they made report to the Grand Committee and the draft approved by the Grand Committee, and then, Mr. Speaker again ascending his Chair, report is made to the House by the Grand Committee, and so the matter resolved by the House" (November 8, 1610 [Titus F IV, f. 131]).

22 Ibid., ff. 200–01.

23 Add. 48119, f. 168. The Privy Councillors and others were probably afraid to have any part in a petition which might anger the King.

24 Add. 48119, ff. 168–168v. One of the many instances of Sandys's influence over the House.

25 Ibid., f. 168v; cf. *CJ*, 1:431.

26 For an instance in 1607 of a subcommittee apparently reporting directly to the House, see the notes of Thomas Wilson in Bowyer, p. 306 n. 2. For a case in 1610, see *CJ*, 1:445, July 3 and 4. A subcommittee of the Grand Committee was named July 3 to report about Impositions. On the next day Martin reported from the subcommittee to the House, or so I would interpret the Clerk's book.

27 *Parl. Debates 1610*, p. 46; cf. *CJ*, 1:434.

28 It will be recalled that Sir John Savile, M.P. for Yorkshire, Sir Roger Owen, and others refused to serve on the subcommittee. Savile did so because he believed that the concessions ought not to be bargained for and the hundred thousand pounds already offered was as much as the subjects could stand (*Parl. Debates 1610*, pp. 46–47).

29 On April 25 Sir Edwin Sandys wished some process devised to get better attendance at the Committee of Grievances. The subject before the Committee was impositions, and the Committee had directed him "to move that the King's Counsel Learned and all other lawyers of the House might be warned to give their attendance which was thought meet by the House" (*HMC House of Lords*, new ser., 11:117).

30 On March 31, 1606, Sir Thomas Holcroft remarked: "It will be a scandal to shew what we have done is done with so small a number" (*CJ*, 1:291). Toward the ends of sessions the number voting was sometimes under 100 and now and then under 50.

31 The writer of the notes on procedure in Titus F IV has some interesting remarks about the value of the committees: "The appointed place was the Parliament House and to sit as a committee without the Speaker. Which was accordingly done, and by that means everyone of the meanest capacity and learning understood th'effect of the records before the matter came to be solemnly argued of. Which was resolved to be at a committee, that if occasion were, there might be often replies, the times every morning till the debates were ended, to begin at 9 of the clock and continue till 12. And that the lawyers might the better attend at the reading of the records, it was ordered that all the lawyers' names should by the Clerk be delivered to one of the House, and he to make report how many were absent, which was accordingly done" (June 23, f. 121). The writer is talking of the Committee of the Whole House for Impositions. Those who had consulted the records, he believed, could in the committee explain them clearly and simply for all. Why such explanation was better in the committee than in the House he does not tell us. But probably it was because those who did not understand could ask questions.

32 In 1610 the House of Lords was using the Committee of the Whole House, which they had begun to use in 1606. On March 31 at 9:00 a.m. the House adjourned till Monday and went into a Committee of the Whole House: "The Lord Chancellor put the Lords in mind of their last purpose to spend this morning as committees, every man to keep his place and to speak by interlocution, and no man to be barred by a first or second speech, but to speak often, as occasion shall require it" (Braye, 61, f. 18v). On March 29 the "Lord Chancellor moved to hear the committee's names that were before used, and then to add as should be thought good. The Lower House first made a committee of more than this whole House; then those committees, after many meetings, reported it to the whole Lower House; then they reported it to your Lordships. Therefore, if it please you, let the whole House be certified. And ordered that this committee *hac vice* only should set in order, as now they do, and he that speaketh to stand, and no other, and the place to be this House, the time Saturday morning at 9, of the clock" (ibid., f. 18).

Chapter 7

THE SPEAKER'S ELECTION AND QUALIFICATIONS

1 *HMC Buccleuch,* 3:79.
2 Justice of Common Pleas in the County Palatine of Lancaster.
3 Those forms of procedure were embodied in rules that were fairly well known by the end of the reign of Elizabeth; some of them were known to Sir Edward. All that was true, yet there were forms of procedure destined to become common practice in the reign of Charles I which were by no means established as yet.
4 June 12, 1607 (*CJ*, 1:382).
5 May 15, 1606 (ibid., 1:309).
6 E.g., April 19, 1604 (*CJ*, 1:178); November 26, 1606 (Bowyer, p. 193 n. 2); April 29, 1607; (Bowyer, p. 274 and n. 1; *CJ*, 1:1037).
7 There were Elizabethan examples of somewhat similar action. On March 19, 1588/89, the bill concerning Hue and Cry was reserved for further consideration in another session (D'Ewes, p. 448). Probably the bill was left with the Clerk. On March 17, 1592/93, T. P. Hoby, asked by the House to deliver two bills (which had been given him by the Clerk), secured the bills from his brother, Sir Edward, and delivered them (ibid., p. 502).

THE SPEAKER AND THE HOUSE

1 "If any of the House be desirous to have any new law made for the reforming of anything that is amiss in the Commonwealth, he may, when he shall perceive the House not to be otherwise employed, make a motion in the House to that effect, declaring the reasons of his desire and praying House to take it into their consideration and to appoint some of the House to pen a law to that purpose" (Exeter, D and C. 4718, f.1; see E. R. Foster, "Speaking in the House of Commons," *Bull. Inst. Hist. Research,* 43 [1970]: 35–55, where the manuscript is identified as the draft of another chapter of William Hakewill's collections on parliamentary procedure and collated with the related manuscripts in the Montagu Papers and the British Museum). Francis Tate,

writing probably in 1581, urged any member who wished to bring in a bill to confer with others and to ask some colleague to join with him in penning the bill (Harl., 253, f. 35).

2   When the bill has been "drawn to the effect of his desire, he may present it to the House to be read, but when such bills are so delivered, the Speaker is not bound then presently to cause them to be read, but may take time till the next day that he may . . . make a breviate for his memory in opening the substance thereof, which he is bound to do upon the reading thereof" (Exeter, D. and C., f. 1). See also a letter from Carleton to Edmondes, June 7, 1610, in which Carleton informed Edmondes that his bill for the naturalization of the children of ambassadors, of which Fuller was in charge, had had a day arranged for it (Birch, 1:115–16).

In determining the order in which bills were to be read, the Speaker might have used his discretion in favor of friends. To exercise such discretion was no sin in that day. In 1581 Lord Thomas Howard wrote William Pytt of Weymouth that it was not possible to do anything in the Parliament: "For when I should have bestowed chargeable sums of money in framing bills, in rewarding them that should speak favorably in them, in gratifying the Speaker and other men of authority, then should I look for a hard passage of the bill by reason that Sir Christopher Hatton's countenance and credit would work much against, and surely would overthrow it when it should come to her Majesty's hands" (*HMC 5th Rep.*, App. 1, p. 579). Hatton was of course a Privy Councillor and had long been on good terms with the Queen. The bills Lord Thomas Howard mentioned may have been private bills. For such bills the Speaker expected fees, and he may have received higher ones for seeing to it that they were read early and advanced to the committee stage and beyond. I know of no evidence of Phelips's having taken money for advancing public bills. He was more interested, I suspect, in offices and honors than in money. About the taking of fees, see *CJ*, 1:197, 1054–55.

3   On March 7, 1592/93, the Speaker "propounds it as an order in the House in such a case for him to ask the parties that would speak, on which side they would speak, whether with him that spake next before, or against him; and the party that speaketh against the last speaker is to be heard first, and so it was ruled" (D'Ewes, p. 493). Cf. June 4, 1607, in *CJ*, 1:232.

4   On February 18, 1588/89, when there was great disorder in the House, men standing up to speak "sometimes three or four together," each one trying to gain the floor and trusting to the acclamation of his fellows to make good his claim, the Speaker pointed out that the House was a court and that judges in other courts did not tolerate such disorders and "such confused courses either of contention, acclamations, or reciprocal bitter and sharp speeches" (D'Ewes, p. 434). On May 2, 1604, it was put to the question "whether Sir Francis Hastings or Sir Richard Leveson should stand up. Resolved, Sir Francis Hastings" *CJ*, 1:963). The Clerk wrote in his finished notes of "being doubtful whether [*sic*] stood up first; put to question, *as the manner is often in the like case*" (*CJ*, 1:197, my italics). I do not know of earlier cases, but the then Clerk had more knowledge than I have now.

5   William Hakewill, *The Manner how Statutes are Enacted in Parliament* (London, 1670), p. 136. The pamphlet was first published in 1641 but had existed in manuscript at least thirty years earlier. Cf. British Museum 8980, f. 3. The Speaker had his rights as against the members; see *CJ*, 1:175. Tey complained that the Speaker disliked his motion and clipped him off. The House compelled Tey to apologize for his manner of writing to the Speaker about the episode. The writer of "Policies in Parliament" declared: "The Speaker may

not be put to the reading and repeating of a bill presently upon the first offering it in the House, if he refuse to do it" *Huntington Library Quarterly,* 15 [1951]: 50.) It is quite possible that the author of "Policies in Parliament" was thinking of the Tey case.

6 D'Ewes, p. 677. Carew would have found it hard to cite a precedent for his statement that they could remove the Speaker.

7 *Commons Debates in 1621,* 6:356. Francis Tate assumed throughout his short discourse on Parliament ca. 1580 (Harl., 253, ff. 32–36v) that the Speaker had a good deal of power with reference to which bills were advanced or held back.

8 See the document *Concerninge the Speaker's Dutie in Putting of Things to the Question* in Catherine S. Sims, "The Speaker of the House of Commons," *AHR,* 45 (1939): 90–95. Mrs. Sims believes with reason that this MS was almost certainly written by William Hakewill. Her footnote (p. 92 n. 7) about this passage is worth reproducing: "This may be a description of what later came to be called the previous question," and there can be no doubt about it. See the *CJ* for May 25, 1604: "Much labor to keep the bill from the question at that time; and agreed at last, that a question should be made, whether the bill shall presently be put to question: and upon question, *Resolved* in the affirmative." John Hatsell cited this as the "first instance I have found of putting the previous question"; see his *Precedents of Proceedings in the House of Commons* (London, 1818), 2:111.

9 An excellent example is to be found in the session of February 28, 1609/10 (*CJ,* 1:403), when the Speaker framed the question from the words used by the Recorder.

10 One would be glad to know Salisbury's real opinion of Phelips.

11 I am inclined to believe that the House was interfering more and more with the Speaker as to how the question should be put.

12 *CJ,* 1:964. Occasionally the leaders did demand a part in framing the question and succeeded in getting the very wording they sought (*CJ,* 1:179). On June 2, 1604, there had been "much wrangle what the question should be." The wrangle had arisen in part because the Commons had just voted on another question, whether or not to confer with the Lords about the proportion of the "composition" (for purveyance), and the Ayes had carried the vote. That decision as to the number of votes on each side, made presumably by the Speaker, was "not agreed unto," and the upshot was that no vote seems to have been recorded (*CJ,* 1:984–85, 231).

13 Elizabethan Speakers had prevented men from speaking by putting the question or by rising and thus ending the proceedings for the day. See also Peter Wentworth's complaints about the Speaker, March 1, 1586/87 (D'Ewes, p. 411).

14 "Agreed for a general rule, if any superfluous motion or tedious speech be offered in the House, the party is to be directed and ordered by Mr. Speaker" (*CJ,* 1:175). Three days earlier Sir Henry Jenkins had been interrupted by the Speaker "to prevent the idle expense of time," and thereupon a rule was conceived "that if any man speak impertinently, or besides the question in hand, it stands with the orders of the House for Mr. Speaker to interrupt him and to know the pleasure of the House whether they will further hear him" (*CJ,* 1:171–72). On May 19, 1604, Sir William Paddy, the well-known physician, made a long speech and was "interrupted and a question offered . . . whether he should go on; by reason the order was peremptory for reading ingrossed bills half an hour after eight. A rule agreed, if any man speak not to the matter in question the Speaker is to moderate" (*CJ,* 1:214).

15 *CJ,* 1:948.

16 D'Ewes, p. 306. Francis Tate, M.P. for Shrewsbury in 1604 (and M.P. in Elizabethan Parliaments probably as early as 1580/81), wrote: "Here is the great difficulty of the Speaker's whole service, to give temper [character, quality?], and yet to avoid opinion of overruling or straitening the liberty of the House. There must be discreet interposing of committees and such good means, and among other, not to be too hasty with reading of those bills that have been found upon a first or second reading to be so long walking fields [getting nowhere?]" (A Discourse Importing the Assembly of a Parliament, in Harl., 253, f. 35).

17 Bowyer, p. 362.

18 Ibid., pp. 305–06. When the Speaker asked permission to interrupt Sir Daniel, he was acting in accordance with the rule already mentioned (*CJ*, 1:172). That the pleasure of the House should be sought was, I suspect, a rather new principle and may have represented one aspect of the encroachment of the Commons upon the powers of the Speaker.

19 *CJ*, 1:162, 941; Elsynge, *Proceedings in Parliament in Passing Bills*, p. 33. Elsynge, who was probably quoting his father's MS, cited the case of April 2, 1604, when the House refused to go back on their decision as to conferring with the Lords. Elsynge had also presented the case of April 27, 1604, when the Commons again declared that a judgment once passed by them could not be reversed. He added that on April 3 of that year the Commons stood by their refusal to confer with the Lords "in a matter private to our own House, *which by rules of order might not be by us revoked.*" The italics are Elsynge's and would seem to point to some practice already recognized.

20 *CJ*, 1:329, 330, 333–34, 1012–13; Bowyer, pp. 207–08.

21 Fuller declared that no notes made at the committee should be read by the Speaker or the Clerk. Doubtless some members were afraid that the Speaker might so word the report as to strengthen the hands of the Peers and that then the report would emerge as a bill. See Bowyer, pp. 207–08.

22 In this respect Phelips was following in a tradition. The Elizabethan Speaker could make himself exceedingly useful to the House. In 1593, when it was disputed whether Thomas Fitzherbert of Staffordshire, who had been outlawed, could serve as a member, the Speaker (Edward Coke) undertook a historical study of the problem and concluded that outlawed men could serve in the Commons but that Fitzherbert had not been returned and therefore could not serve, a judgment the Commons at once accepted.

23 March 14, 1610 (*CJ*, 1:410–11).

24 April 7, 1606 (*CJ*, 1:294).

25 February 27, 1610 (*CJ*, 1:399).

THE EFFECT OF THE SPEAKER ON BILLS AND COMMITTEES

1 When Adrian Stoughton, M.P. for Chichester, moved that the bill for highways in Sussex, Surrey, and Kent be expedited, the Speaker explained that the bill was a private one (being for three shires), although "followed" as a public bill, and that no fees had been paid to the officers, "nor any man took care to answer them." The House supported the Speaker (June 27, 1607 [*CJ*, 1:388, 1054–55]).

2 Ibid., 1:962.

3 About recommitment see Anonymous Journal (Titus F II, ff. 67–70; D'Ewes, pp. 505–07). See also Hakewill's opinion (Add. 8986, f. 7).

4 It was the opinion of Francis Tate that the more committees there were, the longer would be the delay in getting the bill through (Harl., 253, ff. 33–34v).

5 *Huntington Library Quarterly*, 15 (1951): 54.

6 On March 15, 1592/93, Speaker Edward Coke ruled that one who spoke against the body of a bill might be on the committee "and had an order to shew made in the Upper House upon the like doubt" (Titus F II, f. 61). But on November 9, 1601, Speaker John Croke put two questions to the House: (1) whether a man who had spoken against the body of a bill should be on the committee for the bill, and (2) whether a member of the House who had been a member of the committee on the bill when the bill was reported could speak against it. On the first question the House voted No; to the second, Aye, giving a new sanction to what had been fairly established usage. The Speaker wanted such a definite pronouncement (D'Ewes, p. 635).

7 *Huntington Library Quarterly*, 15 (1951): 47.

8 Another possibility must be mentioned. The *Commons Journals* for the reigns of Edward VI and Mary were brief in their records of committees. Not infrequently when the nomination of a committee was set down only one name was given (especially in the mid-Tudor period). The man named may conceivably have been the man to take charge of the bill. He was also sometimes the man who brought the bill back from the committee to the House. I cannot make out, however, that in the reign of James I the first-named member had any special function.

9 When two men discussed a measure with one another, without reference to the Speaker or the House, the Speaker was to intervene: "When . . . someone hath propounded a question to the House about the exposition of some statute, to know their opinion, and how it hath been practiced in the several parts of England, as did Mr. Wiseman in a point concerning bastardy, but to such as sat near him. But against such behavior there hath oftentimes been orders made, and it is the duty of the Speaker to admonish the House" (Exeter, D and C, art. 5).

THE SPEAKER'S FUNCTION IN DEBATES

1 See D'Ewes, pp. 306, 411; cf. Lansd., 43, f. 165.

2 See, for example, the attitude of the Speaker after the Queen's message, May 23, 1572 (D'Ewes, pp. 213–14; also Thomas Cromwell's Journal [Trinity College, Dublin], f. 41). In the Parliament of 1593, when James Morrice, M.P. for Colchester, brought in a bill against the jurisdiction of the bishops, the Speaker spoke of the importance and weight of the bill and asked leave to consider of it. The Speaker was sent for by the Queen, and Morrice was committed to the custody of Sir John Fortescue (Titus F II, ff. 30–34v; cf. D'Ewes, p. 476). On the other hand, Francis Tate, M.P. for Shrewsbury in 1604–1610 and probably an M.P. in 1581 (Harl., 253, ff. 32–36v), assumed that the Speaker looked toward the Crown and the Privy Council (ibid., ff. 33–35). "The good choice of the Speaker," Tate wrote, "being named by the Councillors present, will without doubt be such as her Majesty's service will be well

advanced and the Speaker both may of the Council receive direction for deliverance and assistance for furtherance."

Tate was above all an antiquarian and, when he thought of the Speaker, looked backward rather than forward. Writing in 1580 or thereabouts, it is hardly surprising that he regarded Parliament as working hand in hand with the Privy Council and the Speaker as a faithful servant of the Crown. He recognized, however, that there might be another outlook, that "in some heads there might be a jealousy that a Councillor, being especially sworn to her Majesty's service is not a person so congruent with the liberty of the House" (ibid., f. 32v). In the same Discourse he wrote: "A Councillor being Speaker shall never find and disclose the humors [moods?] of the House as another shall." Tate was on the whole loyal to the sovereign, since it was Elizabeth: "I think it good that a choice be made of bills, wherein this I note that it is not good that anything for choice or admitting or rejecting of bills to be delivered by the Speaker or any Councillor or other, by her Majesty's commandment, for so would by and by be raised by some humorous [odd, fantastic?] body some question of the liberty of the House and of restraining their free consultation, perhaps offensive to her Majesty, and assuredly with long speeches to the troublesome prolonging of the session" (ibid., ff. 33–34).

3 May 7, 1607 (Bowyer, pp. 378–80).
4 June 25, 1604 (*CJ*, 1:997, 245).
5 April 27, 1604 (*CJ*, 1:959, 187).
6 *CJ*, 1:979.
7 Bowyer, pp. 195–98.
8 Ibid., pp. 255–61.
9 Sandys, in a speech on March 7, had proposed the perfect union (Bowyer, pp. 218–23).
10 Ibid., p. 261.

Chapter 7

THE SPEAKER AND THE LORDS

1 E.g., April 19, 1604 (*CJ*, 1:95).
2 March 14, 1606/07 (Bowyer, p. 234).
3 The conference between the two Houses on December 11, 1601, gives little information about the debate but reveals the tension between the two Houses over the proposed Bill for Patents (D'Ewes, pp. 678–79). In the Anonymous Journal for March 2, 1592/93, the conference between the two Houses was "to consider of our dangers and to consult of remedies" (Titus F II, f. 41v), but the Commons had authorized their committeemen "to agree to nothing but only to report to the whole House afterwards what is done and said" (ibid., f. 39v). At a conference on March 24, 1584/85 (Thomas Cromwell's Journal, f. 91 in Trinity Coll. Dublin MS. N. 2.12.), the Commons "stood to the maintenance" of what they had passed, and "neither party seemed satisfied." On May 15, 1572, a conference was arranged between the two Houses "for further direction and a plot to be devised for their manner of proceeding in the matter concerning the Queen of Scots" (D'Ewes, p. 205). On the next day the Commons were consulted as to the general resolution arrived at in the conference for beheading the Duke of Norfolk. All the House favored a resolution for the beheading to be sent to the Queen.

4   D. H. Willson, *The Privy Councillors in the House of Commons, 1604-1629* (Minneapolis, 1940), pp. 223–30.
5   *CJ*, 1:177.
6   Bowyer, p. 197 n. 1.

THE SPEAKER AND THE KING

1   Bowyer, pp. 297–98.
2   *CJ*, 1.976.
3   *CJ*, 1:978.
4   Ibid.
5   *CJ*, 1:980.
6   *CJ*, 1:1053.
7   *CJ*, 1:384–85; Bowyer, pp. 341–42.
8   Bowyer, pp. 343–44.
9   *CJ*, 1:451–52.

Epilogue

1   Birch, 1:176. In 1612 John Chamberlain wrote to Edmondes: "The King is given to understand that he is ill served in the Parliament by reason of the Councillors."
2   Wallace Notestein, *The Winning of the Initiative by the House of Commons*, Raleigh Lecture (London, British Academy, 1924); Willson, *Privy Councillors*.
3   The *DNB* says that Sir Thomas Knyvet (or Knevet), M.P. for Westminster, was made a Privy Councillor late in 1605 or early in 1606. He served on a few committees and made one speech. In July 1607 he was made a peer. I find no contemporary proof that he was made a Privy Councillor, and I doubt it.
4   James had great confidence in his "judgment"—misplaced confidence.
5   The obscure members failed to find places on committees, partly because they did not rise to speak to motions. In the 1604–10 House of Commons there were more than 460 members, of whom, as a rough estimate, 272 made no speech. But the membership rolls are sadly incomplete: not all of those who spoke found a place in the known records, and my memory of those who never spoke is probably at fault. Of the 190 or thereabouts who did speak,

probably two-thirds spoke fewer than three times, and probably fewer than sixty were regular speakers.

6 These are inferences that cannot be proved unless more parliamentary diaries turn up, and possibly not then, but they would explain which committees often arrived at decisions wholly agreeable to the opposition.

7 Townshend, *Historical Collections*, p. 37.

8 Gardiner, in his *DNB* account of James, discounts his timidity and emphasizes his impatience with details. That he listened too often to those courtiers who spoke last and who offered him the opinion he was waiting to hear is, I believe, true. He was a nervous man and did not stop to weigh all the relevant facts, and thus he sometimes—not always—jumped to conclusions.

9 Cecil had spent most of his days in royal courts, where men grew proficient in telling royalty what it wished to hear. As a young man he had been for some time in France, and there he could hardly have failed to hear the doctrine that statesmen should act expediently.

10 The probabilities are that the courtiers rather than the Commons would have prevailed with his Majesty.

11 James was a King from early infancy and was doubtless flattered at every turn. It would not be surprising if, as a child, he became dependent upon flattery to give him confidence. I suspect that his assurance in conversation and in his speeches covered a fundamental timidity.

12 Sandys was the son of an archbishop and was familiar with the language of courts. He was probably not anxious to offend the King, and he was naturally one who could see both sides of a question.

13 We have so few accounts of the debates that our conclusions must be taken with reserve. Those who wrote them up were using longhand and were likely to get the gist of what the better-known speakers said and to leave out much of the close debating, of which there would appear to have been little. But there may have been more than we think. It would seem that each man made his own speech without too much reference to what had been said before.

14 There are examples of what looks like collusion between speakers, as if the debates had been planned. It is hard, at least for me, to suppose that the opposition was not carefully organized, especially in 1610.

15 Some of his statements had so little relation to the facts that one asks how he could have so deceived himself. Possibly sycophantic courtiers had helped him to draft the statements, and they would have had the general public in view.

Index